OUT OF ORDER!
OUT OF ORDER!
OUT OF ORDER!
Coke
OUT OF ORDER!
OUT OF ORDER!
WEATHER BUREAU
OUT OF ORDER!
OUT OF ORDER!
MAD
WAIT
WALK
OUT OF ORDER!
OUT OF ORDER!
OUT OF ORDER!

Dave Berg

Dave Berg MAD logo: cover, MAD #105, Sept. 1966

Dave Berg "foot" self-portrait, date unknown
(we don't know what it means, either)

MAD's GREATEST ARTISTS

Dave Berg

FIVE DECADES OF "THE LIGHTER SIDE OF..."

FOREWORD BY
Drew Friedman

RUNNING PRESS

PHILADELPHIA · LONDON

Acknowledgments

Thanks to Al Feldstein and Nick Meglin, who edited "The Lighter Side of..," and John Putnam and Lenny Brenner, who provided art direction.

Thanks to Tom Richmond, Bill Janocha, Phil Hurd, Claudia Hurd, and *Cartoonist PROfiles* for the Dave Berg interview and related materials.

Additional thanks to Vivian and Nancy Berg, Drew Friedman, Max Korn, Doug Gilford, and Mike Slaubaugh.

Extra special thanks to Diane Nelson.

And thanks to all of Dave's friends, relatives, coworkers (and especially doctors), who inspired his "Berg's-Eye View" of the world.

Books published by Running Press are available at special discounts for bulk purchases in the United States by corporations, institutions, and other organizations. For more information, please contact the Special Markets Department at the Perseus Books Group, 2300 Chestnut Street, Suite 200, Philadelphia, PA 19103, or call (800) 810-4145, ext. 5000, or e-mail special.markets@perseusbooks.com.

9   8   7   6   5   4   3   2   1
Digit on the right indicates the number of this printing

Library of Congress Control Number: 2013934598

ISBN 978-0-7624-5161-6

Cover Art by Dave Berg
Cover and Interior Layouts by Joshua McDonnell
Editor: Jordana Tusman

For E.C. Publications:
Editors: John Ficarra and Charlie Kadau (MAD)
Art Director: Sam Viviano (MAD)

Running Press Book Publishers
2300 Chestnut St.
Philadelphia, Pennsylvania 19103-4371

Visit us on the web!
www.runningpress.com

Visit MAD Magazine on the web:
www.madmagazine.com

CONTENTS

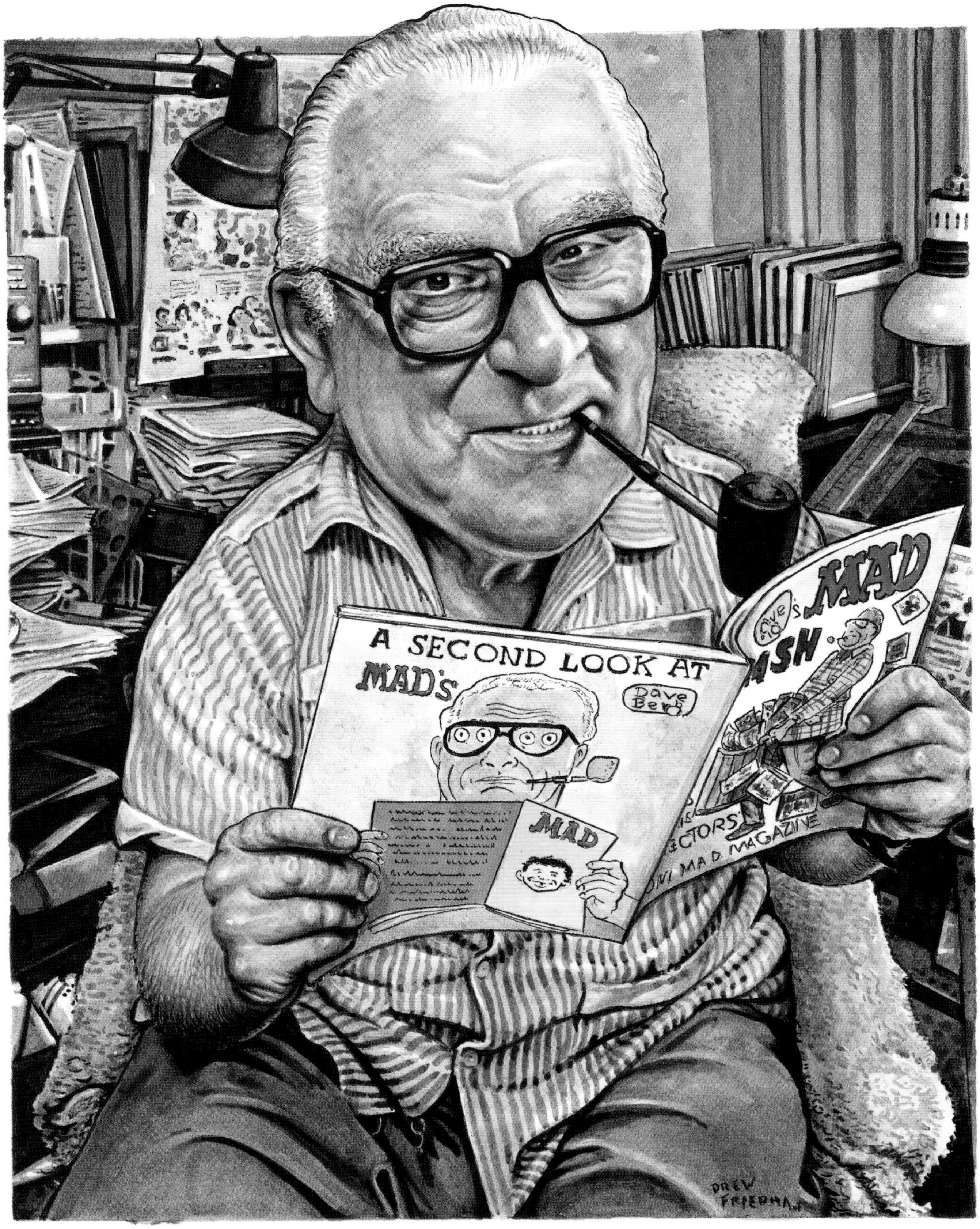
A SECOND LOOK AT
MAD's
MAD
MAD
MAD MAGAZINE
DREW FRIEDMAN

Foreword

Dave Berg saved my life.

Well, not literally, but . . .

I never had much use for school. Yet, despite being forced to attend, I *still* received a good education, thanks to watching *The Three Stooges*, *Soupy Sales*, and *Popeye* cartoons on TV, *and* reading MAD magazine, most significantly, Dave Berg's "The Lighter Side of. . ." With a father and mother who were a bit too preoccupied, respectively, with work and shopping for shoes, Dave Berg was always there for me, reliable and dependable, instructing me with a monthly primer on life within the pages of MAD. "The Lighter Side of. . ." feature literally prepared me and countless other kids for what we could expect from life, be it school, little league, camp, parties, driving, weddings, doctors, winter, spring, summer, fall, religion, and death. The foibles of popular culture and the American scene, finding truth in humor, was Dave Berg's *raison de vivre*, and why I'm so grateful to him for always being there for me. For example: When I was first sent off to summer camp, I had already familiarized myself with Dave Berg's "The Lighter Side of Summer Camp," and so felt totally prepared for whatever nightmares awaited me. (I also made certain that my underwear was *not* Fruit of the Loom.)

"The Lighter Side of. . ." debuted in 1961, a more innocent era of MAD men. Artist/writer Dave Berg's whimsical barbs poked fun at such benign, omnibus topics as men and women (and could he draw some *sexy* women!), dating, young marrieds, children, shopping, car mechanics, household items, and especially Dave Berg himself, in the guise of his square-jawed, pipe smoking alter-ego, the moralizing everyman Roger Kaputnik. The body of brilliant work collected in this book is an accurate, astute, and always funny chronicle of what American life was like back in the mid to late 20th century, a psychological and sociological study of the human condition. Think of it as the only history book you'll ever need.

A perfect example of the enormity of Dave Berg's talent *and* huge influence can be found within his early "A Mad Look at Christmas," which includes a sequence with an adorable little tot in line at a department store, eager to meet Santa Claus. ("I'm gonna see Sandy Claws!") When the tot's turn arrives, Santa reveals his truly horrific face up-close, exclaiming, "Well . . . HO-HO-HO!" The terrified tot runs off screaming. After first seeing that disturbing Santa face, I too became terrified of the very *concept* of Santa Claus. That face haunted me. This seemed more like the *darker* side. Skip several decades ahead to the 1983 holiday classic *A Christmas Story*, and sure enough, when the children are lined up to visit Santa, what they encounter is an exact replica of that horrific close-up of Santa, chanting "HO-HO-HO," the director (Bob Clark) clearly channeling/borrowing from Dave Berg. Such was his influence. Take a look and compare for yourself.

As the 1960s wore on, times were indeed a changin', and Dave Berg found himself dealing with the baffling generation gap: rock and roll, student unrest, war protesters, and perhaps the most difficult concept of all for him to swallow—*hippies*. Still, a determined Dave Berg (Roger Kaputnik) rolled up his plaid sleeves and met the kids head-on, attempting to shepherd them toward the proper path, sometimes sermonizing, sometimes confrontational, but always with his self-mocking sense of humor intact. By the late sixties, his old-fashioned morals and love of country seemed sadly archaic, and Dave Berg was rendered an official *square*. This all changed one morning circa 1970, when portly, crew-cutted MAD publisher William M. Gaines (a familiar character in "The Lighter Side of. . .") woke up one morning and decided he no longer wanted to shave *or* get his hair cut, ostensibly becoming the world's oldest (and fattest) hippie. This seemed to have a profound effect on Dave Berg. It mellowed him (if his very own *boss* could be a hippie), and before long, he too grew sideburns, let his hair get a bit shaggier, wore plaid bell bottoms, Nehru shirts, and finally, donned his iconic safari jacket. I used to speculate about the Dave Berg safari jacket: Did he get them custom made? Did he have a closet filled with them? Did he also wear pith helmets? Did he actually ever *go* on any African safaris?? No matter, Dave Berg was once again officially *hip*.

As the seventies unfurled, the Vietnam War sputtered to an end, Richard Nixon moved to New Jersey, Disco truly sucked, and smelly hippies gave way to smelly punks. Dave Berg soldiered on (in his trusty safari jacket), tackling the important issues of the moment: The Energy Crisis and The Me Generation. When the topics inevitably became narrower, (and perhaps to lighten his load), his "The Lighter Side of. . ." feature was streamlined so he could now jump with ease from topic to topic ("The Doctor," "The Office," etc.) within the same MAD spread. As he grew older, his once beautifully rendered art began to loosen up and his pen line became a bit shakier. Old cartoonists don't die—they fade away—or at least their *ink* fades away. Dave Berg literally grew old within the pages of MAD magazine, finally fading away.

When Dave Berg died in 2002, it was discovered that he had a backlog of "The Lighter Side of. . ." gags he hadn't yet drawn. The MAD editors assigned them to 18 of his fellow MAD artists to bring to life as a sort of tribute to Dave Berg. (This was Jack Davis's last contribution to MAD.) I was assigned "The Office," which for years had featured Bill Gaines as the *boss* of the office. After Gaines died, Dave Berg continued to include him, his head now (disturbingly) mounted within a frame, deerlike, watching over and reacting to the office proceedings beneath him. The two MAD editors, Nick Meglin and John Ficarra, became Berg's new office bosses (naturally, both sharing the same desk).

This was my version of "The Office" by Dave Berg, also featuring art director Sam Viviano, perhaps somewhat *over*-reacting to the Dave Berg punch-line?

THE OFFICE
I think it's time we hired new blood around here!
That would help generate new ideas and bring fresh energy!
Maybe, but you know the main reason for doing it!
Of course! So we'll have someone to blame if business doesn't improve!
PLOP!

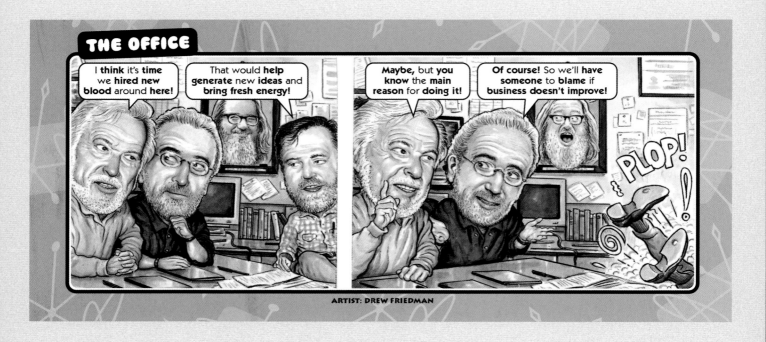

ARTIST: DREW FRIEDMAN

I only met Dave Berg once, in the early '90s, after I began doing regular work for MAD and fulfilling a lifelong goal—becoming one of the "Usual Gang of Idiots." My wife and I were invited to MAD's annual Christmas party at New York's Society of Illustrators. And sure enough, as MAD's *newest* regular contributor (and as a sort of initiation), I was seated with MAD's *oldest* regular contributor, none other than Dave Berg himself. He was a pure delight—upbeat, funny, giddy—almost childlike in his enthusiasm in being there among his fellow idiots. MAD's Dave Berg clearly *loved* being MAD's Dave Berg (he would often wear a T-shirt around his neighborhood which read *MAD's Dave Berg*).

It's that infectious Dave Berg, who not only educated me about life but also welcomed me into the MAD fold as a fellow "idiot," that I attempted to lovingly capture in my portrait.

—Drew Friedman, March 2013

The 1950s

SHOOTING THE GRAND RAPIDS DEPT.

Today, people are "living modern". They're driving modern cars like "Flight Sweep", smoking modern cigarettes like "L&M", running up modern debts like "Installment Plan" and ending up with modern illnesses like "Flap the Lower Lip". Here's one craze that's a major contributor to today's MAD mode of living . . .

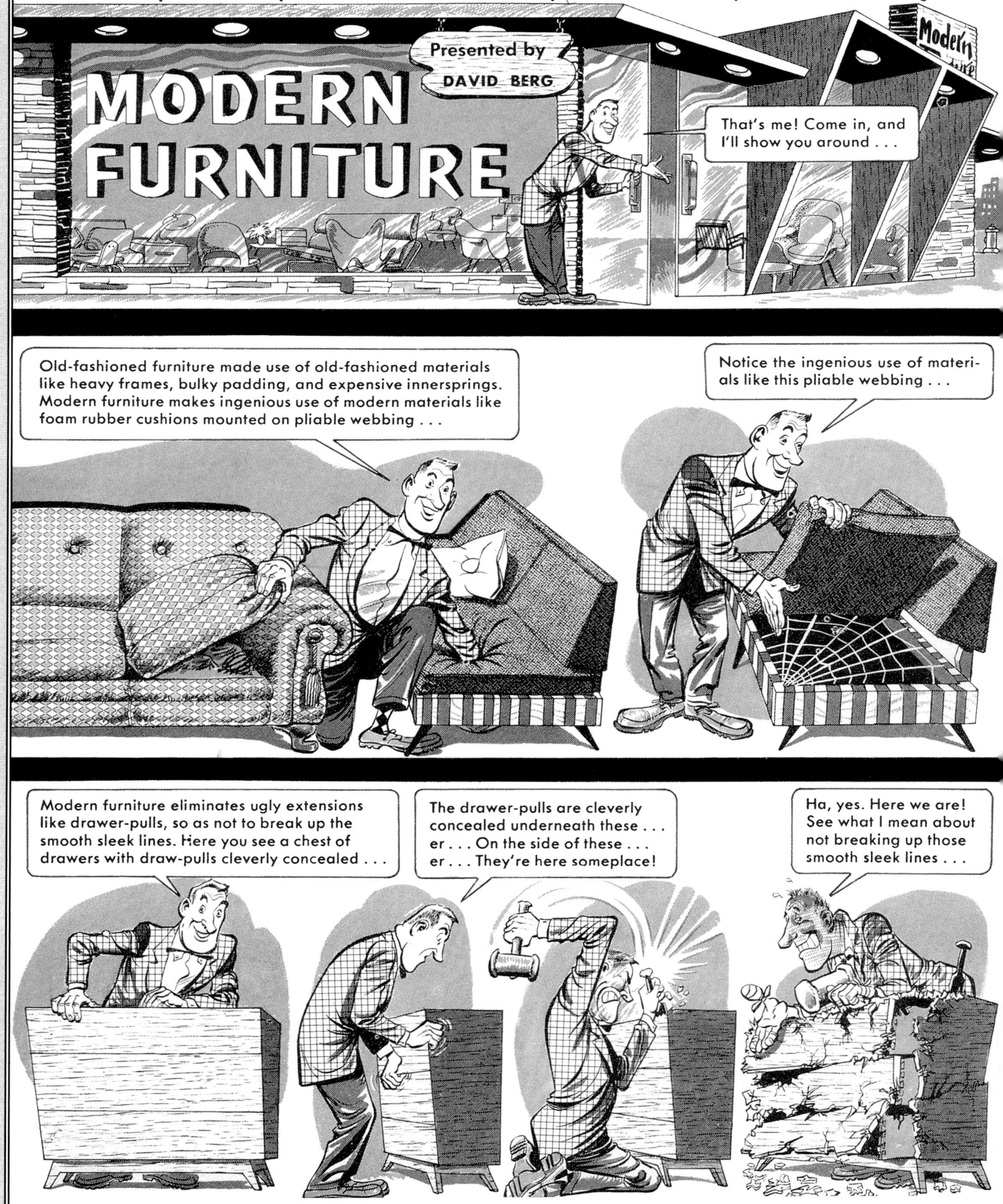
MODERN FURNITURE
Presented by DAVID BERG
That's me! Come in, and I'll show you around . . .
Old-fashioned furniture made use of old-fashioned materials like heavy frames, bulky padding, and expensive innersprings. Modern furniture makes ingenious use of modern materials like foam rubber cushions mounted on pliable webbing . . .
Notice the ingenious use of materials like this pliable webbing . . .
Modern furniture eliminates ugly extensions like drawer-pulls, so as not to break up the smooth sleek lines. Here you see a chest of drawers with draw-pulls cleverly concealed . . .
The drawer-pulls are cleverly concealed underneath these . . . er . . . On the side of these . . . er . . . They're here someplace!
Ha, yes. Here we are! See what I mean about not breaking up those smooth sleek lines . . .

Dave Berg's first published MAD article

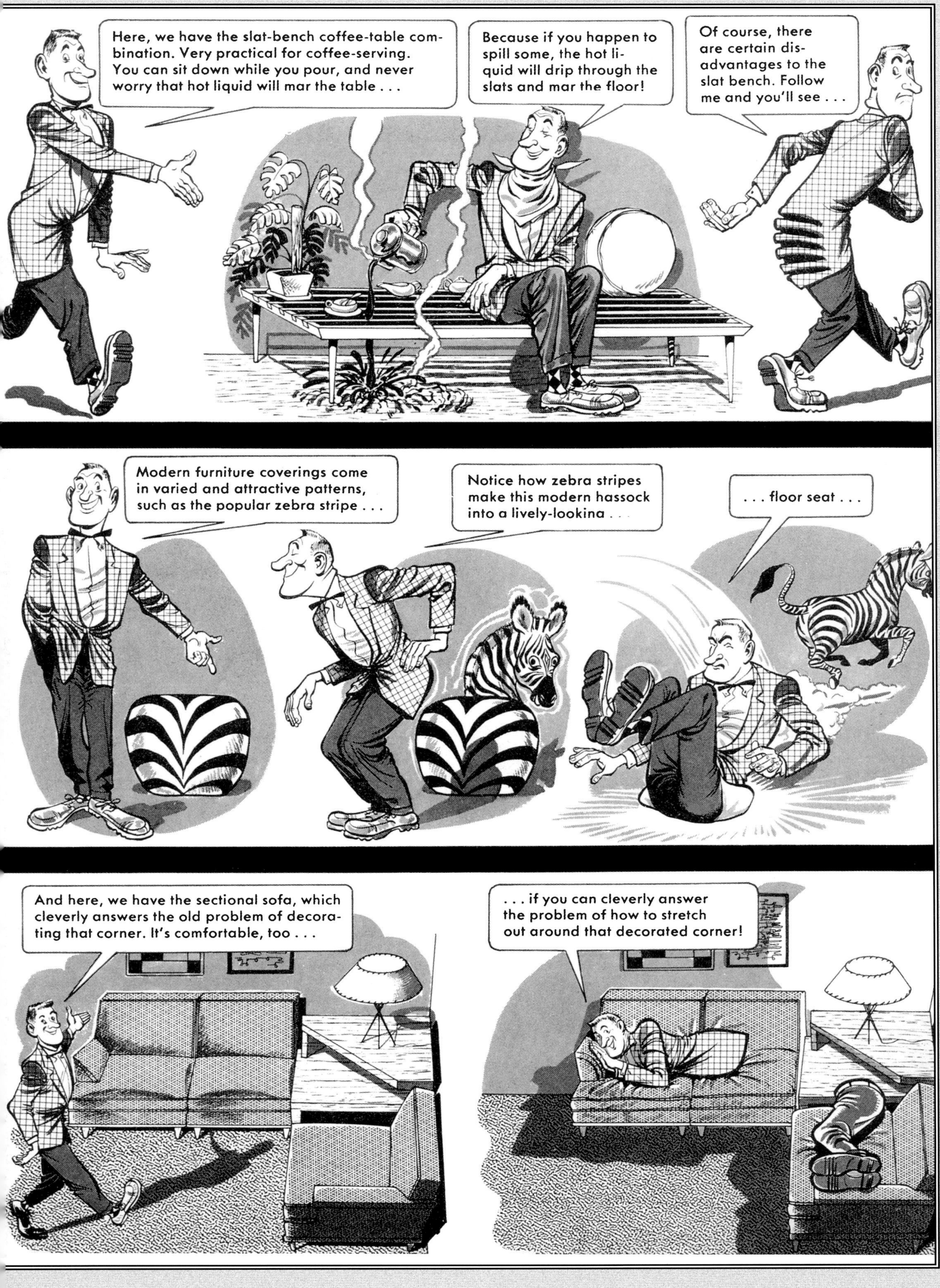
Here, we have the slat-bench coffee-table combination. Very practical for coffee-serving. You can sit down while you pour, and never worry that hot liquid will mar the table . . .
Because if you happen to spill some, the hot liquid will drip through the slats and mar the floor!
Of course, there are certain disadvantages to the slat bench. Follow me and you'll see . . .
Modern furniture coverings come in varied and attractive patterns, such as the popular zebra stripe . . .
Notice how zebra stripes make this modern hassock into a lively-looking . . .
. . . floor seat . . .
And here, we have the sectional sofa, which cleverly answers the old problem of decorating that corner. It's comfortable, too . . .
. . . if you can cleverly answer the problem of how to stretch out around that decorated corner!

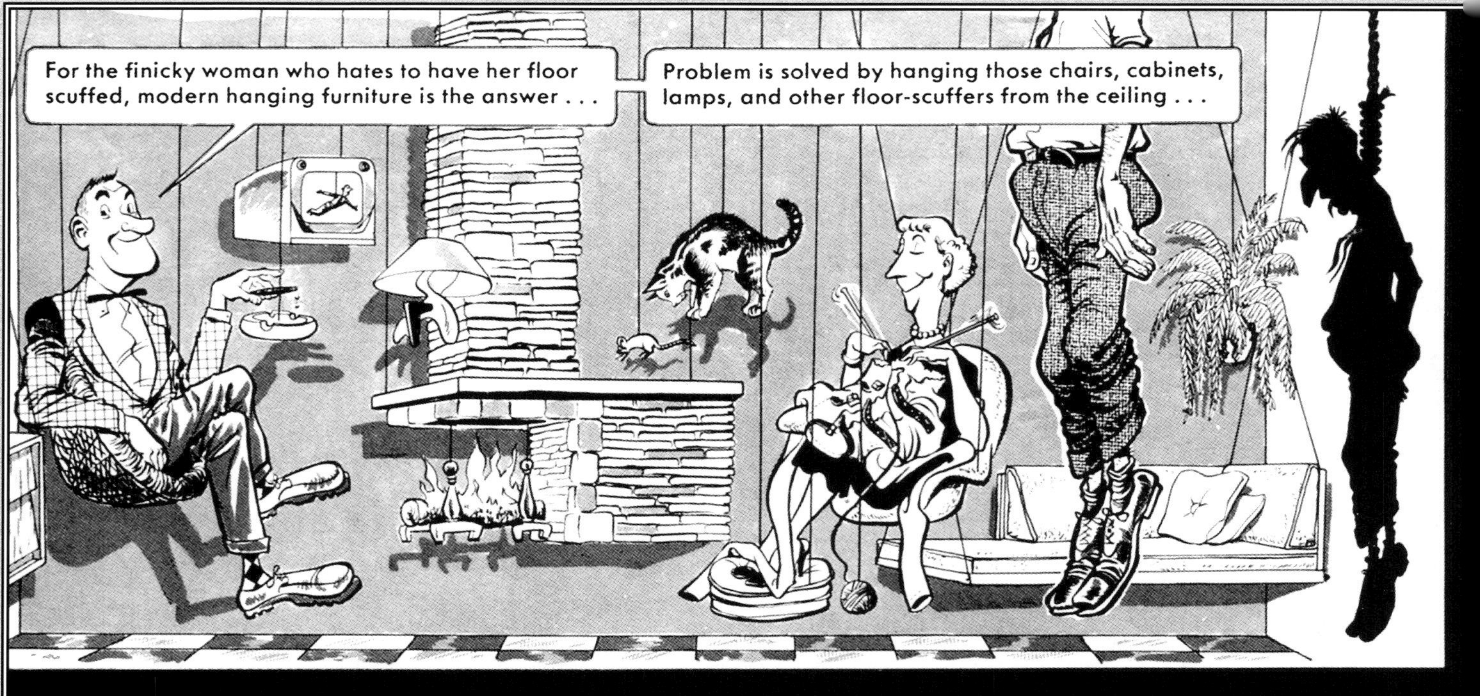
For the finicky woman who hates to have her floor scuffed, modern hanging furniture is the answer . . .
Problem is solved by hanging those chairs, cabinets, lamps, and other floor-scuffers from the ceiling . . .

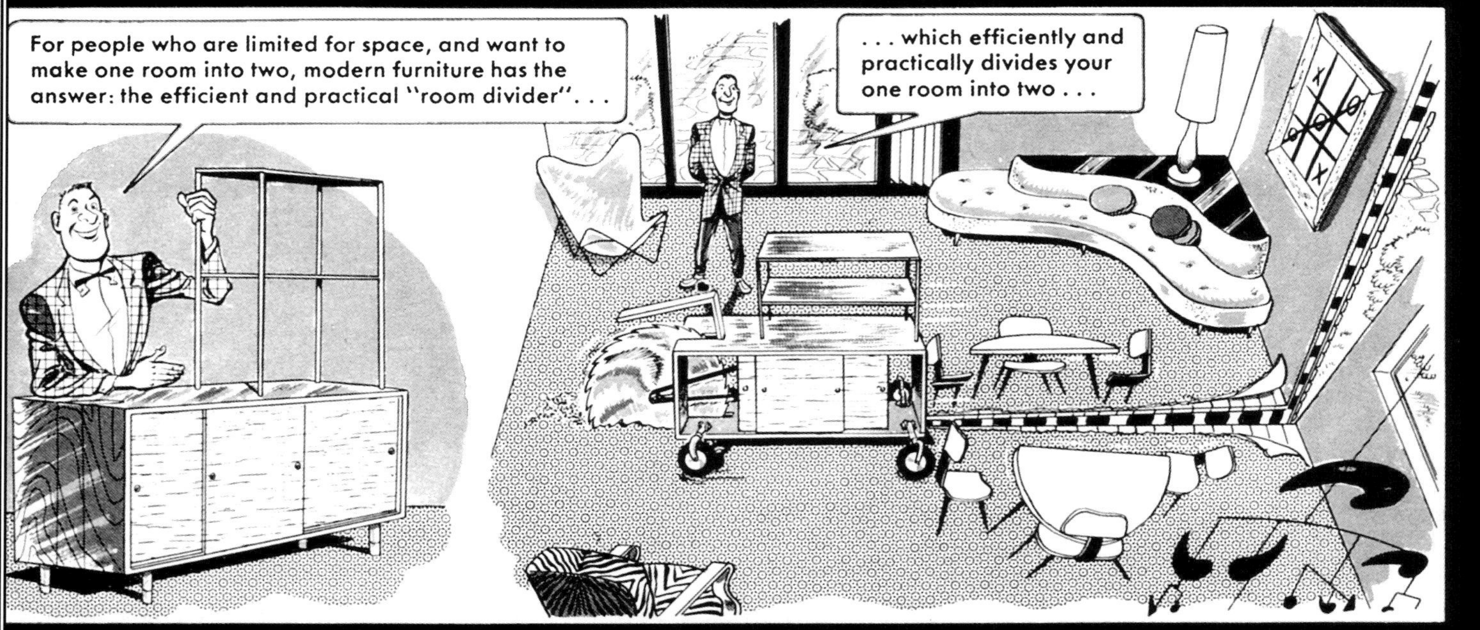
For people who are limited for space, and want to make one room into two, modern furniture has the answer: the efficient and practical "room divider" . . .
. . . which efficiently and practically divides your one room into two . . .

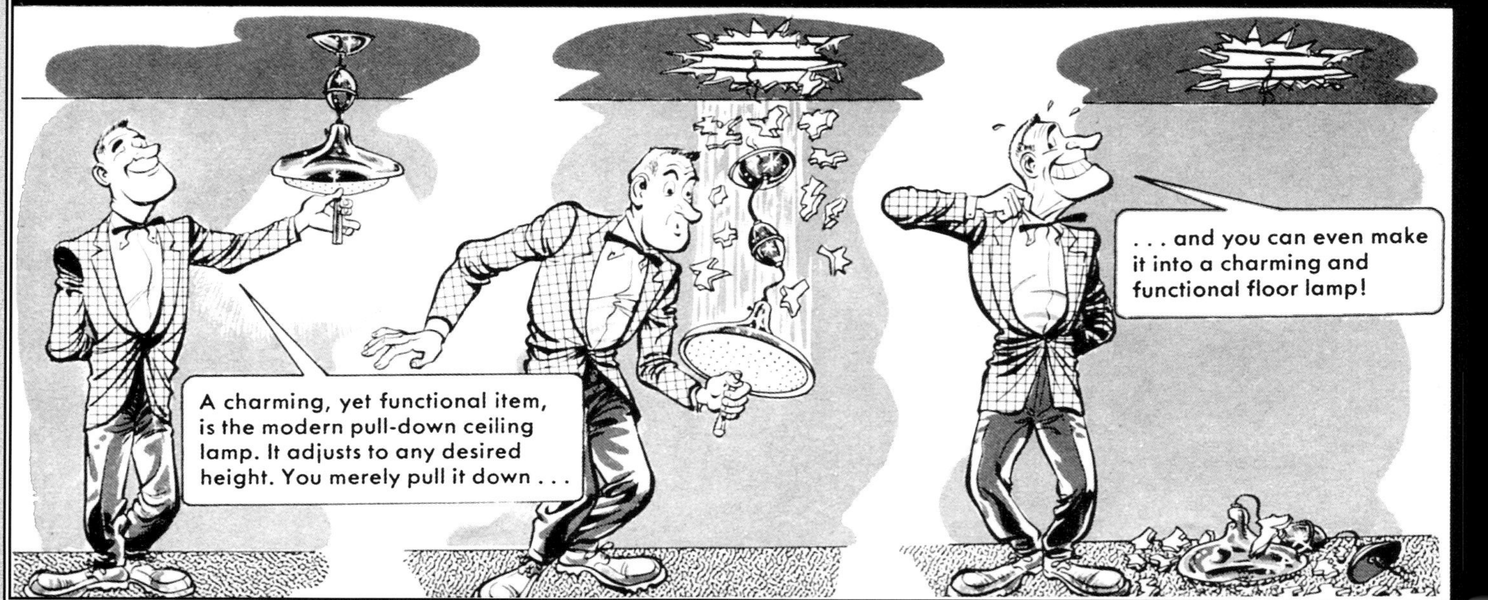
A charming, yet functional item, is the modern pull-down ceiling lamp. It adjusts to any desired height. You merely pull it down . . .
. . . and you can even make it into a charming and functional floor lamp!

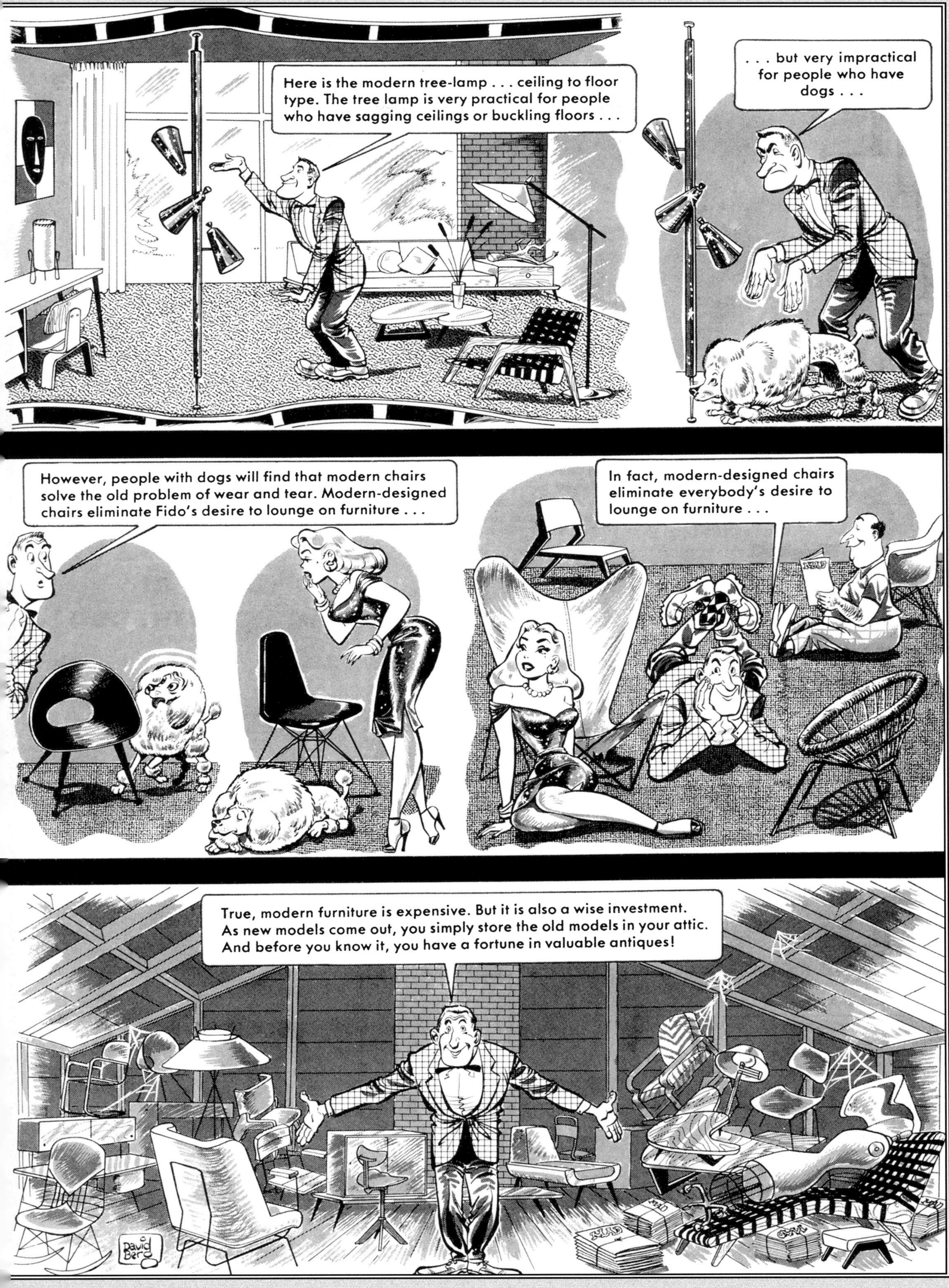
Here is the modern tree-lamp . . . ceiling to floor type. The tree lamp is very practical for people who have sagging ceilings or buckling floors . . .
. . . but very impractical for people who have dogs . . .
However, people with dogs will find that modern chairs solve the old problem of wear and tear. Modern-designed chairs eliminate Fido's desire to lounge on furniture . . .
In fact, modern-designed chairs eliminate everybody's desire to lounge on furniture . . .
True, modern furniture is expensive. But it is also a wise investment. As new models come out, you simply store the old models in your attic. And before you know it, you have a fortune in valuable antiques!
David Berg

PASS ANOTHER NAPKIN DEPT.

Let's face it! The Italians have built a better mouth trap. And now, the world is beating a path to the Pizzeria door. Here, then, is an article about the pie that's rapidly replacing "apple" as our National Pastry...

PIZZA PIE

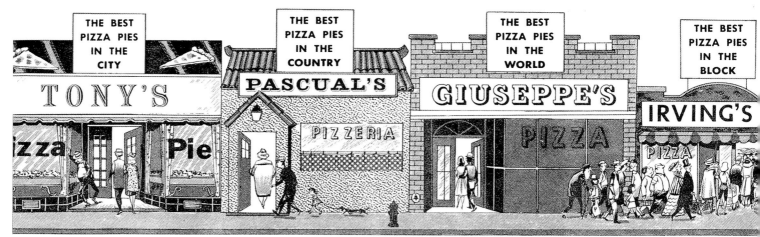

THE BEST PIZZA PIES IN THE CITY
TONY'S
izza
Pie
THE BEST PIZZA PIES IN THE COUNTRY
PASCUAL'S
PIZZERIA
THE BEST PIZZA PIES IN THE WORLD
GIUSEPPE'S
PIZZA
THE BEST PIZZA PIES IN THE BLOCK
IRVING'S
PIZZA

STORY AND PICTURES BY DAVID BERG

INGREDIENTS NEEDED FOR A PIZZA PIE

TOO MANY BROADS SPOIL THE COOK.

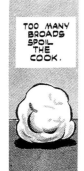

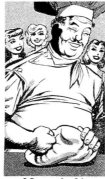

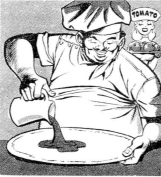

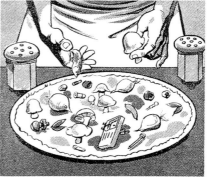

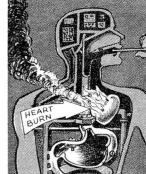

First, dough is needed.

Next, chef is needed ... to knead the dough.

TOMATO

Then, Mozzarella cheese and Tomato sauce are needed ... to spread on the kneaded dough.

Then, anchovies, mushrooms, peppers, sausages or onions are needed to kill the taste of the previous ingredients.

HEART BURN

Finally, a cast-iron stomach is needed to help digest the mess.

MAKING A PIZZA PIE

The chef then places the pie in the oven.

Next, he manipulates pizza with a big wooden paddle. You think he's baking your pie, when actually he's playing shuffleboard.

10 OFF

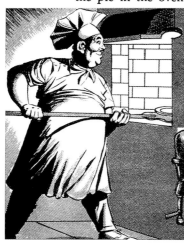

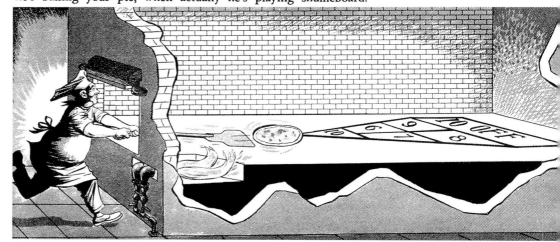

EATING A PIZZA PIE

Grasp hard crust of pizza with thumb and first two fingers of one hand . . .

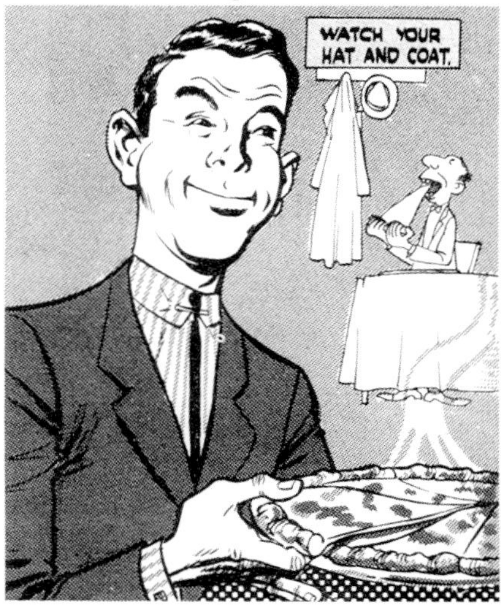
WATCH YOUR HAT AND COAT.

Lift section from rest of pie. With this method, section will flop over . . .

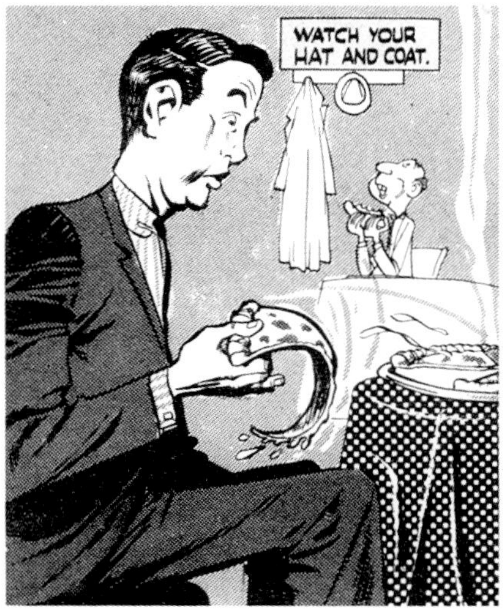
WATCH YOUR HAT AND COAT.

. . . getting icky sticky gook all over your new $49.50 charcoal-gray suit.

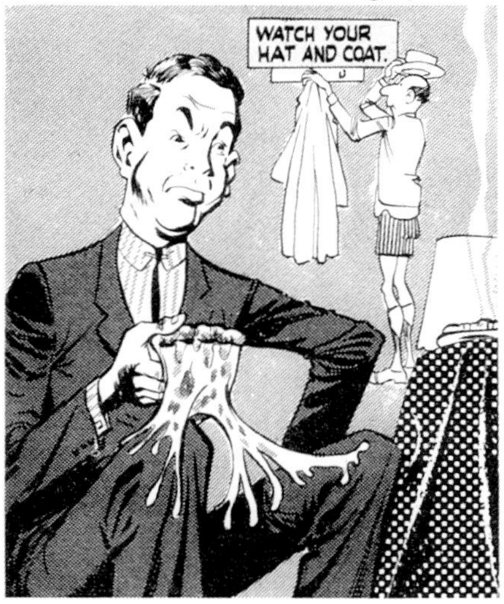
WATCH YOUR HAT AND COAT.

Neatly roll up pizza pie section from point to hard crust as shown above . . .

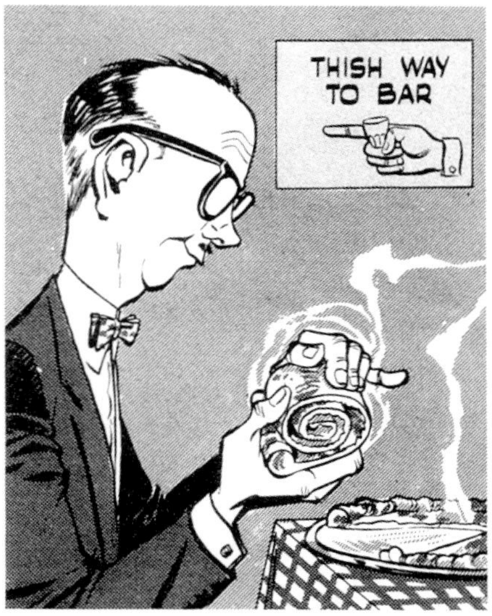
THISH WAY TO BAR

With this method, the ingredients are sure to ooze out from both sides . . .

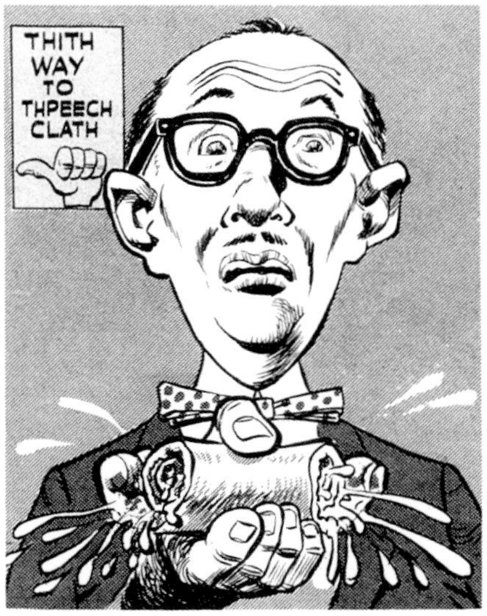
THITH WAY TO THPEECH CLATH

. . . getting icky sticky gook all over your new $49.50 charcoal-gray suit.

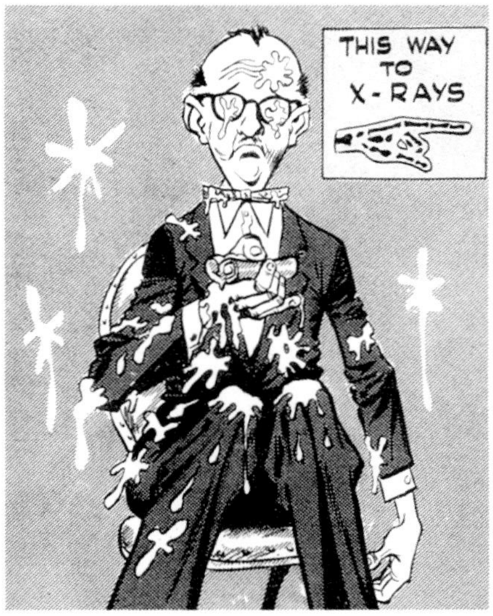
THIS WAY TO X-RAYS

If you are a he-man type pizza eater, grasp whole pie firmly in both hands.

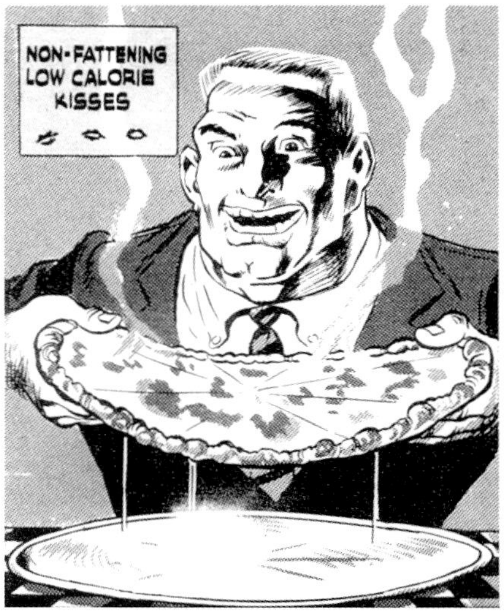
NON-FATTENING LOW CALORIE KISSES

With this method, whole pie will fall apart, as it has been pre-sectioned . . .

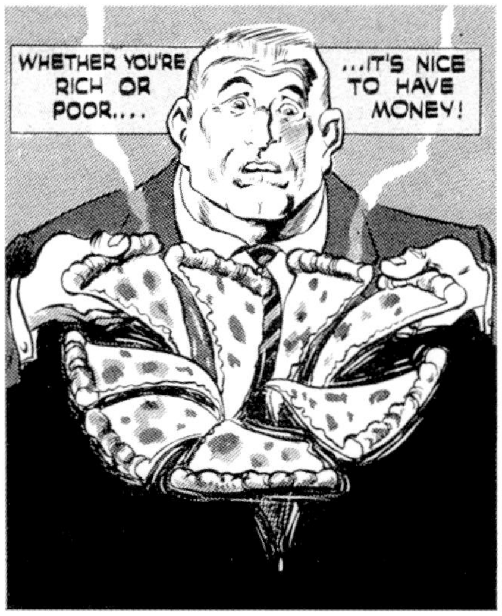
WHETHER YOU'RE RICH OR POOR....
...IT'S NICE TO HAVE MONEY!

. . . getting icky sticky gook all over your new $49.50 charcoal-gray suit.

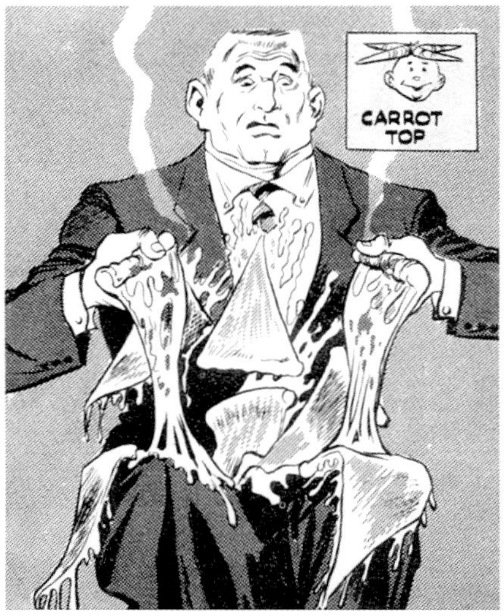
CARROT TOP

PIZZA PIE TAKE-OUT ORDERS

If your family wants to eat Pizza at home, you can always dash down to the nearest Pizzeria for a "take-out" order.

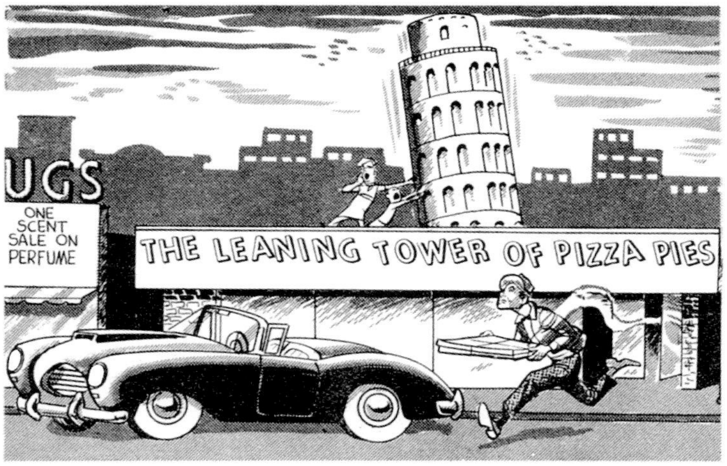
UGS
ONE SCENT SALE ON PERFUME
THE LEANING TOWER OF PIZZA PIES

If you get caught in traffic jam on the way home, you can always set fire to the car seat to keep the Pizza pie hot.

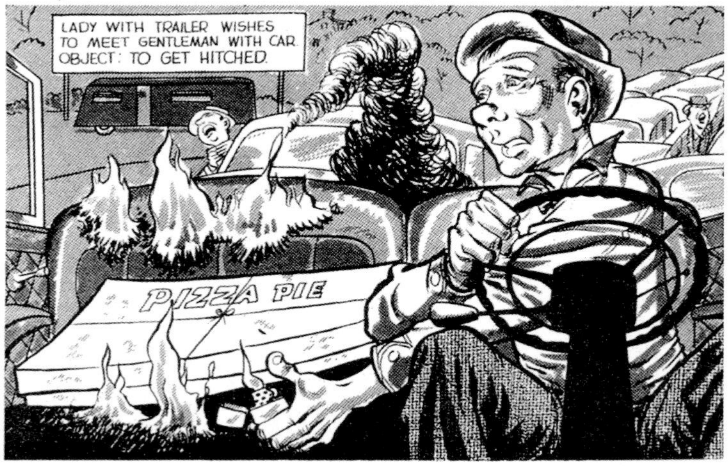
LADY WITH TRAILER WISHES TO MEET GENTLEMAN WITH CAR OBJECT: TO GET HITCHED
PIZZA PIE

If you get caught speeding on the way home, you can always offer piece of Pizza as bribe, known as "Cheezit, the Cop!"

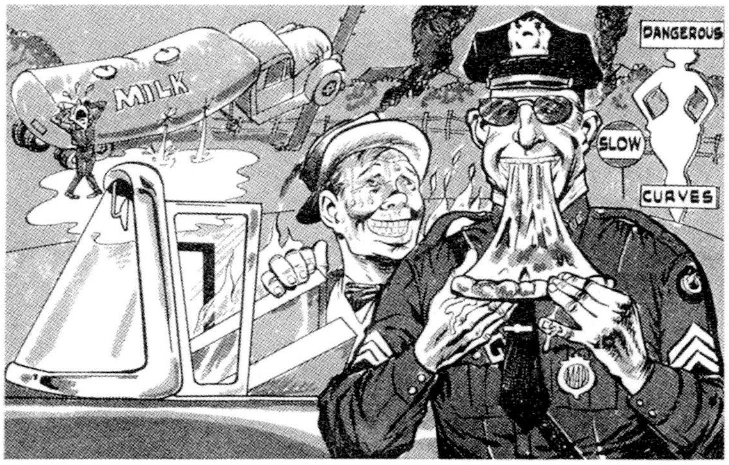
MILK
DANGEROUS
SLOW
CURVES

If you finally get the Pizza home, and it's ice cold... you can always take the family out to a nice Chinese Restaurant.

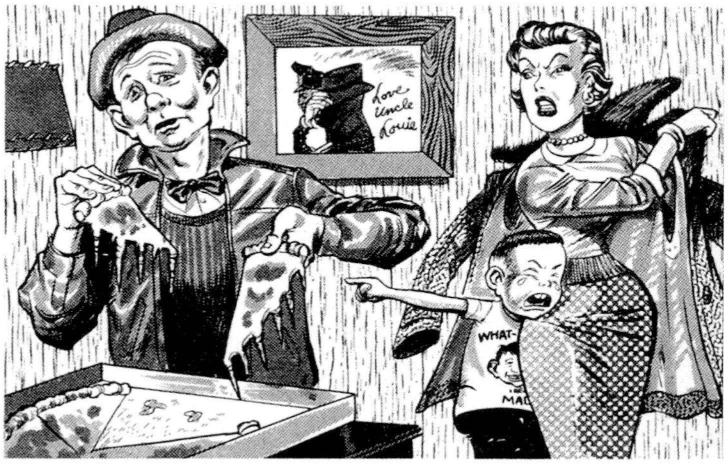
Love Uncle Louie
WHAT-

NEW USES FOR PIZZA PIES

Like all fads, Pizza Pie popularity may fade. When this happens, MAD is ready to save the Pizza Pie makers with these suggested...

Continental-style back for cars

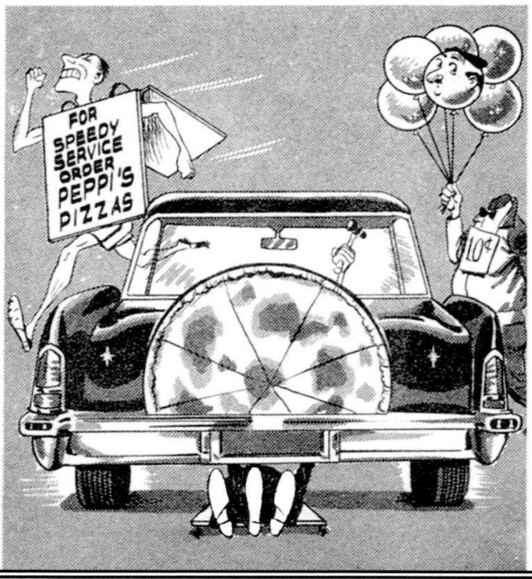
FOR SPEEDY SERVICE ORDER PEPPI'S PIZZAS
10¢

Life nets for firemen

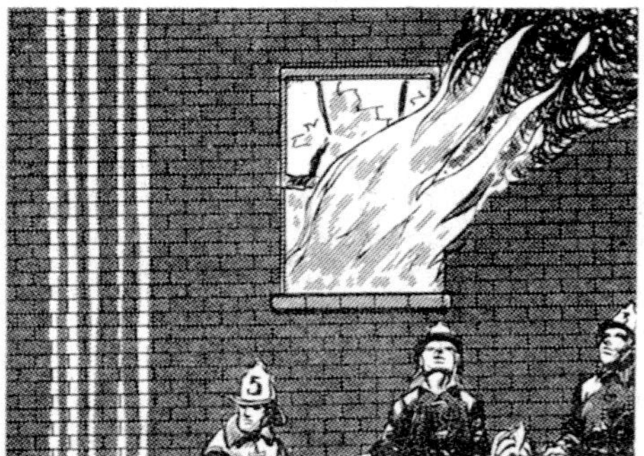

Introduce J. Arthur Rank movies

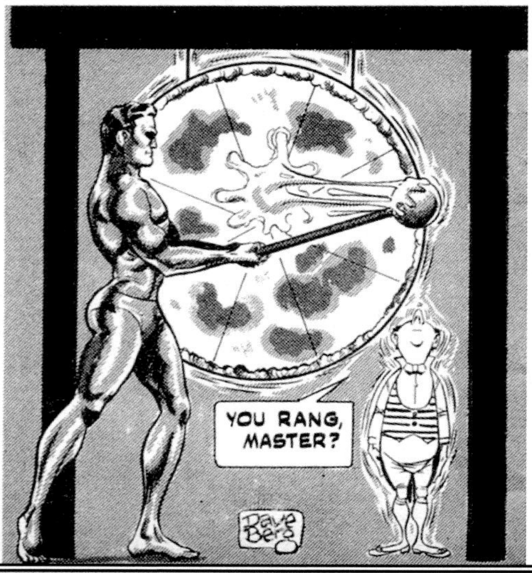
YOU RANG, MASTER?
Dave Berg

ONE-LEGGED BANDIT DEPT.

Wake up, America! Before it's too late! Today our nation is in the grip of a deadly peril more sinister and diabolical than the infamous fifth columns of World War II! These particular columns are made of steel pipe, on top of which are mounted . . .

Parking Meters

Yes, today, mercenary local officials all over the country, in an effort to fill their city's coffers (and perhaps their own pockets), are innocently destroying America's basic security! They are breaking down its morale! Because the every day normal functions of our American way of life are periodically being disrupted by the necessity of our having to drop everything in order to rush out into the street and put another coin into that parking meter. Like f'rinstance . . .

Now, what was that we were doing?

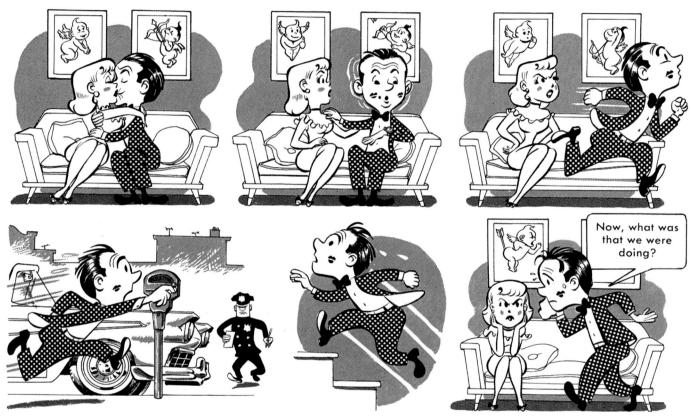

CONTINUITY AND PICTURES BY DAVID BERG

. . . or f'rinstance . . .

BARBER SHOP

. . . or f'rinstance . . .

HOSPITAL

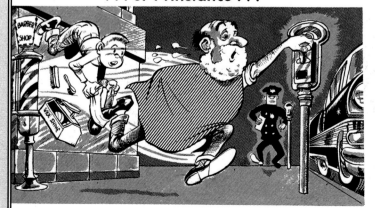

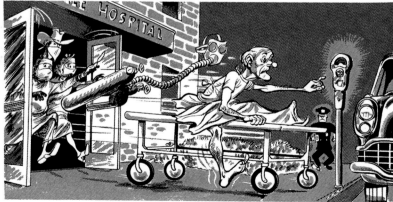

Now, we here at MAD are all for a guy making a quick buck if he can! But we draw the line when it comes to our country's security. Let's take a look at the handwriting on the wall! Prodded by the success of their "automobile" parking meters, these mercenary local jerks are gonna keep going! And before you know it, here's what we'll all be facing!

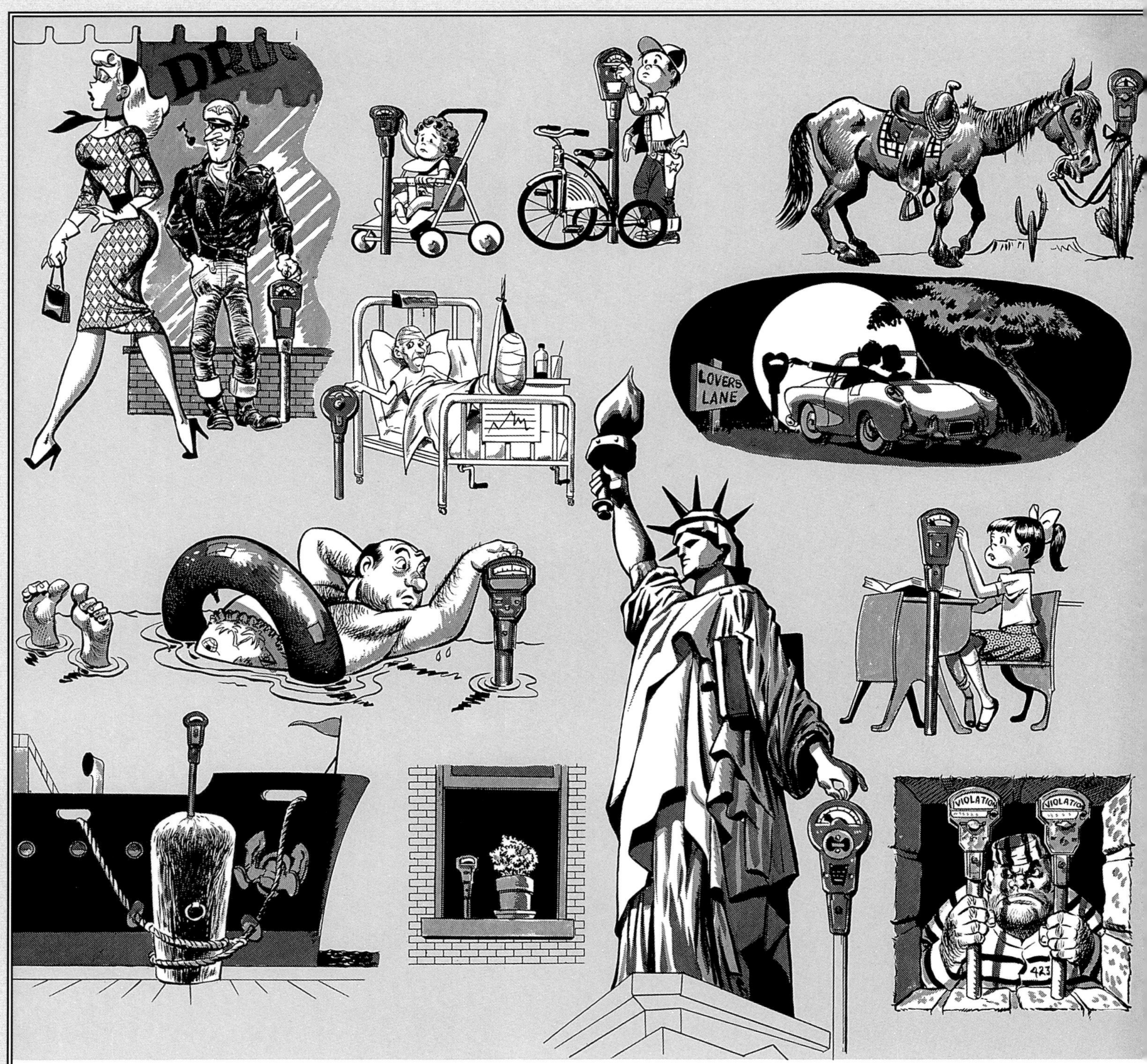
LOVERS
LANE
423

Pretty soon, there'll be so many parking meters for so many different purposes, they'll end up choking off all commerce, and "The American Way of Life" as we know it will come to a grinding, sickening halt.

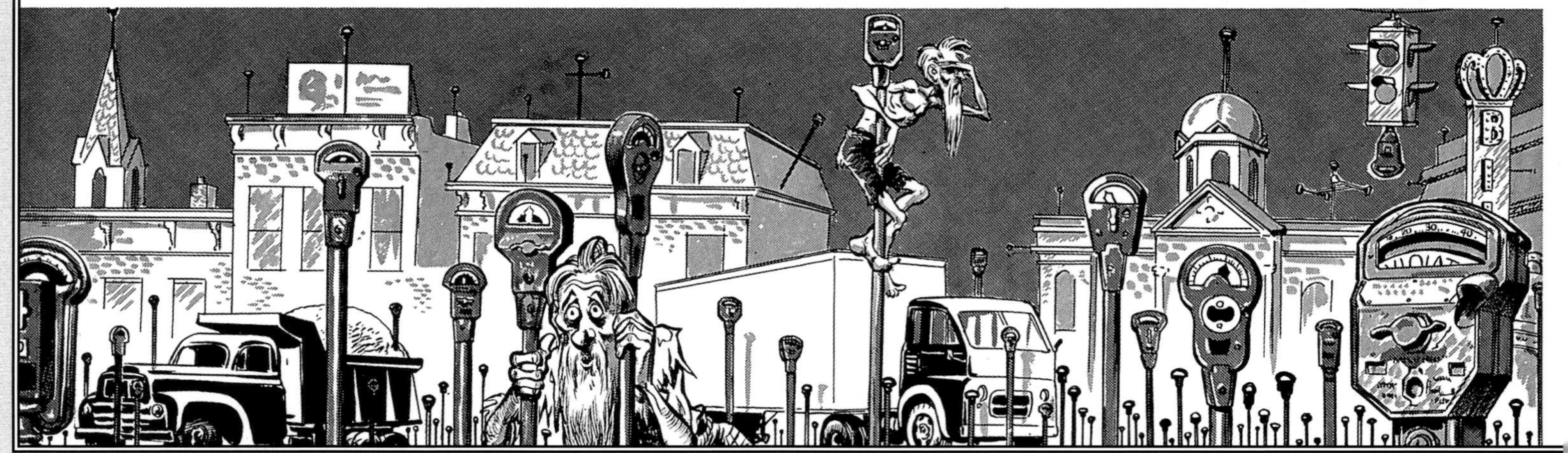

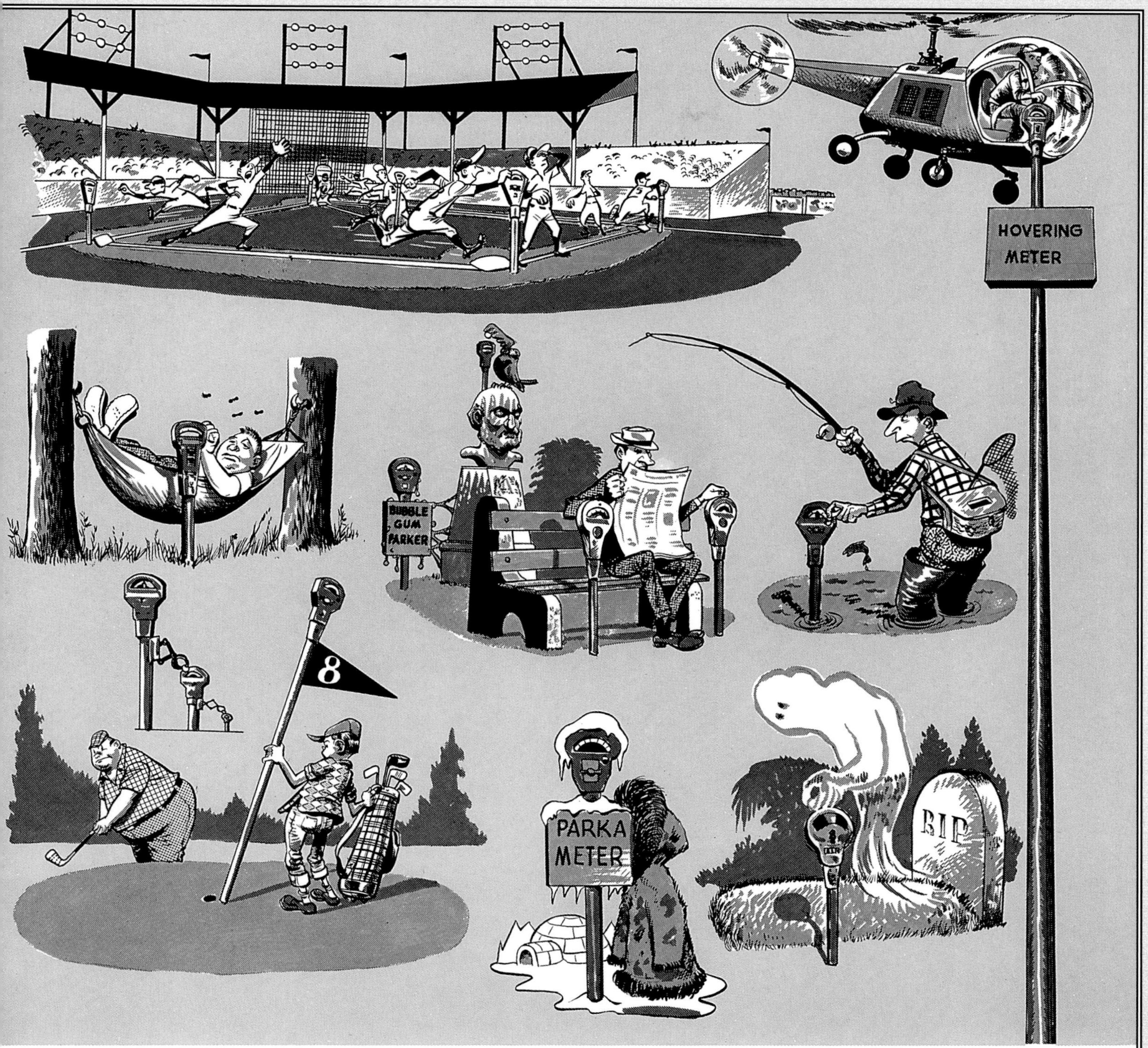
HOVERING
METER
BUBBLE
GUM
PARKER
8
PARKA
METER
RIP

There's only one solution, as we at MAD see it . . . the American male must give up driving the family car, and turn that chore over to the women. Given enough time, the menace will certainly be destroyed. **END**

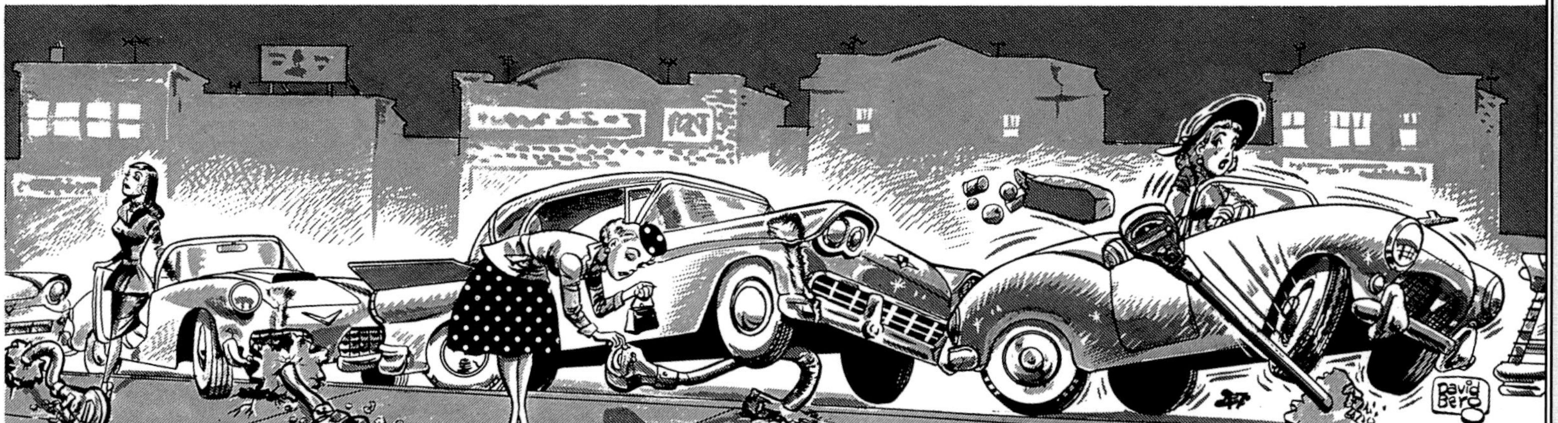
David
Berg

BERG'S-EYE VIEW DEPT.

The trouble with kids today is: they get the wrong conception of what life's all about. They think life is all play, and the world is just one big playground. We figure they get this idea from the very playgrounds they play in. Because today's playgrounds are built for fun, and they don't prepare kids for the miserable adult life they face. Therefore, we at MAD have designed the following playground equipment to prepare kids for adult life. Mainly, now they can be just as miserable as we adults are, suffering in . . .

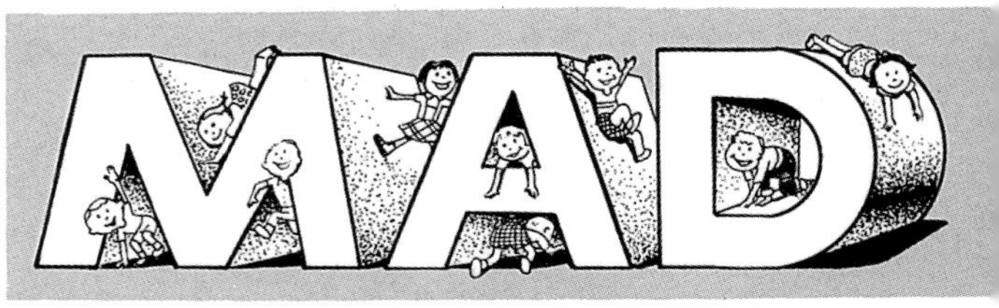
MAD

THAT PREPARE

THE SHOWY PYRAMID Teaches kids the art of "Social Climbing".

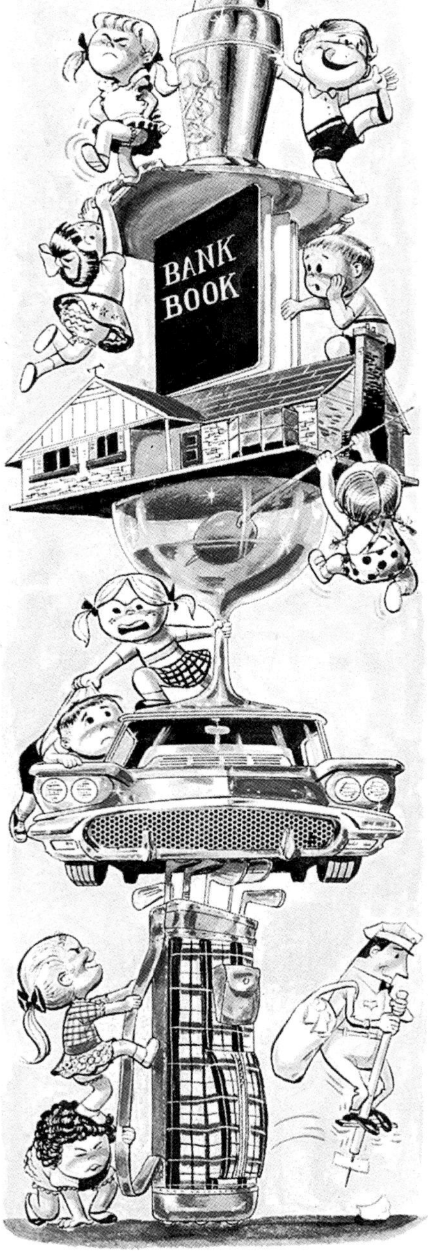
BANK
BOOK

THE SOCIALLY ACCEPTABLE MERRY-GO-ROUND Prepares kids to be good conformists.

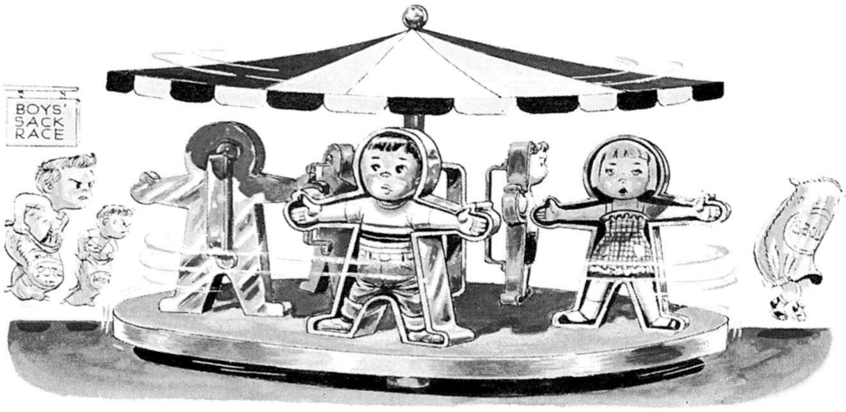
BOYS'
SACK
RACE

THE CONSTANTLY OUT-OF-REACH SWING Teaches kids to face life's frustrations.

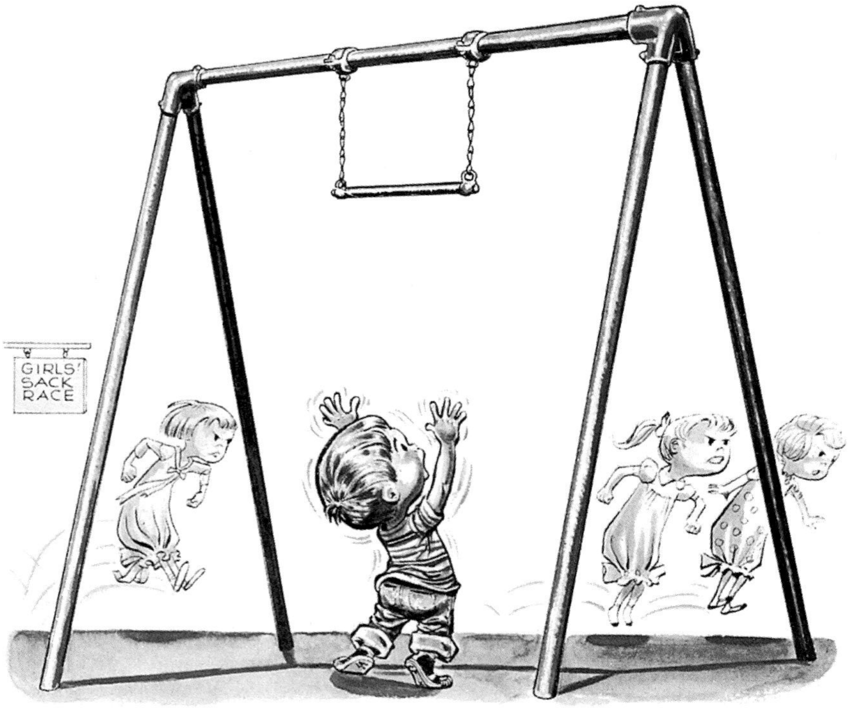
GIRLS'
SACK
RACE

PLAYGROUNDS
KIDS FOR ADULT LIFE

STORY AND ART—DAVID BERG

THE TANK OF SURVIVAL

Teaches kids how to keep their heads above water.

THE LADDERS OF IMPOSSIBILITY

Teaches kids how to get along without any visible means of support.

THE LADDER OF UNREALITY

Prepares kids for living way beyond their means.

THE BUSINESS TREADMILL

Trains kids for the old rat-race.

THE SOCIAL TREADMILL

Gets kids into condition for "keeping up with the Joneses".

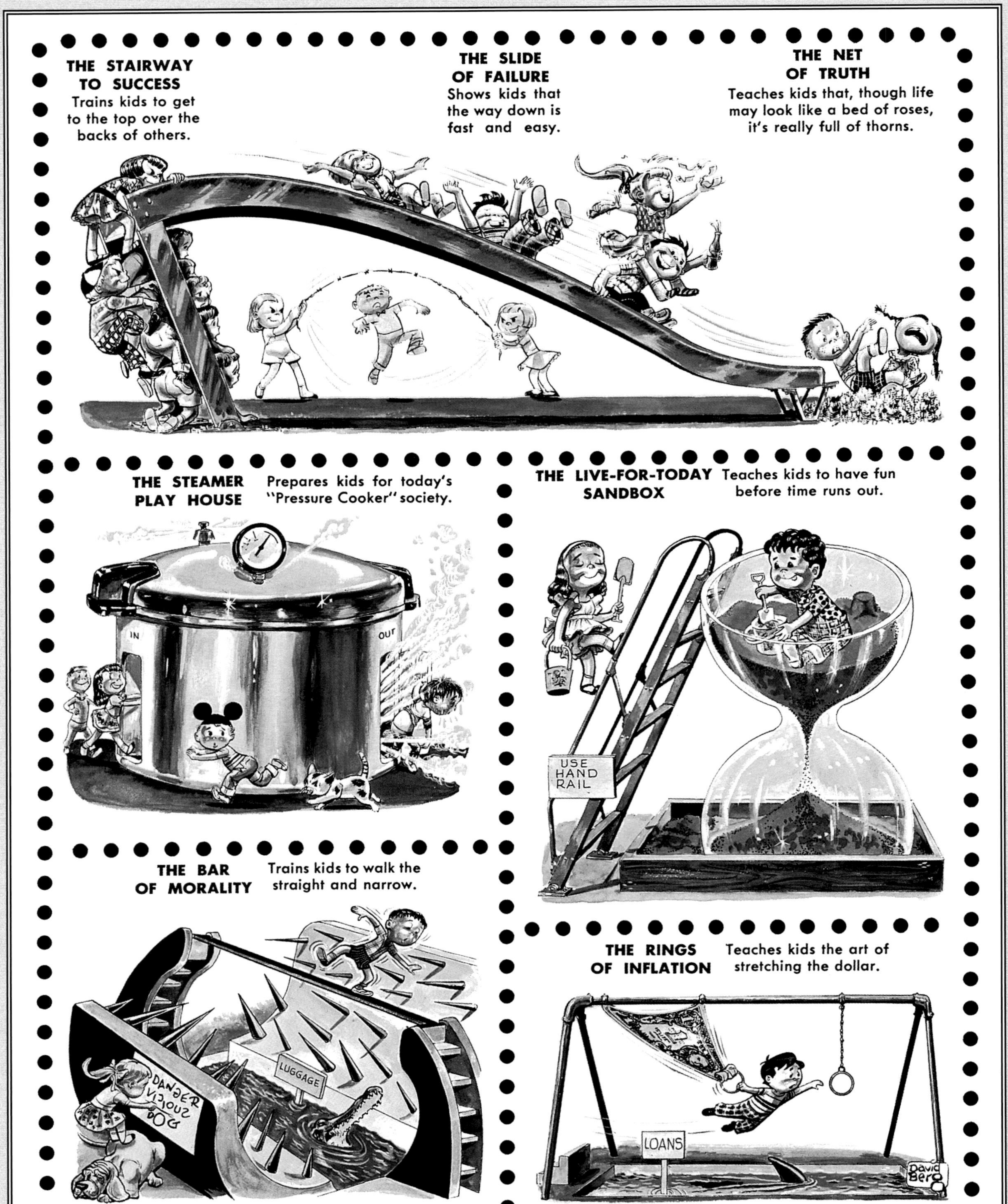
THE STAIRWAY TO SUCCESS
Trains kids to get to the top over the backs of others.
THE SLIDE OF FAILURE
Shows kids that the way down is fast and easy.
THE NET OF TRUTH
Teaches kids that, though life may look like a bed of roses, it's really full of thorns.
THE STEAMER PLAY HOUSE
Prepares kids for today's "Pressure Cooker" society.
IN
OUT
THE LIVE-FOR-TODAY SANDBOX
Teaches kids to have fun before time runs out.
USE HAND RAIL
THE BAR OF MORALITY
Trains kids to walk the straight and narrow.
LUGGAGE
THE RINGS OF INFLATION
Teaches kids the art of stretching the dollar.
LOANS
David Berg

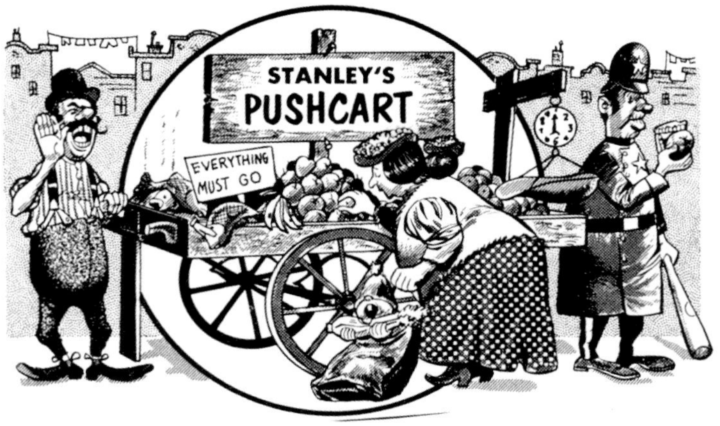
STANLEY'S
PUSHCART
EVERYTHING MUST GO

FOOD FOR THOUGHT DEPT.

In the beginning, man purchased meats, fruits, vegetables, and all the other things he needed to live by means of

PUSHCARTS

But man is creative and must progress, so he gathered up some "Pushcarts" under one roof, and called it a "Store."

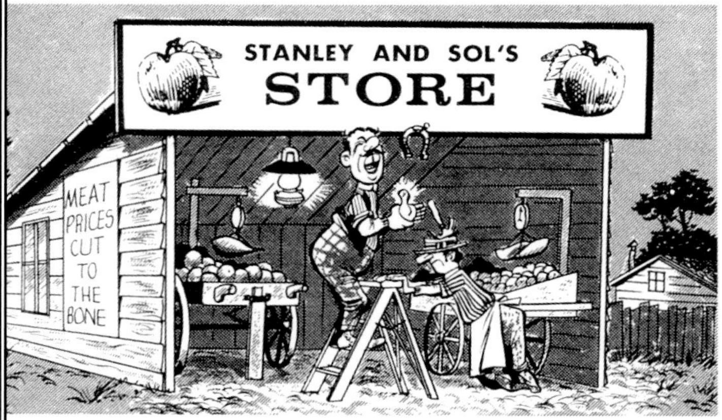
STANLEY AND SOL'S
STORE
MEAT PRICES CUT TO THE BONE

Then man progressed even further. He gathered up some of these "Stores" under one roof, and called it a "Market."

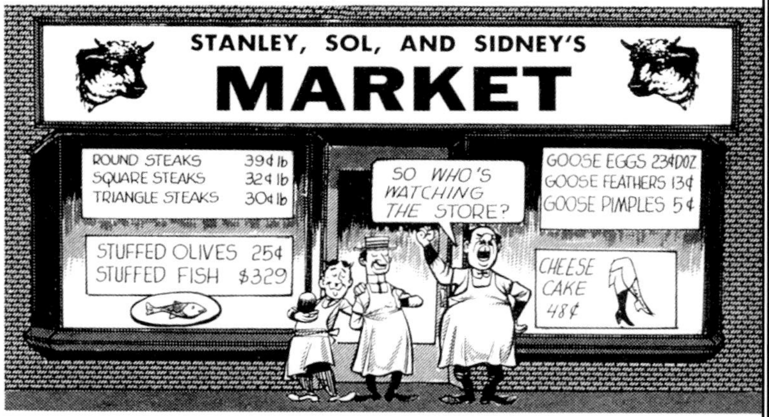
STANLEY, SOL, AND SIDNEY'S
MARKET
ROUND STEAKS 39¢ lb
SQUARE STEAKS 32¢ lb
TRIANGLE STEAKS 30¢ lb
SO WHO'S WATCHING THE STORE?
GOOSE EGGS 23¢ DOZ
GOOSE FEATHERS 13¢
GOOSE PIMPLES 5¢
STUFFED OLIVES 25¢
STUFFED FISH $3.29
CHEESE CAKE 48¢

And still man wasn't satisfied. So he gathered up some of these "Markets" under one big roof, equipped the monster with glass-and-chrome, scientifically-calculated displays, electric-eye door-openers, conveyor belts, cash registers that add, divide and subtract your money, surrounded the place with a parking lot, and called it a "Super Market."

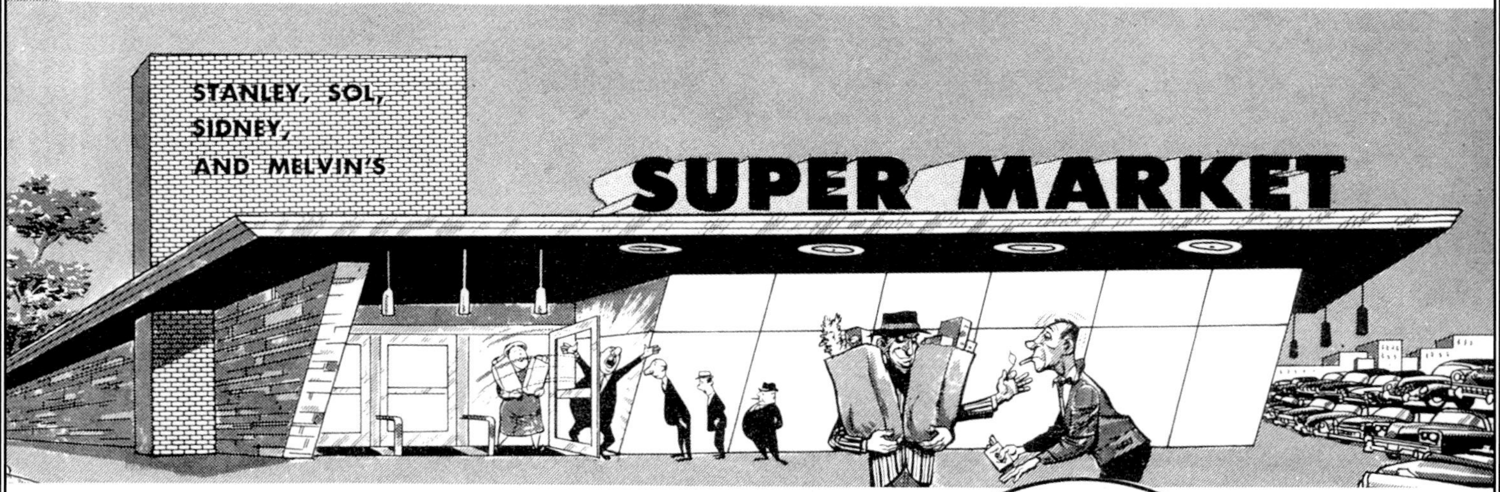
STANLEY, SOL, SIDNEY, AND MELVIN'S
SUPER MARKET

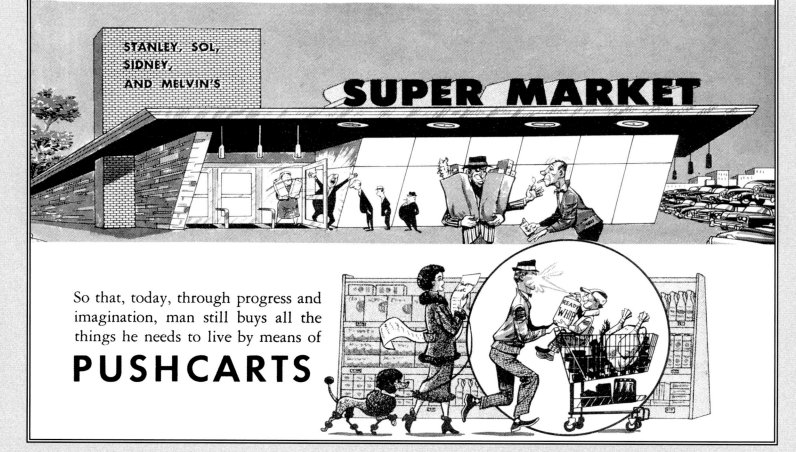

So that, today, through progress and imagination, man still buys all the things he needs to live by means of

PUSHCARTS

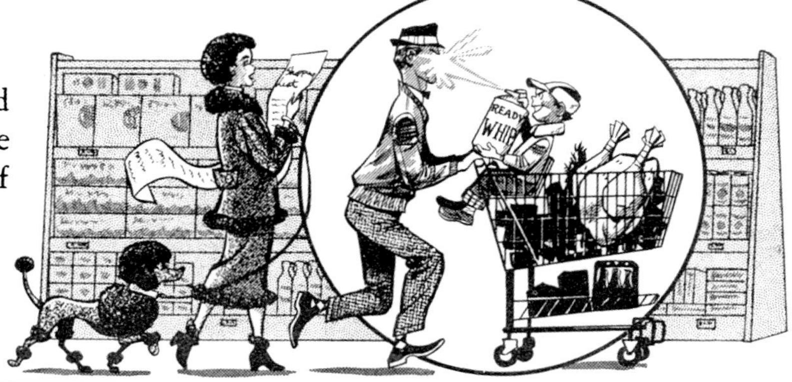
READY WHIP

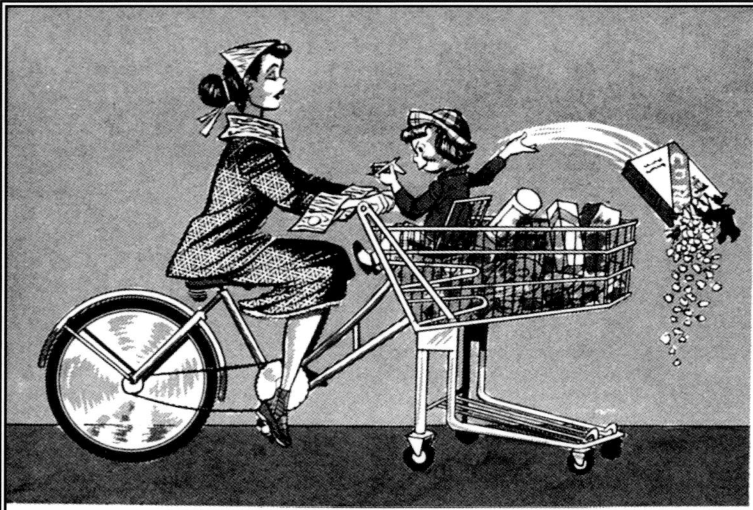

But man's creative genius and desire to progress won't stop there. "Pushcarts" will develop into "Cyclecarts" . . .

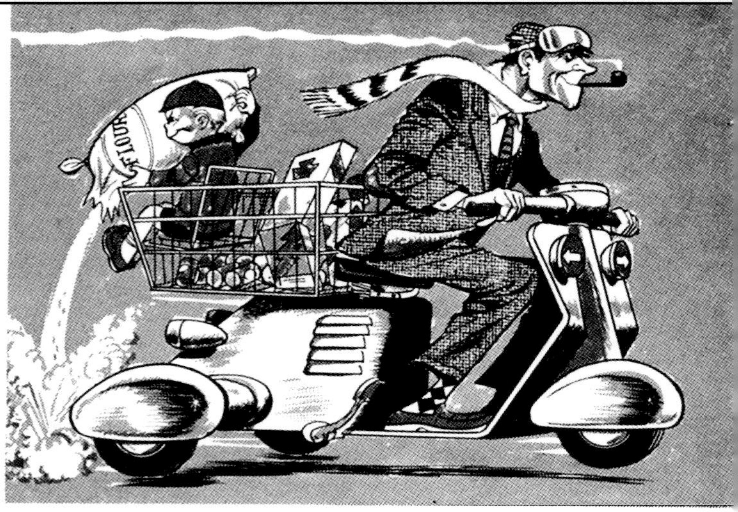

And eventually, man's inventiveness will finally develop the ultimate in shopping convenience . . . the "Motorcart."

Their aisles will stretch for miles, like super highways, signals, speed limits, police patrol units, and all the

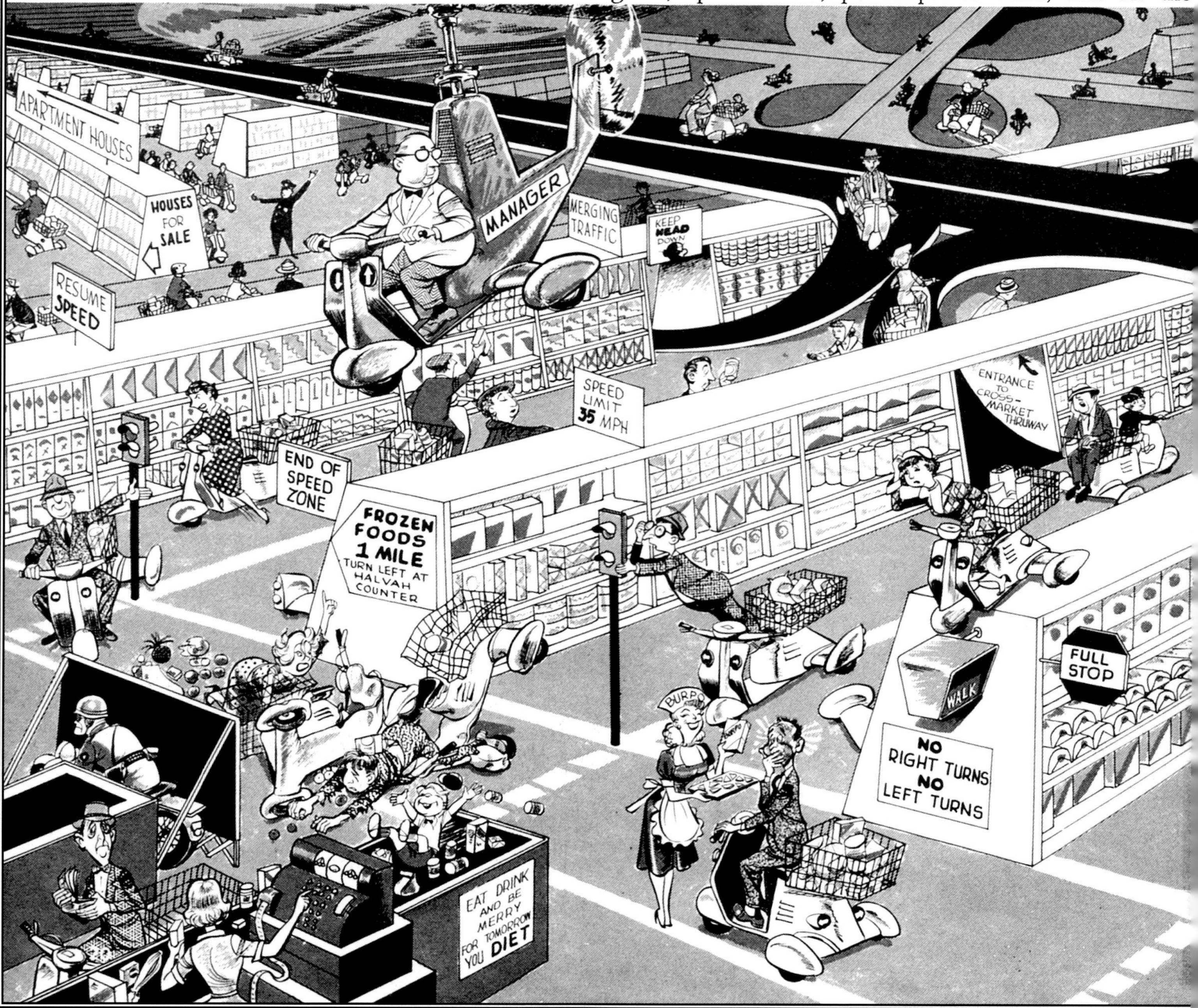
APARTMENT HOUSES
HOUSES FOR SALE
RESUME SPEED
MANAGER
MERGING TRAFFIC
KEEP HEAD DOWN
SPEED LIMIT 35 MPH
END OF SPEED ZONE
FROZEN FOODS 1 MILE TURN LEFT AT HALVAH COUNTER
ENTRANCE TO CROSS-MARKET THRUWAY
FULL STOP
WALK
NO RIGHT TURNS NO LEFT TURNS
BURPO
EAT DRINK AND BE MERRY FOR TOMORROW YOU DIET

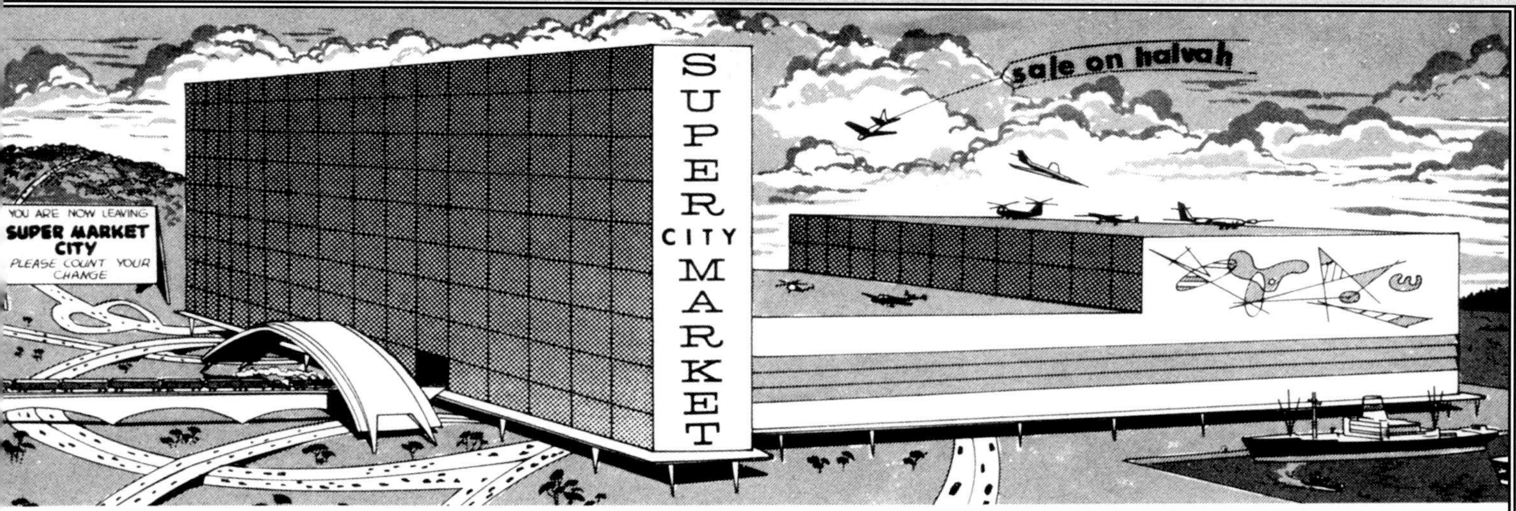
YOU ARE NOW LEAVING
SUPER MARKET CITY
PLEASE COUNT YOUR CHANGE
SUPER CITY MARKET
sale on halvah

This great step, this added mobility to man's purchasing power will open up vast new horizons of progress. "Super-Markets" will spread out over huge tracts of land They will grow so large, they'll become cities in themselves.

vith clover-leaf intersections, full-stop signs, traffic
ɔther regulations modern motorists are now plagued with.

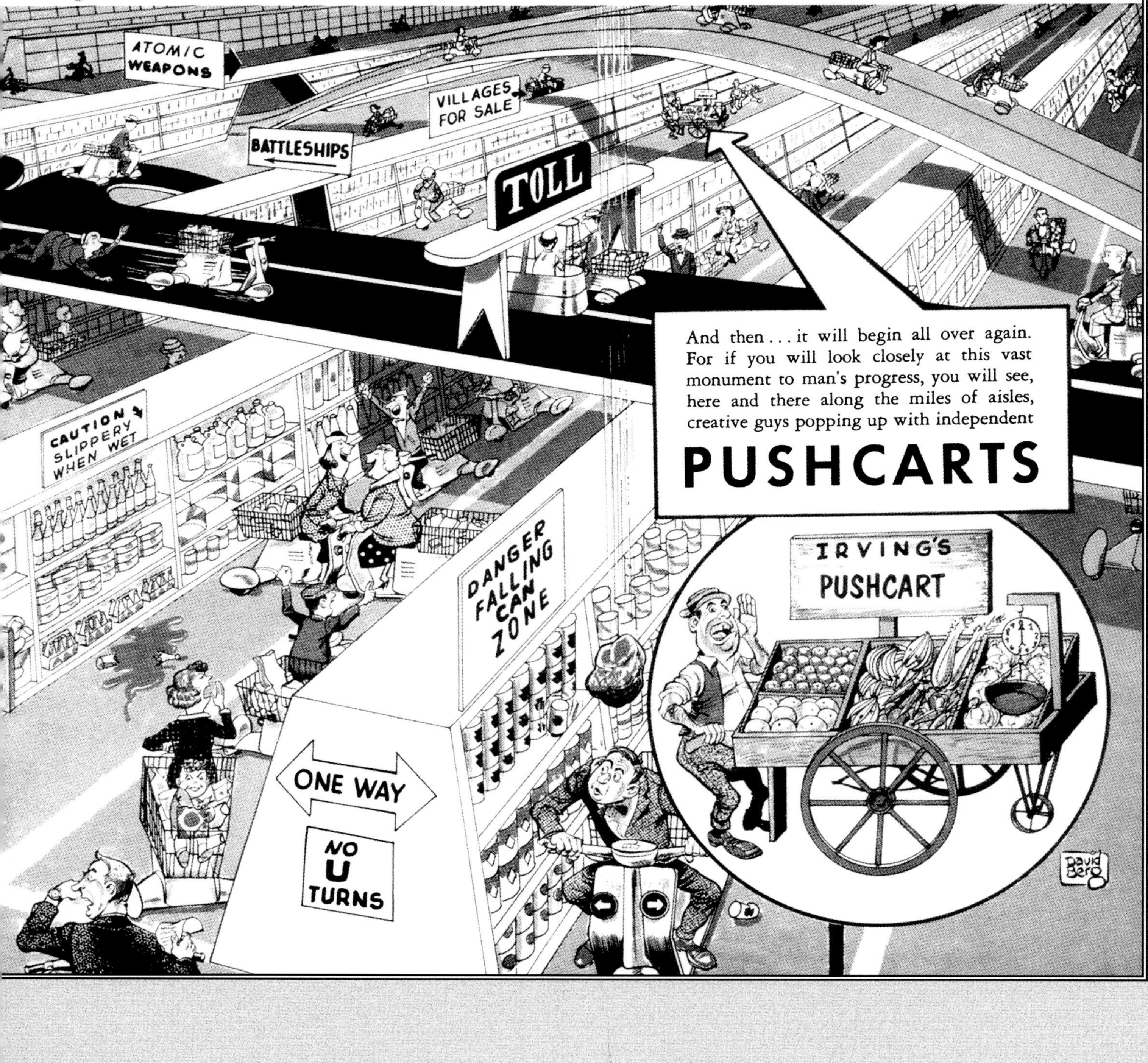
ATOMIC WEAPONS
VILLAGES FOR SALE
BATTLESHIPS
TOLL
And then . . . it will begin all over again. For if you will look closely at this vast monument to man's progress, you will see, here and there along the miles of aisles, creative guys popping up with independent
PUSHCARTS
CAUTION SLIPPERY WHEN WET
DANGER FALLING CAN ZONE
IRVING'S PUSHCART
ONE WAY
NO U TURNS
David Berg

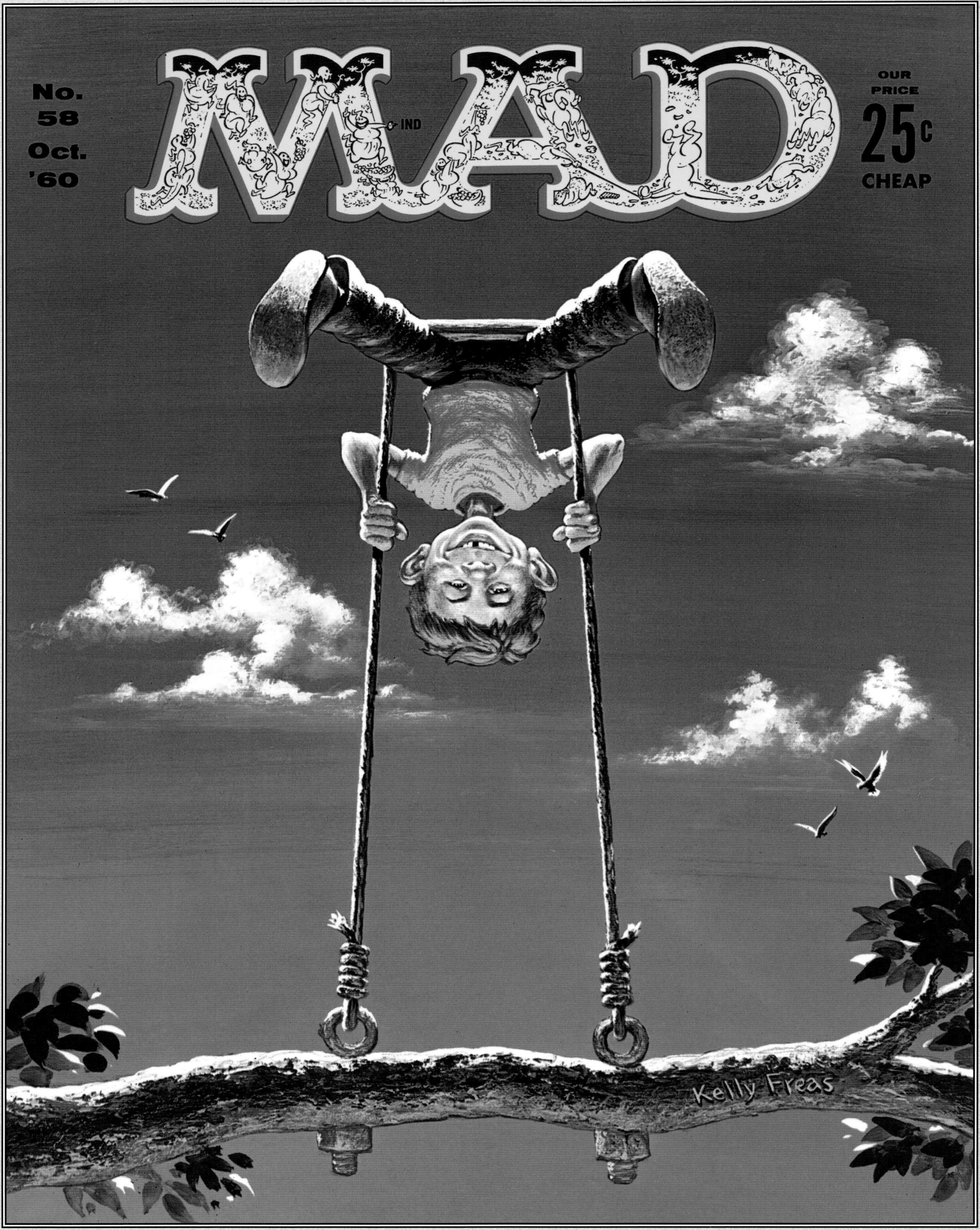
No.
58
Oct.
'60
MAD
IND
OUR
PRICE
25¢
CHEAP
Kelly Freas

Cover idea by Dave Berg, illustrated by Kelly Freas

The 1960s

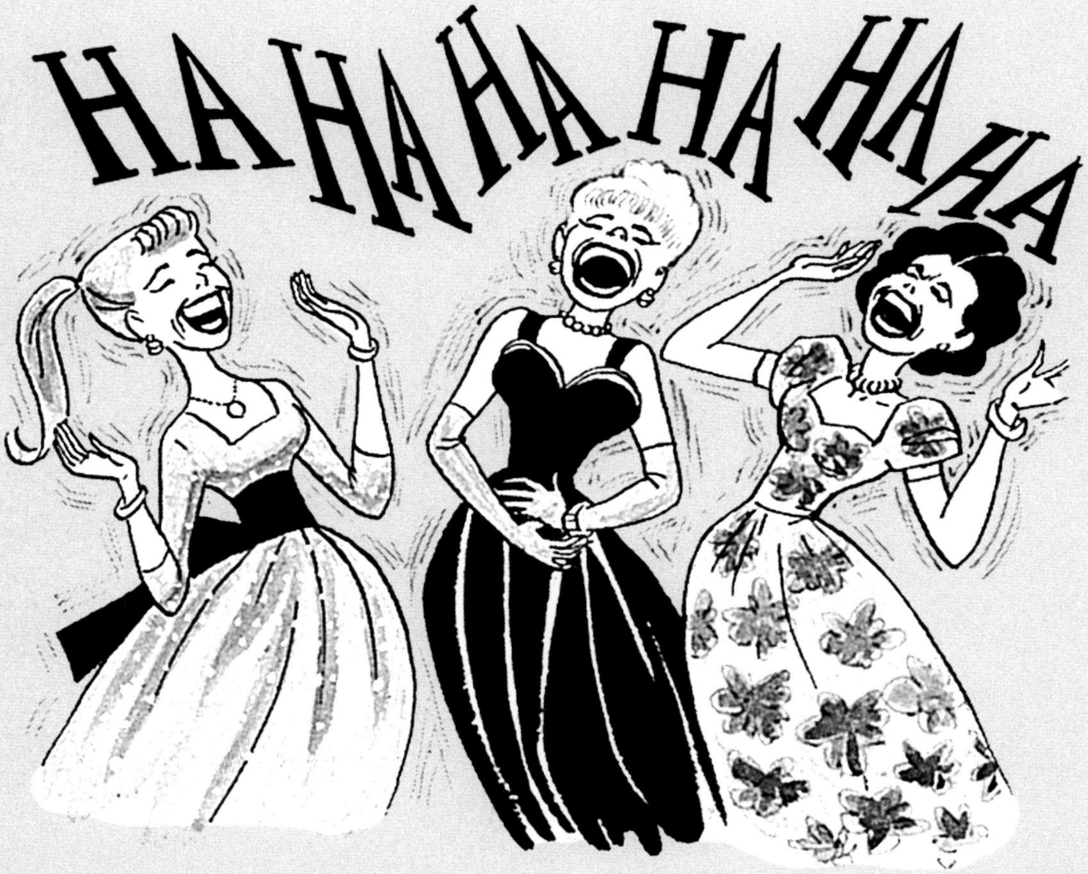
HA HA HA HA HA HA HA HA

BERG'S-EYE VIEW DEPT.

ANCIENT HISTORY TELLS US THAT ROME BECAME THE MOST POWERFUL EMPIRE IN THE CIVILIZED WORLD. AND THEN THE ROMANS STOPPED WALKING, AND TOOK TO RIDING ABOUT IN CONVEYANCES.

INSTANT AMBROSIA
READY MIX NECTAR OF THE GODS

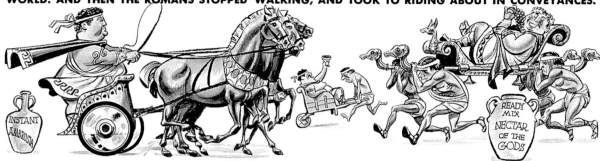

TODAY, THE UNITED STATES HAS BECOME THE MOST POWERFUL NATION IN THE CIVILIZED WORLD. AND LIKE THE ROMANS, WE ARE BECOMING SELF-INDULGENT.

AMERICA IS

SUPER MARKET
Shopping List
1 loaf of bread
1 jug of wine
and thou

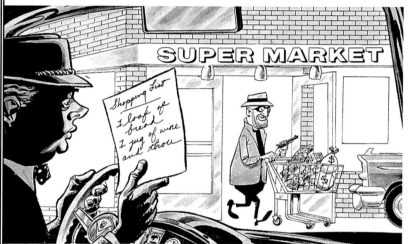

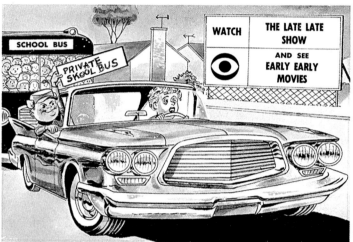

In the old days, when we needed something at the grocer's we walked. Today, we drive to the supermarket in our cars.

SCHOOL BUS
PRIVATE SKOOL BUS
WATCH
THE LATE LATE SHOW
AND SEE
EARLY EARLY MOVIES

Our kids don't even walk to school any more. A bus picks them up at the corner, or Mom drives them the two blocks.

LITTLE BY LITTLE, CONVEYANCES ARE

There was a time when the average, inactive businessman got his exercise out on the golf course, walking around the 18 holes. Today, he rides around in a "Golfmobile".

THE GOLFMOBILE WITH THE FRINGE ON TOP FOR THE GOLFER WITH THE FRINGE ON TOP

The necessity of walking is being eliminated from other sports, too. F'rinstance, skiing. A skier once got good exercise climbing them ski hills. Now, he uses ski lifts.

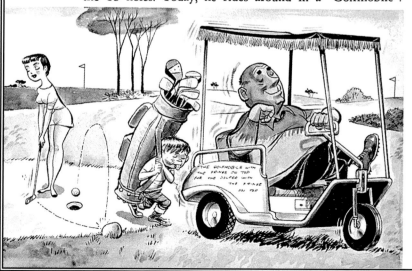

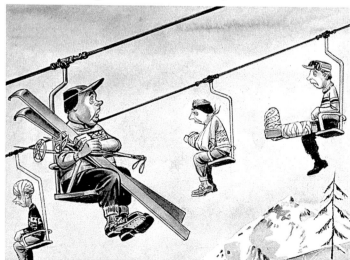

AS A RESULT OF SELF-INDULGENCES SUCH AS THIS, THE ROMANS BECAME SOFT AND FAT. AND SO THEY WERE EASY PUSH-OVERS FOR THE LEAN AND HUNGRY BARBARIAN INVADERS FROM THE NORTH.

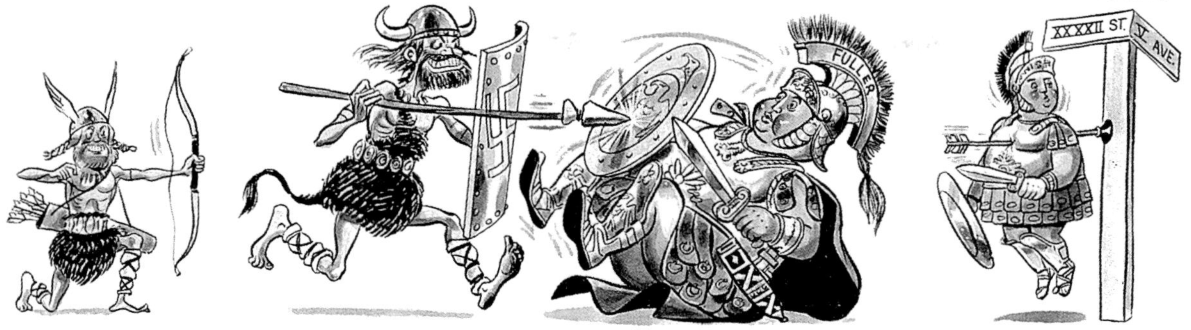
XXXII ST.
FULLER

F'RINSTANCE, LITTLE BY LITTLE, WE HAVE STOPPED WALKING, AND TAKEN TO RIDING ABOUT IN CONVEYANCES. AND SO, AS A RESULT, MAD FEELS THAT . . .

GETTING SOFT

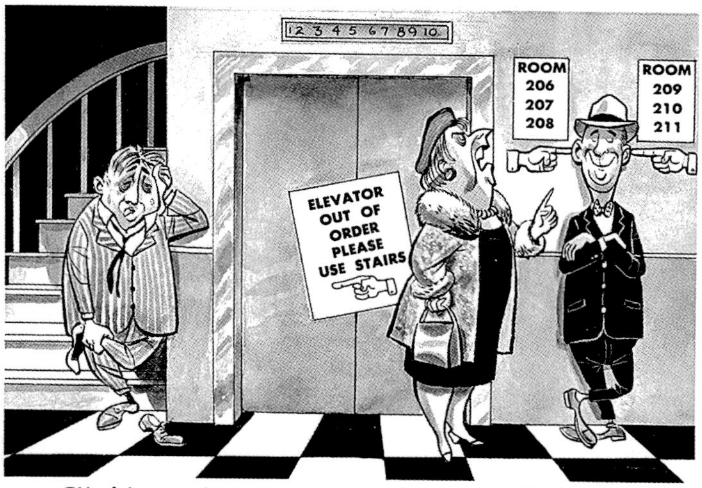
1 2 3 4 5 6 7 8 9 10
ROOM 206 207 208
ROOM 209 210 211
ELEVATOR OUT OF ORDER PLEASE USE STAIRS

Climbing stairs was once good exercise. Today, the only stair-climbing we do is when the elevator's out of order.

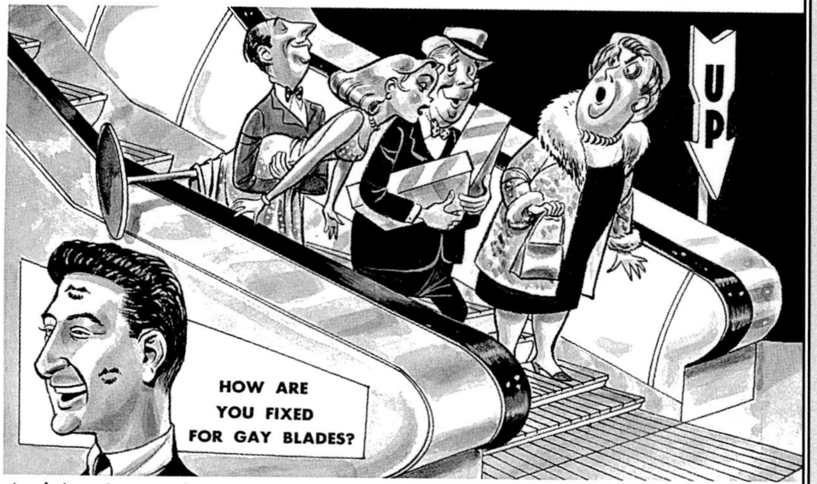
UP
HOW ARE YOU FIXED FOR GAY BLADES?

And in places where elevators would make no sense, like a two-story building, we've replaced stairs with escalators.

ELIMINATING THE NEED FOR WALKING

The inactive man also used to get exercise pushing a lawn mower. Today, the gadget is mechanized. Now, he sits at a desk all week, and sits at the lawn mower on the weekend.

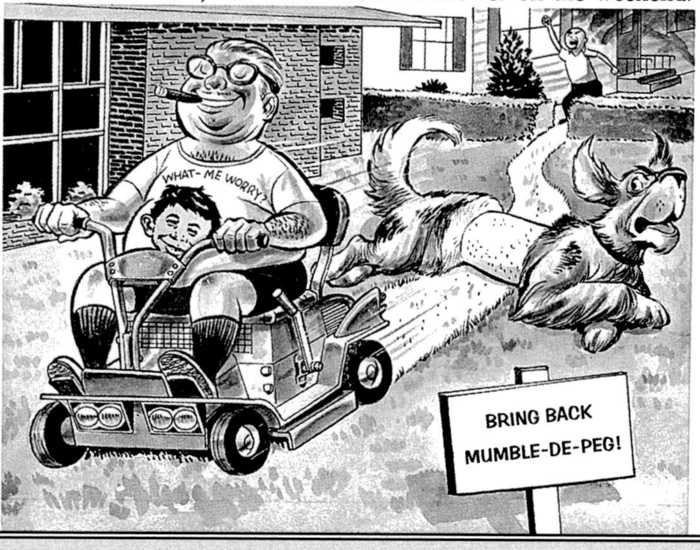
WHAT—ME WORRY?
BRING BACK MUMBLE-DE-PEG!

Recently, the greatest threat of all, mainly the one that threatens to eliminate walking entirely, made its appearance. THE MOTOR SCOOTER! To see its effect, turn page:

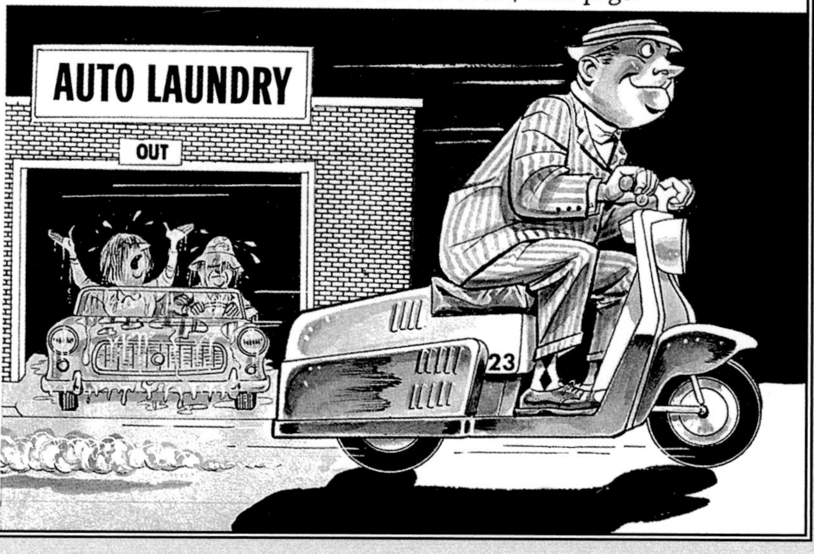
AUTO LAUNDRY
OUT
23

THE MOTOR SCOOTER WILL

IN OUR SPORTS

BASEBALL

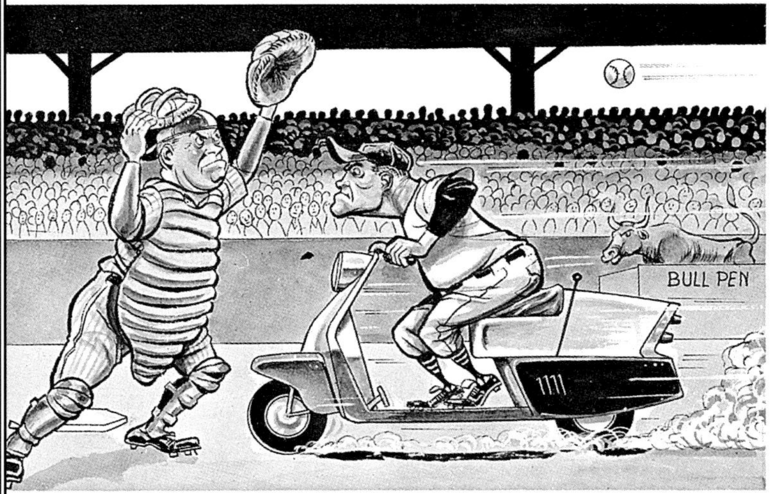
BULL PEN

America's National Pastime will take to wheels as crowds cheer a new version of the home run . . . the "home drive".

FOOTBALL

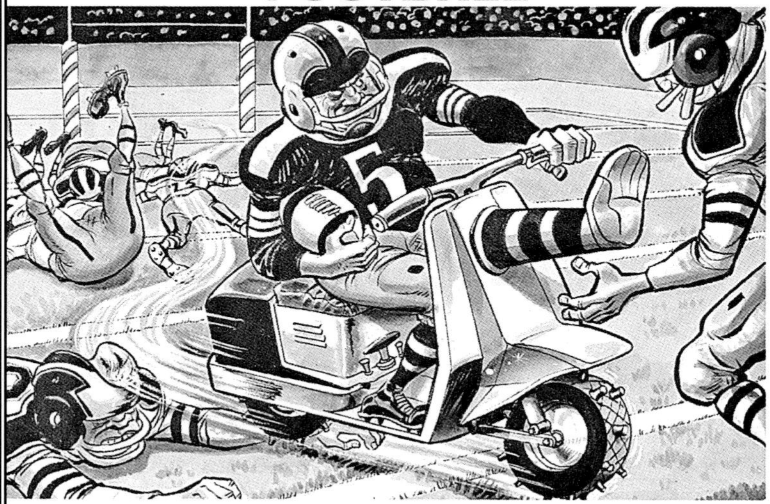

Our exciting Fall spectacles will feature a new gridiron star, the Quarterback affectionately called "snake axles".

BASKETBALL

College and Professional Coaches will search the country for men who can shoot baskets while driving tall scooters.

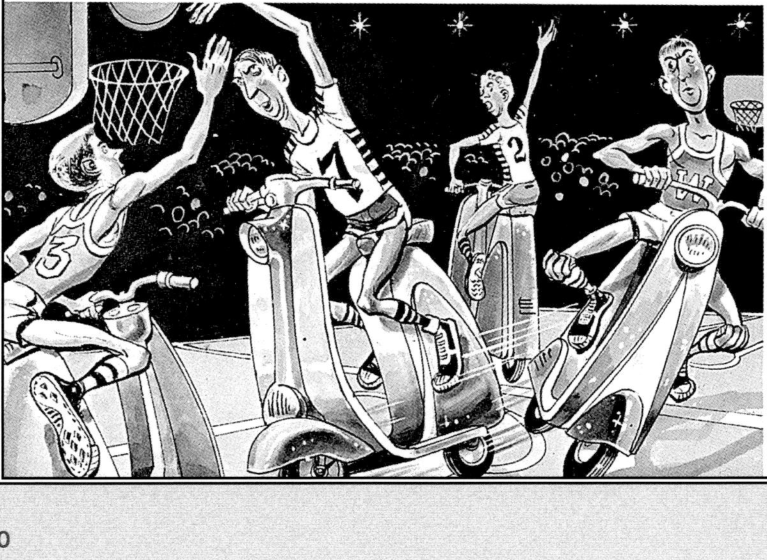

IN OUR

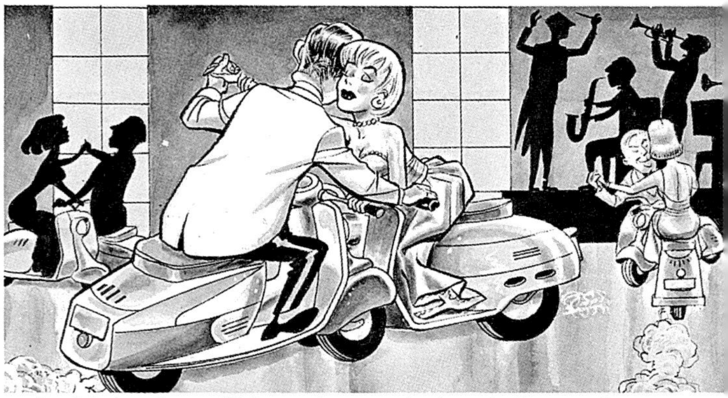

Social dancing will have the new look as ballrooms become death traps for couples who aren't light on their wheels.

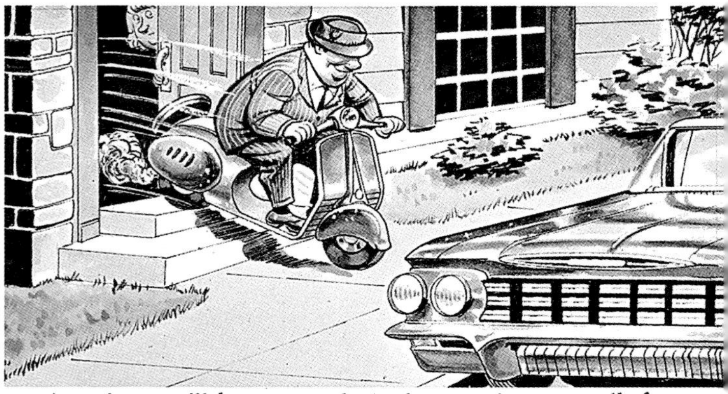

Americans will become so lazy, they won't even walk from the front door to the garage for the car; they'll scooter.

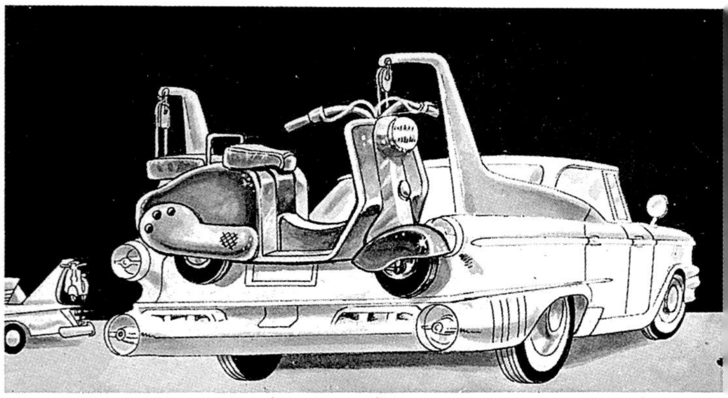

Motor scooters will be carried everywhere, hanging from the back of the family car like a dinghy on a motor yacht.

And as infants grow up in this lazy, self-indulgent world, they'll be taught to scooter instead of learning to walk.

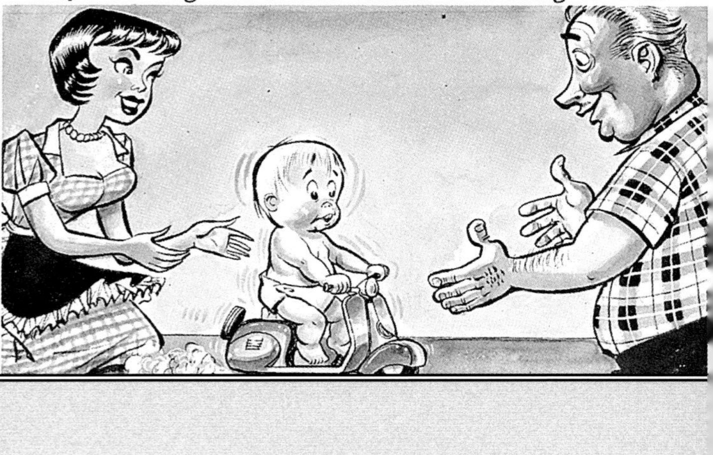

ELIMINATE ALL LEG-WORK

"Have you anything to say before I pronounce sentence on you?

DAILY LIVES

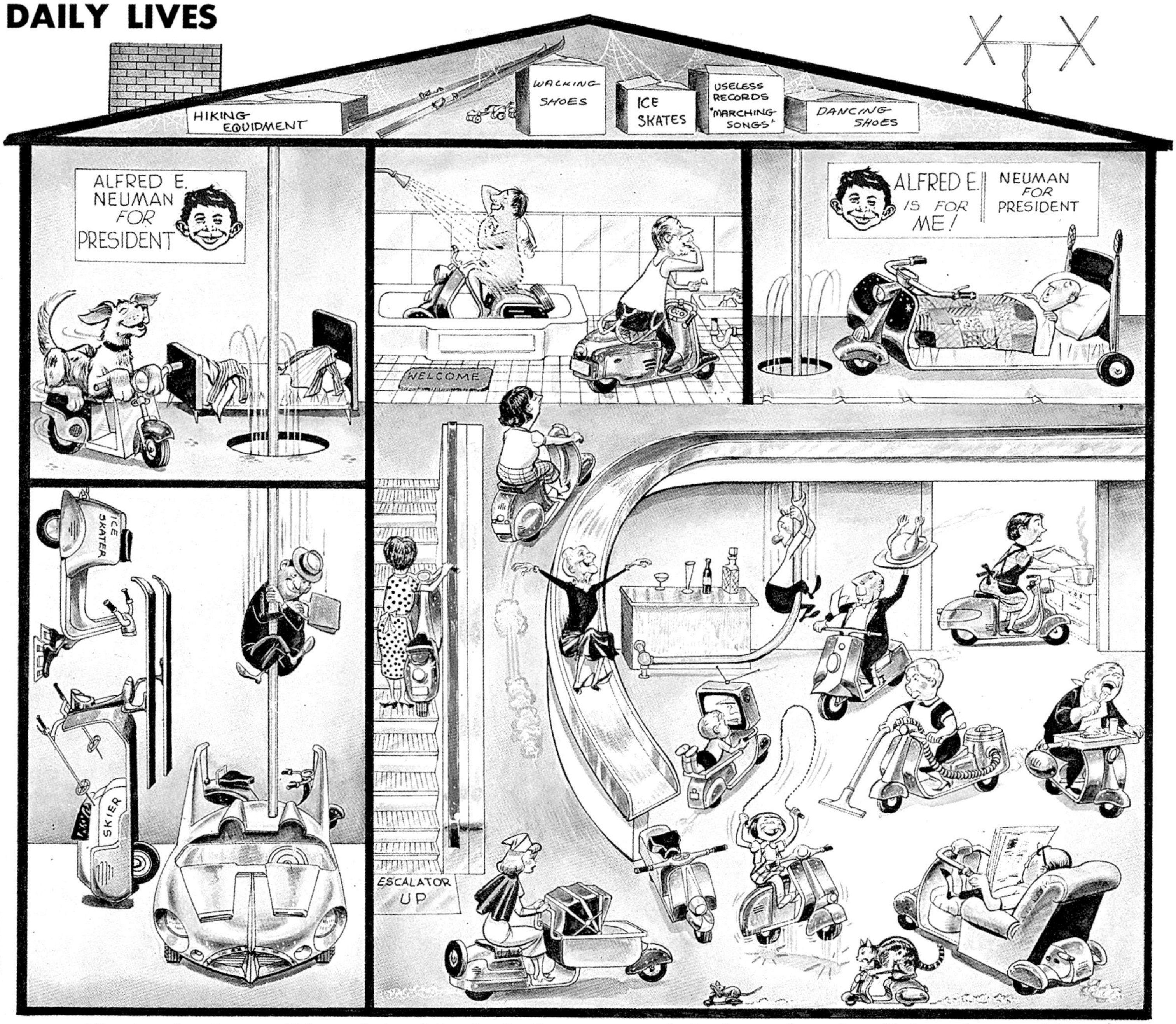
HIKING EQUIPMENT
WALKING SHOES
ICE SKATES
USELESS RECORDS "MARCHING SONGS"
DANCING SHOES
ALFRED E. NEUMAN FOR PRESIDENT
ALFRED E. IS FOR ME!
NEUMAN FOR PRESIDENT
WELCOME
ICE SKATER
SKIER
ESCALATOR UP

The American home will be re-designed for the family on wheels. The patter of little feet will no longer be heard around the house. Instead, we'll hear the screeching of brakes and the clatter of engines as walking disappears.

In time, our legs will become vestigial organs, and we'll end up soft and fat, looking like round-bottom toy dolls.

And round-bottom toy dolls, like the Romans, will be easy push-overs for the lean, hungry barbarians from the East.

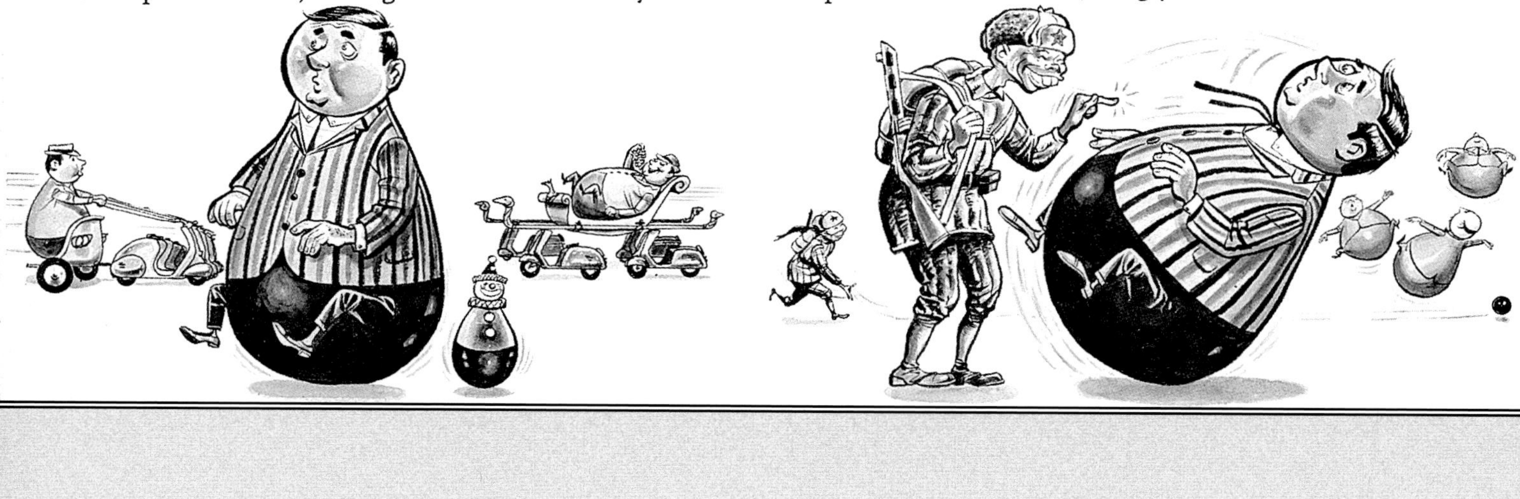

INSIDE-OUCH DEPT.

Today, huge companies spend millions of dollars in advertising and public relations to maintain a "Corporate Image". However, a company's "Corporate Image" isn't always a true picture of what goes on . . . as you'll discover when the Editors bring you

A MAD PEEK BEHIND

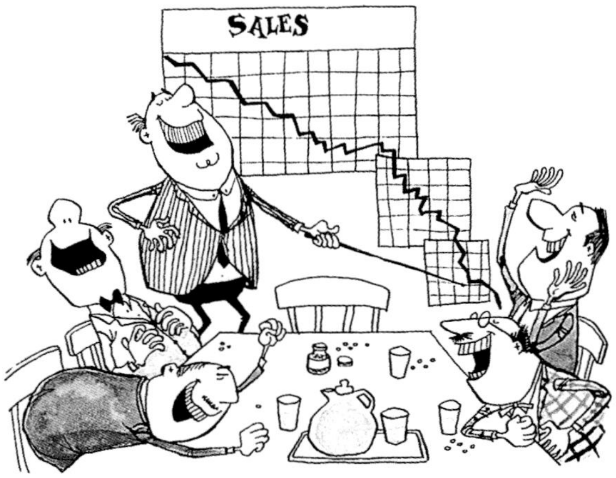
SALES

BOARD MEETING AT THE "MILTOWN TRANQUILIZER" COMPANY

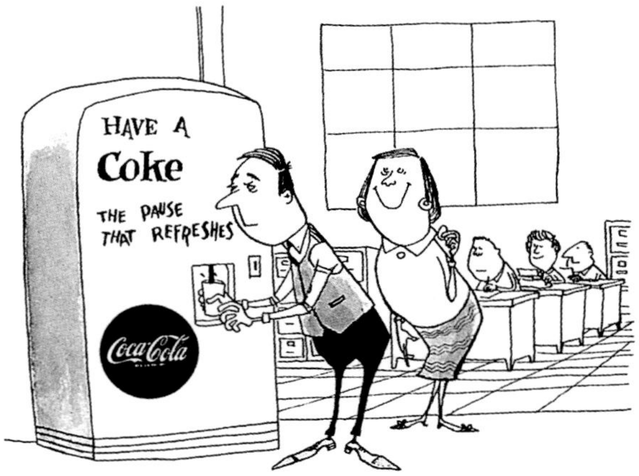
HAVE A
Coke
THE PAUSE THAT REFRESHES
Coca-Cola

THE MAIN OFFICE OF THE "PEPSI-COLA" COMPANY

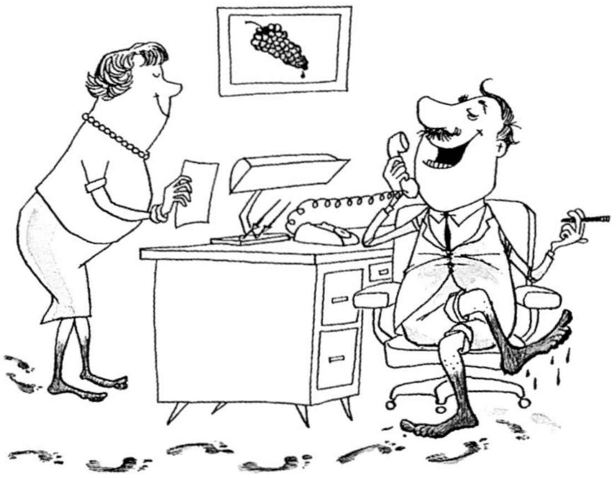

THE OFFICE OF "ITALIAN SWISS COLONY WINES"

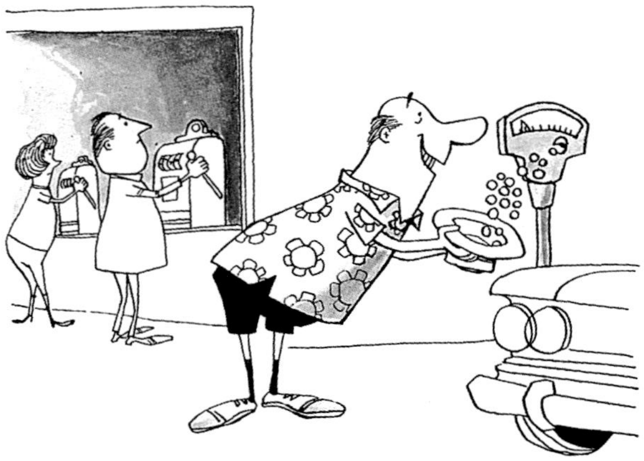

A LAS VEGAS PARKING LOT

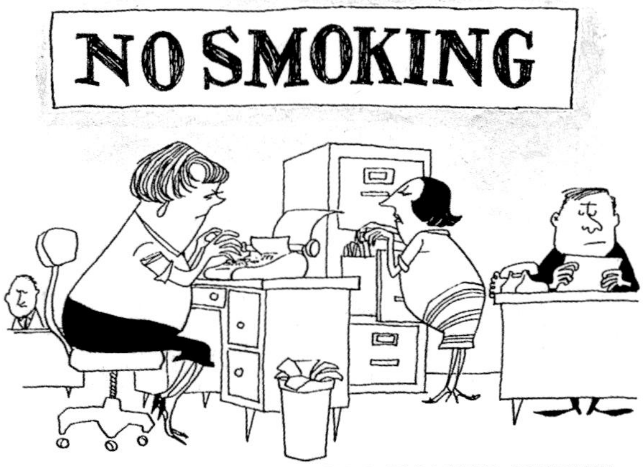
NO SMOKING

THE OFFICE OF THE "REYNOLDS TOBACCO" COMPANY

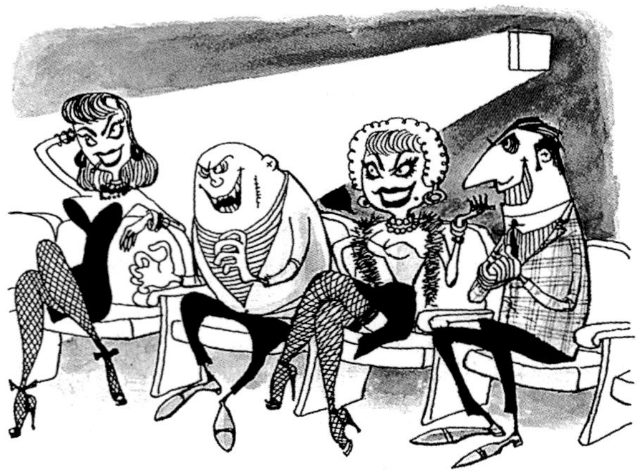

TODAY'S MOTION PICTURE CENSORSHIP BUREAU

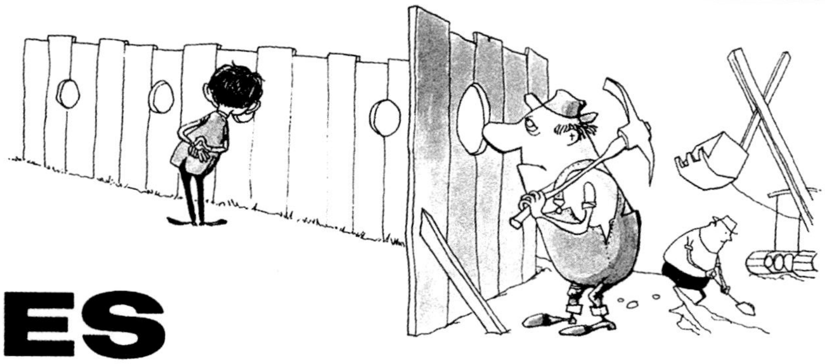

THE SCENES

WRITER & ARTIST: DAVID BERG

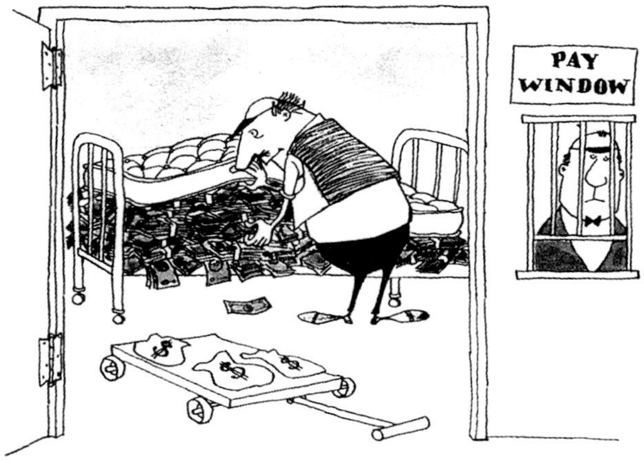
PAY
WINDOW

THE PAYROLL OFFICE AT THE "MOSLER SAFE" COMPANY

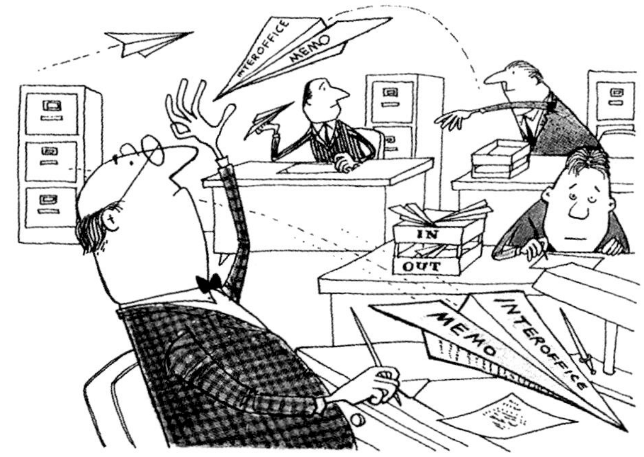
INTEROFFICE
MEMO
IN
OUT
MEMO
INTEROFFICE

THE OFFICE OF "PAN AMERICAN WORLD AIRWAYS"

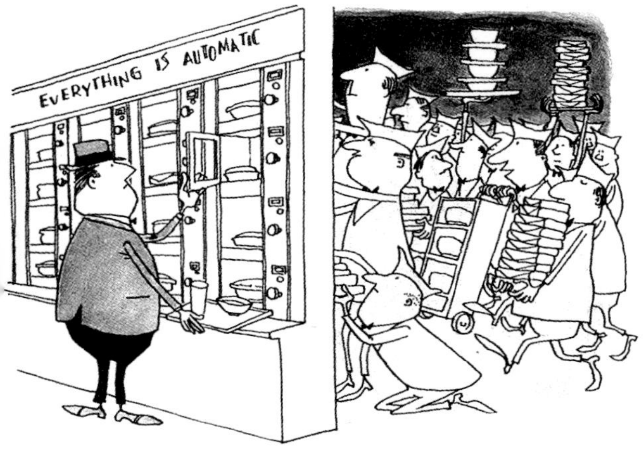
EVERYTHING IS AUTOMATIC

THE AUTOMAT

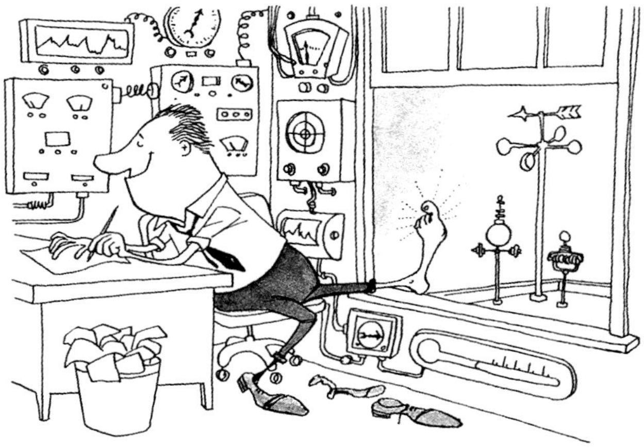

THE UNITED STATES WEATHER BUREAU

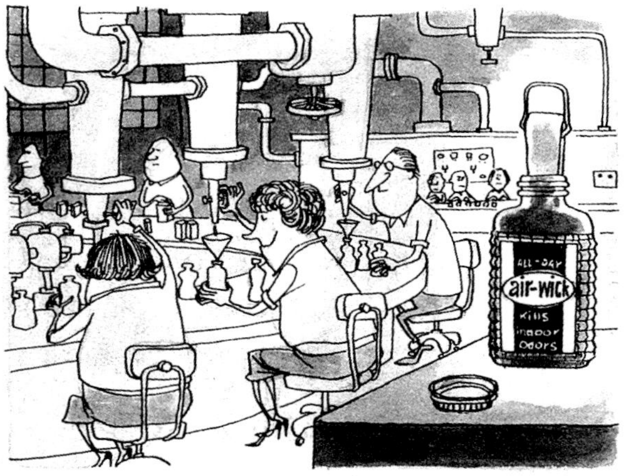
ALL-DAY
air-wick
KILLS
INDOOR
ODORS

THE "ARPEGE PERFUME" FACTORY

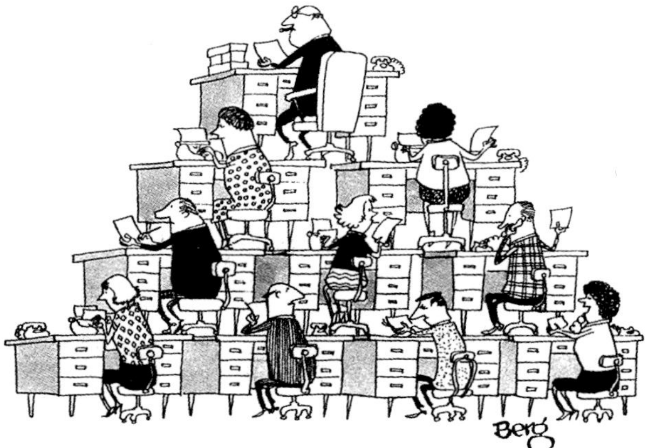
Berg

THE MAIN OFFICE OF THE "A & P"

A TONE FOR OUR SINS DEPT.

WRITER & ARTIST: DAVID BERG

We all take the telephone for granted . . . until we get the bill at the end of the month. That's when we realize a phone is something we keep paying for, but never get to own. Which is why AT & T tells us: "It's fun to phone!" It *is* fun—for *them!* All kidding aside, though, a phone can be a real convenience . . . if you're looking for a convenient way to go crazy! You'll see what we mean as the Editors present

A MAD LOOK AT

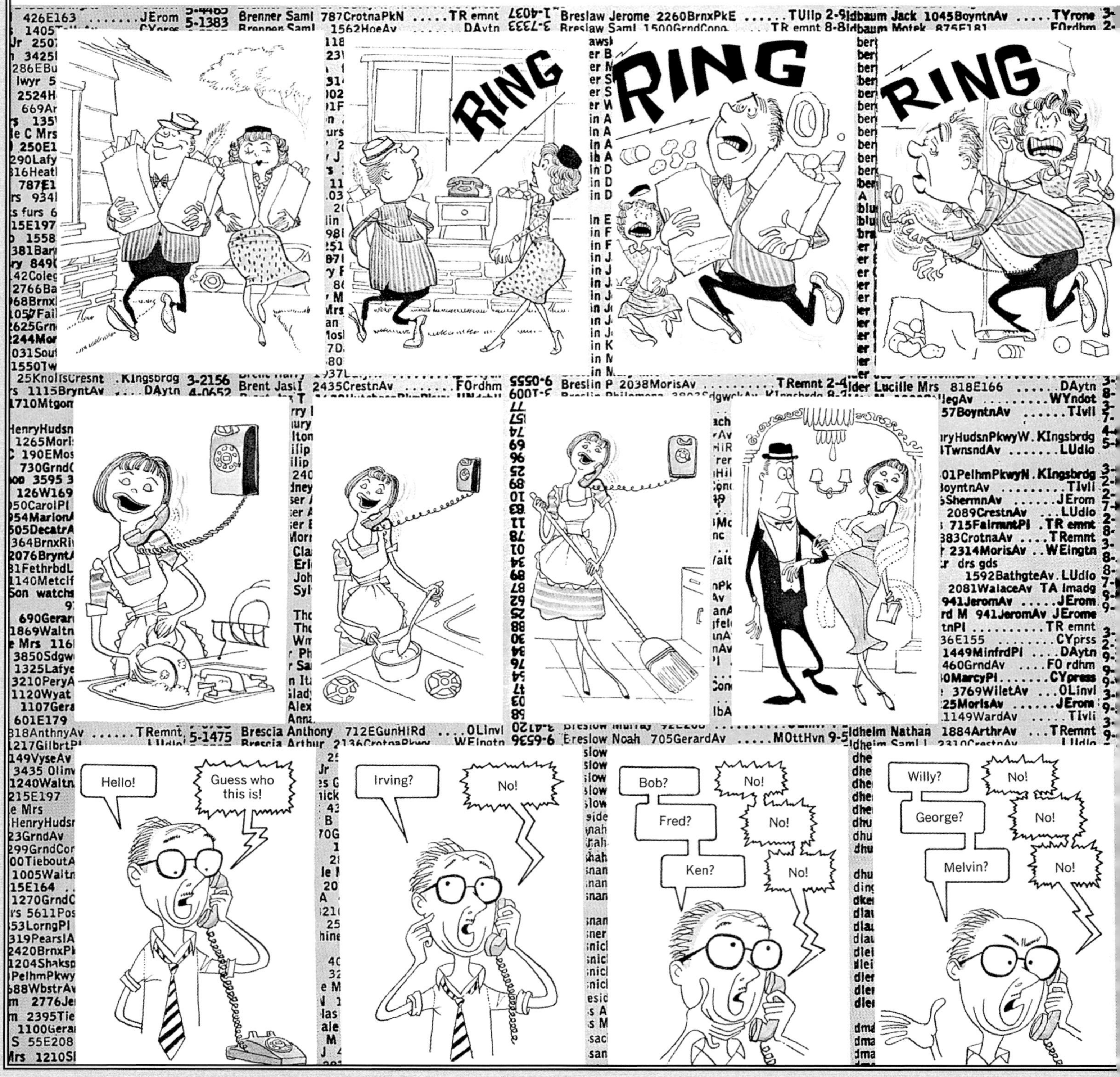
RING
RING
RING
Hello!
Guess who this is!
Irving?
No!
Bob?
No!
Fred?
No!
Ken?
No!
Willy?
No!
George?
No!
Melvin?
No!

This "MAD Look at" was the first by Dave using a format that two issues later would become "The Lighter Side of…"

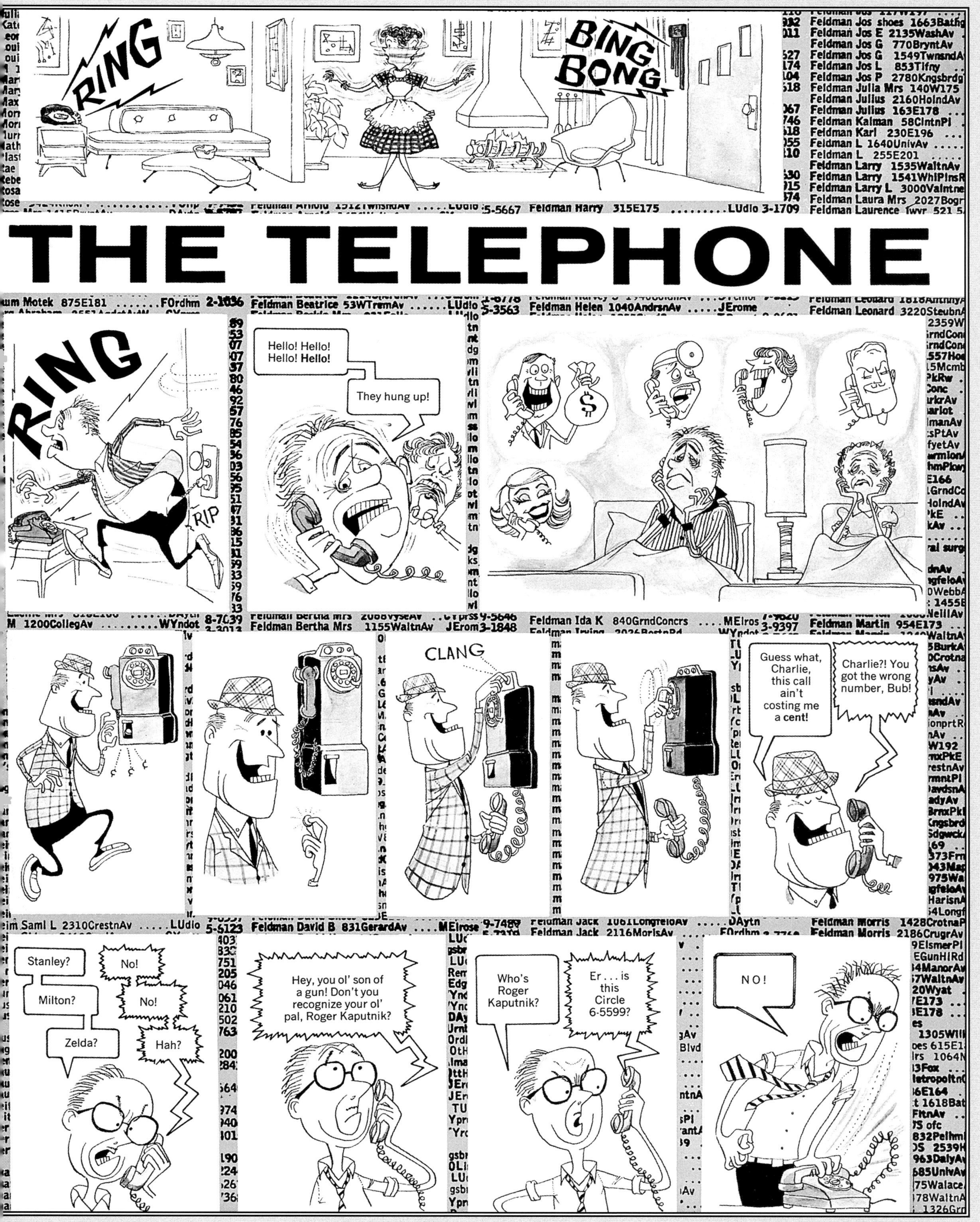
RING
BING BONG
THE TELEPHONE
RING
RIP
Hello! Hello! Hello! Hello!
They hung up!
CLANG
Guess what, Charlie, this call ain't costing me a cent!
Charlie?! You got the wrong number, Bub!
Stanley?
No!
Milton?
No!
Zelda?
Hah?
Hey, you ol' son of a gun! Don't you recognize your ol' pal, Roger Kaputnik?
Who's Roger Kaputnik?
Er . . . is this Circle 6-5599?
NO!

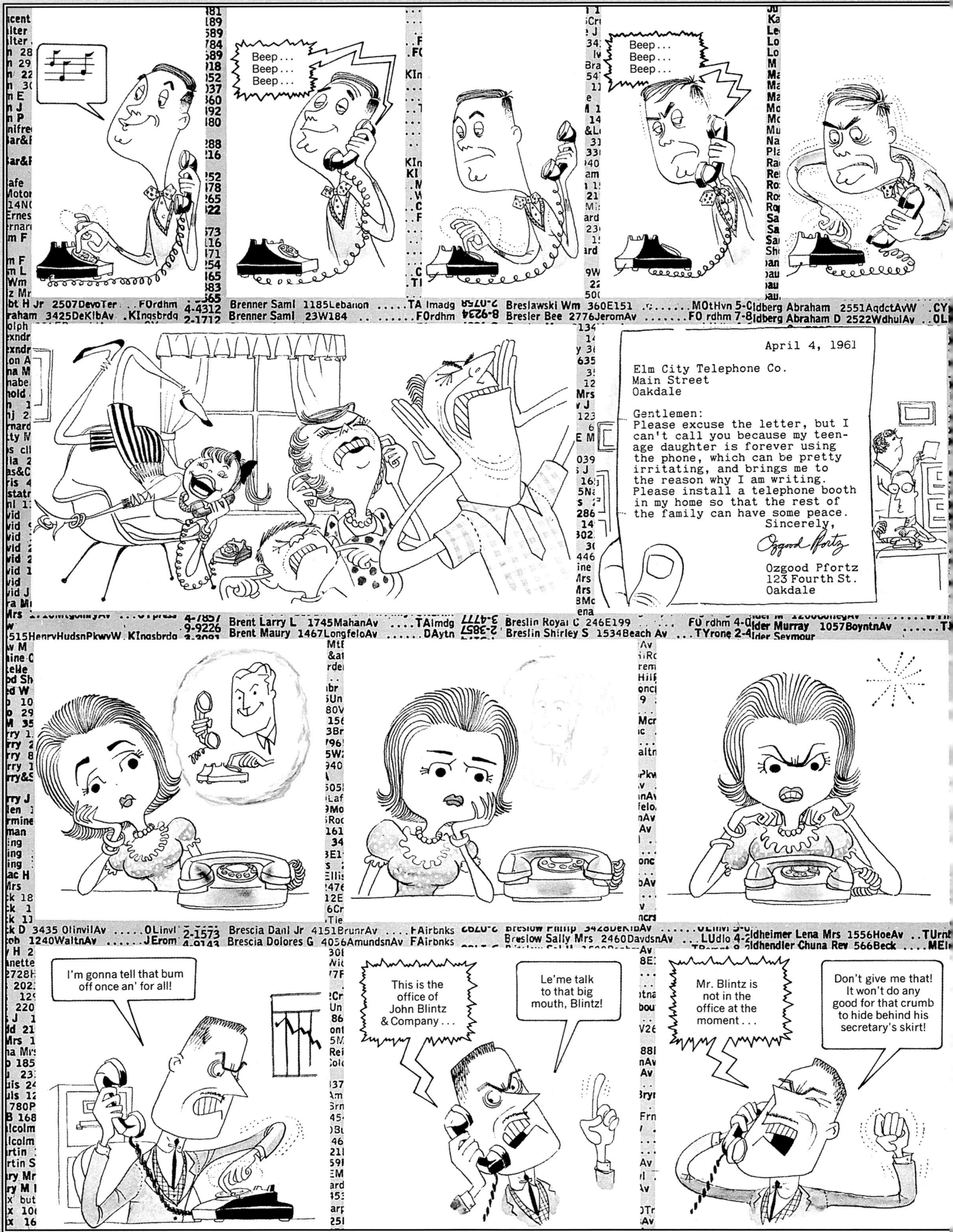
Beep . . .
Beep . . .
Beep . . .
Beep . . .
Beep . . .
Beep . . .
April 4, 1961
Elm City Telephone Co.
Main Street
Oakdale
Gentlemen:
Please excuse the letter, but I can't call you because my teen-age daughter is forever using the phone, which can be pretty irritating, and brings me to the reason why I am writing. Please install a telephone booth in my home so that the rest of the family can have some peace.
Sincerely,
Ozgood Pfortz
Ozgood Pfortz
123 Fourth St.
Oakdale
I'm gonna tell that bum off once an' for all!
This is the office of John Blintz & Company . . .
Le'me talk to that big mouth, Blintz!
Mr. Blintz is not in the office at the moment . . .
Don't give me that! It won't do any good for that crumb to hide behind his secretary's skirt!

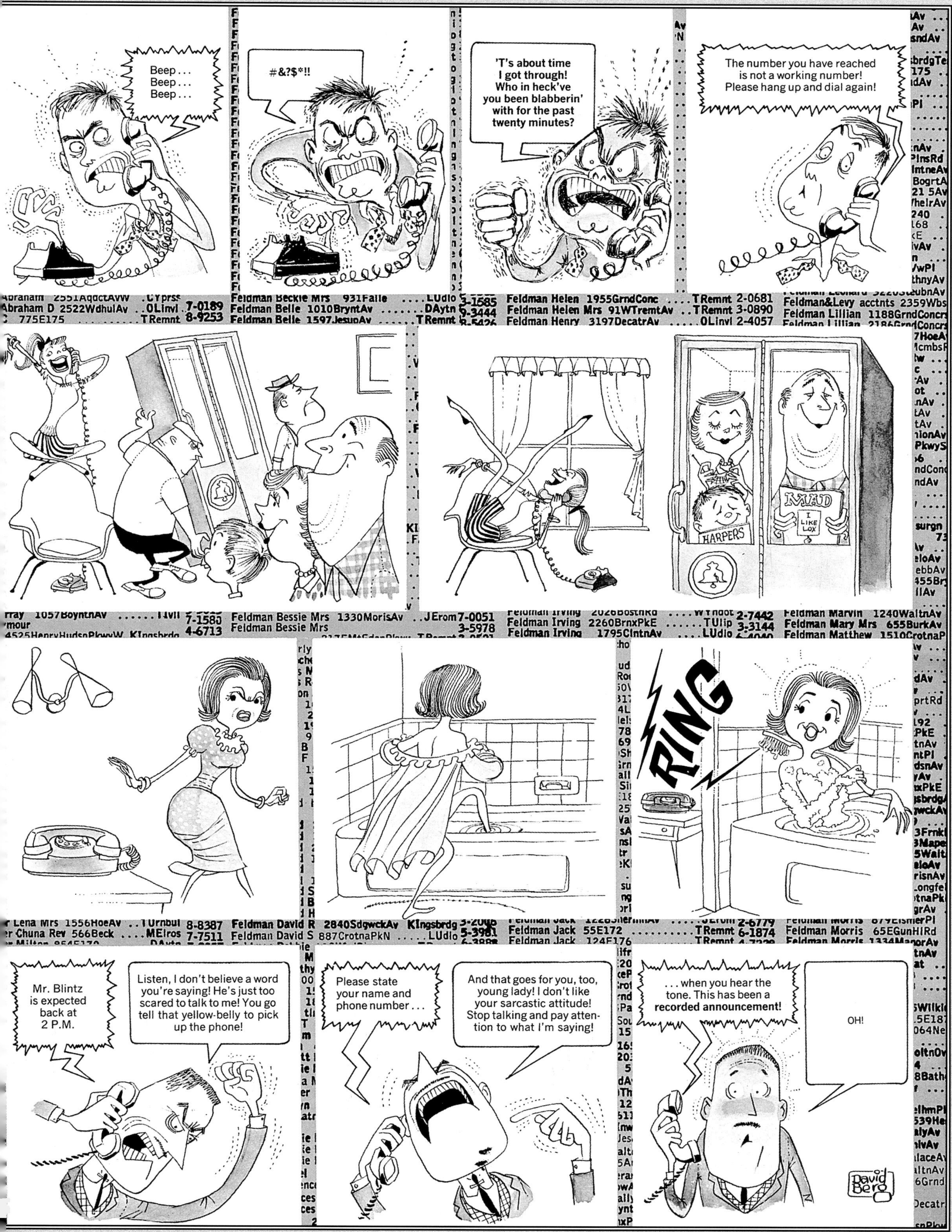
Beep . . .
Beep . . .
Beep . . .
&?$*!!
'T's about time I got through! Who in heck've you been blabberin' with for the past twenty minutes?
The number you have reached is not a working number! Please hang up and dial again!
HARPERS
MAD
I LIKE LOX
RING
Mr. Blintz is expected back at 2 P.M.
Listen, I don't believe a word you're saying! He's just too scared to talk to me! You go tell that yellow-belly to pick up the phone!
Please state your name and phone number . . .
And that goes for you, too, young lady! I don't like your sarcastic attitude! Stop talking and pay attention to what I'm saying!
. . . when you hear the tone. This has been a recorded announcement!
OH!
David Berg

LOONEY-TUNERS DEPT.

Television has only been in general use for about 15 years, and yet it has completely changed our way of life. The TV set has brought the world into our living rooms—as if we didn't have enough troubles already. It has wised-up our young people beyond their years, killed the ancient art of conversation, and reduced the pastime of reading to the pages of "TV Guide." We at MAD have always found television a vulnerable target for our kidding. But somehow, we've limited our fun to the idiotic things that appear on the TV screen, and we've ignored the idiotic things that face the TV screen, mainly, the TV viewers, some of whom can be more ridiculous than all the ridiculous TV programs and TV commercials combined. To them MAD dedicates the following article, which offers . . .

the lighter THE

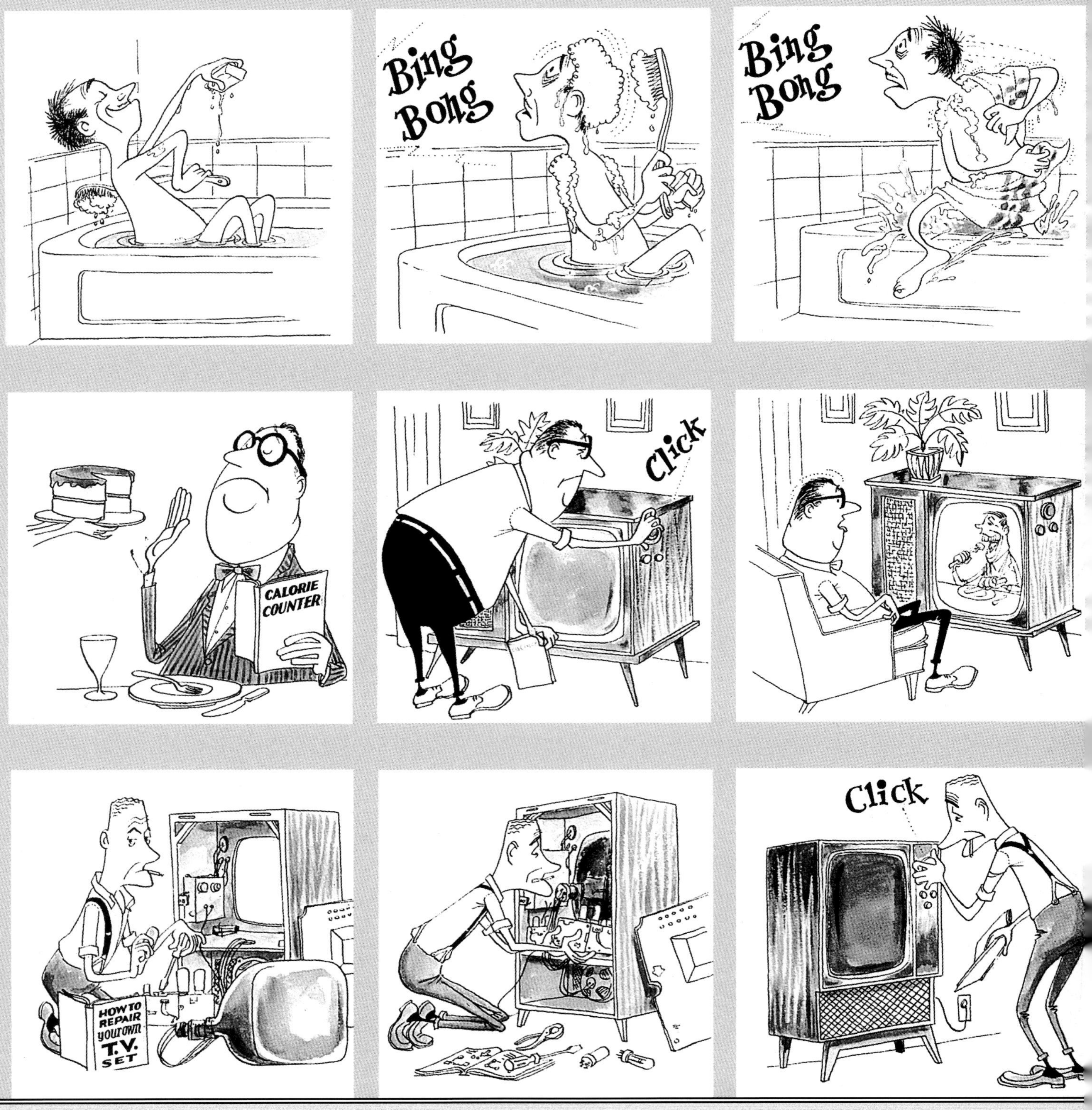
Bing
Bong
Bing
Bong
CALORIE COUNTER
Click
HOW TO REPAIR your own T.V. SET
Click

The first of 333 "The Lighter Side of..." installments

...ide of
TELEVISION SET

...ITER & ARTIST: DAVID BERG

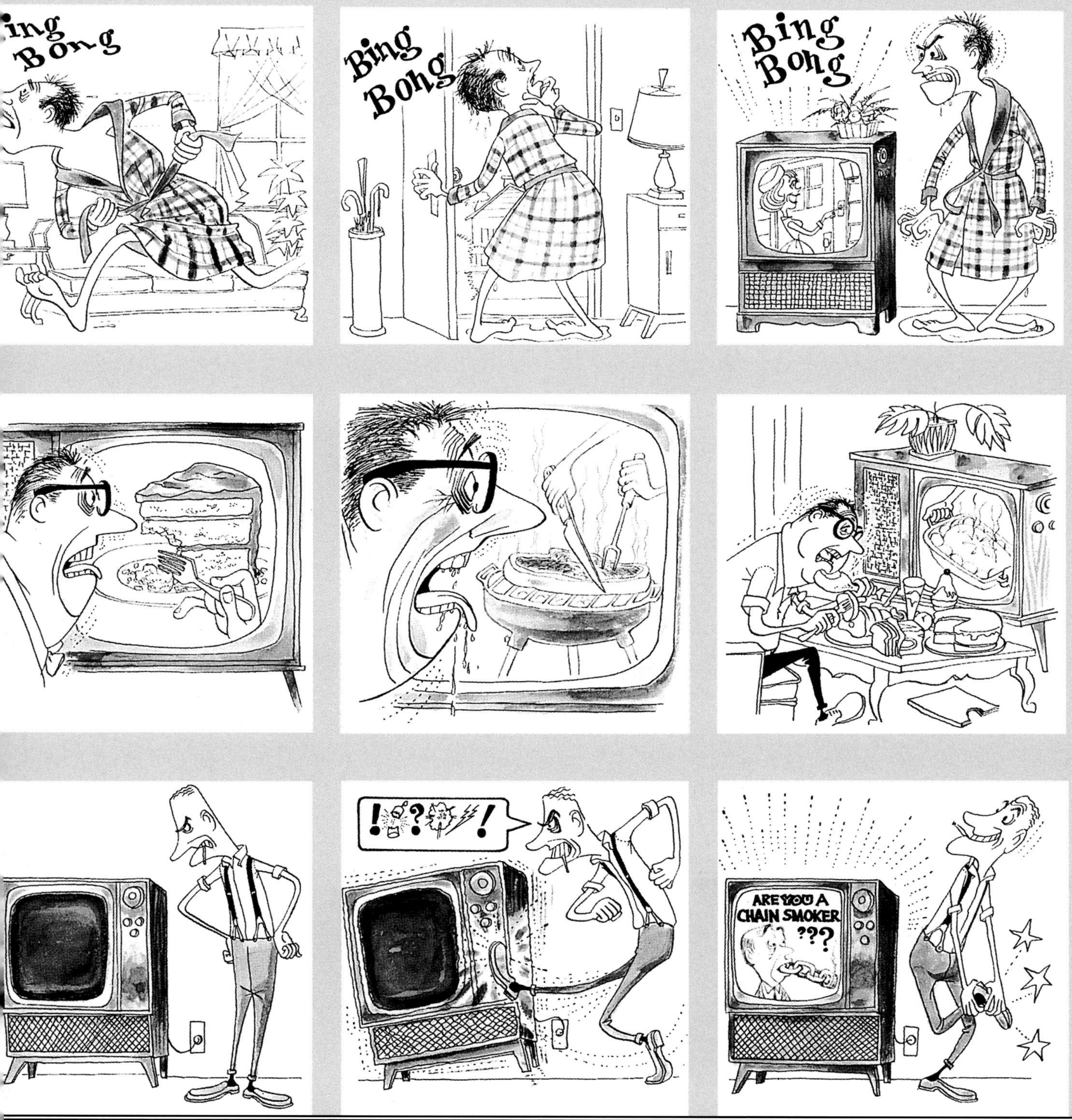
ing Bong
Bing Bong
Bing Bong
!?!
ARE YOU A CHAIN SMOKER ???

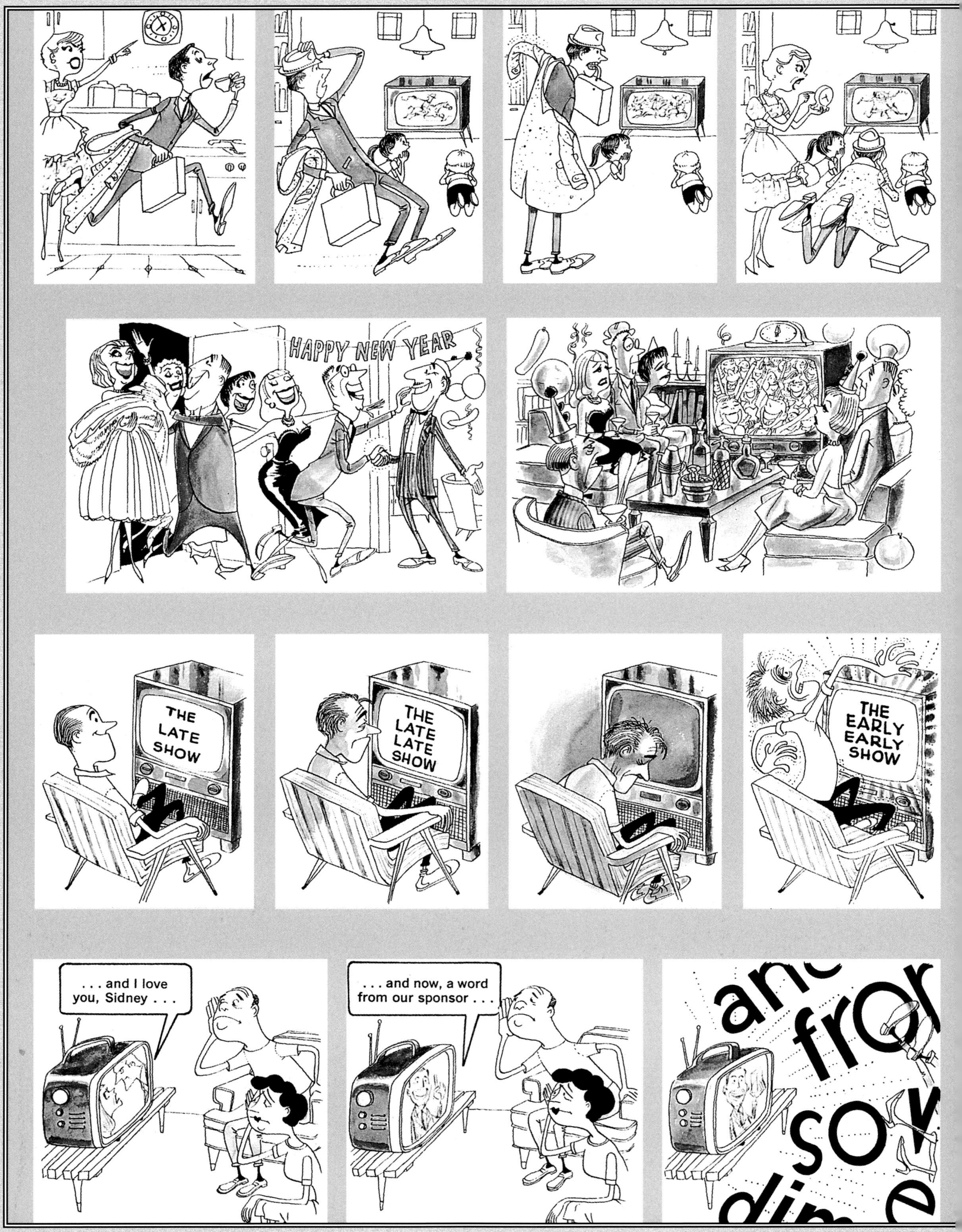
HAPPY NEW YEAR
THE LATE SHOW
THE LATE LATE SHOW
THE EARLY EARLY SHOW
. . . and I love you, Sidney . . .
. . . and now, a word from our sponsor . . .

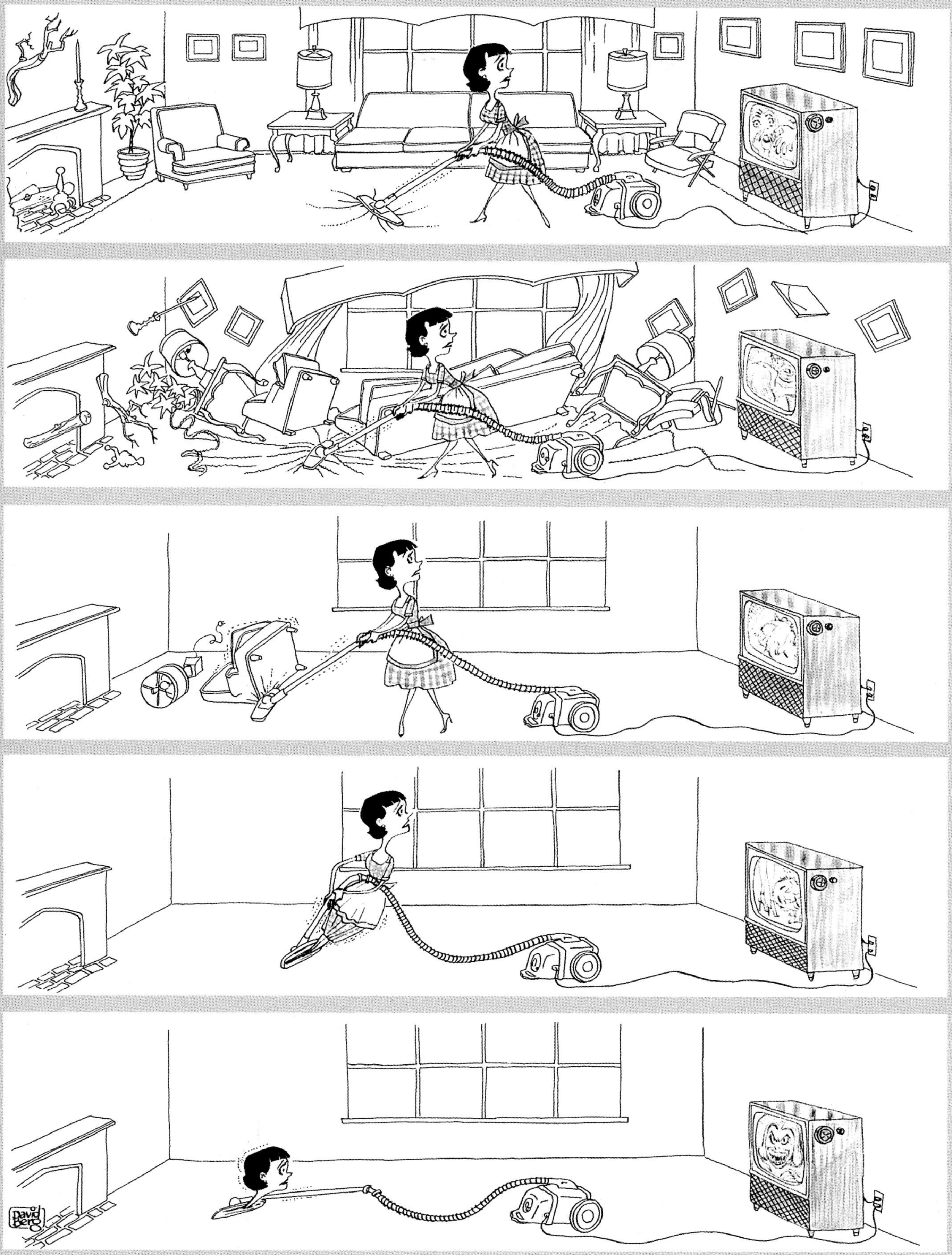
David Berg

WE'LL SEE YOU INHALE DEPT.

DID YOU EVER STOP TO THINK WHAT A RIDICULOUS HABIT "SMOKING" IS? THE TOBACCO COMPANIES AND MADISON AVE, MAKE A FORTUNE WHILE YOU MAKE AN ASH OF YOURSELF! GIVING UP SMOKING IS EASY! MARK TWAIN DID IT A THOUSAND TIMES! MAYBE, AFTER YOU READ THIS ARTICLE, YOU'LL GIVE UP ANOTHER RIDICULOUS HABIT . . . READING MAD! ANYWAY, HERE IS

THE LIGHTER SIDE OF SMO

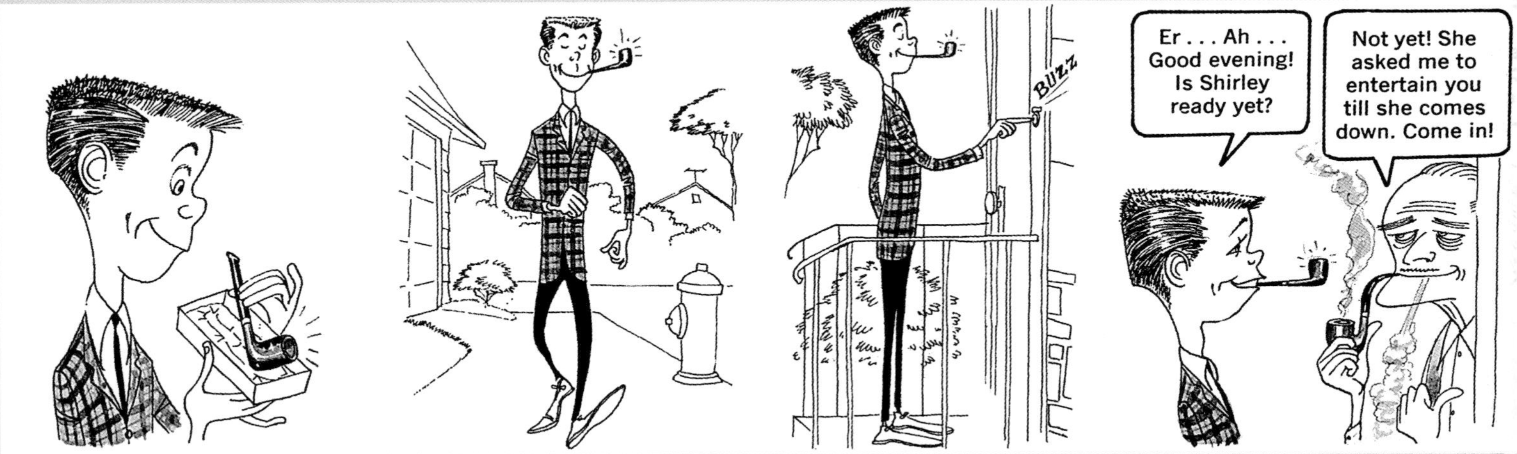
BUZZ
Er . . . Ah . . . Good evening! Is Shirley ready yet?
Not yet! She asked me to entertain you till she comes down. Come in!

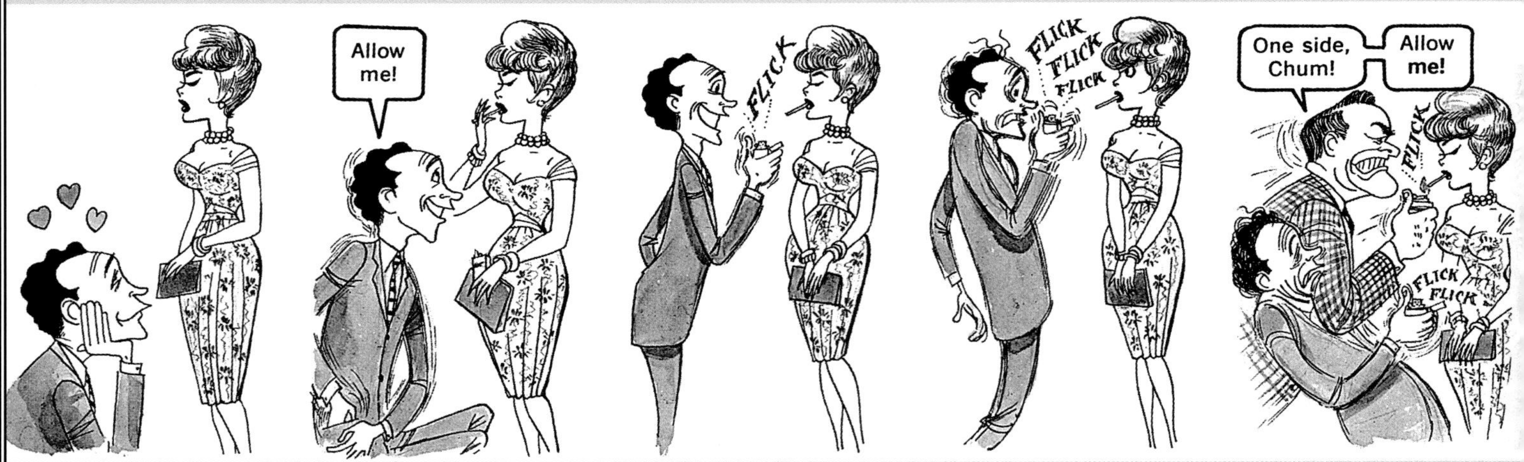
Allow me!
FLICK
FLICK FLICK FLICK
One side, Chum!
Allow me!
FLICK
FLICK FLICK

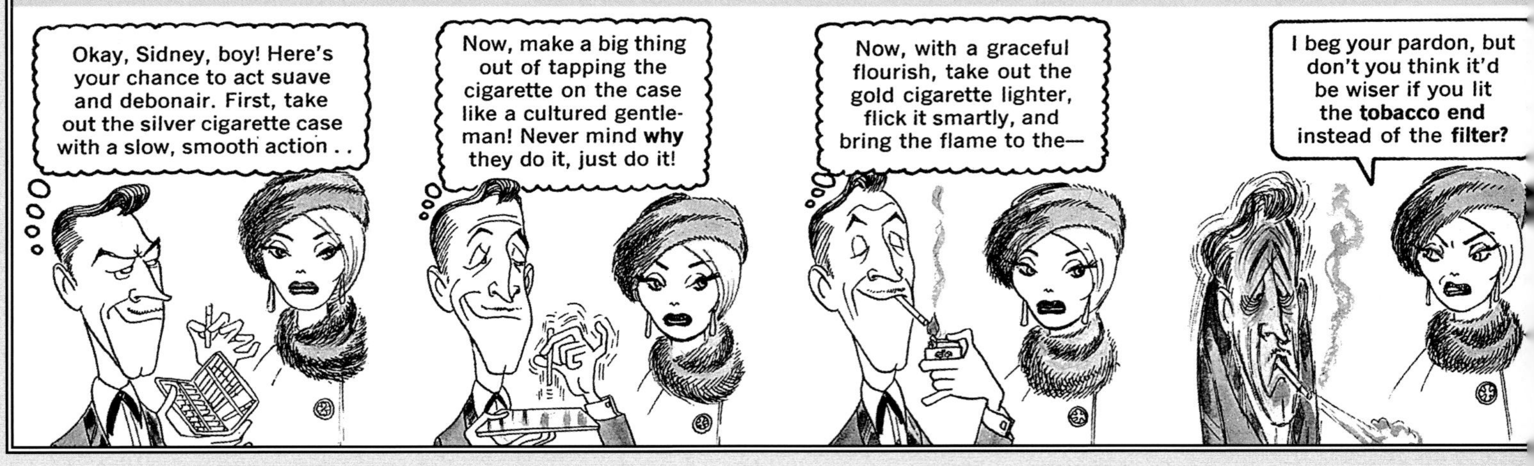
Okay, Sidney, boy! Here's your chance to act suave and debonair. First, take out the silver cigarette case with a slow, smooth action . .
Now, make a big thing out of tapping the cigarette on the case like a cultured gentleman! Never mind why they do it, just do it!
Now, with a graceful flourish, take out the gold cigarette lighter, flick it smartly, and bring the flame to the—
I beg your pardon, but don't you think it'd be wiser if you lit the tobacco end instead of the filter?

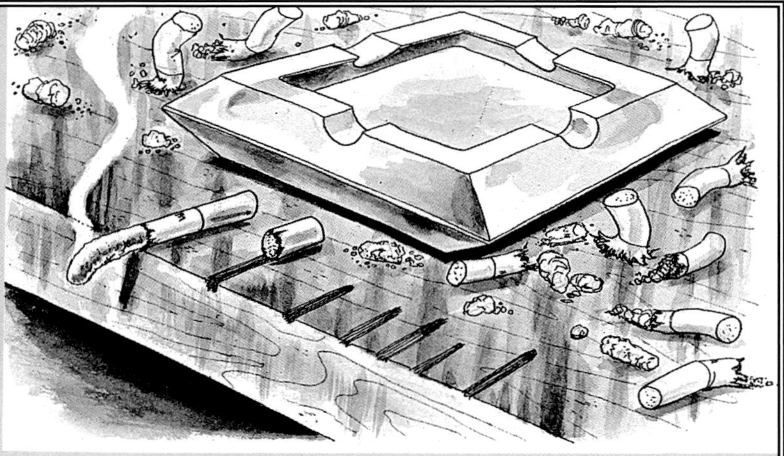

KING

WRITER & ARTIST: DAVID BERG

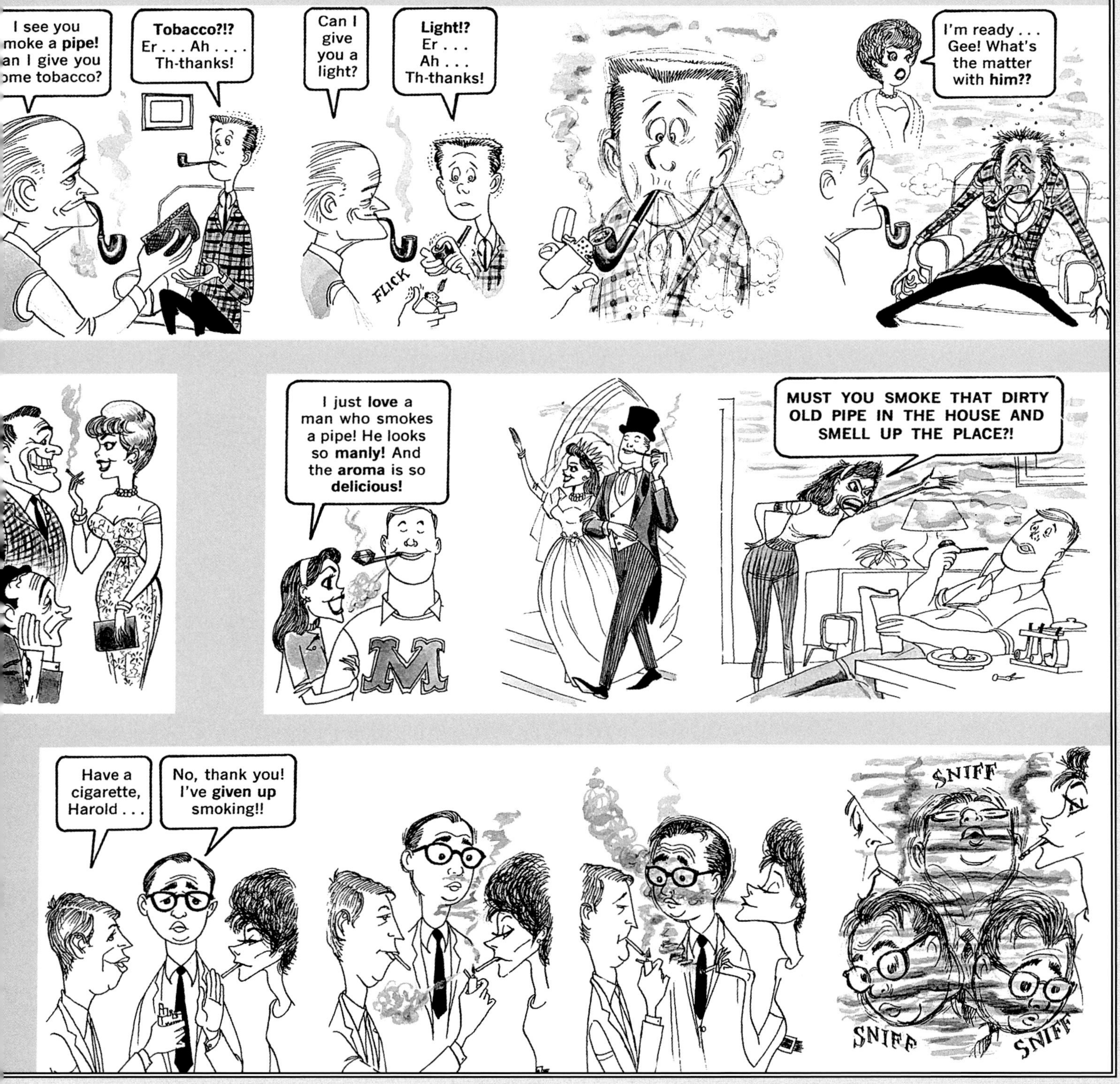
I see you
moke a **pipe!**
an I give you
ome tobacco?
Tobacco?!?
Er . . . Ah . . . .
Th-thanks!
Can I give you a light?
Light!?
Er . . .
Ah . . .
Th-thanks!
FLICK
I'm ready . . .
Gee! What's the matter with **him??**
I just **love** a man who smokes a pipe! He looks so **manly!** And the **aroma** is so **delicious!**
MUST YOU SMOKE THAT DIRTY OLD PIPE IN THE HOUSE AND SMELL UP THE PLACE?!
Have a cigarette, Harold . . .
No, thank you! I've **given up** smoking!!
SNIFF
SNIFF
SNIFF

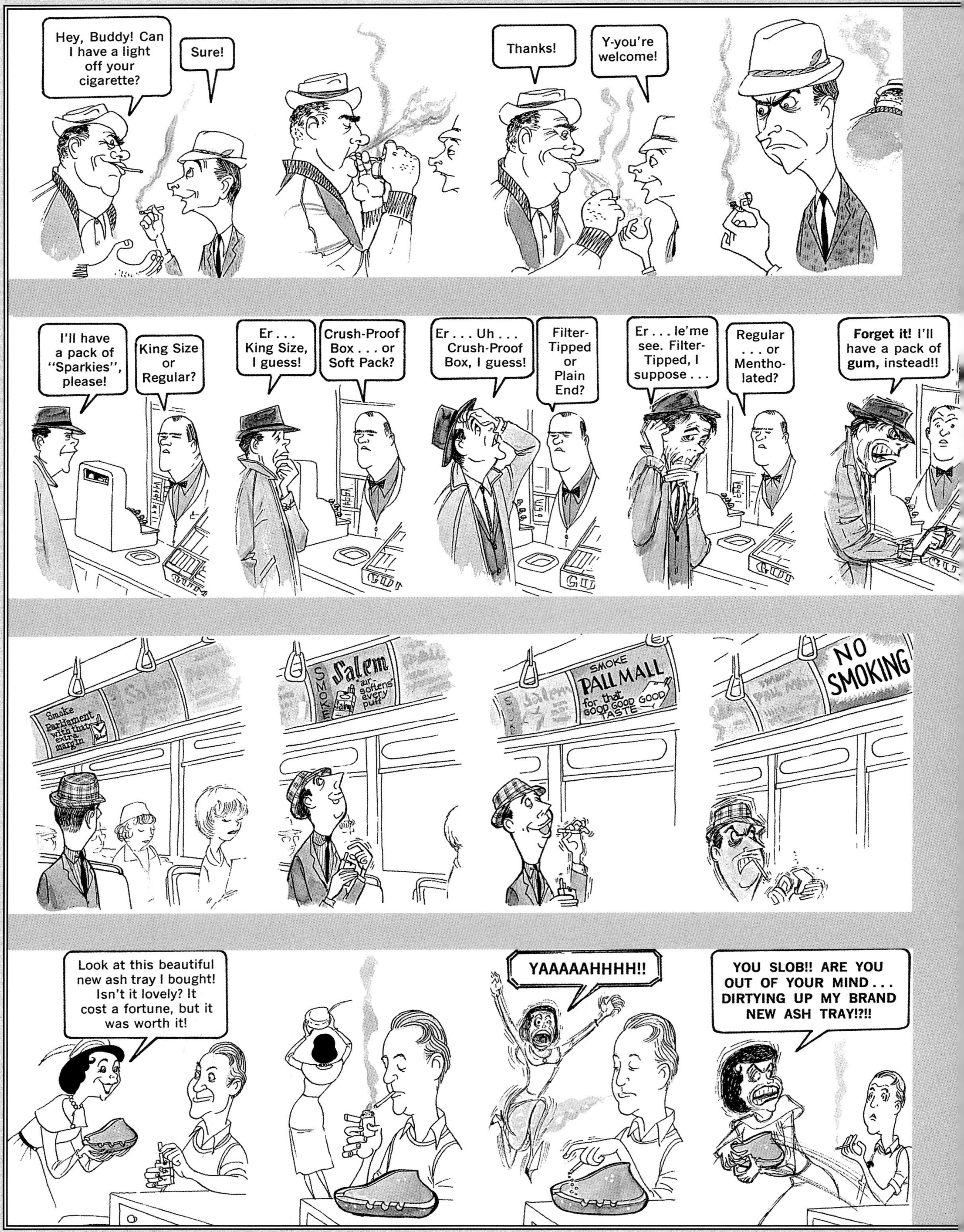

Hey, Buddy! Can I have a light off your cigarette?
Sure!
Thanks!
Y-you're welcome!
I'll have a pack of "Sparkies", please!
King Size or Regular?
Er . . . King Size, I guess!
Crush-Proof Box . . . or Soft Pack?
Er . . . Uh . . . Crush-Proof Box, I guess!
Filter-Tipped or Plain End?
Er . . . le'me see. Filter-Tipped, I suppose . . .
Regular . . . or Mentho-lated?
Forget it! I'll have a pack of gum, instead!!
Smoke Parliament with that extra margin
SMOKE Salem air-softens every puff
SMOKE PALL MALL for that GOOD GOOD GOOD TASTE
NO SMOKING
Look at this beautiful new ash tray I bought! Isn't it lovely? It cost a fortune, but it was worth it!
YAAAAAHHHH!!
YOU SLOB!! ARE YOU OUT OF YOUR MIND . . . DIRTYING UP MY BRAND NEW ASH TRAY!?!!

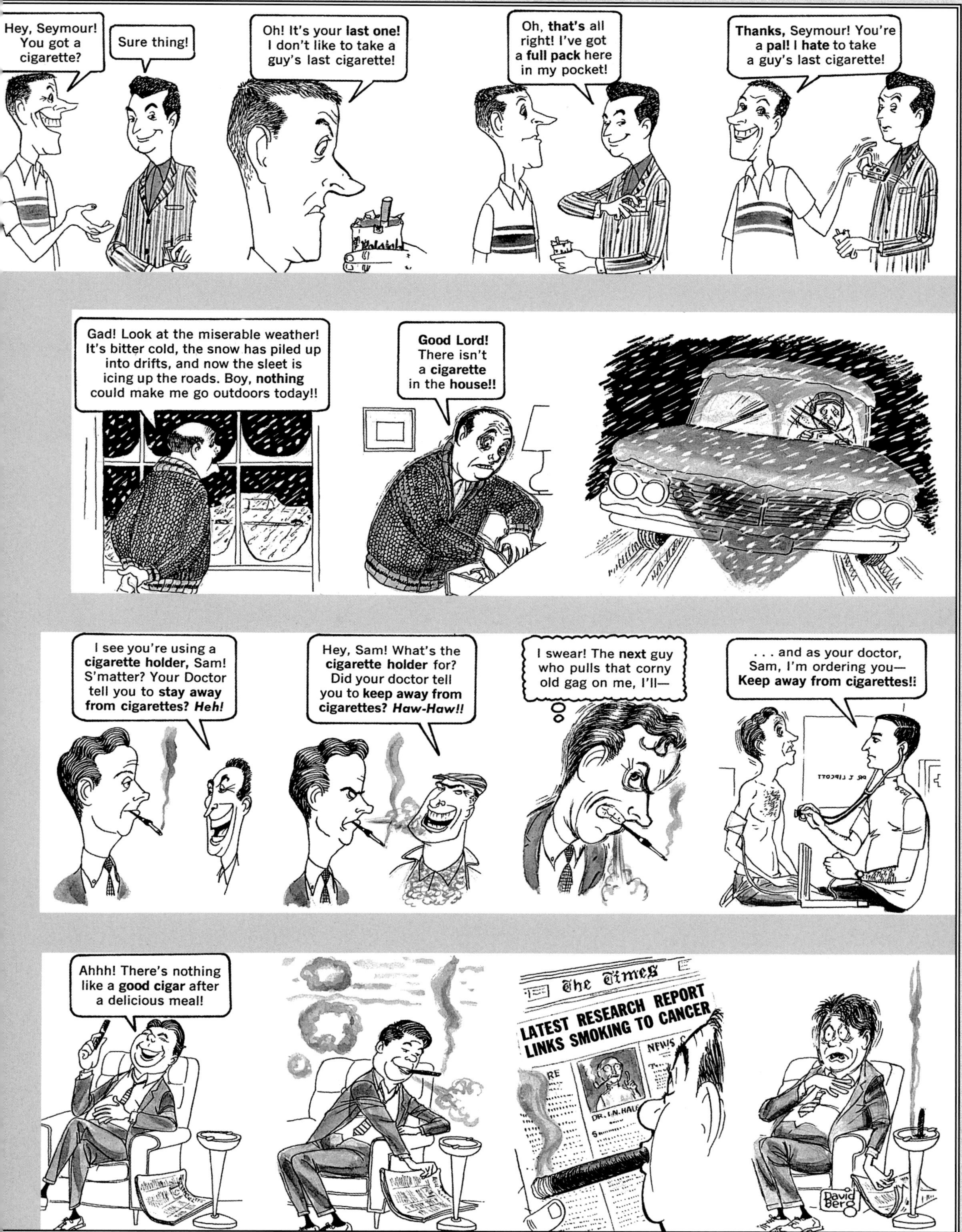
Hey, Seymour! You got a cigarette?
Sure thing!
Oh! It's your **last one!** I don't like to take a guy's last cigarette!
Oh, **that's** all right! I've got a **full pack** here in my pocket!
Thanks, Seymour! You're a **pal!** I **hate** to take a guy's last cigarette!
Gad! Look at the miserable weather! It's bitter cold, the snow has piled up into drifts, and now the sleet is icing up the roads. Boy, **nothing** could make me go outdoors today!!
Good Lord! There isn't a **cigarette** in the **house!!**
I see you're using a **cigarette holder,** Sam! S'matter? Your Doctor tell you to **stay away from cigarettes?** ***Heh!***
Hey, Sam! What's the **cigarette holder** for? Did your doctor tell you to **keep away from cigarettes?** ***Haw-Haw!!***
I swear! The **next** guy who pulls that corny old gag on me, I'll—
. . . and as your doctor, Sam, I'm ordering you— **Keep away from cigarettes!!**
Ahhh! There's nothing like a **good cigar** after a delicious meal!
The Times
LATEST RESEARCH REPORT LINKS SMOKING TO CANCER
David Berg

BERG'S-EYE VIEW DEPT.

Chestnuts roasting on an open fire, Jack Frost nipping at our nose . . . Yep, that frigid season is almost upon us. So, as a special service to all our readers, MAD presents the following feature guaranteed to warm the heart . . . and the hands as well . . . mainly if you put a match to it before you read it. Or better still, use a "lighter" on—

THE LIGHTER SIDE OF WINTER

WRITER & ARTIST: DAVID BERG

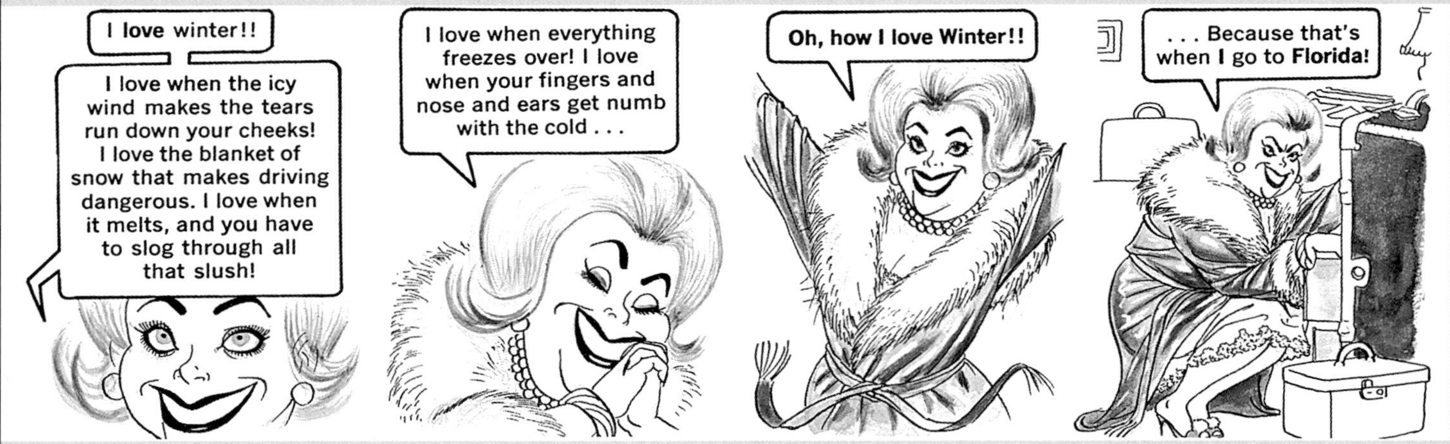
I **love** winter!!
I love when the icy wind makes the tears run down your cheeks! I love the blanket of snow that makes driving dangerous. I love when it melts, and you have to slog through all that slush!
I love when everything freezes over! I love when your fingers and nose and ears get numb with the cold . . .
Oh, how I love Winter!!
. . . Because that's when **I** go to **Florida!**

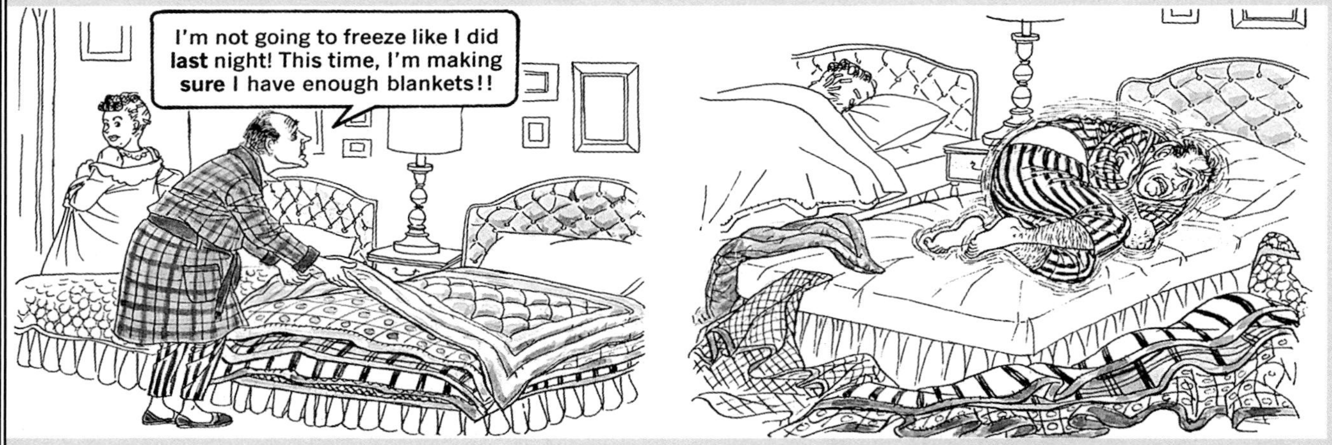
I'm not going to freeze like I did **last** night! This time, I'm making **sure** I have enough blankets!!

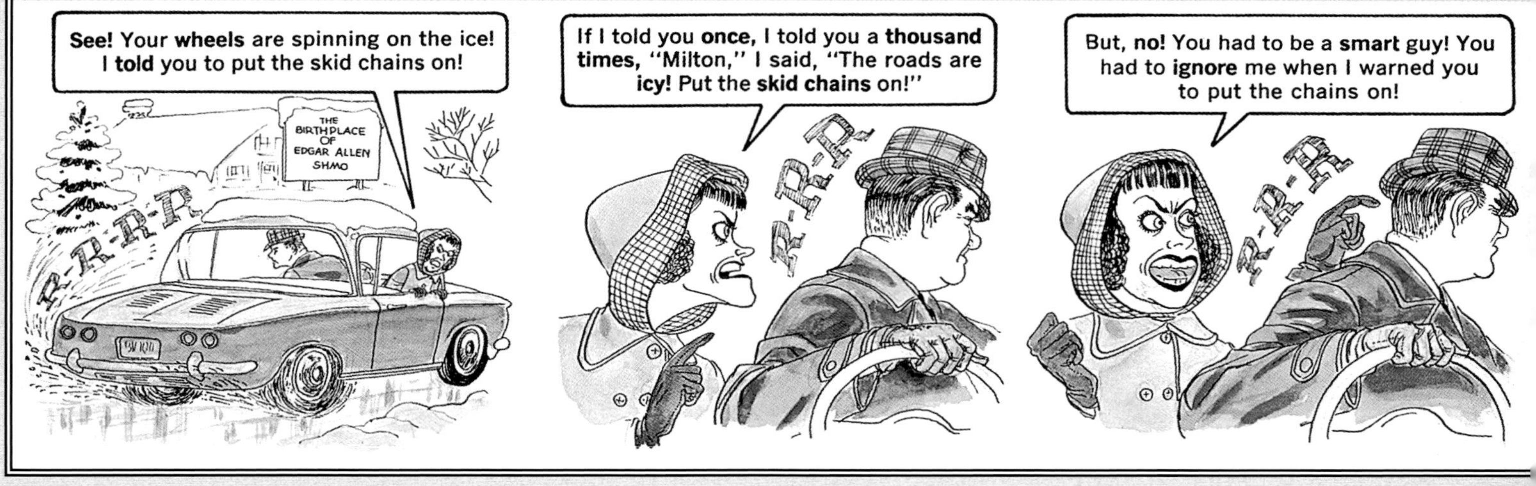
See! Your **wheels** are spinning on the ice! I **told** you to put the skid chains on!
THE BIRTHPLACE OF EDGAR ALLEN SHMO
R-R-R
If I told you **once,** I told you a **thousand times,** "Milton," I said, "The roads are **icy!** Put the **skid chains** on!"
R-R-R
But, **no!** You had to be a **smart** guy! You had to **ignore** me when I warned you to put the chains on!
R-R-R

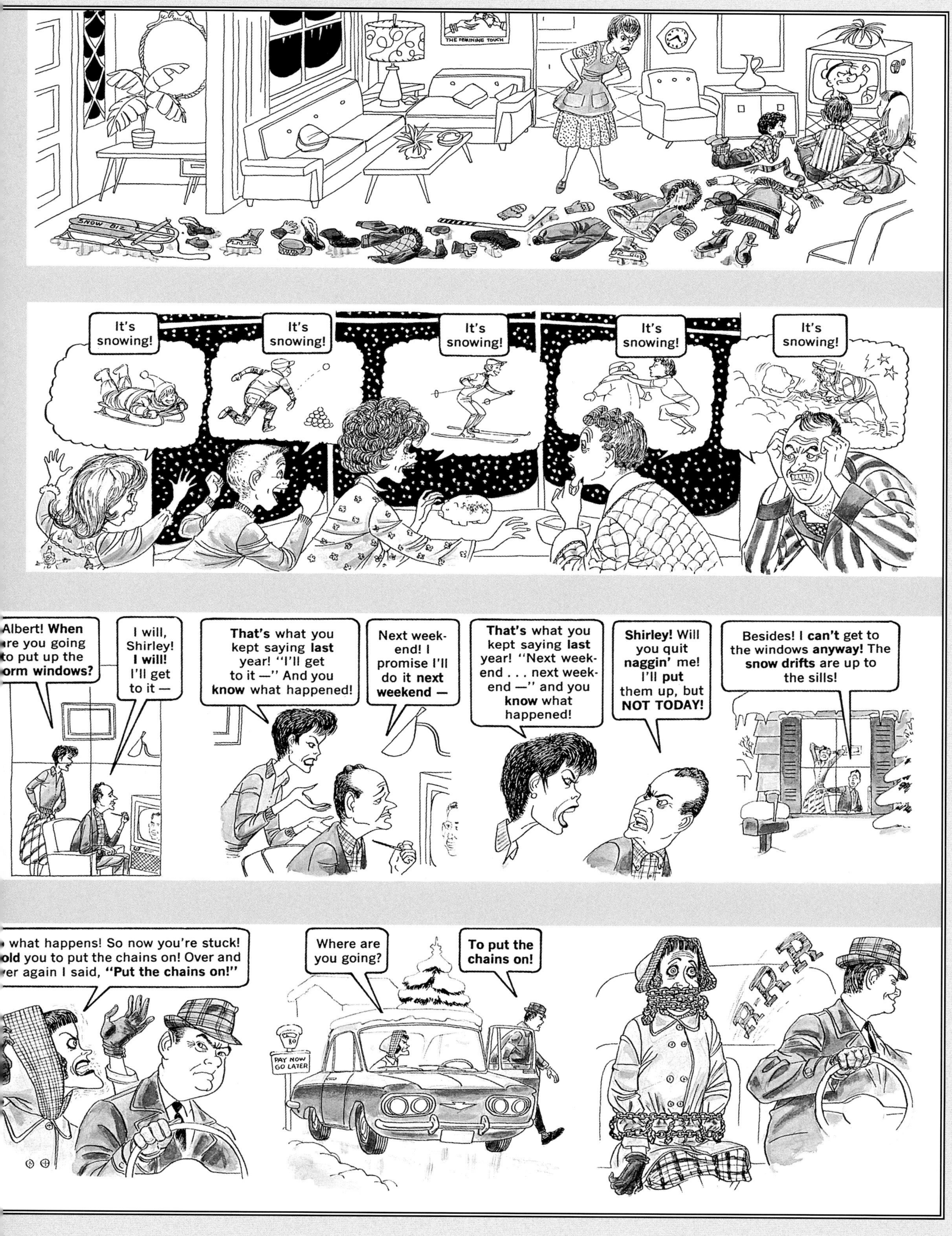
THE FEMININE TOUCH
SNOW BIZ
It's snowing!
It's snowing!
It's snowing!
It's snowing!
It's snowing!
Albert! When
re you going
to put up the
orm windows?
I will, Shirley! I will! I'll get to it —
That's what you kept saying last year! "I'll get to it —" And you know what happened!
Next week-end! I promise I'll do it next weekend —
That's what you kept saying last year! "Next week-end . . . next week-end —" and you know what happened!
Shirley! Will you quit naggin' me! I'll put them up, but NOT TODAY!
Besides! I can't get to the windows anyway! The snow drifts are up to the sills!
what happens! So now you're stuck!
old you to put the chains on! Over and
er again I said, "Put the chains on!"
Where are you going?
To put the chains on!
PAY NOW GO LATER
R-R-R

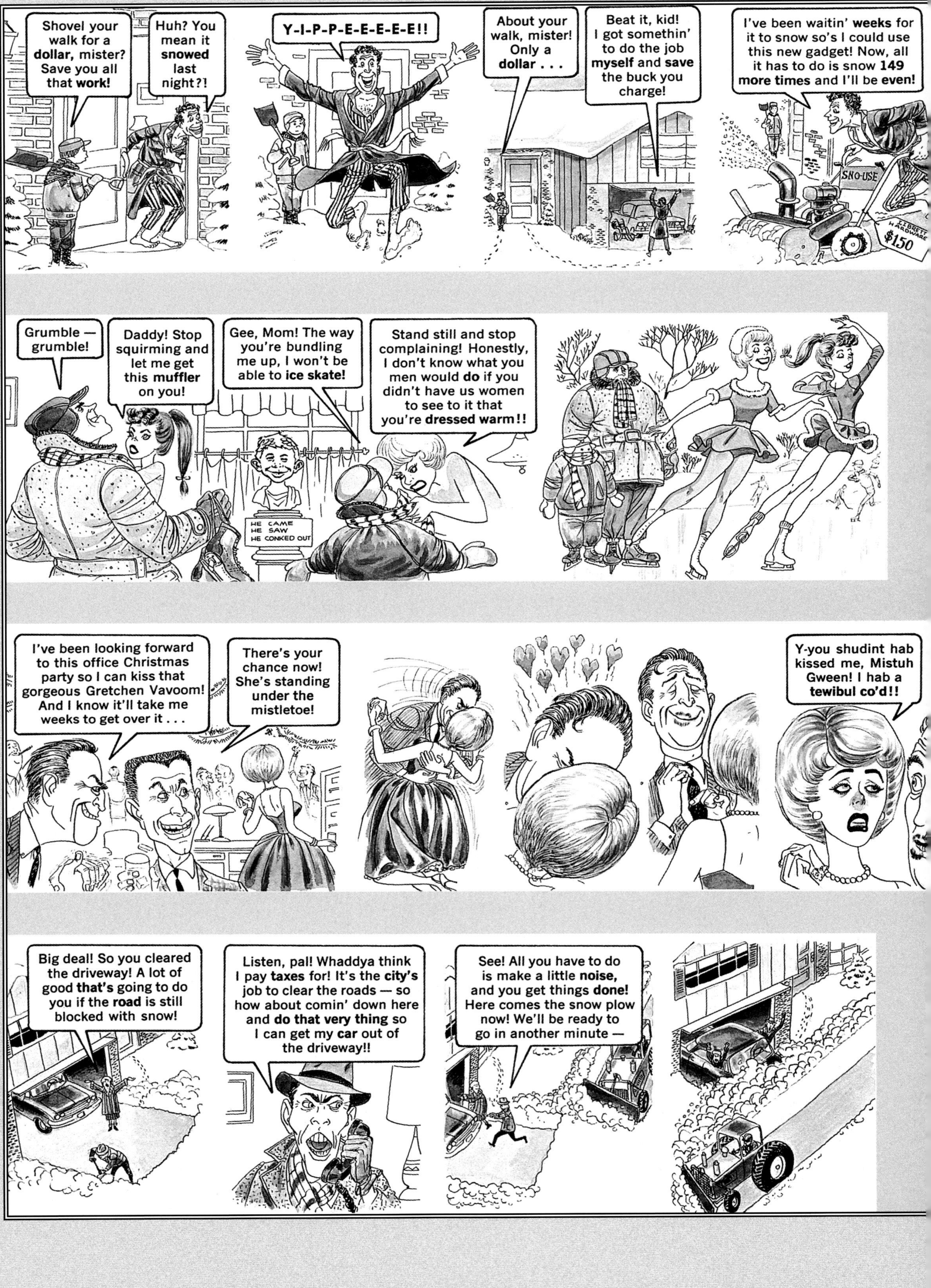
Shovel your walk for a dollar, mister? Save you all that work!
Huh? You mean it snowed last night?!
Y-I-P-P-E-E-E-E-E!!
About your walk, mister! Only a dollar . . .
Beat it, kid! I got somethin' to do the job myself and save the buck you charge!
I've been waitin' weeks for it to snow so's I could use this new gadget! Now, all it has to do is snow 149 more times and I'll be even!
SNO-USE
$150
Grumble — grumble!
Daddy! Stop squirming and let me get this muffler on you!
Gee, Mom! The way you're bundling me up, I won't be able to ice skate!
HE CAME
HE SAW
HE CONKED OUT
Stand still and stop complaining! Honestly, I don't know what you men would do if you didn't have us women to see to it that you're dressed warm!!
I've been looking forward to this office Christmas party so I can kiss that gorgeous Gretchen Vavoom! And I know it'll take me weeks to get over it . . .
There's your chance now! She's standing under the mistletoe!
Y-you shudint hab kissed me, Mistuh Gween! I hab a tewibul co'd!!
Big deal! So you cleared the driveway! A lot of good that's going to do you if the road is still blocked with snow!
Listen, pal! Whaddya think I pay taxes for! It's the city's job to clear the roads — so how about comin' down here and do that very thing so I can get my car out of the driveway!!
See! All you have to do is make a little noise, and you get things done! Here comes the snow plow now! We'll be ready to go in another minute —

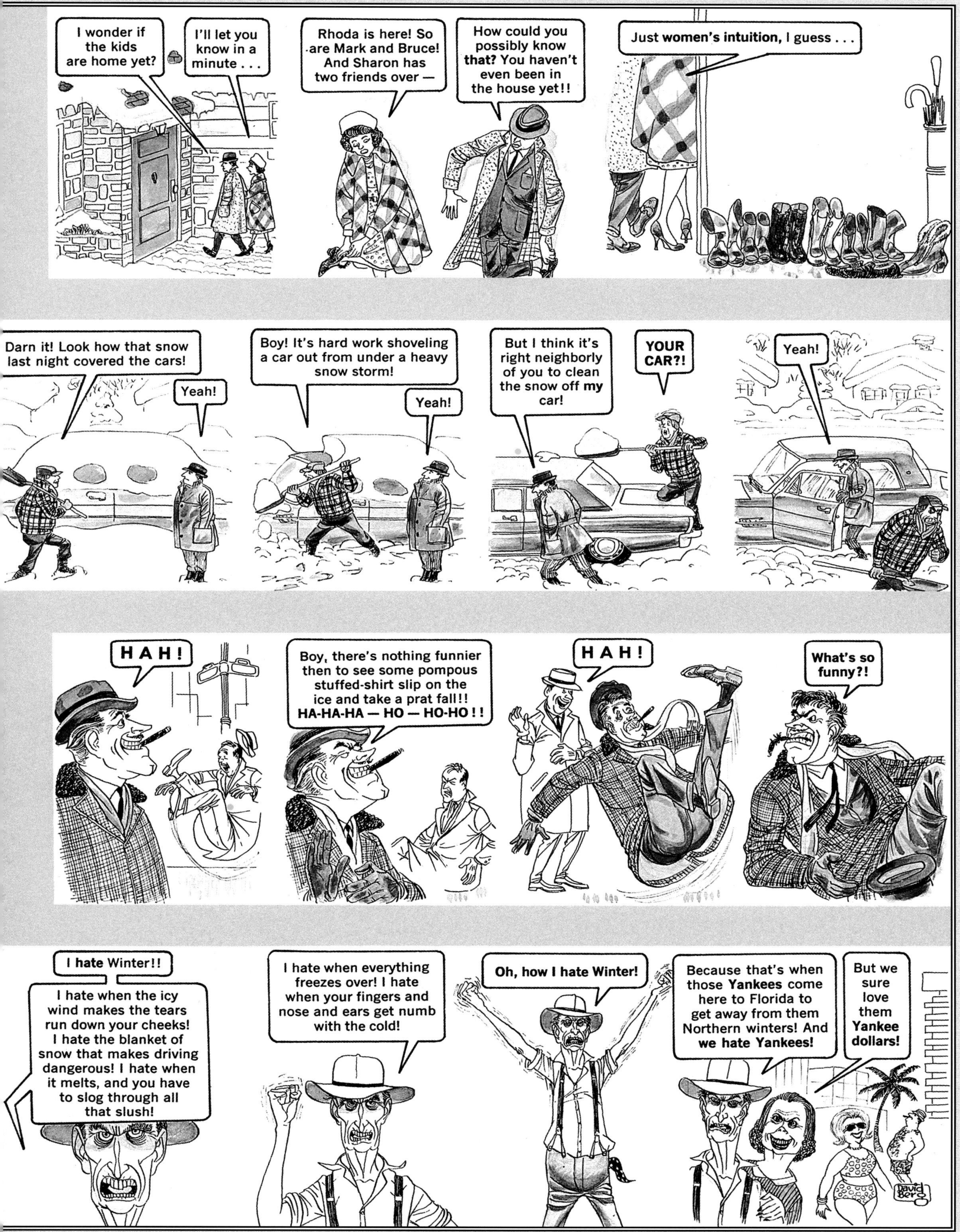
I wonder if the kids are home yet?
I'll let you know in a minute . . .
Rhoda is here! So are Mark and Bruce! And Sharon has two friends over —
How could you possibly know that? You haven't even been in the house yet!!
Just women's intuition, I guess . . .
Darn it! Look how that snow last night covered the cars!
Yeah!
Boy! It's hard work shoveling a car out from under a heavy snow storm!
Yeah!
But I think it's right neighborly of you to clean the snow off my car!
YOUR CAR?!
Yeah!
HAH!
Boy, there's nothing funnier then to see some pompous stuffed-shirt slip on the ice and take a prat fall!! HA-HA-HA — HO — HO-HO!!
HAH!
What's so funny?!
I hate Winter!!
I hate when the icy wind makes the tears run down your cheeks! I hate the blanket of snow that makes driving dangerous! I hate when it melts, and you have to slog through all that slush!
I hate when everything freezes over! I hate when your fingers and nose and ears get numb with the cold!
Oh, how I hate Winter!
Because that's when those Yankees come here to Florida to get away from them Northern winters! And we hate Yankees!
But we sure love them Yankee dollars!
David Berg

BERG'S-EYE VIEW DEPT.

The author of the following article has agreed to take full responsibility for it . . . mainly because the rest of us are "chicken", and we'd like to stay on the good side of our wives, girl friends and other members of the opposite sex who might not see anything funny about . . .

THE LIGHTER SIDE OF

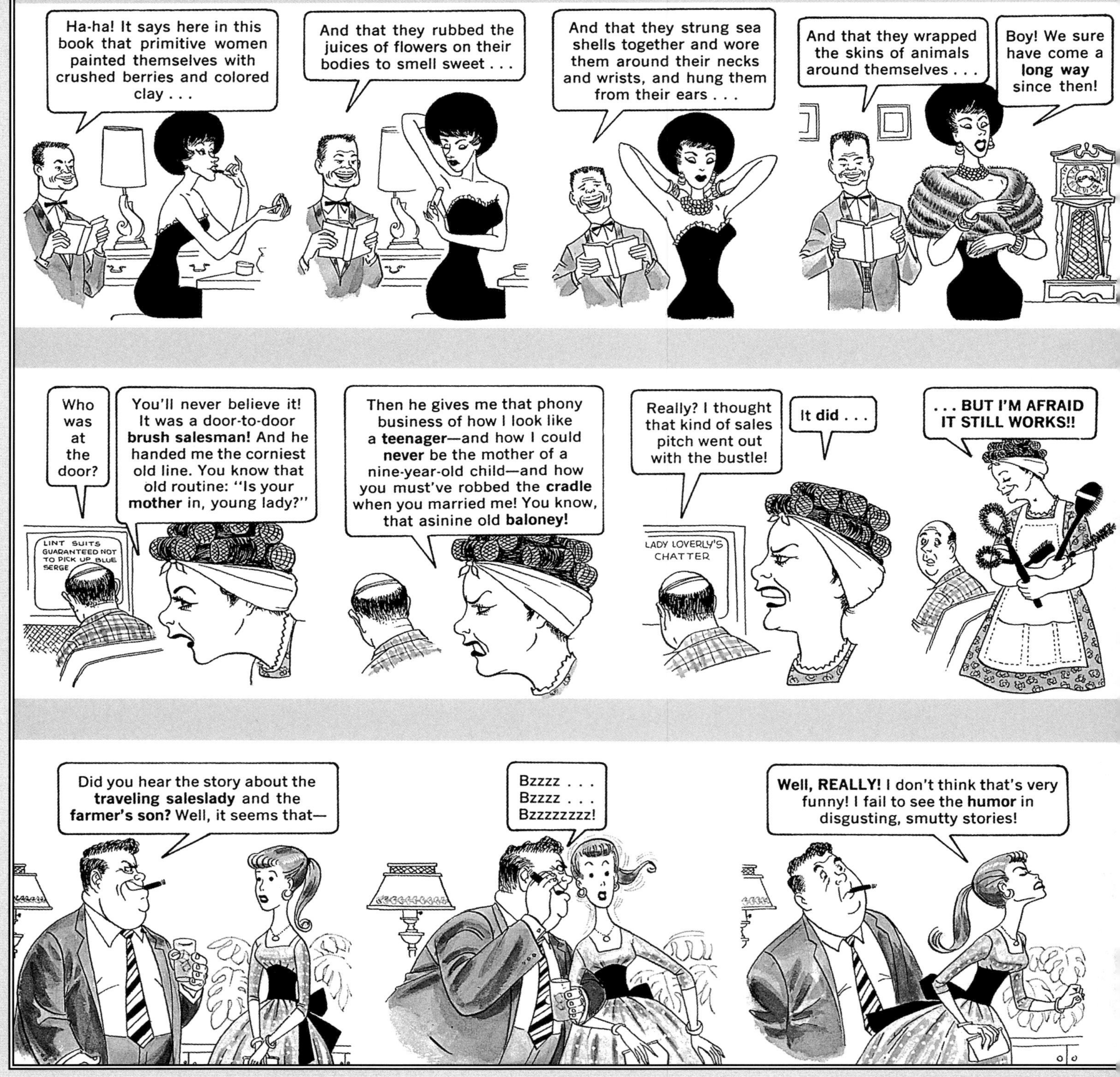

Ha-ha! It says here in this book that primitive women painted themselves with crushed berries and colored clay . . .
And that they rubbed the juices of flowers on their bodies to smell sweet . . .
And that they strung sea shells together and wore them around their necks and wrists, and hung them from their ears . . .
And that they wrapped the skins of animals around themselves . . .
Boy! We sure have come a **long way** since then!
Who was at the door?
You'll never believe it! It was a door-to-door **brush salesman!** And he handed me the corniest old line. You know that old routine: "Is your **mother** in, young lady?"
LINT SUITS GUARANTEED NOT TO PICK UP BLUE SERGE
Then he gives me that phony business of how I look like a **teenager**—and how I could **never** be the mother of a nine-year-old child—and how you must've robbed the **cradle** when you married me! You know, that asinine old **baloney!**
Really? I thought that kind of sales pitch went out with the bustle!
LADY LOVERLY'S CHATTER
It **did** . . .
. . . BUT I'M AFRAID IT STILL WORKS!!
Did you hear the story about the **traveling saleslady** and the **farmer's son?** Well, it seems that—
Bzzzz . . .
Bzzzz . . .
Bzzzzzzzz!
Well, REALLY! I don't think that's very funny! I fail to see the **humor** in disgusting, smutty stories!

Women

WRITER & ARTIST: DAVID BERG

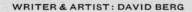
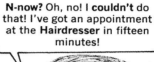

Doctor, I can't stand it! I've got this terrible toothache!!

Please! Please! Can you give me an appointment for today??

Okay! If you come down right now, I'll squeeze you in!

N-now? Oh, no! I couldn't do that! I've got an appointment at the Hairdresser in fifteen minutes!

What a day I had! I'm so tired I can hardly talk!

I know! I know!

My hand aches, and my throat is sore—

I know! I know!

WHAT DO YOU MEAN—YOU KNOW—YOU KNOW?

I mean I know you've had a hard day! I've been trying to call you since 10:00 A.M. this morning . . . and the line's been constantly busy!!

The nerve of that Sidney Gruber! He just told me the filthiest story! It seems there was this traveling saleslady . . .

Bzzzz . . . Bzzzz . . . Bzzzzzzzz!

HA HA HA HA HA HA

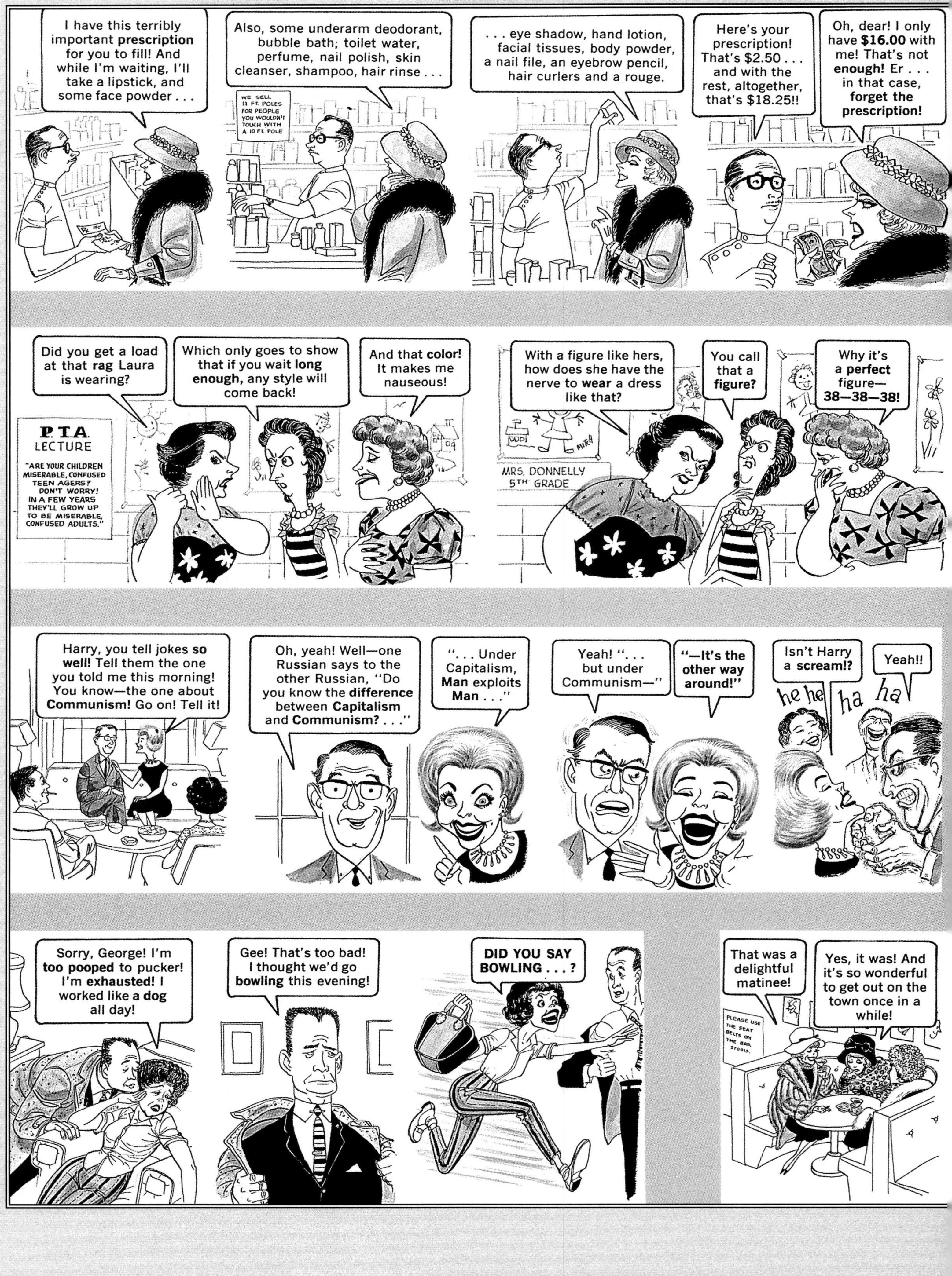
I have this terribly important **prescription** for you to fill! And while I'm waiting, I'll take a lipstick, and some face powder . . .
WE SELL 11 FT. POLES FOR PEOPLE YOU WOULDN'T TOUCH WITH A 10 FT. POLE
Also, some underarm deodorant, bubble bath; toilet water, perfume, nail polish, skin cleanser, shampoo, hair rinse . . .
. . . eye shadow, hand lotion, facial tissues, body powder, a nail file, an eyebrow pencil, hair curlers and a rouge.
Here's your prescription! That's $2.50 . . . and with the rest, altogether, that's $18.25!!
Oh, dear! I only have **$16.00** with me! That's not **enough!** Er . . . in that case, **forget the prescription!**
P.T.A. LECTURE
"ARE YOUR CHILDREN MISERABLE, CONFUSED TEEN AGERS? DON'T WORRY! IN A FEW YEARS THEY'LL GROW UP TO BE MISERABLE, CONFUSED ADULTS."
Did you get a load at that **rag** Laura is wearing?
Which only goes to show that if you wait **long enough,** any style will come back!
And that **color!** It makes me nauseous!
With a figure like hers, how does she have the nerve to **wear** a dress like that?
MRS. DONNELLY 5TH GRADE
You call that a **figure?**
Why it's a **perfect** figure— **38—38—38!**
Harry, you tell jokes **so well!** Tell them the one you told me this morning! You know—the one about **Communism!** Go on! Tell it!
Oh, yeah! Well—one Russian says to the other Russian, "Do you know the **difference** between **Capitalism** and **Communism?** . . ."
". . . Under Capitalism, **Man** exploits **Man** . . ."
Yeah! ". . . but under Communism—"
"—It's the other way around!"
Isn't Harry a **scream!?**
Yeah!!
he he
ha ha
Sorry, George! I'm **too pooped** to pucker! I'm **exhausted!** I worked like a **dog** all day!
Gee! That's too bad! I thought we'd go **bowling** this evening!
DID YOU SAY BOWLING . . . ?
That was a delightful matinee!
PLEASE USE THE SEAT BELTS ON THE BAR STOOLS.
Yes, it was! And it's so wonderful to get out on the town once in a while!

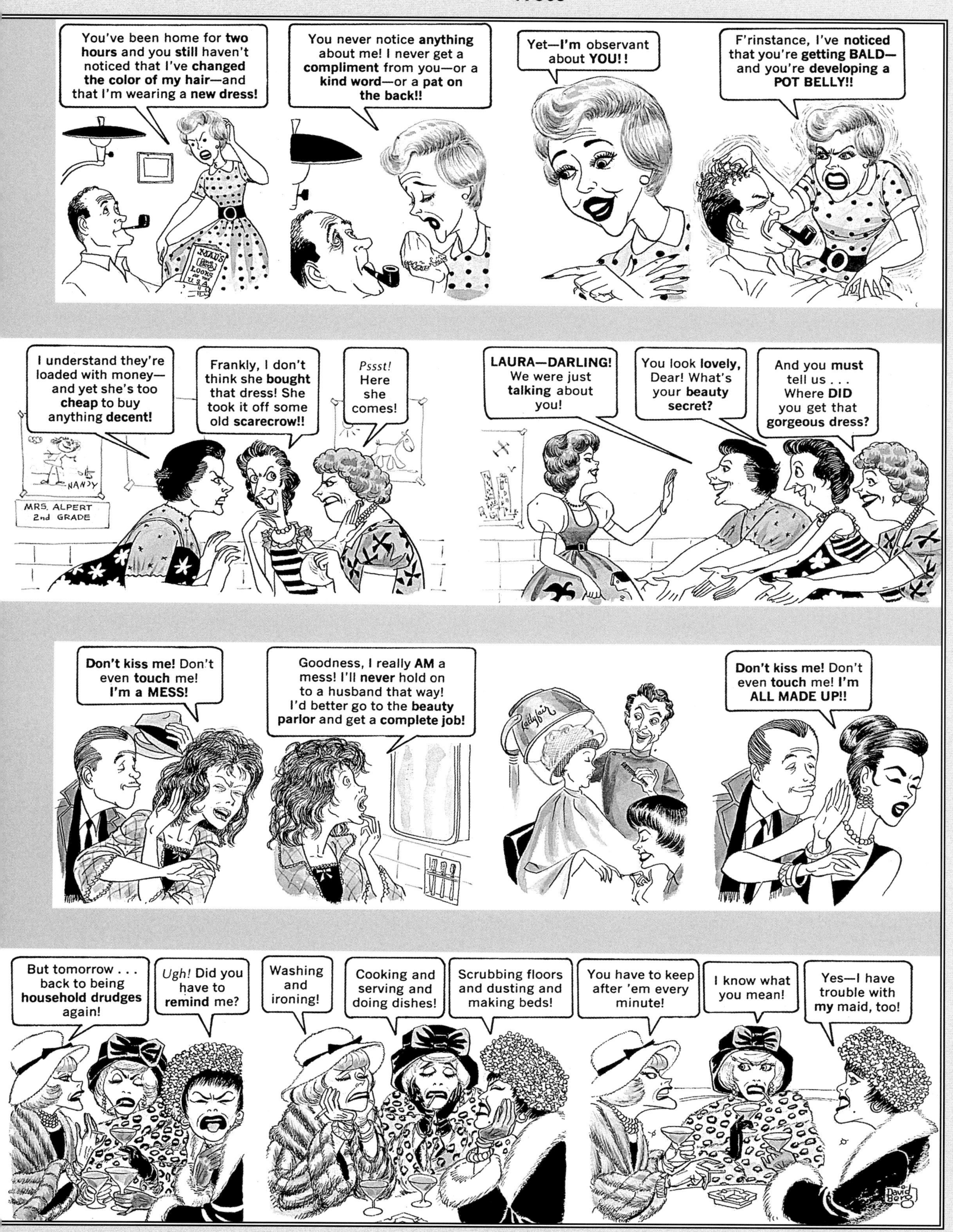
You've been home for two hours and you still haven't noticed that I've changed the color of my hair—and that I'm wearing a new dress!
You never notice anything about me! I never get a compliment from you—or a kind word—or a pat on the back!!
Yet—I'm observant about YOU!!
F'rinstance, I've noticed that you're getting BALD—and you're developing a POT BELLY!!
I understand they're loaded with money—and yet she's too cheap to buy anything decent!
Frankly, I don't think she bought that dress! She took it off some old scarecrow!!
Pssst! Here she comes!
MRS. ALPERT 2nd GRADE
LAURA—DARLING! We were just talking about you!
You look lovely, Dear! What's your beauty secret?
And you must tell us . . . Where DID you get that gorgeous dress?
Don't kiss me! Don't even touch me! I'm a MESS!
Goodness, I really AM a mess! I'll never hold on to a husband that way! I'd better go to the beauty parlor and get a complete job!
Don't kiss me! Don't even touch me! I'm ALL MADE UP!!
But tomorrow . . . back to being household drudges again!
Ugh! Did you have to remind me?
Washing and ironing!
Cooking and serving and doing dishes!
Scrubbing floors and dusting and making beds!
You have to keep after 'em every minute!
I know what you mean!
Yes—I have trouble with my maid, too!
David Berg

BERG'S-EYE VIEW DEPT.

The following article by David Berg is about dogs and their owners, and although you may not be interested in either, you will read the article and begin to laugh as soon as the bell rings. Get that? You will read the article and begin to laugh as soon as the bell rings! Understand? Okay, ring the bell, Mr. Pavlov . . .

THE LIGHTER SIDE OF

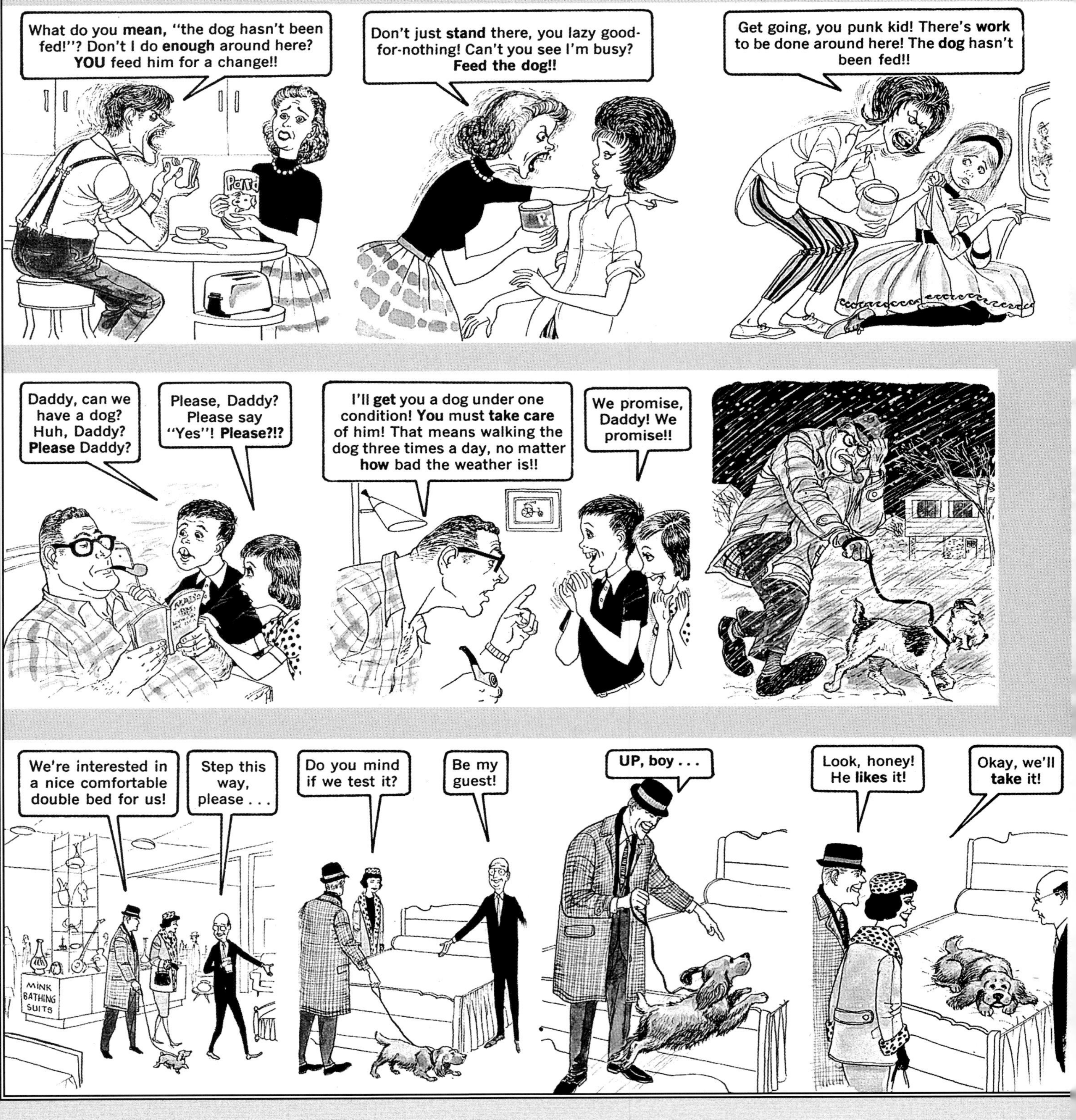
What do you mean, "the dog hasn't been fed!"? Don't I do enough around here? YOU feed him for a change!!
Don't just stand there, you lazy good-for-nothing! Can't you see I'm busy? Feed the dog!!
Get going, you punk kid! There's work to be done around here! The dog hasn't been fed!!
Daddy, can we have a dog? Huh, Daddy? Please Daddy?
Please, Daddy? Please say "Yes"! Please?!?
I'll get you a dog under one condition! You must take care of him! That means walking the dog three times a day, no matter how bad the weather is!!
We promise, Daddy! We promise!!
We're interested in a nice comfortable double bed for us!
Step this way, please . . .
MINK BATHING SUITS
Do you mind if we test it?
Be my guest!
UP, boy . . .
Look, honey! He likes it!
Okay, we'll take it!

DOG OWNERS

WRITER & ARTIST: DAVID BERG

It's **your turn** to feed the **dog** tonight, stupid! **Move!**

Go feed the dog, or I'll tell Mom who cracked that vase . . .

Bad dog! 'Cause of you, I'm always in trouble! Just for that you don't get any supper!!

"The Washington Post" isn't bad!

Neither is "The Chicago Tribune"

Personally, I like "The Denver Post"!

That's okay, but "The Philadelphia Inquirer" is better!

But best of all is the "Sunday New York Times!"

You said it!

You get 8 pounds of news-paper all at once!

Yep! When it comes to **PAPER-TRAINING A PUPPY,** you can't beat "The New York Times"!

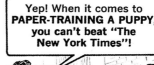

I'm **warning** you kids **right now!** There'll be **no deserts** unless you finish everything on your plates . . .

Well, **that's** more like it!!

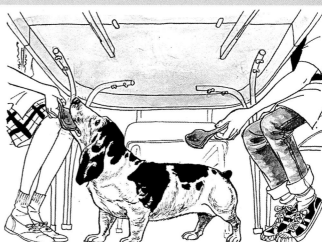

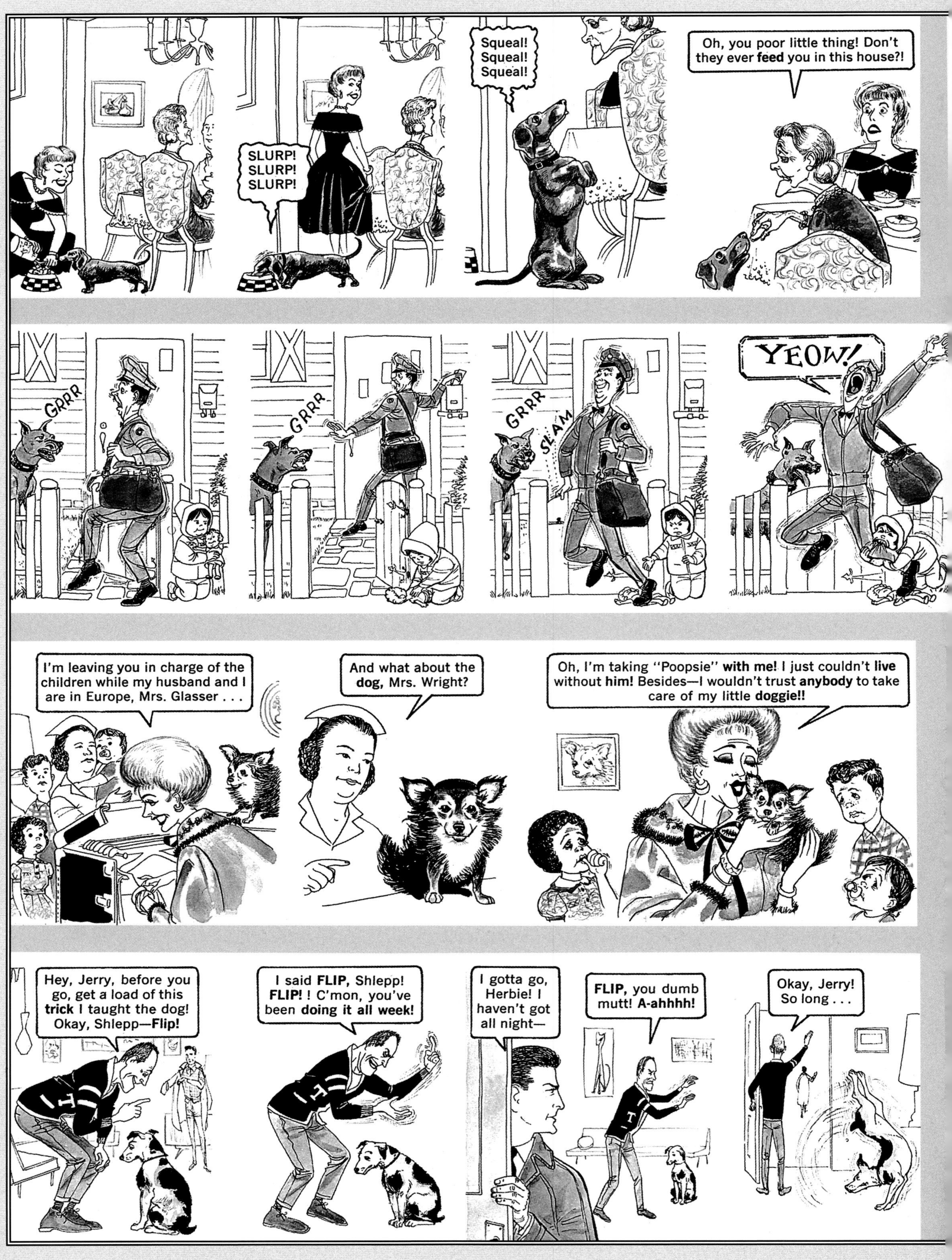
SLURP!
SLURP!
SLURP!
Squeal!
Squeal!
Squeal!
Oh, you poor little thing! Don't they ever **feed** you in this house?!
GRRR
GRRR
GRRR
SLAM
YEOW!
I'm leaving you in charge of the children while my husband and I are in Europe, Mrs. Glasser . . .
And what about the **dog**, Mrs. Wright?
Oh, I'm taking "Poopsie" **with me!** I just couldn't **live** without **him!** Besides—I wouldn't trust **anybody** to take care of my little **doggie!!**
Hey, Jerry, before you go, get a load of this **trick** I taught the dog! Okay, Shlepp—**Flip!**
I said **FLIP,** Shlepp! **FLIP!** ! C'mon, you've been **doing it all week!**
I gotta go, Herbie! I haven't got all night—
FLIP, you dumb mutt! **A-ahhhh!**
Okay, Jerry! So long . . .

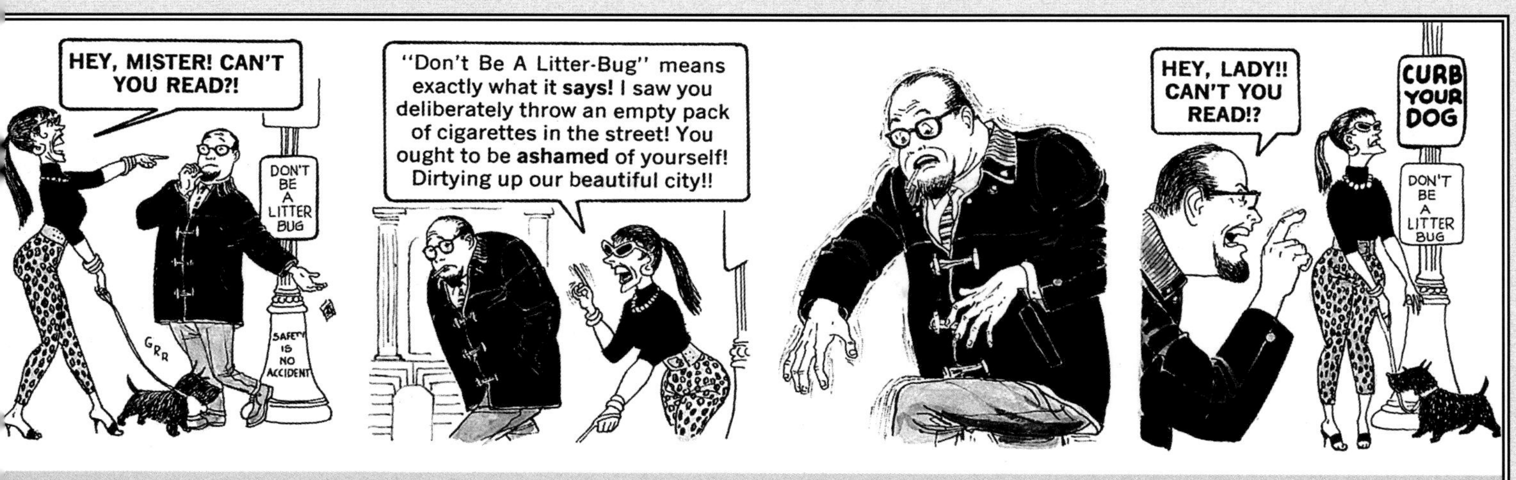
HEY, MISTER! CAN'T YOU READ?!
DON'T BE A LITTER BUG
SAFETY IS NO ACCIDENT
GRR
"Don't Be A Litter-Bug" means exactly what it says! I saw you deliberately throw an empty pack of cigarettes in the street! You ought to be ashamed of yourself! Dirtying up our beautiful city!!
HEY, LADY!! CAN'T YOU READ!?
CURB YOUR DOG
DON'T BE A LITTER BUG

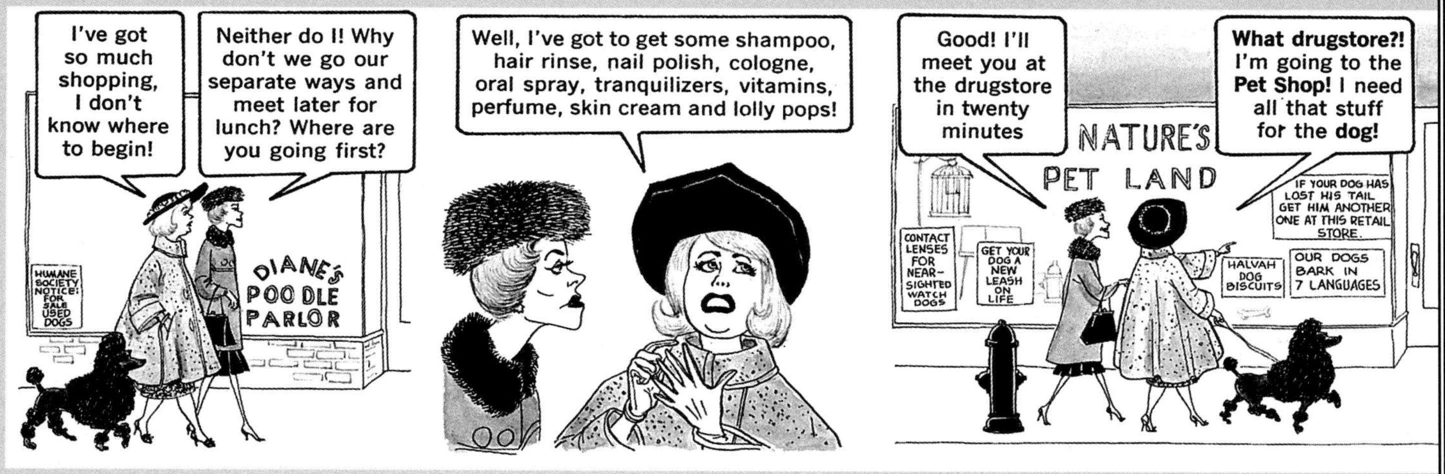
I've got so much shopping, I don't know where to begin!
Neither do I! Why don't we go our separate ways and meet later for lunch? Where are you going first?
HUMANE SOCIETY NOTICE: FOR SALE USED DOGS
DIANE'S POODLE PARLOR
Well, I've got to get some shampoo, hair rinse, nail polish, cologne, oral spray, tranquilizers, vitamins, perfume, skin cream and lolly pops!
Good! I'll meet you at the drugstore in twenty minutes
What drugstore?! I'm going to the Pet Shop! I need all that stuff for the dog!
NATURE'S PET LAND
IF YOUR DOG HAS LOST HIS TAIL GET HIM ANOTHER ONE AT THIS RETAIL STORE.
CONTACT LENSES FOR NEAR-SIGHTED WATCH DOGS
GET YOUR DOG A NEW LEASH ON LIFE
HALVAH DOG BISCUITS
OUR DOGS BARK IN 7 LANGUAGES

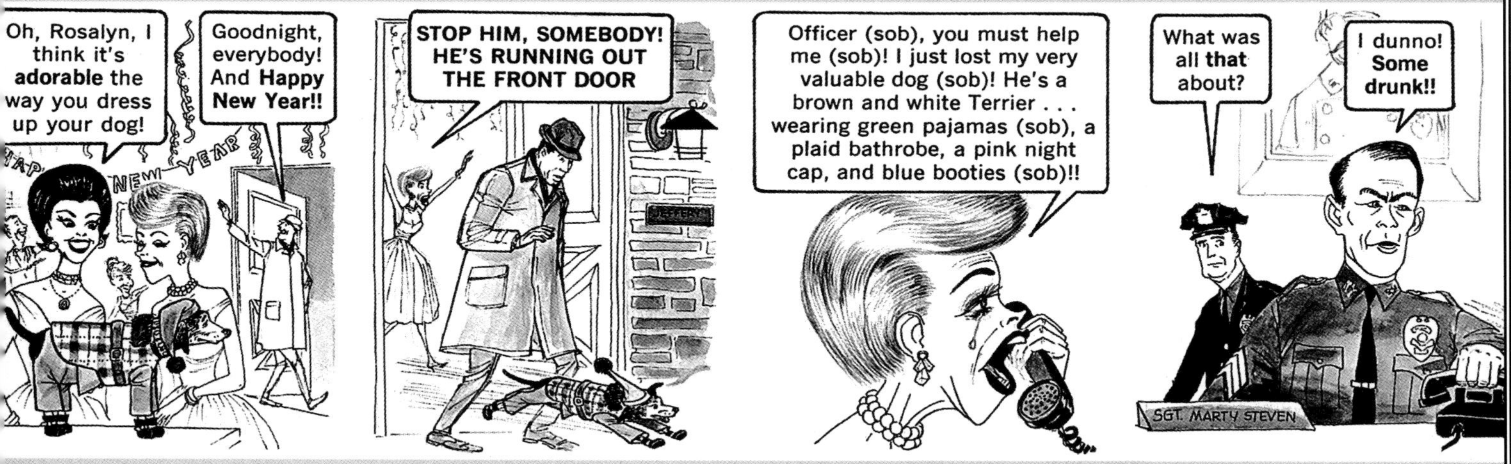
Oh, Rosalyn, I think it's adorable the way you dress up your dog!
Goodnight, everybody! And Happy New Year!!
STOP HIM, SOMEBODY! HE'S RUNNING OUT THE FRONT DOOR
Officer (sob), you must help me (sob)! I just lost my very valuable dog (sob)! He's a brown and white Terrier . . . wearing green pajamas (sob), a plaid bathrobe, a pink night cap, and blue booties (sob)!!
What was all that about?
I dunno! Some drunk!!
SGT. MARTY STEVEN

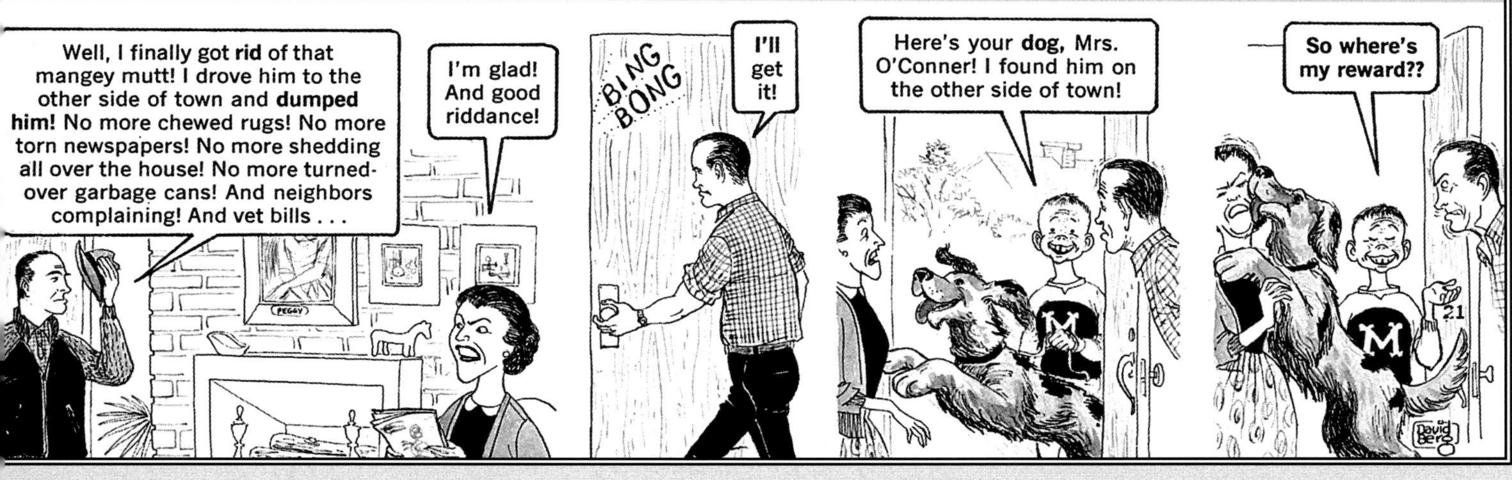
Well, I finally got rid of that mangey mutt! I drove him to the other side of town and dumped him! No more chewed rugs! No more torn newspapers! No more shedding all over the house! No more turned-over garbage cans! And neighbors complaining! And vet bills . . .
I'm glad! And good riddance!
BING BONG
I'll get it!
Here's your dog, Mrs. O'Conner! I found him on the other side of town!
So where's my reward??

BERG'S-EYE VIEW DEPT.

THE LIGHTER SIDE OF SUMMER

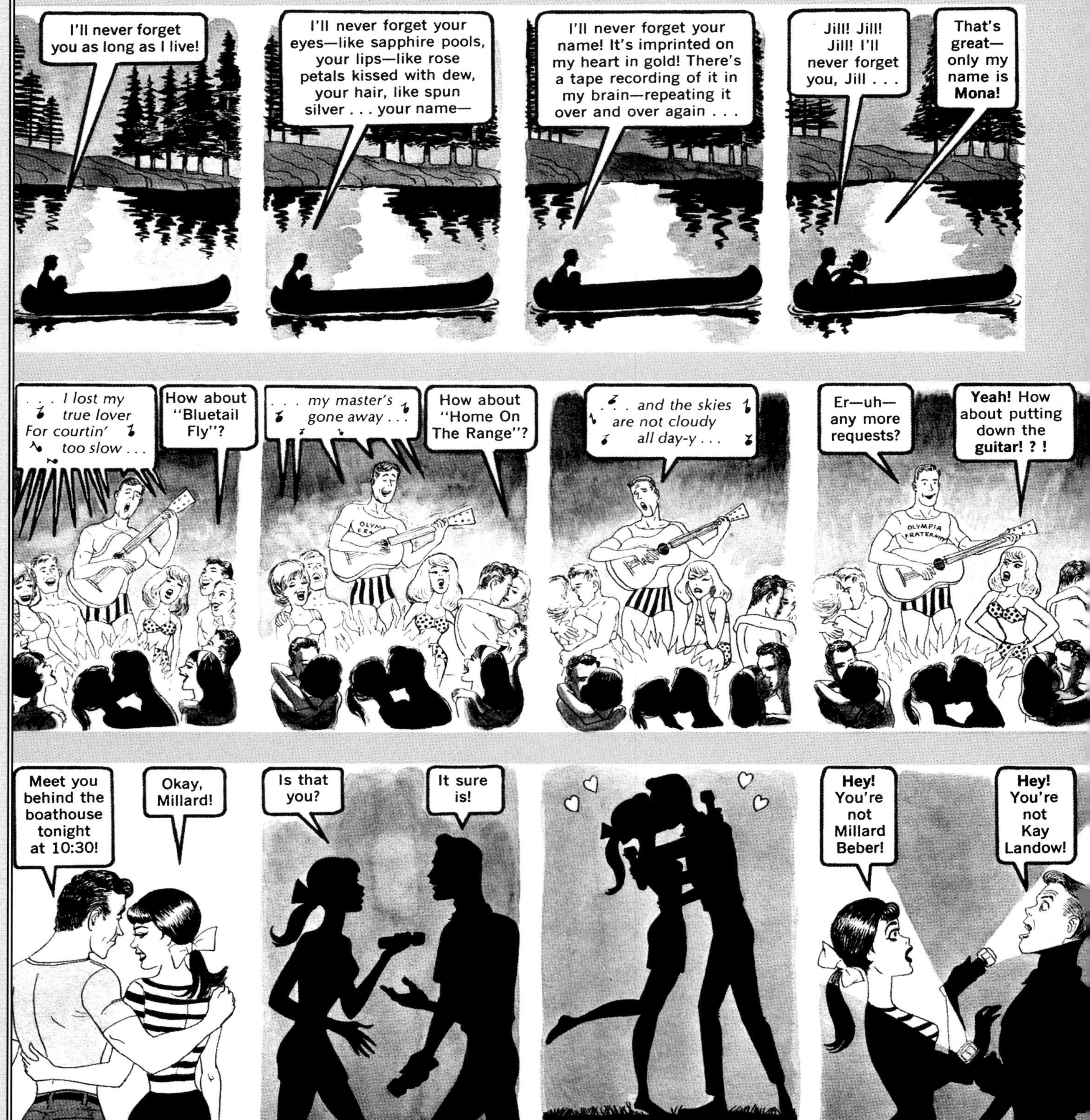
I'll never forget you as long as I live!
I'll never forget your eyes—like sapphire pools, your lips—like rose petals kissed with dew, your hair, like spun silver . . . your name—
I'll never forget your name! It's imprinted on my heart in gold! There's a tape recording of it in my brain—repeating it over and over again . . .
Jill! Jill! Jill! I'll never forget you, Jill . . .
That's great—only my name is **Mona!**
. . . *I lost my true lover For courtin' too slow . . .*
How about "Bluetail Fly"?
. . . *my master's gone away . . .*
How about "Home On The Range"?
. . . *and the skies are not cloudy all day-y . . .*
Er—uh—any more requests?
Yeah! How about putting down the **guitar! ? !**
Meet you behind the boathouse tonight at 10:30!
Okay, Millard!
Is that you?
It sure is!
Hey! You're not Millard Beber!
Hey! You're not Kay Landow!

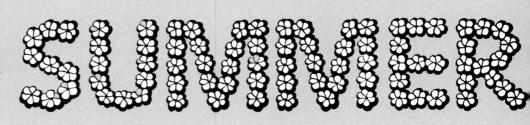

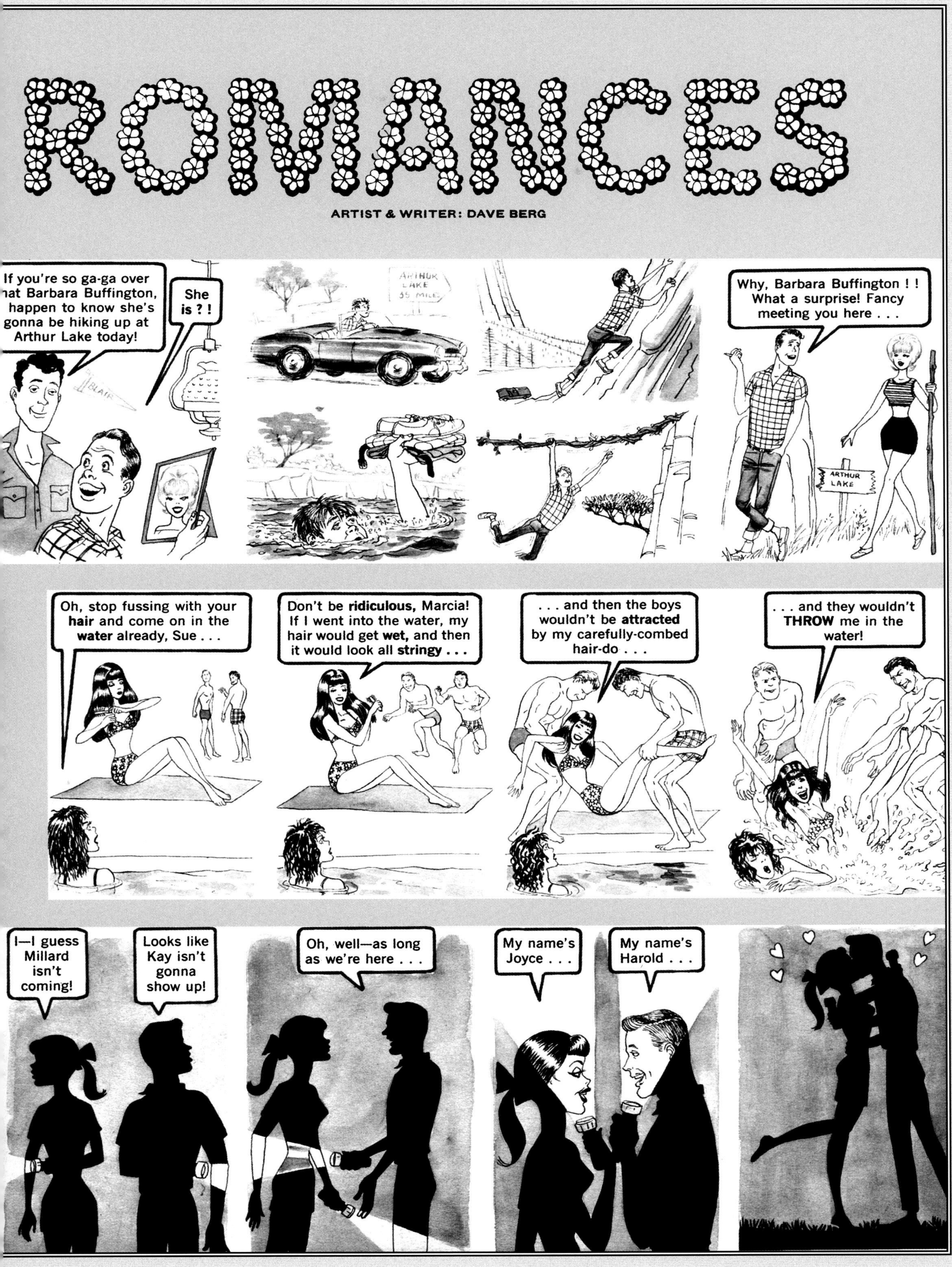
ROMANCES
ARTIST & WRITER: DAVE BERG
If you're so ga-ga over hat Barbara Buffington, happen to know she's gonna be hiking up at Arthur Lake today!
She is ? !
BLAIR
ARTHUR LAKE 35 MILES
Why, Barbara Buffington ! ! What a surprise! Fancy meeting you here . . .
ARTHUR LAKE
Oh, stop fussing with your **hair** and come on in the **water** already, Sue . . .
Don't be **ridiculous,** Marcia! If I went into the water, my hair would get **wet,** and then it would look all **stringy . . .**
. . . and then the boys wouldn't be **attracted** by my carefully-combed hair-do . . .
. . . and they wouldn't **THROW** me in the water!
I—I guess Millard isn't coming!
Looks like Kay isn't gonna show up!
Oh, well—as long as we're here . . .
My name's Joyce . . .
My name's Harold . . .

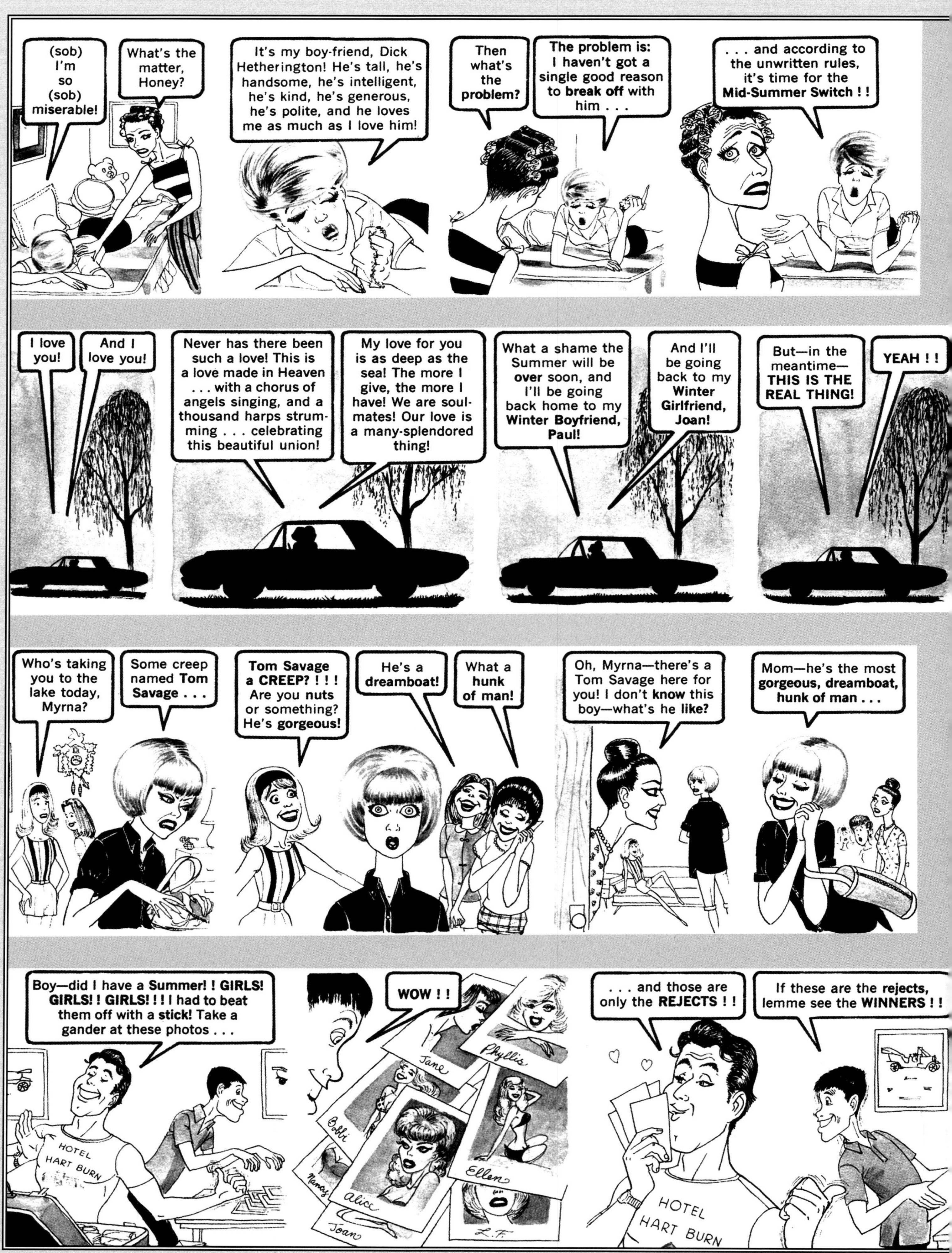
(sob) I'm so (sob) miserable!
What's the matter, Honey?
It's my boy-friend, Dick Hetherington! He's tall, he's handsome, he's intelligent, he's kind, he's generous, he's polite, and he loves me as much as I love him!
Then what's the problem?
The problem is: I haven't got a single good reason to break off with him . . .
. . . and according to the unwritten rules, it's time for the Mid-Summer Switch ! !
I love you!
And I love you!
Never has there been such a love! This is a love made in Heaven . . . with a chorus of angels singing, and a thousand harps strumming . . . celebrating this beautiful union!
My love for you is as deep as the sea! The more I give, the more I have! We are soul-mates! Our love is a many-splendored thing!
What a shame the Summer will be over soon, and I'll be going back home to my Winter Boyfriend, Paul!
And I'll be going back to my Winter Girlfriend, Joan!
But—in the meantime— THIS IS THE REAL THING!
YEAH ! !
Who's taking you to the lake today, Myrna?
Some creep named Tom Savage . . .
Tom Savage a CREEP? ! ! ! Are you nuts or something? He's gorgeous!
He's a dreamboat!
What a hunk of man!
Oh, Myrna—there's a Tom Savage here for you! I don't know this boy—what's he like?
Mom—he's the most gorgeous, dreamboat, hunk of man . . .
Boy—did I have a Summer! ! GIRLS! GIRLS! ! GIRLS! ! ! I had to beat them off with a stick! Take a gander at these photos . . .
HOTEL HART BURN
WOW ! !
Jane
Phyllis
Bobbi
Ellen
Nancy
Alice
Joan
. . . and those are only the REJECTS ! !
If these are the rejects, lemme see the WINNERS ! !
HOTEL HART BURN

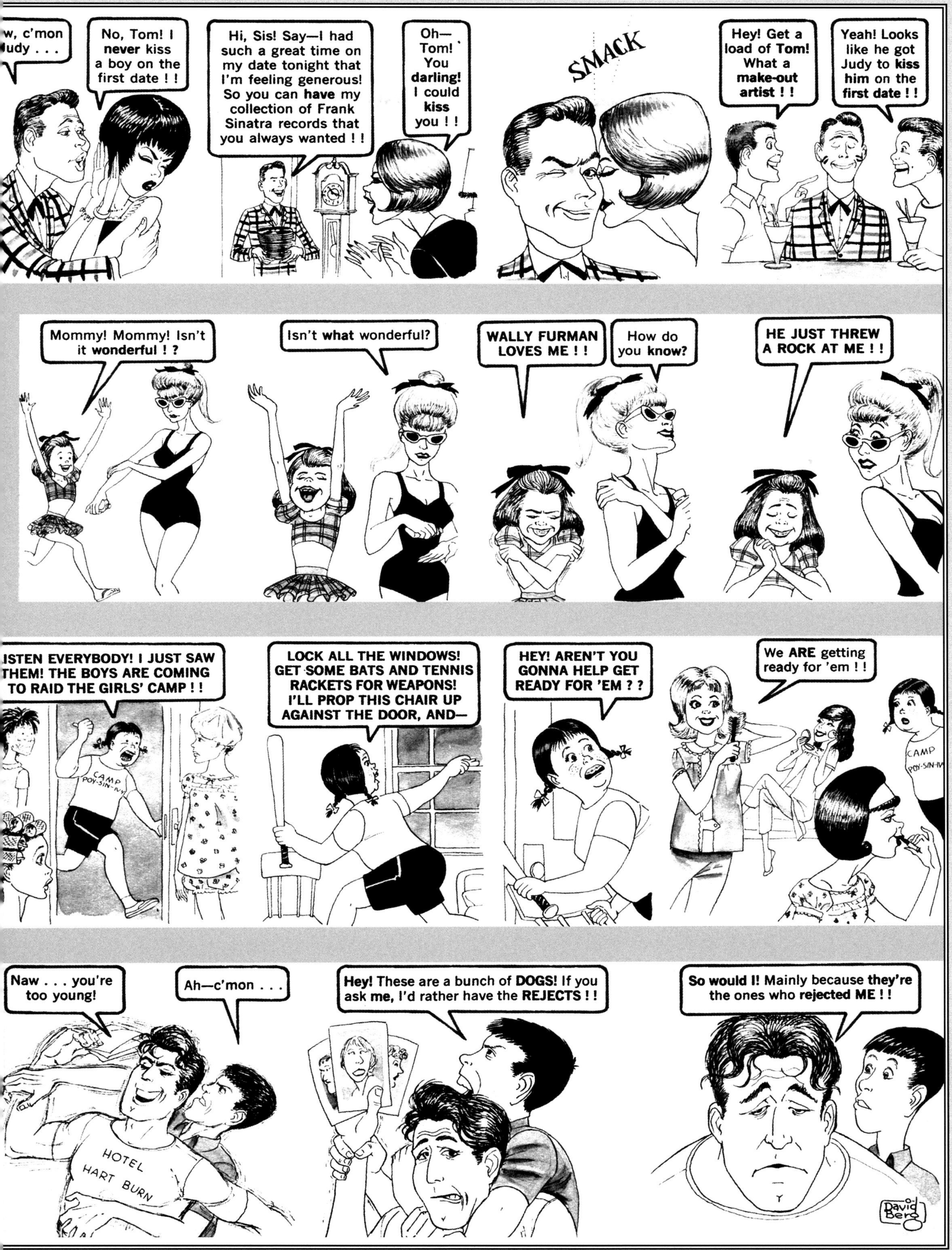
w, c'mon
udy . . .
No, Tom! I never kiss a boy on the first date ! !
Hi, Sis! Say—I had such a great time on my date tonight that I'm feeling generous! So you can have my collection of Frank Sinatra records that you always wanted ! !
Oh— Tom! You darling! I could kiss you ! !
SMACK
Hey! Get a load of Tom! What a make-out artist ! !
Yeah! Looks like he got Judy to kiss him on the first date ! !
Mommy! Mommy! Isn't it wonderful ! ?
Isn't what wonderful?
WALLY FURMAN LOVES ME ! !
How do you know?
HE JUST THREW A ROCK AT ME ! !
ISTEN EVERYBODY! I JUST SAW THEM! THE BOYS ARE COMING TO RAID THE GIRLS' CAMP ! !
CAMP POY-SIN-IVY
LOCK ALL THE WINDOWS! GET SOME BATS AND TENNIS RACKETS FOR WEAPONS! I'LL PROP THIS CHAIR UP AGAINST THE DOOR, AND—
HEY! AREN'T YOU GONNA HELP GET READY FOR 'EM ? ?
We ARE getting ready for 'em ! !
CAMP POY-SIN-IVY
Naw . . . you're too young!
Ah—c'mon . . .
HOTEL HART BURN
Hey! These are a bunch of DOGS! If you ask me, I'd rather have the REJECTS ! !
So would I! Mainly because they're the ones who rejected ME ! !
David Berg

BERG'S-EYE VIEW DEPT.

THE LIGHTER SIDE OF

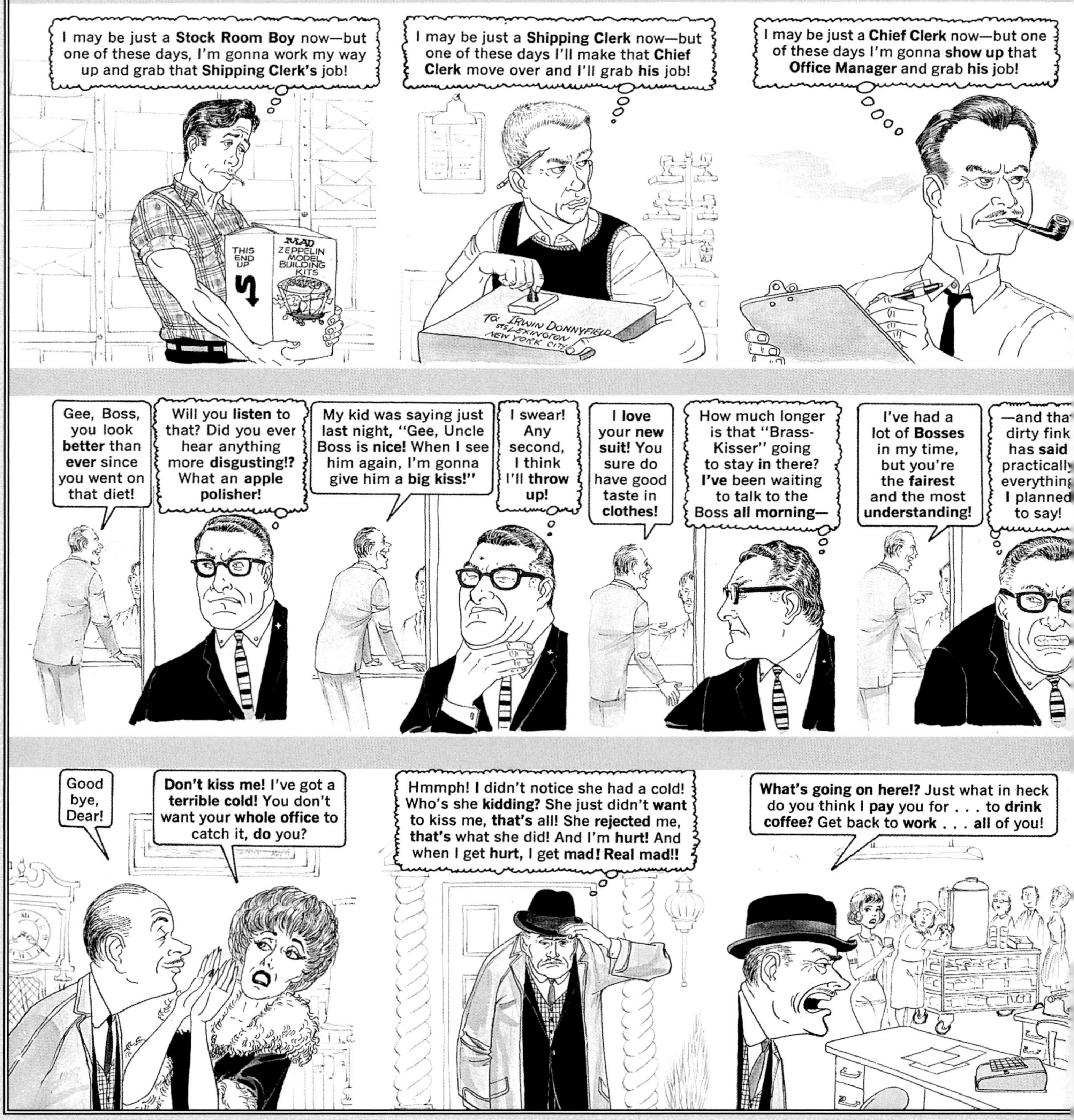
I may be just a **Stock Room Boy** now—but one of these days, I'm gonna work my way up and grab that **Shipping Clerk's** job!
THIS END UP
MAD ZEPPELIN MODEL BUILDING KITS
I may be just a **Shipping Clerk** now—but one of these days I'll make that **Chief Clerk** move over and I'll grab **his** job!
TO: IRWIN DONNYFIELD 575 LEXINGTON NEW YORK CITY
I may be just a **Chief Clerk** now—but one of these days I'm gonna **show up** that **Office Manager** and grab **his** job!
Gee, Boss, you look **better** than **ever** since you went on that diet!
Will you **listen** to that? Did you ever hear anything more **disgusting!?** What an **apple polisher!**
My kid was saying just last night, "Gee, Uncle Boss is **nice!** When I see him again, I'm gonna give him a **big kiss!**"
I swear! Any second, I think I'll **throw up!**
I **love** your **new suit!** You sure do have good taste in **clothes!**
How much longer is that "Brass-Kisser" going to stay **in** there? **I've** been waiting to talk to the Boss **all morning—**
I've had a lot of **Bosses** in my time, but you're the **fairest** and the most **understanding!**
—and tha dirty fink has **said** practically everythin **I** planned to say!
Good bye, Dear!
Don't kiss me! I've got a **terrible cold!** You don't want your **whole office** to catch it, **do** you?
Hmmph! **I** didn't notice she had a cold! Who's she **kidding?** She just didn't **want** to kiss me, **that's** all! She **rejected** me, **that's** what she did! And I'm **hurt!** And when I get **hurt**, I get **mad! Real mad!!**
What's going on here!? Just what in heck do you think **I pay** you for . . . to **drink coffee?** Get back to **work** . . . **all** of you!

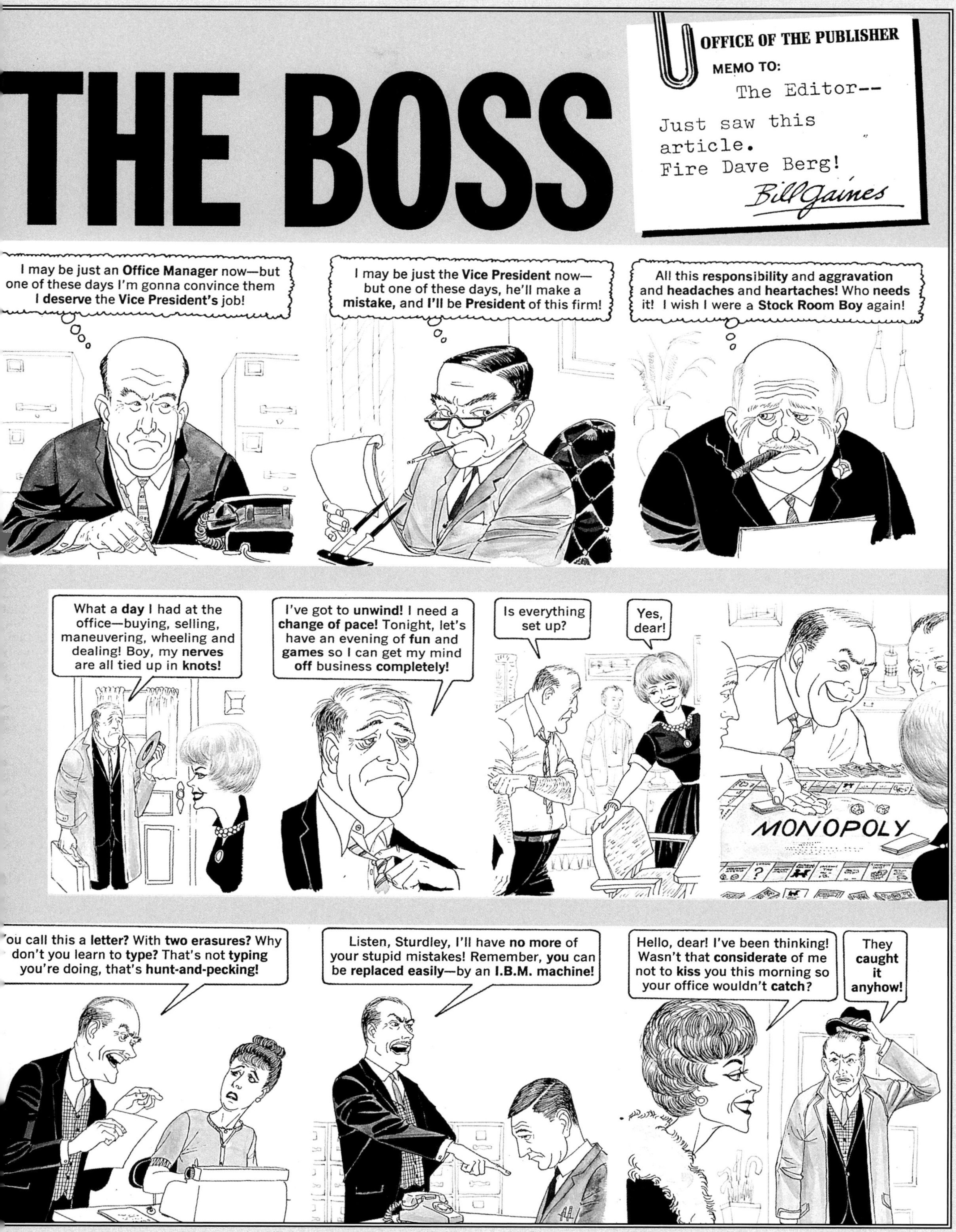
THE BOSS
OFFICE OF THE PUBLISHER
MEMO TO:
The Editor--
Just saw this article.
Fire Dave Berg!
Bill Gaines
I may be just an Office Manager now—but one of these days I'm gonna convince them I deserve the Vice President's job!
I may be just the Vice President now—but one of these days, he'll make a mistake, and I'll be President of this firm!
All this responsibility and aggravation and headaches and heartaches! Who needs it! I wish I were a Stock Room Boy again!
What a day I had at the office—buying, selling, maneuvering, wheeling and dealing! Boy, my nerves are all tied up in knots!
I've got to unwind! I need a change of pace! Tonight, let's have an evening of fun and games so I can get my mind off business completely!
Is everything set up?
Yes, dear!
MONOPOLY
'ou call this a letter? With two erasures? Why don't you learn to type? That's not typing you're doing, that's hunt-and-pecking!
Listen, Sturdley, I'll have no more of your stupid mistakes! Remember, you can be replaced easily—by an I.B.M. machine!
Hello, dear! I've been thinking! Wasn't that considerate of me not to kiss you this morning so your office wouldn't catch?
They caught it anyhow!

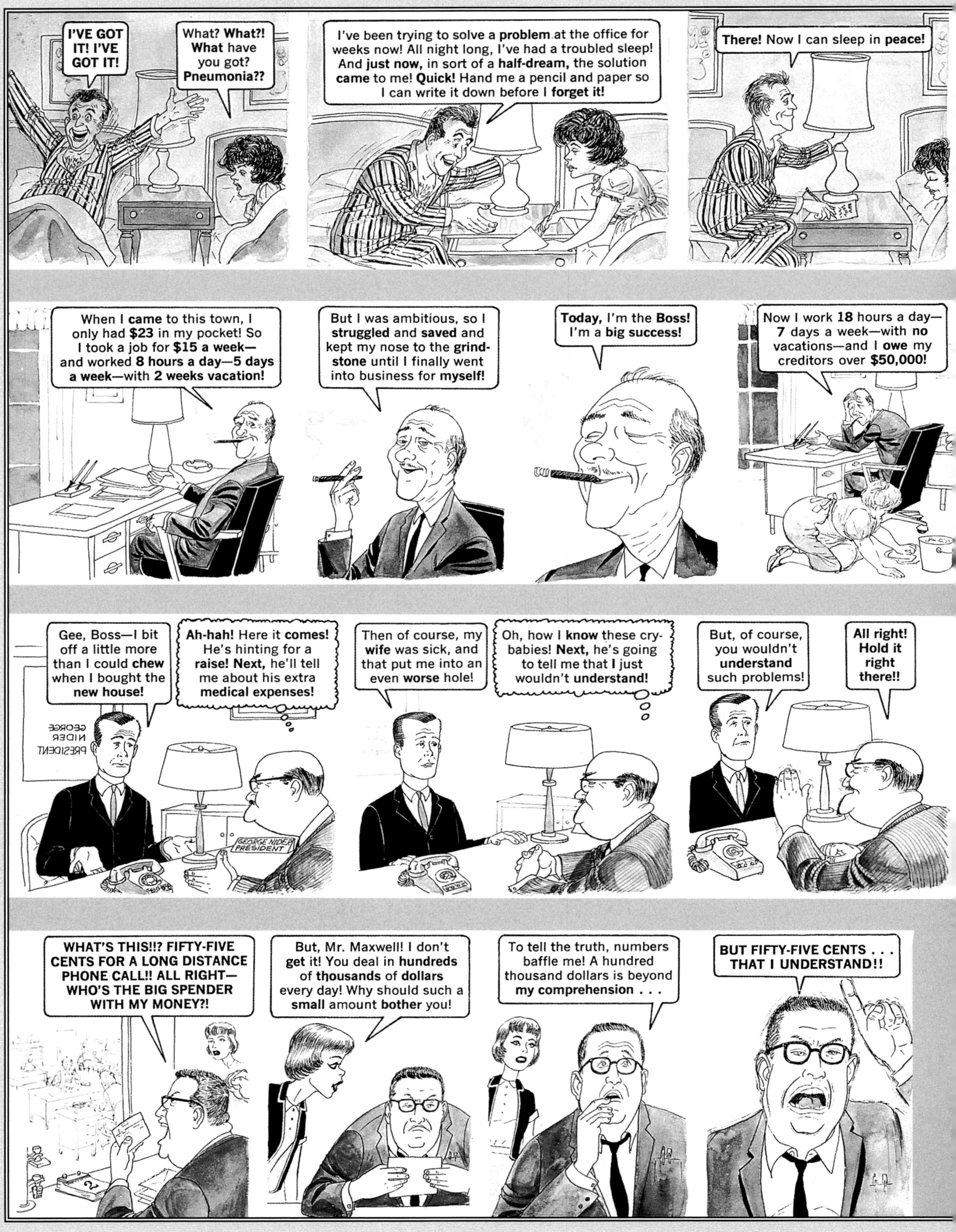
I'VE GOT IT! I'VE GOT IT!
What? What?! What have you got? Pneumonia??
I've been trying to solve a problem at the office for weeks now! All night long, I've had a troubled sleep! And just now, in sort of a half-dream, the solution came to me! Quick! Hand me a pencil and paper so I can write it down before I forget it!
There! Now I can sleep in peace!
When I came to this town, I only had $23 in my pocket! So I took a job for $15 a week—and worked 8 hours a day—5 days a week—with 2 weeks vacation!
But I was ambitious, so I struggled and saved and kept my nose to the grind-stone until I finally went into business for myself!
Today, I'm the Boss! I'm a big success!
Now I work 18 hours a day—7 days a week—with no vacations—and I owe my creditors over $50,000!
Gee, Boss—I bit off a little more than I could chew when I bought the new house!
Ah-hah! Here it comes! He's hinting for a raise! Next, he'll tell me about his extra medical expenses!
GEORGE NIDER PRESIDENT
Then of course, my wife was sick, and that put me into an even worse hole!
Oh, how I know these cry-babies! Next, he's going to tell me that I just wouldn't understand!
But, of course, you wouldn't understand such problems!
All right! Hold it right there!!
WHAT'S THIS!!? FIFTY-FIVE CENTS FOR A LONG DISTANCE PHONE CALL!! ALL RIGHT—WHO'S THE BIG SPENDER WITH MY MONEY?!
But, Mr. Maxwell! I don't get it! You deal in hundreds of thousands of dollars every day! Why should such a small amount bother you!
To tell the truth, numbers baffle me! A hundred thousand dollars is beyond my comprehension . . .
BUT FIFTY-FIVE CENTS . . . THAT I UNDERSTAND!!

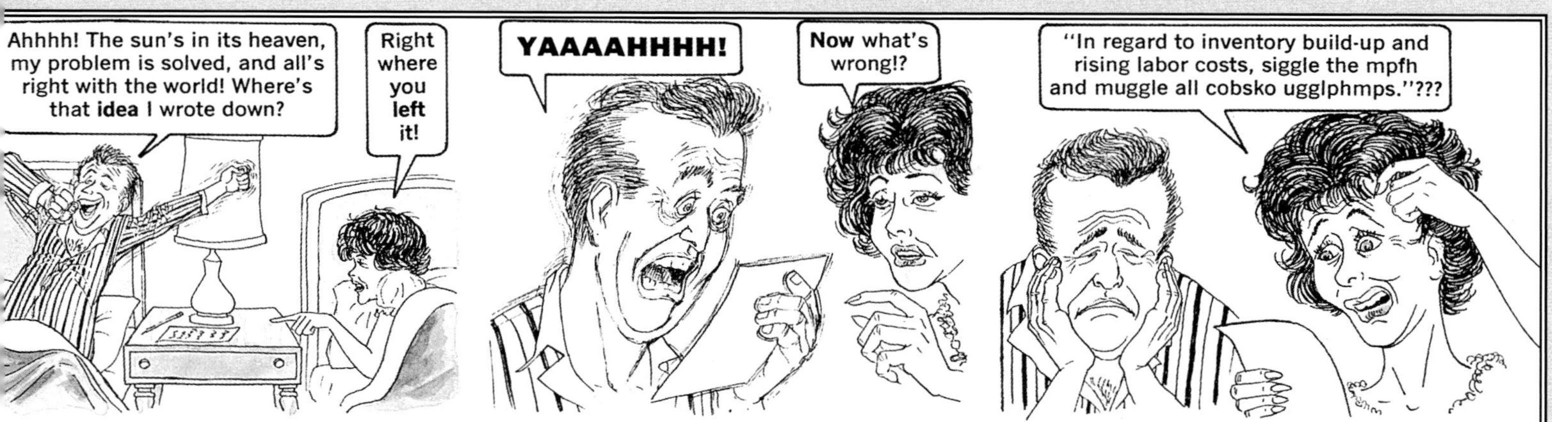
Ahhhh! The sun's in its heaven, my problem is solved, and all's right with the world! Where's that **idea** I wrote down?
Right where you **left** it!
YAAAAHHHH!
Now what's wrong!?
"In regard to inventory build-up and rising labor costs, siggle the mpfh and muggle all cobsko ugglphmps."???

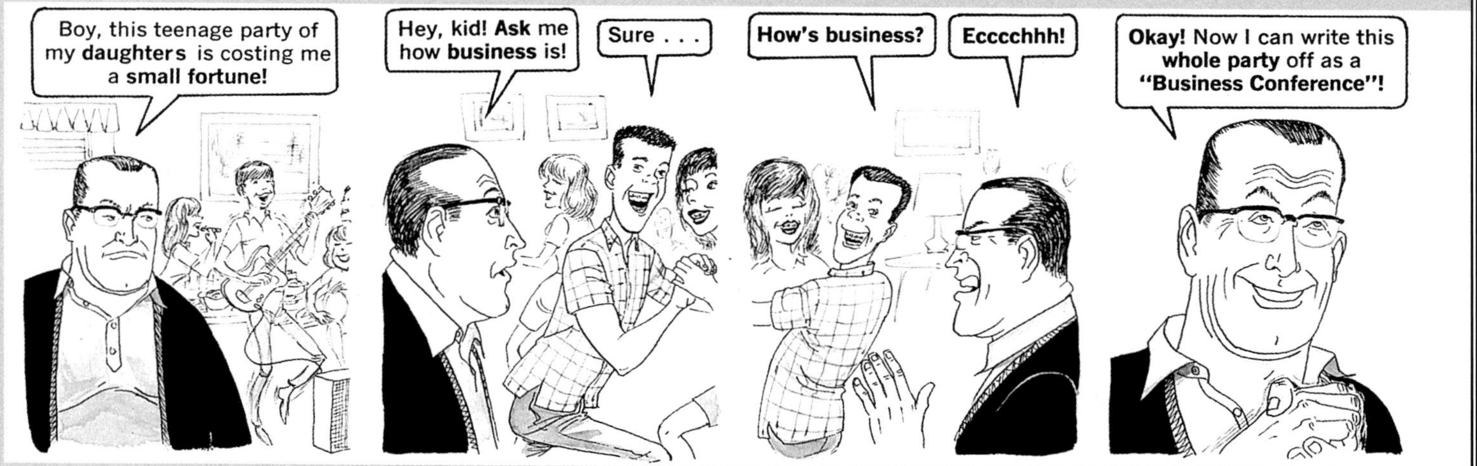
Boy, this teenage party of my **daughters** is costing me a **small fortune!**
Hey, kid! **Ask** me how **business** is!
Sure . . .
How's business?
Ecccchhh!
Okay! Now I can write this **whole party** off as a **"Business Conference"!**

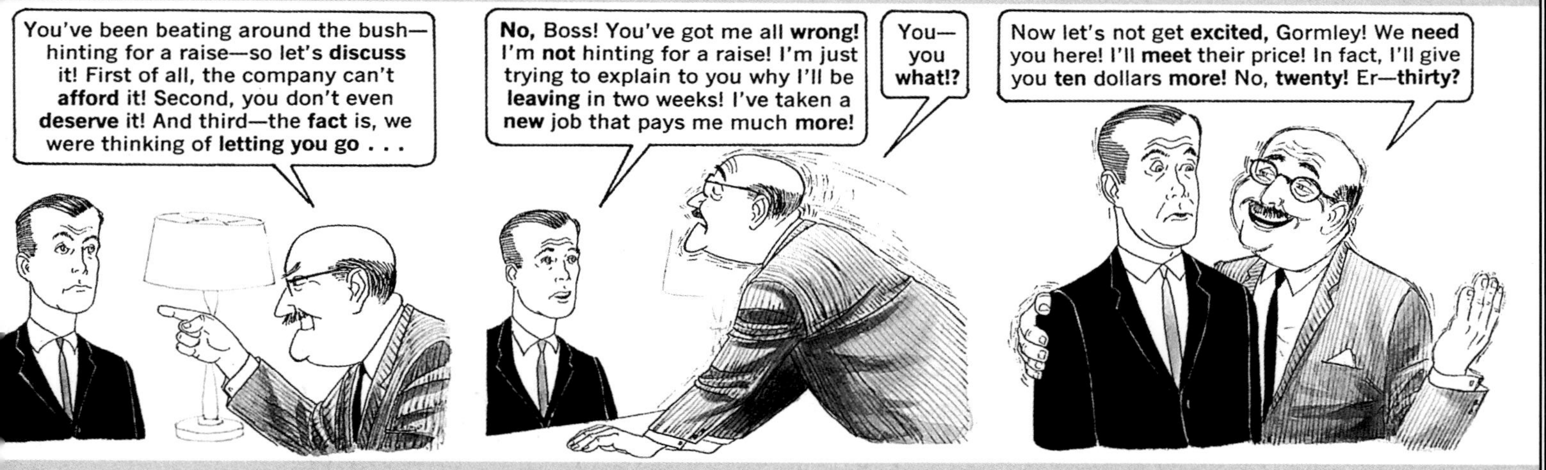
You've been beating around the bush—hinting for a raise—so let's **discuss** it! First of all, the company can't **afford** it! Second, you don't even **deserve** it! And third—the **fact** is, we were thinking of **letting you go . . .**
No, Boss! You've got me all **wrong!** I'm **not** hinting for a raise! I'm just trying to explain to you why I'll be **leaving** in two weeks! I've taken a **new** job that pays me much **more!**
You—you **what!?**
Now let's not get **excited**, Gormley! We **need** you here! I'll **meet** their price! In fact, I'll give you **ten dollars more!** No, **twenty!** Er—**thirty?**

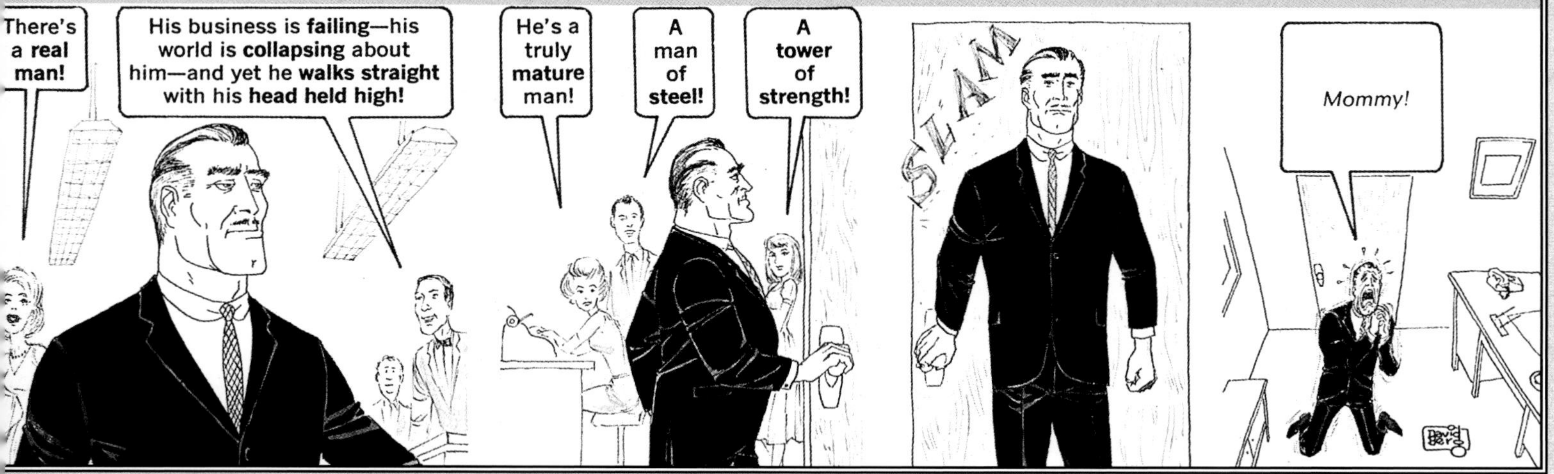
There's a **real man!**
His business is **failing**—his world is **collapsing** about him—and yet he **walks straight** with his **head held high!**
He's a truly **mature** man!
A man of steel!
A tower of strength!
Mommy!

BERG'S-EYE VIEW DEPT.

THE LIGHTER SIDE OF

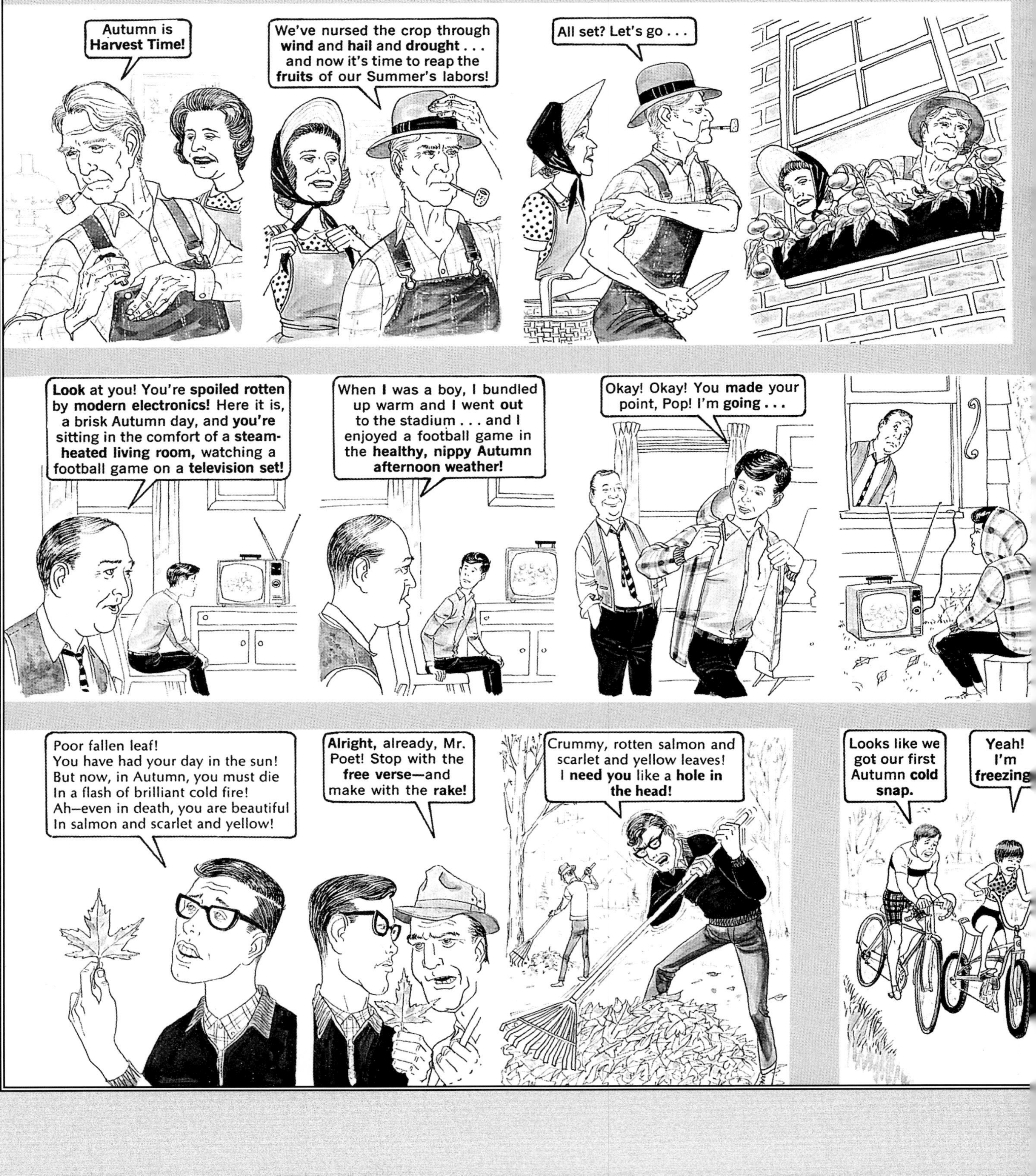
Autumn is Harvest Time!
We've nursed the crop through wind and hail and drought . . . and now it's time to reap the fruits of our Summer's labors!
All set? Let's go . . .
Look at you! You're spoiled rotten by modern electronics! Here it is, a brisk Autumn day, and you're sitting in the comfort of a steam-heated living room, watching a football game on a television set!
When I was a boy, I bundled up warm and I went out to the stadium . . . and I enjoyed a football game in the healthy, nippy Autumn afternoon weather!
Okay! Okay! You made your point, Pop! I'm going . . .
Poor fallen leaf! You have had your day in the sun! But now, in Autumn, you must die In a flash of brilliant cold fire! Ah—even in death, you are beautiful In salmon and scarlet and yellow!
Alright, already, Mr. Poet! Stop with the free verse—and make with the rake!
Crummy, rotten salmon and scarlet and yellow leaves! I need you like a hole in the head!
Looks like we got our first Autumn cold snap.
Yeah! I'm freezing

AUTUMN

WRITER & ARTIST: DAVID BERG

Trick or treat!

It's **blackmail,** that's what this Halloween business is! **Blackmail!** I wonder what would happen if, just once, I **refused** to **give in** to it?

Trick or treat!

TRICK!!

WAAA!

D-d-don't cry, kids! I-I was only **kidding!** Here! Here— take the **whole bowl** of candy!

You can't buck the **system!**

Before we eat, I'd like to say a few words about "Thanksgiving"! Too often, we **forget** the real **idea** of this holiday! Now is the time when we should **count our blessings!**

We may not be **wealthy** . . . but as long as we have our **lives** and our **health,** we are indeed **very rich!**

Yes, I would say that **everybody** at this table has a **great deal** to be thankful for!

Except the **turkey!**

So am **I!** Neither of us are **dressed** warm enough! It's all because of that **darn undependable Telephone Weather Forecasting Service!**

Did **they** goof again? Boy, they **never** get it right! Why do you even bother to **call** them?

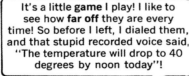

It's a little **game** I play! I like to see how **far off** they are every time! So before I left, I dialed them, and that stupid recorded voice said, "The temperature will drop to 40 degrees by noon today"!

Huh? But they were **right!** Why didn't you **take along** some warm clothes?

Because I **never believe** them!

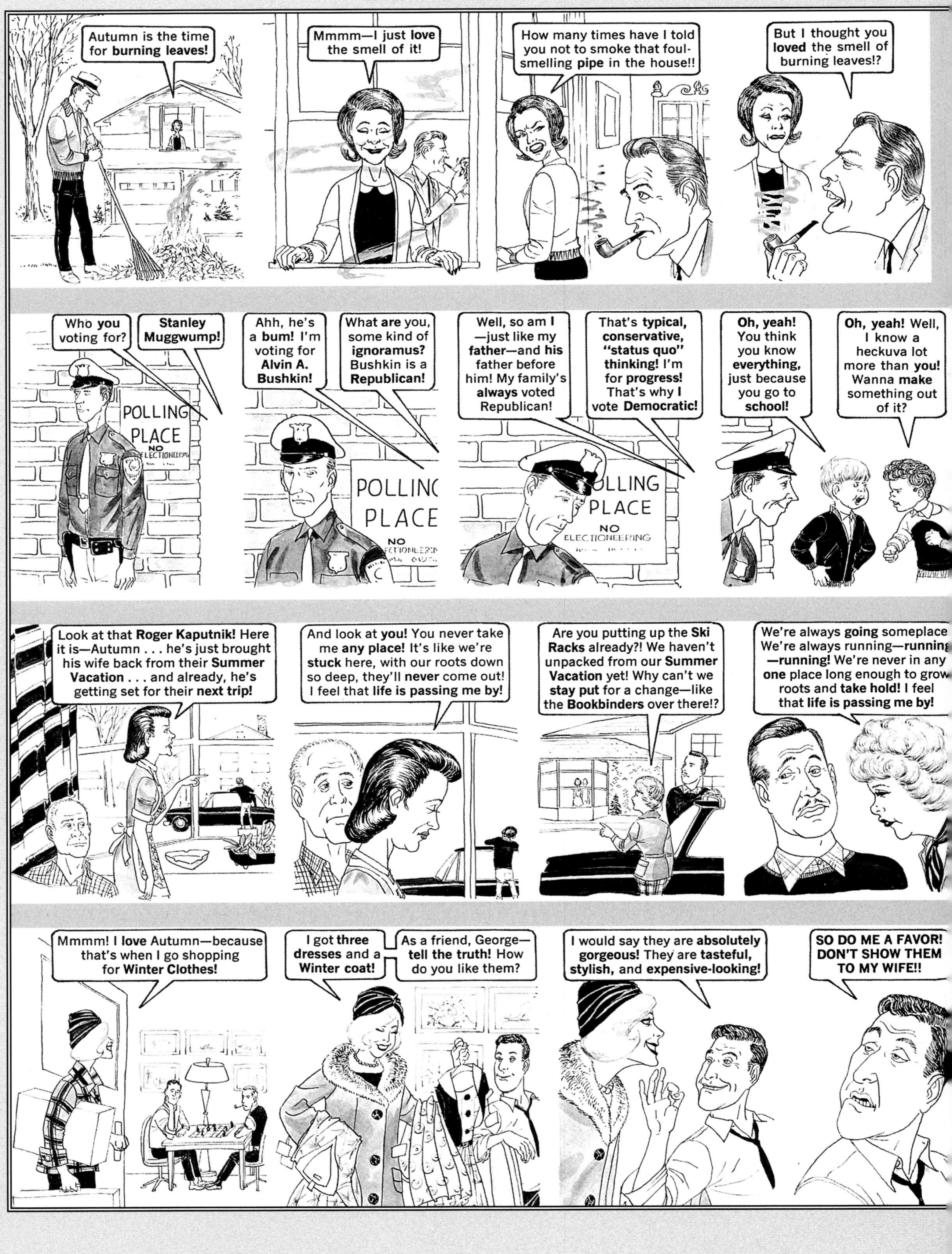
Autumn is the time for burning leaves!
Mmmm—I just love the smell of it!
How many times have I told you not to smoke that foul-smelling pipe in the house!!
But I thought you loved the smell of burning leaves!?
Who you voting for?
Stanley Muggwump!
POLLING PLACE
NO ELECTIONEERING
Ahh, he's a bum! I'm voting for Alvin A. Bushkin!
What are you, some kind of ignoramus? Bushkin is a Republican!
POLLING PLACE
Well, so am I—just like my father—and his father before him! My family's always voted Republican!
That's typical, conservative, "status quo" thinking! I'm for progress! That's why I vote Democratic!
PLACE
NO ELECTIONEERING
Oh, yeah! You think you know everything, just because you go to school!
Oh, yeah! Well, I know a heckuva lot more than you! Wanna make something out of it?
Look at that Roger Kaputnik! Here it is—Autumn . . . he's just brought his wife back from their Summer Vacation . . . and already, he's getting set for their next trip!
And look at you! You never take me any place! It's like we're stuck here, with our roots down so deep, they'll never come out! I feel that life is passing me by!
Are you putting up the Ski Racks already?! We haven't unpacked from our Summer Vacation yet! Why can't we stay put for a change—like the Bookbinders over there!?
We're always going someplace We're always running—running—running! We're never in any one place long enough to grow roots and take hold! I feel that life is passing me by!
Mmmm! I love Autumn—because that's when I go shopping for Winter Clothes!
I got three dresses and a Winter coat!
As a friend, George—tell the truth! How do you like them?
I would say they are absolutely gorgeous! They are tasteful, stylish, and expensive-looking!
SO DO ME A FAVOR! DON'T SHOW THEM TO MY WIFE!!

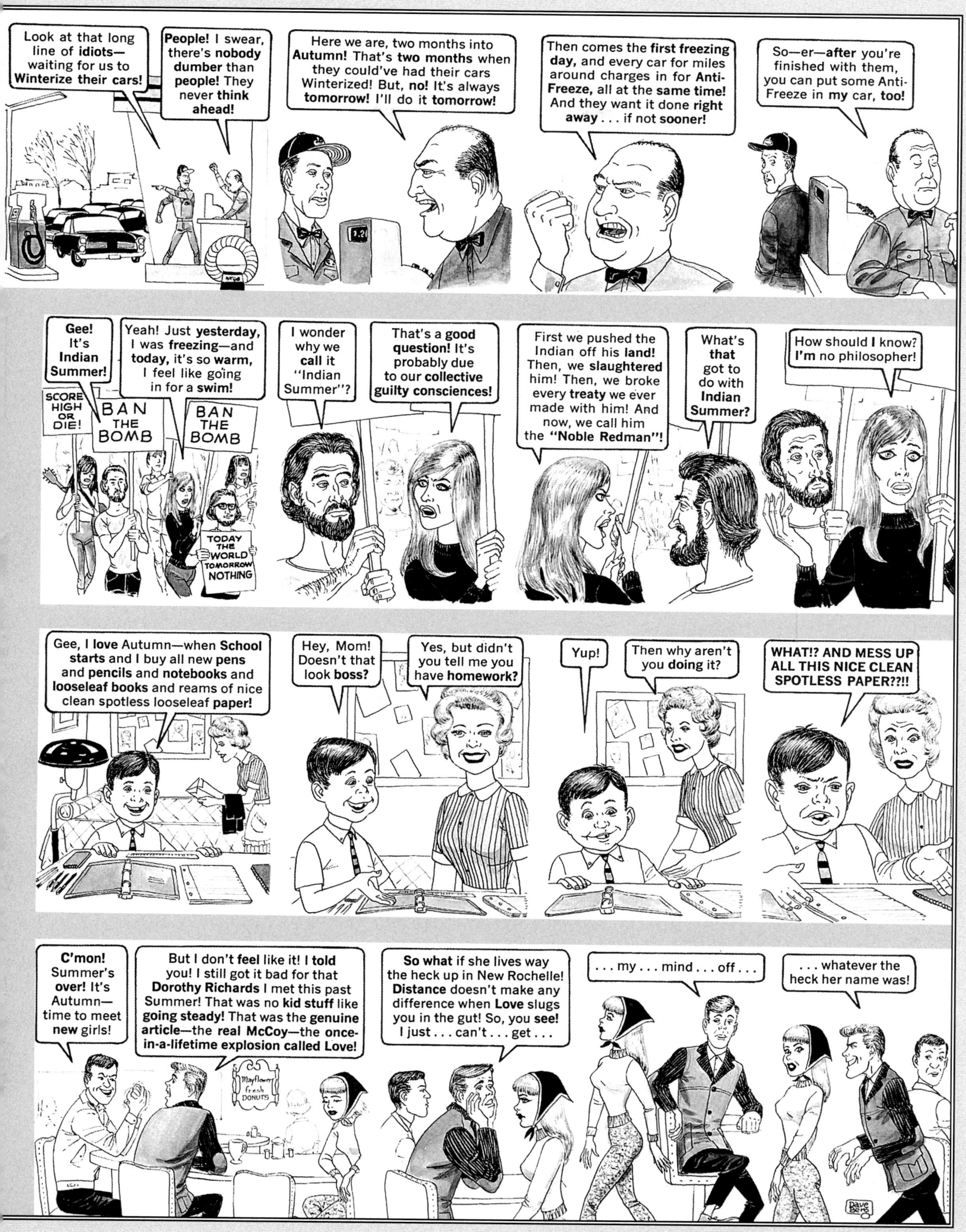
Look at that long line of idiots—waiting for us to Winterize their cars!
People! I swear, there's nobody dumber than people! They never think ahead!
Here we are, two months into Autumn! That's two months when they could've had their cars Winterized! But, no! It's always tomorrow! I'll do it tomorrow!
Then comes the first freezing day, and every car for miles around charges in for Anti-Freeze, all at the same time! And they want it done right away . . . if not sooner!
So—er—after you're finished with them, you can put some Anti-Freeze in my car, too!
Gee! It's Indian Summer!
Yeah! Just yesterday, I was freezing—and today, it's so warm, I feel like going in for a swim!
SCORE HIGH OR DIE!
BAN THE BOMB
BAN THE BOMB
TODAY THE WORLD TOMORROW NOTHING
I wonder why we call it "Indian Summer"?
That's a good question! It's probably due to our collective guilty consciences!
First we pushed the Indian off his land! Then, we slaughtered him! Then, we broke every treaty we ever made with him! And now, we call him the "Noble Redman"!
What's that got to do with Indian Summer?
How should I know? I'm no philosopher!
Gee, I love Autumn—when School starts and I buy all new pens and pencils and notebooks and looseleaf books and reams of nice clean spotless looseleaf paper!
Hey, Mom! Doesn't that look boss?
Yes, but didn't you tell me you have homework?
Yup!
Then why aren't you doing it?
WHAT!? AND MESS UP ALL THIS NICE CLEAN SPOTLESS PAPER??!!
C'mon! Summer's over! It's Autumn—time to meet new girls!
But I don't feel like it! I told you! I still got it bad for that Dorothy Richards I met this past Summer! That was no kid stuff like going steady! That was the genuine article—the real McCoy—the once-in-a-lifetime explosion called Love!
Mayflower fresh DONUTS
So what if she lives way the heck up in New Rochelle! Distance doesn't make any difference when Love slugs you in the gut! So, you see! I just . . . can't . . . get . . .
. . . my . . . mind . . . off . . .
. . . whatever the heck her name was!
Dave Berg

BERG'S-EYE VIEW DEPT.

THE LIGHTER SIDE OF... CAME

DON'T JUST STAND THERE! **DO SOMETHING!!**

THIS IS A MOVIE CAMERA! RUN! JUMP! LAUGH! ANYTHING!!

Forget it! I'll go in the house and get my "still" camera!

DON'T JUST DO SOMETHING! **STAND THERE!!**

Joe, baby! I've got a **surprise** for you! I'm gonna show you my **movies!**

Oh, that's quite a surprise!

This is me in front of my girl-friend's house . . . And this is me diving into her pool . . . And this is me in my brand new car . . .

This is me playing with my dog . . . This is me rowing a boat . . . This is me taking a snooze . . . This is me—

Hey, **Joe,** baby! What are you **doing?**

This is me . . . LEAVING!

Do you realize this is the **last day** of our **vacation,** and I haven't got **one picture** of **us together!?** And what's more, I've only got **one shot left!**

Why don't you ask someone to **help** us, dear?

Pardon me, Sir—would you be kind enough to take a picture of my wife and I together?

Sure, thing!

No, **wait!** You're **too far away!** Tell you what . . . you stand here where I am, and I'll set things up for you!

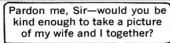

RA-BUGS
WRITER & ARTIST: DAVID BERG
I'm going on a trip and I'll need a lot of film! Give me 10 cartridges of Kodak Instamatic Film for Color Prints!
At 98¢ each—that will be $9.80 plus tax!
My goodness, that's expensive!
And that does NOT include developing—which is another $3.90 for each cartridge!
WOW! It'll cost me a fortune just to have my pictures developed!
Of course. if the pictures don't come out, there'll be no charge!
Maybe I'll get lucky and ruin the whole batch!
Camera Craft
Hi, there, Marvin! I understand you just got back from Europe!
Yup!
They tell me you saw the entire continent through the viewfinder of a camera!
Yup!
Did you have a good time?
I dunno!
I haven't gotten my pictures back yet!
Okay, this is the spot! I've got the exposure set, the focus set, and the shutter cocked. All you have to do is stand here, look through the viewfinder, and press this button like . . .
. . . this!
CLICK

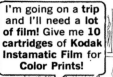

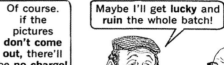

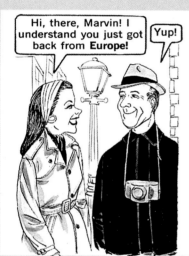

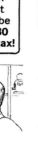

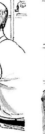

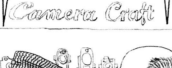

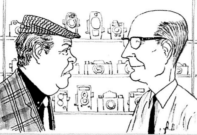

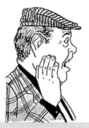

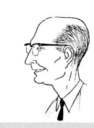

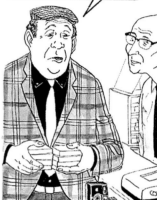

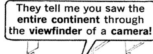

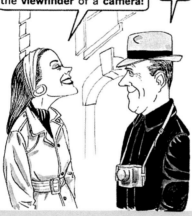

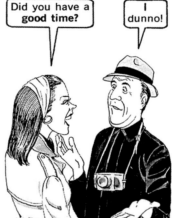

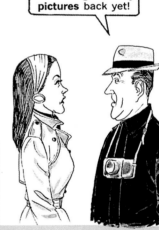

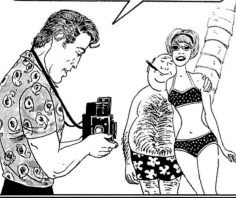

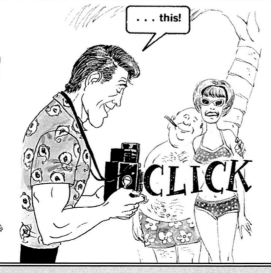

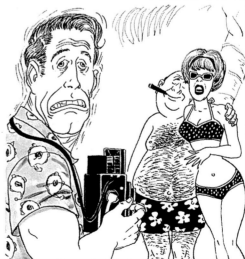

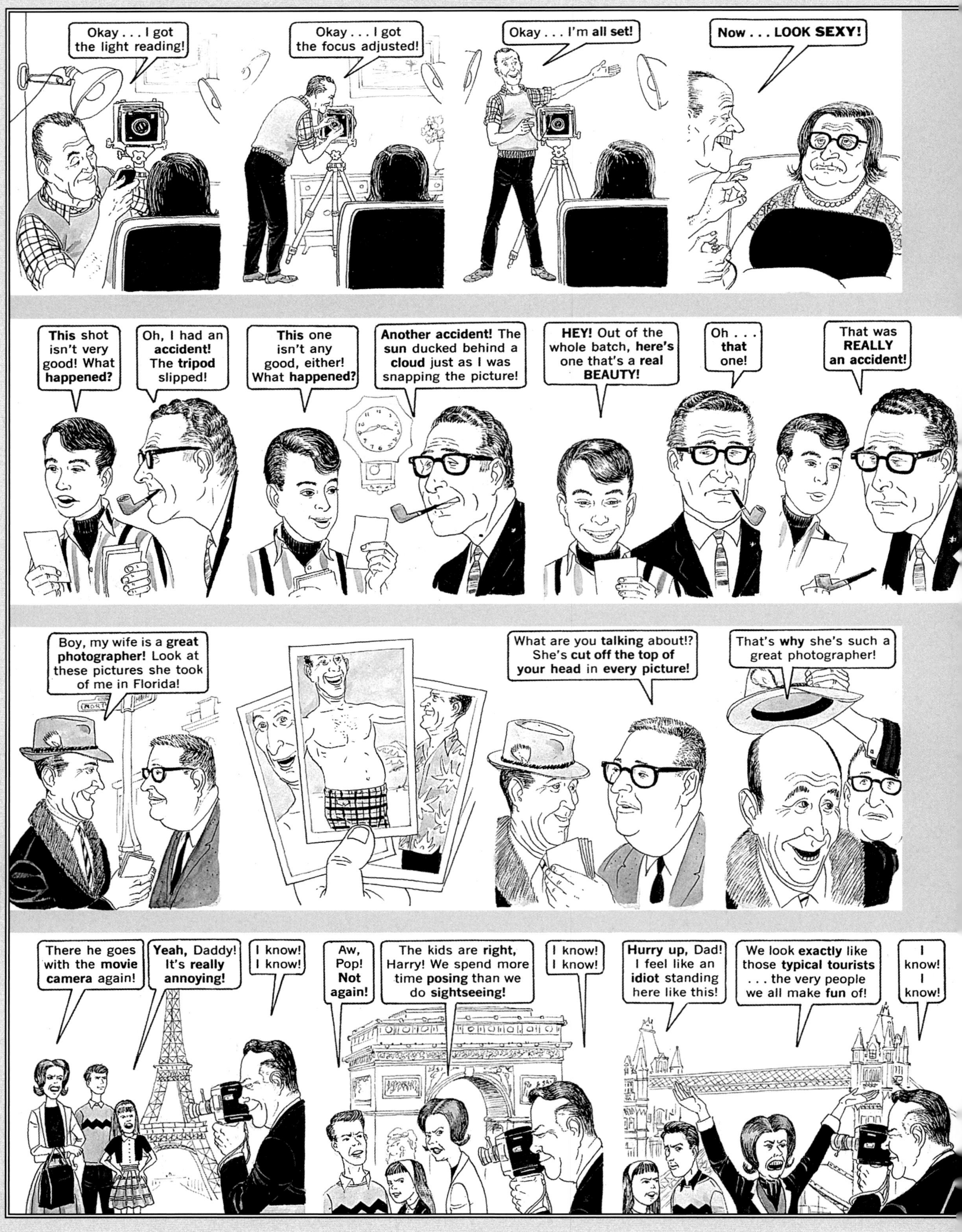
Okay . . . I got the light reading!
Okay . . . I got the focus adjusted!
Okay . . . I'm all set!
Now . . . LOOK SEXY!
This shot isn't very good! What happened?
Oh, I had an accident! The tripod slipped!
This one isn't any good, either! What happened?
Another accident! The sun ducked behind a cloud just as I was snapping the picture!
HEY! Out of the whole batch, here's one that's a real BEAUTY!
Oh . . . that one!
That was REALLY an accident!
Boy, my wife is a great photographer! Look at these pictures she took of me in Florida!
What are you talking about!? She's cut off the top of your head in every picture!
That's why she's such a great photographer!
There he goes with the movie camera again!
Yeah, Daddy! It's really annoying!
I know! I know!
Aw, Pop! Not again!
The kids are right, Harry! We spend more time posing than we do sightseeing!
I know! I know!
Hurry up, Dad! I feel like an idiot standing here like this!
We look exactly like those typical tourists . . . the very people we all make fun of!
I know! I know!

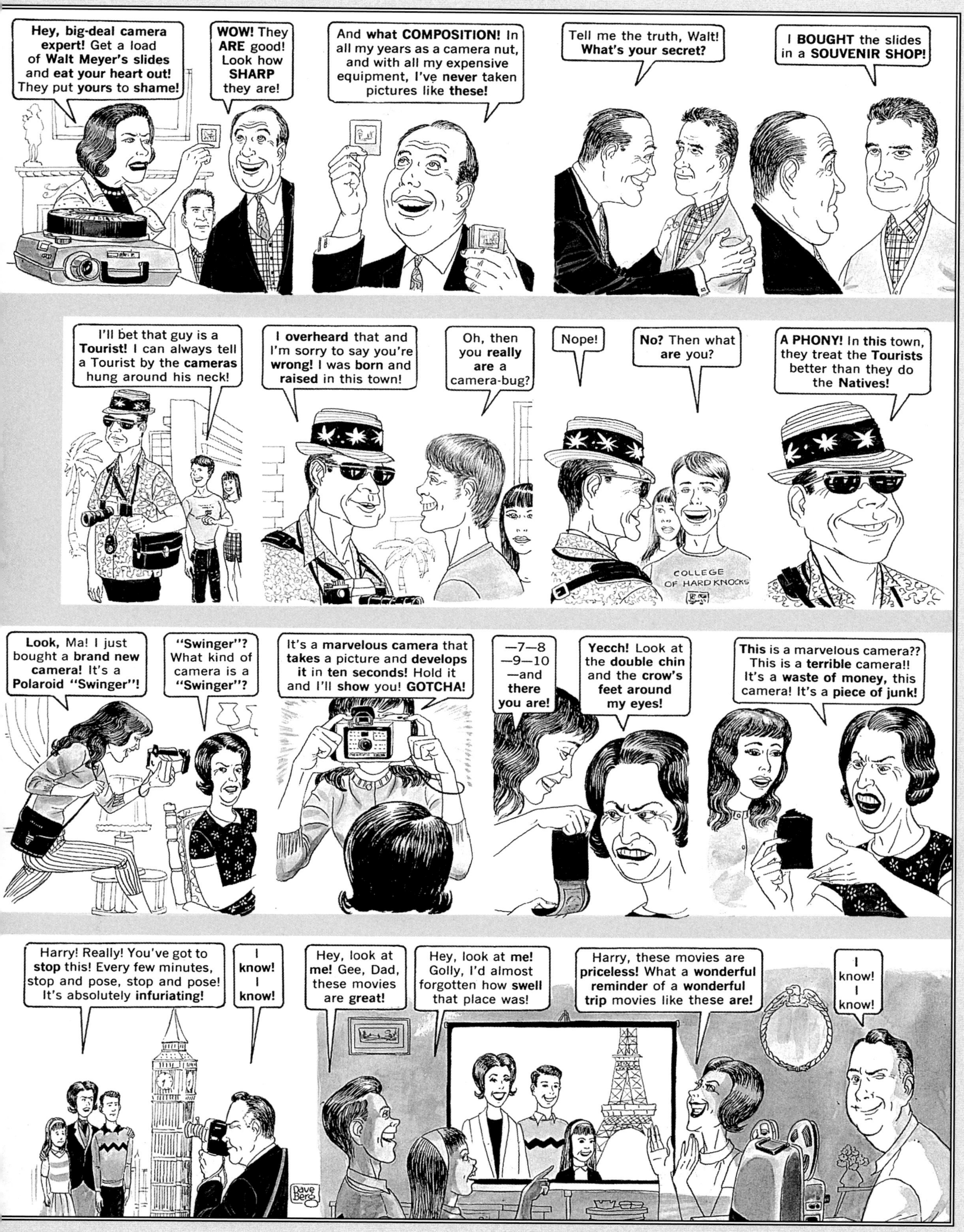
Hey, big-deal camera expert! Get a load of Walt Meyer's slides and eat your heart out! They put yours to shame!
WOW! They ARE good! Look how SHARP they are!
And what COMPOSITION! In all my years as a camera nut, and with all my expensive equipment, I've never taken pictures like these!
Tell me the truth, Walt! What's your secret?
I BOUGHT the slides in a SOUVENIR SHOP!
I'll bet that guy is a Tourist! I can always tell a Tourist by the cameras hung around his neck!
I overheard that and I'm sorry to say you're wrong! I was born and raised in this town!
Oh, then you really are a camera-bug?
Nope!
No? Then what are you?
A PHONY! In this town, they treat the Tourists better than they do the Natives!
COLLEGE OF HARD KNOCKS
Look, Ma! I just bought a brand new camera! It's a Polaroid "Swinger"!
"Swinger"? What kind of camera is a "Swinger"?
It's a marvelous camera that takes a picture and develops it in ten seconds! Hold it and I'll show you! GOTCHA!
—7—8 —9—10 —and there you are!
Yecch! Look at the double chin and the crow's feet around my eyes!
This is a marvelous camera?? This is a terrible camera!! It's a waste of money, this camera! It's a piece of junk!
Harry! Really! You've got to stop this! Every few minutes, stop and pose, stop and pose! It's absolutely infuriating!
I know! I know!
Hey, look at me! Gee, Dad, these movies are great!
Hey, look at me! Golly, I'd almost forgotten how swell that place was!
Harry, these movies are priceless! What a wonderful reminder of a wonderful trip movies like these are!
I know! I know!
Dave Berg

BERG'S EYE-VIEW DEPT.

THE LIGHTER SIDE OF... FR

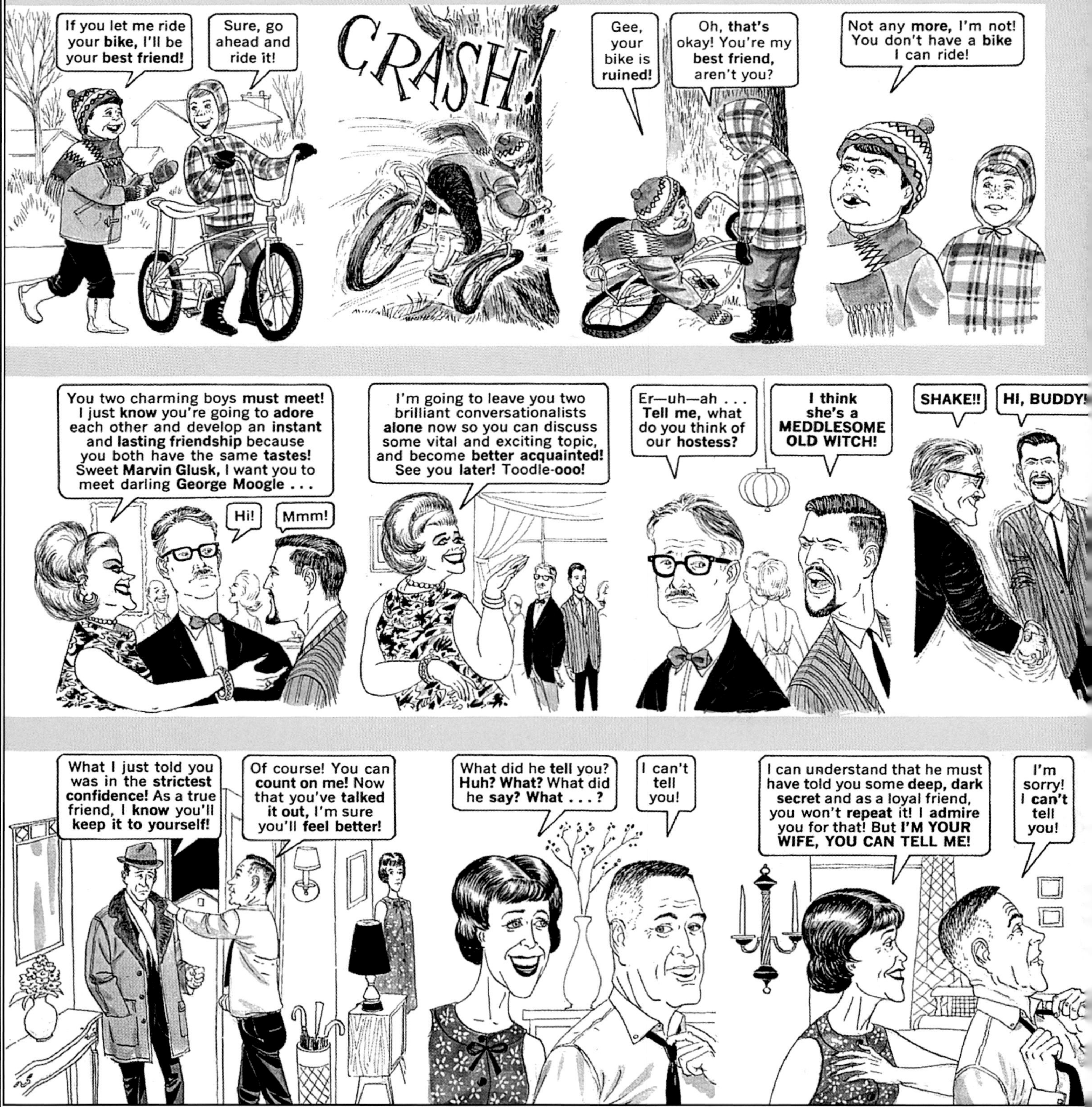
If you let me ride your bike, I'll be your best friend!
Sure, go ahead and ride it!
CRASH!
Gee, your bike is ruined!
Oh, that's okay! You're my best friend, aren't you?
Not any more, I'm not! You don't have a bike I can ride!
You two charming boys must meet! I just know you're going to adore each other and develop an instant and lasting friendship because you both have the same tastes! Sweet Marvin Glusk, I want you to meet darling George Moogle . . .
Hi!
Mmm!
I'm going to leave you two brilliant conversationalists alone now so you can discuss some vital and exciting topic, and become better acquainted! See you later! Toodle-ooo!
Er—uh—ah . . . Tell me, what do you think of our hostess?
I think she's a MEDDLESOME OLD WITCH!
SHAKE!!
HI, BUDDY!
What I just told you was in the strictest confidence! As a true friend, I know you'll keep it to yourself!
Of course! You can count on me! Now that you've talked it out, I'm sure you'll feel better!
What did he tell you? Huh? What? What did he say? What . . . ?
I can't tell you!
I can understand that he must have told you some deep, dark secret and as a loyal friend, you won't repeat it! I admire you for that! But I'M YOUR WIFE, YOU CAN TELL ME!
I'm sorry! I can't tell you!

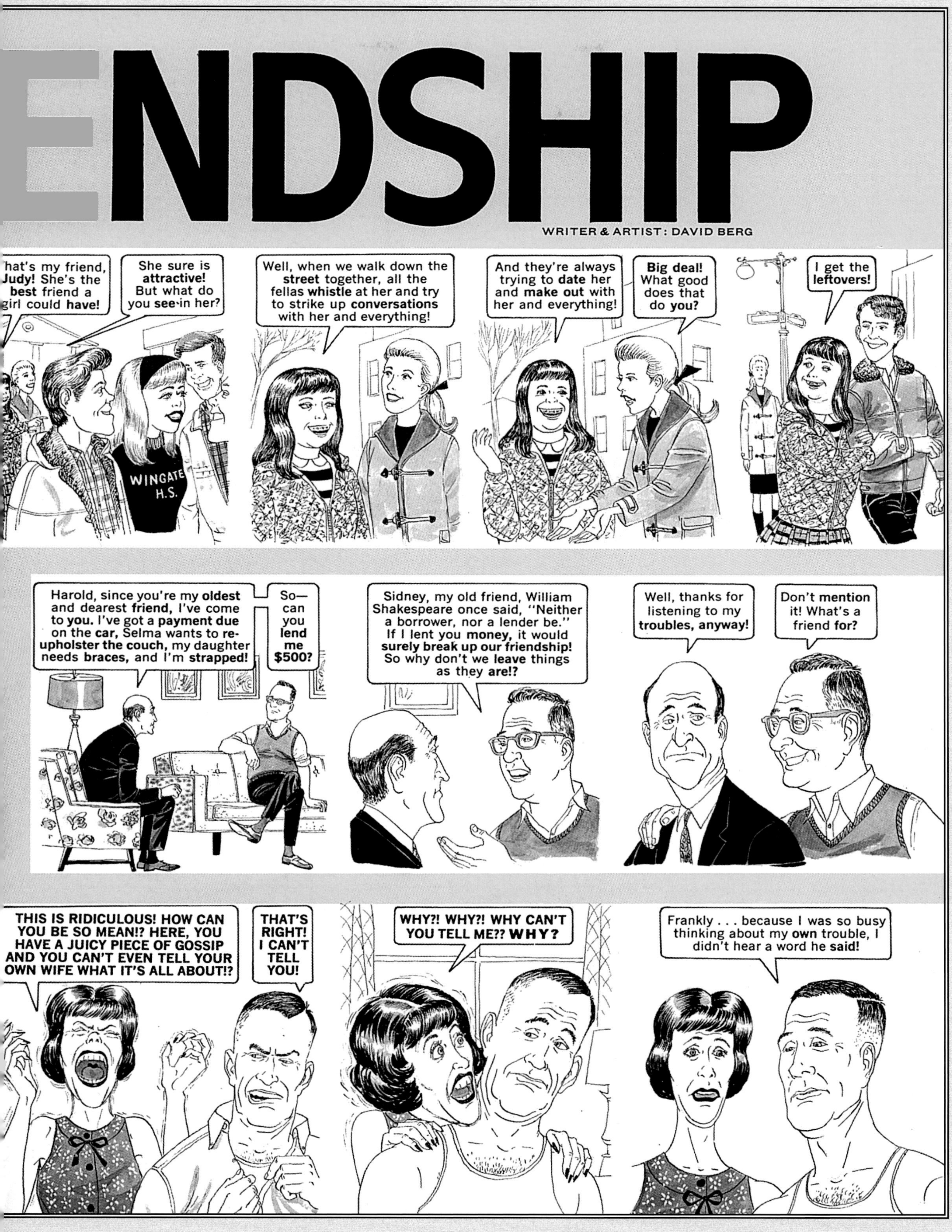
NDSHIP
WRITER & ARTIST: DAVID BERG
hat's my friend, Judy! She's the best friend a girl could have!
She sure is attractive! But what do you see in her?
WINGATE H.S.
Well, when we walk down the street together, all the fellas whistle at her and try to strike up conversations with her and everything!
And they're always trying to date her and make out with her and everything!
Big deal! What good does that do you?
I get the leftovers!
Harold, since you're my oldest and dearest friend, I've come to you. I've got a payment due on the car, Selma wants to re-upholster the couch, my daughter needs braces, and I'm strapped!
So—can you lend me $500?
Sidney, my old friend, William Shakespeare once said, "Neither a borrower, nor a lender be." If I lent you money, it would surely break up our friendship! So why don't we leave things as they are!?
Well, thanks for listening to my troubles, anyway!
Don't mention it! What's a friend for?
THIS IS RIDICULOUS! HOW CAN YOU BE SO MEAN!? HERE, YOU HAVE A JUICY PIECE OF GOSSIP AND YOU CAN'T EVEN TELL YOUR OWN WIFE WHAT IT'S ALL ABOUT!?
THAT'S RIGHT! I CAN'T TELL YOU!
WHY?! WHY?! WHY CAN'T YOU TELL ME?? WHY?
Frankly . . . because I was so busy thinking about my own trouble, I didn't hear a word he said!

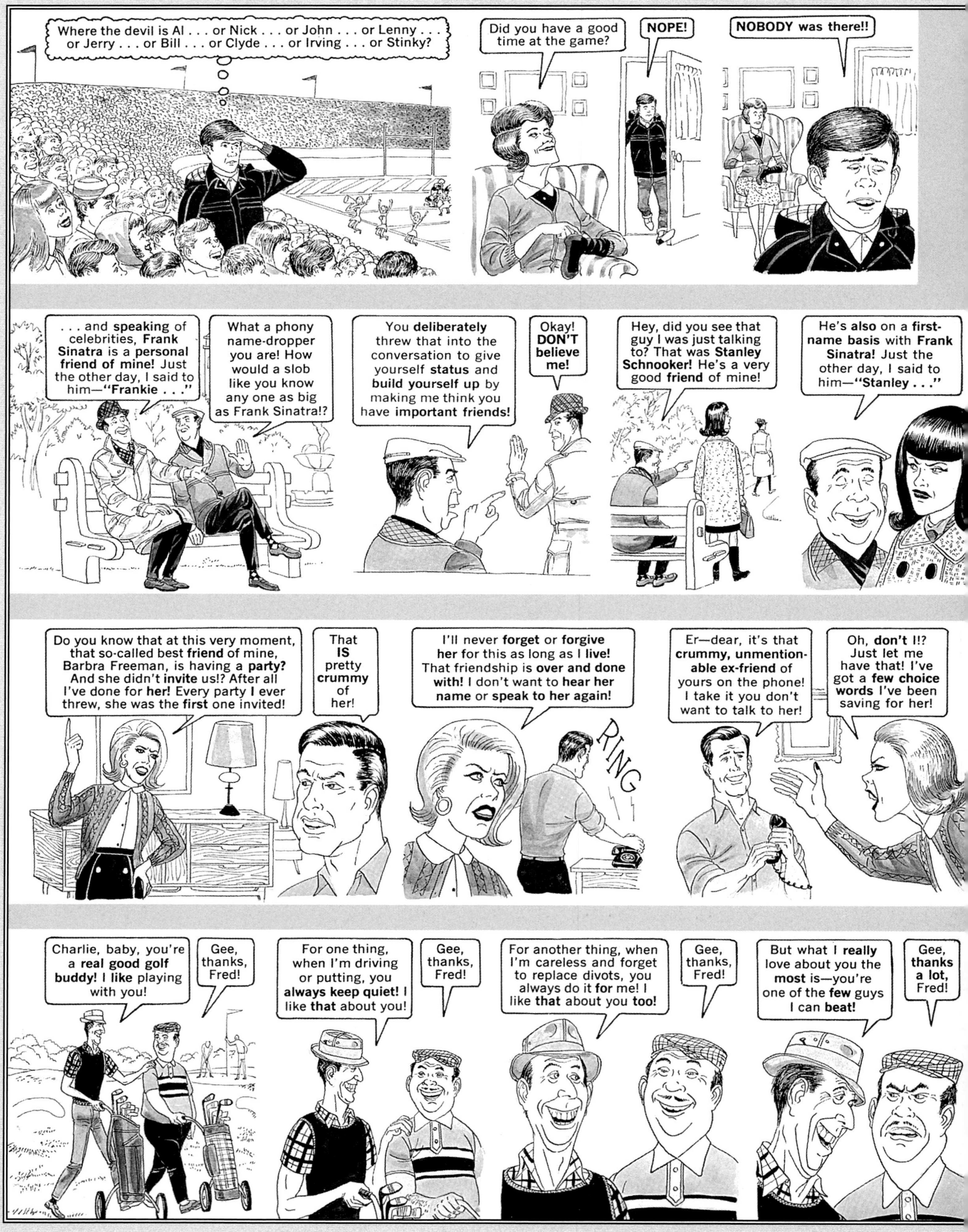

Where the devil is Al . . . or Nick . . . or John . . . or Lenny . . . or Jerry . . . or Bill . . . or Clyde . . . or Irving . . . or Stinky?
Did you have a good time at the game?
NOPE!
NOBODY was there!!
. . . and speaking of celebrities, Frank Sinatra is a personal friend of mine! Just the other day, I said to him—"Frankie . . ."
What a phony name-dropper you are! How would a slob like you know any one as big as Frank Sinatra!?
You deliberately threw that into the conversation to give yourself status and build yourself up by making me think you have important friends!
Okay! DON'T believe me!
Hey, did you see that guy I was just talking to? That was Stanley Schnooker! He's a very good friend of mine!
He's also on a first-name basis with Frank Sinatra! Just the other day, I said to him—"Stanley . . ."
Do you know that at this very moment, that so-called best friend of mine, Barbra Freeman, is having a party? And she didn't invite us!? After all I've done for her! Every party I ever threw, she was the first one invited!
That IS pretty crummy of her!
I'll never forget or forgive her for this as long as I live! That friendship is over and done with! I don't want to hear her name or speak to her again!
RING
Er—dear, it's that crummy, unmentionable ex-friend of yours on the phone! I take it you don't want to talk to her!
Oh, don't I!? Just let me have that! I've got a few choice words I've been saving for her!
Charlie, baby, you're a real good golf buddy! I like playing with you!
Gee, thanks, Fred!
For one thing, when I'm driving or putting, you always keep quiet! I like that about you!
Gee, thanks, Fred!
For another thing, when I'm careless and forget to replace divots, you always do it for me! I like that about you too!
Gee, thanks, Fred!
But what I really love about you the most is—you're one of the few guys I can beat!
Gee, thanks a lot, Fred!

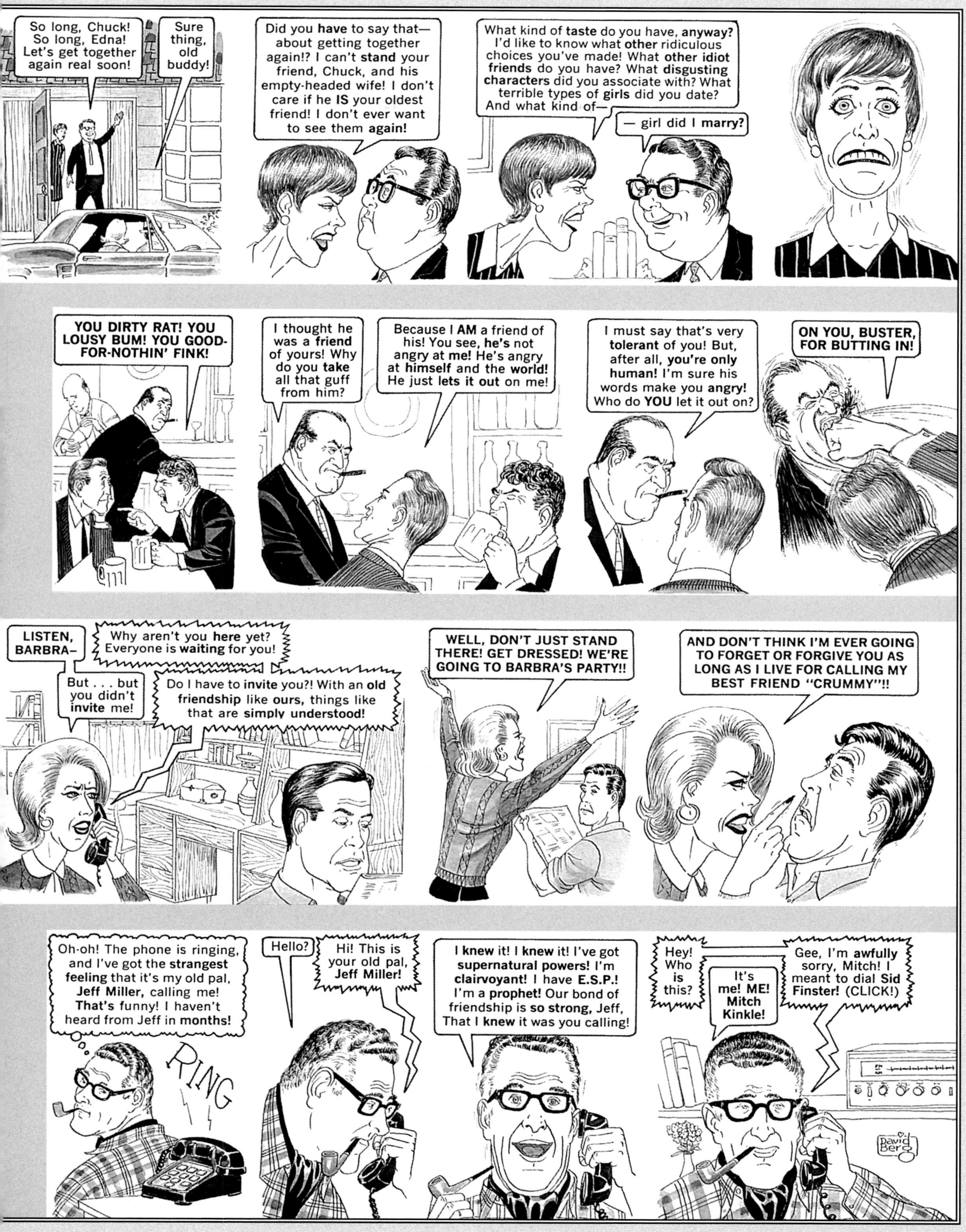
So long, Chuck! So long, Edna! Let's get together again real soon!
Sure thing, old buddy!
Did you have to say that—about getting together again!? I can't stand your friend, Chuck, and his empty-headed wife! I don't care if he IS your oldest friend! I don't ever want to see them again!
What kind of taste do you have, anyway? I'd like to know what other ridiculous choices you've made! What other idiot friends do you have? What disgusting characters did you associate with? What terrible types of girls did you date? And what kind of—
— girl did I marry?
YOU DIRTY RAT! YOU LOUSY BUM! YOU GOOD-FOR-NOTHIN' FINK!
I thought he was a friend of yours! Why do you take all that guff from him?
Because I AM a friend of his! You see, he's not angry at me! He's angry at himself and the world! He just lets it out on me!
I must say that's very tolerant of you! But, after all, you're only human! I'm sure his words make you angry! Who do YOU let it out on?
ON YOU, BUSTER, FOR BUTTING IN!
LISTEN, BARBRA–
Why aren't you here yet? Everyone is waiting for you!
But . . . but you didn't invite me!
Do I have to invite you?! With an old friendship like ours, things like that are simply understood!
WELL, DON'T JUST STAND THERE! GET DRESSED! WE'RE GOING TO BARBRA'S PARTY!!
AND DON'T THINK I'M EVER GOING TO FORGET OR FORGIVE YOU AS LONG AS I LIVE FOR CALLING MY BEST FRIEND "CRUMMY"!!
Oh-oh! The phone is ringing, and I've got the strangest feeling that it's my old pal, Jeff Miller, calling me! That's funny! I haven't heard from Jeff in months!
RING
Hello?
Hi! This is your old pal, Jeff Miller!
I knew it! I knew it! I've got supernatural powers! I'm clairvoyant! I have E.S.P.! I'm a prophet! Our bond of friendship is so strong, Jeff, That I knew it was you calling!
Hey! Who is this?
It's me! ME! Mitch Kinkle!
Gee, I'm awfully sorry, Mitch! I meant to dial Sid Finster! (CLICK!)
David Berg

BERG'S-EYE VIEW DEPT.

THE LIGHTER SIDE OF

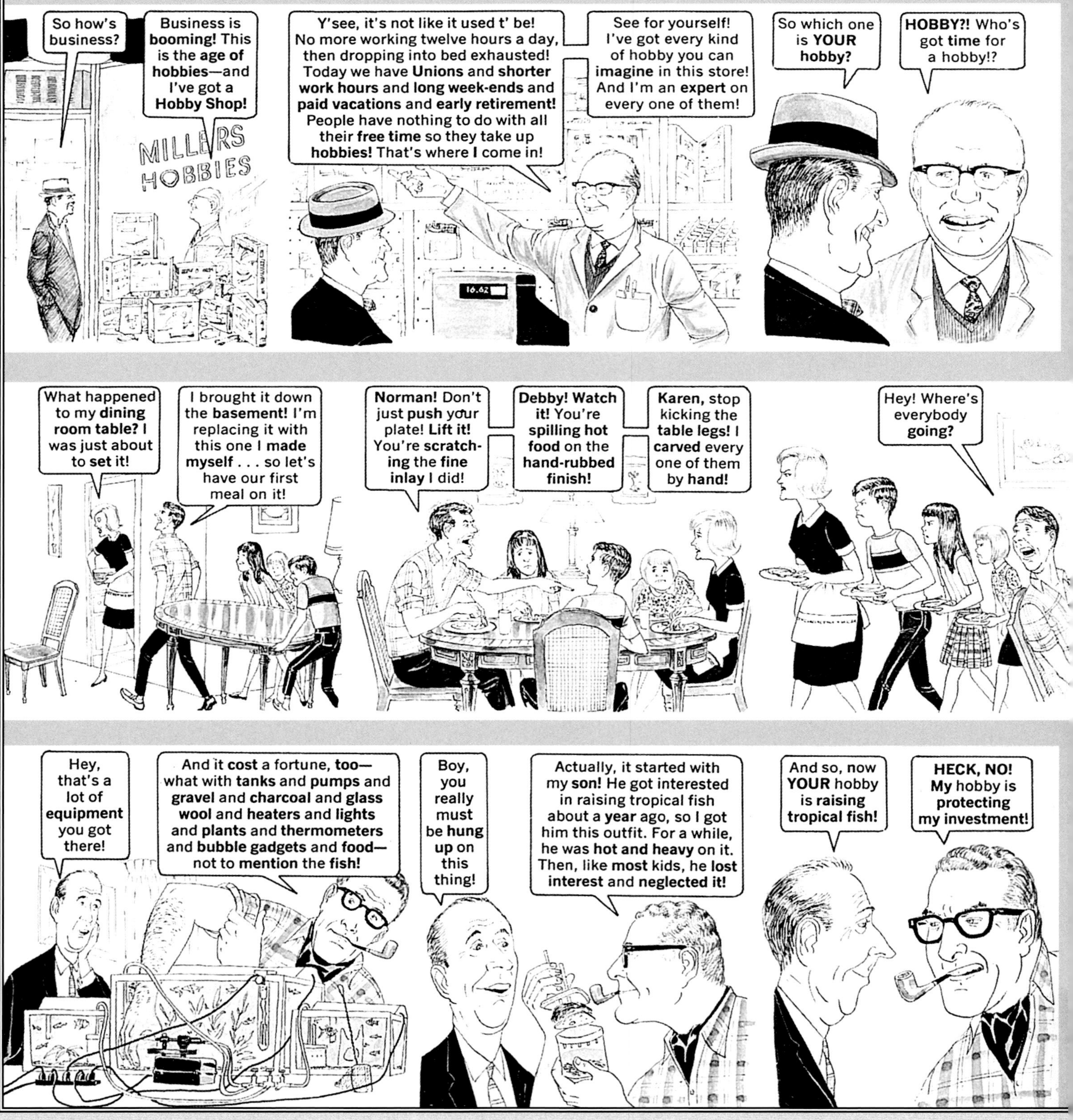
So how's business?
Business is booming! This is the age of hobbies—and I've got a Hobby Shop!
MILLERS HOBBIES
Y'see, it's not like it used t' be! No more working twelve hours a day, then dropping into bed exhausted! Today we have Unions and shorter work hours and long week-ends and paid vacations and early retirement! People have nothing to do with all their free time so they take up hobbies! That's where I come in!
See for yourself! I've got every kind of hobby you can imagine in this store! And I'm an expert on every one of them!
So which one is YOUR hobby?
HOBBY?! Who's got time for a hobby!?
What happened to my dining room table? I was just about to set it!
I brought it down the basement! I'm replacing it with this one I made myself . . . so let's have our first meal on it!
Norman! Don't just push your plate! Lift it! You're scratching the fine inlay I did!
Debby! Watch it! You're spilling hot food on the hand-rubbed finish!
Karen, stop kicking the table legs! I carved every one of them by hand!
Hey! Where's everybody going?
Hey, that's a lot of equipment you got there!
And it cost a fortune, too—what with tanks and pumps and gravel and charcoal and glass wool and heaters and lights and plants and thermometers and bubble gadgets and food—not to mention the fish!
Boy, you really must be hung up on this thing!
Actually, it started with my son! He got interested in raising tropical fish about a year ago, so I got him this outfit. For a while, he was hot and heavy on it. Then, like most kids, he lost interest and neglected it!
And so, now YOUR hobby is raising tropical fish!
HECK, NO! My hobby is protecting my investment!

HOBBIES

ARTIST & WRITER: DAVE BERG

Well, Eric—it's almost your **birthday!** Is there anything special you'd like as a **gift?**

I'll say there is!

I'd like a set of **electric trains**—H-O gauge, terminal track, 18-inch radius—with an 18-volt transformer and Santa Fe cars . . . plus four switches, a trestle, and an automatic crossing gate!

But you've got all that! Your father **bought** an electric train set when you were only three . . . and he's **added to it** and kept it in good condition and **worked on it** and run it all these years!

Sure! That's **just it!** Now I want a set **for MYSELF!**

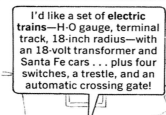

Finished!

FINISHED!?? We started making the same model at the **same time** and I'm only **half** done! How can you **possibly** be finished so fast?

It's **very simple!** I am extremely **dexterous,** I work **systematically** and **rapidly**—my **mind** racing ahead to the **next step,** I have **mastered** the technique of applying **just the right amount of cement** . . .

. . . and I leave out a great many parts!

This is the **worst** service I've **ever** had! Look at that **waiter!** All he seems to be interested in is **counting his tip money!**

Well, if you're **so** annoyed, **don't leave him a tip!**

No, I've got a **better** idea! I'll leave him just **one lousy penny!** That'll show him **exactly** what I think of him!

Look, he's picking it up! He's studying it! He can't believe his eyes! Heh-heh! You gotta give me **credit!** I sure know how to **hurt a guy!**

YAHOO!! It's a 1909 S VDB Lincoln Head—worth about **two hundred dollars!**

Yep, you sure know how to **hurt a guy**—especially if he's a **coin collector!**

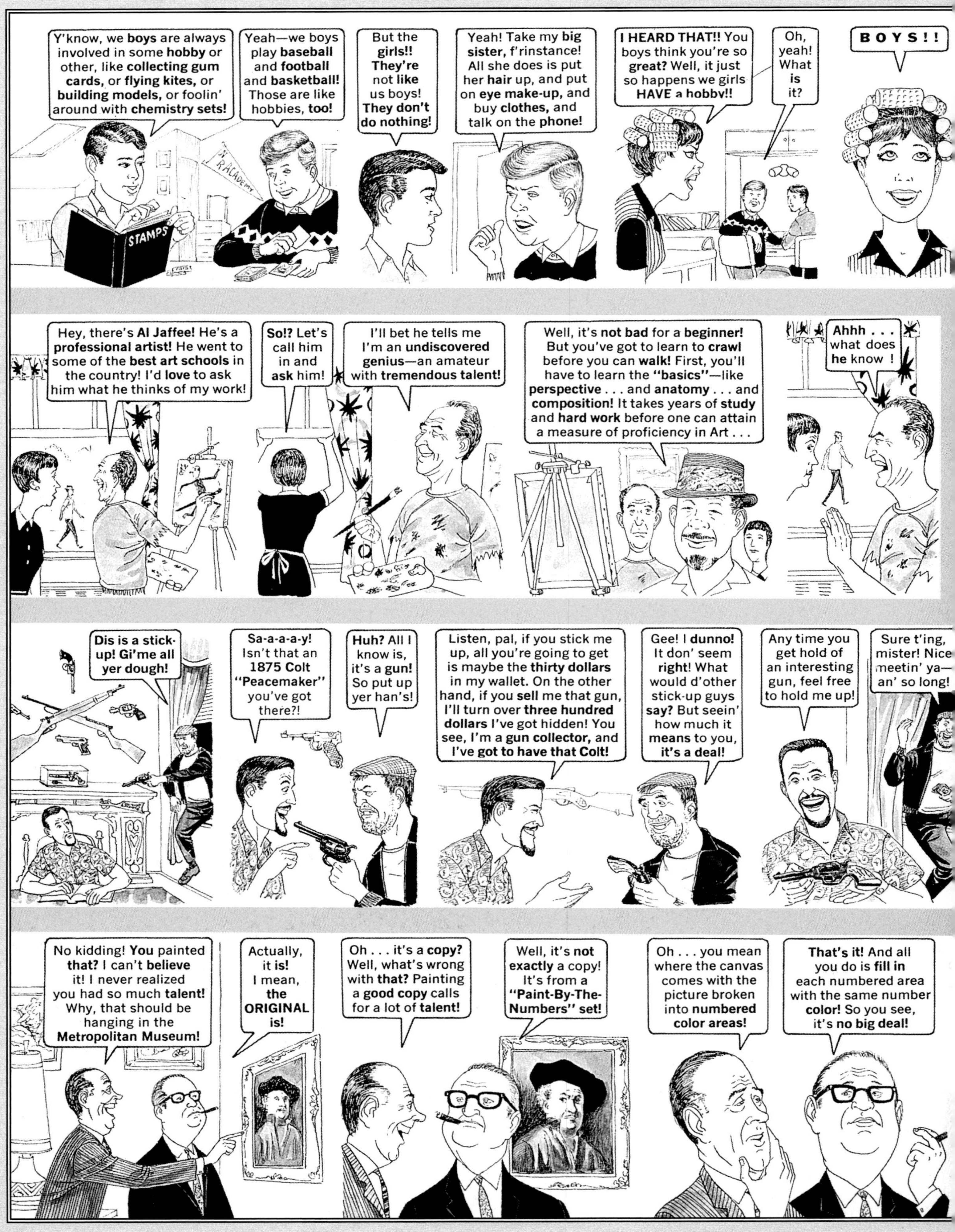
Y'know, we boys are always involved in some hobby or other, like collecting gum cards, or flying kites, or building models, or foolin' around with chemistry sets!
STAMPS
Yeah—we boys play baseball and football and basketball! Those are like hobbies, too!
But the girls!! They're not like us boys! They don't do nothing!
Yeah! Take my big sister, f'rinstance! All she does is put her hair up, and put on eye make-up, and buy clothes, and talk on the phone!
I HEARD THAT!! You boys think you're so great? Well, it just so happens we girls HAVE a hobby!!
Oh, yeah! What is it?
BOYS!!
Hey, there's Al Jaffee! He's a professional artist! He went to some of the best art schools in the country! I'd love to ask him what he thinks of my work!
So!? Let's call him in and ask him!
I'll bet he tells me I'm an undiscovered genius—an amateur with tremendous talent!
Well, it's not bad for a beginner! But you've got to learn to crawl before you can walk! First, you'll have to learn the "basics"—like perspective . . . and anatomy . . . and composition! It takes years of study and hard work before one can attain a measure of proficiency in Art . . .
Ahhh . . . what does he know !
Dis is a stick-up! Gi'me all yer dough!
Sa-a-a-a-y! Isn't that an 1875 Colt "Peacemaker" you've got there?!
Huh? All I know is, it's a gun! So put up yer han's!
Listen, pal, if you stick me up, all you're going to get is maybe the thirty dollars in my wallet. On the other hand, if you sell me that gun, I'll turn over three hundred dollars I've got hidden! You see, I'm a gun collector, and I've got to have that Colt!
Gee! I dunno! It don' seem right! What would d'other stick-up guys say? But seein' how much it means to you, it's a deal!
Any time you get hold of an interesting gun, feel free to hold me up!
Sure t'ing, mister! Nice meetin' ya—an' so long!
No kidding! You painted that? I can't believe it! I never realized you had so much talent! Why, that should be hanging in the Metropolitan Museum!
Actually, it is! I mean, the ORIGINAL is!
Oh . . . it's a copy? Well, what's wrong with that? Painting a good copy calls for a lot of talent!
Well, it's not exactly a copy! It's from a "Paint-By-The-Numbers" set!
Oh . . . you mean where the canvas comes with the picture broken into numbered color areas!
That's it! And all you do is fill in each numbered area with the same number color! So you see, it's no big deal!

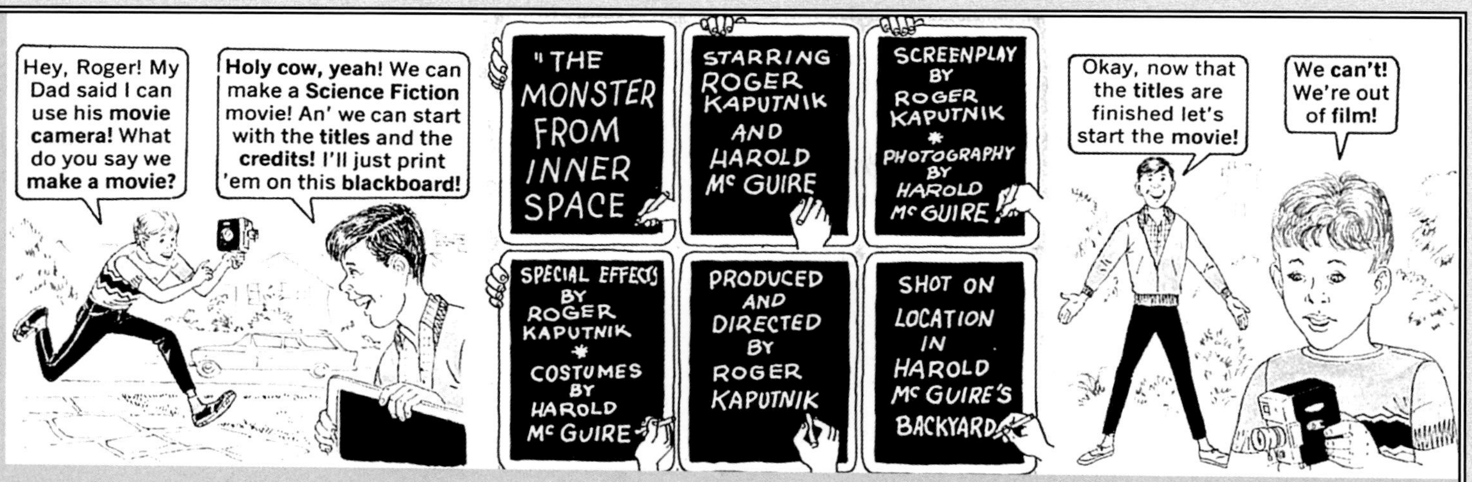
Hey, Roger! My Dad said I can use his **movie camera!** What do you say we **make a movie?**
Holy cow, yeah! We can make a **Science Fiction** movie! An' we can start with the **titles** and the **credits!** I'll just print 'em on this **blackboard!**
"THE MONSTER FROM INNER SPACE
STARRING ROGER KAPUTNIK AND HAROLD Mc GUIRE
SCREENPLAY BY ROGER KAPUTNIK * PHOTOGRAPHY BY HAROLD Mc GUIRE
SPECIAL EFFECTS BY ROGER KAPUTNIK * COSTUMES BY HAROLD Mc GUIRE
PRODUCED AND DIRECTED BY ROGER KAPUTNIK
SHOT ON LOCATION IN HAROLD Mc GUIRE'S BACKYARD
Okay, now that the **titles** are finished let's start the **movie!**
We can't! We're out of film!

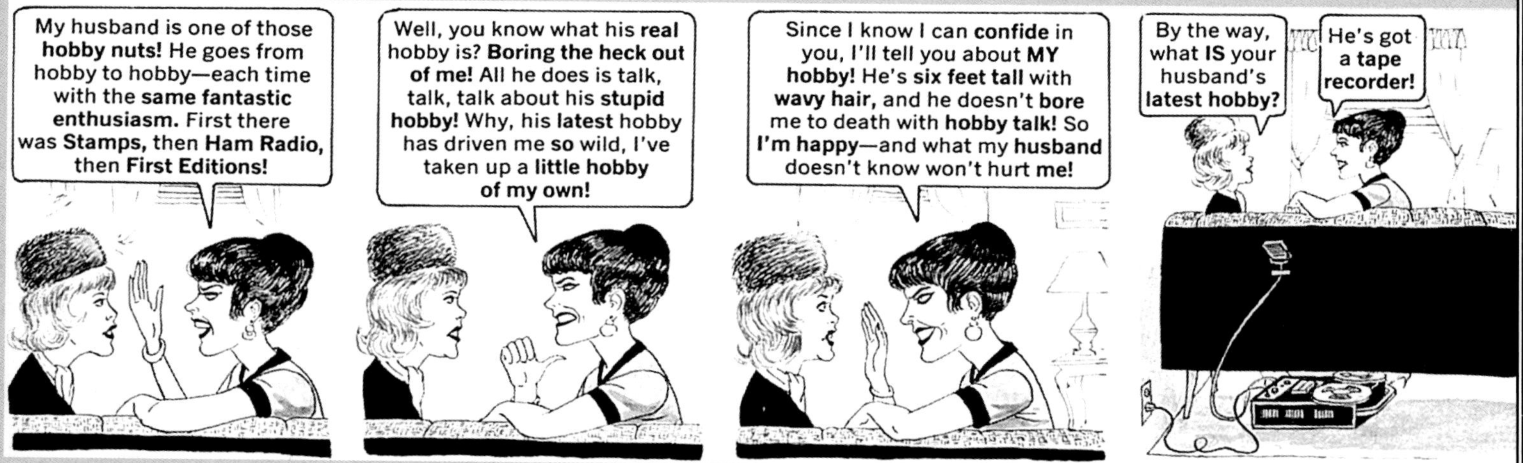
My husband is one of those **hobby nuts!** He goes from hobby to hobby—each time with the **same fantastic enthusiasm.** First there was **Stamps,** then **Ham Radio,** then **First Editions!**
Well, you know what his **real** hobby is? **Boring the heck out of me!** All he does is talk, talk, talk about his **stupid hobby!** Why, his **latest** hobby has driven me **so** wild, I've taken up a **little hobby of my own!**
Since I know I can **confide** in you, I'll tell you about **MY hobby!** He's **six feet tall** with **wavy hair,** and he doesn't **bore** me to death with **hobby talk!** So **I'm happy**—and what my **husband** doesn't know won't hurt **me!**
By the way, what **IS** your husband's **latest hobby?**
He's got **a tape recorder!**

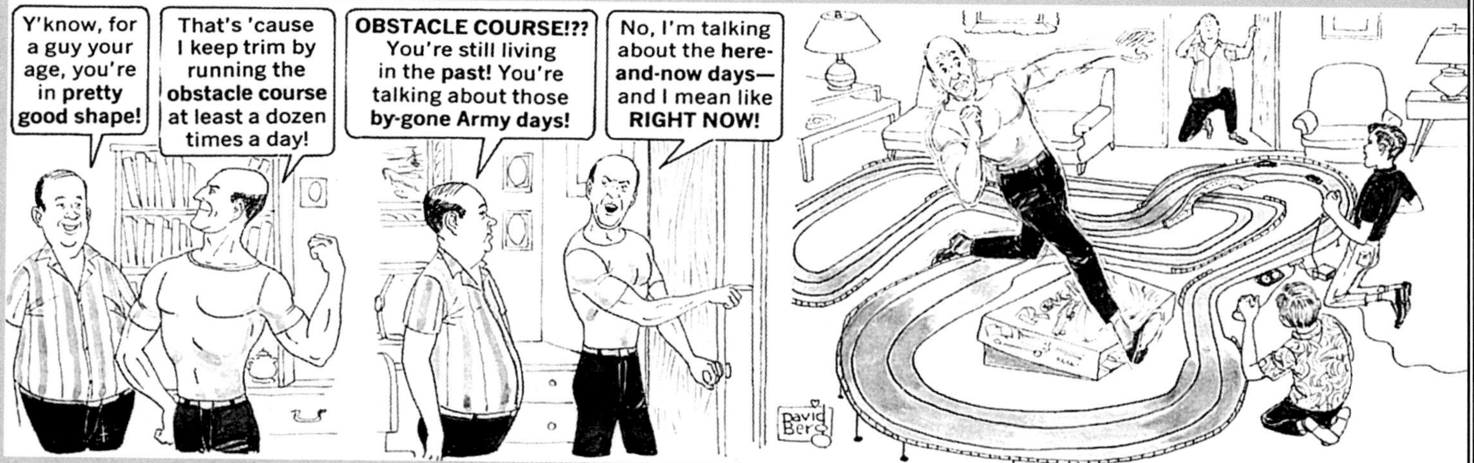
Y'know, for a guy your age, you're in **pretty good shape!**
That's 'cause I keep trim by running the **obstacle course** at least a dozen times a day!
OBSTACLE COURSE!?? You're still living in the **past!** You're talking about those **by-gone Army days!**
No, I'm talking about the **here-and-now days**—and I mean like **RIGHT NOW!**
David Berg

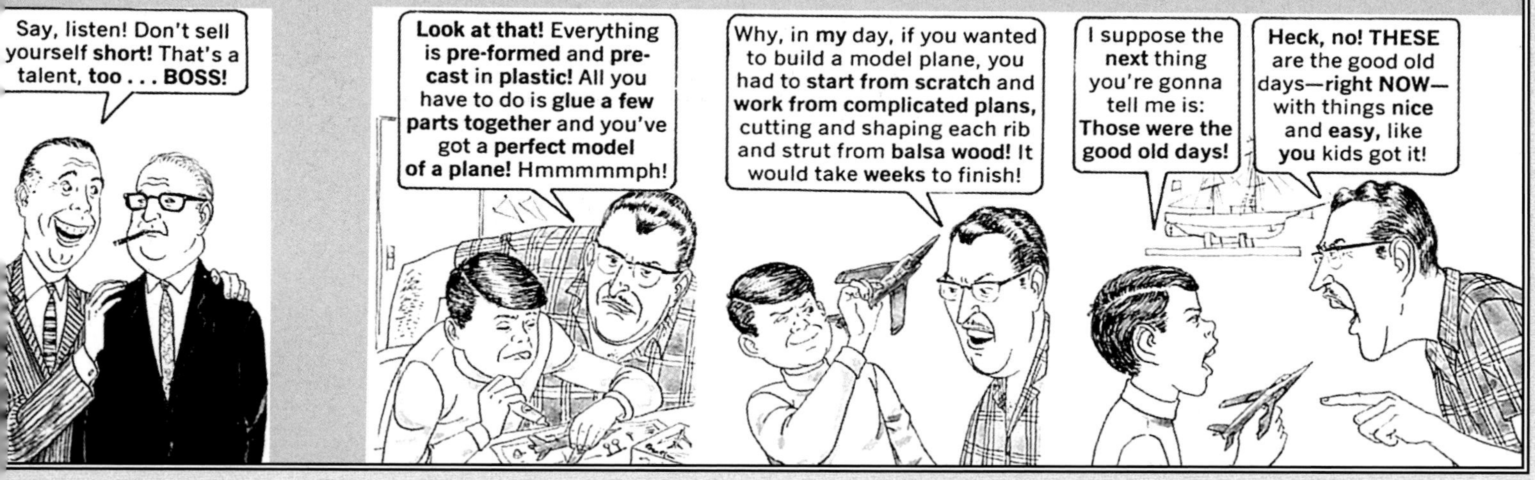
Say, listen! Don't sell yourself **short!** That's a talent, **too . . . BOSS!**
Look at that! Everything is **pre-formed** and **pre-cast in plastic!** All you have to do is **glue a few parts together** and you've got a **perfect model of a plane!** Hmmmmmph!
Why, in **my** day, if you wanted to build a model plane, you had to **start from scratch** and **work from complicated plans,** cutting and shaping each rib and strut from **balsa wood!** It would take **weeks** to finish!
I suppose the **next** thing you're gonna tell me is: **Those were the good old days!**
Heck, no! THESE are the good old days—**right NOW**—with things **nice** and **easy,** like **you kids got it!**

BERG'S-EYE VIEW DEPT.

THE LIGHTER SIDE OF

Plucking
Trimming
Cutting
Shaping
Shaving
Shampooing
Coloring
Curling
Setting
Drying
Brushing
Combing
Straightening
Faking
Growing and
Removing...

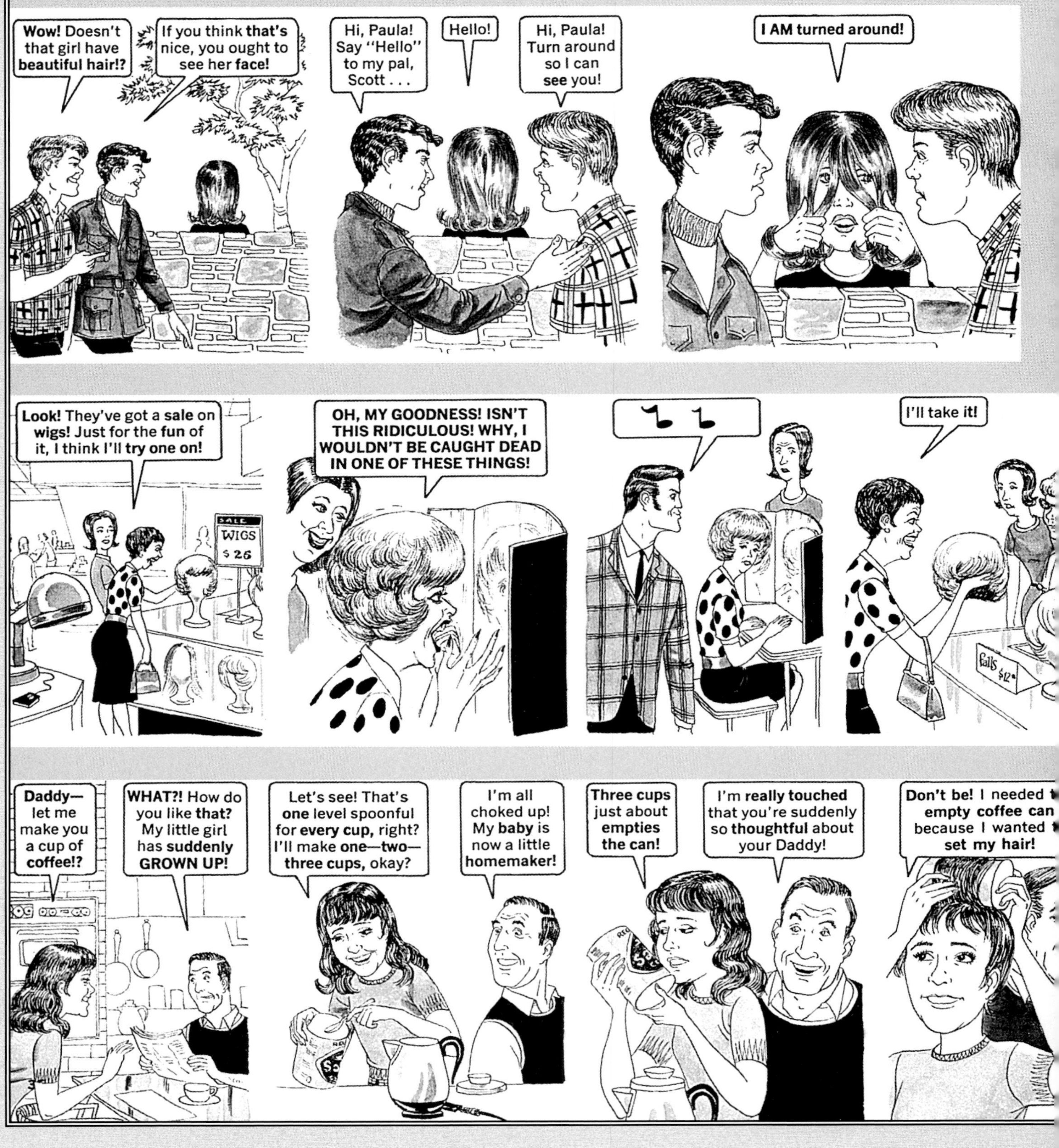
Wow! Doesn't that girl have beautiful hair!?
If you think that's nice, you ought to see her face!
Hi, Paula! Say "Hello" to my pal, Scott . . .
Hello!
Hi, Paula! Turn around so I can see you!
I AM turned around!
Look! They've got a sale on wigs! Just for the fun of it, I think I'll try one on!
SALE
WIGS
$26
OH, MY GOODNESS! ISN'T THIS RIDICULOUS! WHY, I WOULDN'T BE CAUGHT DEAD IN ONE OF THESE THINGS!
I'll take it!
Falls $12
Daddy— let me make you a cup of coffee!?
WHAT?! How do you like that? My little girl has suddenly GROWN UP!
Let's see! That's one level spoonful for every cup, right? I'll make one—two— three cups, okay?
I'm all choked up! My baby is now a little homemaker!
Three cups just about empties the can!
I'm really touched that you're suddenly so thoughtful about your Daddy!
Don't be! I needed t empty coffee can because I wanted t set my hair!

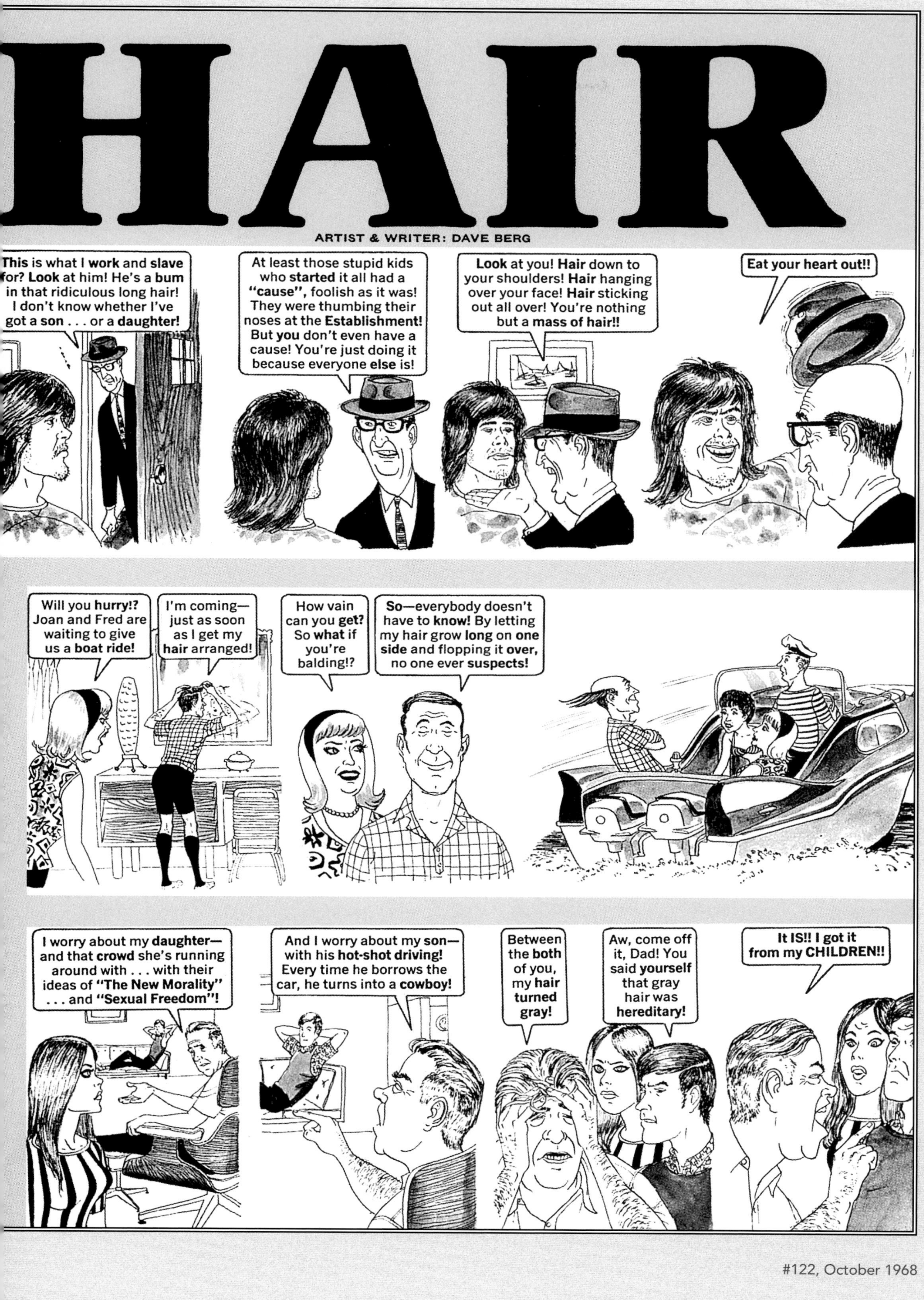
HAIR
ARTIST & WRITER: DAVE BERG
This is what I work and slave for? Look at him! He's a bum in that ridiculous long hair! I don't know whether I've got a son . . . or a daughter!
At least those stupid kids who started it all had a "cause", foolish as it was! They were thumbing their noses at the Establishment! But you don't even have a cause! You're just doing it because everyone else is!
Look at you! Hair down to your shoulders! Hair hanging over your face! Hair sticking out all over! You're nothing but a mass of hair!!
Eat your heart out!!
Will you hurry!? Joan and Fred are waiting to give us a boat ride!
I'm coming—just as soon as I get my hair arranged!
How vain can you get? So what if you're balding!?
So—everybody doesn't have to know! By letting my hair grow long on one side and flopping it over, no one ever suspects!
I worry about my daughter—and that crowd she's running around with . . . with their ideas of "The New Morality" . . . and "Sexual Freedom"!
And I worry about my son—with his hot-shot driving! Every time he borrows the car, he turns into a cowboy!
Between the both of you, my hair turned gray!
Aw, come off it, Dad! You said yourself that gray hair was hereditary!
It IS!! I got it from my CHILDREN!!

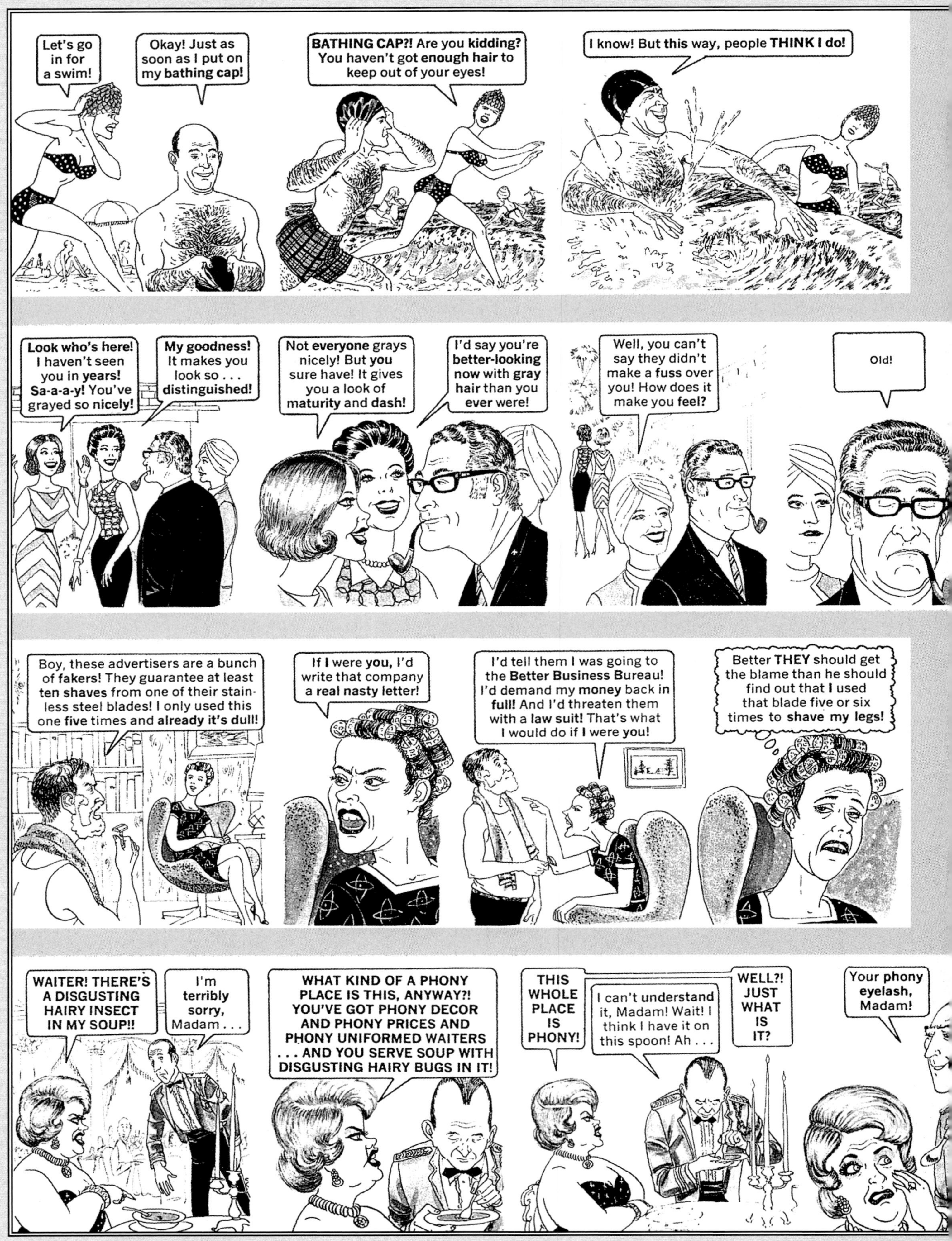
Let's go in for a swim!
Okay! Just as soon as I put on my bathing cap!
BATHING CAP?! Are you kidding? You haven't got enough hair to keep out of your eyes!
I know! But this way, people THINK I do!
Look who's here! I haven't seen you in years! Sa-a-a-y! You've grayed so nicely!
My goodness! It makes you look so . . . distinguished!
Not everyone grays nicely! But you sure have! It gives you a look of maturity and dash!
I'd say you're better-looking now with gray hair than you ever were!
Well, you can't say they didn't make a fuss over you! How does it make you feel?
Old!
Boy, these advertisers are a bunch of fakers! They guarantee at least ten shaves from one of their stainless steel blades! I only used this one five times and already it's dull!
If I were you, I'd write that company a real nasty letter!
I'd tell them I was going to the Better Business Bureau! I'd demand my money back in full! And I'd threaten them with a law suit! That's what I would do if I were you!
Better THEY should get the blame than he should find out that I used that blade five or six times to shave my legs!
WAITER! THERE'S A DISGUSTING HAIRY INSECT IN MY SOUP!!
I'm terribly sorry, Madam . . .
WHAT KIND OF A PHONY PLACE IS THIS, ANYWAY?! YOU'VE GOT PHONY DECOR AND PHONY PRICES AND PHONY UNIFORMED WAITERS . . . AND YOU SERVE SOUP WITH DISGUSTING HAIRY BUGS IN IT!
THIS WHOLE PLACE IS PHONY!
I can't understand it, Madam! Wait! I think I have it on this spoon! Ah . . .
WELL?! JUST WHAT IS IT?
Your phony eyelash, Madam!

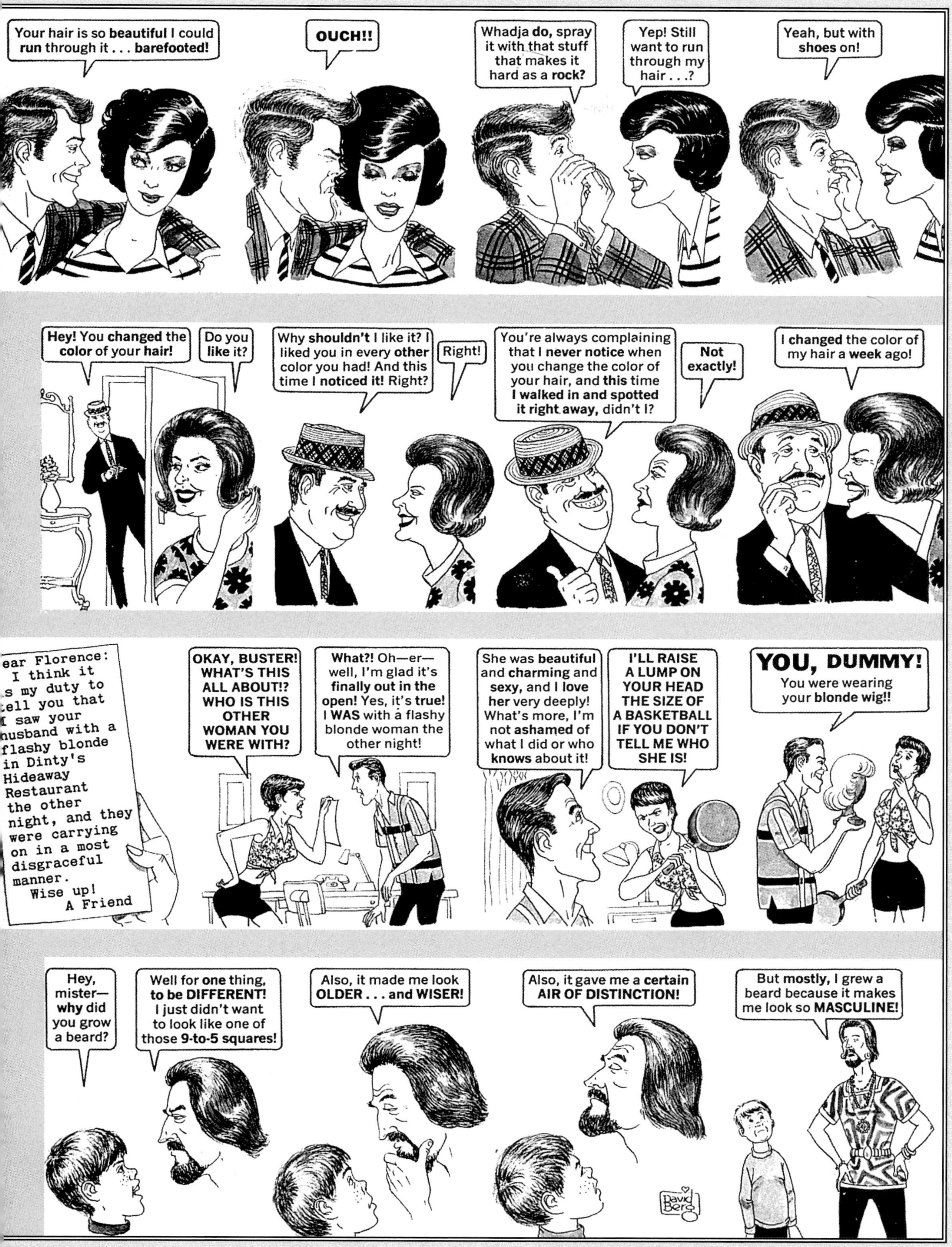
Your hair is so beautiful I could run through it . . . barefooted!
OUCH!!
Whadja do, spray it with that stuff that makes it hard as a rock?
Yep! Still want to run through my hair . . .?
Yeah, but with shoes on!
Hey! You changed the color of your hair!
Do you like it?
Why shouldn't I like it? I liked you in every other color you had! And this time I noticed it! Right?
Right!
You're always complaining that I never notice when you change the color of your hair, and this time I walked in and spotted it right away, didn't I?
Not exactly!
I changed the color of my hair a week ago!
ear Florence:
I think it
s my duty to
ell you that
I saw your
husband with a
flashy blonde
in Dinty's
Hideaway
Restaurant
the other
night, and they
were carrying
on in a most
disgraceful
manner.
Wise up!
A Friend
OKAY, BUSTER! WHAT'S THIS ALL ABOUT!? WHO IS THIS OTHER WOMAN YOU WERE WITH?
What?! Oh—er—well, I'm glad it's finally out in the open! Yes, it's true! I WAS with a flashy blonde woman the other night!
She was beautiful and charming and sexy, and I love her very deeply! What's more, I'm not ashamed of what I did or who knows about it!
I'LL RAISE A LUMP ON YOUR HEAD THE SIZE OF A BASKETBALL IF YOU DON'T TELL ME WHO SHE IS!
YOU, DUMMY! You were wearing your blonde wig!!
Hey, mister—why did you grow a beard?
Well for one thing, to be DIFFERENT! I just didn't want to look like one of those 9-to-5 squares!
Also, it made me look OLDER . . . and WISER!
Also, it gave me a certain AIR OF DISTINCTION!
But mostly, I grew a beard because it makes me look so MASCULINE!
David Berg

BERG'S-EYE-VIEW DEPT.

THE LIGHTER SIDE OF... STATUS

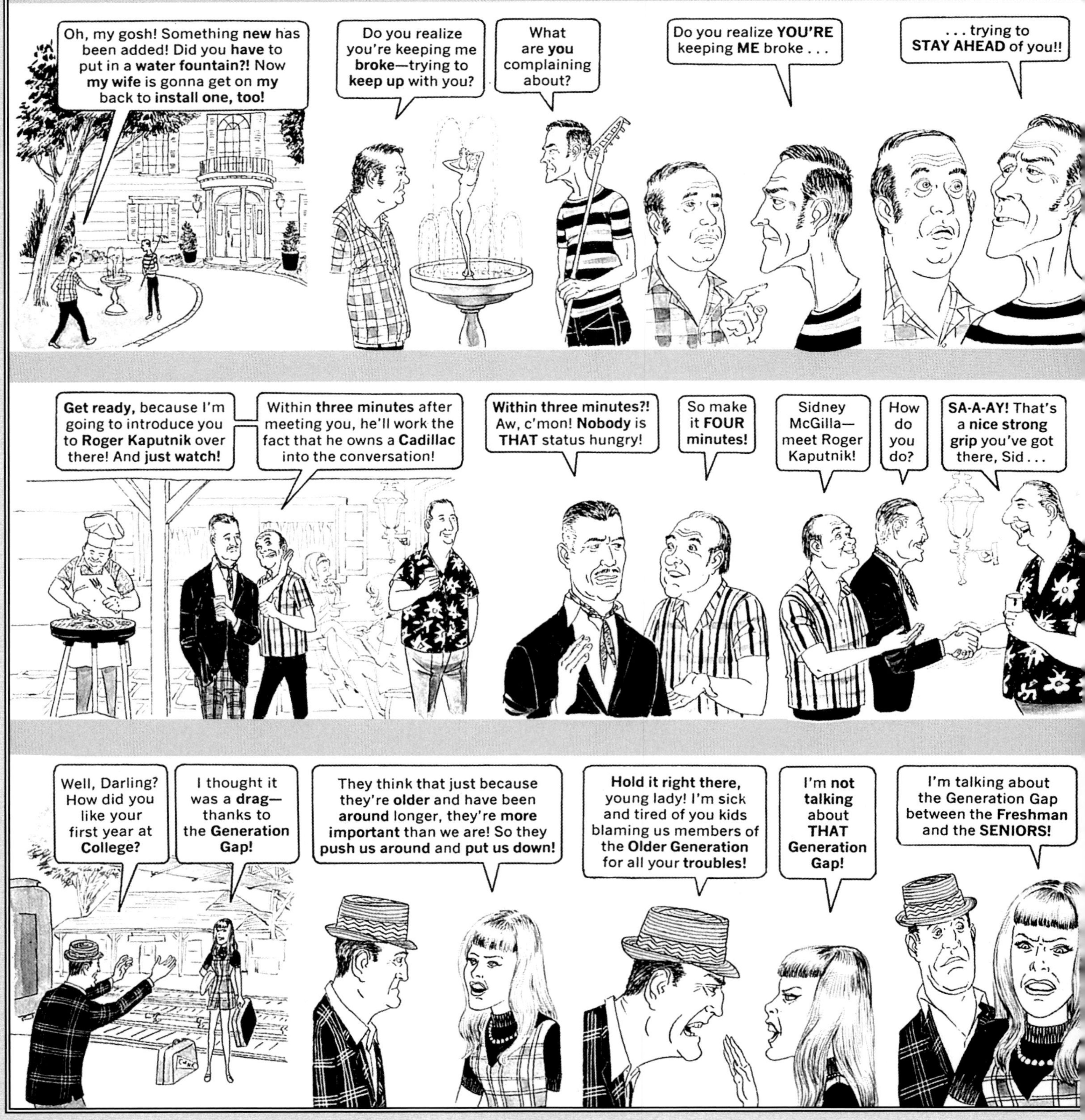
Oh, my gosh! Something new has been added! Did you have to put in a water fountain?! Now my wife is gonna get on my back to install one, too!
Do you realize you're keeping me broke—trying to keep up with you?
What are you complaining about?
Do you realize YOU'RE keeping ME broke . . .
. . . trying to STAY AHEAD of you!!
Get ready, because I'm going to introduce you to Roger Kaputnik over there! And just watch!
Within three minutes after meeting you, he'll work the fact that he owns a Cadillac into the conversation!
Within three minutes?! Aw, c'mon! Nobody is THAT status hungry!
So make it FOUR minutes!
Sidney McGilla—meet Roger Kaputnik!
How do you do?
SA-A-AY! That's a nice strong grip you've got there, Sid . . .
Well, Darling? How did you like your first year at College?
I thought it was a drag—thanks to the Generation Gap!
They think that just because they're older and have been around longer, they're more important than we are! So they push us around and put us down!
Hold it right there, young lady! I'm sick and tired of you kids blaming us members of the Older Generation for all your troubles!
I'm not talking about THAT Generation Gap!
I'm talking about the Generation Gap between the Freshman and the SENIORS!

SEEKING

ARTIST & WRITER:
DAVE BERG

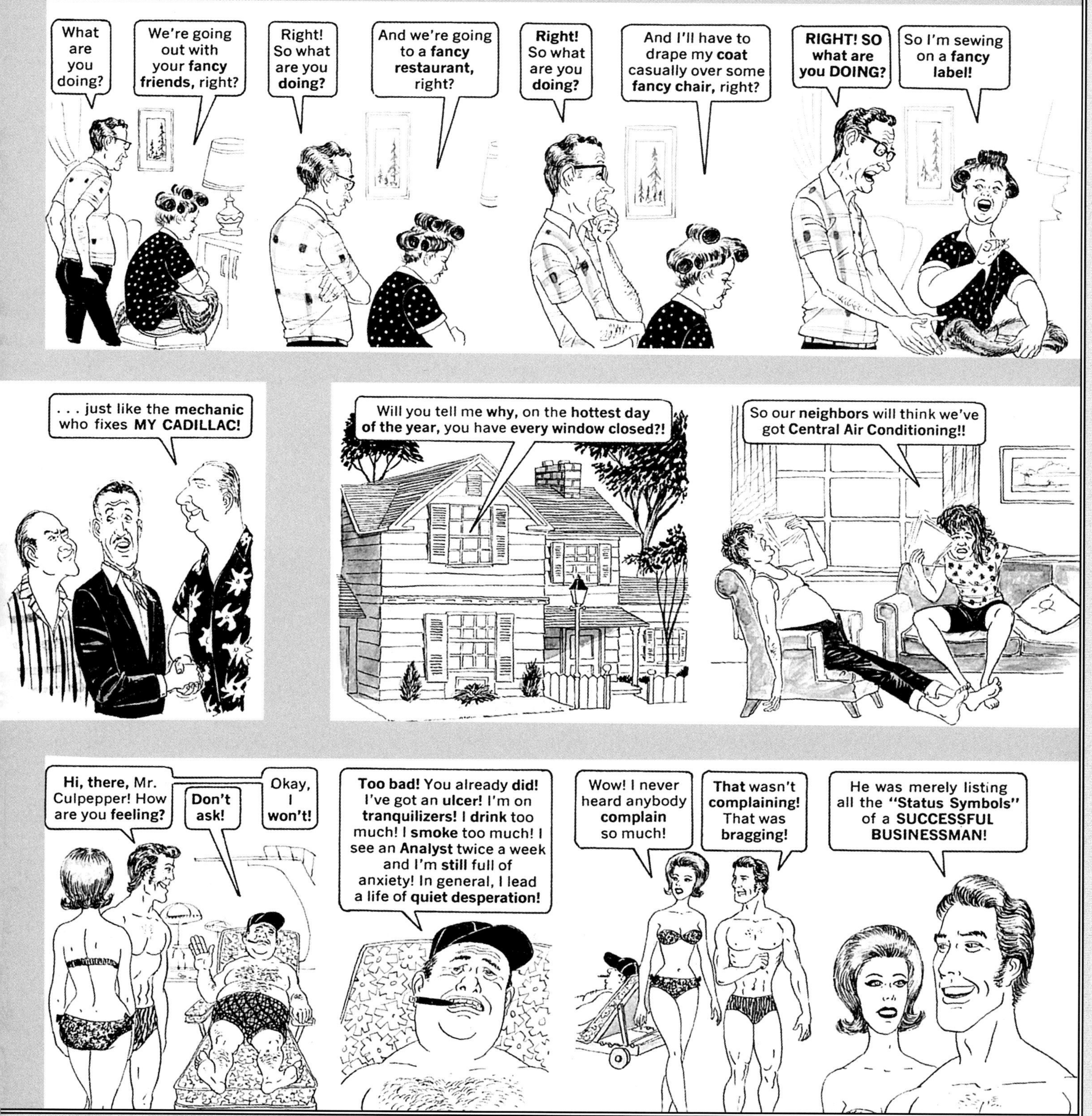
What are you doing?
We're going out with your fancy friends, right?
Right! So what are you doing?
And we're going to a fancy restaurant, right?
Right! So what are you doing?
And I'll have to drape my coat casually over some fancy chair, right?
RIGHT! SO what are you DOING?
So I'm sewing on a fancy label!
. . . just like the mechanic who fixes MY CADILLAC!
Will you tell me why, on the hottest day of the year, you have every window closed?!
So our neighbors will think we've got Central Air Conditioning!!
Hi, there, Mr. Culpepper! How are you feeling?
Don't ask!
Okay, I won't!
Too bad! You already did! I've got an ulcer! I'm on tranquilizers! I drink too much! I smoke too much! I see an Analyst twice a week and I'm still full of anxiety! In general, I lead a life of quiet desperation!
Wow! I never heard anybody complain so much!
That wasn't complaining! That was bragging!
He was merely listing all the "Status Symbols" of a SUCCESSFUL BUSINESSMAN!

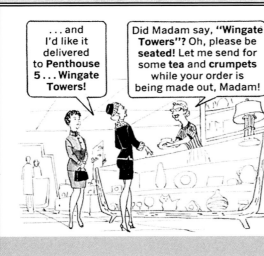

...and I'd like it delivered to Penthouse 5...Wingate Towers!

Did Madam say, "Wingate Towers"? Oh, please be seated! Let me send for some tea and crumpets while your order is being made out, Madam!

Perhaps you'd care for some Champagne? It's Bollinger—'61, a vintage year.

Perhaps some hors d'oeuvres?

Wow! What service! They were falling all over themselves like you were royalty!

Living at that address gets 'em every time!

Yeah...but you're the MAID there!!

Honey, this is my friend, Doris!

How do you do, Doris?

Hello! Oh...I hope my $1800 ring didn't scratch you!

I bought it in St. Thomas while I was on a $5000 cruise to the Caribbean! I remember I was in a chic little $300 chiffon, and the clerk said it would go just perfectly with my $2000 necklace!

Of course, what really makes the difference is my $3000 pair of matching earrings which I got—Oh, you'll have to pardon me! There's my husband...the one wearing the $250 suit and driving the $7500 Lincoln! Nice meeting you!

Hello? All I've got to say to you, Donna Doyle is... NYEAH! NYEAH! NYEAHHH!!

You're not the only twelve-year-old who has a phone of her own! My folks just gave me one, too...and you're getting the first call! So, all I've got to say to you, Donna Doyle, is... NYEAH! NYEAH! NOW WE'RE EVEN!!

I'm sorry, but Miss Doyle is not at home! Would you care to leave a message?

Hey! You're not Donna! Who IS this?

This is her ANSWERING SERVICE!

How about this?! It's another award for my work with the Boy Scouts!

Y'know what I just figured out? All these years that you've been telling me you were in Scouting for the sake of "Boyhood" you were handing me a big fat lie! You've really been in it for only one reason...to inflate your ego!

You've been doing it for prestige, status and awards! All this talk about doing it for "Boyhood" is baloney!

I am SO doing it for "Boyhood"!

And I'm the "Boy"!!

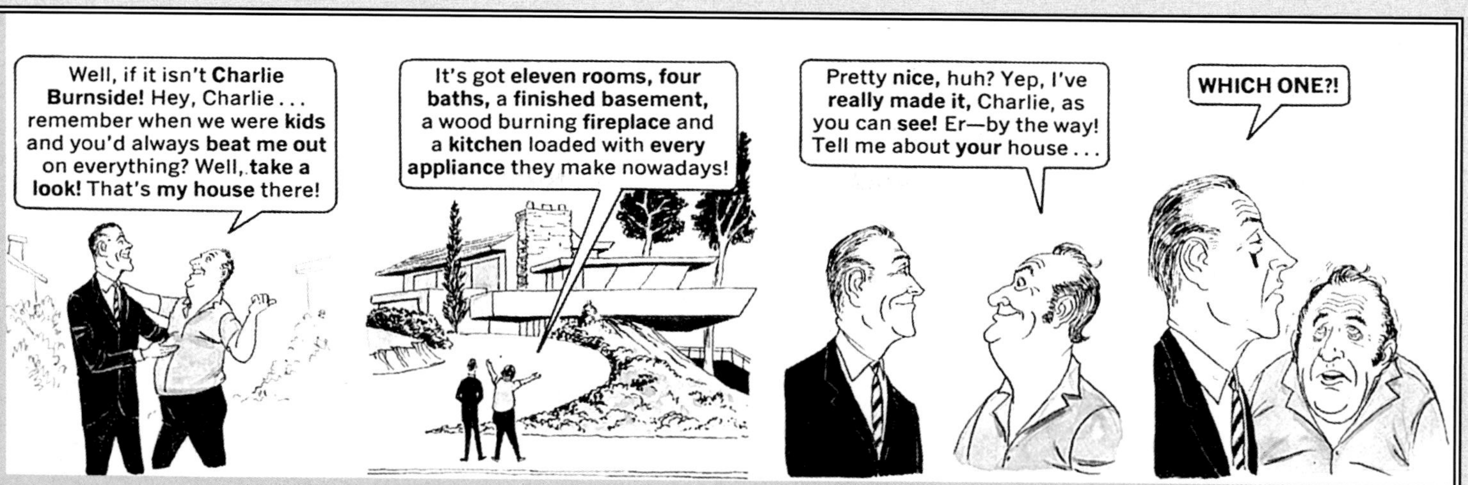
Well, if it isn't Charlie Burnside! Hey, Charlie . . . remember when we were kids and you'd always beat me out on everything? Well, take a look! That's my house there!
It's got eleven rooms, four baths, a finished basement, a wood burning fireplace and a kitchen loaded with every appliance they make nowadays!
Pretty nice, huh? Yep, I've really made it, Charlie, as you can see! Er—by the way! Tell me about your house . . .
WHICH ONE?!

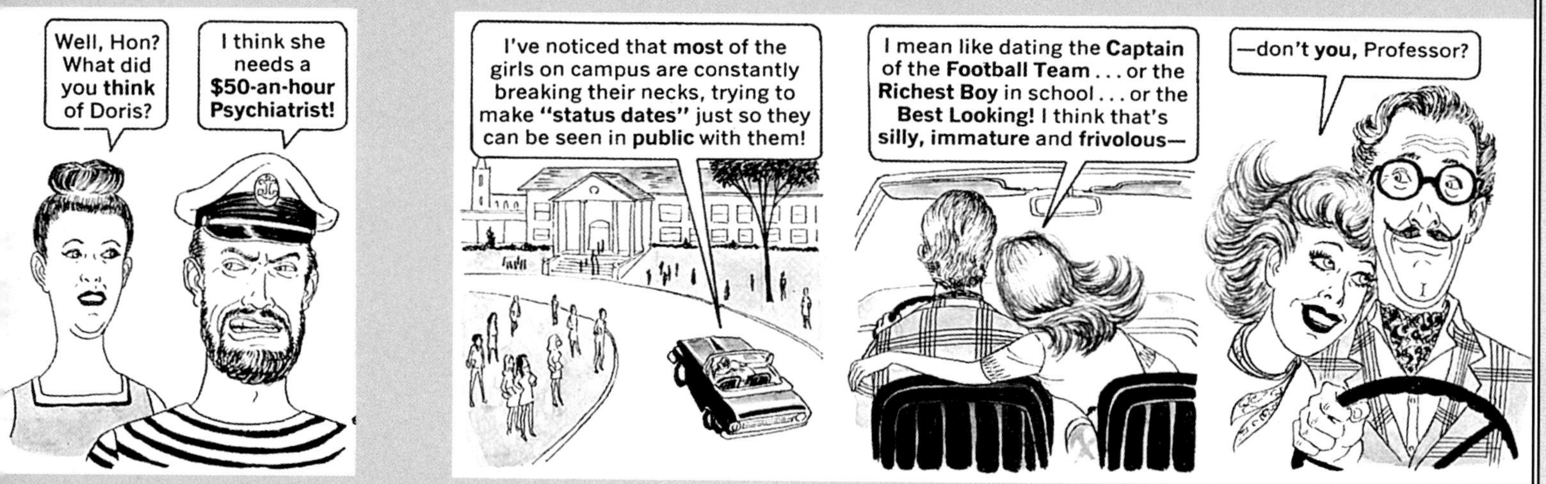
Well, Hon? What did you think of Doris?
I think she needs a $50-an-hour Psychiatrist!
I've noticed that most of the girls on campus are constantly breaking their necks, trying to make "status dates" just so they can be seen in public with them!
I mean like dating the Captain of the Football Team . . . or the Richest Boy in school . . . or the Best Looking! I think that's silly, immature and frivolous—
—don't you, Professor?

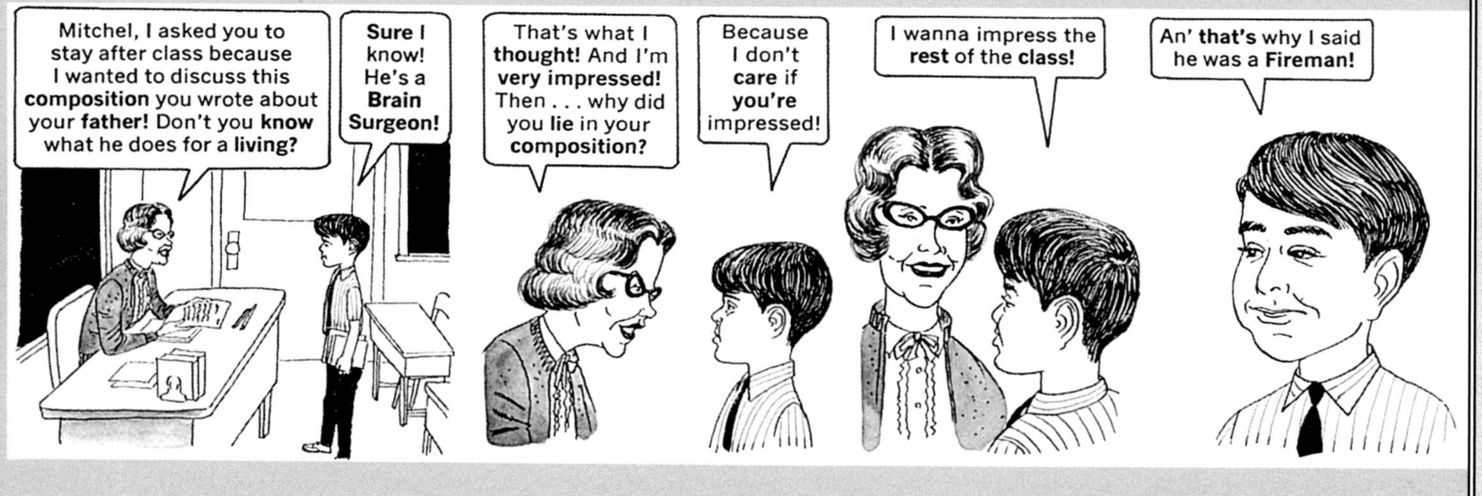
Mitchel, I asked you to stay after class because I wanted to discuss this composition you wrote about your father! Don't you know what he does for a living?
Sure I know! He's a Brain Surgeon!
That's what I thought! And I'm very impressed! Then . . . why did you lie in your composition?
Because I don't care if you're impressed!
I wanna impress the rest of the class!
An' that's why I said he was a Fireman!

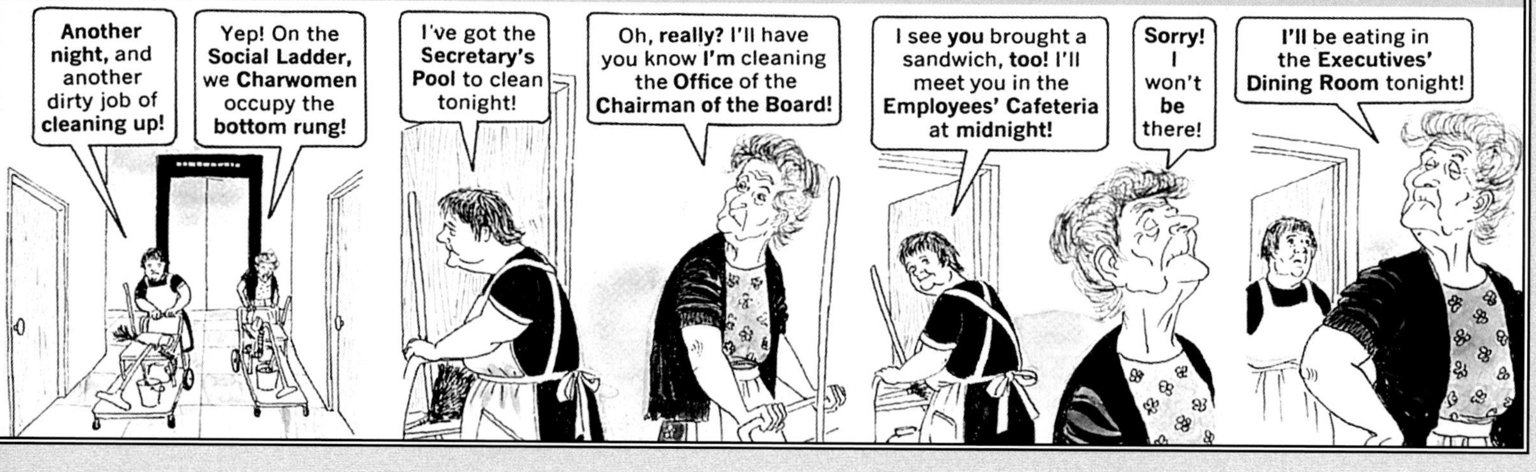
Another night, and another dirty job of cleaning up!
Yep! On the Social Ladder, we Charwomen occupy the bottom rung!
I've got the Secretary's Pool to clean tonight!
Oh, really? I'll have you know I'm cleaning the Office of the Chairman of the Board!
I see you brought a sandwich, too! I'll meet you in the Employees' Cafeteria at midnight!
Sorry! I won't be there!
I'll be eating in the Executives' Dining Room tonight!

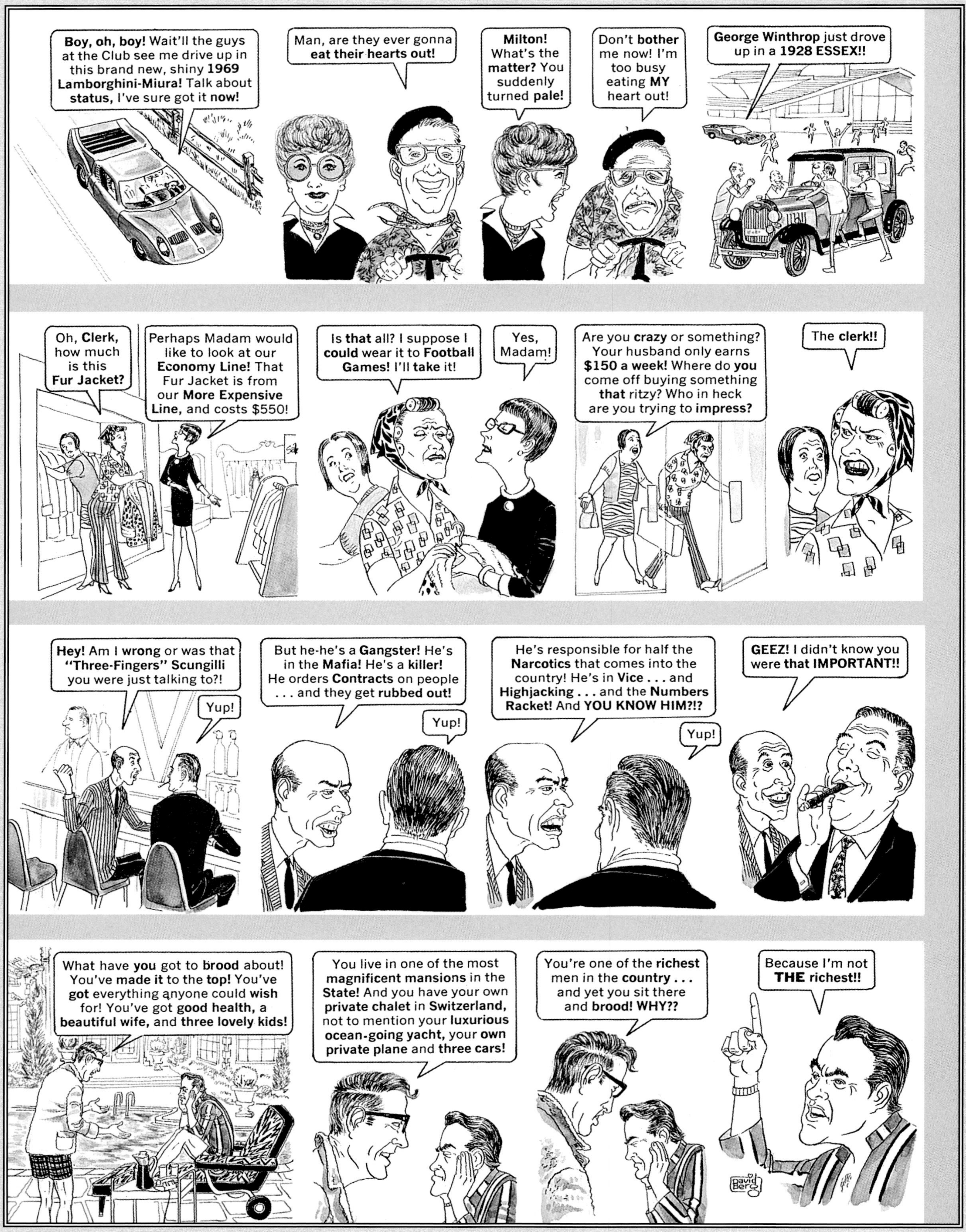
Boy, oh, boy! Wait'll the guys at the Club see me drive up in this brand new, shiny 1969 Lamborghini-Miura! Talk about status, I've sure got it now!
Man, are they ever gonna eat their hearts out!
Milton! What's the matter? You suddenly turned pale!
Don't bother me now! I'm too busy eating MY heart out!
George Winthrop just drove up in a 1928 ESSEX!!
Oh, Clerk, how much is this Fur Jacket?
Perhaps Madam would like to look at our Economy Line! That Fur Jacket is from our More Expensive Line, and costs $550!
Is that all? I suppose I could wear it to Football Games! I'll take it!
Yes, Madam!
Are you crazy or something? Your husband only earns $150 a week! Where do you come off buying something that ritzy? Who in heck are you trying to impress?
The clerk!!
Hey! Am I wrong or was that "Three-Fingers" Scungilli you were just talking to?!
Yup!
But he-he's a Gangster! He's in the Mafia! He's a killer! He orders Contracts on people . . . and they get rubbed out!
Yup!
He's responsible for half the Narcotics that comes into the country! He's in Vice . . . and Highjacking . . . and the Numbers Racket! And YOU KNOW HIM?!?
Yup!
GEEZ! I didn't know you were that IMPORTANT!!
What have you got to brood about! You've made it to the top! You've got everything anyone could wish for! You've got good health, a beautiful wife, and three lovely kids!
You live in one of the most magnificent mansions in the State! And you have your own private chalet in Switzerland, not to mention your luxurious ocean-going yacht, your own private plane and three cars!
You're one of the richest men in the country . . . and yet you sit there and brood! WHY??
Because I'm not THE richest!!
david Berg

The 1970s

BERG'S-EYE-VIEW DEPT.

THE LIGHTER SIDE OF... FAMILY

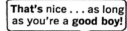

Wow! Will you get a load of this **spread** your Cousin made for the Cousins' Club . . .

I think it's **terrible**!

What are you **talking** about!? It's even **more beautiful, more varied,** and **more expensive** than the spread **YOU** made last time!

That's what I **mean**! I think it's **terrible**!

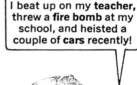

Why do they alla time put us kids at a **separate table** at these family functions?

And the adults never **pay attention** to us! I don't even think they **listen** to anything we **say** to them!

Just watch!

Well, there! How's my **Nephew?**

I've been off **pot** for a **while** now, because I've been **mainlining**! And I've had a couple of **bad LSD trips**!

I beat up on my **teacher,** threw a **fire bomb** at my school, and heisted a couple of **cars** recently!

That's nice . . . as long as you're a **good boy**!

What did you say?

GATHERINGS

ARTIST & WRITER: DAVE BERG

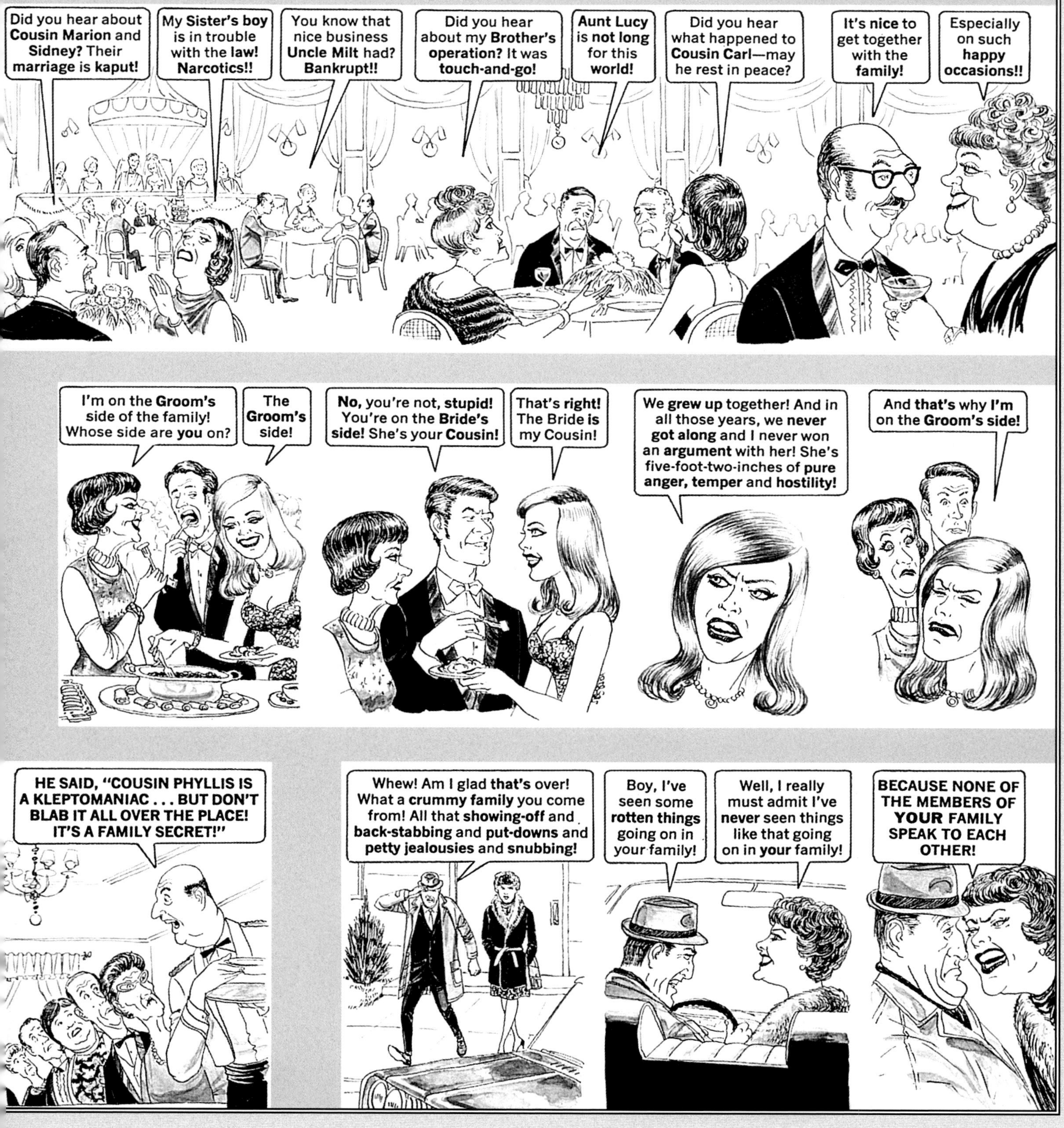
Did you hear about Cousin Marion and Sidney? Their marriage is kaput!
My Sister's boy is in trouble with the law! Narcotics!!
You know that nice business Uncle Milt had? Bankrupt!!
Did you hear about my Brother's operation? It was touch-and-go!
Aunt Lucy is not long for this world!
Did you hear what happened to Cousin Carl—may he rest in peace?
It's nice to get together with the family!
Especially on such happy occasions!!
I'm on the Groom's side of the family! Whose side are you on?
The Groom's side!
No, you're not, stupid! You're on the Bride's side! She's your Cousin!
That's right! The Bride is my Cousin!
We grew up together! And in all those years, we never got along and I never won an argument with her! She's five-foot-two-inches of pure anger, temper and hostility!
And that's why I'm on the Groom's side!
HE SAID, "COUSIN PHYLLIS IS A KLEPTOMANIAC . . . BUT DON'T BLAB IT ALL OVER THE PLACE! IT'S A FAMILY SECRET!"
Whew! Am I glad that's over! What a crummy family you come from! All that showing-off and back-stabbing and put-downs and petty jealousies and snubbing!
Boy, I've seen some rotten things going on in your family!
Well, I really must admit I've never seen things like that going on in your family!
BECAUSE NONE OF THE MEMBERS OF YOUR FAMILY SPEAK TO EACH OTHER!

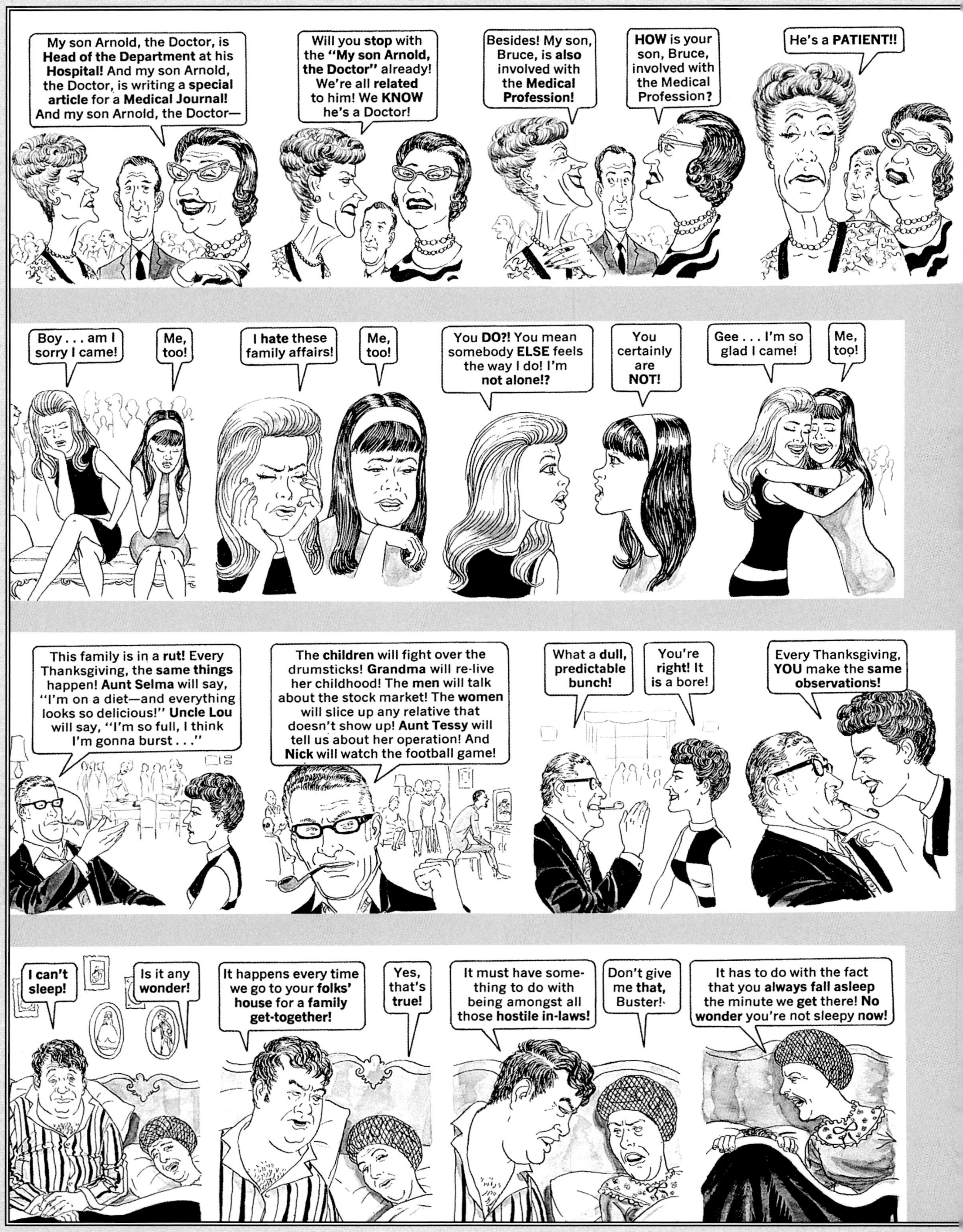
My son Arnold, the Doctor, is Head of the Department at his Hospital! And my son Arnold, the Doctor, is writing a special article for a Medical Journal! And my son Arnold, the Doctor—
Will you stop with the "My son Arnold, the Doctor" already! We're all related to him! We KNOW he's a Doctor!
Besides! My son, Bruce, is also involved with the Medical Profession!
HOW is your son, Bruce, involved with the Medical Profession?
He's a PATIENT!!
Boy . . . am I sorry I came!
Me, too!
I hate these family affairs!
Me, too!
You DO?! You mean somebody ELSE feels the way I do! I'm not alone!?
You certainly are NOT!
Gee . . . I'm so glad I came!
Me, too!
This family is in a rut! Every Thanksgiving, the same things happen! Aunt Selma will say, "I'm on a diet—and everything looks so delicious!" Uncle Lou will say, "I'm so full, I think I'm gonna burst . . ."
The children will fight over the drumsticks! Grandma will re-live her childhood! The men will talk about the stock market! The women will slice up any relative that doesn't show up! Aunt Tessy will tell us about her operation! And Nick will watch the football game!
What a dull, predictable bunch!
You're right! It is a bore!
Every Thanksgiving, YOU make the same observations!
I can't sleep!
Is it any wonder!
It happens every time we go to your folks' house for a family get-together!
Yes, that's true!
It must have something to do with being amongst all those hostile in-laws!
Don't give me that, Buster!
It has to do with the fact that you always fall asleep the minute we get there! No wonder you're not sleepy now!

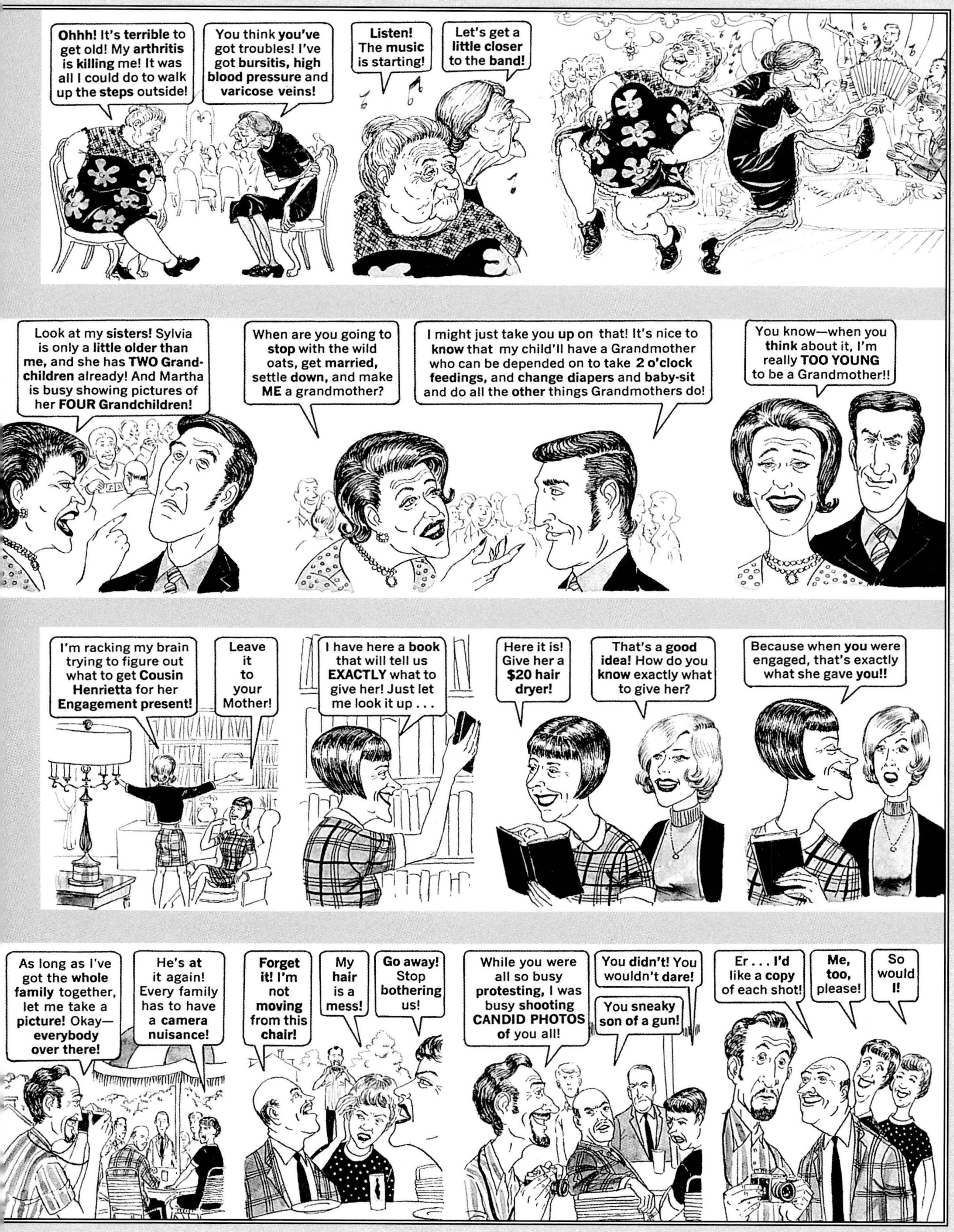
Ohhh! It's terrible to get old! My arthritis is killing me! It was all I could do to walk up the steps outside!
You think you've got troubles! I've got bursitis, high blood pressure and varicose veins!
Listen! The music is starting!
Let's get a little closer to the band!
Look at my sisters! Sylvia is only a little older than me, and she has TWO Grandchildren already! And Martha is busy showing pictures of her FOUR Grandchildren!
When are you going to stop with the wild oats, get married, settle down, and make ME a grandmother?
I might just take you up on that! It's nice to know that my child'll have a Grandmother who can be depended on to take 2 o'clock feedings, and change diapers and baby-sit and do all the other things Grandmothers do!
You know—when you think about it, I'm really TOO YOUNG to be a Grandmother!!
I'm racking my brain trying to figure out what to get Cousin Henrietta for her Engagement present!
Leave it to your Mother!
I have here a book that will tell us EXACTLY what to give her! Just let me look it up . . .
Here it is! Give her a $20 hair dryer!
That's a good idea! How do you know exactly what to give her?
Because when you were engaged, that's exactly what she gave you!!
As long as I've got the whole family together, let me take a picture! Okay—everybody over there!
He's at it again! Every family has to have a camera nuisance!
Forget it! I'm not moving from this chair!
My hair is a mess!
Go away! Stop bothering us!
While you were all so busy protesting, I was busy shooting CANDID PHOTOS of you all!
You didn't! You wouldn't dare!
You sneaky son of a gun!
Er . . . I'd like a copy of each shot!
Me, too, please!
So would I!

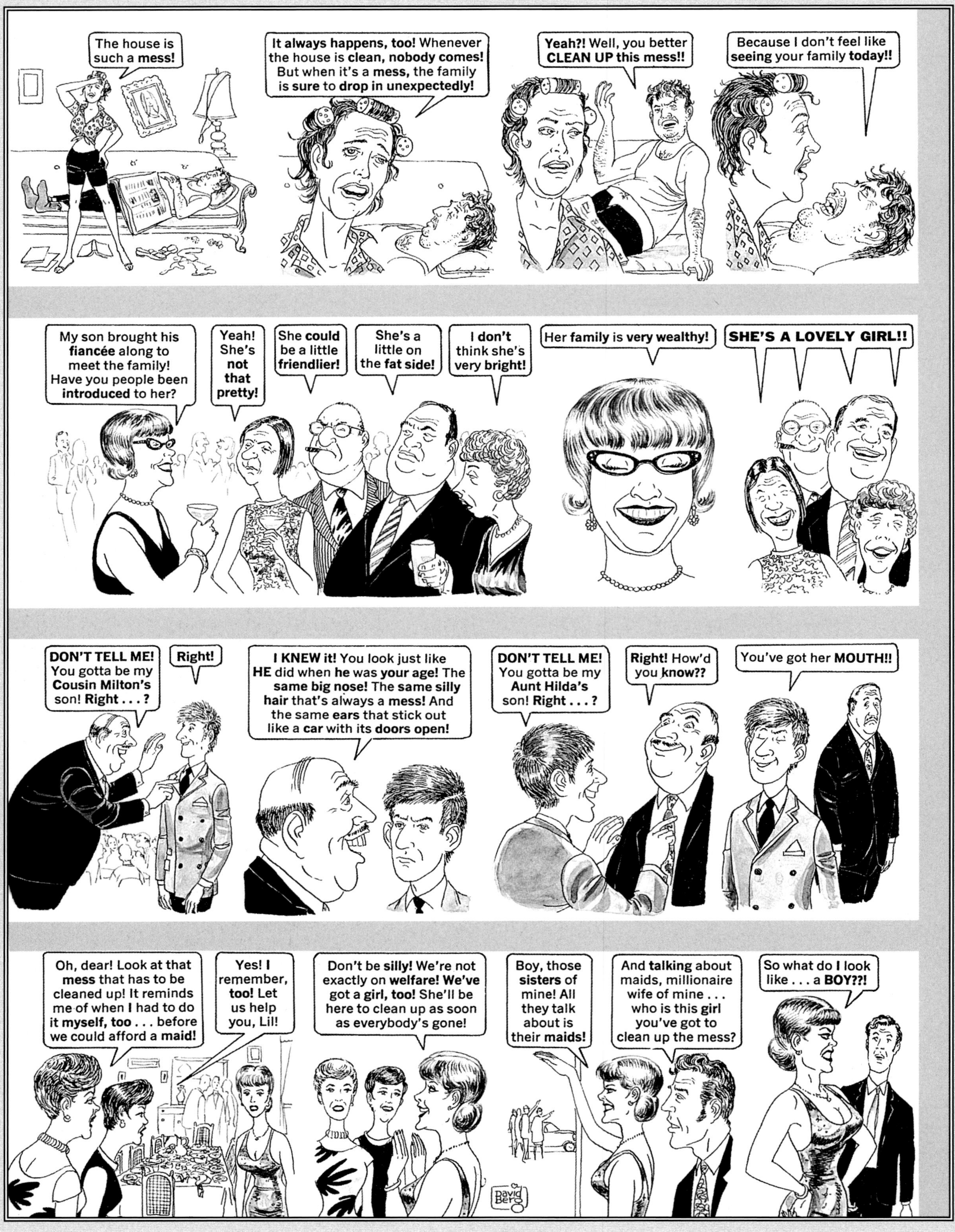
The house is such a **mess!**
It always happens, too! Whenever the house is **clean, nobody comes!** But when it's a **mess,** the family is **sure** to **drop in unexpectedly!**
Yeah?! Well, you better **CLEAN UP this mess!!**
Because I don't feel like **seeing** your family **today!!**
My son brought his **fiancée** along to meet the family! Have you people been **introduced** to her?
Yeah! She's **not that pretty!**
She **could** be a little **friendlier!**
She's a little on the **fat side!**
I **don't** think she's **very bright!**
Her **family** is **very wealthy!**
SHE'S A LOVELY GIRL!!
DON'T TELL ME! You gotta be my **Cousin Milton's** son! **Right . . . ?**
Right!
I KNEW it! You look just like **HE** did when **he** was **your age!** The **same big nose!** The **same silly hair** that's always a **mess!** And the same **ears** that stick out like a **car** with its **doors open!**
DON'T TELL ME! You gotta be my **Aunt Hilda's** son! **Right . . . ?**
Right! How'd you **know??**
You've got her **MOUTH!!**
Oh, dear! Look at that **mess** that has to be cleaned up! It reminds me of when **I** had to do it **myself, too . . .** before we could afford a **maid!**
Yes! I remember, **too!** Let us help you, Lil!
Don't be **silly!** We're not exactly on **welfare! We've** got a **girl, too!** She'll be here to clean up as soon as everybody's gone!
Boy, those **sisters** of mine! All they talk about is their **maids!**
And **talking** about maids, millionaire wife of mine . . . who is this **girl** you've got to clean up the mess?
So what do **I** look like . . . a **BOY??!**

An Interview with Dave Berg

The following are excerpts from an interview conducted by editor/publisher Jud Hurd that appeared in the January 1970 issue of his journal *Cartoonist PROfiles*.

Jud Hurd: You use a tape recorder a good deal in gathering material for the stories and cartoons you do for MAD, don't you?

Dave Berg: Yeah, I get a lot of mail that says, "How do you know so much?" Well, the truth is, I don't know so much. I go around interviewing people with a tape recorder, like yours. People are very willing and they even beg, "When are you going to interview me?" Perhaps it's because I'll put their name in the cartoon. Then they'll go out and buy 1,000 copies and say, "Look, I made MAD Magazine!"

JH: What type of person do you make a point of interviewing?

DB: The average—basically I'm writing about the middle class—suburbia, I suppose, which is really the biggest part of the country now. I live in the suburbs and I want to "get" Mr. Average. People stop me on the street and say, "I have a story just for your thing." Very often it's good—I sometimes have to rewrite it. The basic truth will be there, but the point is to make the gag line at the end, which is the hardest thing of all. Gathering material is easy—it's a workmanlike job, it's a correspondent's job—and I was a correspondent in World War II. I know how to ferret out a story, I know how to research a story. And then, I gather all the material in front of me and then go make it funny—and that is the hard part.

JH: Supposing you were going to do several pages of cartoons about students nowadays. How would you go about interviewing some average ones?

DB: I have, but tell one student that I know and there will be a crowd, either at my house, or somebody will throw a party for the occasion. It's astonishing—they'll invite their friends over, they'll serve refreshments, and I'll put the mike down and just let them talk—whatever the subject happens to be. They forget the mike is there after a while and they just go on—their hearts come out.

JH: Is there a possibility that people who have never seen your MAD cartoons will consciously try to be funny during these tapings?

From the Berg Family Collection

DB: No, they forget about the mike. I think a good example is one in connection with an upcoming series of mine about family gatherings. I got a family gathering together and they said, "Well, we have no trouble in our family—it's a wonderfully loving family." I probed some more and by the time I was finished, all the venom of the family came out—all the conversation was full of rage and anger. What they were saying at first was sweetness, and before long, they were telling all the inside stuff, catty stuff. The tape was going all the time while this family was talking and I still have it.

JH: Although most of us cartoonists became interested in drawing at an early age, I believe you've said that you began even much earlier than most. Is that right?

DB: Well, as far as my talent, it was shown at the age of three. They knew I was going to be an artist—I started to draw a little beyond the usual. They used to call me Wunderkind, which is the German term for Wonder Child, although it was far from the truth! It was just that I was rebellious—I was letting out all my hostility on paper—which I'm still doing to this day.

JH: Did your parents encourage you?

DB: My parents were immigrants from Lithuania. I used to think I was a deprived kid—I grew up in Brooklyn in a ghetto. I was born in a tenement house and everyone thought it was a terrible thing. Everybody has something that's bugging him and my drive was to get out of the ghetto, and once I'd gotten out, I realized that I'd come from something utterly magnificent. There was only poverty there, but the culture was so fantastically high that even among the poverty, we had all sorts of music schools, art school, and museums. At the age of ten, I was sent to a special school, an ethnic cultural school. It's amazing that a poor neighborhood would have had a school like that.

JH: What kind of art were you interested in during your early years?

DB: I had thorough training in fine arts, but I kept gravitating toward caricature. I call the stuff I do now "caricature" rather than "cartooning" because it's very close to realism. It's slightly exaggerated—even the writing itself is a caricature—it's truth exaggerated.

JH: What was the next step after you finished high school?

DB: I kept going toward art, but that was the least of it for me. The art was nothing more than a key to open the door. And still, to this day, it opens doors. I don't like being an artist, I get no thrill out of it, even though I have a very thorough education in it. I'm not interested in being an artist—I think it's a lesser thing. But the thing I admire is writing.

As a child I drew constantly. I was a radio nut and, as I was listening, I'd draw what was happening on the radio in my own imagination. Although I never put into words the idea that I might become a writer, it probably was always in the sub-basement of my mind. I was writing humorous poetry in the beginning, and then sometime around the junior high period I began writing short stories. They fascinated me—I loved them—and at the time short stories were very popular.

One of the short pieces I wrote in high school was about a kid who steals from the candy counter, and it turns out that what he stole were free samples. I've recently incorporated it into one of my MAD books because I thought it was a good plot.

JH: What art school training did you have after high school?

DB: I got a scholarship at Cooper Union and went there for two years. I had a full-time job as a professional artist during the day and went to school in the evening. I was one of those early artist-writers for the comic books during the day. I started originally with Will Eisner doing backgrounds for *The Spirit* and then he gave me a feature in *Military Comics*, which he produced. I eventually went on to *Captain Marvel*, which I wrote and illustrated.

In art school, by the way, I took a course in architecture which, at the time, I didn't think I'd ever need. But years later I did a whole series on architecture in MAD based on what I'd learned. It was actually picked up and reprinted in several architecture magazines! The feature I wrote and drew for Will Eisner was *Death Patrol*.

JH: Were you with MAD from the first?

DB: The original group who started MAD—we were all friends—and we shared a studio together: Harvey Kurztman, Will Elder, and the whole group. When they started the magazine they asked me to come along. I had a good job, so I kept refusing. But I saw it was catching on and switched. I sold them a script and they've been demanding their money back ever since!

Now, I'm astonished at what's happening with MAD! It's so popular, it's translated into six languages, I think. Every year I get letters from students in all grades saying they want to write a term paper on me. They're studying my work as satire, and as art in art classes.

JH: What do you do in the way of reading, etc., to keep up on what's going on in the world?

DB: I'm constantly frustrated—there aren't enough hours in the day. As far as reading, I've got my mean old wife! She reads a book a day. She's an avid reader and she's brilliant. And she'll give me a synopsis of what she's read. I give her reading assignments, and I'll go out and do the interviews to research the subject further.

One of the hardest things I had to write was an article called "The Generation Gap." My wife went to the library and got everything she could find about it. Then she gave me a verbal synopsis of every book she'd read. I did the story on a 50-50 basis, one half from the parents' point of view, and the other half from the children's point of view. Most of the mail said it was fair. It's so complicated! As much as I've read—as much as I'm living it—as much as I try to analyze it—I don't fully understand it. That's why when kids tell me that I'm "with it," I don't know what they're talking about!

When I lecture at colleges, the kids feel that I understand "the Gap." But I don't know—I'm guessing! I might say that

I'm neither right nor left nor middle—my feet are firmly planted in mid-air and I'm looking down and seeing what everyone's doing wrong. And there's also a very large mirror next to me and I see what *I'm* doing wrong.

Being self-critical is very important, I think. I draw myself in a number of MAD sequences for a very important reason. I'm not standing on a pedestal saying, "I am holier than thou." I'm saying that I'm no good either! That's why I'll always put myself in the cartoons in a negative fashion. I have to show that I'm no better. I detest the type of writers who sit in judgment.

JH: You said that you'd rather write than draw. Any further comments on that?

DB: Well, I'd much rather write a daily column with no drawings. Something like what Art Buchwald does. I think I should say this about humor: with me it's a science. It's a trick—and I understand the trick, but I'm not personally funny. I like funny people around me, like Al Jaffee, whom I've known for 30 years.

JH: How much time do you spend on the artwork for, say, a five-page story for MAD?

DB: All of the artwork takes two weeks and the writing sometimes takes more than that. I write double the amount of material which actually appears. The editors pick the best ones. And those which are still good are put aside for a book, and I'm on my fifth book now.

JH: Do you carry a sketchpad around?

DB: From my late teens till well into my twenties I carried one everywhere. But I don't have the patience to do it these days. But I have piles and piles of photos of types that I've cut out of newspapers and magazines for future reference. Another trick of mine is to sketch celebrities, change the features just a bit, and then use the faces in my cartoons so people will say, "Hey, he looks familiar but I can't quite place him."

JH: MAD comes out approximately every six weeks, doesn't it?

DB: Yes, and I allow about four weeks for the MAD material and two weeks for my books. Actually, I never stop working—I can't even go to a party and relax. I carry paper wherever I go and put down ideas when something happens.

JH: What reactions do you get from readers you haven't mentioned previously?

DB: They say, "I feel I know your people—they're real." They play a game in my hometown, Who Have I Put in the Cartoon? I actually don't put in that many local people, but they still love to play the game. I live in a town which I consider pretty typical—New Rochelle, New York. While it's a generally wealthy area, it has its poverty, but it's mostly middle-class. I'm middle-class myself, mentally if not financially—you never get out of that!—and it's the middle-class that I'm trying to portray.

JH: Would you say something about the lecturing you've done at colleges?

DB: I was invited to lecture at the University of Toronto. By the way, Bill Gaines, MAD's publisher, went to the University of Toronto. I took a long time in writing this speech because I'd been invited a long time in advance—I wrote it very carefully. As far as delivering speeches, I've been involved with community work and I've had to speak on a number of occasions. As far as the content, I had a lot of serious things to say, but I made sure that each paragraph ended with a punch line or gag. I was told to expect no more than 150 kids—600 showed up. I was astonished—it was standing room only.

When I was finished, I had one of the most fantastic things that ever happened to me—I got a standing ovation! And I've been knocking myself out ever since trying to figure out what happened. The only thing I could think of is that I was representing a magazine that's very popular with them. I don't think it was me, or any kind of charisma—it's what I represented. Since then I've been besieged with requests to speak at other colleges and universities and I don't even like speaking! A lecture bureau is now taking care of all this, but let's not mention which one because I already have more than I can handle! One of the pleasant things about going to Toronto was that Bill Gaines went with me and we had fun—we're like two kids together.

JH: Any final comments you'd like to add?

DB: Even though my work has a lot of love in it, I'm really rather negative about the human animal. I believe that God has a tremendous sense of humor and that this is his idea of a practical joke on the human animal. And I think we *are* animals and I don't think we've reached civilization yet. My principle is moderation itself—even moderation itself! I think that a true humorist is a sad person. I think one of the greatest crimes in this world is stupidity. And somebody else pointed out that the thing about MAD Magazine is that we don't say things are evil—we say they're *stupid!* MAD has been following this idea and so have I, but we didn't know it! A reverend had to tell us—he's writing a book about it! People sometimes refer to me as a "zany prophet." A prophet is not a supernatural being—he's just an ordinary man who says, "Cut it out! This is wrong!"

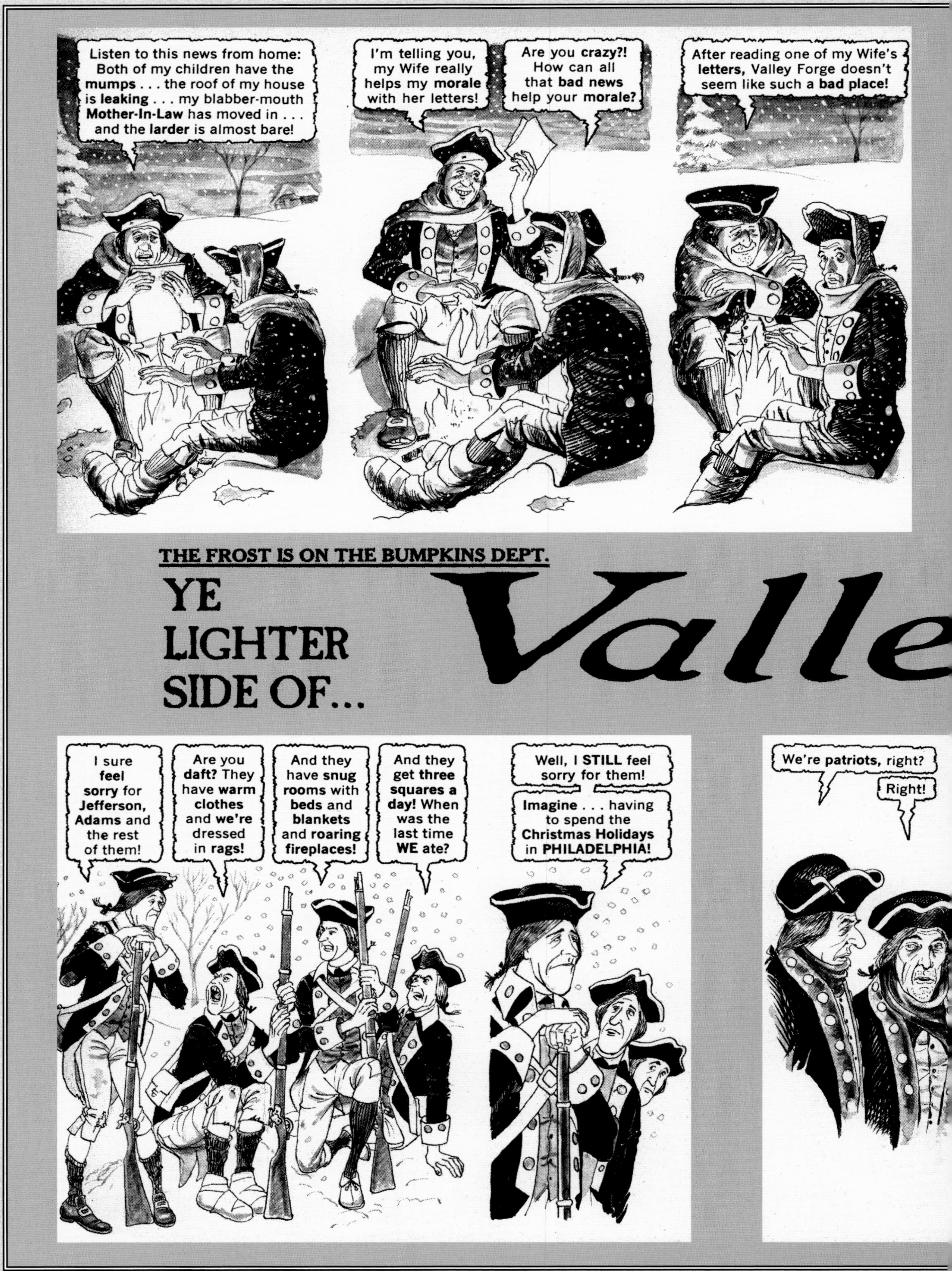

Listen to this news from home: Both of my children have the mumps . . . the roof of my house is leaking . . . my blabber-mouth Mother-In-Law has moved in . . . and the larder is almost bare!
I'm telling you, my Wife really helps my morale with her letters!
Are you crazy?! How can all that bad news help your morale?
After reading one of my Wife's letters, Valley Forge doesn't seem like such a bad place!
THE FROST IS ON THE BUMPKINS DEPT.
YE LIGHTER SIDE OF...
Valle
I sure feel sorry for Jefferson, Adams and the rest of them!
Are you daft? They have warm clothes and we're dressed in rags!
And they have snug rooms with beds and blankets and roaring fireplaces!
And they get three squares a day! When was the last time WE ate?
Well, I STILL feel sorry for them!
Imagine . . . having to spend the Christmas Holidays in PHILADELPHIA!
We're patriots, right?
Right!

In 1976, MAD's artists and writers envisioned a Revolutionary-era version of the magazine. Dave's contribution is excerpted here.

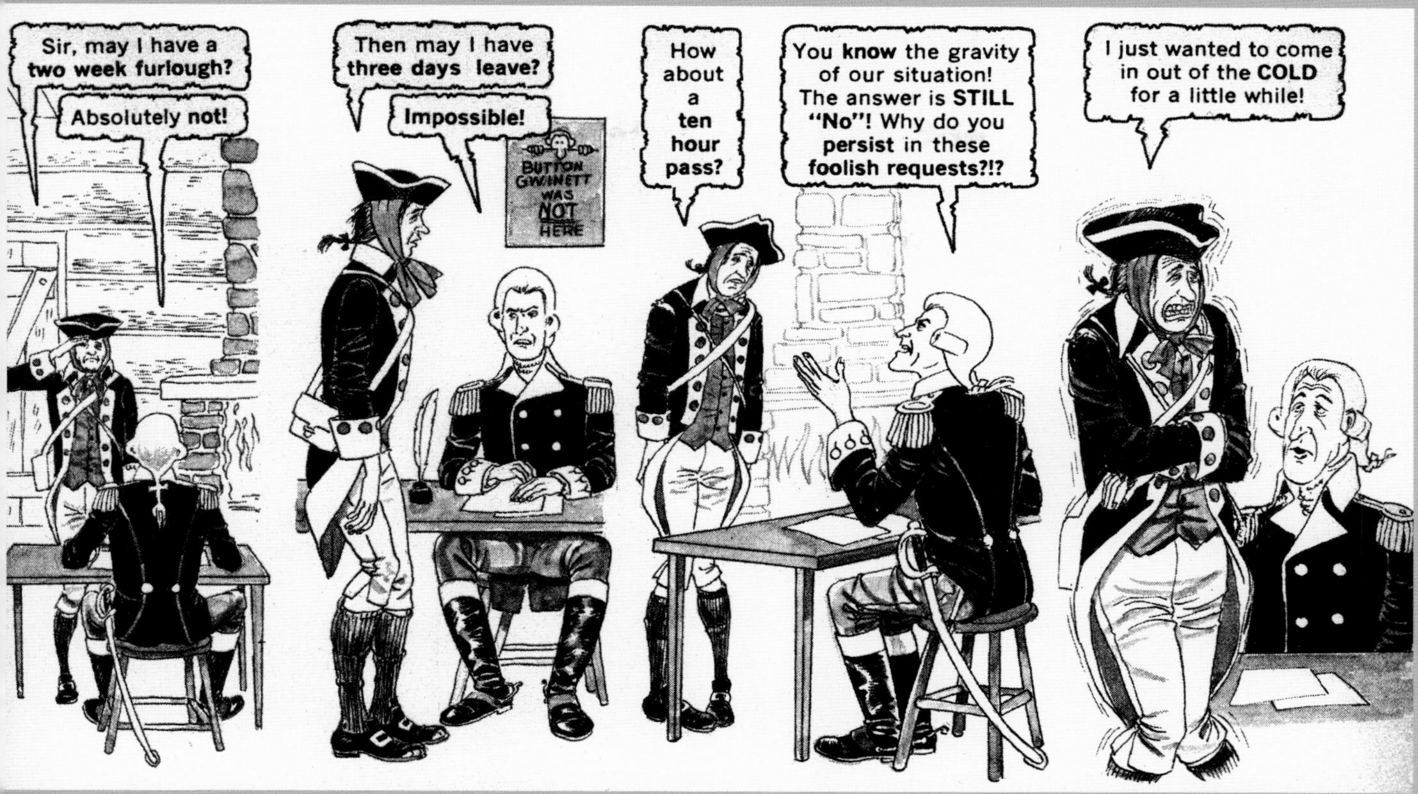
Sir, may I have a two week furlough?
Absolutely not!
Then may I have three days leave?
Impossible!
BUTTON GWINETT WAS NOT HERE
How about a ten hour pass?
You know the gravity of our situation! The answer is STILL "No"! Why do you persist in these foolish requests?!?
I just wanted to come in out of the COLD for a little while!

y Forge

SCRIVENER & DELINEATOR: DAVID BERG

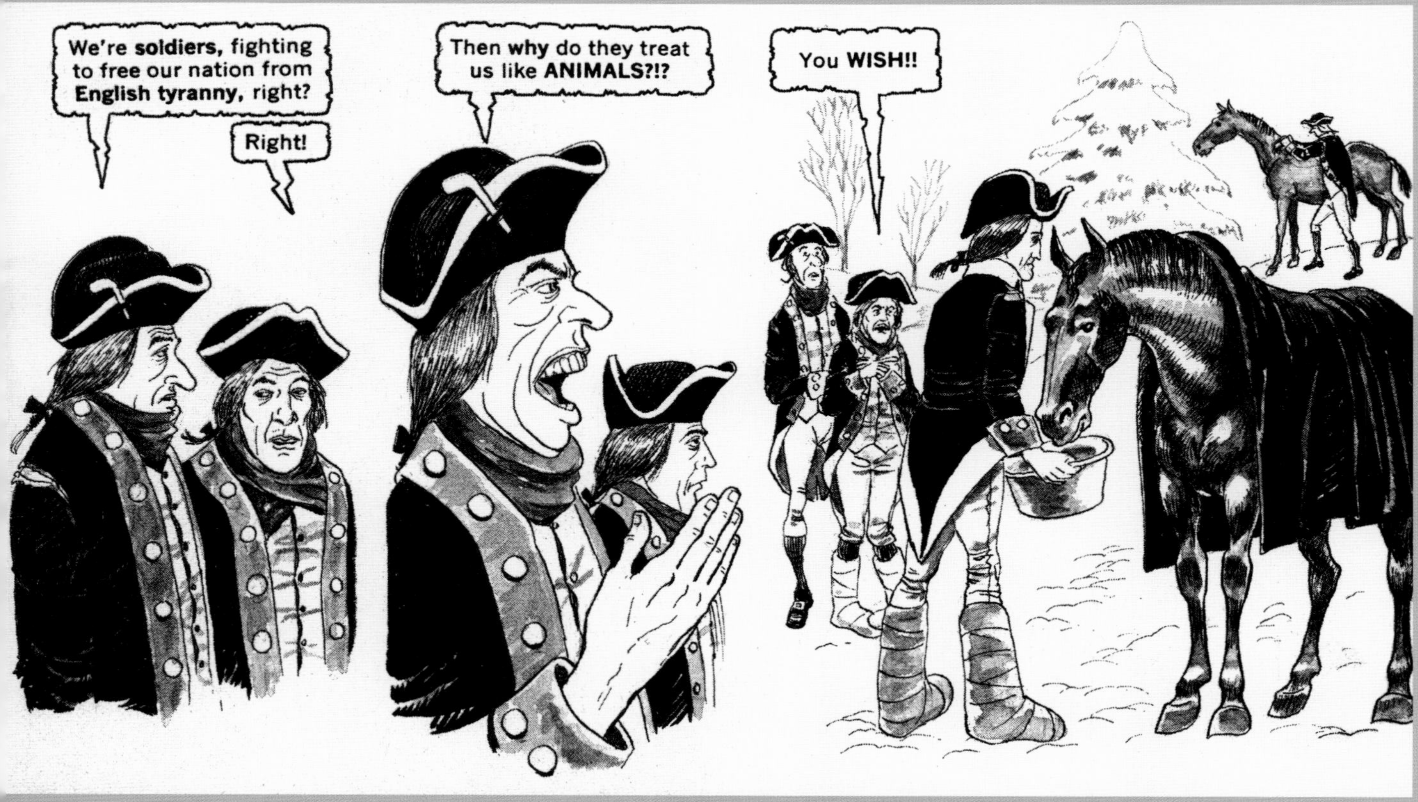
We're soldiers, fighting to free our nation from English tyranny, right?
Right!
Then why do they treat us like ANIMALS?!?
You WISH!!

BERG'S-EYE-VIEW DEPT.

THE LIGHTER SIDE OF... MO

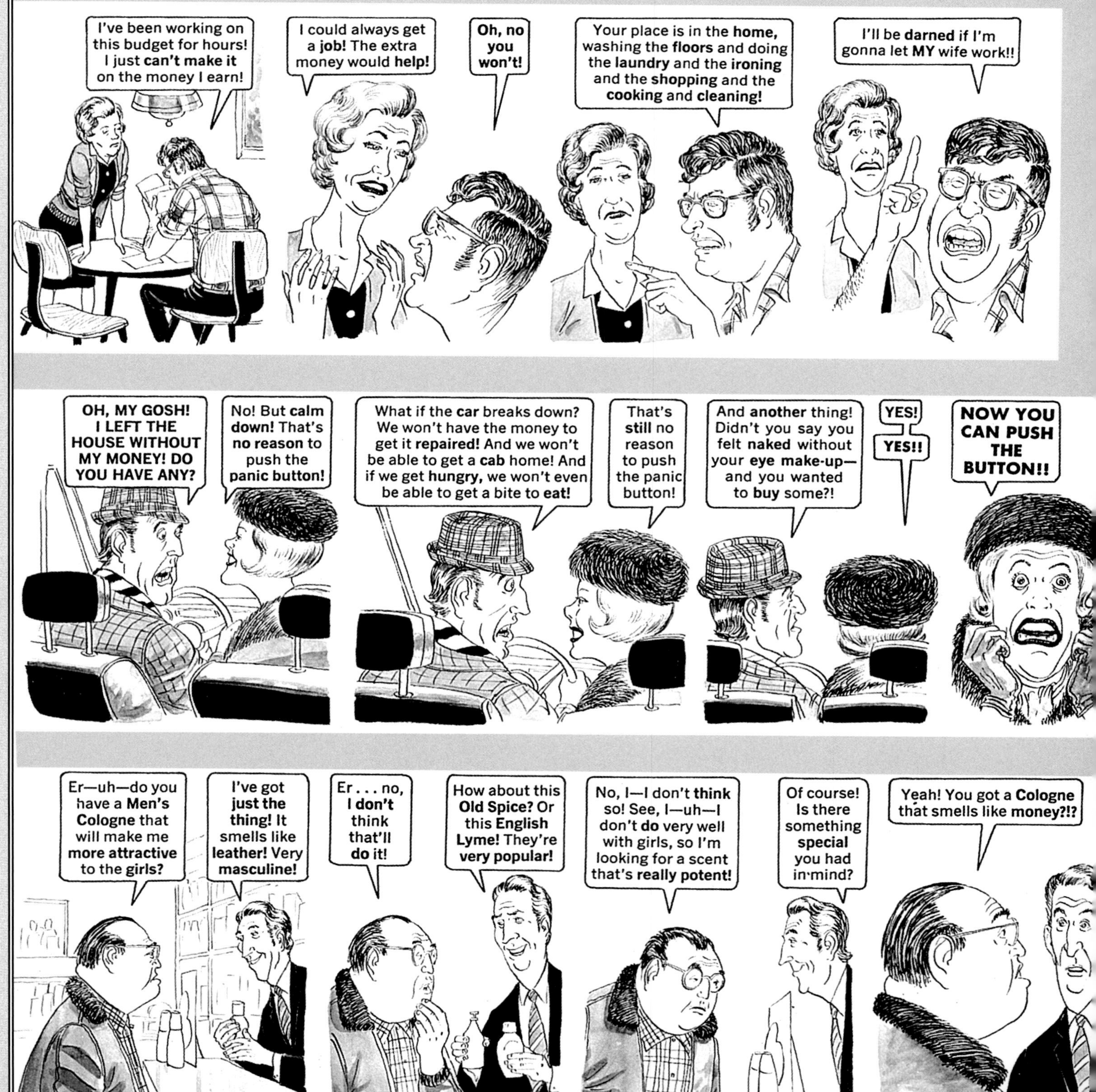
I've been working on this budget for hours! I just can't make it on the money I earn!
I could always get a job! The extra money would help!
Oh, no you won't!
Your place is in the home, washing the floors and doing the laundry and the ironing and the shopping and the cooking and cleaning!
I'll be darned if I'm gonna let MY wife work!!
OH, MY GOSH! I LEFT THE HOUSE WITHOUT MY MONEY! DO YOU HAVE ANY?
No! But calm down! That's no reason to push the panic button!
What if the car breaks down? We won't have the money to get it repaired! And we won't be able to get a cab home! And if we get hungry, we won't even be able to get a bite to eat!
That's still no reason to push the panic button!
And another thing! Didn't you say you felt naked without your eye make-up—and you wanted to buy some?!
YES!
YES!!
NOW YOU CAN PUSH THE BUTTON!!
Er—uh—do you have a Men's Cologne that will make me more attractive to the girls?
I've got just the thing! It smells like leather! Very masculine!
Er . . . no, I don't think that'll do it!
How about this Old Spice? Or this English Lyme! They're very popular!
No, I—I don't think so! See, I—uh—I don't do very well with girls, so I'm looking for a scent that's really potent!
Of course! Is there something special you had in mind?
Yeah! You got a Cologne that smells like money?!?

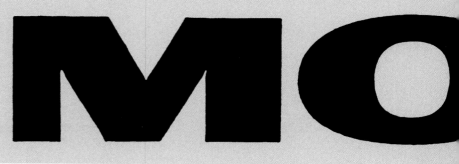

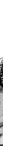

NEY

ARTIST & WRITER: DAVE BERG

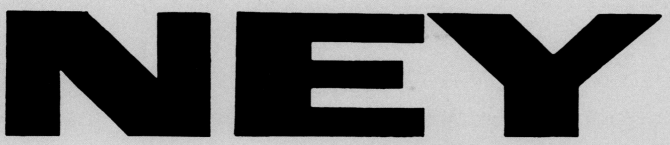

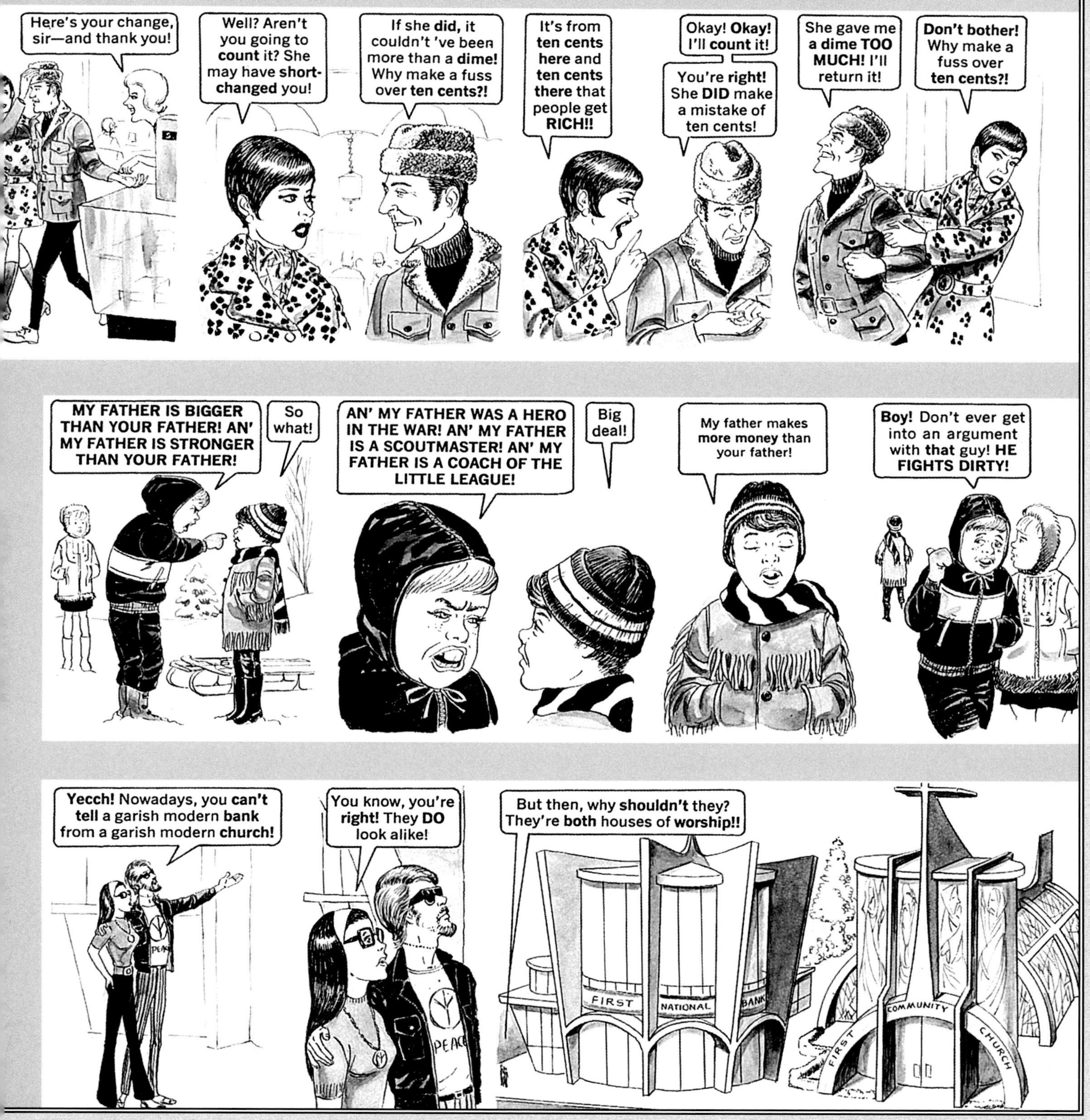
Here's your change, sir—and thank you!
Well? Aren't you going to count it? She may have short-changed you!
If she did, it couldn't 've been more than a dime! Why make a fuss over ten cents?!
It's from ten cents here and ten cents there that people get RICH!!
Okay! Okay! I'll count it!
You're right! She DID make a mistake of ten cents!
She gave me a dime TOO MUCH! I'll return it!
Don't bother! Why make a fuss over ten cents?!
MY FATHER IS BIGGER THAN YOUR FATHER! AN' MY FATHER IS STRONGER THAN YOUR FATHER!
So what!
AN' MY FATHER WAS A HERO IN THE WAR! AN' MY FATHER IS A SCOUTMASTER! AN' MY FATHER IS A COACH OF THE LITTLE LEAGUE!
Big deal!
My father makes more money than your father!
Boy! Don't ever get into an argument with that guy! HE FIGHTS DIRTY!
Yecch! Nowadays, you can't tell a garish modern bank from a garish modern church!
You know, you're right! They DO look alike!
But then, why shouldn't they? They're both houses of worship!!
PEACE
PEACE
FIRST NATIONAL BANK
FIRST COMMUNITY CHURCH

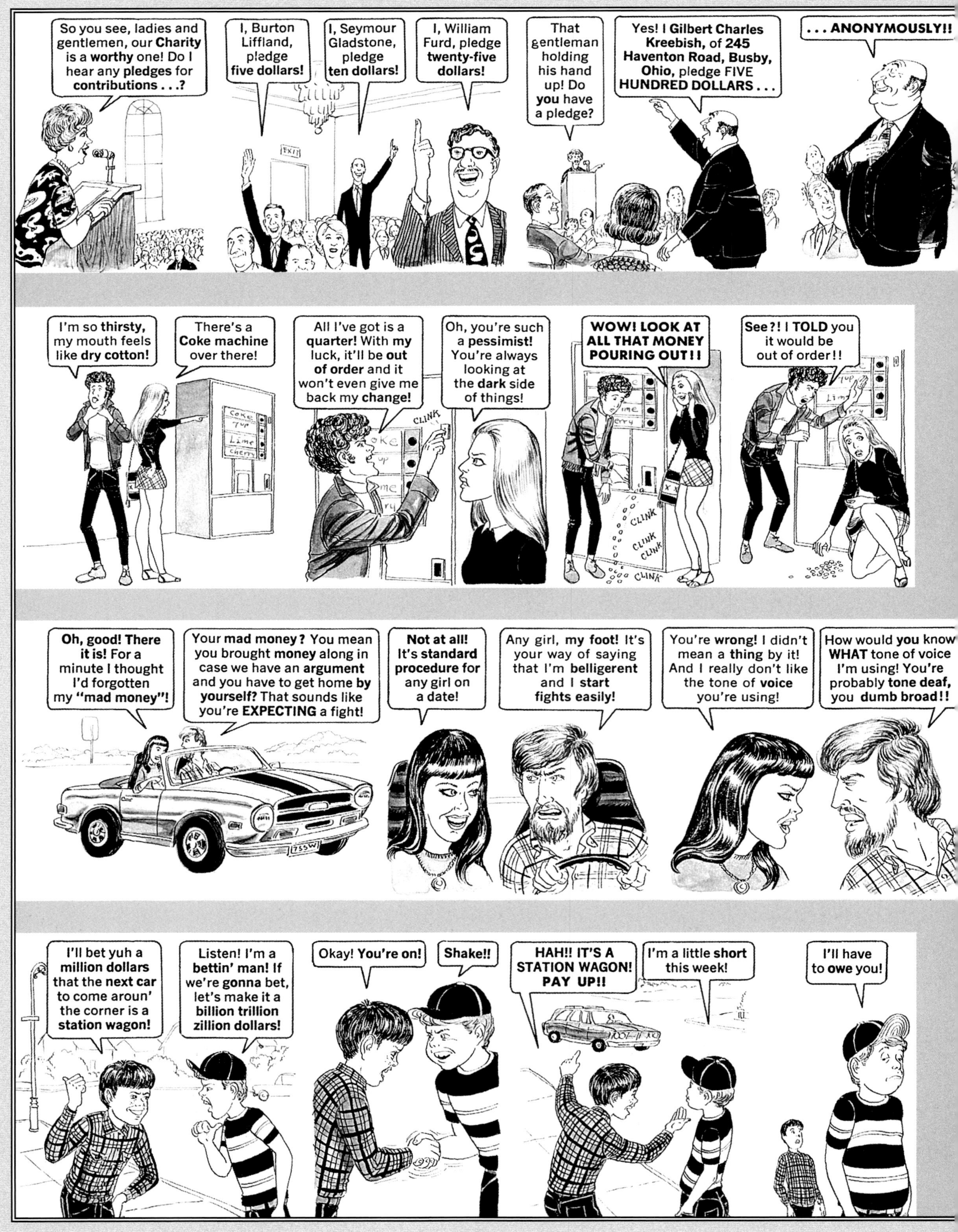
So you see, ladies and gentlemen, our Charity is a worthy one! Do I hear any pledges for contributions . . .?
I, Burton Liffland, pledge five dollars!
I, Seymour Gladstone, pledge ten dollars!
I, William Furd, pledge twenty-five dollars!
That gentleman holding his hand up! Do you have a pledge?
Yes! I Gilbert Charles Kreebish, of 245 Haventon Road, Busby, Ohio, pledge FIVE HUNDRED DOLLARS . . .
. . . ANONYMOUSLY!!
I'm so thirsty, my mouth feels like dry cotton!
There's a Coke machine over there!
All I've got is a quarter! With my luck, it'll be out of order and it won't even give me back my change!
CLINK
Oh, you're such a pessimist! You're always looking at the dark side of things!
WOW! LOOK AT ALL THAT MONEY POURING OUT!!
CLINK
CLINK
CLINK
CLINK
See?! I TOLD you it would be out of order!!
Oh, good! There it is! For a minute I thought I'd forgotten my "mad money"!
Your mad money? You mean you brought money along in case we have an argument and you have to get home by yourself? That sounds like you're EXPECTING a fight!
Not at all! It's standard procedure for any girl on a date!
Any girl, my foot! It's your way of saying that I'm belligerent and I start fights easily!
You're wrong! I didn't mean a thing by it! And I really don't like the tone of voice you're using!
How would you know WHAT tone of voice I'm using! You're probably tone deaf, you dumb broad!!
I'll bet yuh a million dollars that the next car to come aroun' the corner is a station wagon!
Listen! I'm a bettin' man! If we're gonna bet, let's make it a billion trillion zillion dollars!
Okay! You're on!
Shake!!
HAH!! IT'S A STATION WAGON! PAY UP!!
I'm a little short this week!
I'll have to owe you!

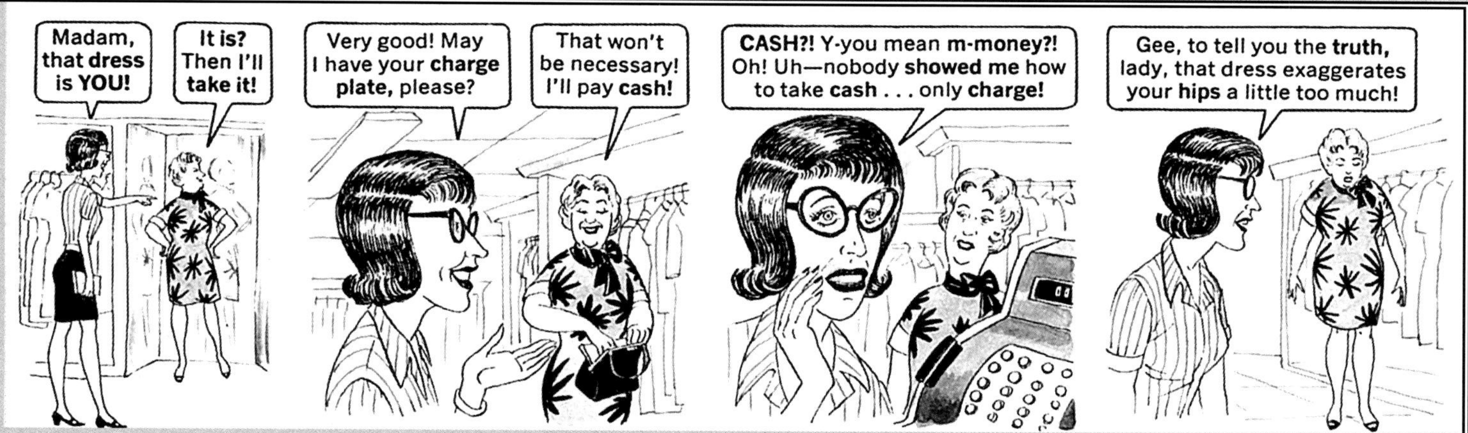
Madam, that dress is YOU!
It is? Then I'll take it!
Very good! May I have your charge plate, please?
That won't be necessary! I'll pay cash!
CASH?! Y-you mean m-money?! Oh! Uh—nobody showed me how to take cash . . . only charge!
Gee, to tell you the truth, lady, that dress exaggerates your hips a little too much!

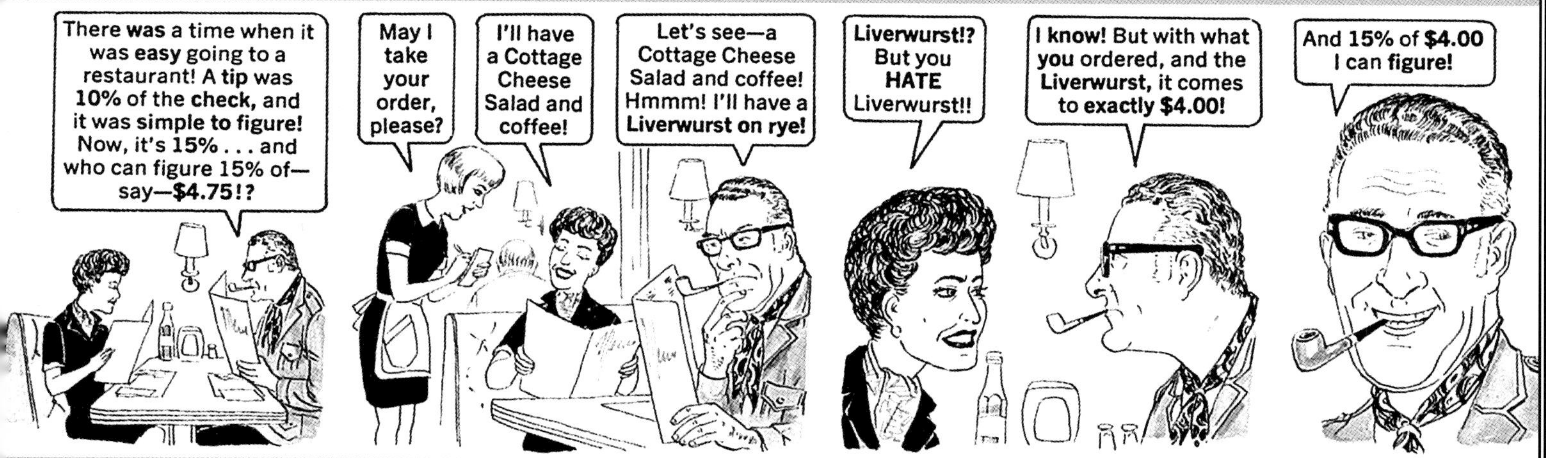
There was a time when it was easy going to a restaurant! A tip was 10% of the check, and it was simple to figure! Now, it's 15% . . . and who can figure 15% of—say—$4.75!?
May I take your order, please?
I'll have a Cottage Cheese Salad and coffee!
Let's see—a Cottage Cheese Salad and coffee! Hmmm! I'll have a Liverwurst on rye!
Liverwurst!? But you HATE Liverwurst!!
I know! But with what you ordered, and the Liverwurst, it comes to exactly $4.00!
And 15% of $4.00 I can figure!

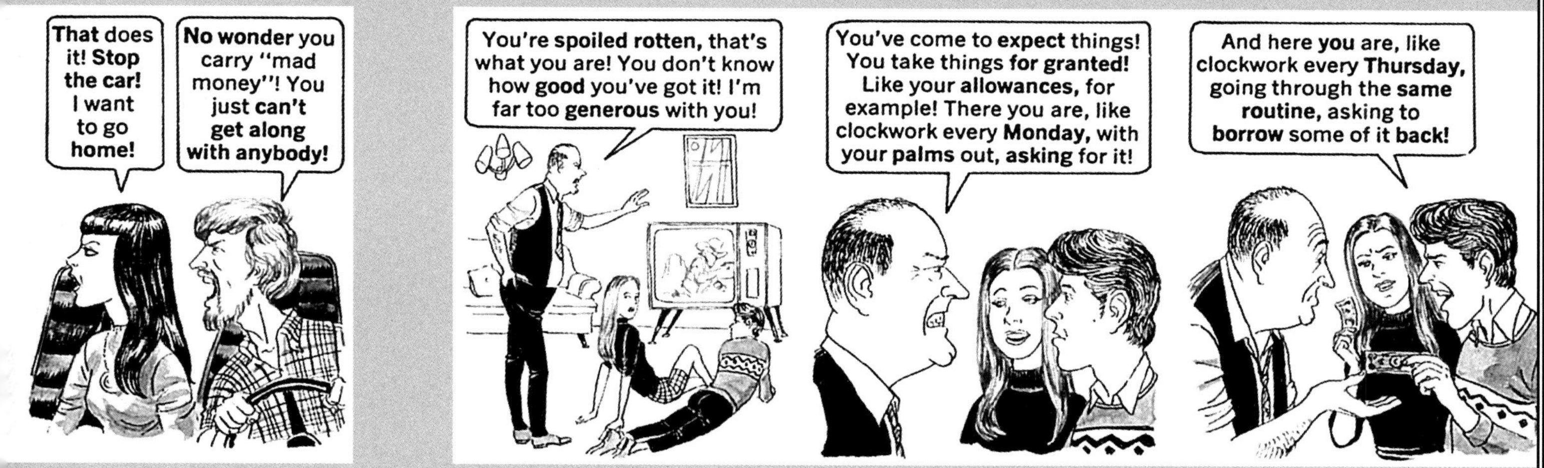
That does it! Stop the car! I want to go home!
No wonder you carry "mad money"! You just can't get along with anybody!
You're spoiled rotten, that's what you are! You don't know how good you've got it! I'm far too generous with you!
You've come to expect things! You take things for granted! Like your allowances, for example! There you are, like clockwork every Monday, with your palms out, asking for it!
And here you are, like clockwork every Thursday, going through the same routine, asking to borrow some of it back!

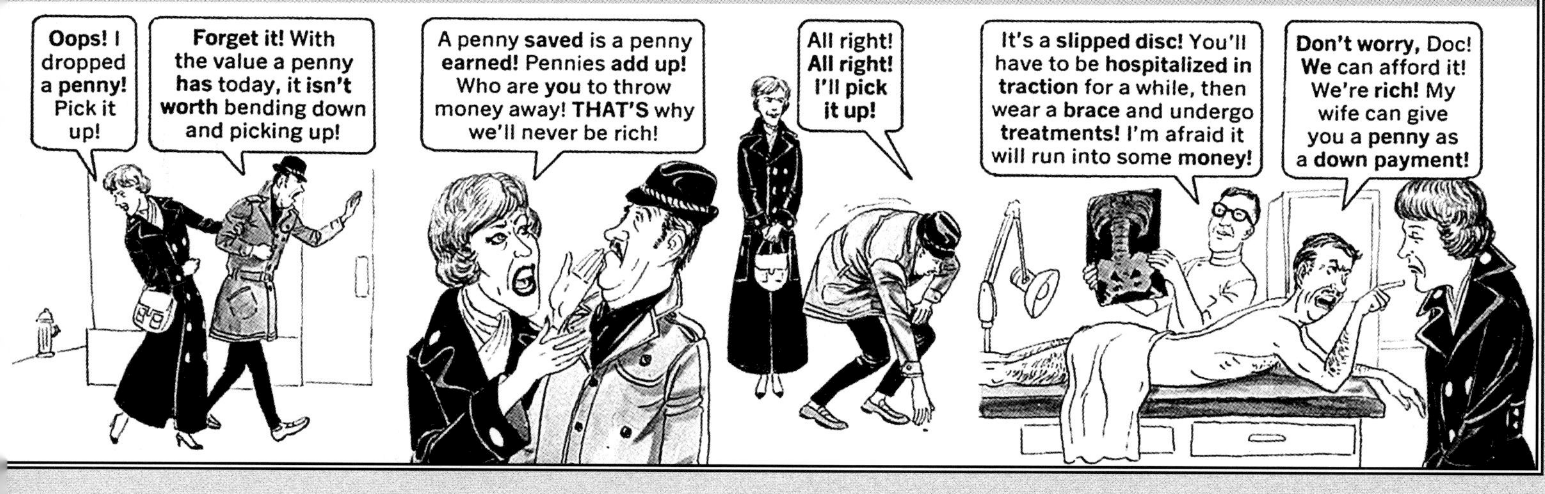
Oops! I dropped a penny! Pick it up!
Forget it! With the value a penny has today, it isn't worth bending down and picking up!
A penny saved is a penny earned! Pennies add up! Who are you to throw money away! THAT'S why we'll never be rich!
All right! All right! I'll pick it up!
It's a slipped disc! You'll have to be hospitalized in traction for a while, then wear a brace and undergo treatments! I'm afraid it will run into some money!
Don't worry, Doc! We can afford it! We're rich! My wife can give you a penny as a down payment!

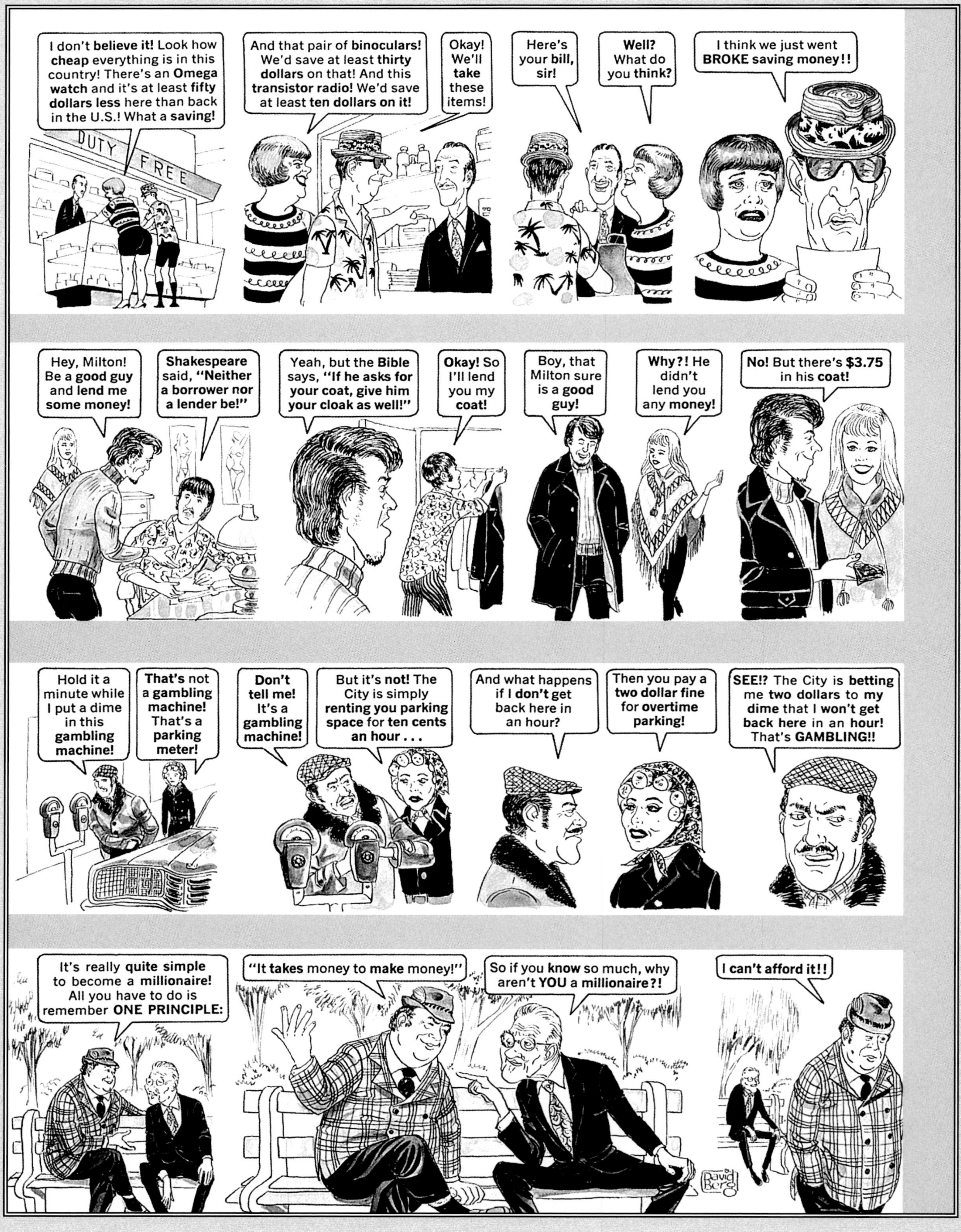
I don't believe it! Look how cheap everything is in this country! There's an Omega watch and it's at least fifty dollars less here than back in the U.S.! What a saving!
DUTY FREE
And that pair of binoculars! We'd save at least thirty dollars on that! And this transistor radio! We'd save at least ten dollars on it!
Okay! We'll take these items!
Here's your bill, sir!
Well? What do you think?
I think we just went BROKE saving money!!
Hey, Milton! Be a good guy and lend me some money!
Shakespeare said, "Neither a borrower nor a lender be!"
Yeah, but the Bible says, "If he asks for your coat, give him your cloak as well!"
Okay! So I'll lend you my coat!
Boy, that Milton sure is a good guy!
Why?! He didn't lend you any money!
No! But there's $3.75 in his coat!
Hold it a minute while I put a dime in this gambling machine!
That's not a gambling machine! That's a parking meter!
Don't tell me! It's a gambling machine!
But it's not! The City is simply renting you parking space for ten cents an hour . . .
And what happens if I don't get back here in an hour?
Then you pay a two dollar fine for overtime parking!
SEE!? The City is betting me two dollars to my dime that I won't get back here in an hour! That's GAMBLING!!
It's really quite simple to become a millionaire! All you have to do is remember ONE PRINCIPLE:
"It takes money to make money!"
So if you know so much, why aren't YOU a millionaire?!
I can't afford it!!
David Berg

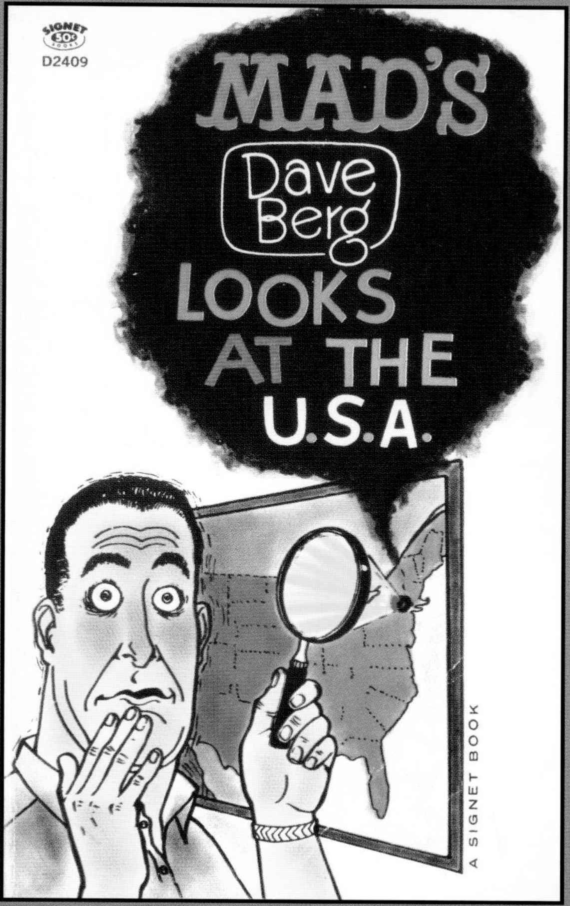
SIGNET 50¢
D2409
MAD'S
Dave Berg
LOOKS
AT THE
U.S.A.
A SIGNET BOOK

1964

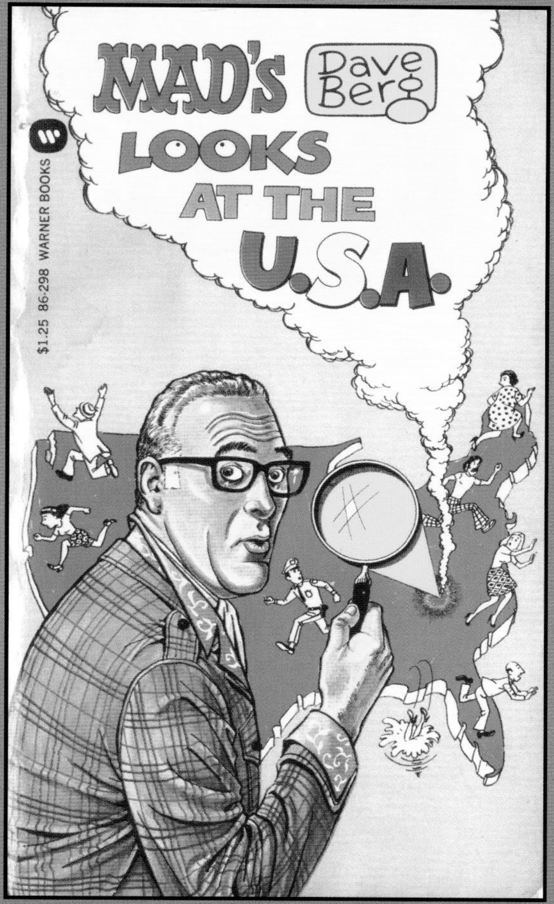
MAD's
Dave Berg
LOOKS
AT THE
U.S.A.
$1.25 86-298 WARNER BOOKS

reprint cover 1977

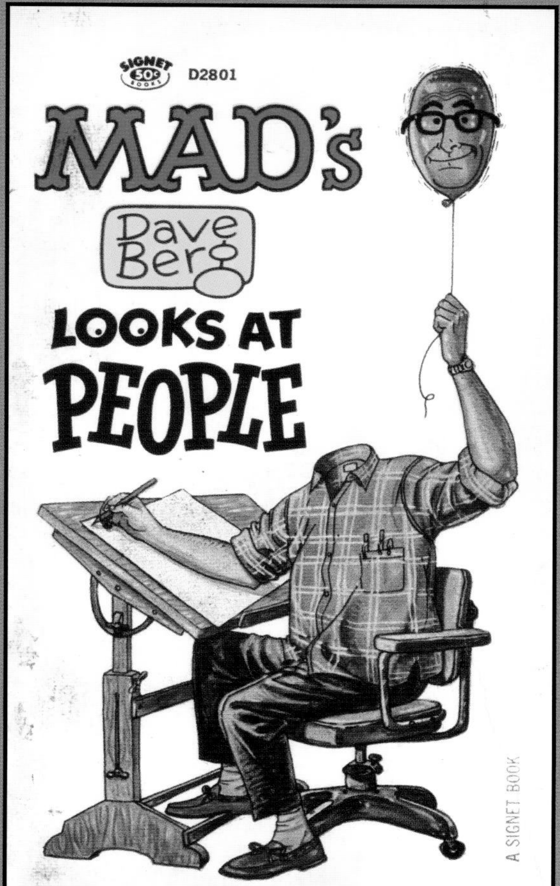
SIGNET 50¢
D2801
MAD's
Dave Berg
LOOKS AT
PEOPLE
A SIGNET BOOK

1966

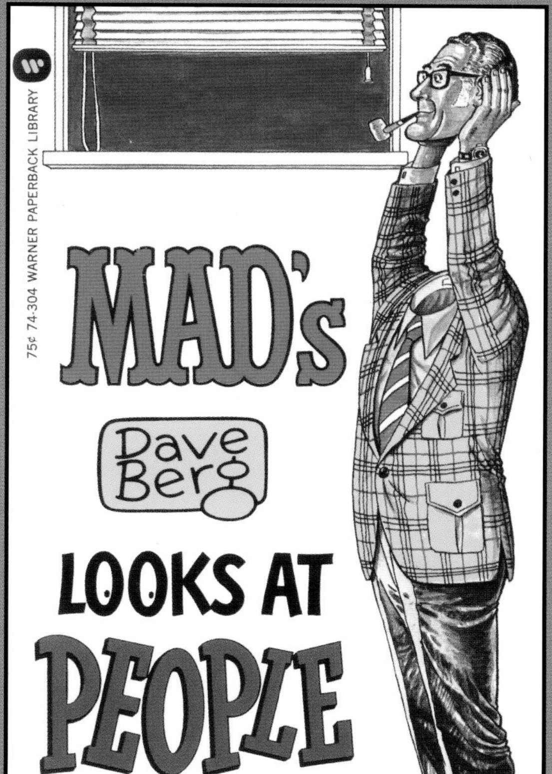
75¢ 74-304 WARNER PAPERBACK LIBRARY
MAD's
Dave Berg
LOOKS AT
PEOPLE

reprint cover 1973

BERG'S-EYE VIEW DEPT.

THE LIGHTER SIDE

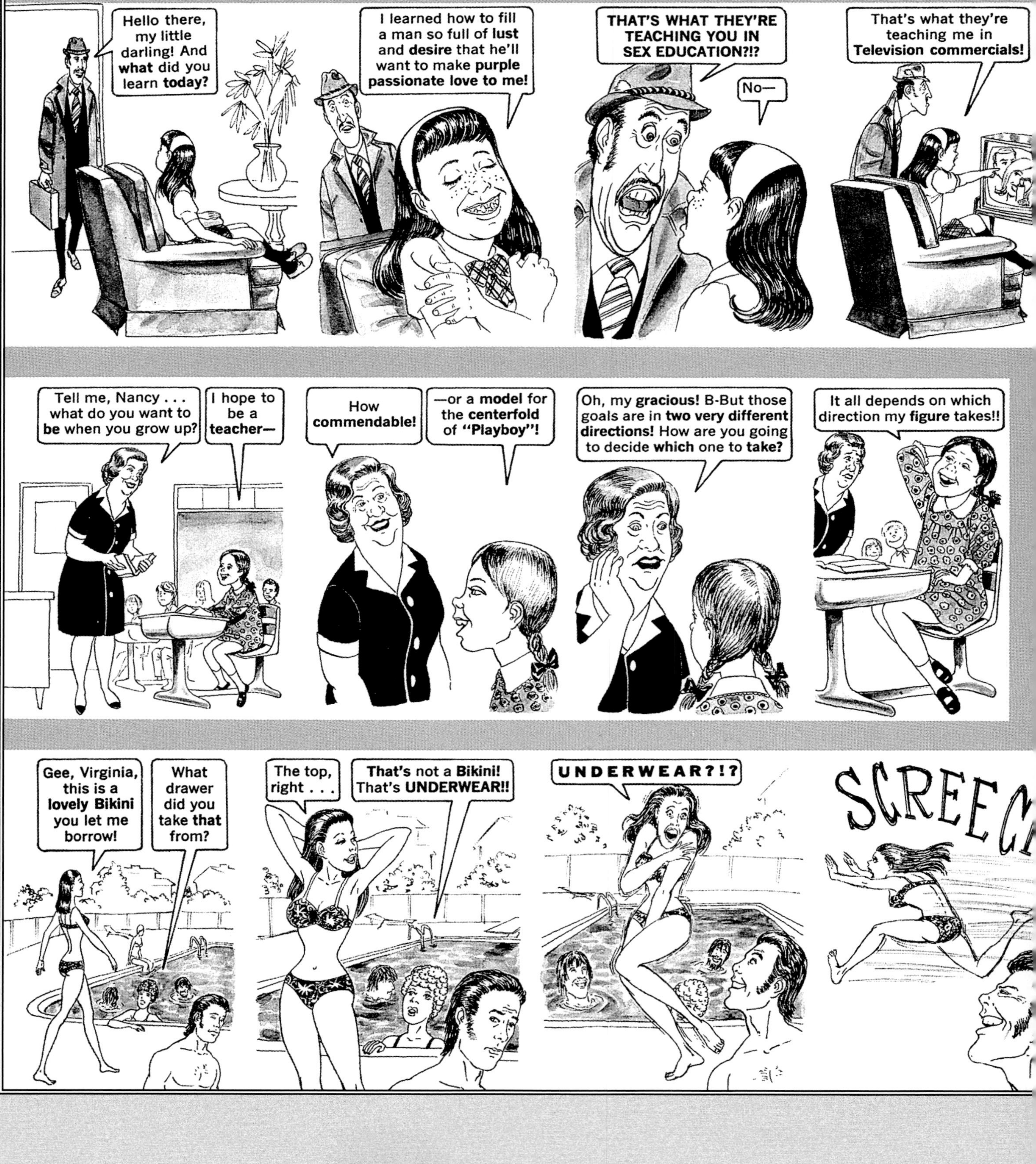
Hello there, my little darling! And what did you learn today?
I learned how to fill a man so full of lust and desire that he'll want to make purple passionate love to me!
THAT'S WHAT THEY'RE TEACHING YOU IN SEX EDUCATION?!?
No—
That's what they're teaching me in Television commercials!
Tell me, Nancy . . . what do you want to be when you grow up?
I hope to be a teacher—
How commendable!
—or a model for the centerfold of "Playboy"!
Oh, my gracious! B-But those goals are in two very different directions! How are you going to decide which one to take?
It all depends on which direction my figure takes!!
Gee, Virginia, this is a lovely Bikini you let me borrow!
What drawer did you take that from?
The top, right . . .
That's not a Bikini! That's UNDERWEAR!!
UNDERWEAR?!?
SCREEC

OF... SEX

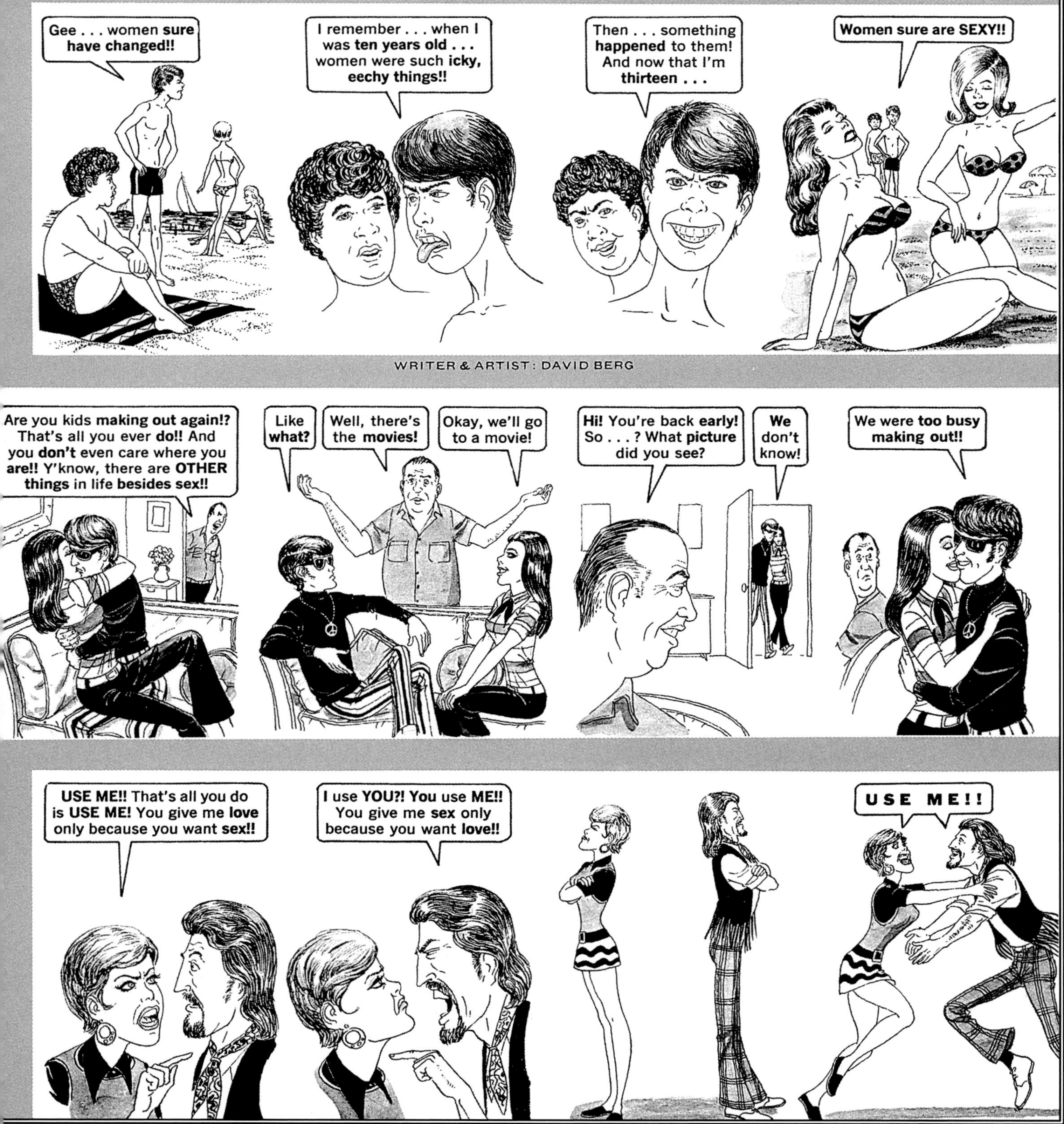

Gee . . . women sure have changed!!
I remember . . . when I was ten years old . . . women were such icky, eechy things!!
Then . . . something happened to them! And now that I'm thirteen . . .
Women sure are SEXY!!
Are you kids making out again!? That's all you ever do!! And you don't even care where you are!! Y'know, there are OTHER things in life besides sex!!
Like what?
Well, there's the movies!
Okay, we'll go to a movie!
Hi! You're back early! So . . . ? What picture did you see?
We don't know!
We were too busy making out!!
USE ME!! That's all you do is USE ME! You give me love only because you want sex!!
I use YOU?! You use ME!! You give me sex only because you want love!!
USE ME!!

WRITER & ARTIST: DAVID BERG

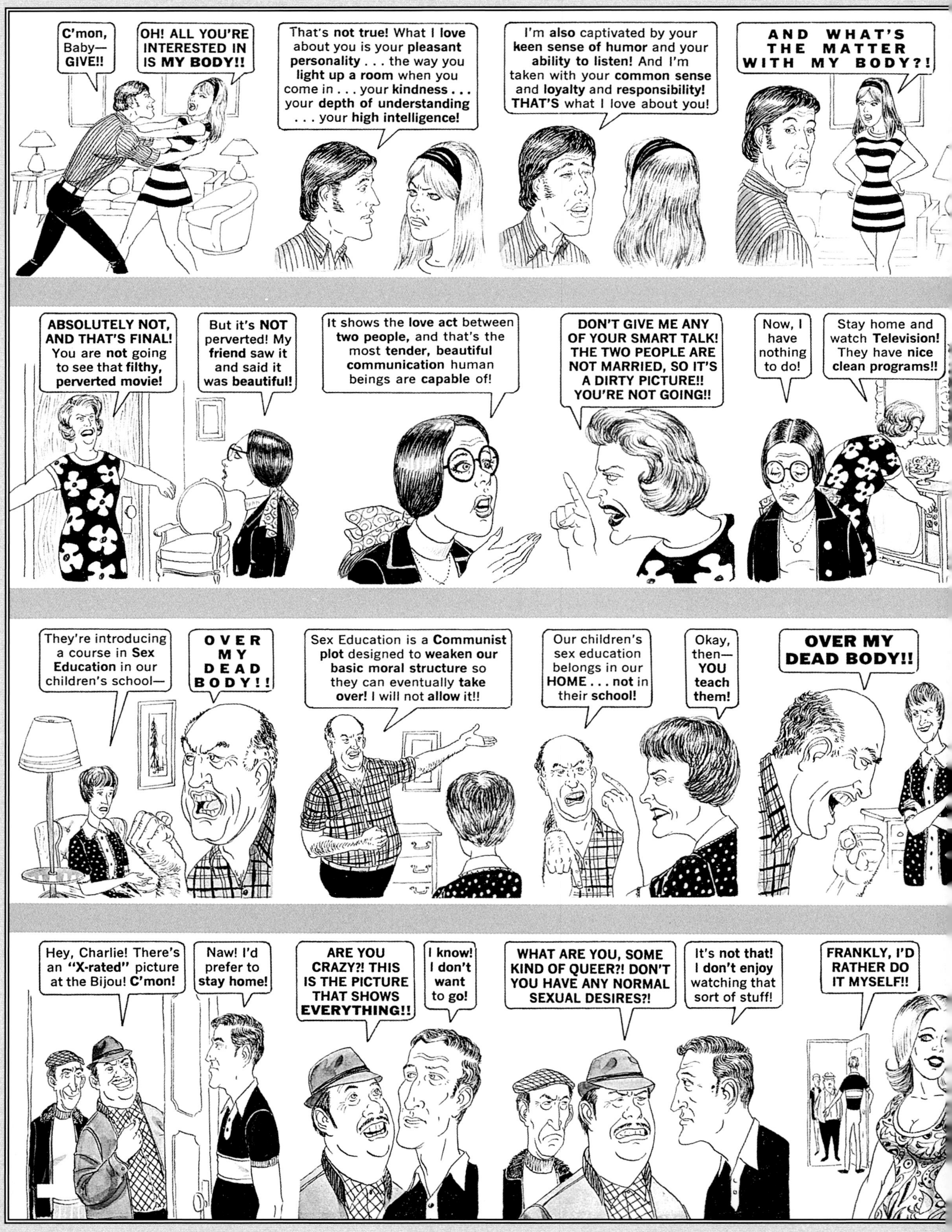
C'mon, Baby— GIVE!!
OH! ALL YOU'RE INTERESTED IN IS MY BODY!!
That's not true! What I love about you is your pleasant personality . . . the way you light up a room when you come in . . . your kindness . . . your depth of understanding . . . your high intelligence!
I'm also captivated by your keen sense of humor and your ability to listen! And I'm taken with your common sense and loyalty and responsibility! THAT'S what I love about you!
AND WHAT'S THE MATTER WITH MY BODY?!
ABSOLUTELY NOT, AND THAT'S FINAL! You are not going to see that filthy, perverted movie!
But it's NOT perverted! My friend saw it and said it was beautiful!
It shows the love act between two people, and that's the most tender, beautiful communication human beings are capable of!
DON'T GIVE ME ANY OF YOUR SMART TALK! THE TWO PEOPLE ARE NOT MARRIED, SO IT'S A DIRTY PICTURE!! YOU'RE NOT GOING!!
Now, I have nothing to do!
Stay home and watch Television! They have nice clean programs!!
They're introducing a course in Sex Education in our children's school—
OVER MY DEAD BODY!!
Sex Education is a Communist plot designed to weaken our basic moral structure so they can eventually take over! I will not allow it!!
Our children's sex education belongs in our HOME . . . not in their school!
Okay, then— YOU teach them!
OVER MY DEAD BODY!!
Hey, Charlie! There's an "X-rated" picture at the Bijou! C'mon!
Naw! I'd prefer to stay home!
ARE YOU CRAZY?! THIS IS THE PICTURE THAT SHOWS EVERYTHING!!
I know! I don't want to go!
WHAT ARE YOU, SOME KIND OF QUEER?! DON'T YOU HAVE ANY NORMAL SEXUAL DESIRES?!
It's not that! I don't enjoy watching that sort of stuff!
FRANKLY, I'D RATHER DO IT MYSELF!!

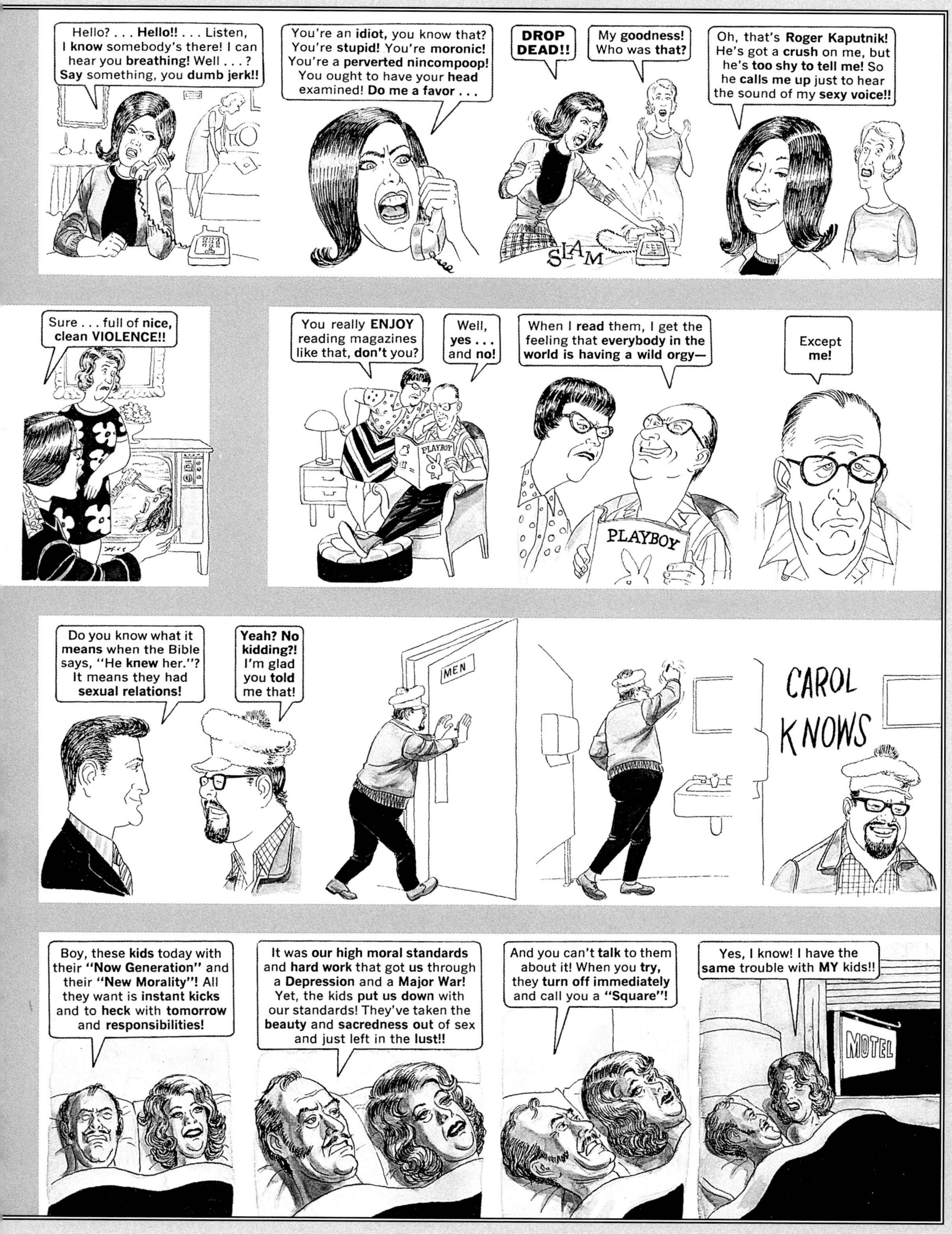
Hello? . . . Hello!! . . . Listen, I know somebody's there! I can hear you breathing! Well . . . ? Say something, you dumb jerk!!
You're an idiot, you know that? You're stupid! You're moronic! You're a perverted nincompoop! You ought to have your head examined! Do me a favor . . .
DROP DEAD!!
My goodness! Who was that?
SLAM
Oh, that's Roger Kaputnik! He's got a crush on me, but he's too shy to tell me! So he calls me up just to hear the sound of my sexy voice!!
Sure . . . full of nice, clean VIOLENCE!!
You really ENJOY reading magazines like that, don't you?
Well, yes . . . and no!
PLAYBOY
When I read them, I get the feeling that everybody in the world is having a wild orgy—
PLAYBOY
Except me!
Do you know what it means when the Bible says, "He knew her."? It means they had sexual relations!
Yeah? No kidding?! I'm glad you told me that!
MEN
CAROL KNOWS
Boy, these kids today with their "Now Generation" and their "New Morality"! All they want is instant kicks and to heck with tomorrow and responsibilities!
It was our high moral standards and hard work that got us through a Depression and a Major War! Yet, the kids put us down with our standards! They've taken the beauty and sacredness out of sex and just left in the lust!!
And you can't talk to them about it! When you try, they turn off immediately and call you a "Square"!
Yes, I know! I have the same trouble with MY kids!!
MOTEL

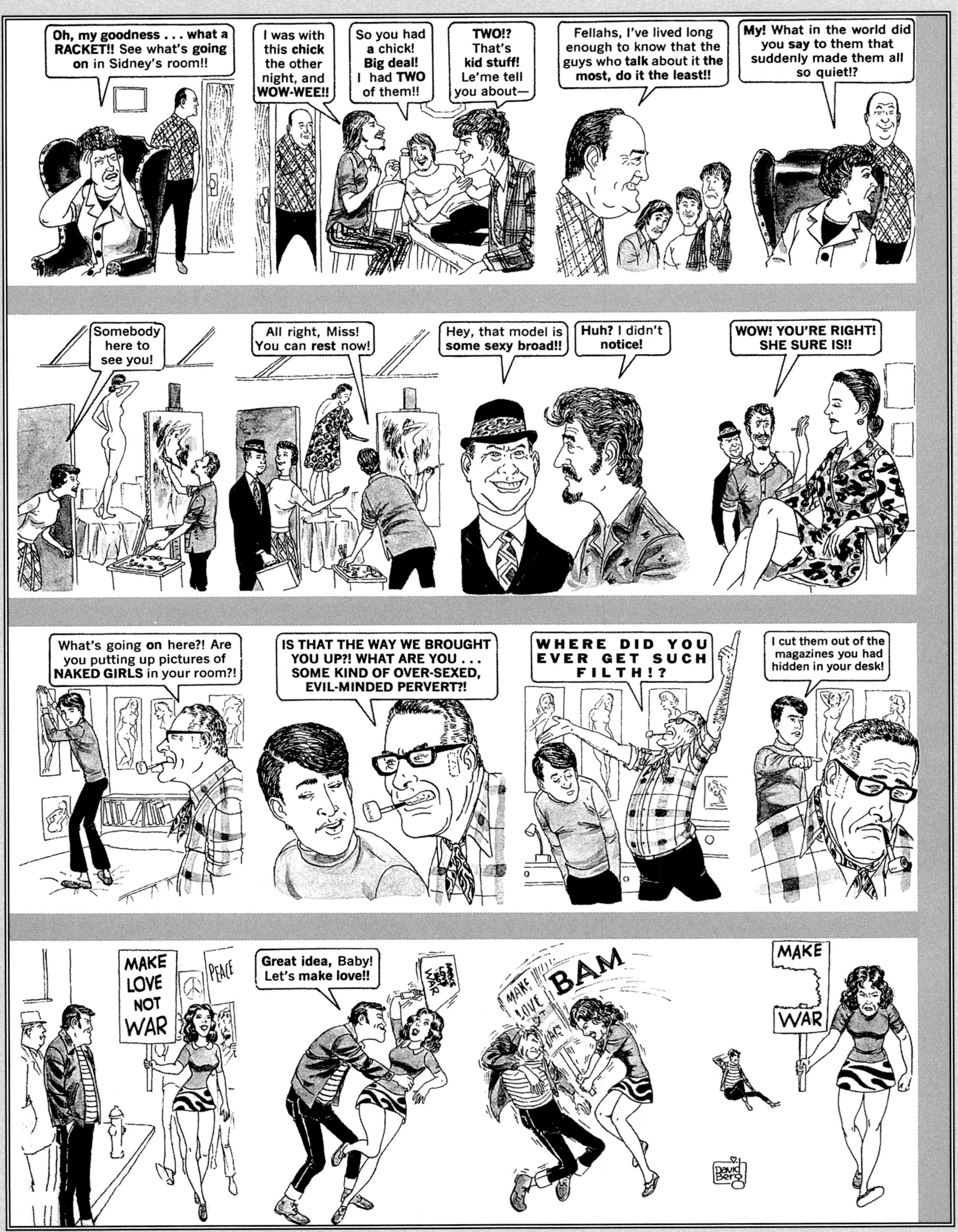
Oh, my goodness . . . what a RACKET!! See what's going on in Sidney's room!!
I was with this chick the other night, and WOW-WEE!!
So you had a chick! Big deal! I had TWO of them!!
TWO!? That's kid stuff! Le'me tell you about—
Fellahs, I've lived long enough to know that the guys who talk about it the most, do it the least!!
My! What in the world did you say to them that suddenly made them all so quiet!?
Somebody here to see you!
All right, Miss! You can rest now!
Hey, that model is some sexy broad!!
Huh? I didn't notice!
WOW! YOU'RE RIGHT! SHE SURE IS!!
What's going on here?! Are you putting up pictures of NAKED GIRLS in your room?!
IS THAT THE WAY WE BROUGHT YOU UP?! WHAT ARE YOU . . . SOME KIND OF OVER-SEXED, EVIL-MINDED PERVERT?!
WHERE DID YOU EVER GET SUCH FILTH!?
I cut them out of the magazines you had hidden in your desk!
MAKE LOVE NOT WAR
PEACE
Great idea, Baby! Let's make love!!
BAM
MAKE
WAR
David Berg

THE CALL OF THE MILD

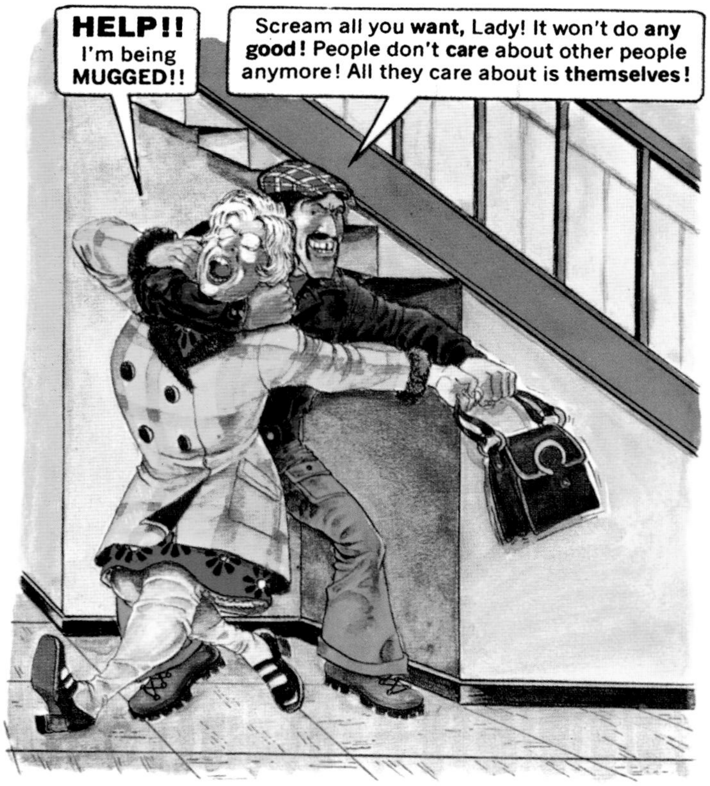

HELP!! I'm being MUGGED!!
Scream all you want, Lady! It won't do any good! People don't care about other people anymore! All they care about is themselves!

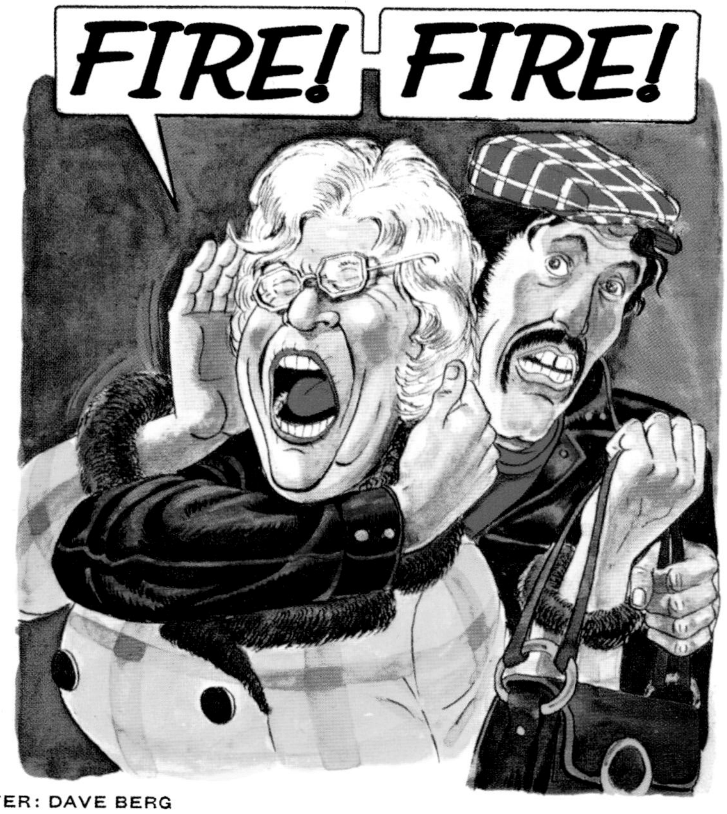

FIRE! FIRE!

ARTIST & WRITER: DAVE BERG

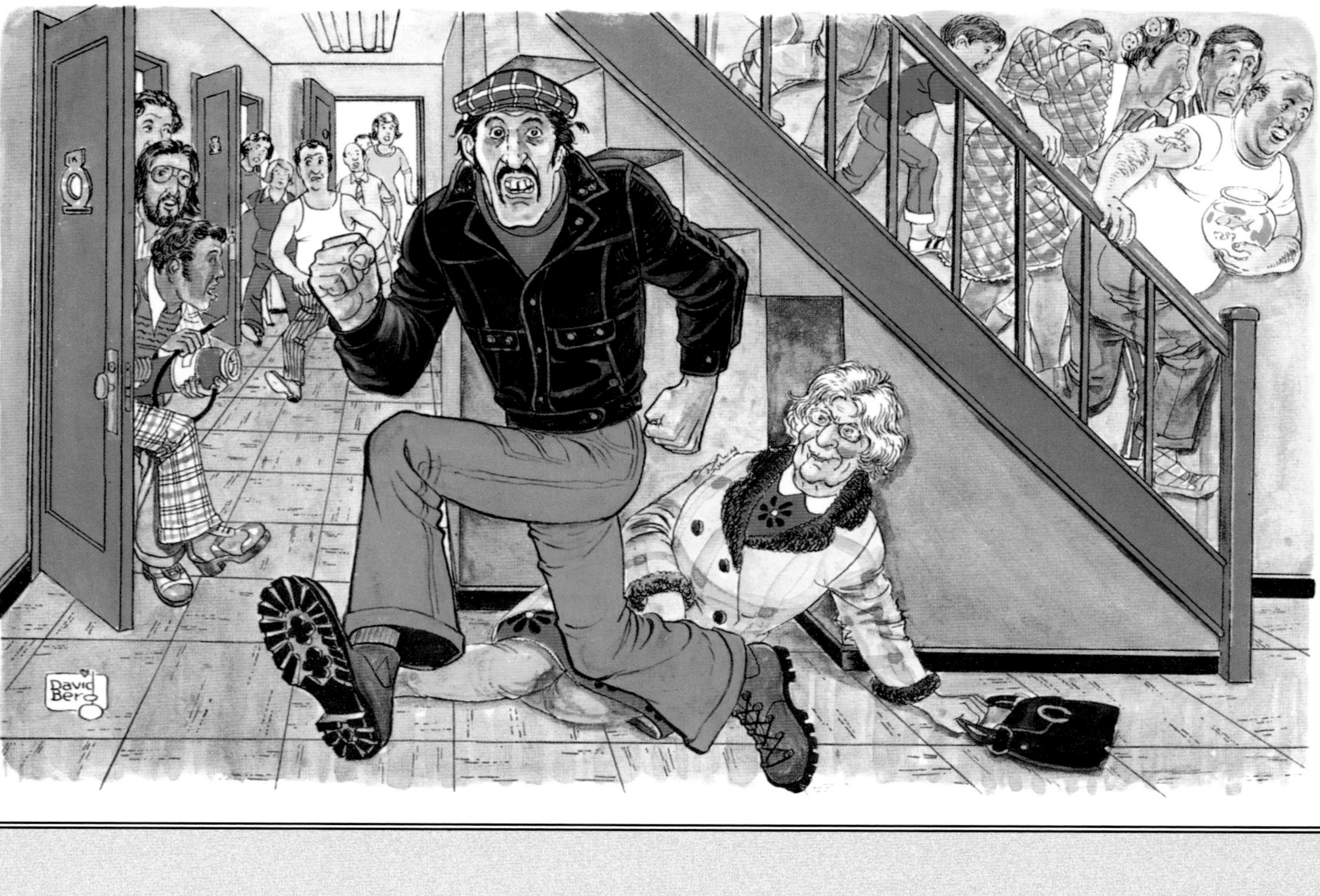

David Berg

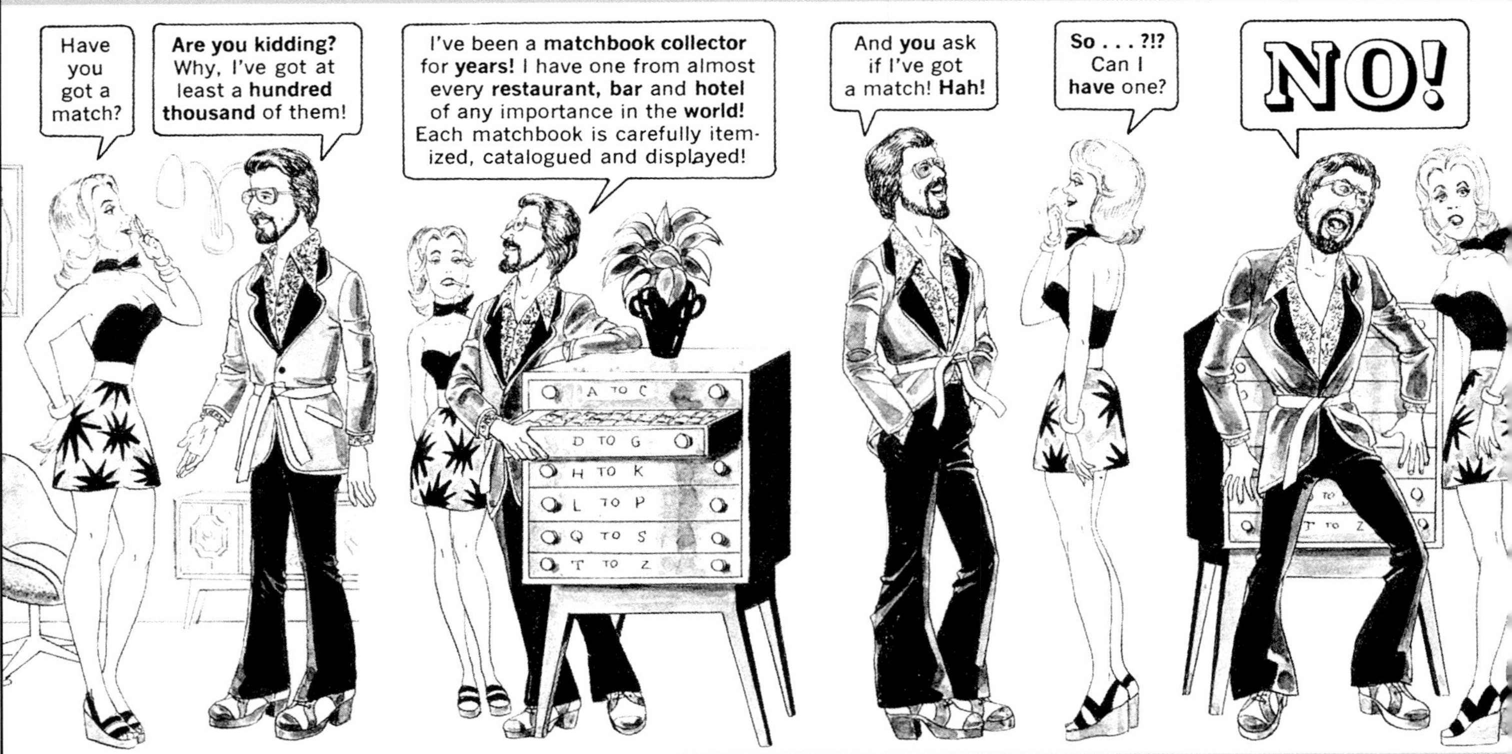
Have you got a match?
Are you kidding? Why, I've got at least a hundred thousand of them!
I've been a matchbook collector for years! I have one from almost every restaurant, bar and hotel of any importance in the world! Each matchbook is carefully itemized, catalogued and displayed!
A TO C
D TO G
H TO K
L TO P
Q TO S
T TO Z
And you ask if I've got a match! Hah!
So . . . ?!? Can I have one?
NO!

BERG'S-EYE VIEW DEPT.

THE LIGHTER SIDE OF... COL

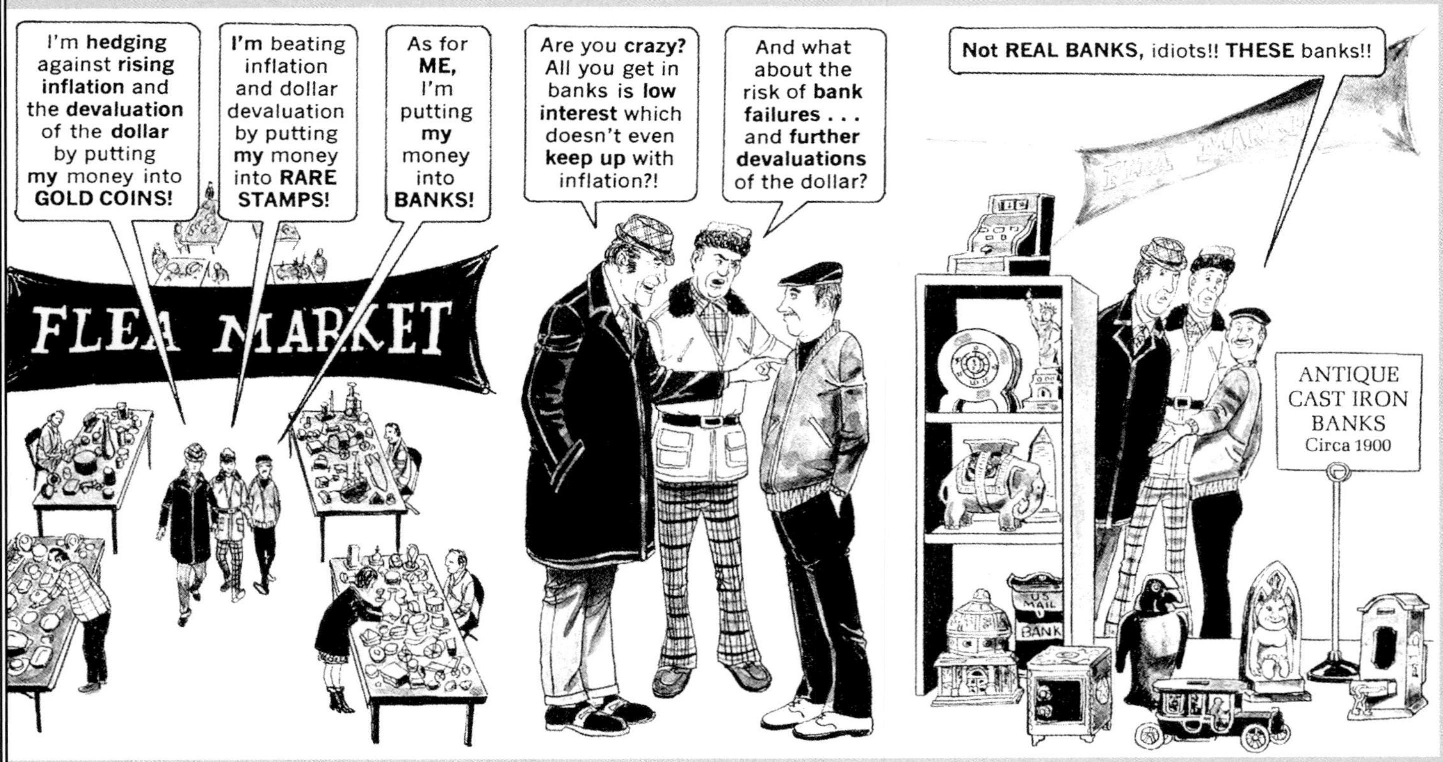
I'm hedging against rising inflation and the devaluation of the dollar by putting my money into GOLD COINS!
I'm beating inflation and dollar devaluation by putting my money into RARE STAMPS!
As for ME, I'm putting my money into BANKS!
FLEA MARKET
Are you crazy? All you get in banks is low interest which doesn't even keep up with inflation?!
And what about the risk of bank failures . . . and further devaluations of the dollar?
Not REAL BANKS, idiots!! THESE banks!!
ANTIQUE CAST IRON BANKS Circa 1900
BANK

Oh . . . I see you're collecting pennies! Tell me, what makes something into a "collectable"?
Anything that's rare . . . or that isn't made any more . . . or that there's a shortage of becomes a valuable collectable!
That's right! I hear that some banks are giving a DOLLAR TWENTY-FIVE for a dollar's worth of pennies! So there really must be a terrible shortage of them!
Yeah . . . I know . . .
. . . because I created the shortage!!

LECTING

ARTIST & WRITER: DAVE BERG

Why the heck don't you throw out all this junk?!
I'm AFRAID to!! With this current "nostalgia" craze, it's really hard to figure out what's JUNK . . . and what's VALUABLE!!
Today, people are paying good money for Big Little Books and Shirley Temple Dolls and Mickey Mouse Watches and Little Orphan Annie Shake-Up Mugs!!
SKIPPY
Now that you mention it, looking at this stuff DOES bring back a flood of nostalgic memories!
It's kinda NICE, isn't it?
Oh, yeah?!? Well, what's so NICE about memories of "THE GREAT DEPRESSION". . . and "WORLD WAR II"?!?

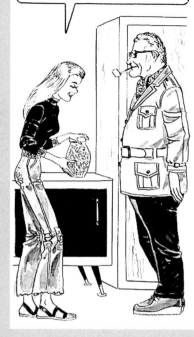

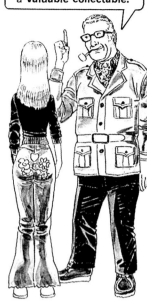

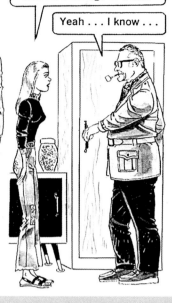

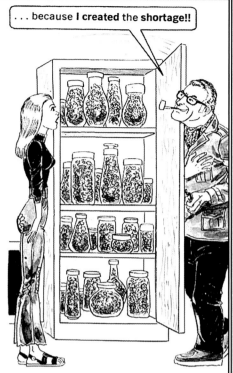

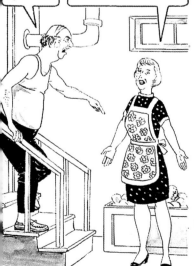

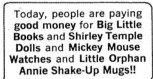

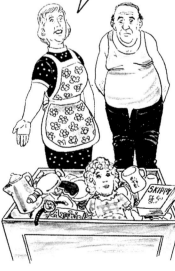

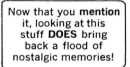

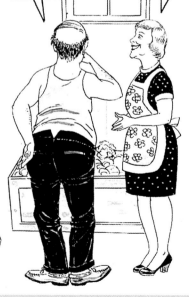

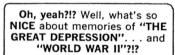

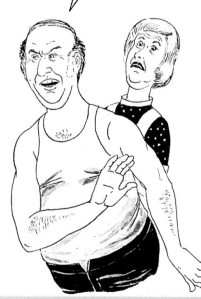

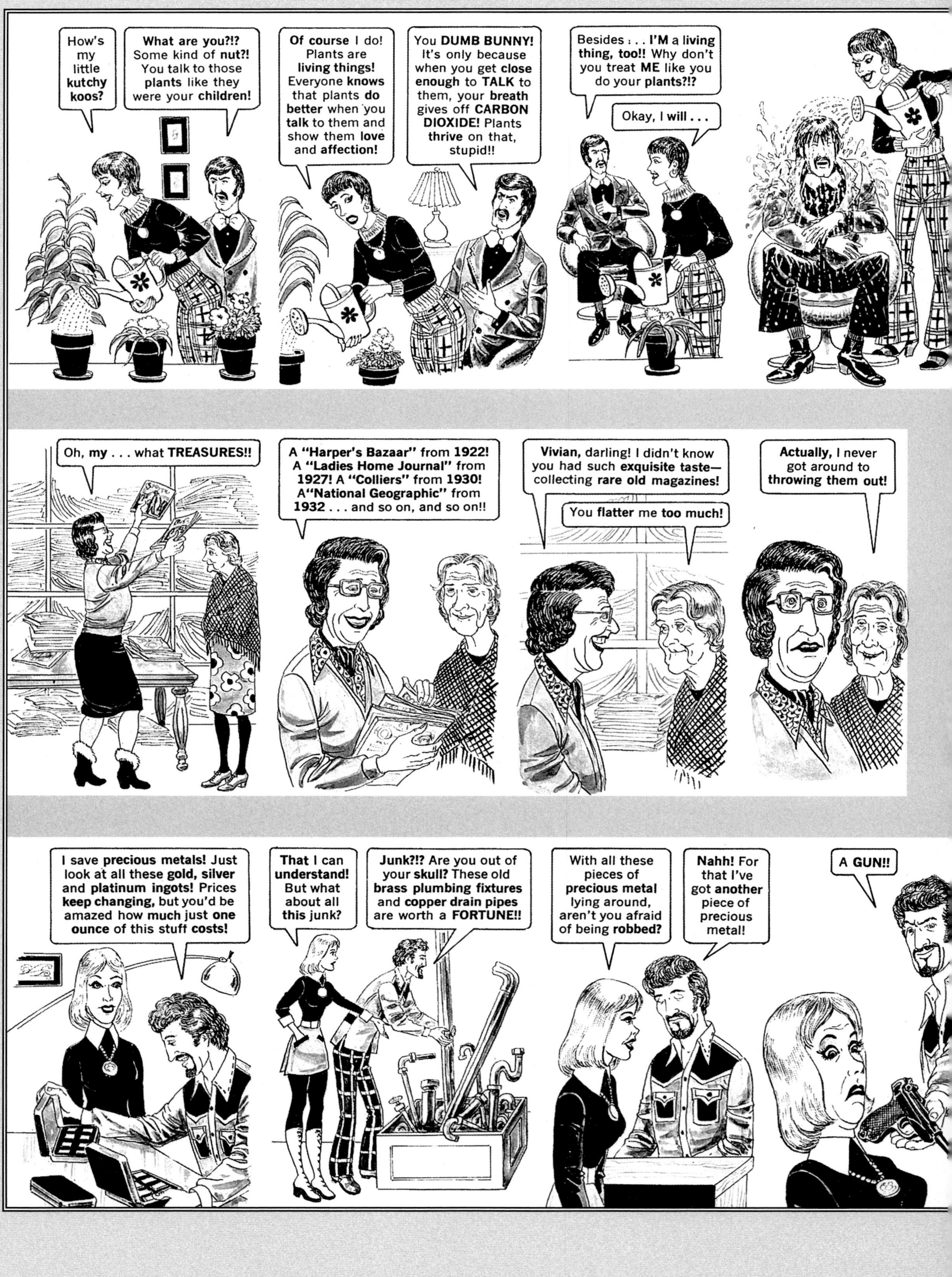
How's my little kutchy koos?
What are you?!? Some kind of nut?! You talk to those plants like they were your children!
Of course I do! Plants are living things! Everyone knows that plants do better when you talk to them and show them love and affection!
You DUMB BUNNY! It's only because when you get close enough to TALK to them, your breath gives off CARBON DIOXIDE! Plants thrive on that, stupid!!
Besides . . . I'M a living thing, too!! Why don't you treat ME like you do your plants?!?
Okay, I will . . .
Oh, my . . . what TREASURES!!
A "Harper's Bazaar" from 1922! A "Ladies Home Journal" from 1927! A "Colliers" from 1930! A "National Geographic" from 1932 . . . and so on, and so on!!
Vivian, darling! I didn't know you had such exquisite taste—collecting rare old magazines!
You flatter me too much!
Actually, I never got around to throwing them out!
I save precious metals! Just look at all these gold, silver and platinum ingots! Prices keep changing, but you'd be amazed how much just one ounce of this stuff costs!
That I can understand! But what about all this junk?
Junk?!? Are you out of your skull? These old brass plumbing fixtures and copper drain pipes are worth a FORTUNE!!
With all these pieces of precious metal lying around, aren't you afraid of being robbed?
Nahh! For that I've got another piece of precious metal!
A GUN!!

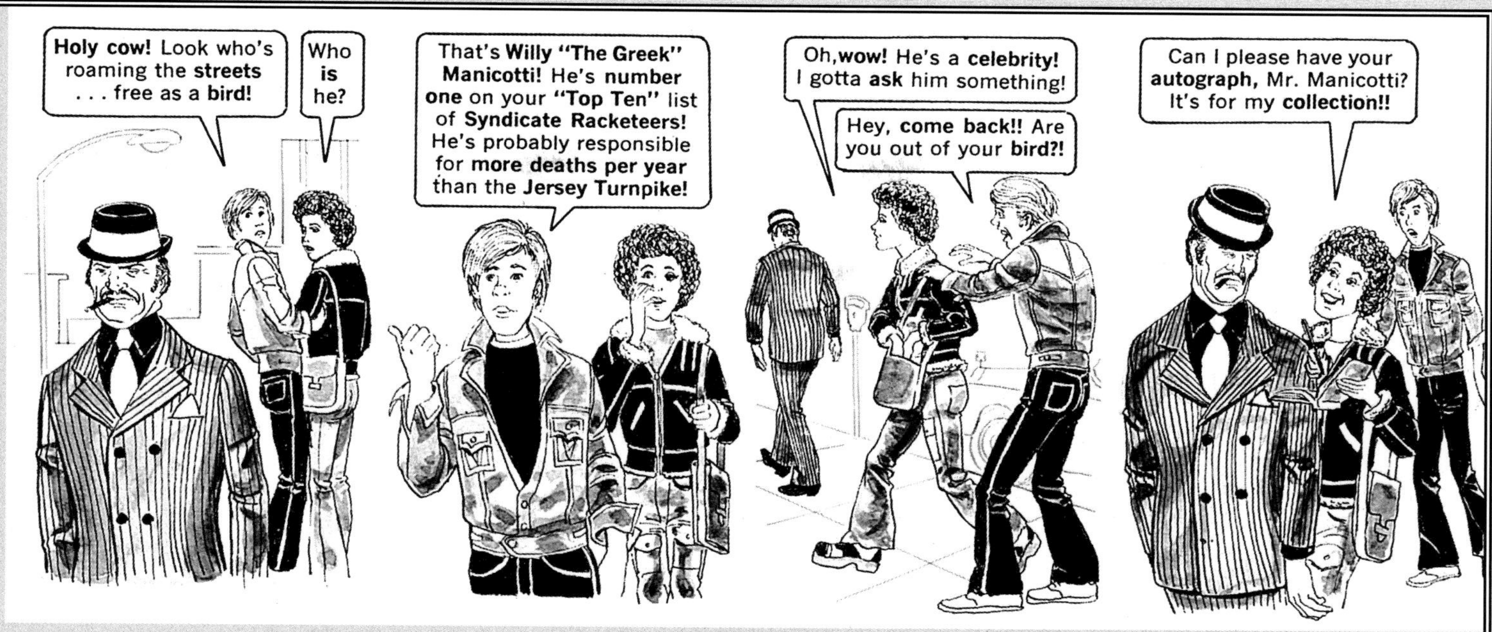
Holy cow! Look who's roaming the streets . . . free as a bird!
Who is he?
That's Willy "The Greek" Manicotti! He's number one on your "Top Ten" list of Syndicate Racketeers! He's probably responsible for more deaths per year than the Jersey Turnpike!
Oh, wow! He's a celebrity! I gotta ask him something!
Hey, come back!! Are you out of your bird?!
Can I please have your autograph, Mr. Manicotti? It's for my collection!!

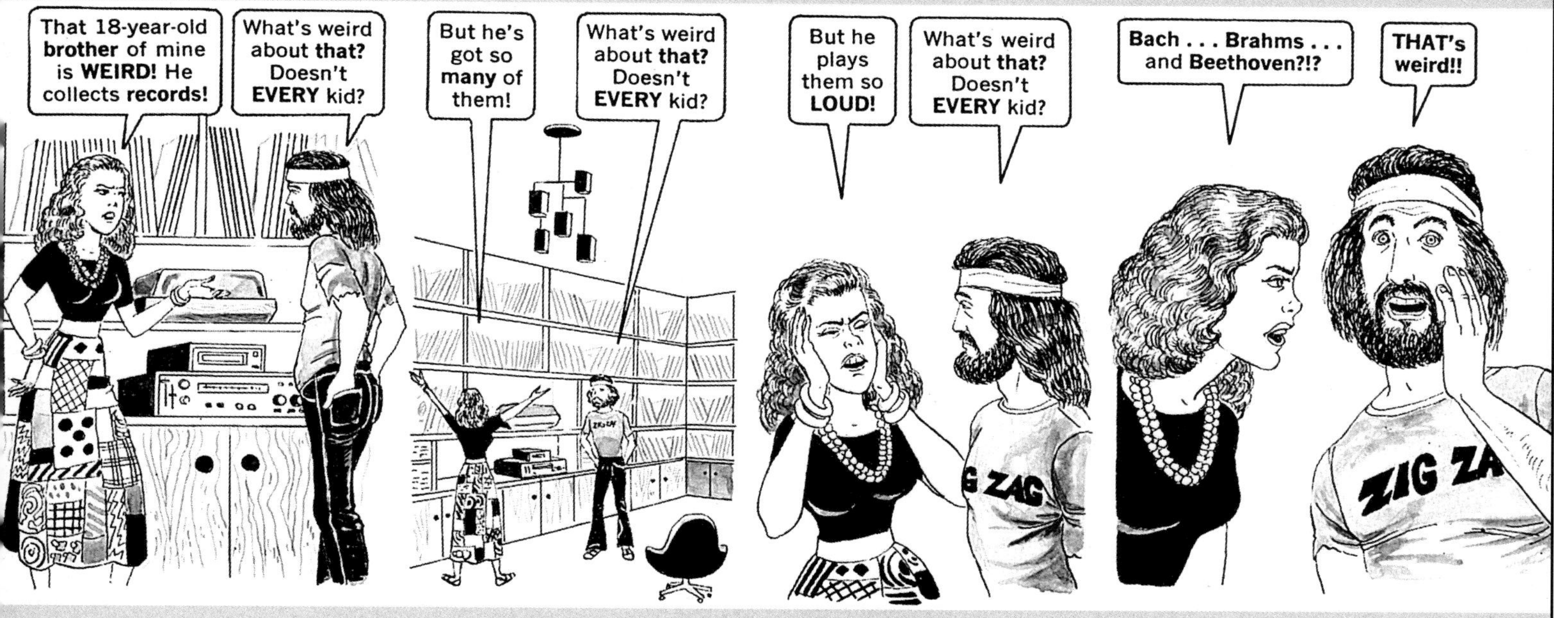
That 18-year-old brother of mine is WEIRD! He collects records!
What's weird about that? Doesn't EVERY kid?
But he's got so many of them!
What's weird about that? Doesn't EVERY kid?
But he plays them so LOUD!
What's weird about that? Doesn't EVERY kid?
Bach . . . Brahms . . . and Beethoven?!?
THAT's weird!!
ZIG ZAG

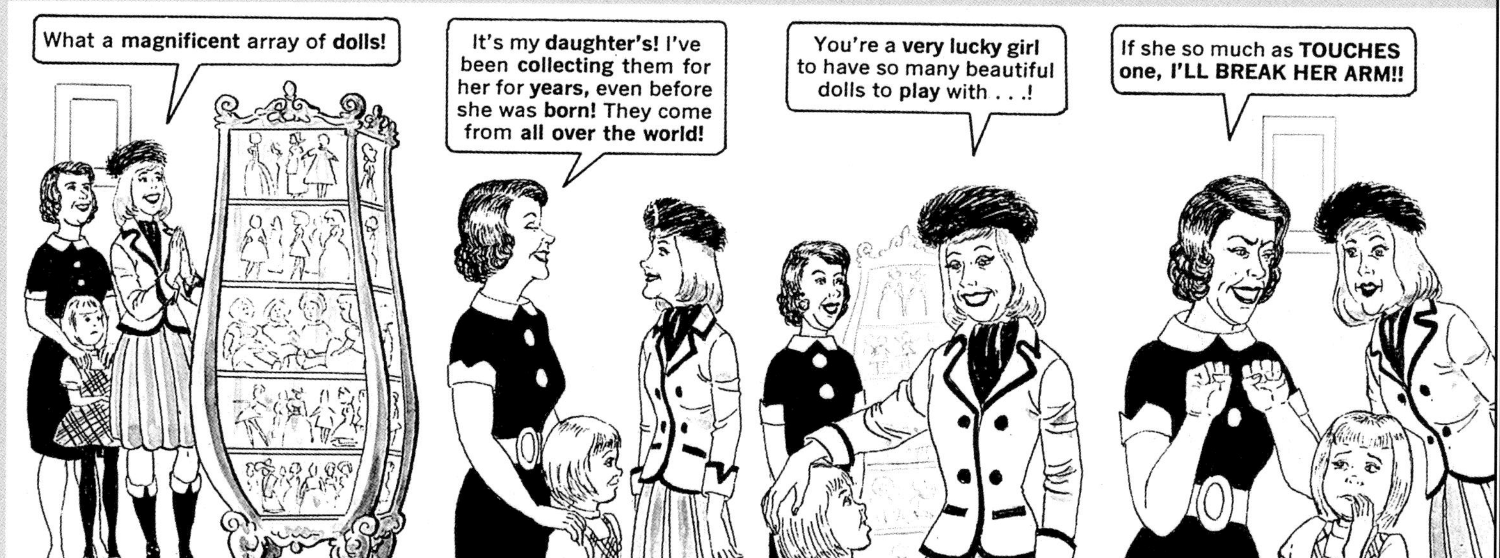
What a magnificent array of dolls!
It's my daughter's! I've been collecting them for her for years, even before she was born! They come from all over the world!
You're a very lucky girl to have so many beautiful dolls to play with . . .!
If she so much as TOUCHES one, I'LL BREAK HER ARM!!

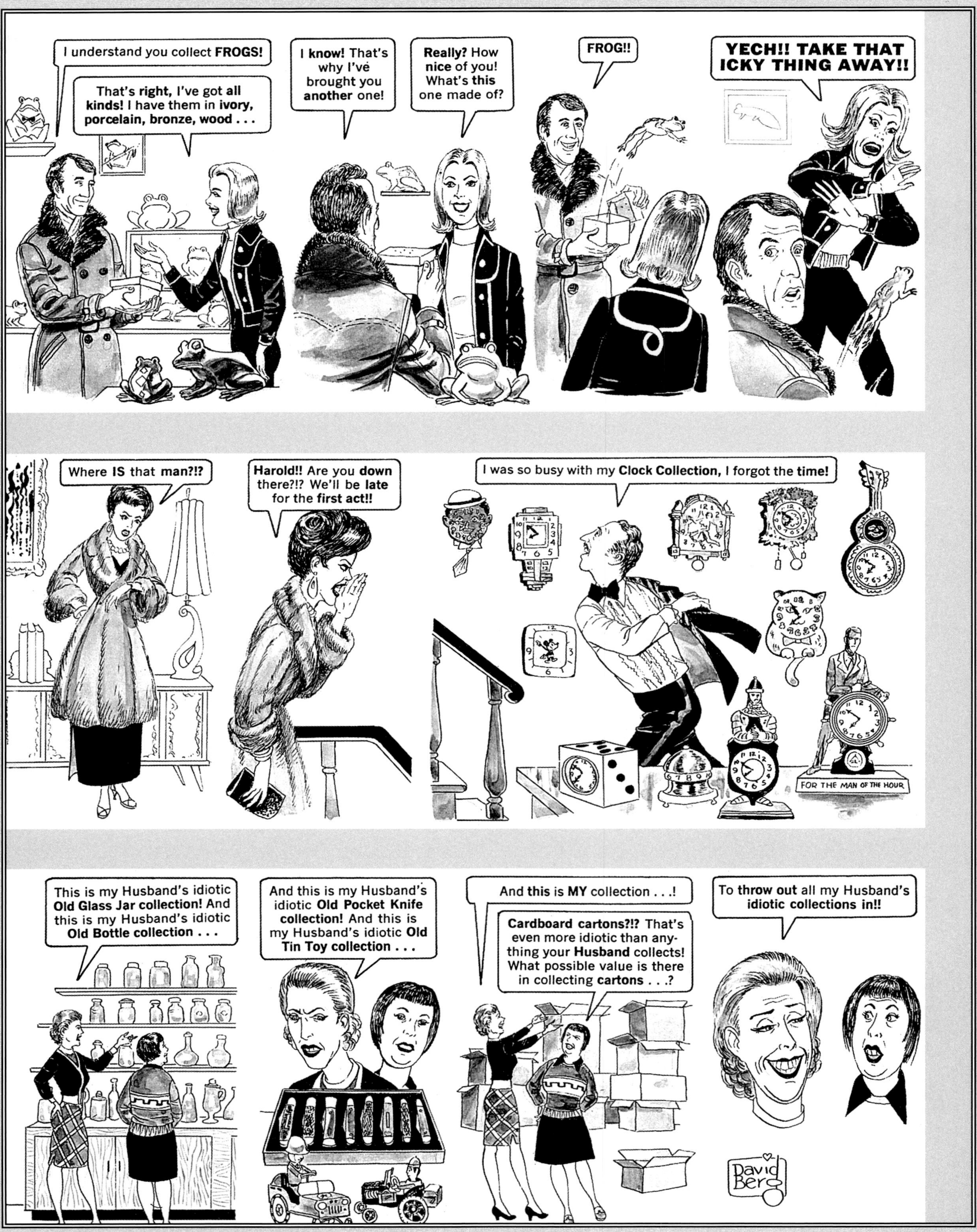
I understand you collect FROGS!
That's right, I've got all kinds! I have them in ivory, porcelain, bronze, wood . . .
I know! That's why I've brought you another one!
Really? How nice of you! What's this one made of?
FROG!!
YECH!! TAKE THAT ICKY THING AWAY!!
Where IS that man?!?
Harold!! Are you down there?!? We'll be late for the first act!!
I was so busy with my Clock Collection, I forgot the time!
FOR THE MAN OF THE HOUR
This is my Husband's idiotic Old Glass Jar collection! And this is my Husband's idiotic Old Bottle collection . . .
And this is my Husband's idiotic Old Pocket Knife collection! And this is my Husband's idiotic Old Tin Toy collection . . .
And this is MY collection . . .!
Cardboard cartons?!? That's even more idiotic than anything your Husband collects! What possible value is there in collecting cartons . . .?
To throw out all my Husband's idiotic collections in!!
David Berg

Paperback Book Covers II

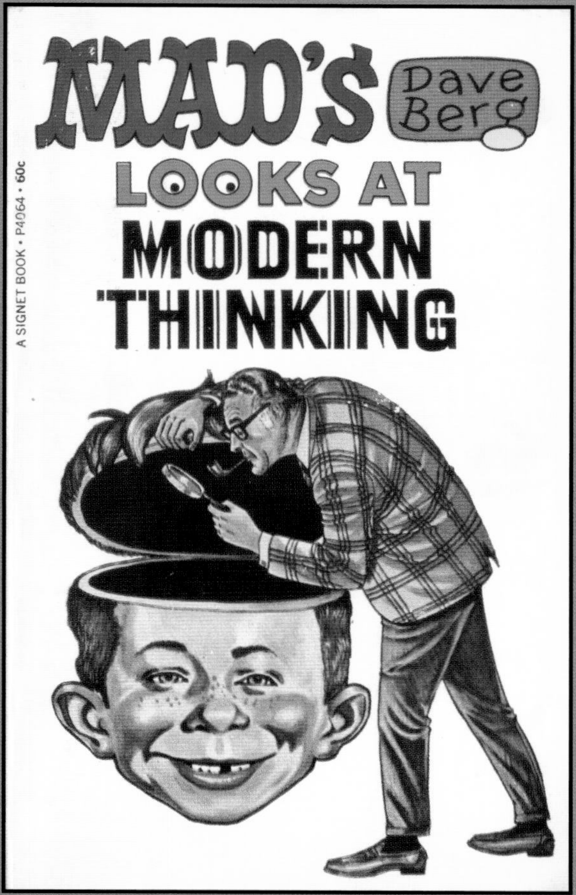

MAD's
Dave Berg
LOOKS AT
MODERN
THINKING
A SIGNET BOOK • P4064 • 60c

1969

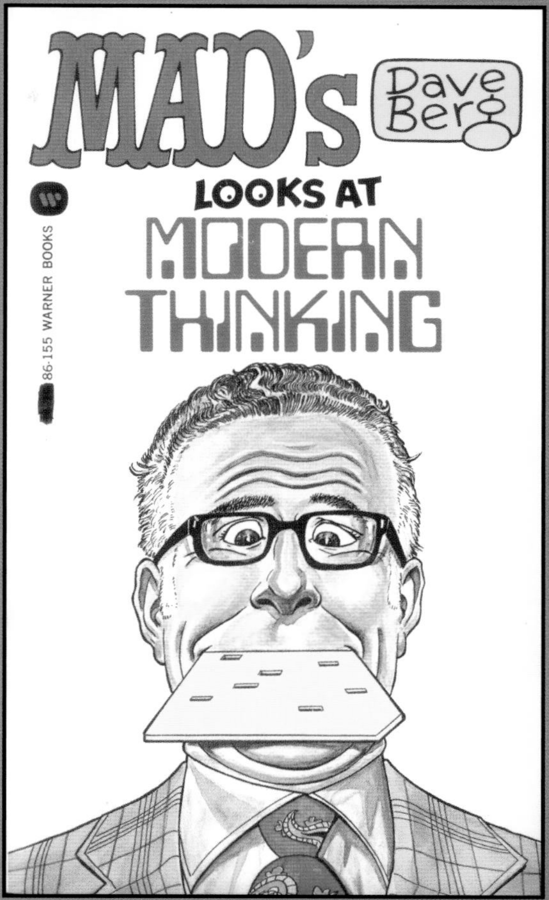

MAD's
Dave Berg
LOOKS AT
MODERN
THINKING
86-155 WARNER BOOKS

reprint cover 1976

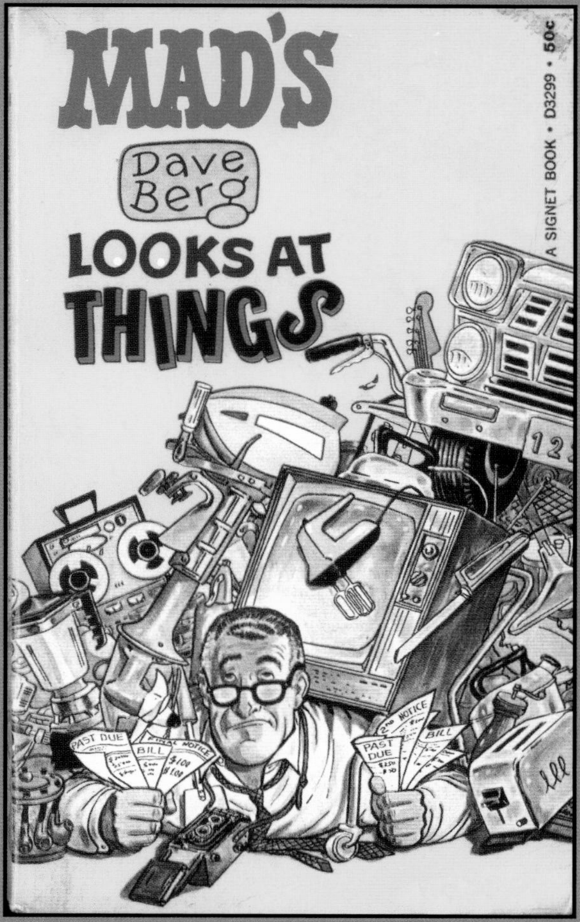

MAD's
Dave Berg
LOOKS AT
THINGS
A SIGNET BOOK • D3299 • 50c
PAST DUE
BILL
FINAL NOTICE
PAST DUE
BILL

1967

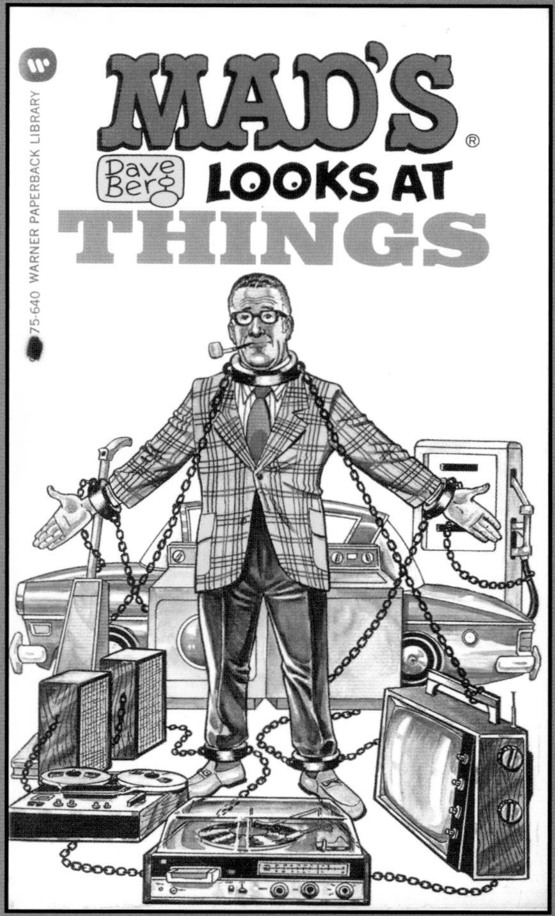

MAD's
Dave Berg
LOOKS AT
THINGS
75-640 WARNER PAPERBACK LIBRARY

reprint cover 1974

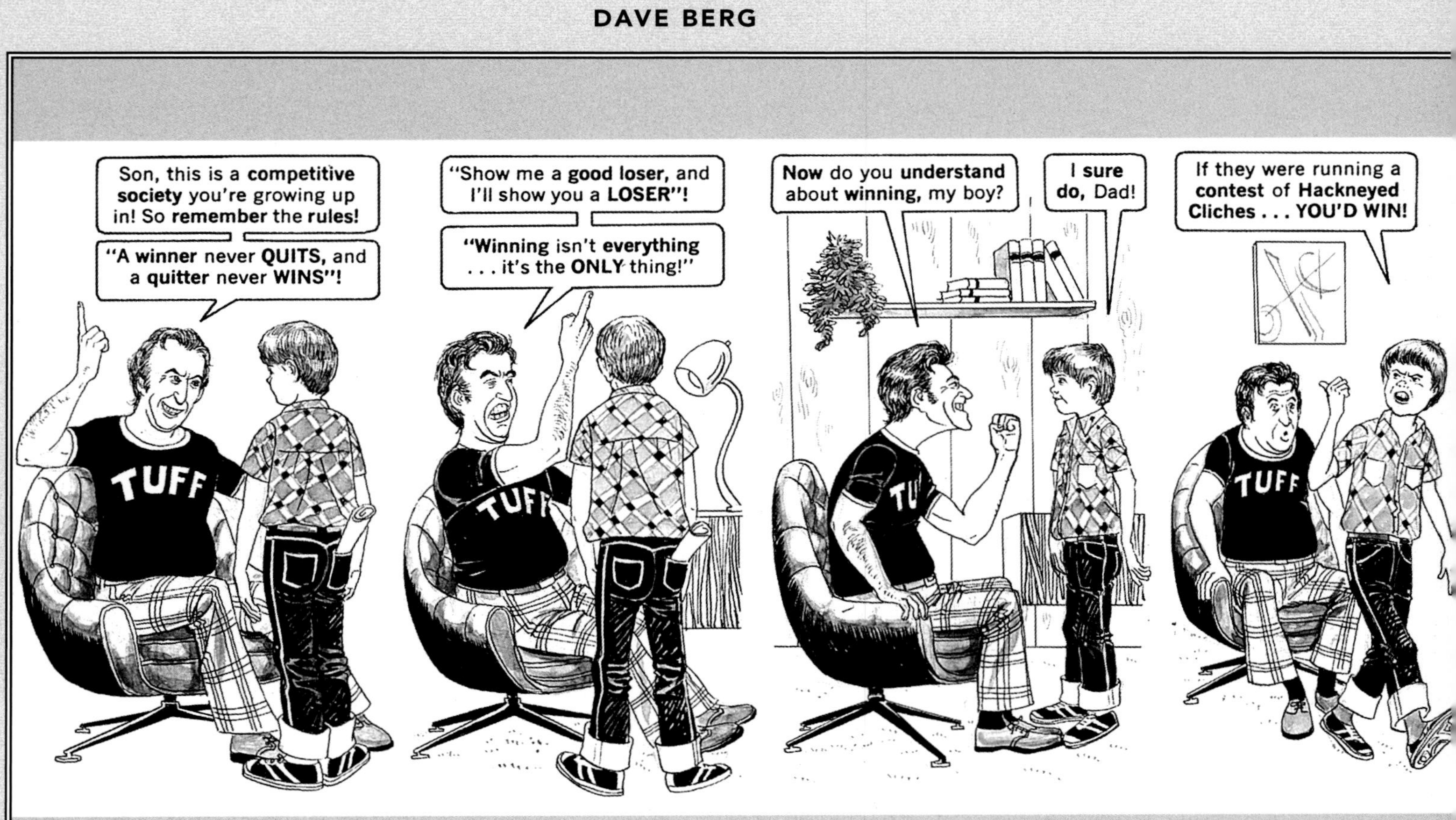
Son, this is a competitive society you're growing up in! So remember the rules!
"A winner never QUITS, and a quitter never WINS"!
"Show me a good loser, and I'll show you a LOSER"!
"Winning isn't everything . . . it's the ONLY thing!"
Now do you understand about winning, my boy?
I sure do, Dad!
If they were running a contest of Hackneyed Cliches . . . YOU'D WIN!
TUFF

BERG'S-EYE VIEW DEPT.

THE LIGHTER SIDE OF... WIN

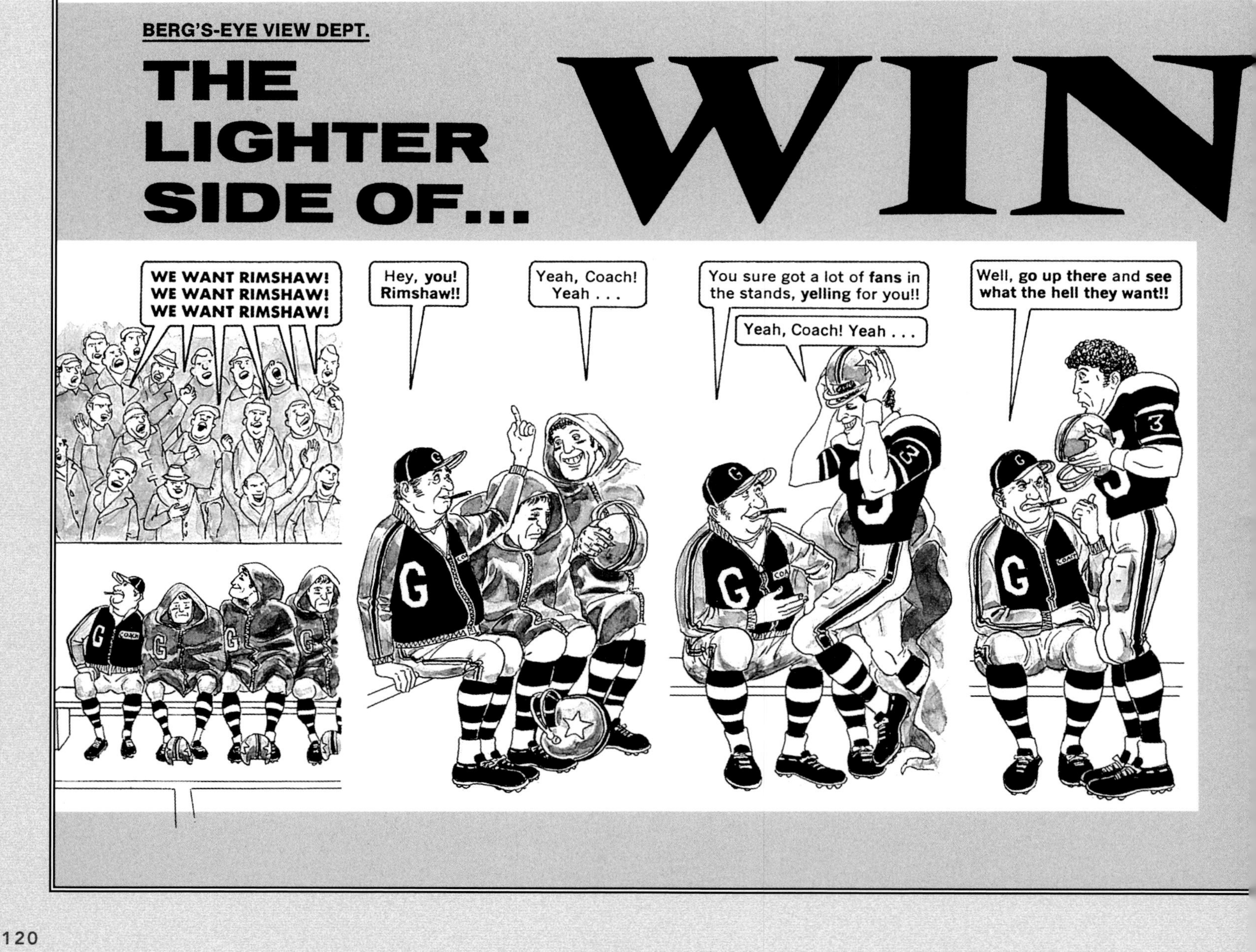
WE WANT RIMSHAW! WE WANT RIMSHAW! WE WANT RIMSHAW!
Hey, you! Rimshaw!!
Yeah, Coach! Yeah . . .
You sure got a lot of fans in the stands, yelling for you!!
Yeah, Coach! Yeah . . .
Well, go up there and see what the hell they want!!

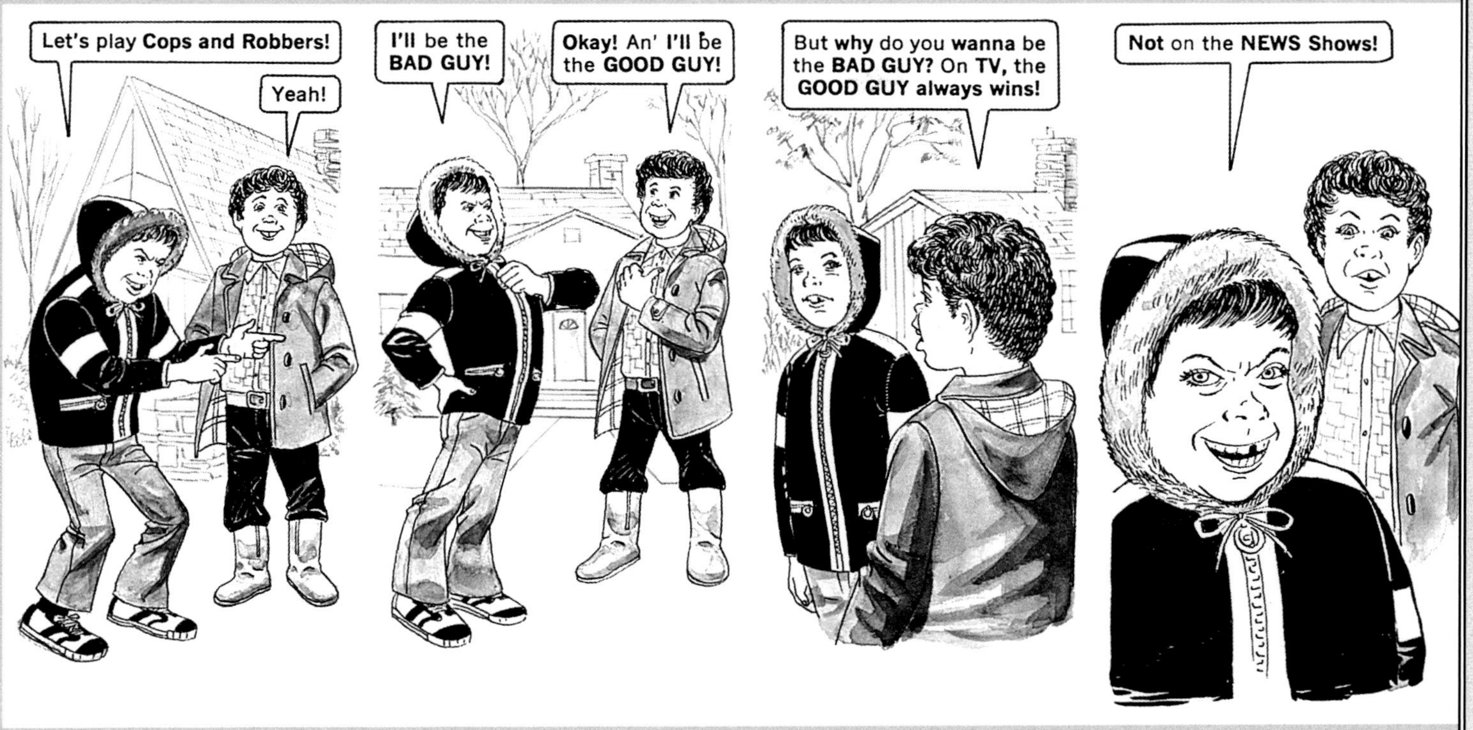
Let's play Cops and Robbers!
Yeah!
I'll be the BAD GUY!
Okay! An' I'll be the GOOD GUY!
But why do you wanna be the BAD GUY? On TV, the GOOD GUY always wins!
Not on the NEWS Shows!

NING

ARTIST & WRITER:
DAVE BERG

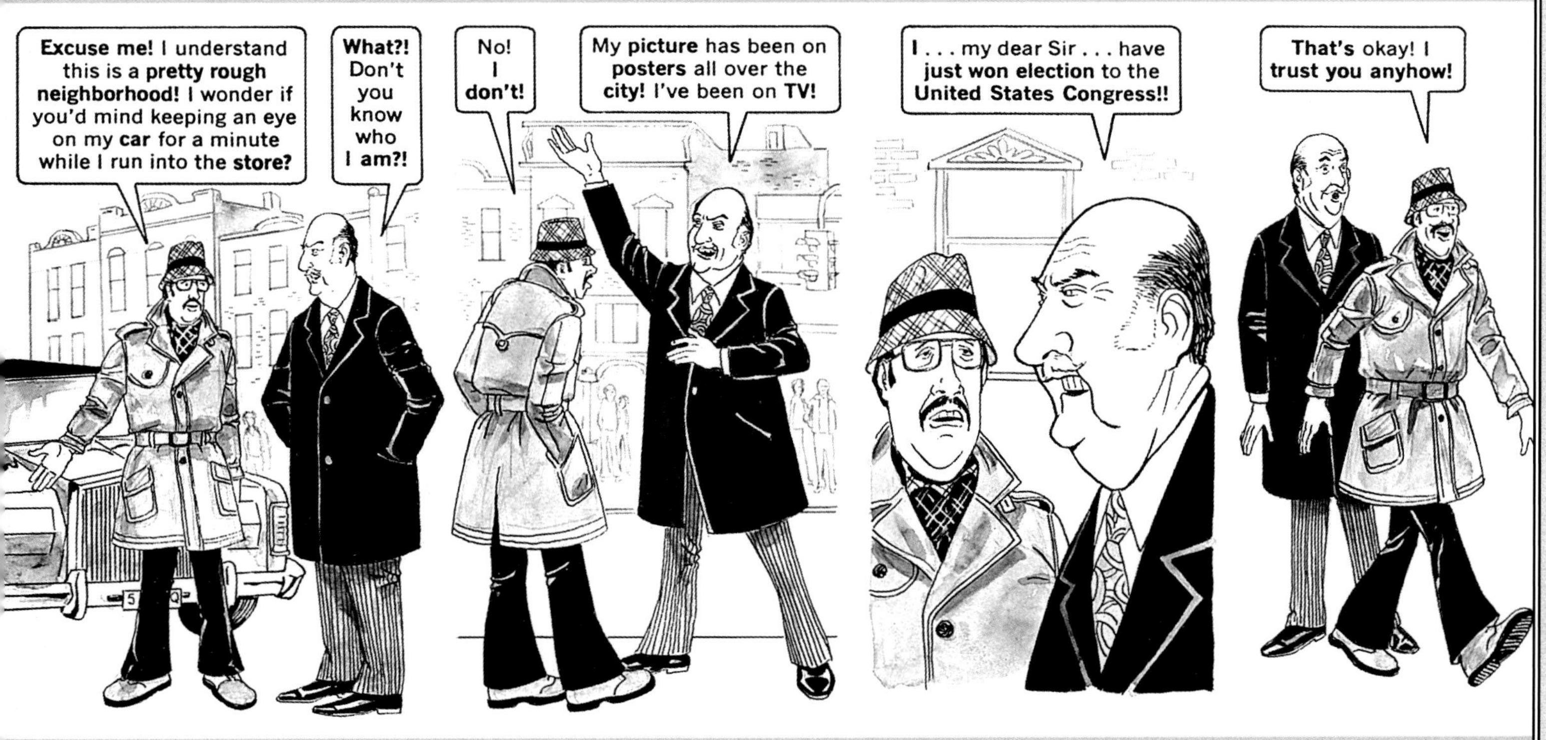
Excuse me! I understand this is a pretty rough neighborhood! I wonder if you'd mind keeping an eye on my car for a minute while I run into the store?
What?! Don't you know who I am?!
No! I don't!
My picture has been on posters all over the city! I've been on TV!
I . . . my dear Sir . . . have just won election to the United States Congress!!
That's okay! I trust you anyhow!

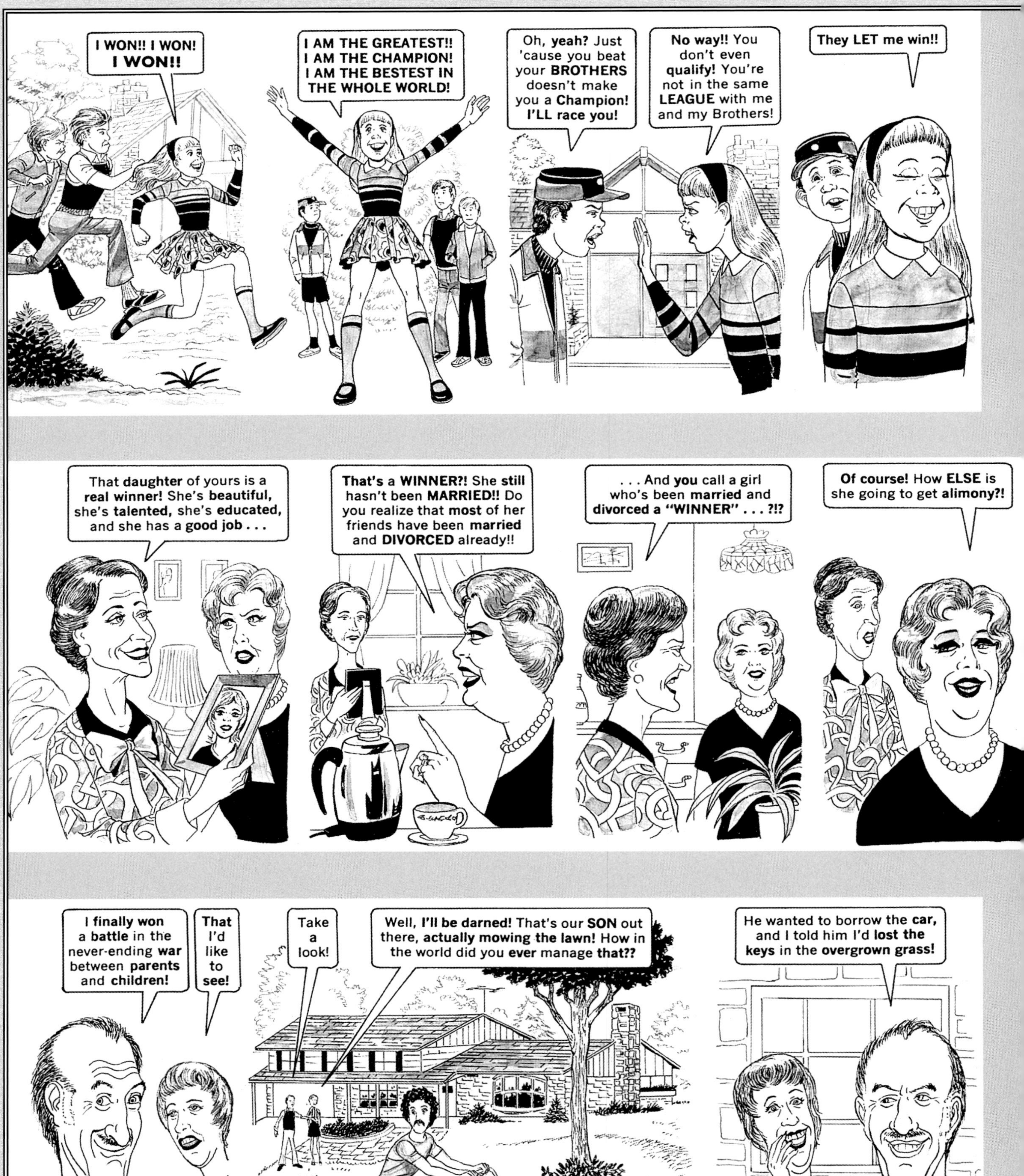
I WON!! I WON!
I WON!!
I AM THE GREATEST!! I AM THE CHAMPION! I AM THE BESTEST IN THE WHOLE WORLD!
Oh, yeah? Just 'cause you beat your BROTHERS doesn't make you a Champion! I'LL race you!
No way!! You don't even qualify! You're not in the same LEAGUE with me and my Brothers!
They LET me win!!
That daughter of yours is a real winner! She's beautiful, she's talented, she's educated, and she has a good job . . .
That's a WINNER?! She still hasn't been MARRIED!! Do you realize that most of her friends have been married and DIVORCED already!!
. . . And you call a girl who's been married and divorced a "WINNER" . . . ?!?
Of course! How ELSE is she going to get alimony?!
I finally won a battle in the never-ending war between parents and children!
That I'd like to see!
Take a look!
Well, I'll be darned! That's our SON out there, actually mowing the lawn! How in the world did you ever manage that??
He wanted to borrow the car, and I told him I'd lost the keys in the overgrown grass!

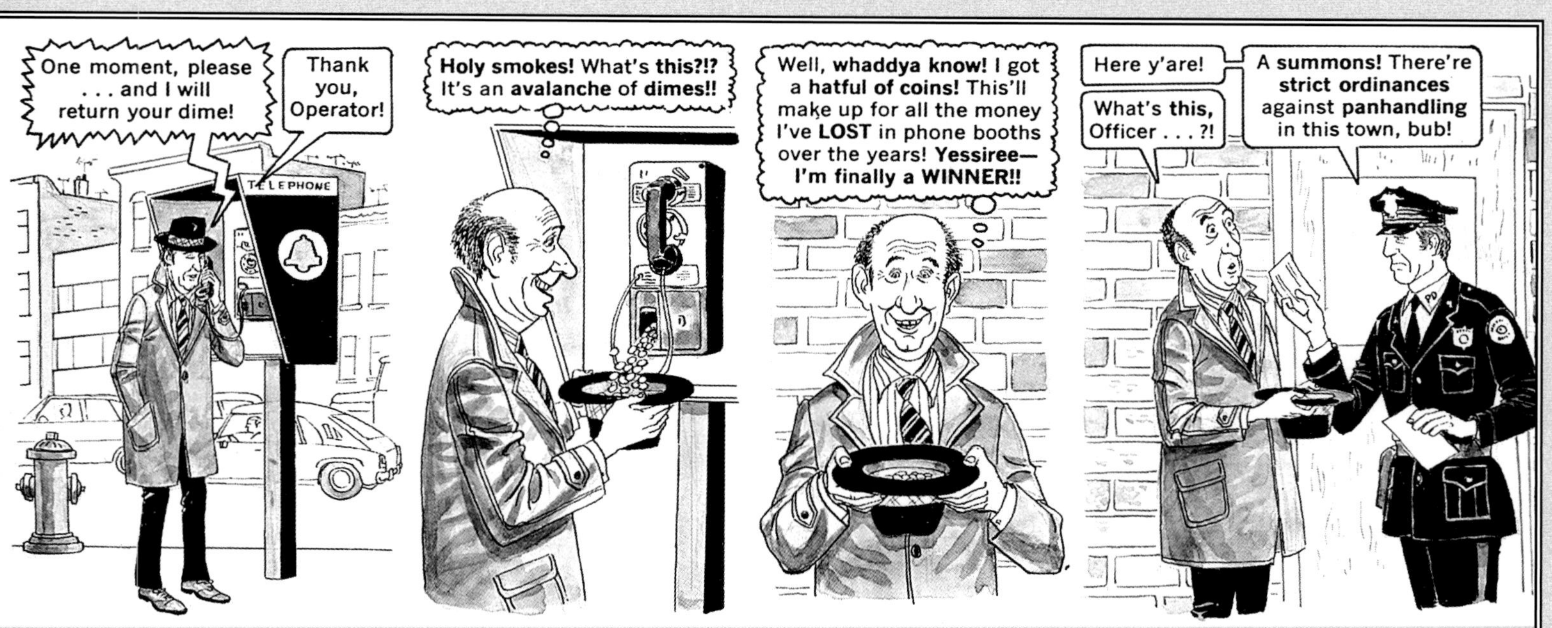
One moment, please . . . and I will return your dime!
Thank you, Operator!
TELEPHONE
Holy smokes! What's this?!? It's an avalanche of dimes!!
Well, whaddya know! I got a hatful of coins! This'll make up for all the money I've LOST in phone booths over the years! Yessiree— I'm finally a WINNER!!
Here y'are!
What's this, Officer . . . ?!
A summons! There're strict ordinances against panhandling in this town, bub!

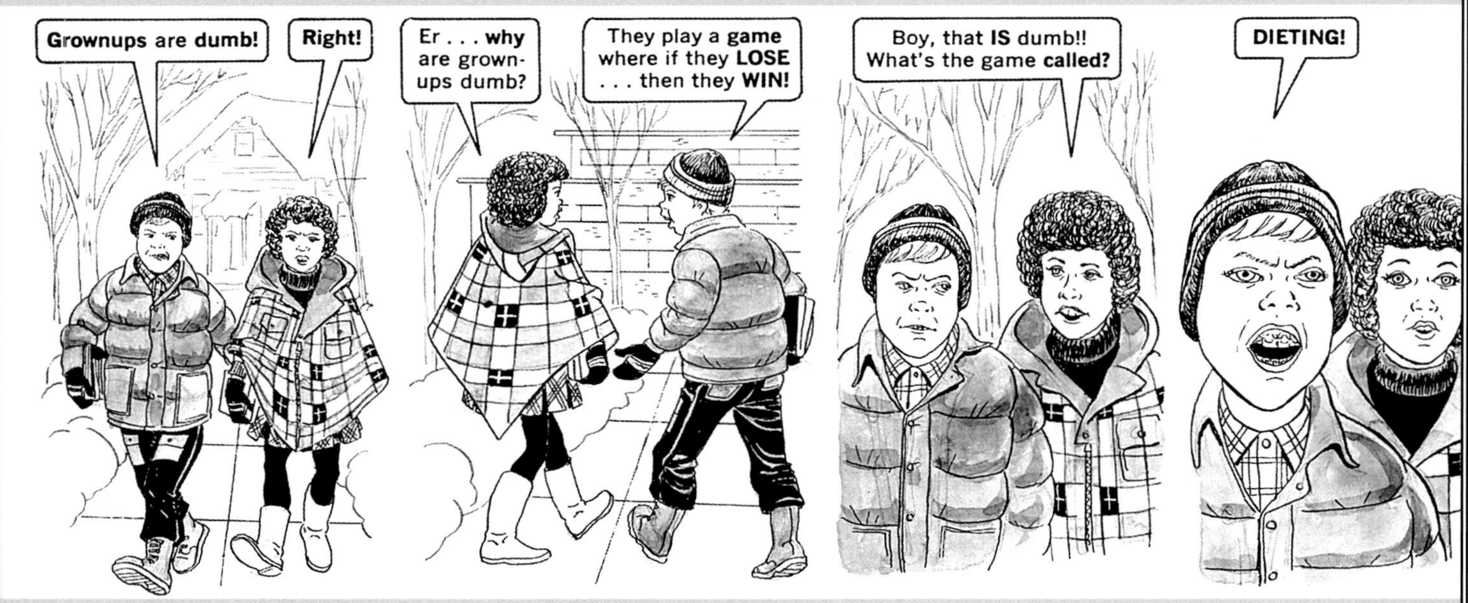
Grownups are dumb!
Right!
Er . . . why are grown-ups dumb?
They play a game where if they LOSE . . . then they WIN!
Boy, that IS dumb!! What's the game called?
DIETING!

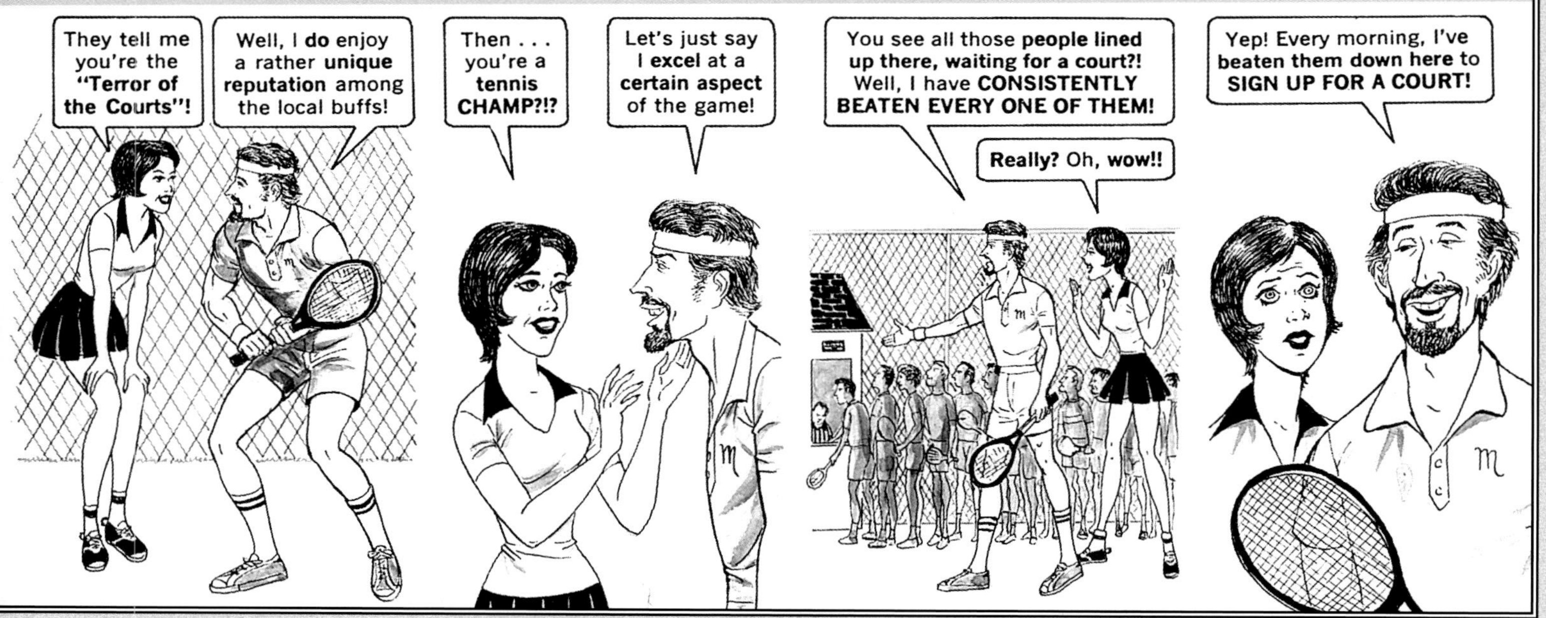
They tell me you're the "Terror of the Courts"!
Well, I do enjoy a rather unique reputation among the local buffs!
Then . . . you're a tennis CHAMP?!?
Let's just say I excel at a certain aspect of the game!
You see all those people lined up there, waiting for a court?! Well, I have CONSISTENTLY BEATEN EVERY ONE OF THEM!
Really? Oh, wow!!
Yep! Every morning, I've beaten them down here to SIGN UP FOR A COURT!

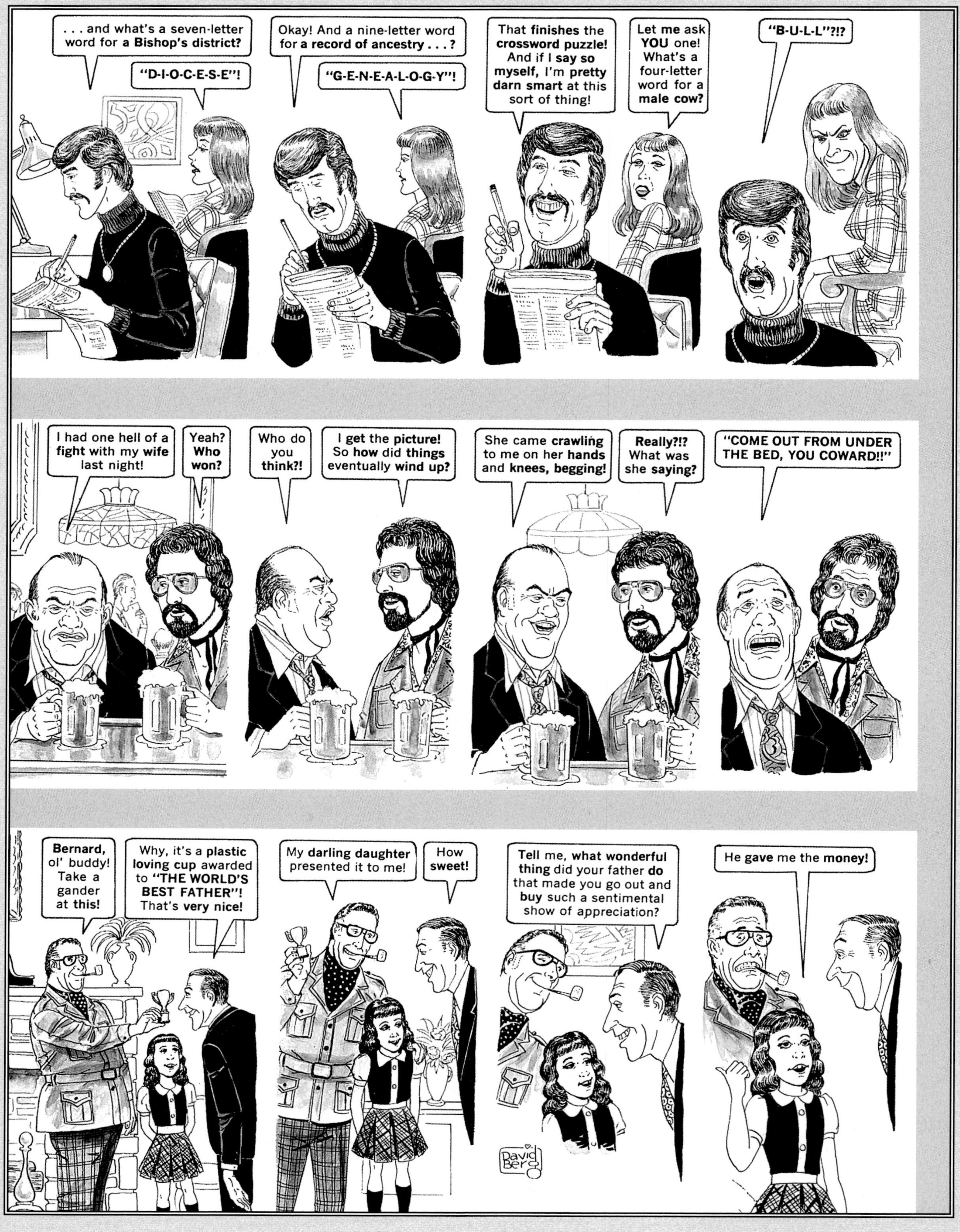
. . . and what's a seven-letter word for a Bishop's district?
"D-I-O-C-E-S-E"!
Okay! And a nine-letter word for a record of ancestry . . . ?
"G-E-N-E-A-L-O-G-Y"!
That finishes the crossword puzzle! And if I say so myself, I'm pretty darn smart at this sort of thing!
Let me ask YOU one! What's a four-letter word for a male cow?
"B-U-L-L"?!?
I had one hell of a fight with my wife last night!
Yeah? Who won?
Who do you think?!
I get the picture! So how did things eventually wind up?
She came crawling to me on her hands and knees, begging!
Really?!? What was she saying?
"COME OUT FROM UNDER THE BED, YOU COWARD!!"
Bernard, ol' buddy! Take a gander at this!
Why, it's a plastic loving cup awarded to "THE WORLD'S BEST FATHER"! That's very nice!
My darling daughter presented it to me!
How sweet!
Tell me, what wonderful thing did your father do that made you go out and buy such a sentimental show of appreciation?
David Berg
He gave me the money!

ROUGHS AND FINISHES

Examples of Dave's initial rough sketches, with added editor's marks and how the final strips appeared in the pages of MAD.

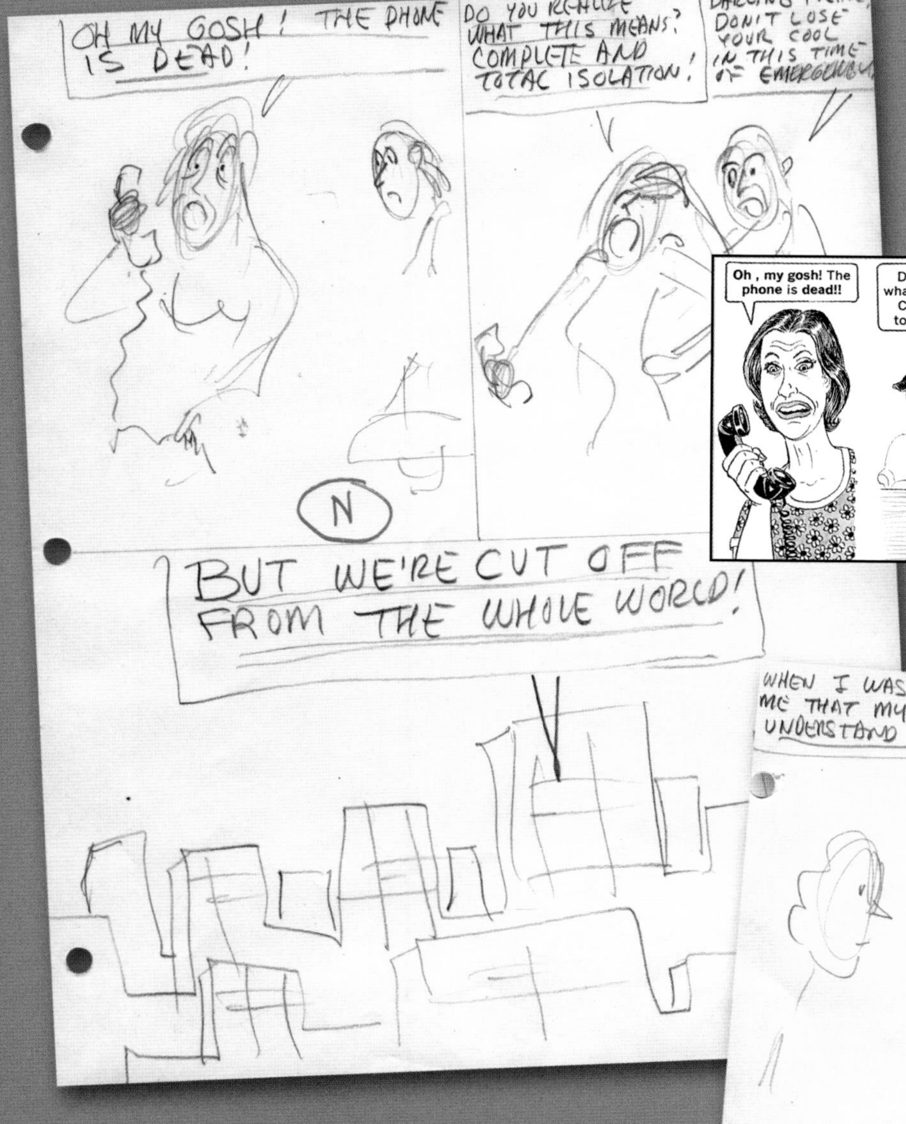
OH MY GOSH! THE PHONE IS DEAD!
DO YOU REALIZE WHAT THIS MEANS? COMPLETE AND TOTAL ISOLATION!
DARLING PLEASE, DON'T LOSE YOUR COOL IN THIS TIME
N
BUT WE'RE CUT OFF FROM THE WHOLE WORLD!

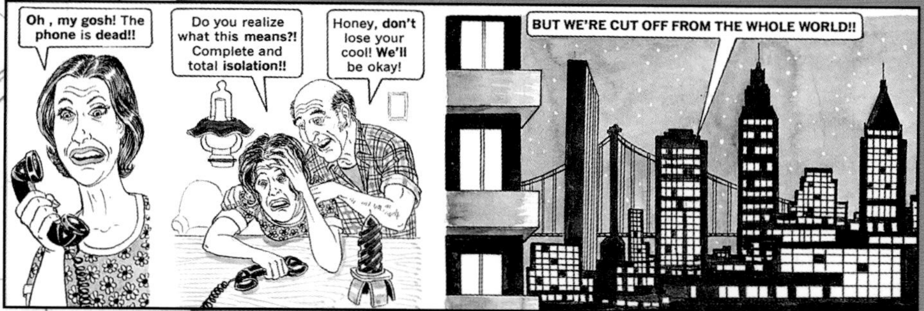
Oh, my gosh! The phone is dead!!
Do you realize what this means?! Complete and total isolation!!
Honey, don't lose your cool! We'll be okay!
BUT WE'RE CUT OFF FROM THE WHOLE WORLD!!

The Lighter Side of... Modern Technology
MAD #151, June 1972

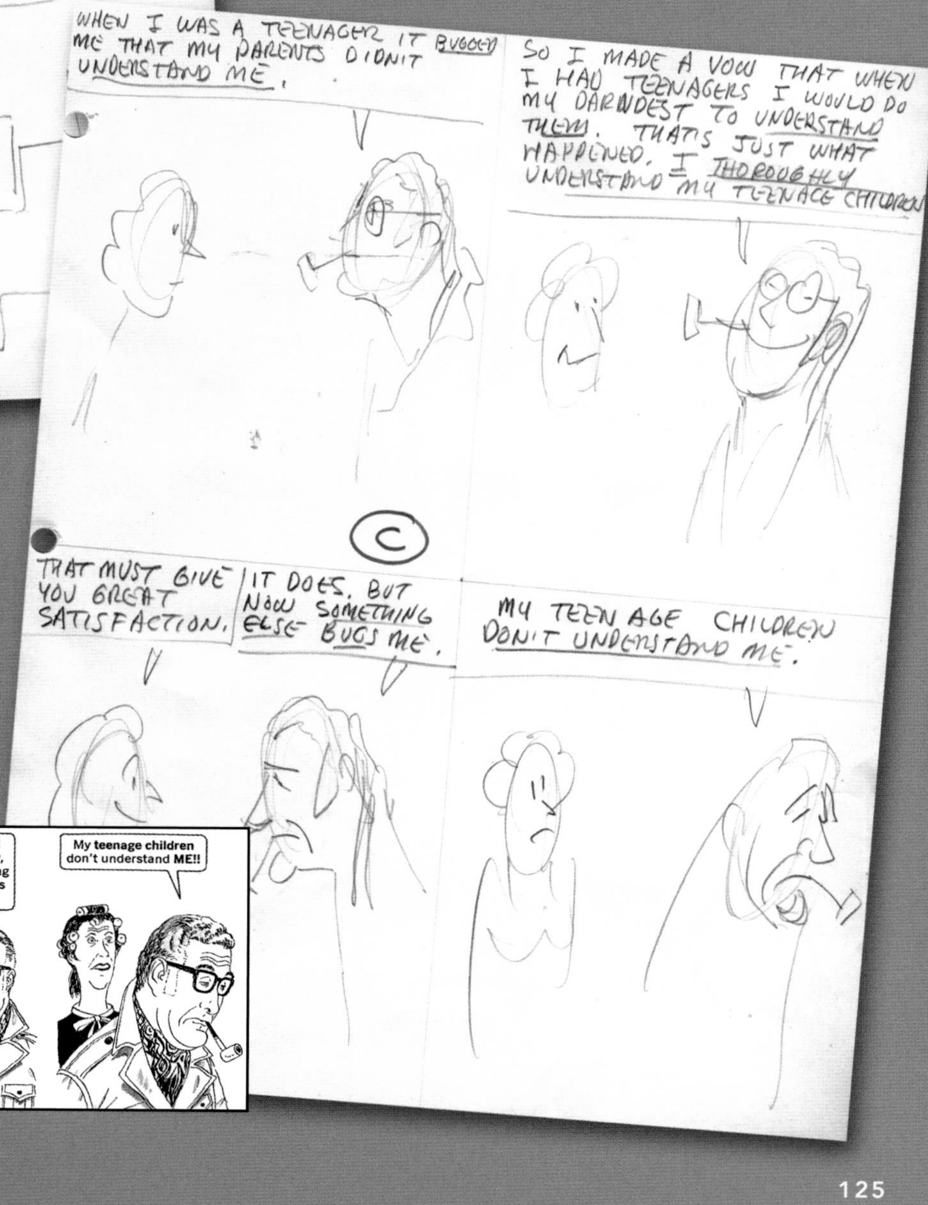
WHEN I WAS A TEENAGER IT BUGGED ME THAT MY PARENTS DIDN'T UNDERSTAND ME.
SO I MADE A VOW THAT WHEN I HAD TEENAGERS I WOULD DO MY DARNDEST TO UNDERSTAND THEM. THAT'S JUST WHAT HAPPENED. I THOROUGHLY UNDERSTAND MY TEENAGE CHILDREN
C
THAT MUST GIVE YOU GREAT SATISFACTION.
IT DOES. BUT NOW SOMETHING ELSE BUGS ME.
MY TEEN AGE CHILDREN DON'T UNDERSTAND ME.

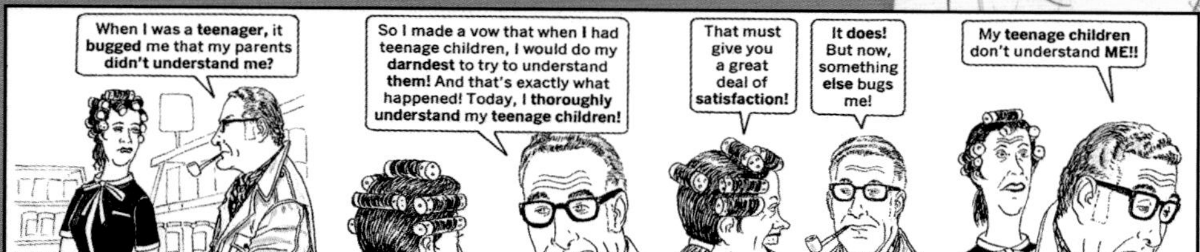
When I was a teenager, it bugged me that my parents didn't understand me?
So I made a vow that when I had teenage children, I would do my darndest to try to understand them! And that's exactly what happened! Today, I thoroughly understand my teenage children!
That must give you a great deal of satisfaction!
It does! But now, something else bugs me!
My teenage children don't understand ME!!

The Lighter Side of... Hang-Ups
MAD #154, Oct. 1972

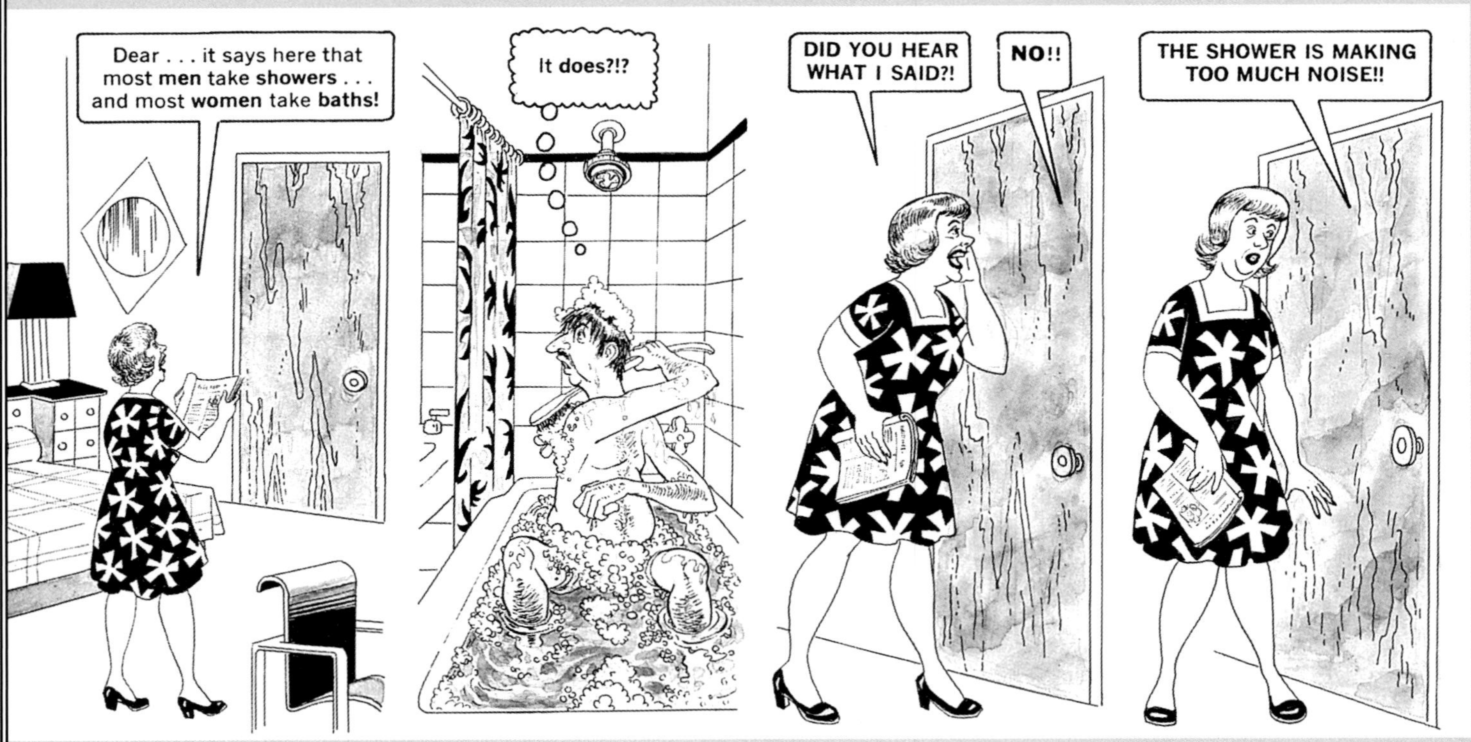
Dear . . . it says here that most men take showers . . . and most women take baths!
It does?!?
DID YOU HEAR WHAT I SAID?!
NO!!
THE SHOWER IS MAKING TOO MUCH NOISE!!

BERG'S-EYE VIEW DEPT.

THE LIGHTER SIDE OF... WA

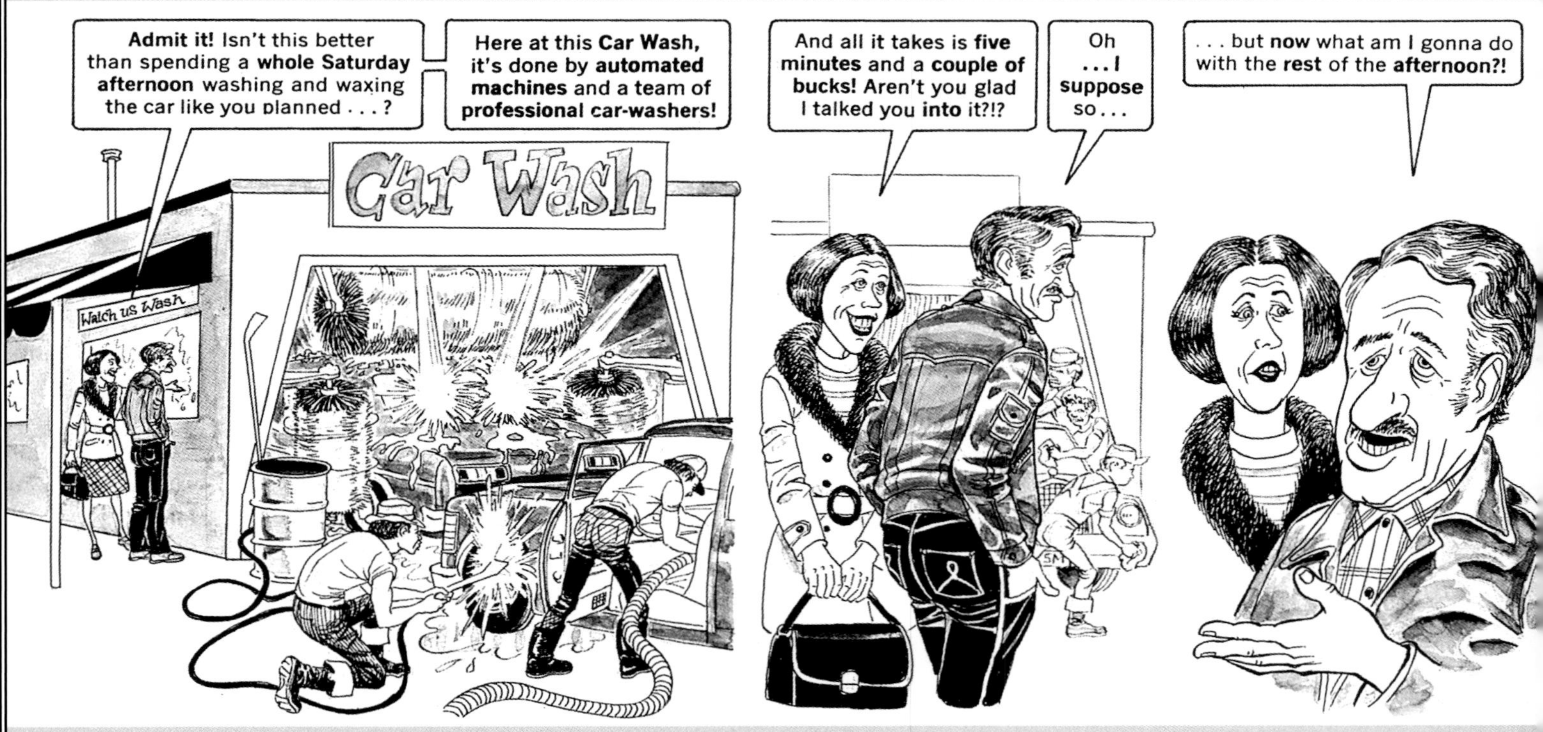
Admit it! Isn't this better than spending a whole Saturday afternoon washing and waxing the car like you planned . . . ?
Here at this Car Wash, it's done by automated machines and a team of professional car-washers!
Car Wash
Watch us Wash
And all it takes is five minutes and a couple of bucks! Aren't you glad I talked you into it?!?
Oh . . . I suppose so . . .
. . . but now what am I gonna do with the rest of the afternoon?!

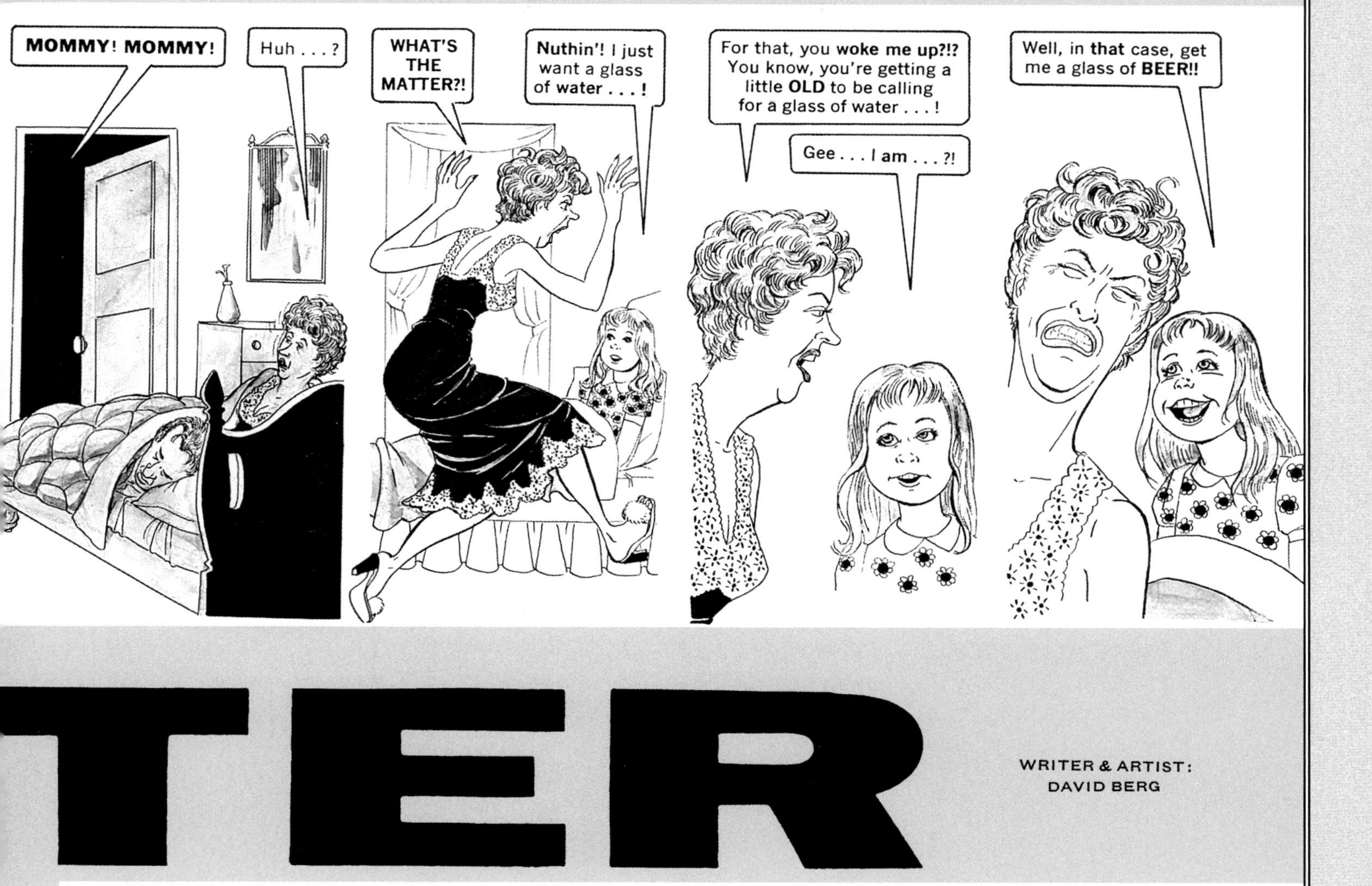
MOMMY! MOMMY!
Huh . . . ?
WHAT'S THE MATTER?!
Nuthin'! I just want a glass of water . . . !
For that, you woke me up?!? You know, you're getting a little OLD to be calling for a glass of water . . . !
Gee . . . I am . . . ?!
Well, in that case, get me a glass of BEER!!

TER

WRITER & ARTIST:
DAVID BERG

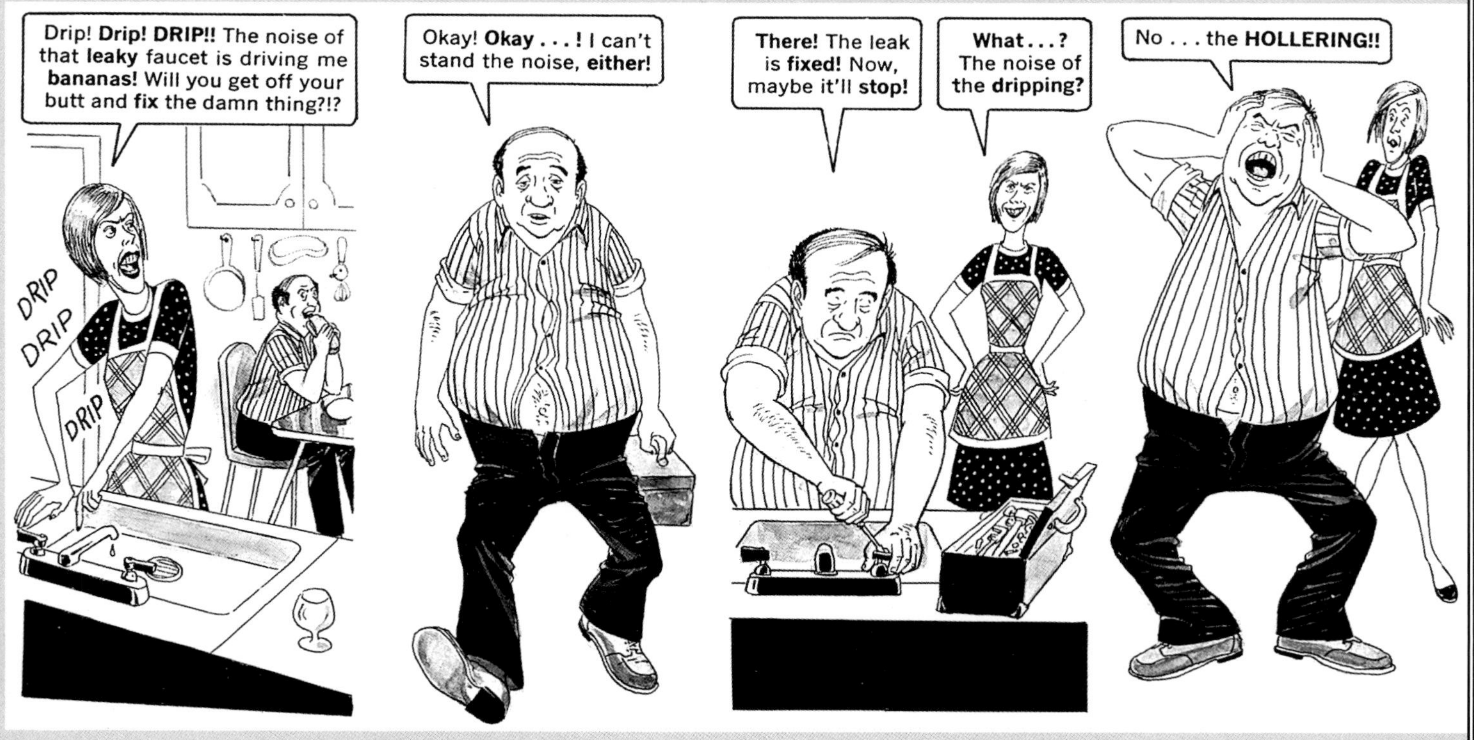
Drip! Drip! DRIP!! The noise of that leaky faucet is driving me bananas! Will you get off your butt and fix the damn thing?!?
DRIP
DRIP
DRIP
Okay! Okay . . . ! I can't stand the noise, either!
There! The leak is fixed! Now, maybe it'll stop!
What . . . ? The noise of the dripping?
No . . . the HOLLERING!!

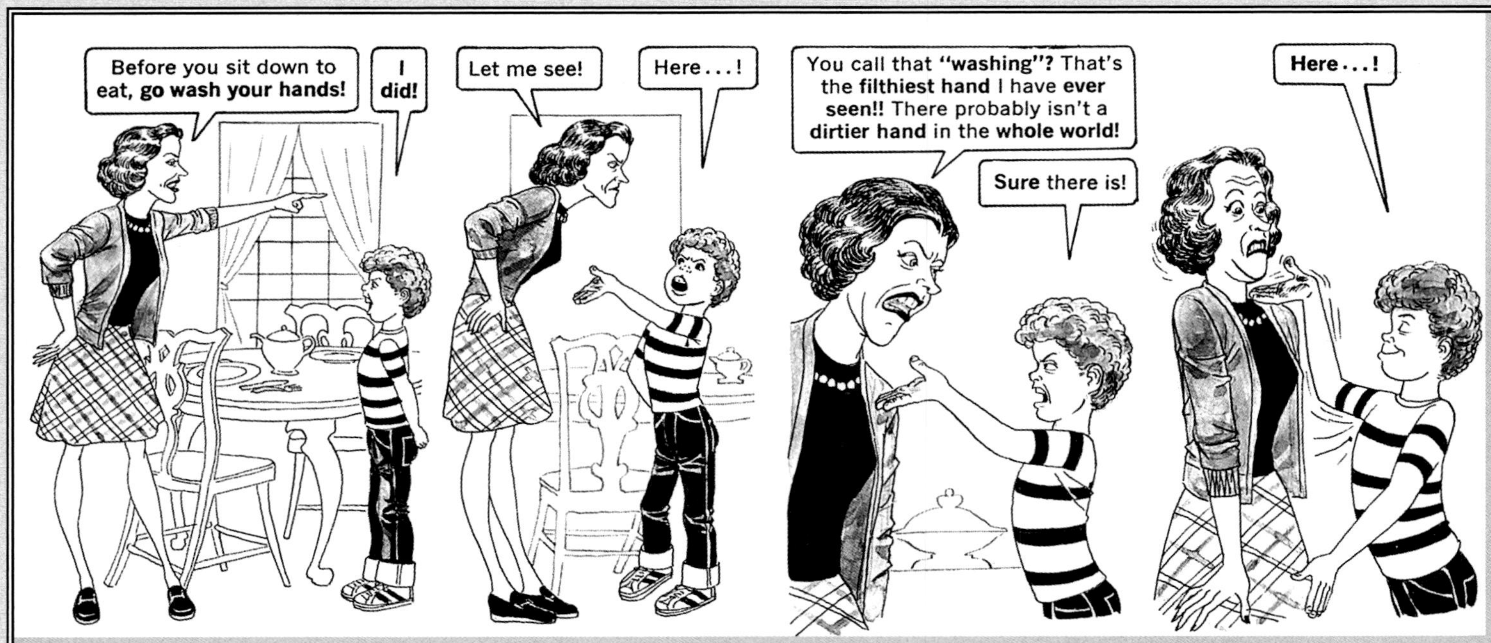
Before you sit down to eat, go wash your hands!
I did!
Let me see!
Here . . . !
You call that "washing"? That's the filthiest hand I have ever seen!! There probably isn't a dirtier hand in the whole world!
Sure there is!
Here . . . !

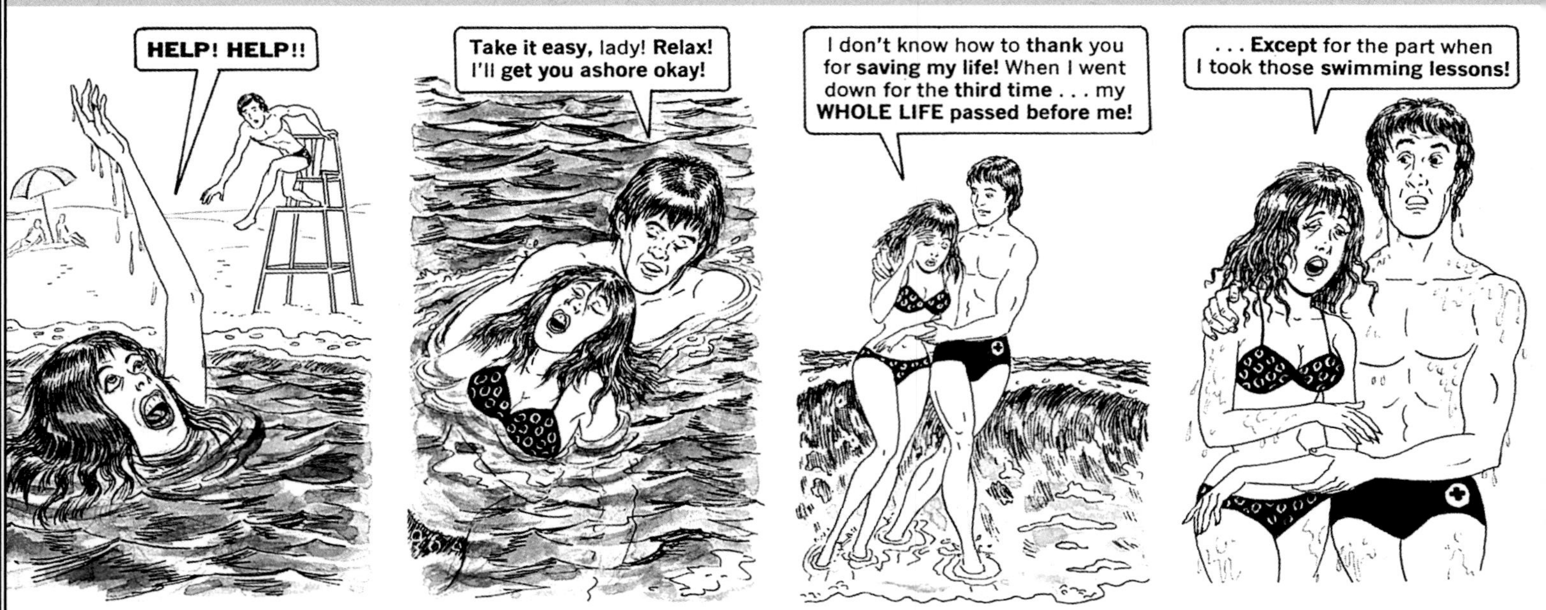
HELP! HELP!!
Take it easy, lady! Relax! I'll get you ashore okay!
I don't know how to thank you for saving my life! When I went down for the third time . . . my WHOLE LIFE passed before me!
. . . Except for the part when I took those swimming lessons!

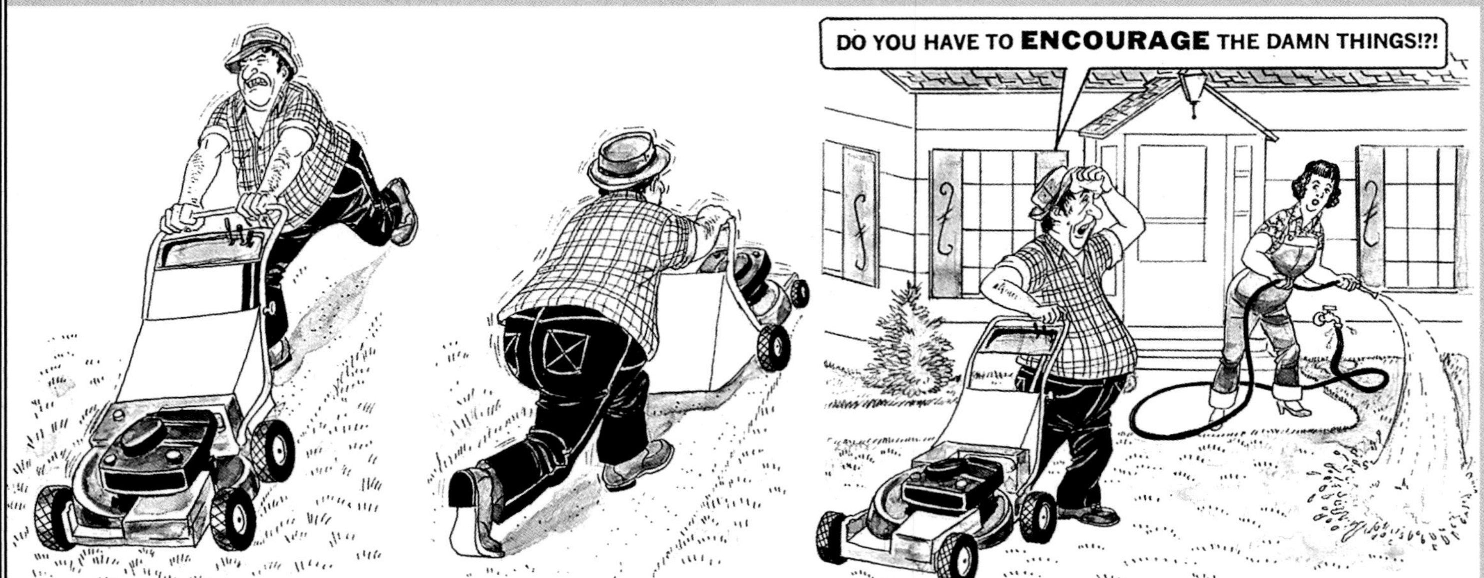
DO YOU HAVE TO ENCOURAGE THE DAMN THINGS!?!

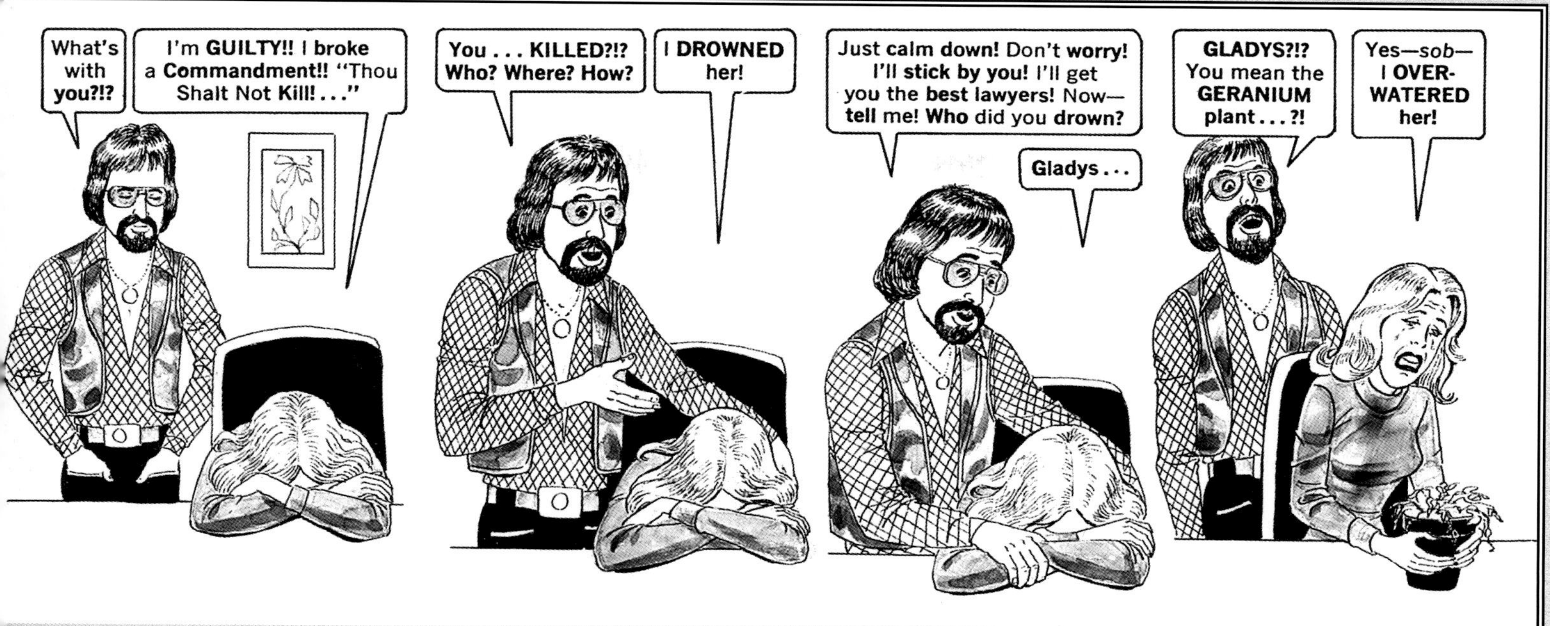
What's with you?!?
I'm GUILTY!! I broke a Commandment!! "Thou Shalt Not Kill!..."
You... KILLED?!? Who? Where? How?
I DROWNED her!
Just calm down! Don't worry! I'll stick by you! I'll get you the best lawyers! Now—tell me! Who did you drown?
Gladys...
GLADYS?!? You mean the GERANIUM plant...?!
Yes—sob—I OVER-WATERED her!

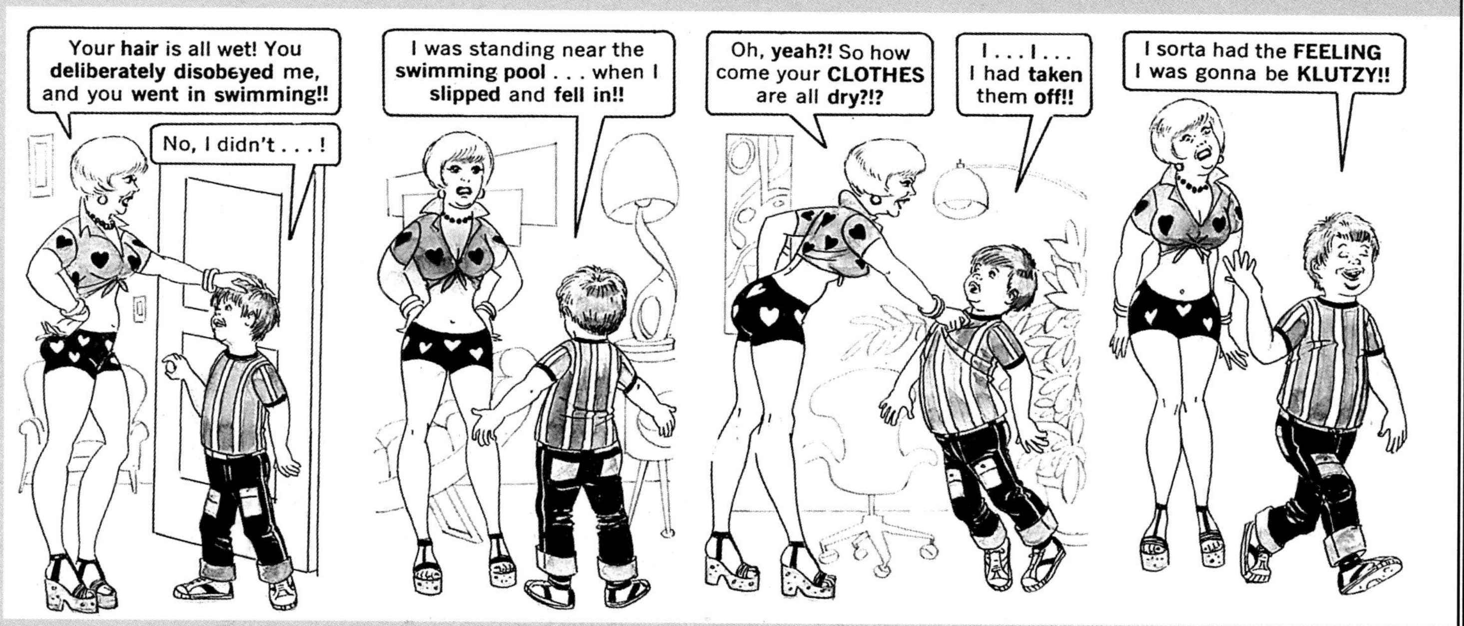
Your hair is all wet! You deliberately disobeyed me, and you went in swimming!!
No, I didn't...!
I was standing near the swimming pool... when I slipped and fell in!!
Oh, yeah?! So how come your CLOTHES are all dry?!?
I... I... I had taken them off!!
I sorta had the FEELING I was gonna be KLUTZY!!

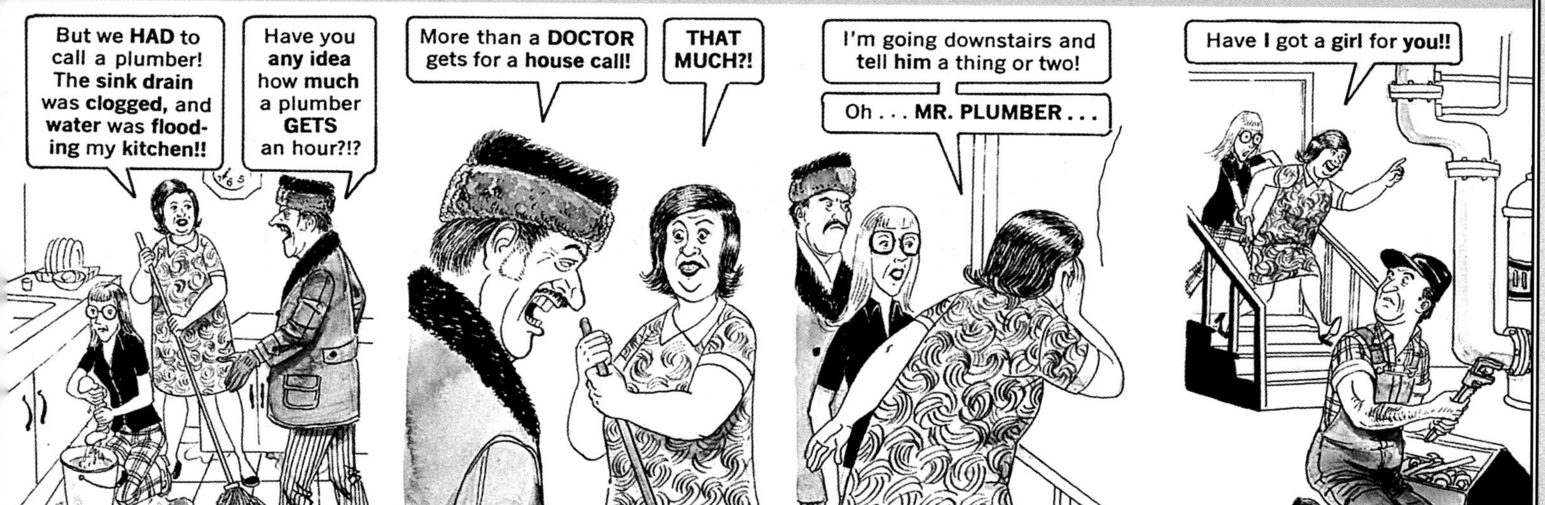
But we HAD to call a plumber! The sink drain was clogged, and water was flooding my kitchen!!
Have you any idea how much a plumber GETS an hour?!?
More than a DOCTOR gets for a house call!
THAT MUCH?!
I'm going downstairs and tell him a thing or two!
Oh... MR. PLUMBER...
Have I got a girl for you!!

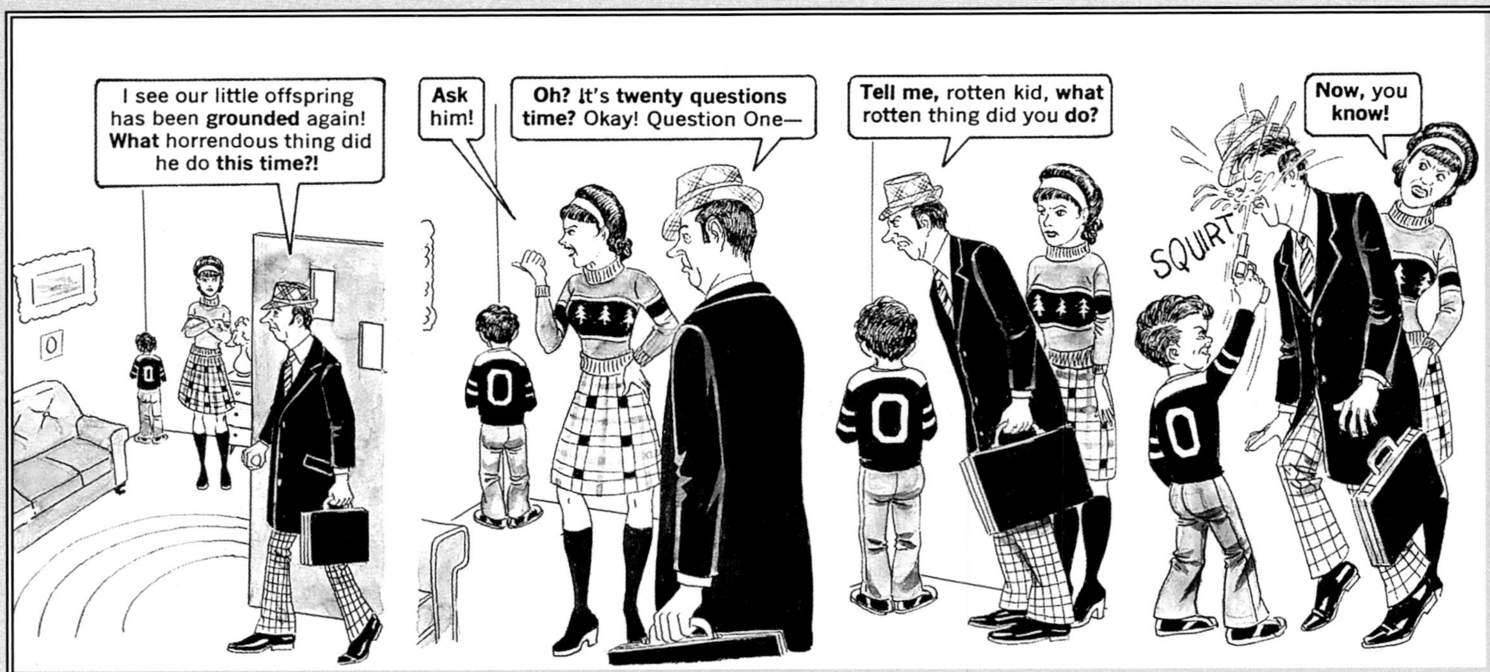
I see our little offspring has been grounded again! What horrendous thing did he do this time?!
Ask him!
Oh? It's twenty questions time? Okay! Question One—
Tell me, rotten kid, what rotten thing did you do?
SQUIRT
Now, you know!

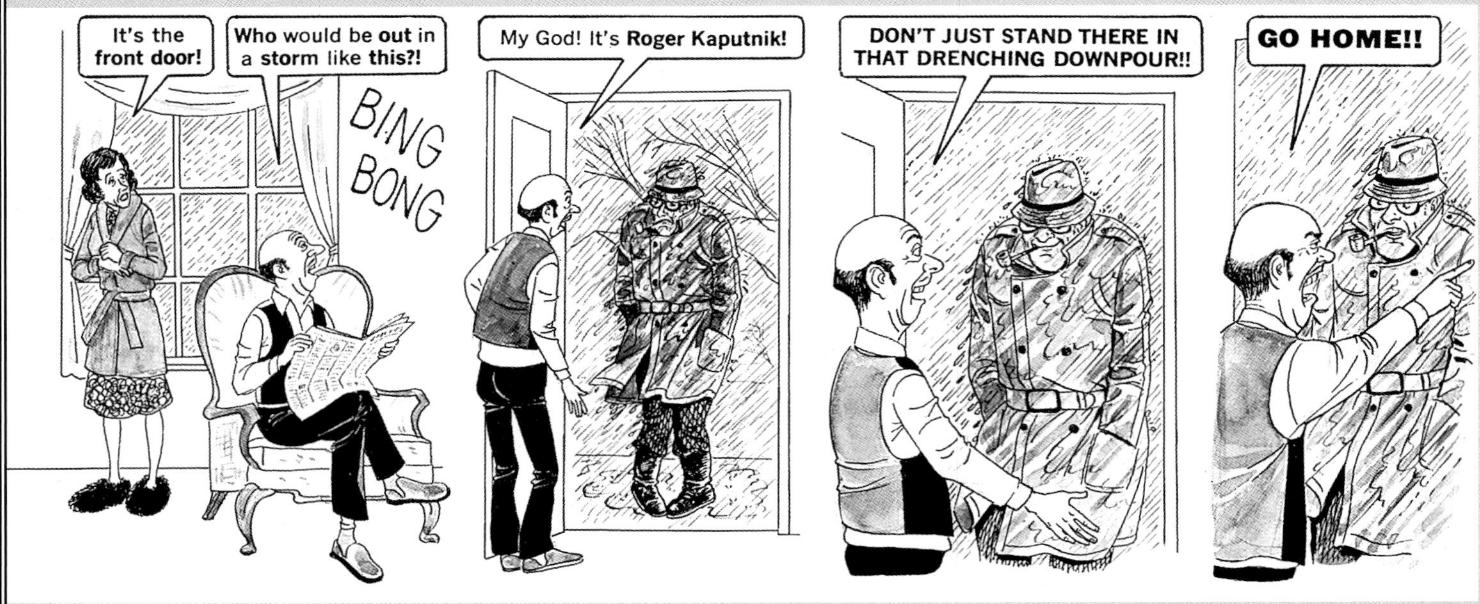
It's the front door!
Who would be out in a storm like this?!
BING BONG
My God! It's Roger Kaputnik!
DON'T JUST STAND THERE IN THAT DRENCHING DOWNPOUR!!
GO HOME!!

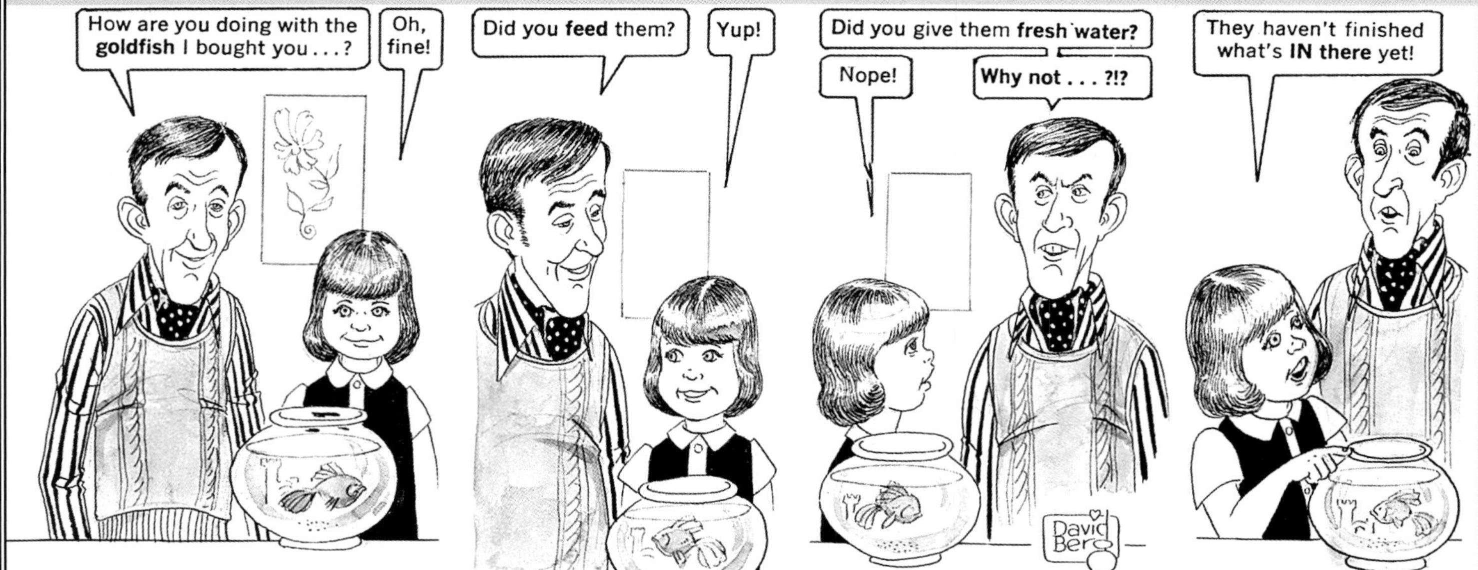
How are you doing with the goldfish I bought you . . . ?
Oh, fine!
Did you feed them?
Yup!
Did you give them fresh water?
Nope!
Why not . . . ?!?
They haven't finished what's IN there yet!

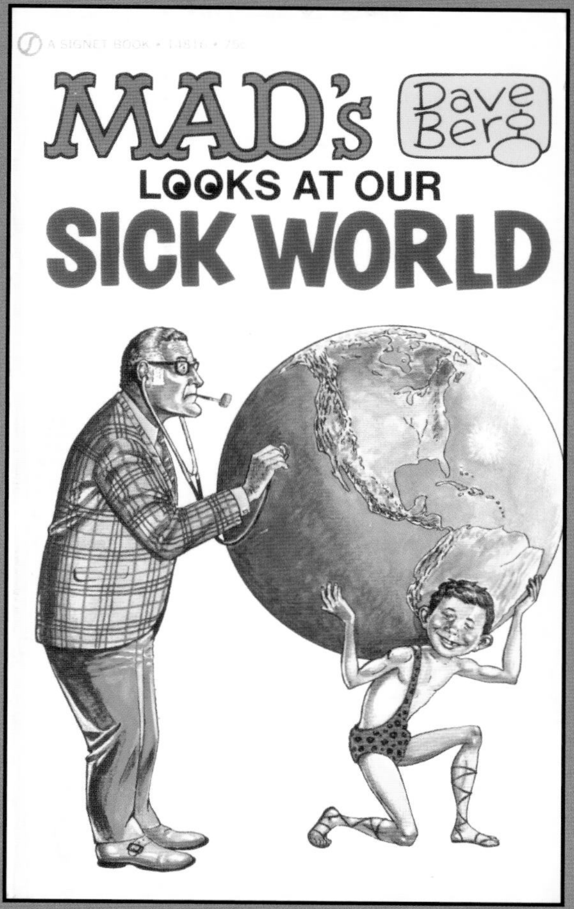
MAD's
Dave Berg
LOOKS AT OUR
SICK WORLD

1971

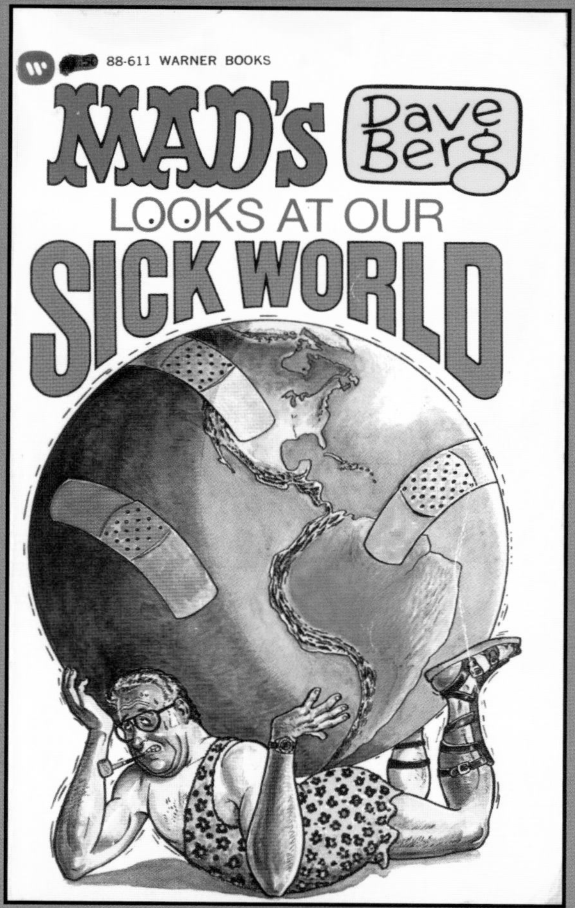
88-611 WARNER BOOKS
MAD's
Dave Berg
LOOKS AT OUR
SICK WORLD

reprint cover 1978

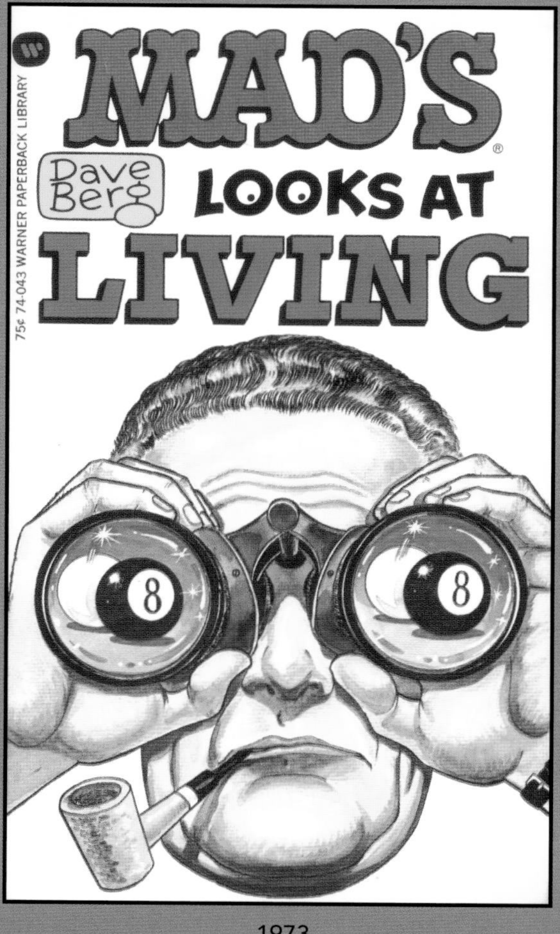
75¢ 74-043 WARNER PAPERBACK LIBRARY
MAD'S
Dave Berg
LOOKS AT
LIVING

1973

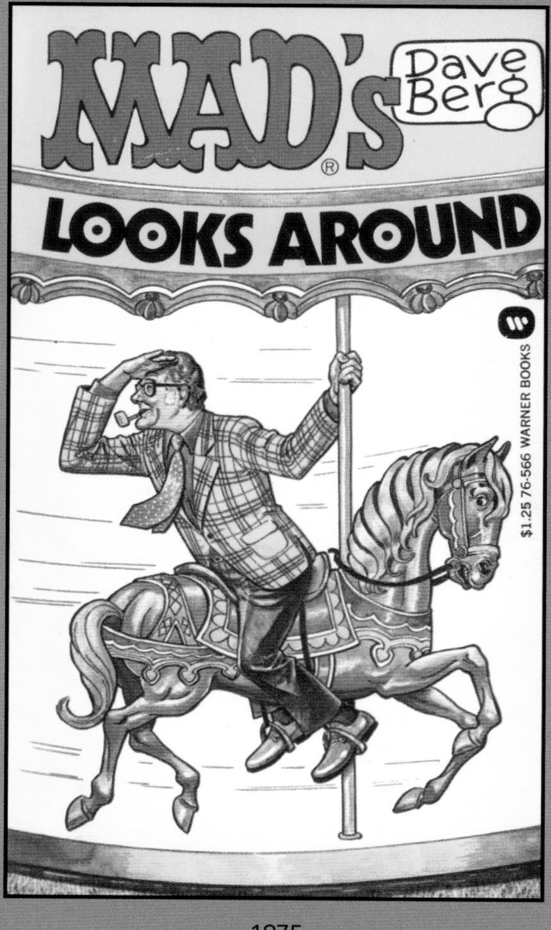
MAD's
Dave Berg
LOOKS AROUND
$1.25 76-566 WARNER BOOKS

1975

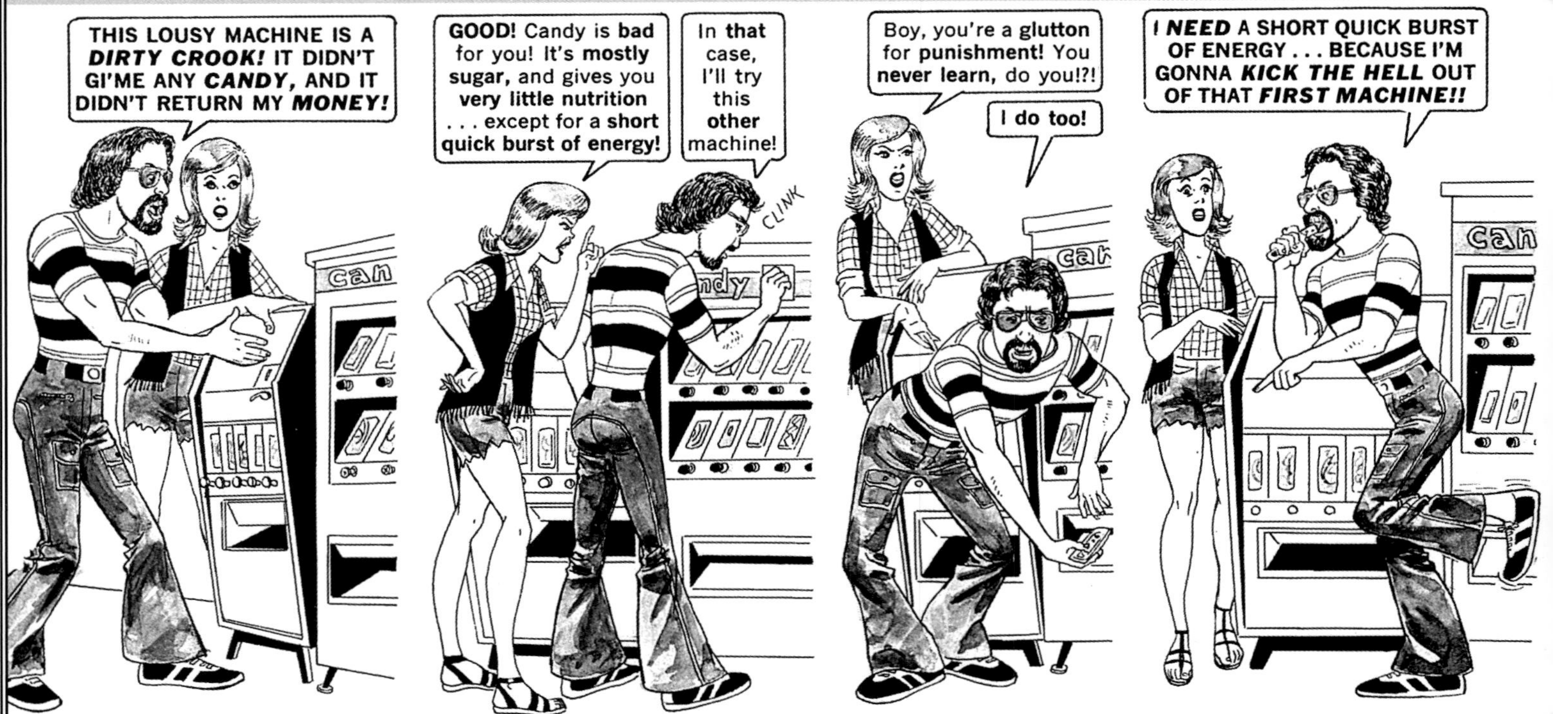
THIS LOUSY MACHINE IS A DIRTY CROOK! IT DIDN'T GI'ME ANY CANDY, AND IT DIDN'T RETURN MY MONEY!
GOOD! Candy is bad for you! It's mostly sugar, and gives you very little nutrition . . . except for a short quick burst of energy!
In that case, I'll try this other machine!
CLINK
Boy, you're a glutton for punishment! You never learn, do you!?!
I do too!
I NEED A SHORT QUICK BURST OF ENERGY . . . BECAUSE I'M GONNA KICK THE HELL OUT OF THAT FIRST MACHINE!!

BERG'S-EYE VIEW DEPT.

THE LIGHTER SIDE OF... OVER-

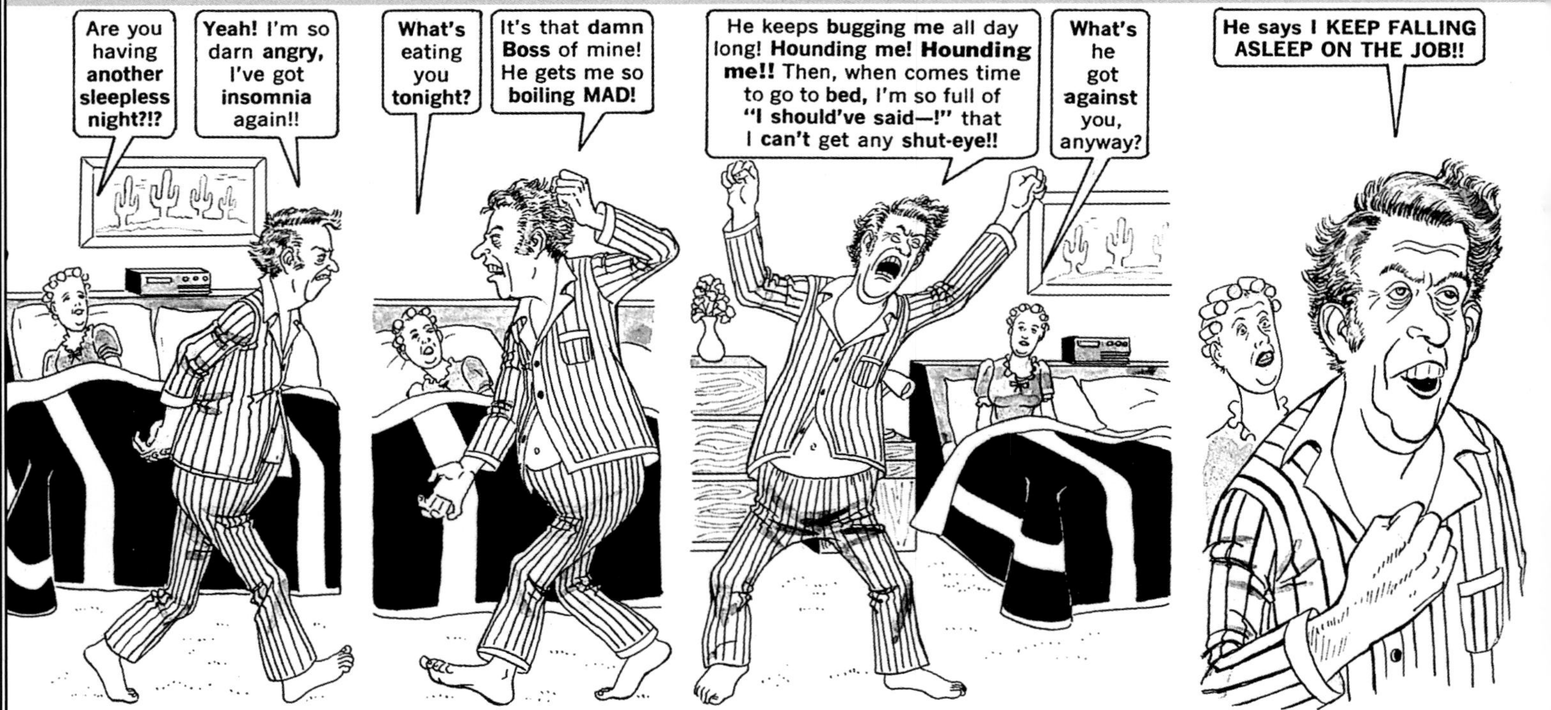
Are you having another sleepless night?!?
Yeah! I'm so darn angry, I've got insomnia again!!
What's eating you tonight?
It's that damn Boss of mine! He gets me so boiling MAD!
He keeps bugging me all day long! Hounding me! Hounding me!! Then, when comes time to go to bed, I'm so full of "I should've said—!" that I can't get any shut-eye!!
What's he got against you, anyway?
He says I KEEP FALLING ASLEEP ON THE JOB!!

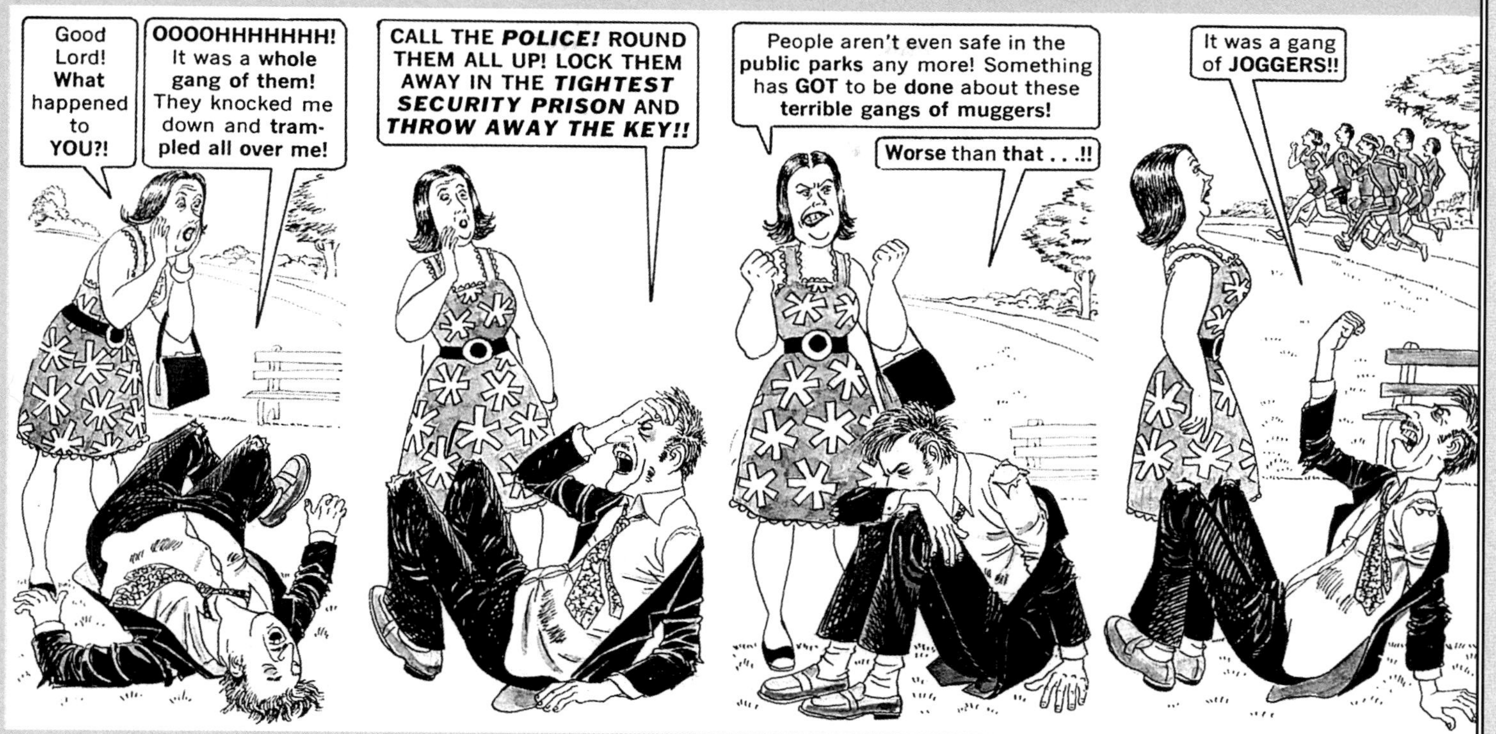
Good Lord! **What** happened to **YOU?!**
OOOOHHHHHHH! It was a **whole gang of them!** They knocked me down and **trampled all over me!**
CALL THE ***POLICE!*** ROUND THEM ALL UP! LOCK THEM AWAY IN THE ***TIGHTEST SECURITY PRISON*** AND ***THROW AWAY THE KEY!!***
People aren't even safe in the **public parks** any more! Something has **GOT** to be **done** about these **terrible gangs of muggers!**
Worse than **that . . .!!**
It was a gang of **JOGGERS!!**

REACTING

ARTIST & WRITER: DAVE BERG

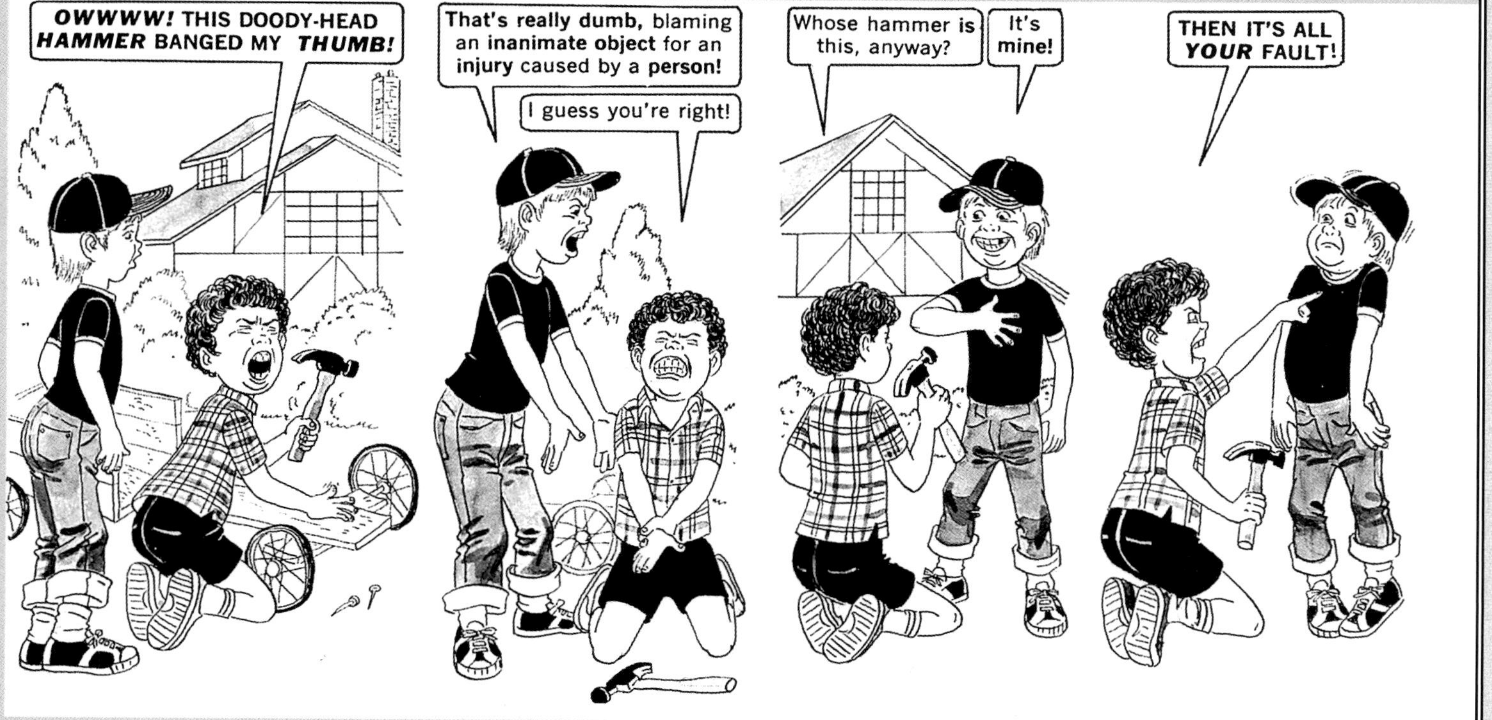
OWWWWW! THIS DOODY-HEAD ***HAMMER*** BANGED MY ***THUMB!***
That's **really dumb,** blaming an **inanimate object** for an **injury** caused by a **person!**
I guess you're right!
Whose hammer **is** this, anyway?
It's **mine!**
THEN IT'S ALL ***YOUR*** FAULT!

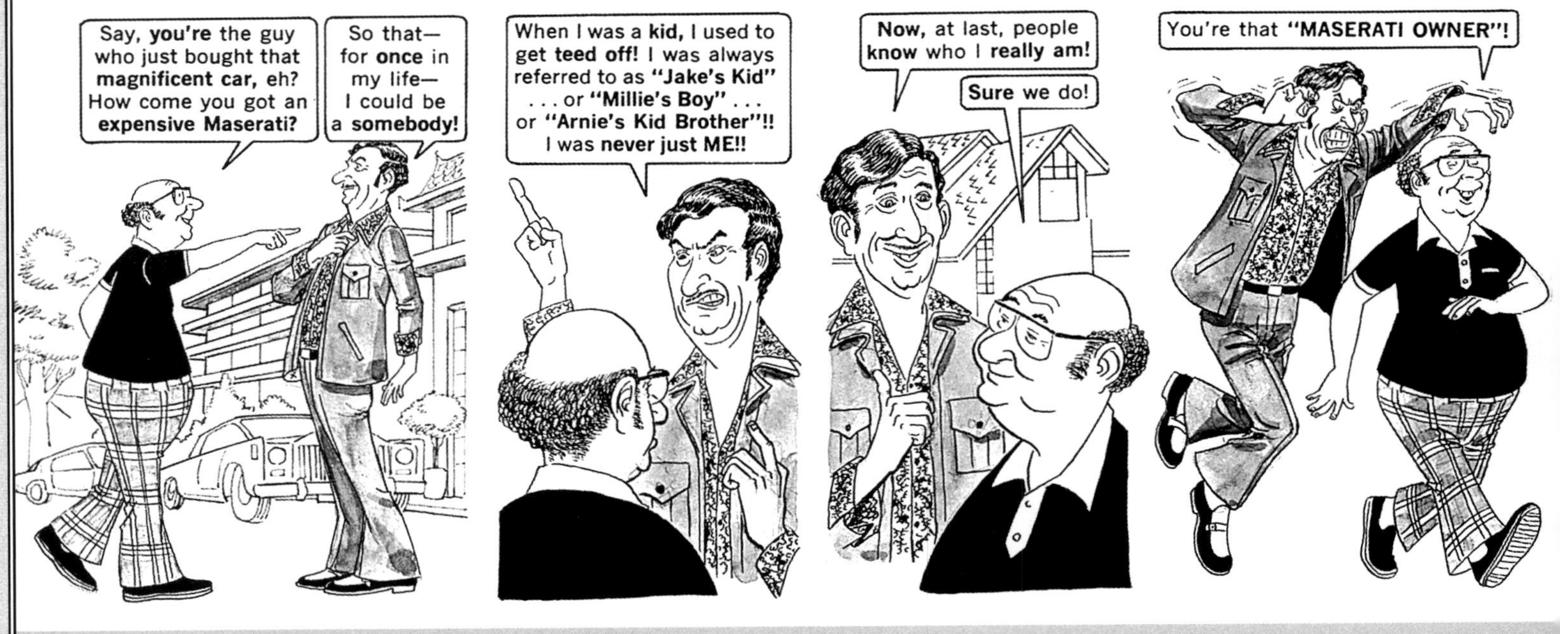
Say, **you're** the guy who just bought that **magnificent car,** eh? How come you got an **expensive Maserati?**
So that— for **once** in my life— I could be a **somebody!**
When I was a **kid,** I used to get **teed off!** I was always referred to as **"Jake's Kid"** . . . or **"Millie's Boy"** . . . or **"Arnie's Kid Brother"!!** I was **never just ME!!**
Now, at last, people **know** who I **really am!**
Sure we do!
You're that **"MASERATI OWNER"!**

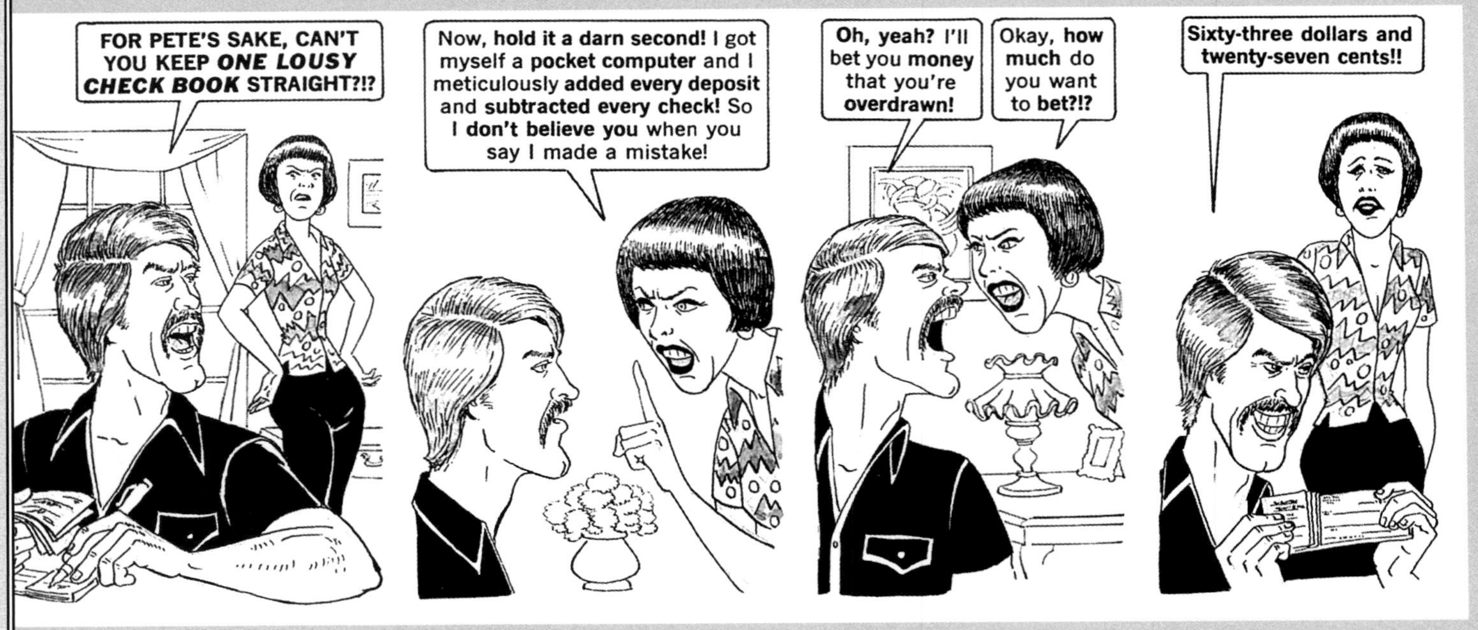
FOR PETE'S SAKE, CAN'T YOU KEEP ***ONE LOUSY CHECK BOOK*** STRAIGHT?!?
Now, **hold it a darn second!** I got myself a **pocket computer** and I meticulously **added every deposit** and **subtracted every check!** So **I don't believe you** when you say I made a mistake!
Oh, yeah? I'll bet you **money** that you're **overdrawn!**
Okay, **how** much do you want to **bet?!?**
Sixty-three dollars and twenty-seven cents!!

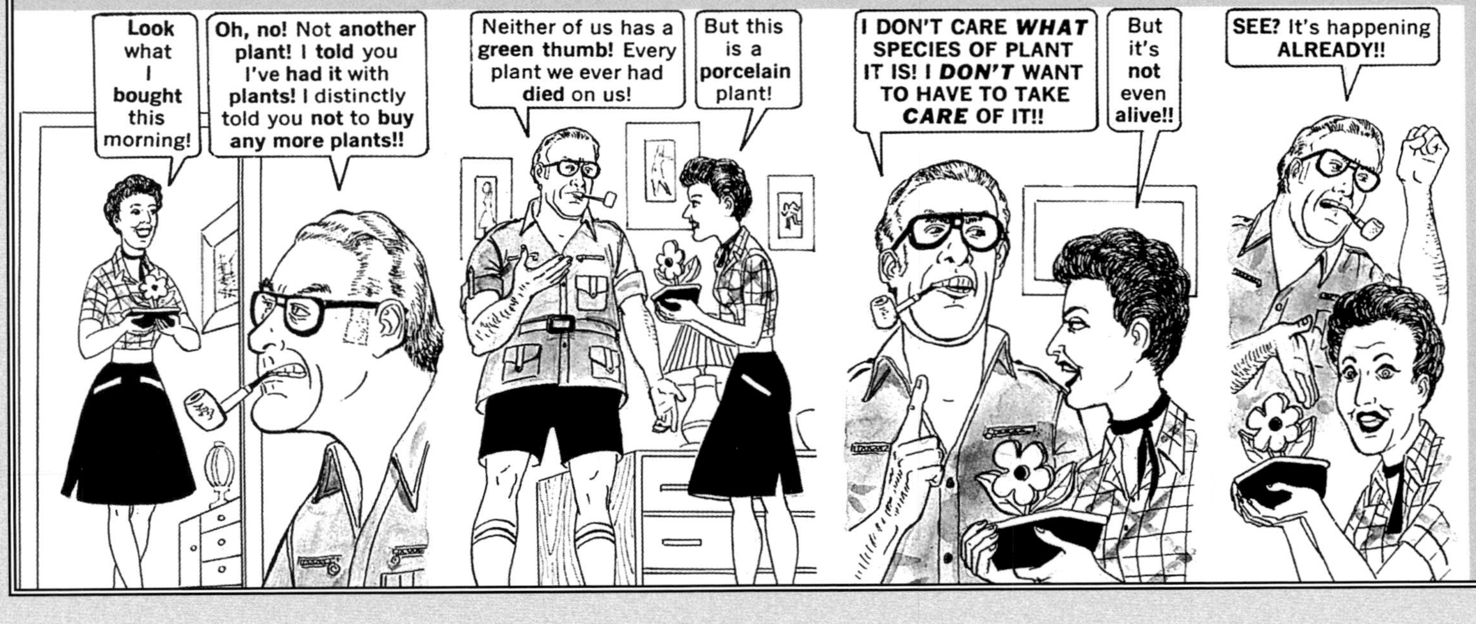
Look what **I bought** this morning!
Oh, no! Not **another plant! I told** you I've **had it** with **plants!** I distinctly told you **not to buy any more plants!!**
Neither of us has a **green thumb!** Every plant we ever had **died** on us!
But this is a **porcelain** plant!
I DON'T CARE ***WHAT*** SPECIES OF PLANT IT IS! I ***DON'T*** WANT TO HAVE TO TAKE ***CARE*** OF IT!!
But it's **not** even **alive!!**
SEE? It's happening **ALREADY!!**

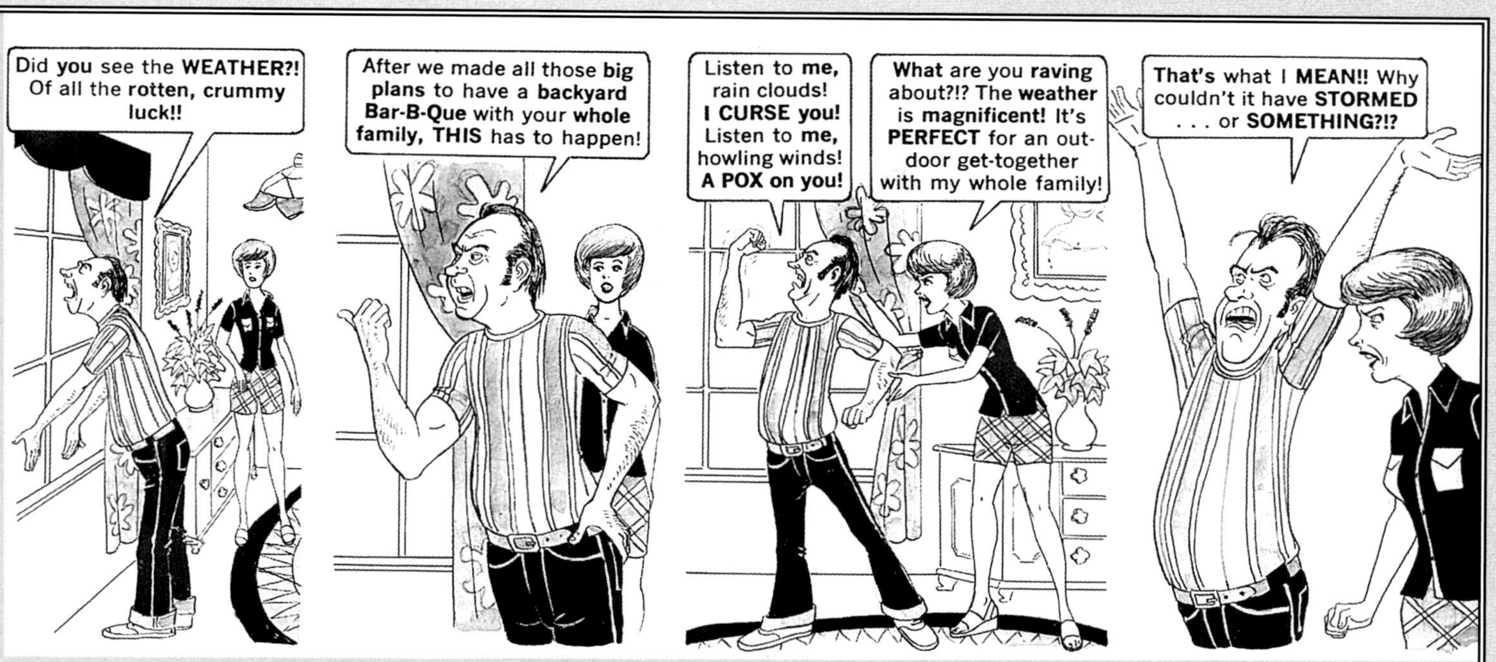
Did you see the WEATHER?! Of all the rotten, crummy luck!!
After we made all those big plans to have a backyard Bar-B-Que with your whole family, THIS has to happen!
Listen to me, rain clouds! I CURSE you! Listen to me, howling winds! A POX on you!
What are you raving about?!? The weather is magnificent! It's PERFECT for an out-door get-together with my whole family!
That's what I MEAN!! Why couldn't it have STORMED . . . or SOMETHING?!?

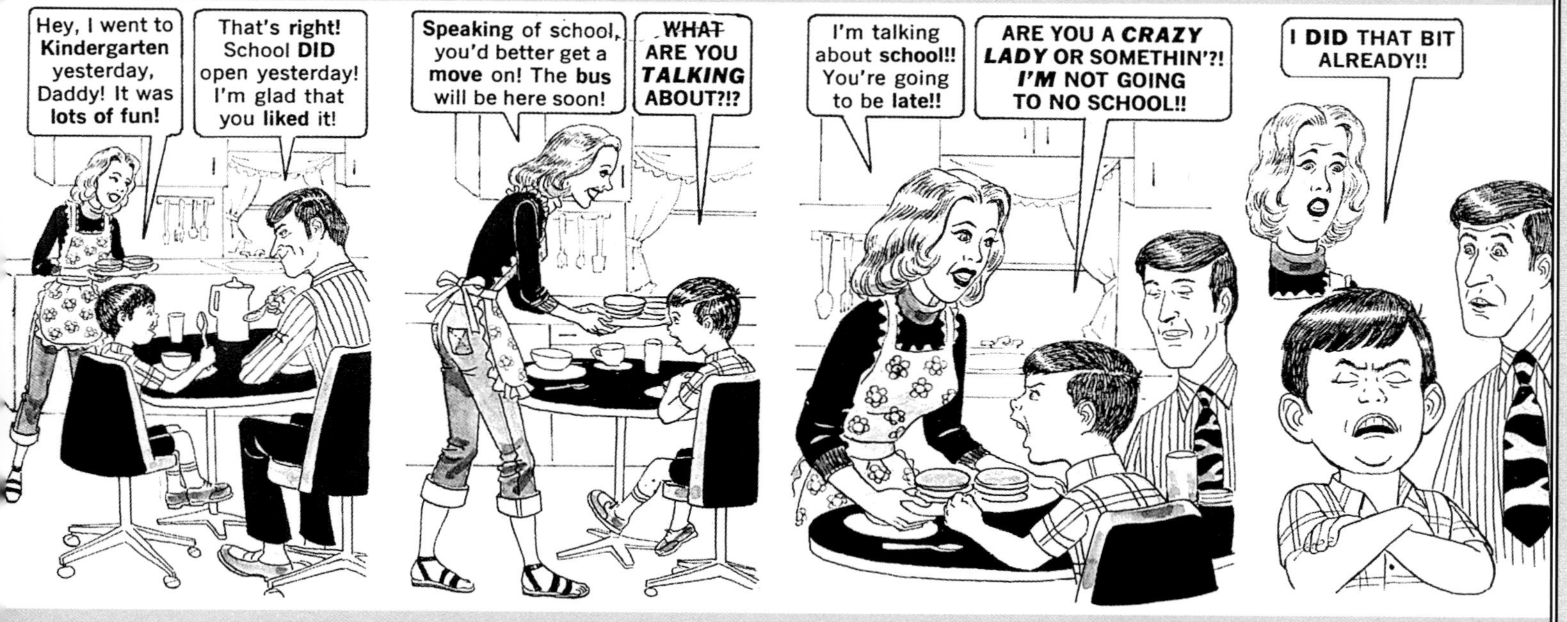
Hey, I went to Kindergarten yesterday, Daddy! It was lots of fun!
That's right! School DID open yesterday! I'm glad that you liked it!
Speaking of school, you'd better get a move on! The bus will be here soon!
WHAT ARE YOU TALKING ABOUT?!?
I'm talking about school!! You're going to be late!!
ARE YOU A CRAZY LADY OR SOMETHIN'?! I'M NOT GOING TO NO SCHOOL!!
I DID THAT BIT ALREADY!!

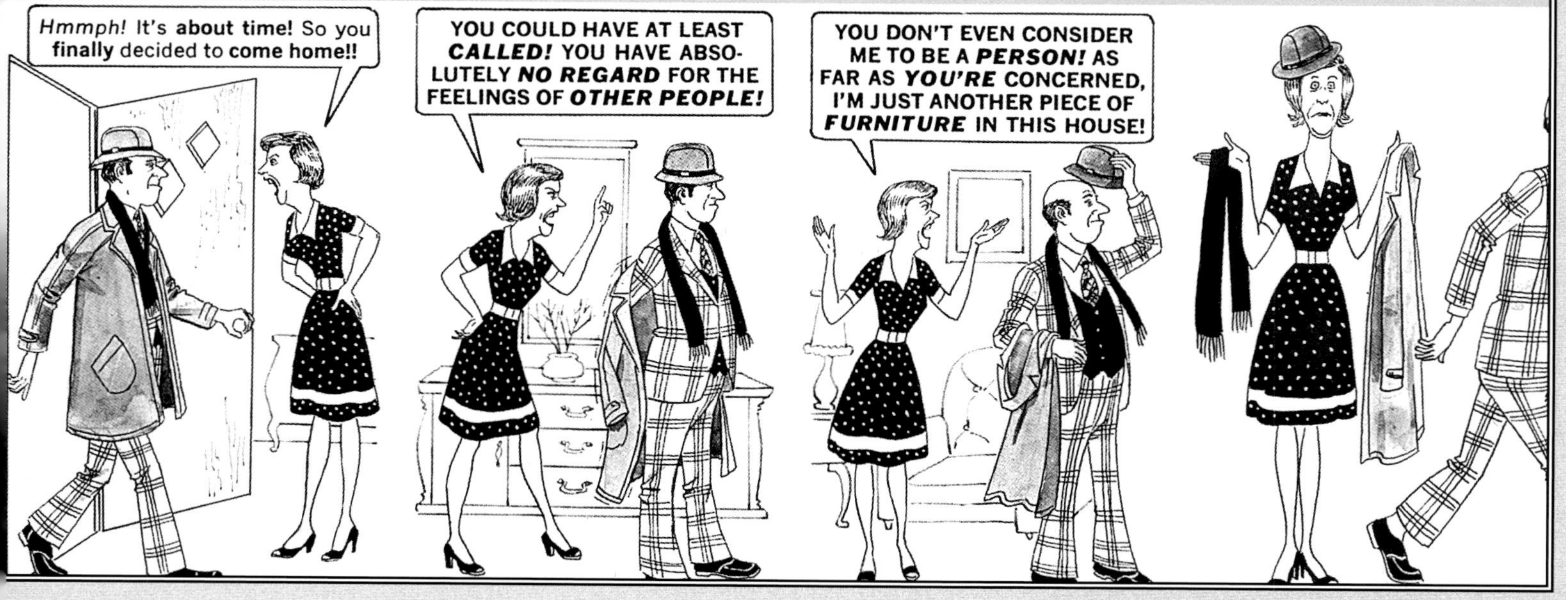
Hmmph! It's about time! So you finally decided to come home!!
YOU COULD HAVE AT LEAST CALLED! YOU HAVE ABSOLUTELY NO REGARD FOR THE FEELINGS OF OTHER PEOPLE!
YOU DON'T EVEN CONSIDER ME TO BE A PERSON! AS FAR AS YOU'RE CONCERNED, I'M JUST ANOTHER PIECE OF FURNITURE IN THIS HOUSE!

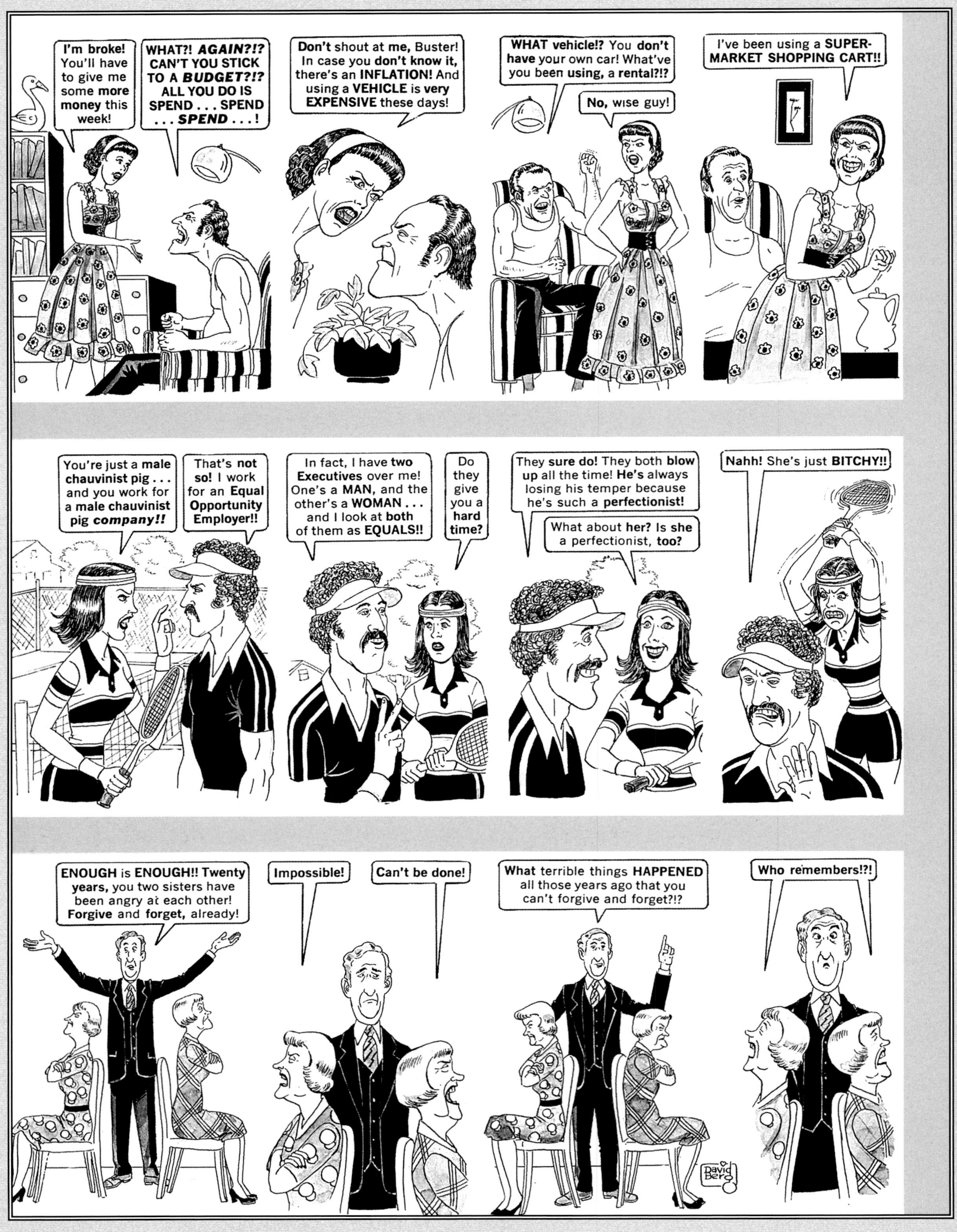
I'm broke! You'll have to give me some more money this week!
WHAT?! AGAIN?!? CAN'T YOU STICK TO A BUDGET?!? ALL YOU DO IS SPEND . . . SPEND . . . SPEND . . . !
Don't shout at me, Buster! In case you don't know it, there's an INFLATION! And using a VEHICLE is very EXPENSIVE these days!
WHAT vehicle!? You don't have your own car! What've you been using, a rental?!?
No, wise guy!
I've been using a SUPER-MARKET SHOPPING CART!!
You're just a male chauvinist pig . . . and you work for a male chauvinist pig company!!
That's not so! I work for an Equal Opportunity Employer!!
In fact, I have two Executives over me! One's a MAN, and the other's a WOMAN . . . and I look at both of them as EQUALS!!
Do they give you a hard time?
They sure do! They both blow up all the time! He's always losing his temper because he's such a perfectionist!
What about her? Is she a perfectionist, too?
Nahh! She's just BITCHY!!
ENOUGH is ENOUGH!! Twenty years, you two sisters have been angry at each other! Forgive and forget, already!
Impossible!
Can't be done!
What terrible things HAPPENED all those years ago that you can't forgive and forget?!?
Who remembers!?!
David Berg

Dave Berg, MAD Model

MAD contributors are often tapped to serve as models in photo shoots for the magazine, and Dave was no exception.

Dave portrays "The Shmo" in this page from "Popular Photo-Monotony," written by Dick DeBartolo, photography by Irving Schild, MAD #175, June 1975

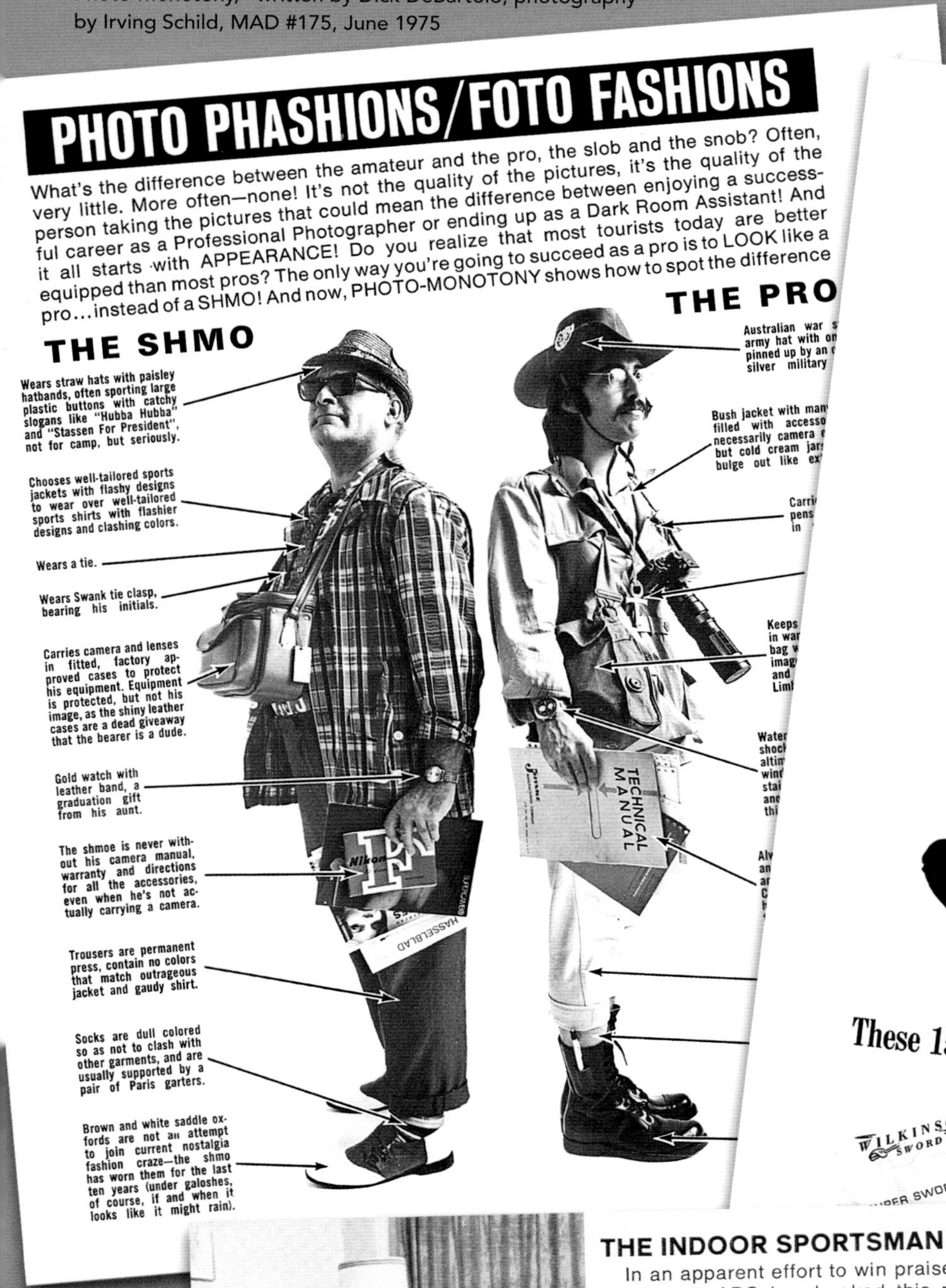

PHOTO PHASHIONS/FOTO FASHIONS
What's the difference between the amateur and the pro, the slob and the snob? Often, very little. More often—none! It's not the quality of the pictures, it's the quality of the person taking the pictures that could mean the difference between enjoying a successful career as a Professional Photographer or ending up as a Dark Room Assistant! And it all starts with APPEARANCE! Do you realize that most tourists today are better equipped than most pros? The only way you're going to succeed as a pro is to LOOK like a pro...instead of a SHMO! And now, PHOTO-MONOTONY shows how to spot the difference
THE SHMO
THE PRO
Wears straw hats with paisley hatbands, often sporting large plastic buttons with catchy slogans like "Hubba Hubba" and "Stassen For President", not for camp, but seriously.
Chooses well-tailored sports jackets with flashy designs to wear over well-tailored sports shirts with flashier designs and clashing colors.
Wears a tie.
Wears Swank tie clasp, bearing his initials.
Carries camera and lenses in fitted, factory approved cases to protect his equipment. Equipment is protected, but not his image, as the shiny leather cases are a dead giveaway that the bearer is a dude.
Gold watch with leather band, a graduation gift from his aunt.
The shmoe is never without his camera manual, warranty and directions for all the accessories, even when he's not actually carrying a camera.
Trousers are permanent press, contain no colors that match outrageous jacket and gaudy shirt.
Socks are dull colored so as not to clash with other garments, and are usually supported by a pair of Paris garters.
Brown and white saddle oxfords are not an attempt to join current nostalgia fashion craze—the shmo has worn them for the last ten years (under galoshes, of course, if and when it looks like it might rain).
Nikon
HASSELBLAD
TECHNICAL MANUAL

Dave is kneeling on the right, in a "Wilkinson Super Sword-Edge Blades," ad parody that included fellow MAD men Bob Clarke, George Woodbridge, John Putnam, Jerry DeFuccio, Sergio Aragonés, Lenny Brenner and Al Jaffee, among others. From MAD #86, April, 1964

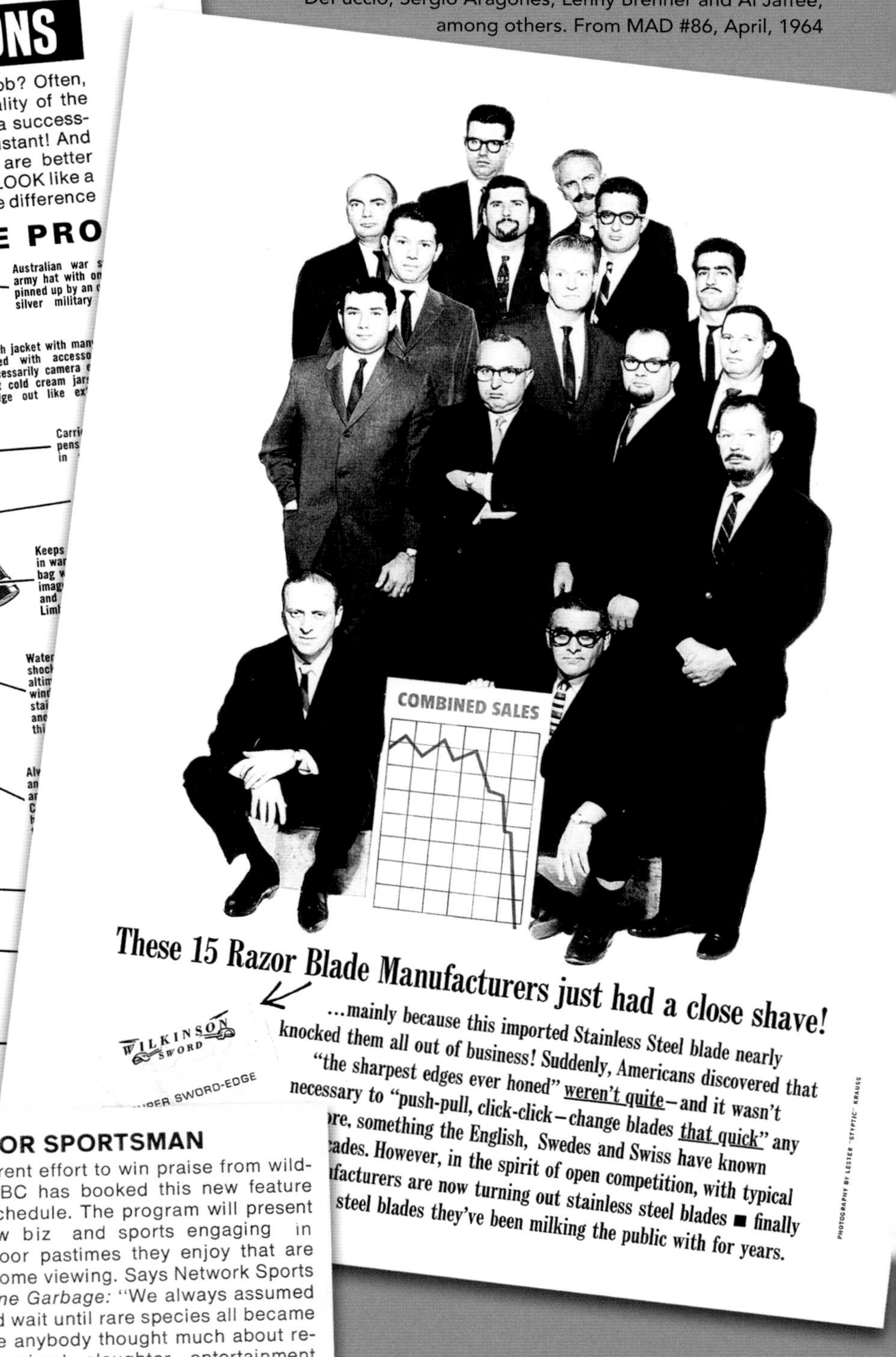

COMBINED SALES
These 15 Razor Blade Manufacturers just had a close shave!
WILKINSON SWORD
...mainly because this imported Stainless Steel blade nearly knocked them all out of business! Suddenly, Americans discovered that "the sharpest edges ever honed" weren't quite–and it wasn't necessary to "push-pull, click-click–change blades that quick" any
PHOTOGRAPHY BY LESTER "STYPTIC" KRAUSS

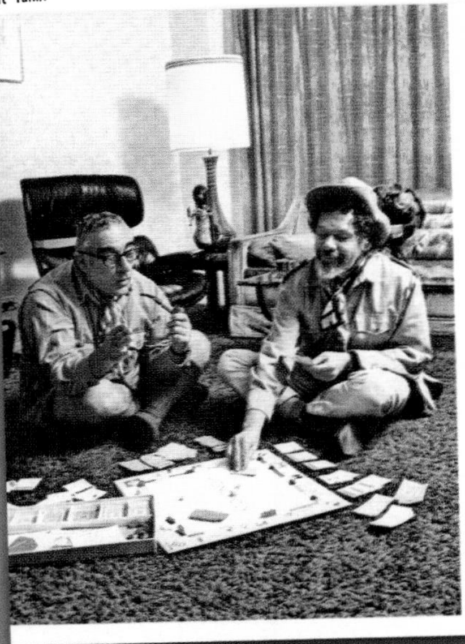

THE INDOOR SPORTSMAN

In an apparent effort to win praise from wildlife lovers, ABC has booked this new feature into its fall schedule. The program will present stars of show biz and sports engaging in whatever indoor pastimes they enjoy that are suitable for home viewing. Says Network Sports Director *Roone Garbage:* "We always assumed that TV would wait until rare species all became extinct before anybody thought much about replacing its animal slaughter entertainment shows. But recent surveys indicate that when you've seen one wart hog stalked by Phil Harris, you've seen them all."

Slated for early guest appearances on "The Indoor Sportsman" are *Frank Sinatra* trying to make six the hard way in Las Vegas, *Jackie Gleason* going after a new pizza consumption record in Miami Beach, *Hugh Hefner* fishing for bunnies in his Chicago office and *Charles Manson* playing solitaire on Death Row at San Quentin.

Saturday, 4 P.M.

Adventurer Dave shares a game of Monopoly with Al Jaffee in The Indoor Sportsman, part of a "TV Guise" parody written by Tom Koch and photographed by Irving Schild, MAD Super Special #8, Winter 1972

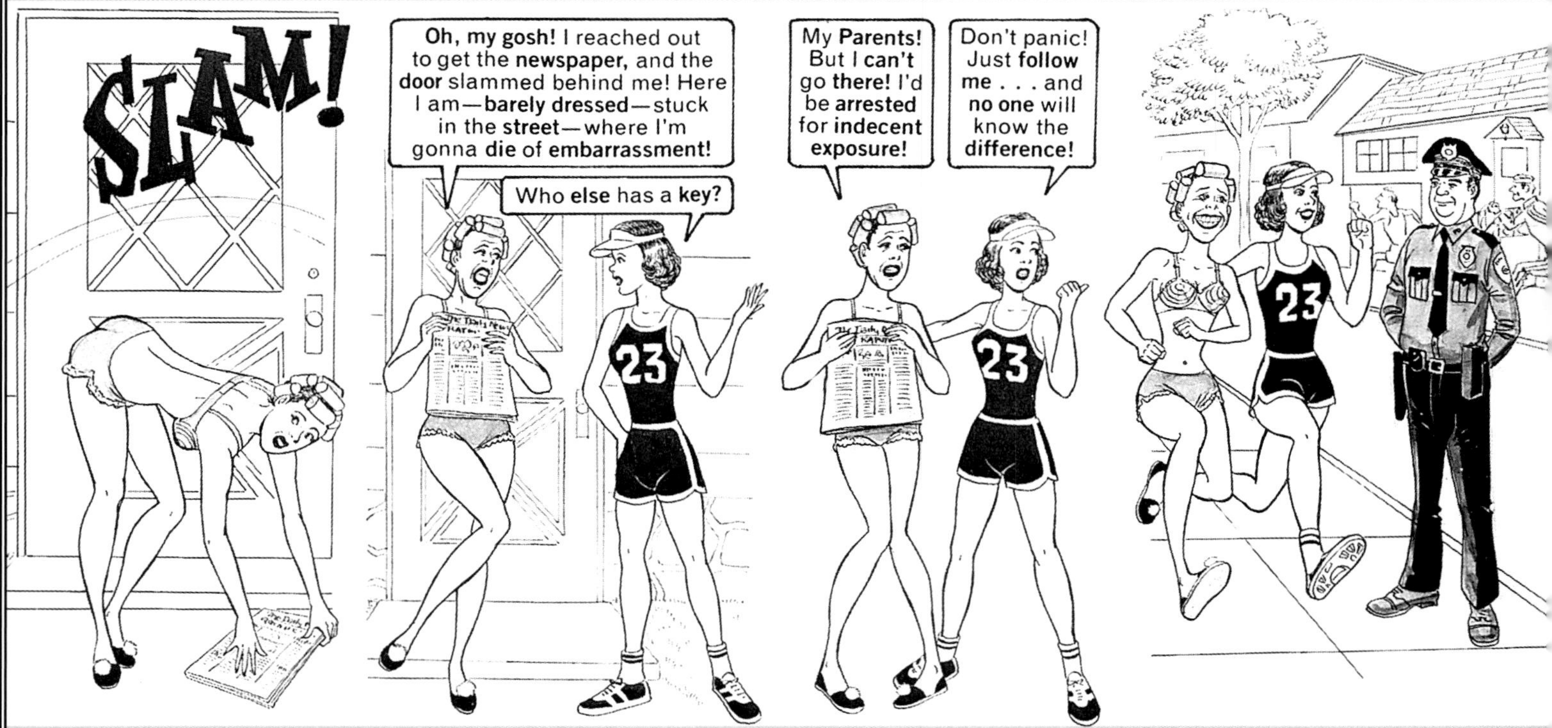
SLAM!
Oh, my gosh! I reached out to get the newspaper, and the door slammed behind me! Here I am—barely dressed—stuck in the street—where I'm gonna die of embarrassment!
Who else has a key?
My Parents! But I can't go there! I'd be arrested for indecent exposure!
Don't panic! Just follow me . . . and no one will know the difference!
23
23
23

BERG'S-EYE VIEW DEPT.

THE LIGHTER SIDE OF... BO

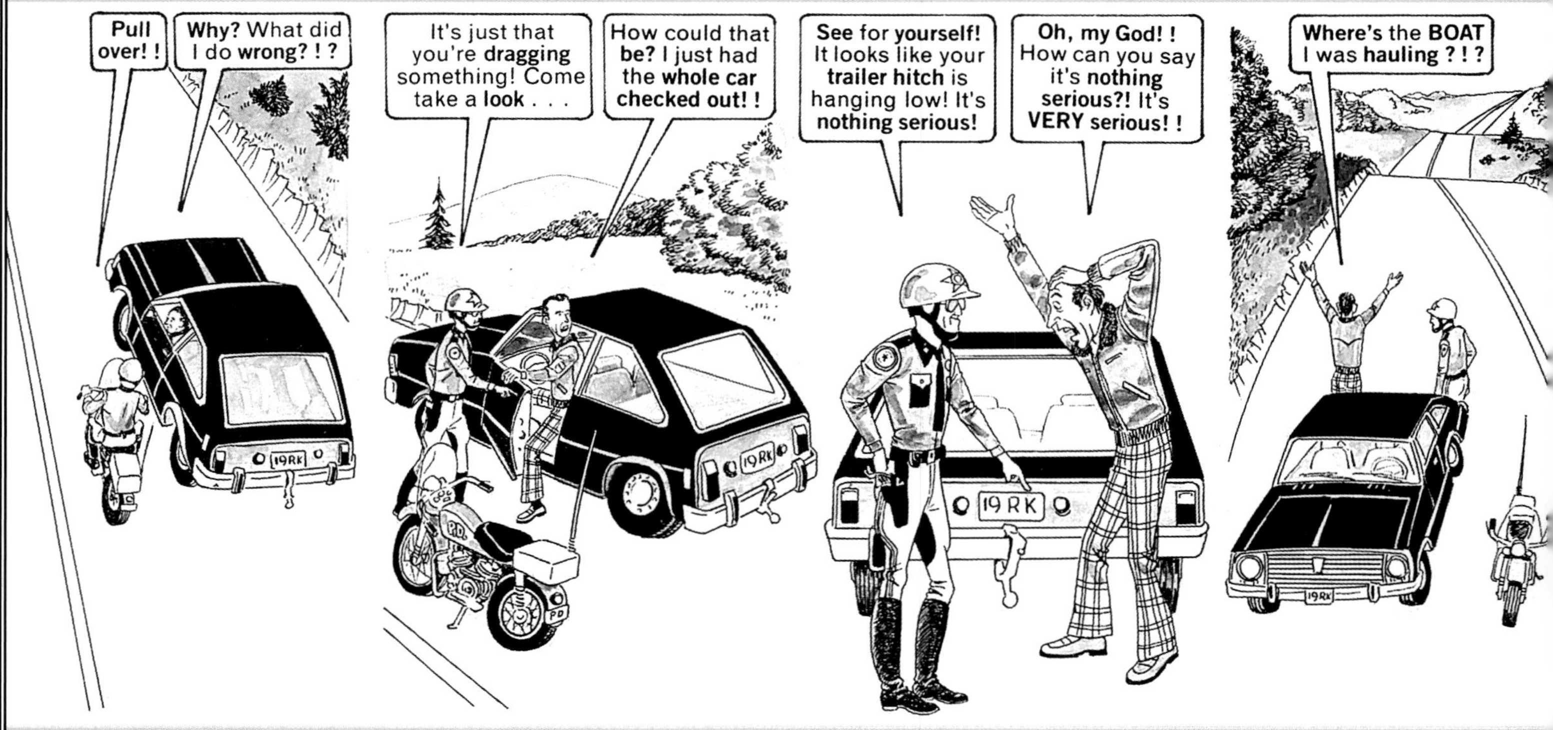
Pull over! !
Why? What did I do wrong? ! ?
It's just that you're dragging something! Come take a look . . .
How could that be? I just had the whole car checked out! !
See for yourself! It looks like your trailer hitch is hanging low! It's nothing serious!
Oh, my God! ! How can you say it's nothing serious?! It's VERY serious! !
Where's the BOAT I was hauling ? ! ?
19RK
19 RK

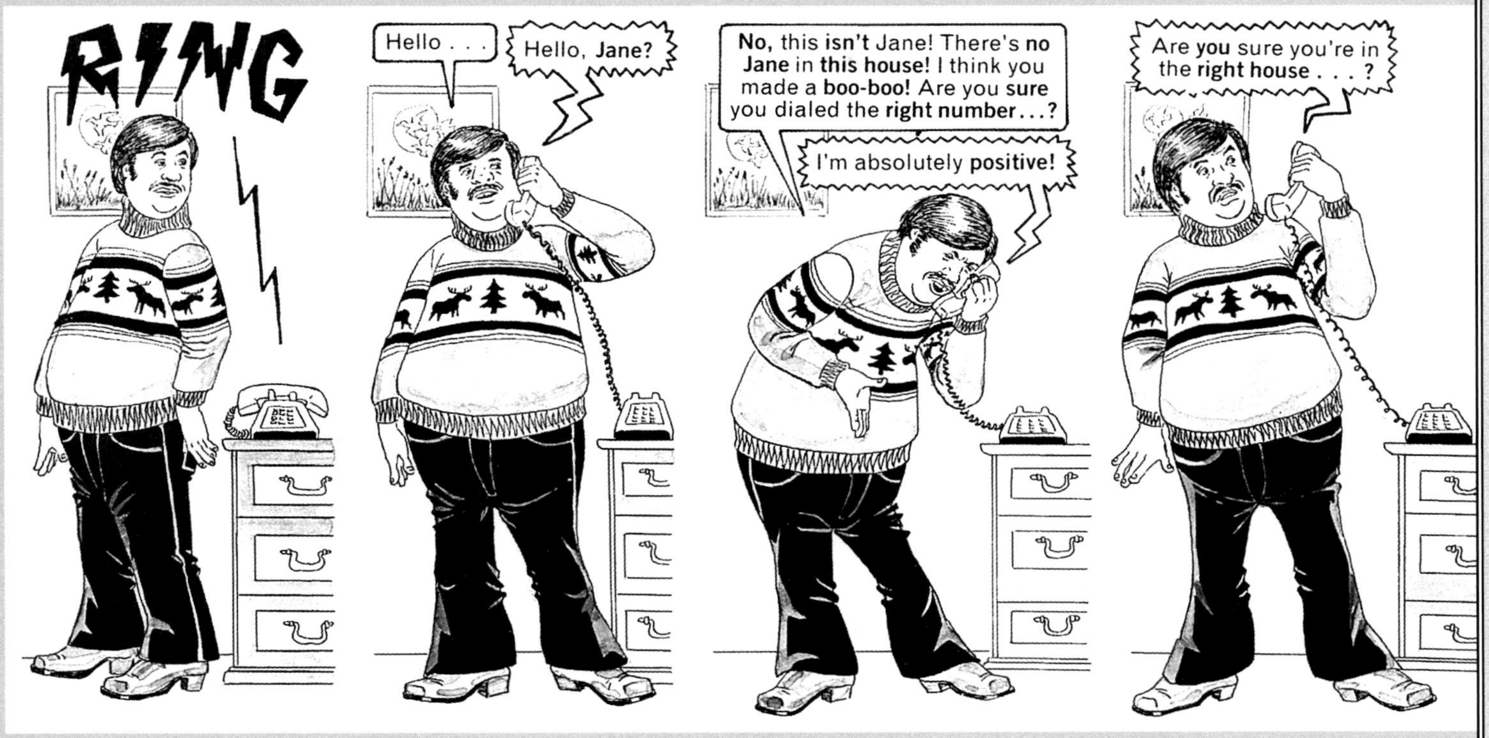
RING
Hello . . .
Hello, Jane?
No, this isn't Jane! There's no Jane in this house! I think you made a boo-boo! Are you sure you dialed the right number . . . ?
I'm absolutely positive!
Are you sure you're in the right house . . . ?

O-BOOS

ARTIST & WRITER:
DAVE BERG

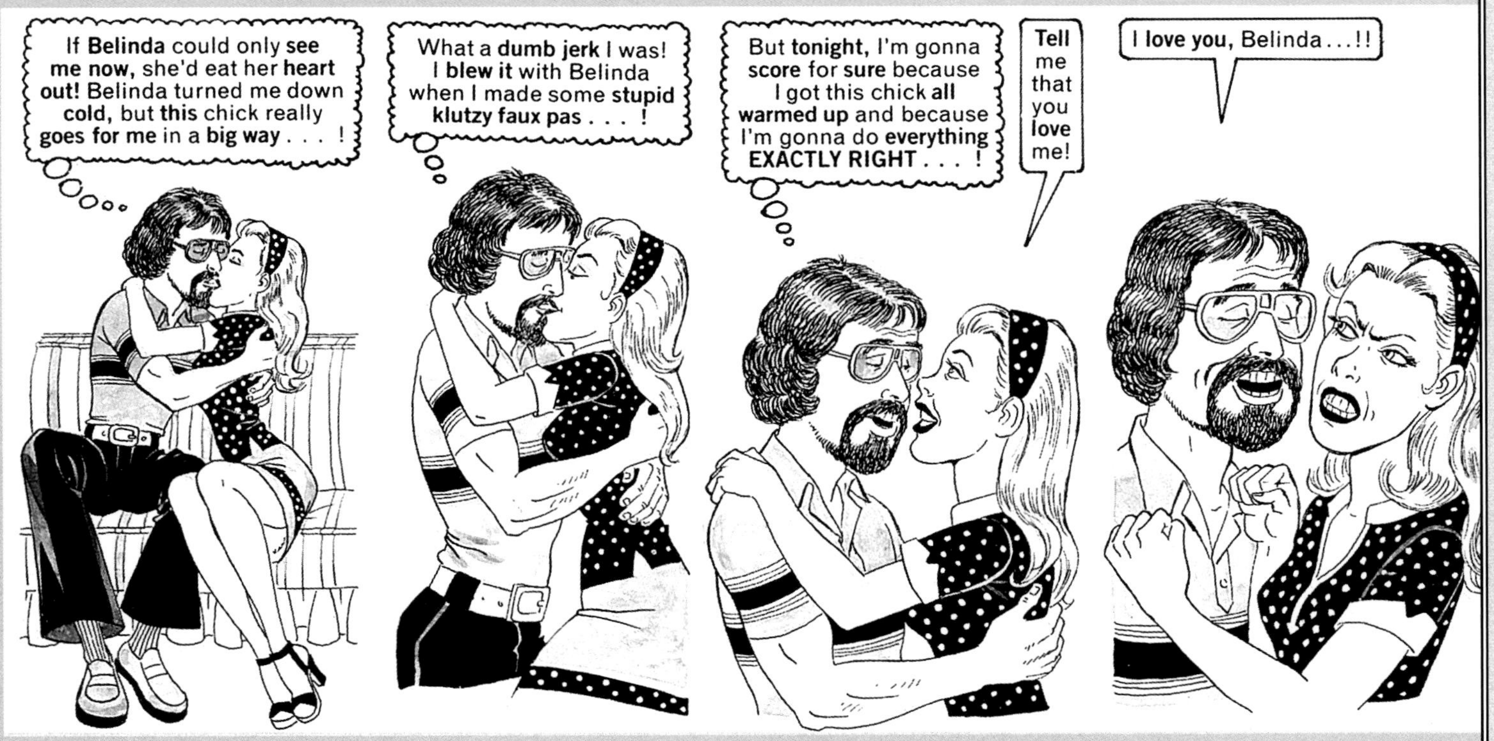
If Belinda could only see me now, she'd eat her heart out! Belinda turned me down cold, but this chick really goes for me in a big way . . . !
What a dumb jerk I was! I blew it with Belinda when I made some stupid klutzy faux pas . . . !
But tonight, I'm gonna score for sure because I got this chick all warmed up and because I'm gonna do everything EXACTLY RIGHT . . . !
Tell me that you love me!
I love you, Belinda . . . !!

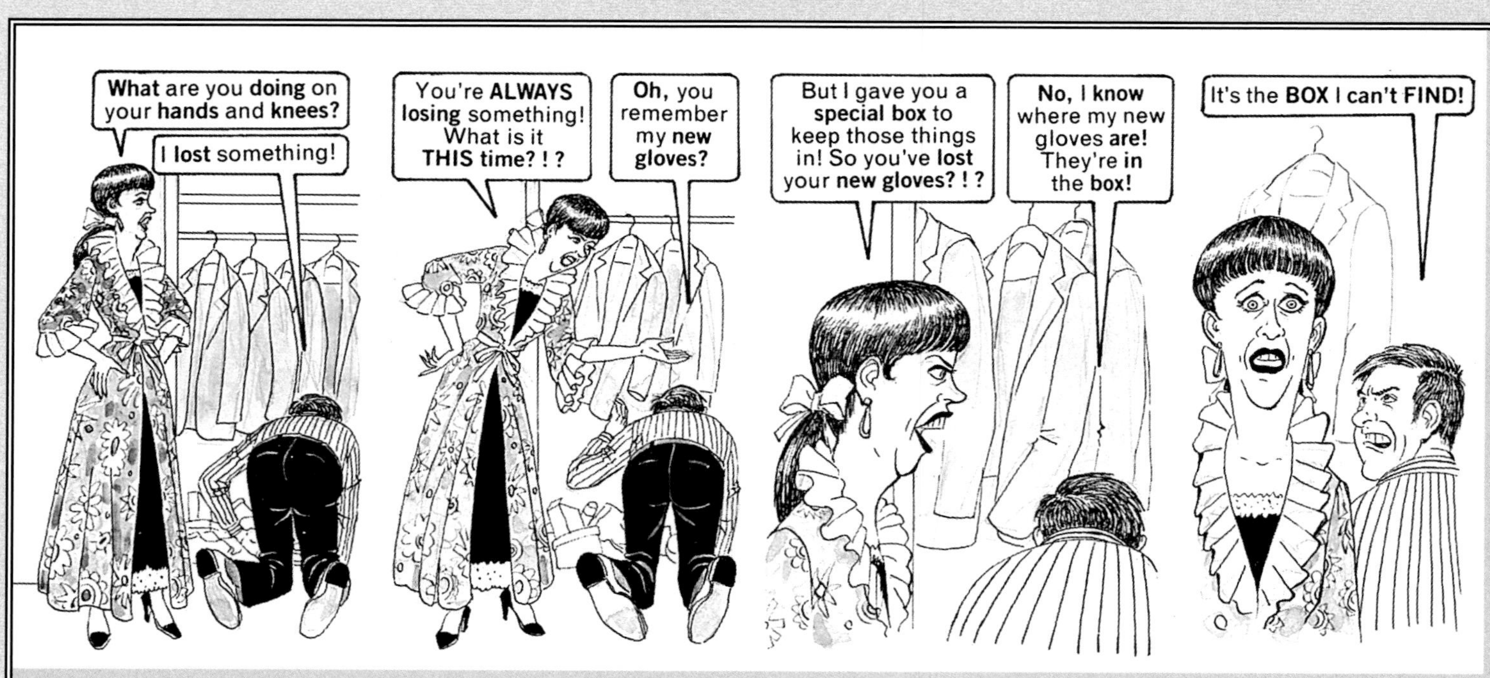
What are you doing on your hands and knees?
I lost something!
You're ALWAYS losing something! What is it THIS time? ! ?
Oh, you remember my new gloves?
But I gave you a special box to keep those things in! So you've lost your new gloves? ! ?
No, I know where my new gloves are! They're in the box!
It's the BOX I can't FIND!

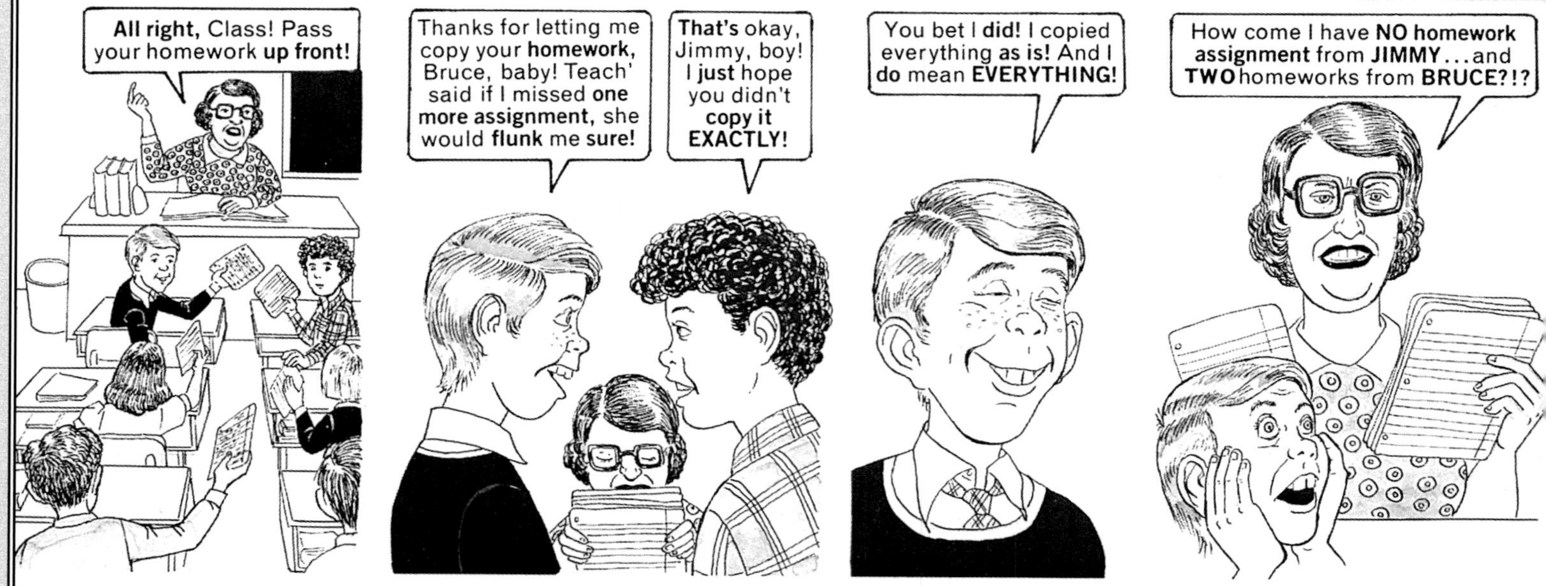
All right, Class! Pass your homework up front!
Thanks for letting me copy your homework, Bruce, baby! Teach' said if I missed one more assignment, she would flunk me sure!
That's okay, Jimmy, boy! I just hope you didn't copy it EXACTLY!
You bet I did! I copied everything as is! And I do mean EVERYTHING!
How come I have NO homework assignment from JIMMY...and TWO homeworks from BRUCE?!?

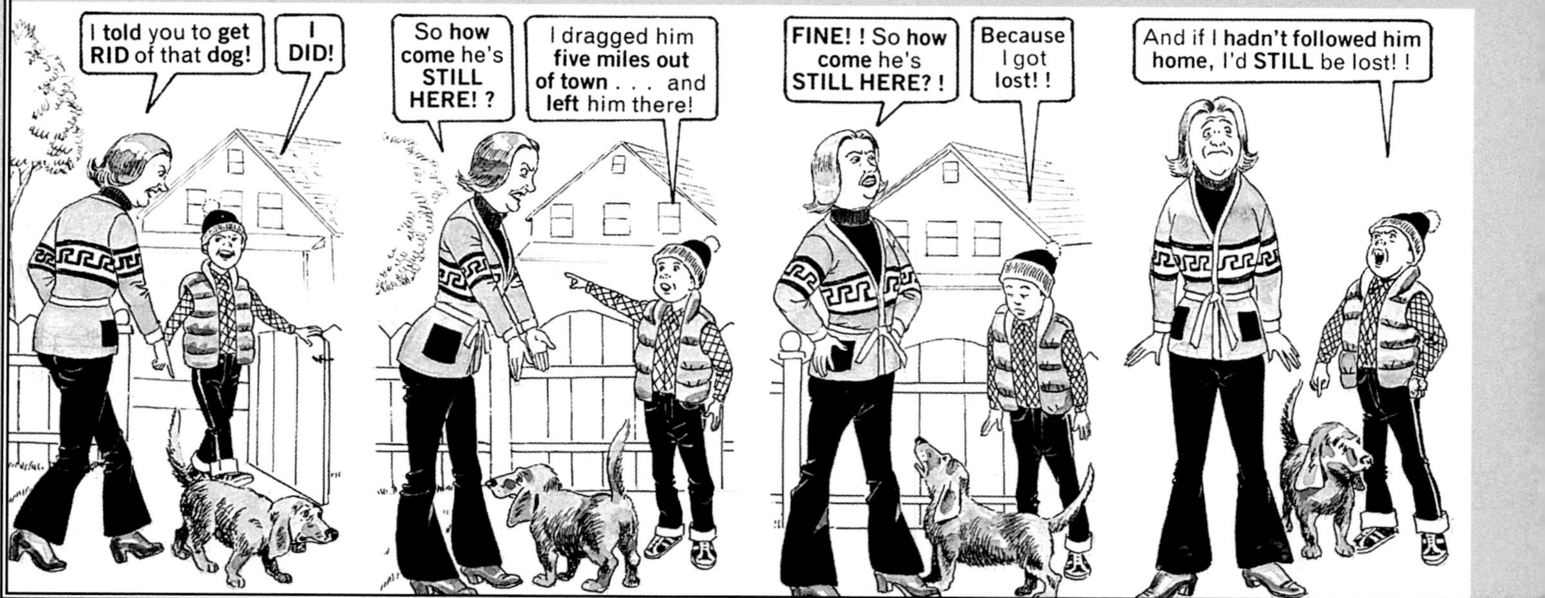
I told you to get RID of that dog!
I DID!
So how come he's STILL HERE! ?
I dragged him five miles out of town . . . and left him there!
FINE! ! So how come he's STILL HERE? !
Because I got lost! !
And if I hadn't followed him home, I'd STILL be lost! !

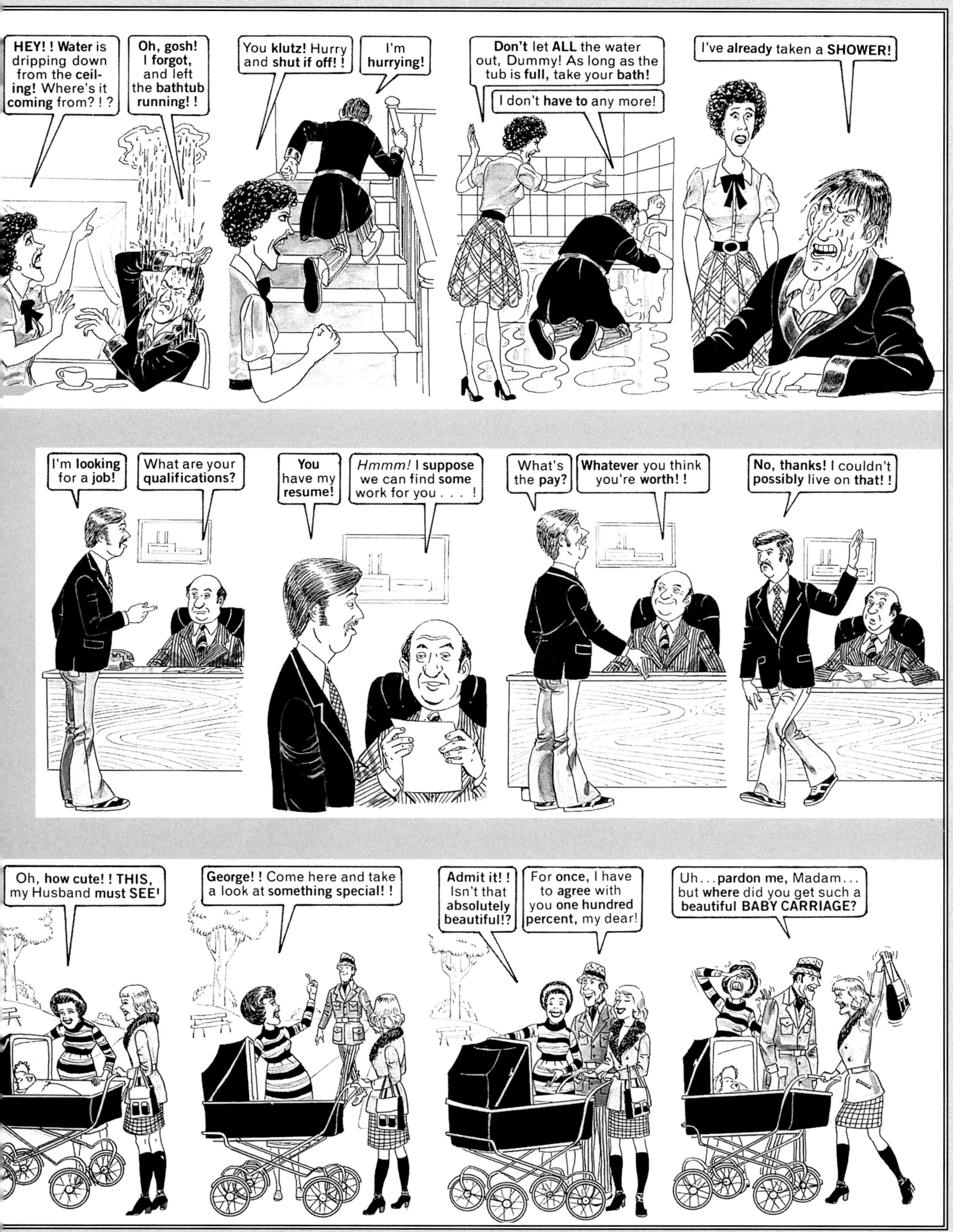
HEY! ! Water is dripping down from the ceil-ing! Where's it coming from? ! ?
Oh, gosh! I forgot, and left the bathtub running! !
You klutz! Hurry and shut if off! !
I'm hurrying!
Don't let ALL the water out, Dummy! As long as the tub is full, take your bath!
I don't have to any more!
I've already taken a SHOWER!
I'm looking for a job!
What are your qualifications?
You have my resume!
Hmmm! I suppose we can find some work for you . . . !
What's the pay?
Whatever you think you're worth! !
No, thanks! I couldn't possibly live on that! !
Oh, how cute! ! THIS, my Husband must SEE!
George! ! Come here and take a look at something special! !
Admit it! ! Isn't that absolutely beautiful!?
For once, I have to agree with you one hundred percent, my dear!
Uh...pardon me, Madam... but where did you get such a beautiful BABY CARRIAGE?

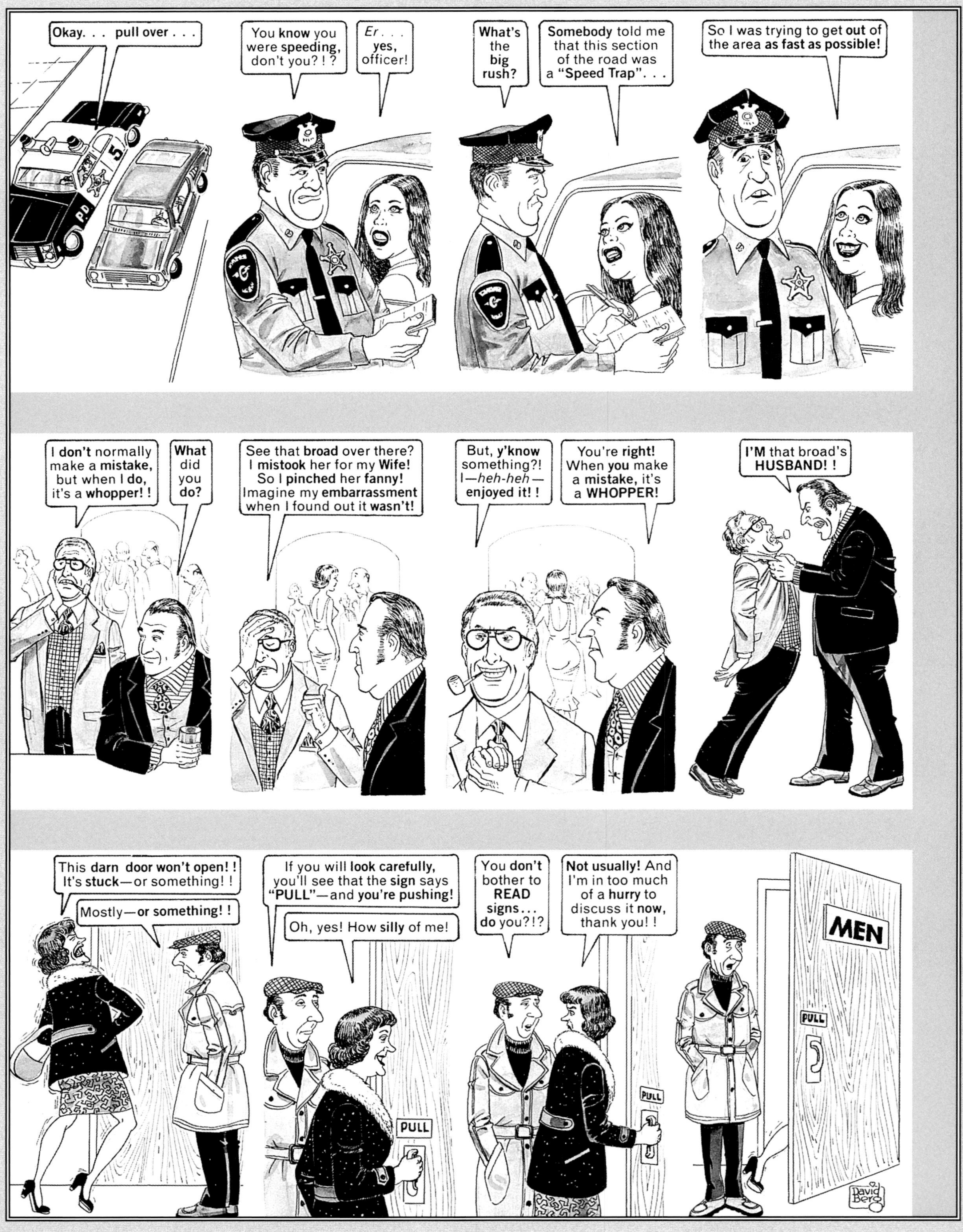
Okay. . . pull over . . .
You know you were speeding, don't you? ! ?
Er . . . yes, officer!
What's the big rush?
Somebody told me that this section of the road was a "Speed Trap". . .
So I was trying to get out of the area as fast as possible!
I don't normally make a mistake, but when I do, it's a whopper! !
What did you do?
See that broad over there? I mistook her for my Wife! So I pinched her fanny! Imagine my embarrassment when I found out it wasn't!
But, y'know something?! I—heh-heh—enjoyed it! !
You're right! When you make a mistake, it's a WHOPPER!
I'M that broad's HUSBAND! !
This darn door won't open! ! It's stuck—or something! !
Mostly—or something! !
If you will look carefully, you'll see that the sign says "PULL"—and you're pushing!
Oh, yes! How silly of me!
You don't bother to READ signs... do you?!?
Not usually! And I'm in too much of a hurry to discuss it now, thank you! !
PULL
PULL
MEN
PULL
David Berg

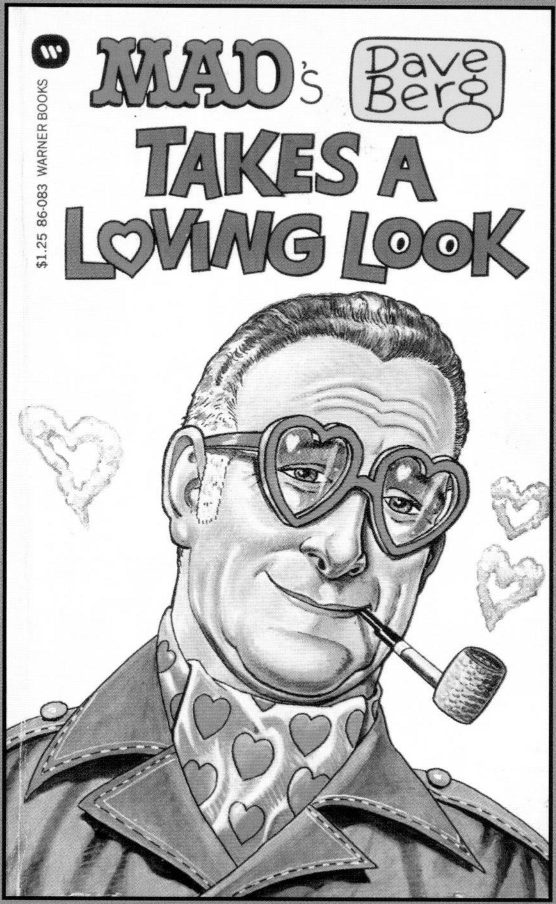
$1.25 86-083 WARNER BOOKS
MAD's Dave Berg
TAKES A LOVING LOOK

1977

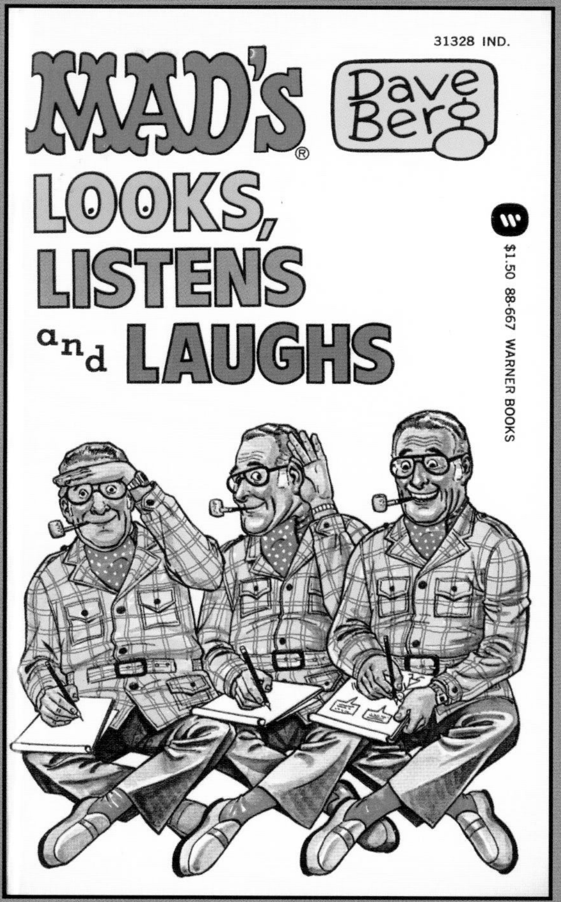
31328 IND.
MAD's® Dave Berg
LOOKS, LISTENS and LAUGHS
$1.50 88-667 WARNER BOOKS

1979

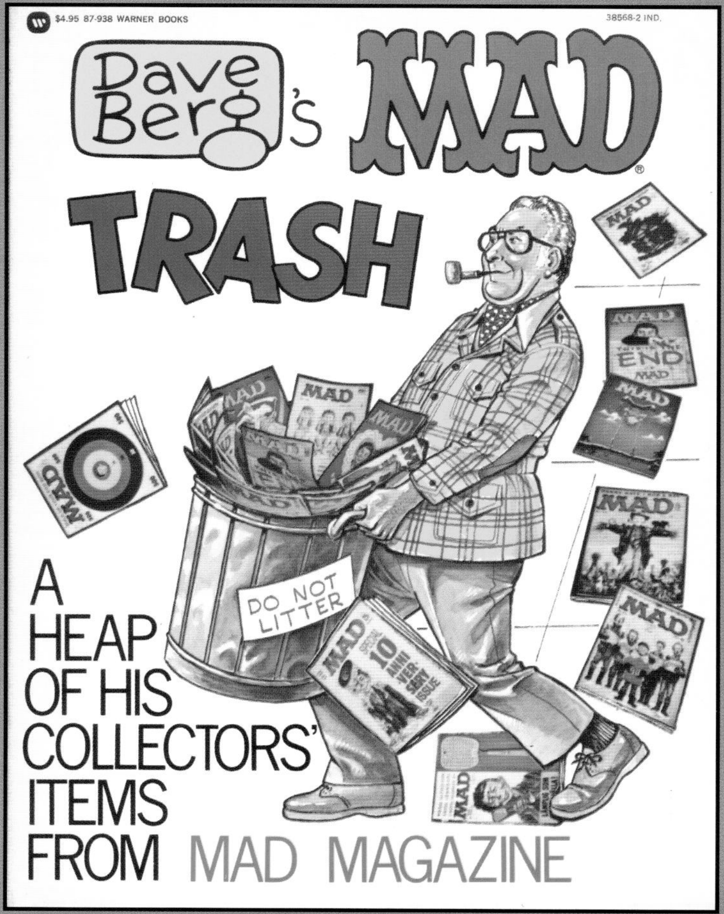
$4.95 87-938 WARNER BOOKS
38568-2 IND.
Dave Berg's MAD® TRASH
DO NOT LITTER
A HEAP OF HIS COLLECTORS' ITEMS FROM MAD MAGAZINE

1977

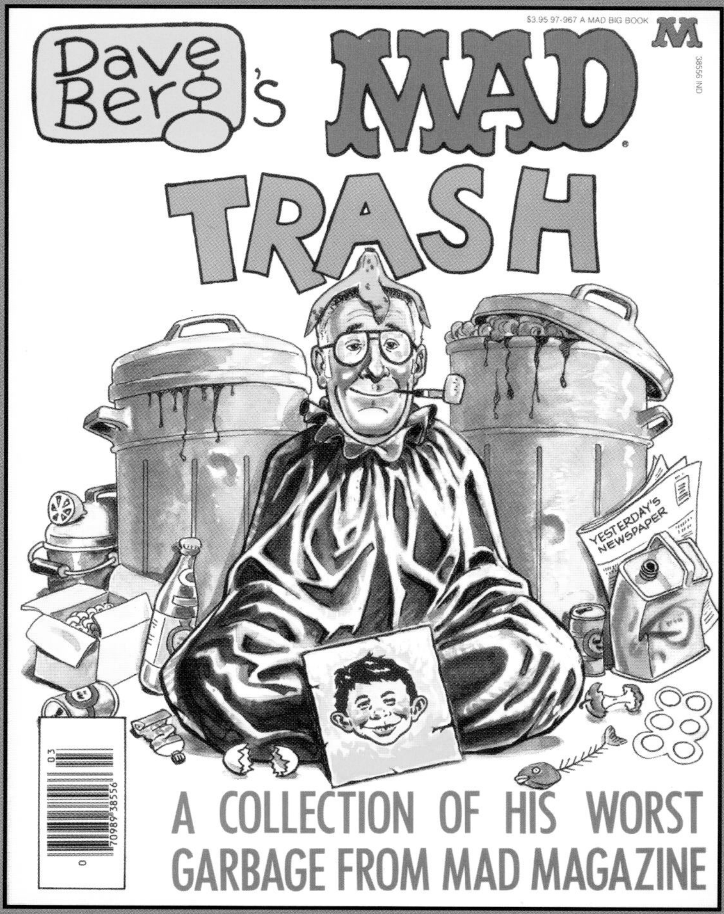
$3.95 97-967 A MAD BIG BOOK
38556 IND
Dave Berg's MAD® TRASH
YESTERDAY'S NEWSPAPER
A COLLECTION OF HIS WORST GARBAGE FROM MAD MAGAZINE

reprint cover 1981

Darn it! We had a surprise test in **Chemistry** today!

I hate when Teachers pull sneaky things like that! They must have **sadistic streaks!** The **least** they could do is give a little **warning!**

We had a **TWO WEEK** warning! We **reviewed** the entire mess of un-intelligible material **every day!** We dealt in **formulas** and **symbols** and **elements!** Most of the time, I didn't know what in heck the Teacher was **talking** about!

And every night, I sweated over **homework** on the same impossible subject matter!

So **why** do you call it a "surprise test"?!?

Because **I PASSED!!**

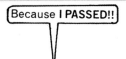

BERG'S-EYE-VIEW DEPT.

THE LIGHTER SIDE OF...

SUR

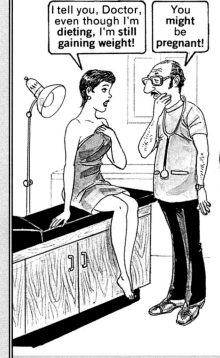

I tell you, Doctor, even though I'm dieting, I'm **still** gaining weight!

You **might** be pregnant!

WHAT?! THAT CAN'T BE!! I USE BIRTH CONTROL PILLS!

That's not a hundred percent certain!

Then **what** is?!

Abstinence!

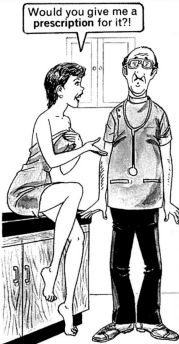

Would you give me a **prescription** for it?!

144

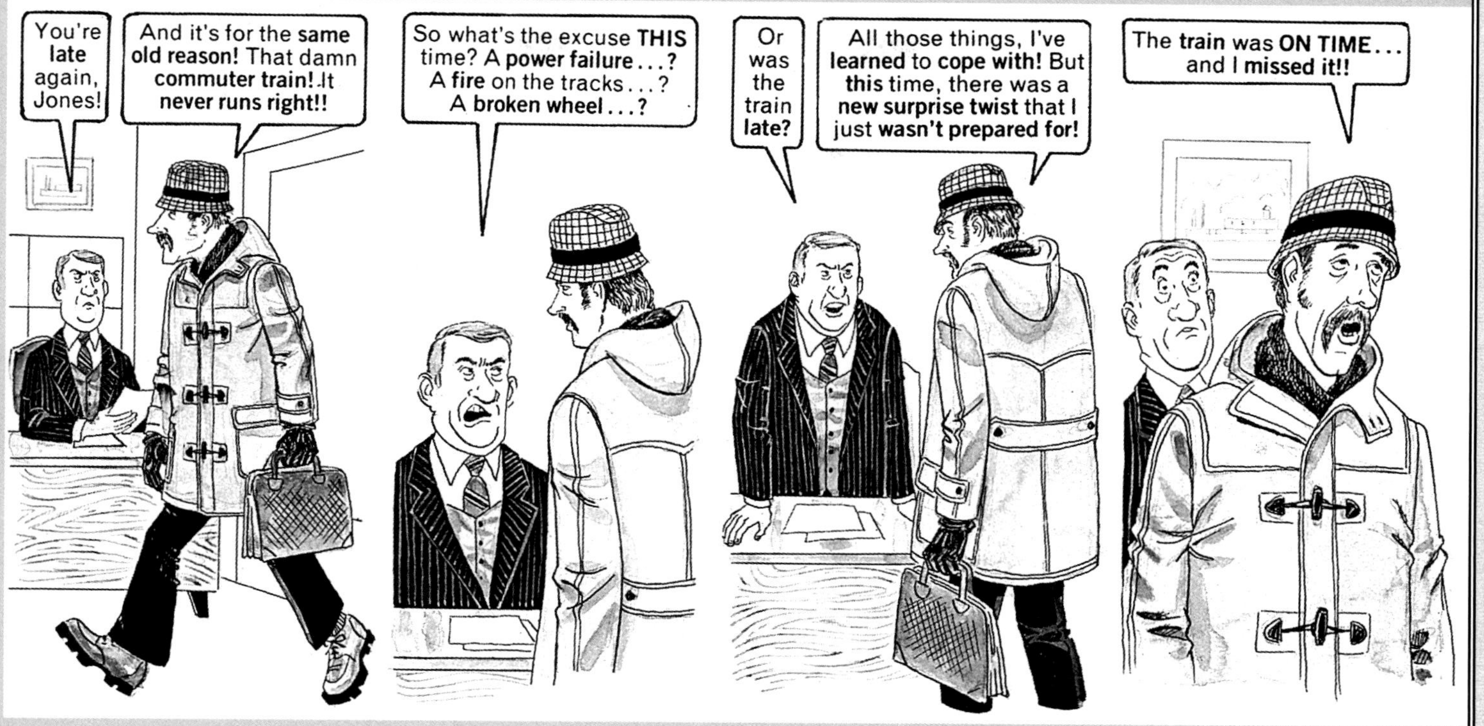
You're late again, Jones!
And it's for the same old reason! That damn commuter train! It never runs right!!
So what's the excuse THIS time? A power failure . . . ? A fire on the tracks . . . ? A broken wheel . . . ?
Or was the train late?
All those things, I've learned to cope with! But this time, there was a new surprise twist that I just wasn't prepared for!
The train was ON TIME . . . and I missed it!!

PRISES

ARTIST & WRITER:
DAVE BERG

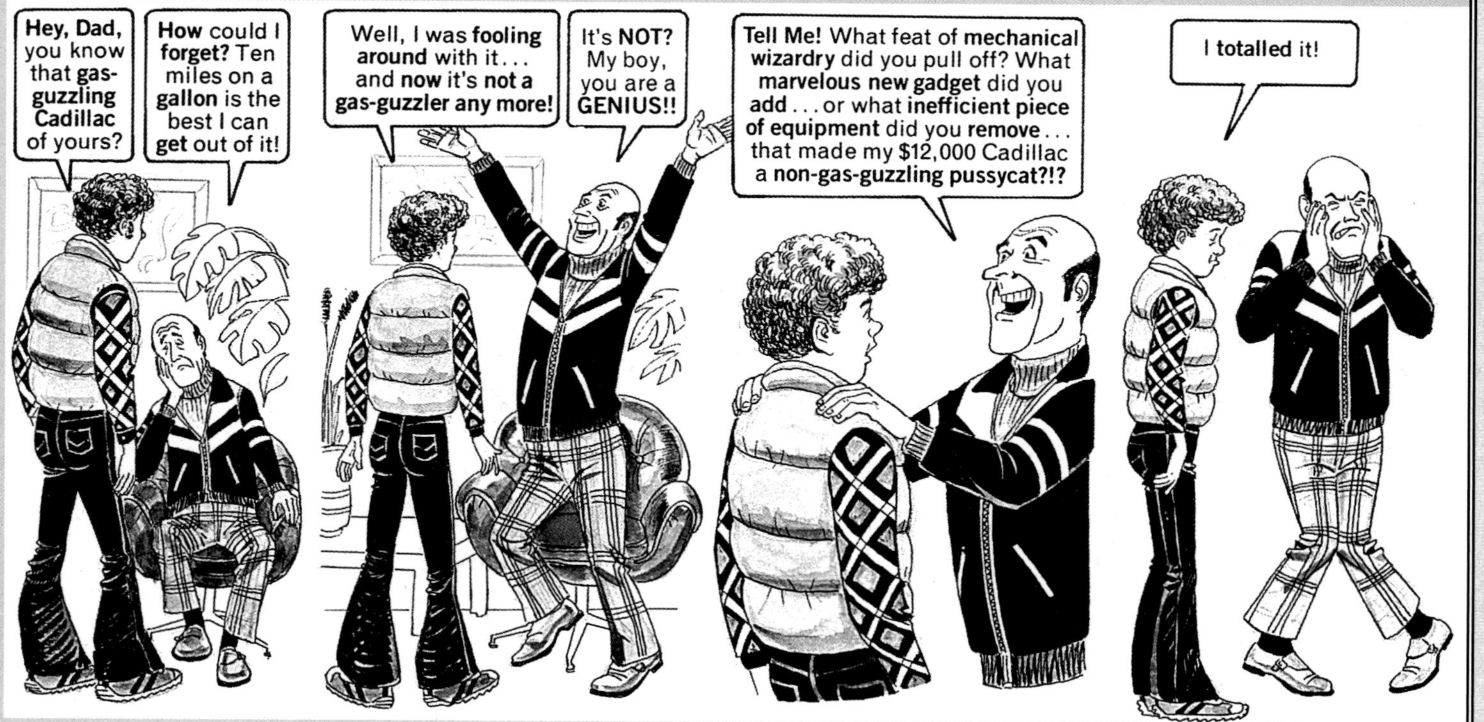
Hey, Dad, you know that gas-guzzling Cadillac of yours?
How could I forget? Ten miles on a gallon is the best I can get out of it!
Well, I was fooling around with it . . . and now it's not a gas-guzzler any more!
It's NOT? My boy, you are a GENIUS!!
Tell Me! What feat of mechanical wizardry did you pull off? What marvelous new gadget did you add . . . or what inefficient piece of equipment did you remove . . . that made my $12,000 Cadillac a non-gas-guzzling pussycat?!?
I totalled it!

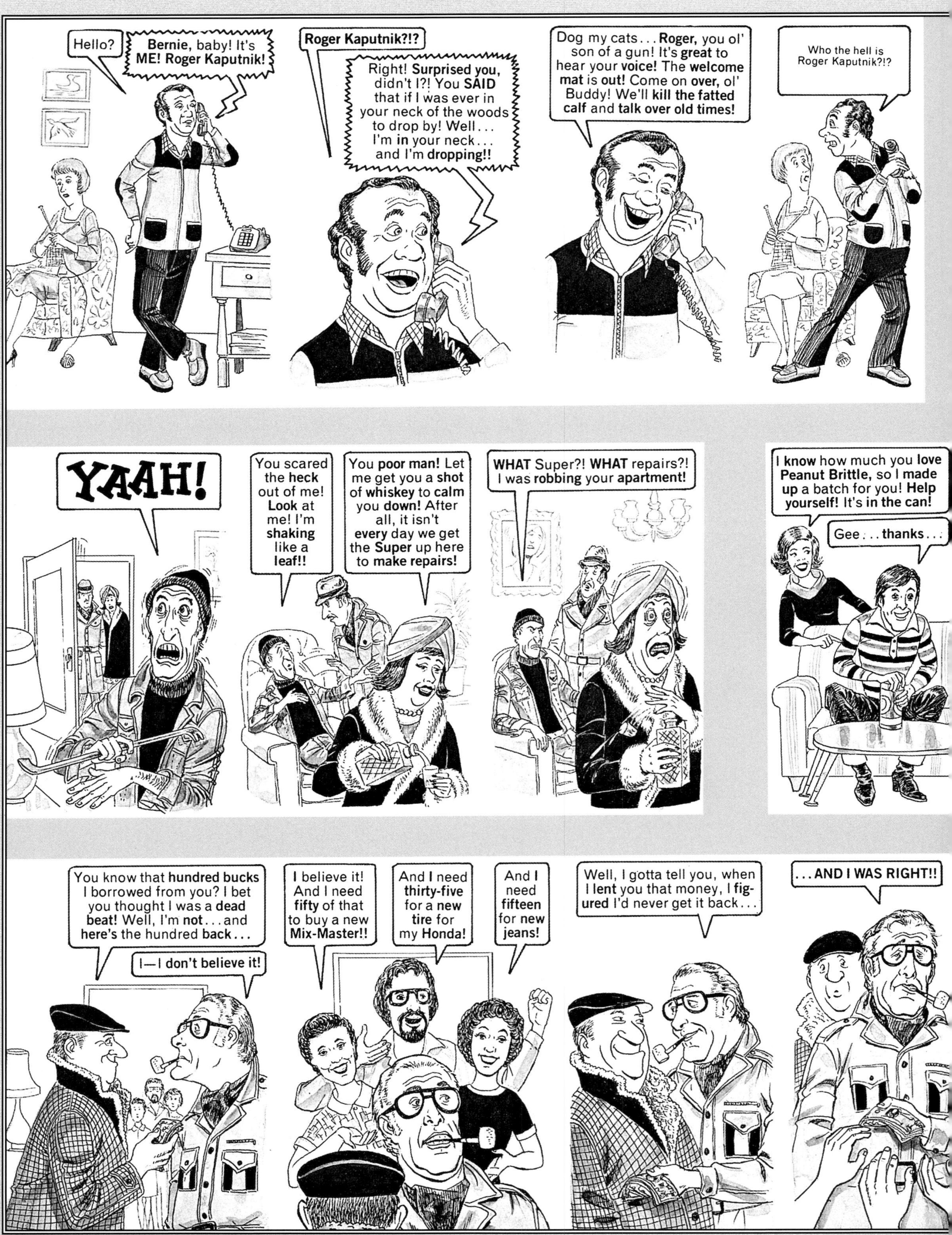
Hello?
Bernie, baby! It's ME! Roger Kaputnik!
Roger Kaputnik?!?
Right! Surprised you, didn't I?! You SAID that if I was ever in your neck of the woods to drop by! Well... I'm in your neck... and I'm dropping!!
Dog my cats... Roger, you ol' son of a gun! It's great to hear your voice! The welcome mat is out! Come on over, ol' Buddy! We'll kill the fatted calf and talk over old times!
Who the hell is Roger Kaputnik?!?
YAAH!
You scared the heck out of me! Look at me! I'm shaking like a leaf!!
You poor man! Let me get you a shot of whiskey to calm you down! After all, it isn't every day we get the Super up here to make repairs!
WHAT Super?! WHAT repairs?! I was robbing your apartment!
I know how much you love Peanut Brittle, so I made up a batch for you! Help yourself! It's in the can!
Gee... thanks...
You know that hundred bucks I borrowed from you? I bet you thought I was a dead beat! Well, I'm not... and here's the hundred back...
I—I don't believe it!
I believe it! And I need fifty of that to buy a new Mix-Master!!
And I need thirty-five for a new tire for my Honda!
And I need fifteen for new jeans!
Well, I gotta tell you, when I lent you that money, I figured I'd never get it back...
... AND I WAS RIGHT!!

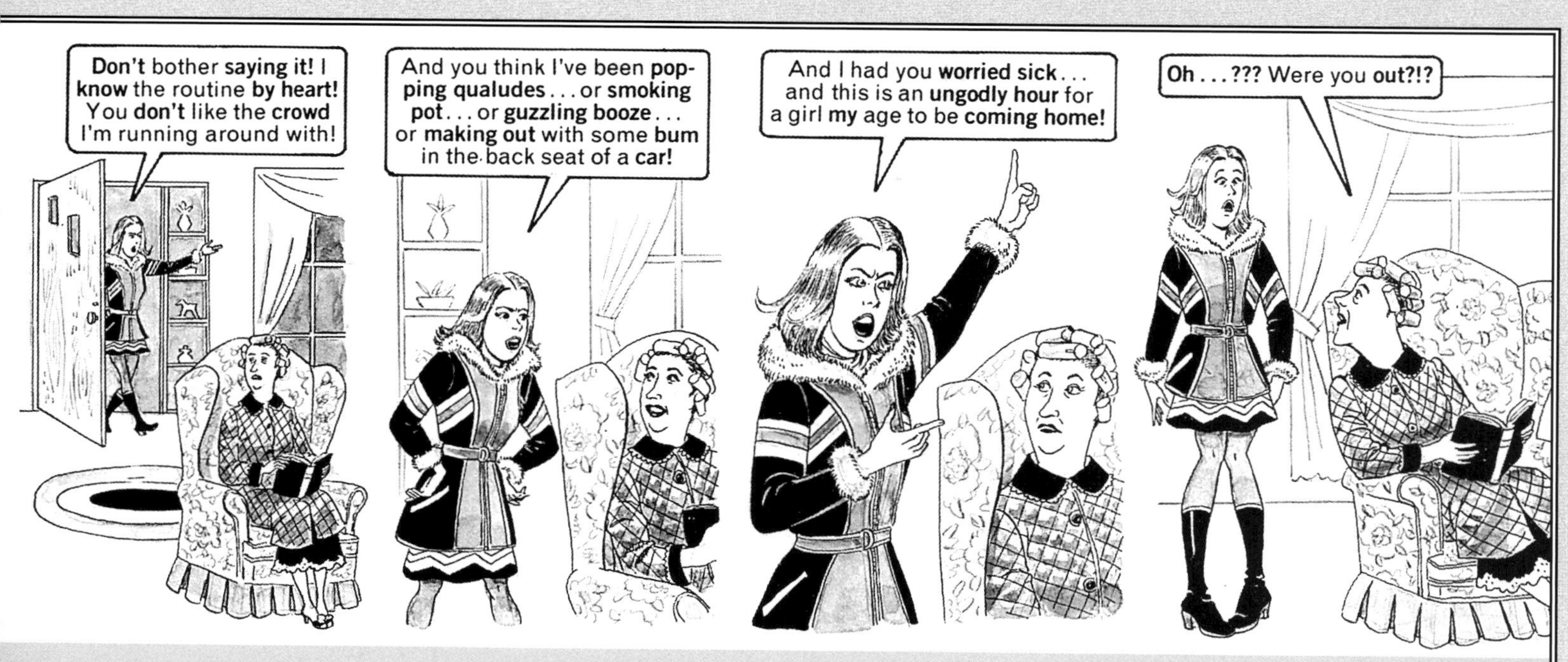
Don't bother saying it! I know the routine by heart! You don't like the crowd I'm running around with!
And you think I've been popping qualudes . . . or smoking pot . . . or guzzling booze . . . or making out with some bum in the back seat of a car!
And I had you worried sick . . . and this is an ungodly hour for a girl my age to be coming home!
Oh . . . ??? Were you out?!?

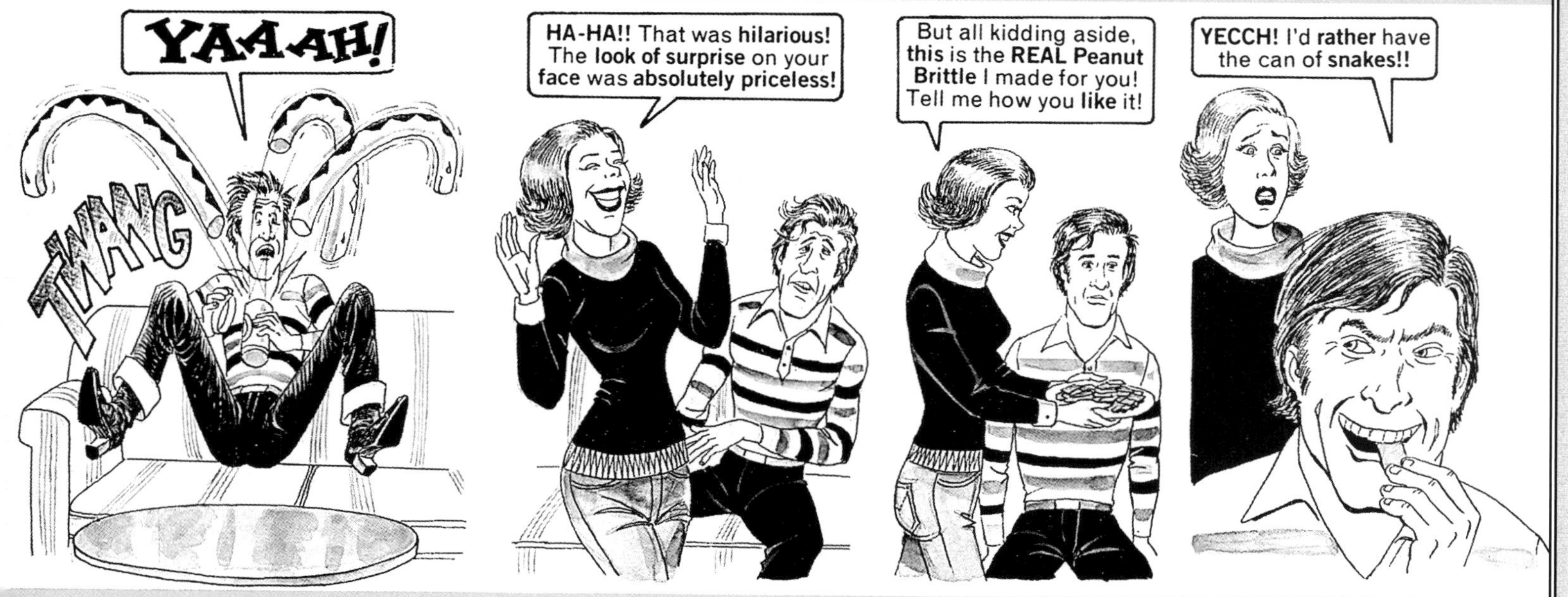
YAAAH!
TWANG
HA-HA!! That was hilarious! The look of surprise on your face was absolutely priceless!
But all kidding aside, this is the REAL Peanut Brittle I made for you! Tell me how you like it!
YECCH! I'd rather have the can of snakes!!

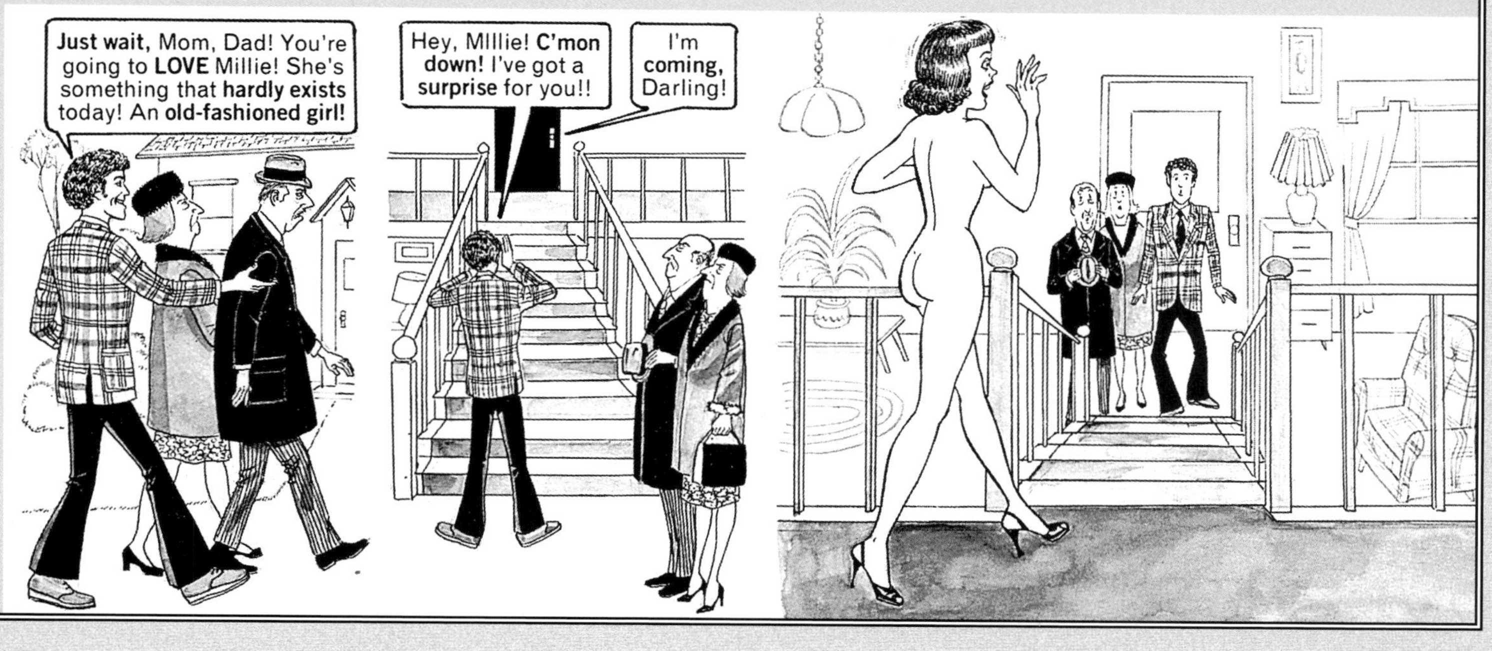
Just wait, Mom, Dad! You're going to LOVE Millie! She's something that hardly exists today! An old-fashioned girl!
Hey, Millie! C'mon down! I've got a surprise for you!!
I'm coming, Darling!

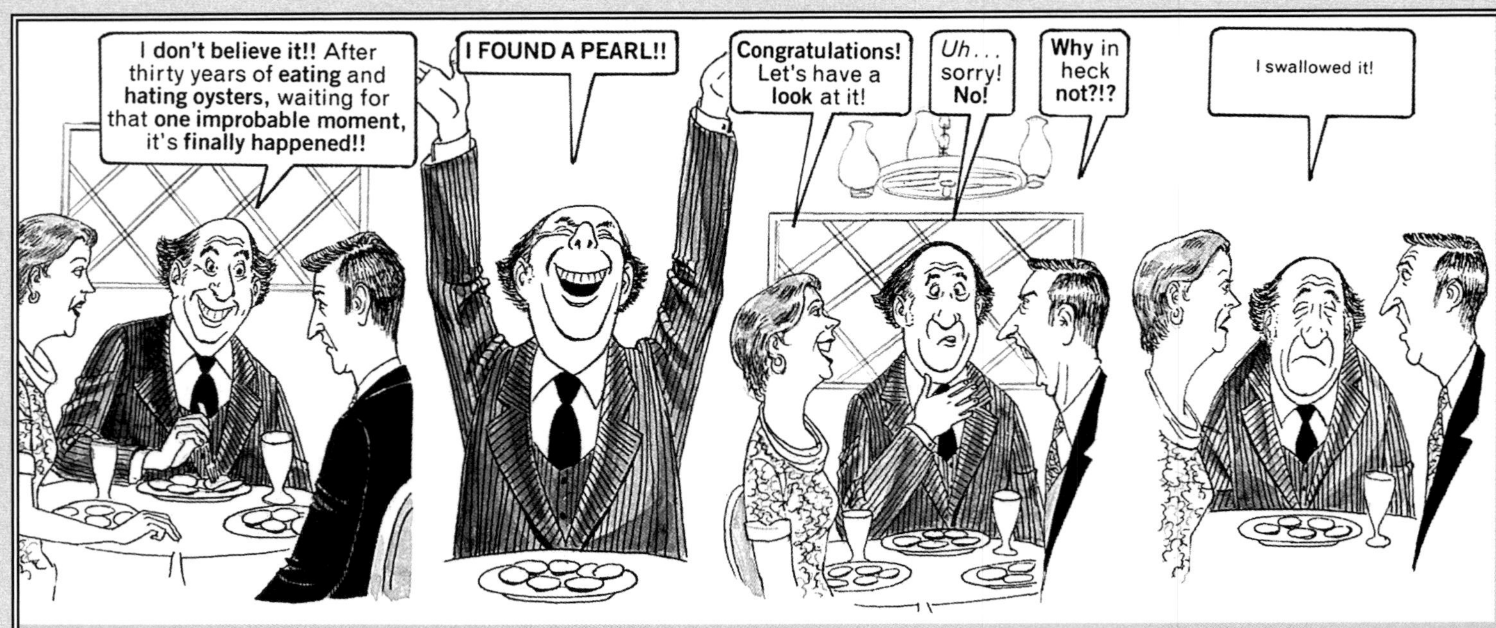
I don't believe it!! After thirty years of eating and hating oysters, waiting for that one improbable moment, it's finally happened!!
I FOUND A PEARL!!
Congratulations! Let's have a look at it!
Uh . . . sorry! No!
Why in heck not?!?
I swallowed it!

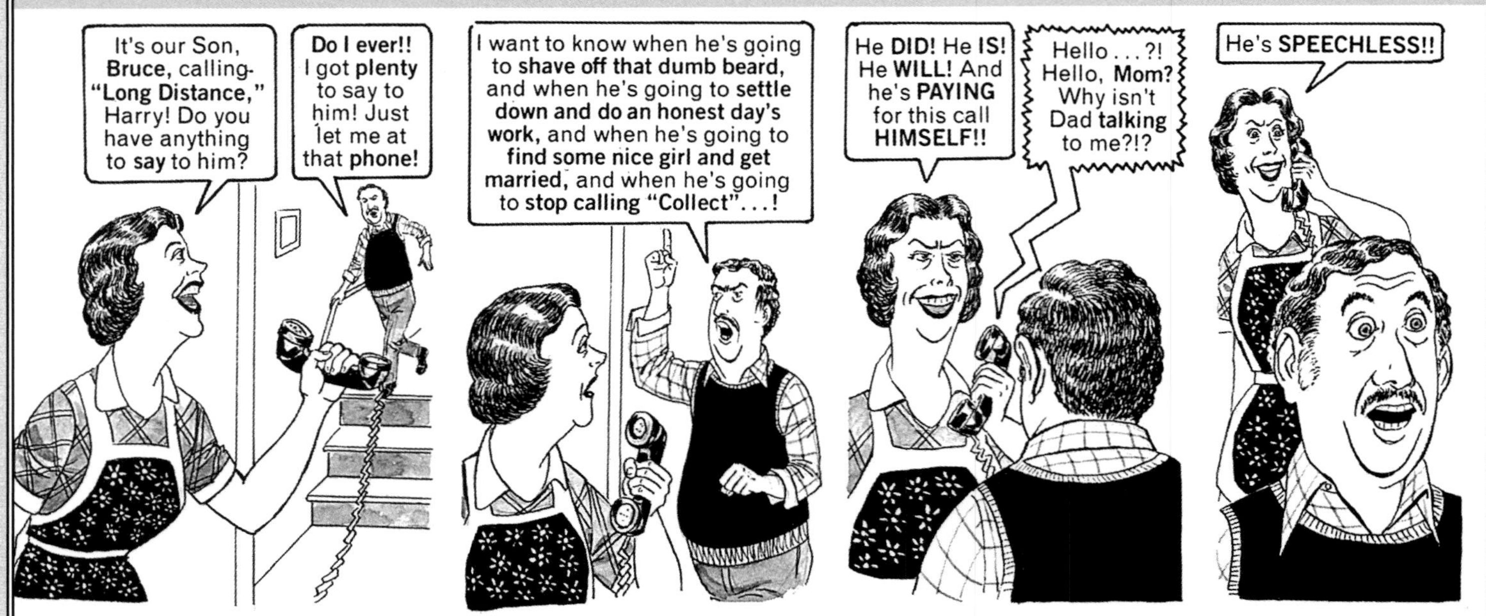
It's our Son, Bruce, calling "Long Distance," Harry! Do you have anything to say to him?
Do I ever!! I got plenty to say to him! Just let me at that phone!
I want to know when he's going to shave off that dumb beard, and when he's going to settle down and do an honest day's work, and when he's going to find some nice girl and get married, and when he's going to stop calling "Collect". . . !
He DID! He IS! He WILL! And he's PAYING for this call HIMSELF!!
Hello . . . ?! Hello, Mom? Why isn't Dad talking to me?!?
He's SPEECHLESS!!

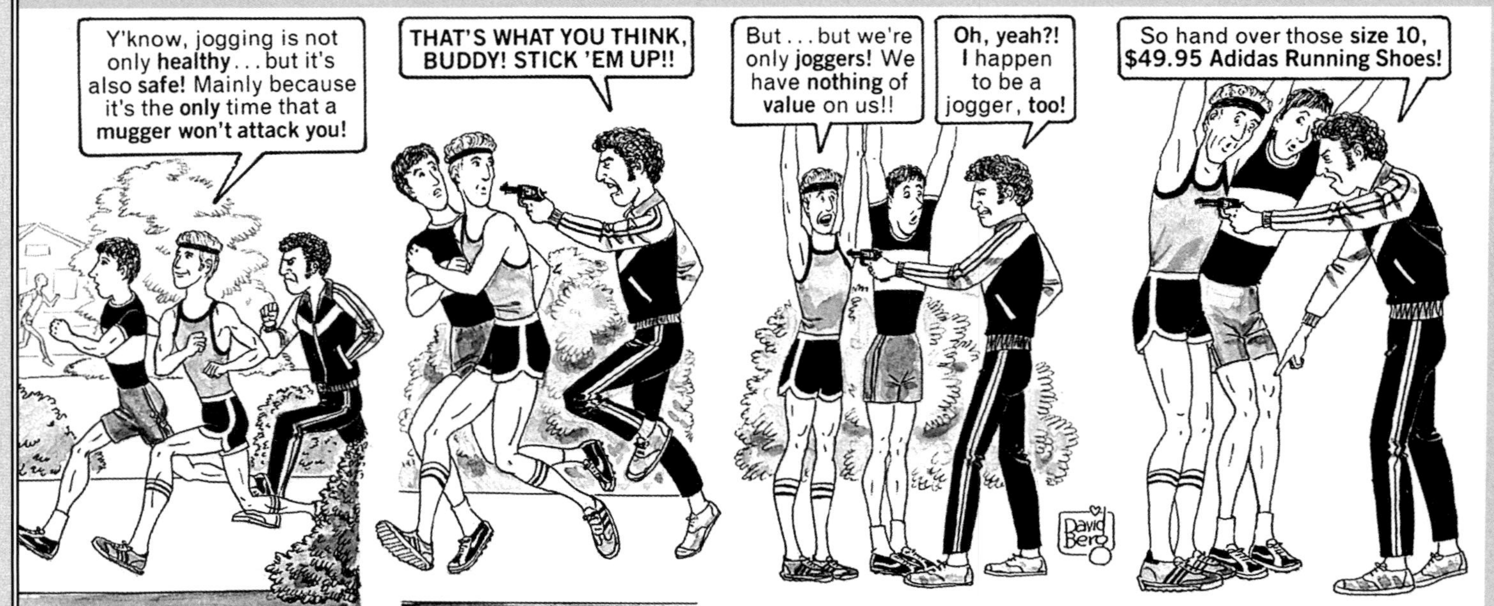
Y'know, jogging is not only healthy . . . but it's also safe! Mainly because it's the only time that a mugger won't attack you!
THAT'S WHAT YOU THINK, BUDDY! STICK 'EM UP!!
But . . . but we're only joggers! We have nothing of value on us!!
Oh, yeah?! I happen to be a jogger, too!
So hand over those size 10, $49.95 Adidas Running Shoes!
David Berg

The 1980s

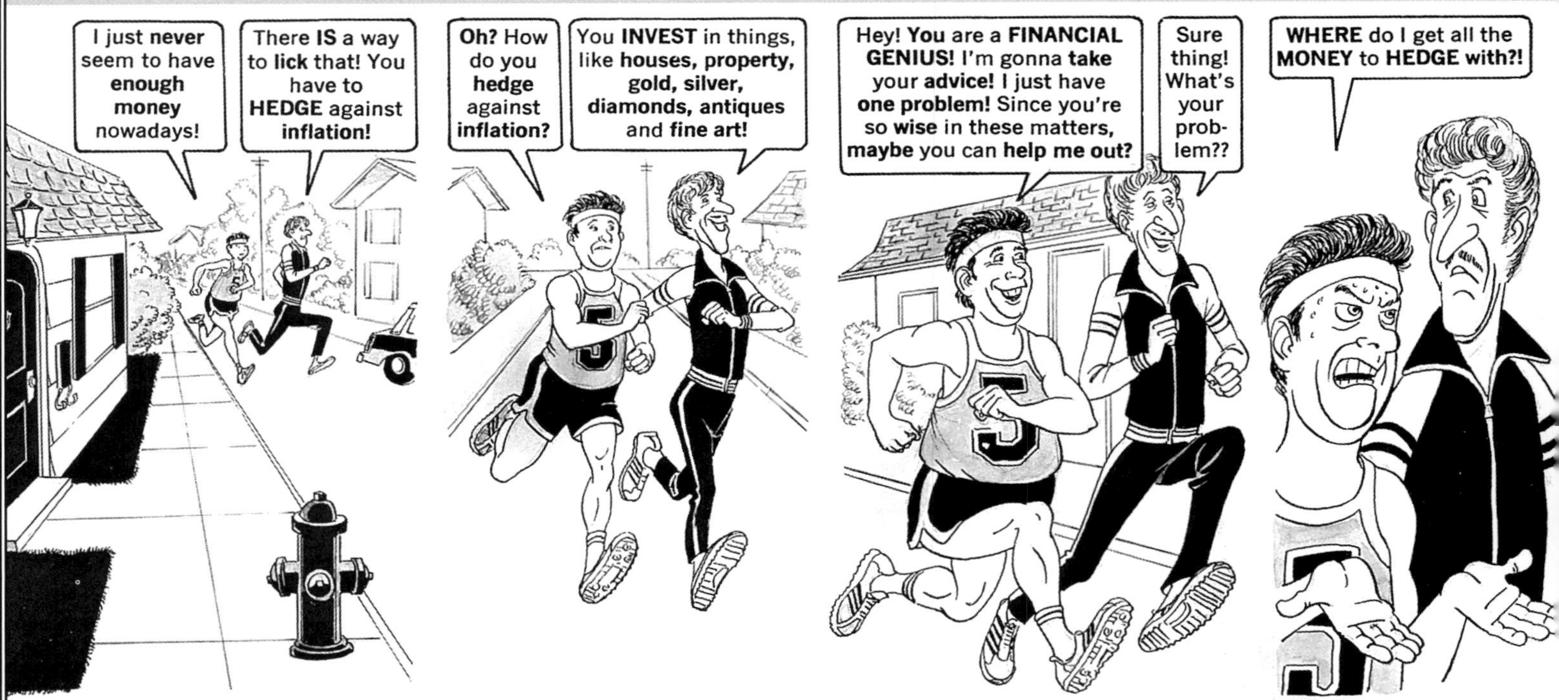
I just never seem to have enough money nowadays!
There IS a way to lick that! You have to HEDGE against inflation!
Oh? How do you hedge against inflation?
You INVEST in things, like houses, property, gold, silver, diamonds, antiques and fine art!
Hey! You are a FINANCIAL GENIUS! I'm gonna take your advice! I just have one problem! Since you're so wise in these matters, maybe you can help me out?
Sure thing! What's your prob-lem??
WHERE do I get all the MONEY to HEDGE with?!

BERG'S-EYE VIEW DEPT.

THE LIGHTER SIDE OF... INF

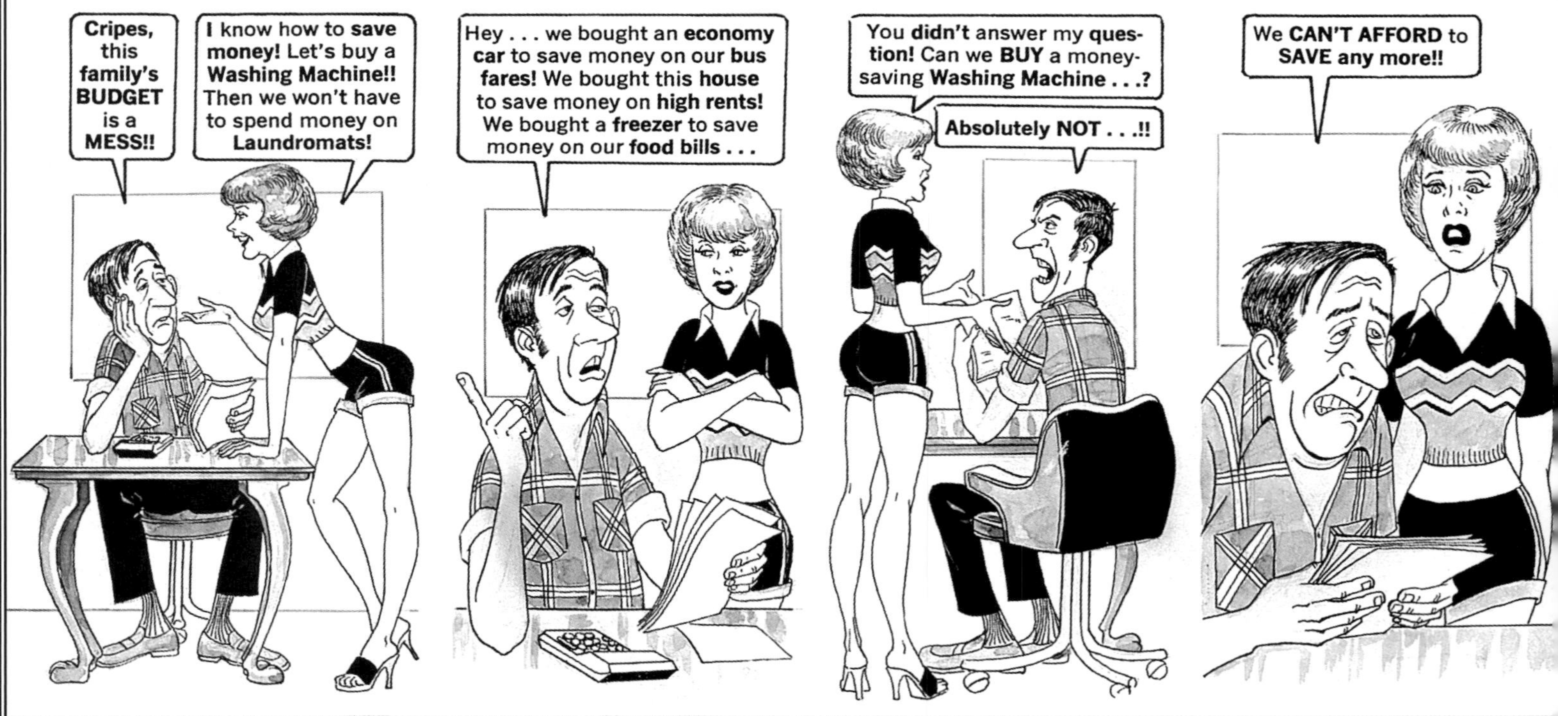
Cripes, this family's BUDGET is a MESS!!
I know how to save money! Let's buy a Washing Machine!! Then we won't have to spend money on Laundromats!
Hey . . . we bought an economy car to save money on our bus fares! We bought this house to save money on high rents! We bought a freezer to save money on our food bills . . .
You didn't answer my ques-tion! Can we BUY a money-saving Washing Machine . . .?
Absolutely NOT . . .!!
We CAN'T AFFORD to SAVE any more!!

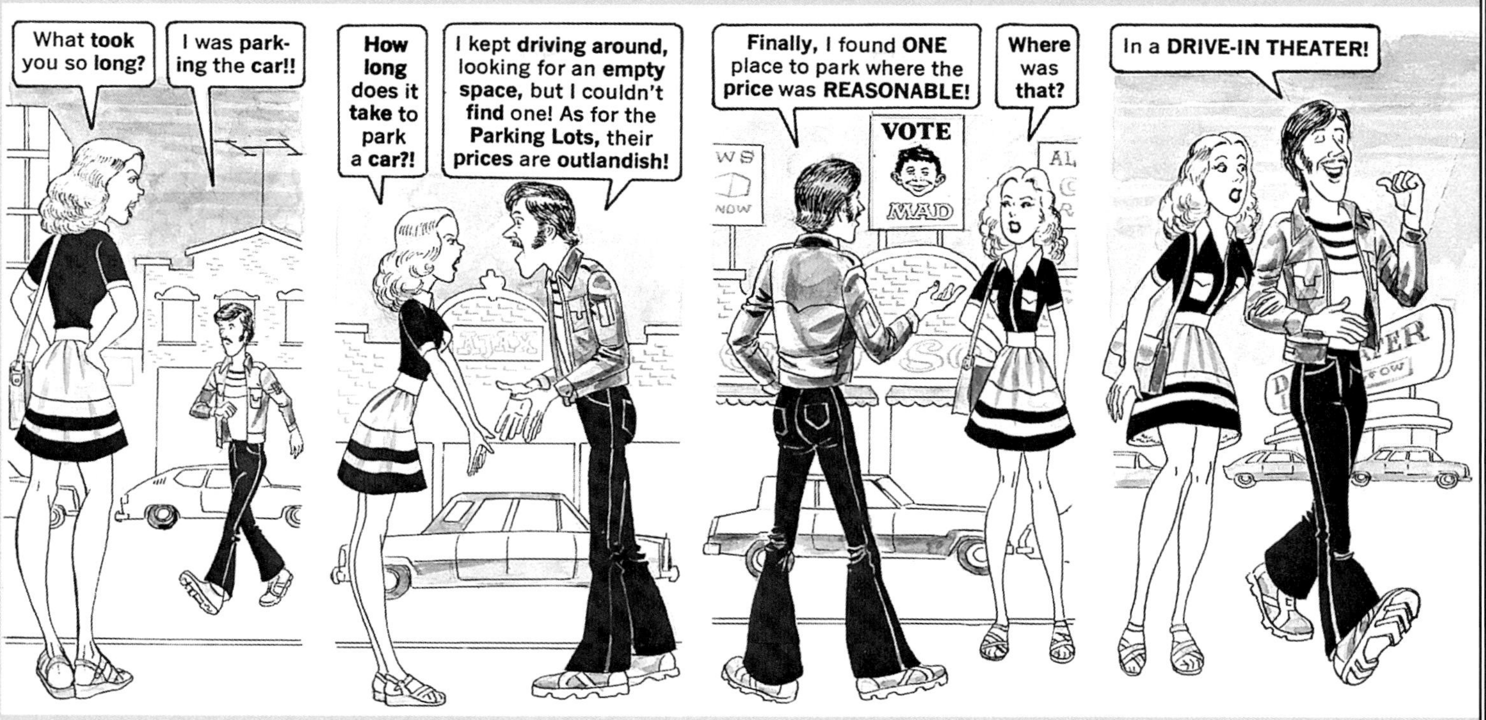
What took you so long?
I was parking the car!!
How long does it take to park a car?!
I kept driving around, looking for an empty space, but I couldn't find one! As for the Parking Lots, their prices are outlandish!
Finally, I found ONE place to park where the price was REASONABLE!
VOTE
MAD
Where was that?
In a DRIVE-IN THEATER!

LATION

ARTIST & WRITER:
DAVE BERG

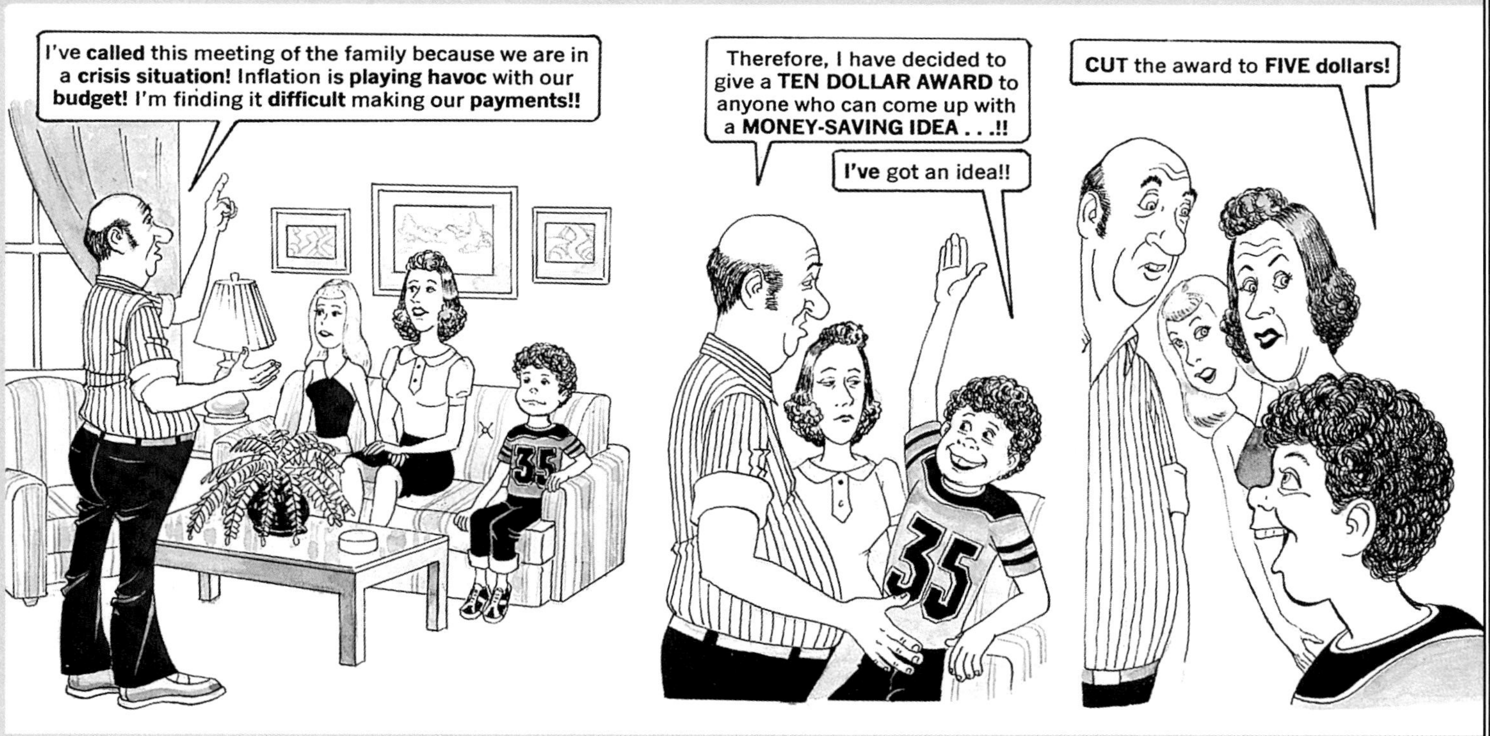
I've called this meeting of the family because we are in a crisis situation! Inflation is playing havoc with our budget! I'm finding it difficult making our payments!!
Therefore, I have decided to give a TEN DOLLAR AWARD to anyone who can come up with a MONEY-SAVING IDEA . . .!!
I've got an idea!!
CUT the award to FIVE dollars!

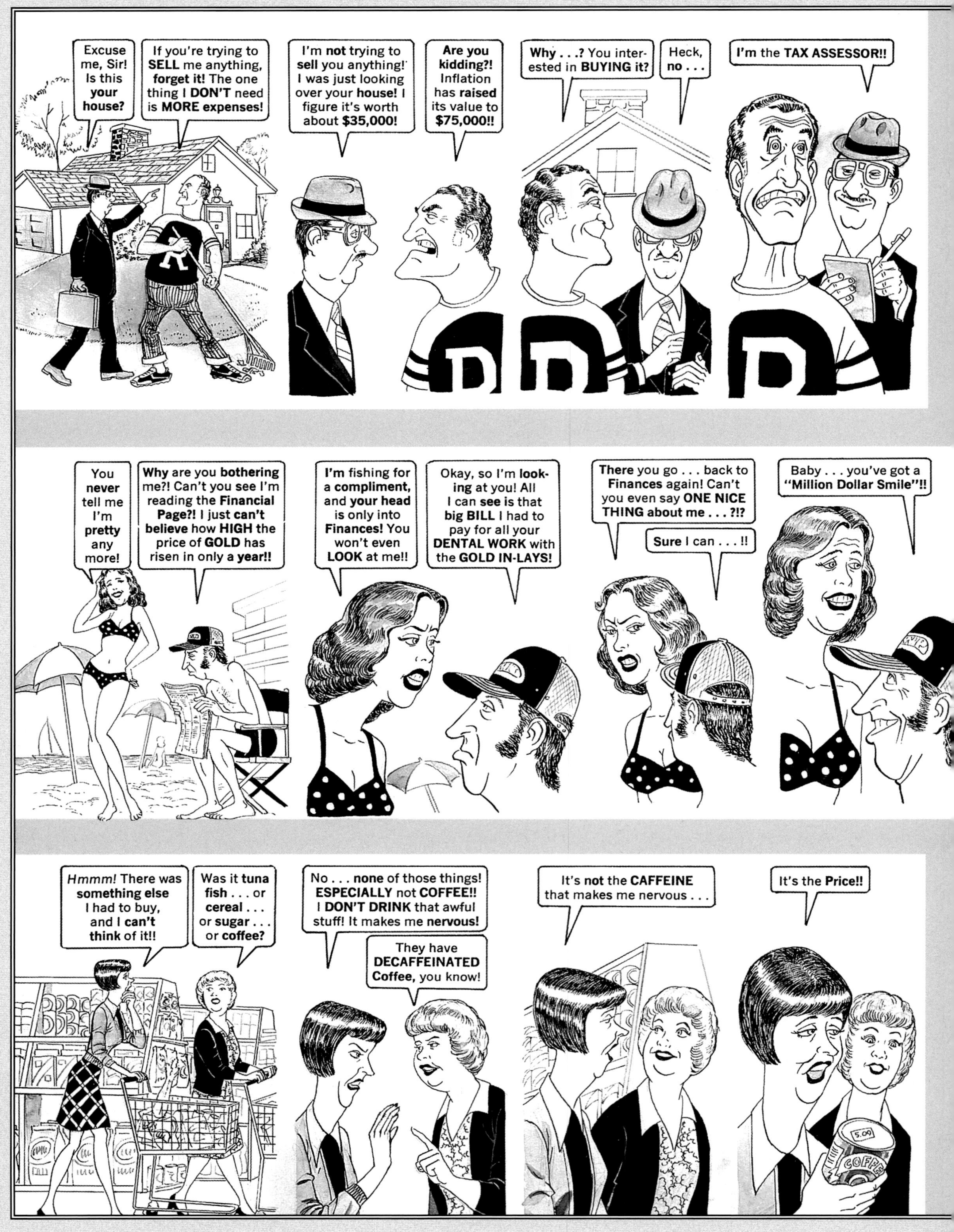
Excuse me, Sir! Is this your house?
If you're trying to SELL me anything, forget it! The one thing I DON'T need is MORE expenses!
I'm not trying to sell you anything! I was just looking over your house! I figure it's worth about $35,000!
Are you kidding?! Inflation has raised its value to $75,000!!
Why . . .? You interested in BUYING it?
Heck, no . . .
I'm the TAX ASSESSOR!!
You never tell me I'm pretty any more!
Why are you bothering me?! Can't you see I'm reading the Financial Page?! I just can't believe how HIGH the price of GOLD has risen in only a year!!
I'm fishing for a compliment, and your head is only into Finances! You won't even LOOK at me!!
Okay, so I'm looking at you! All I can see is that big BILL I had to pay for all your DENTAL WORK with the GOLD IN-LAYS!
There you go . . . back to Finances again! Can't you even say ONE NICE THING about me . . . ?!?
Sure I can . . . !!
Baby . . . you've got a "Million Dollar Smile"!!
Hmmm! There was something else I had to buy, and I can't think of it!!
Was it tuna fish . . . or cereal . . . or sugar . . . or coffee?
No . . . none of those things! ESPECIALLY not COFFEE!! I DON'T DRINK that awful stuff! It makes me nervous!
They have DECAFFEINATED Coffee, you know!
It's not the CAFFEINE that makes me nervous . . .
It's the Price!!
5.09
COFFEE

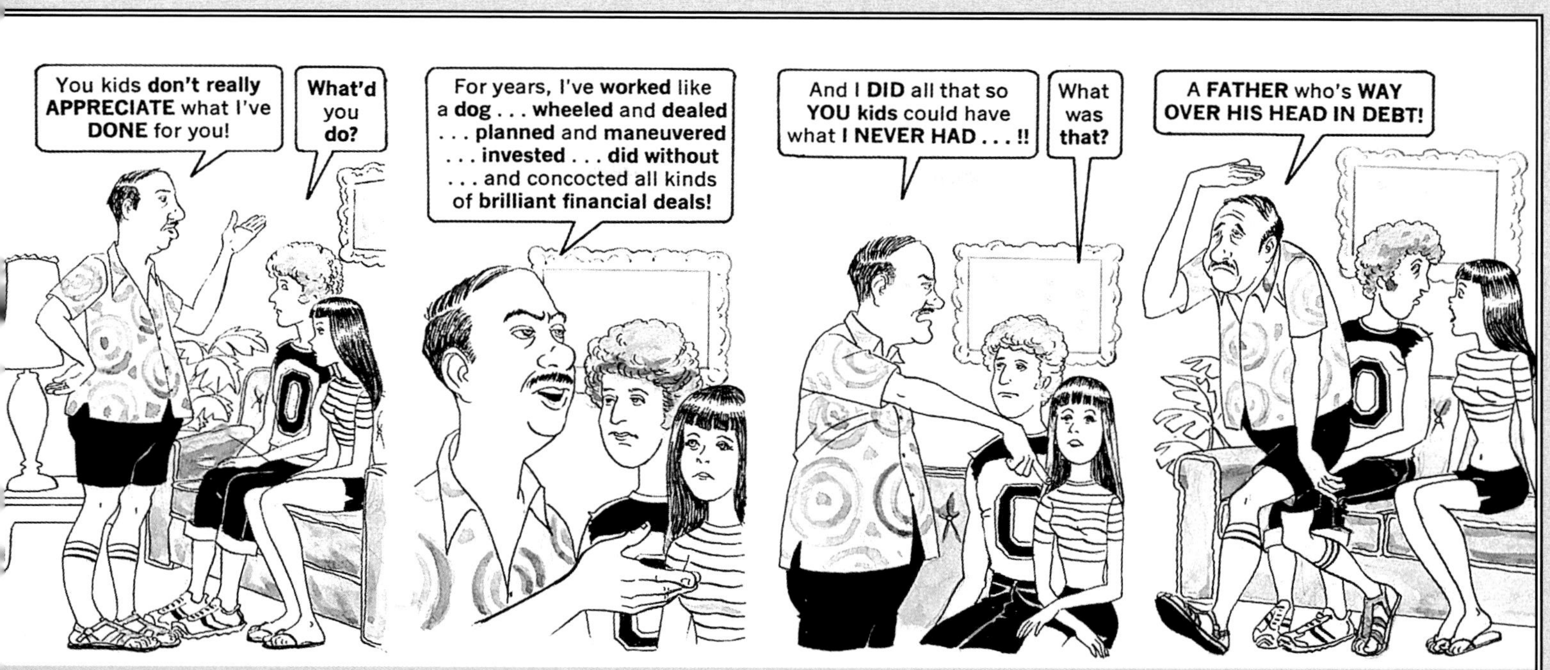
You kids don't really APPRECIATE what I've DONE for you!
What'd you do?
For years, I've worked like a dog . . . wheeled and dealed . . . planned and maneuvered . . . invested . . . did without . . . and concocted all kinds of brilliant financial deals!
And I DID all that so YOU kids could have what I NEVER HAD . . . !!
What was that?
A FATHER who's WAY OVER HIS HEAD IN DEBT!

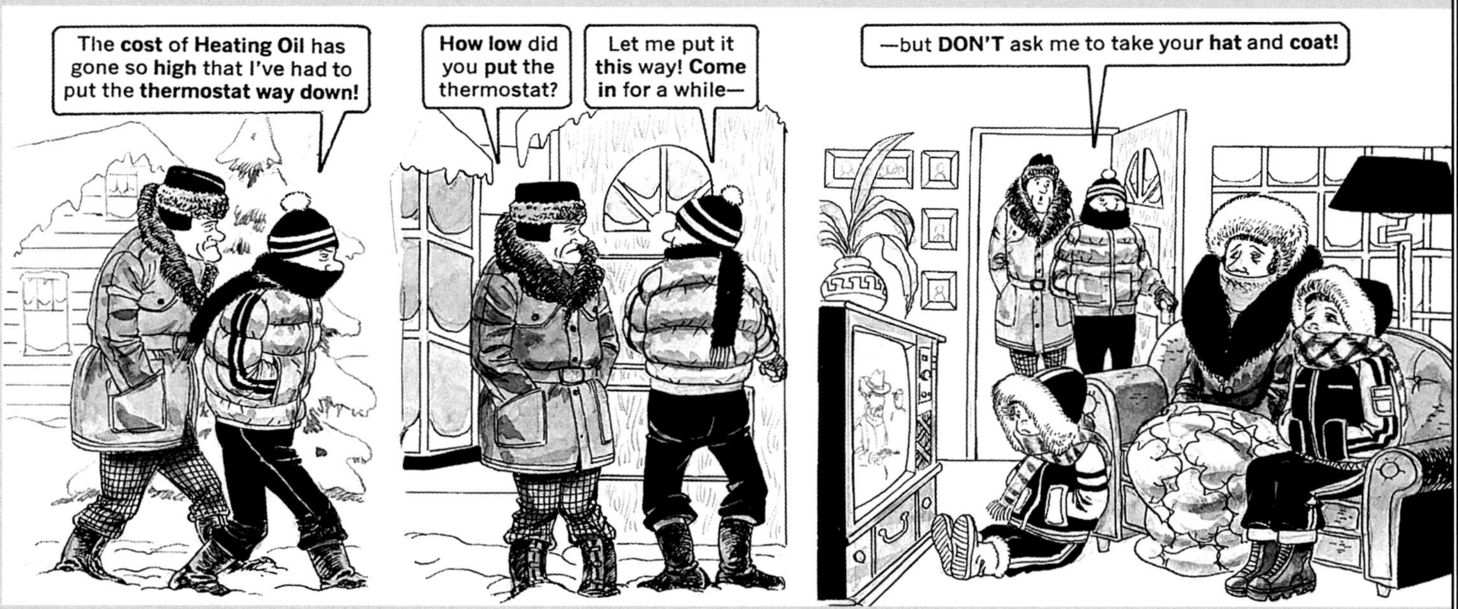
The cost of Heating Oil has gone so high that I've had to put the thermostat way down!
How low did you put the thermostat?
Let me put it this way! Come in for a while—
—but DON'T ask me to take your hat and coat!

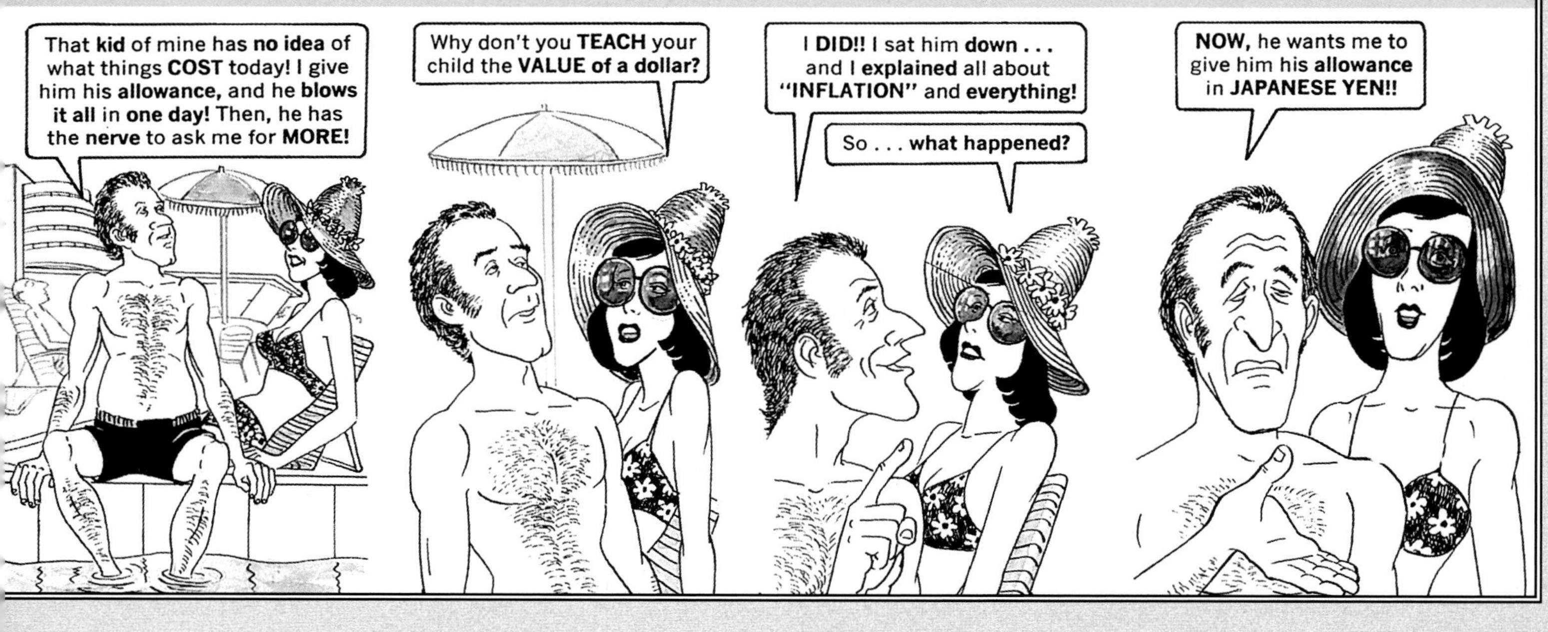
That kid of mine has no idea of what things COST today! I give him his allowance, and he blows it all in one day! Then, he has the nerve to ask me for MORE!
Why don't you TEACH your child the VALUE of a dollar?
I DID!! I sat him down . . . and I explained all about "INFLATION" and everything!
So . . . what happened?
NOW, he wants me to give him his allowance in JAPANESE YEN!!

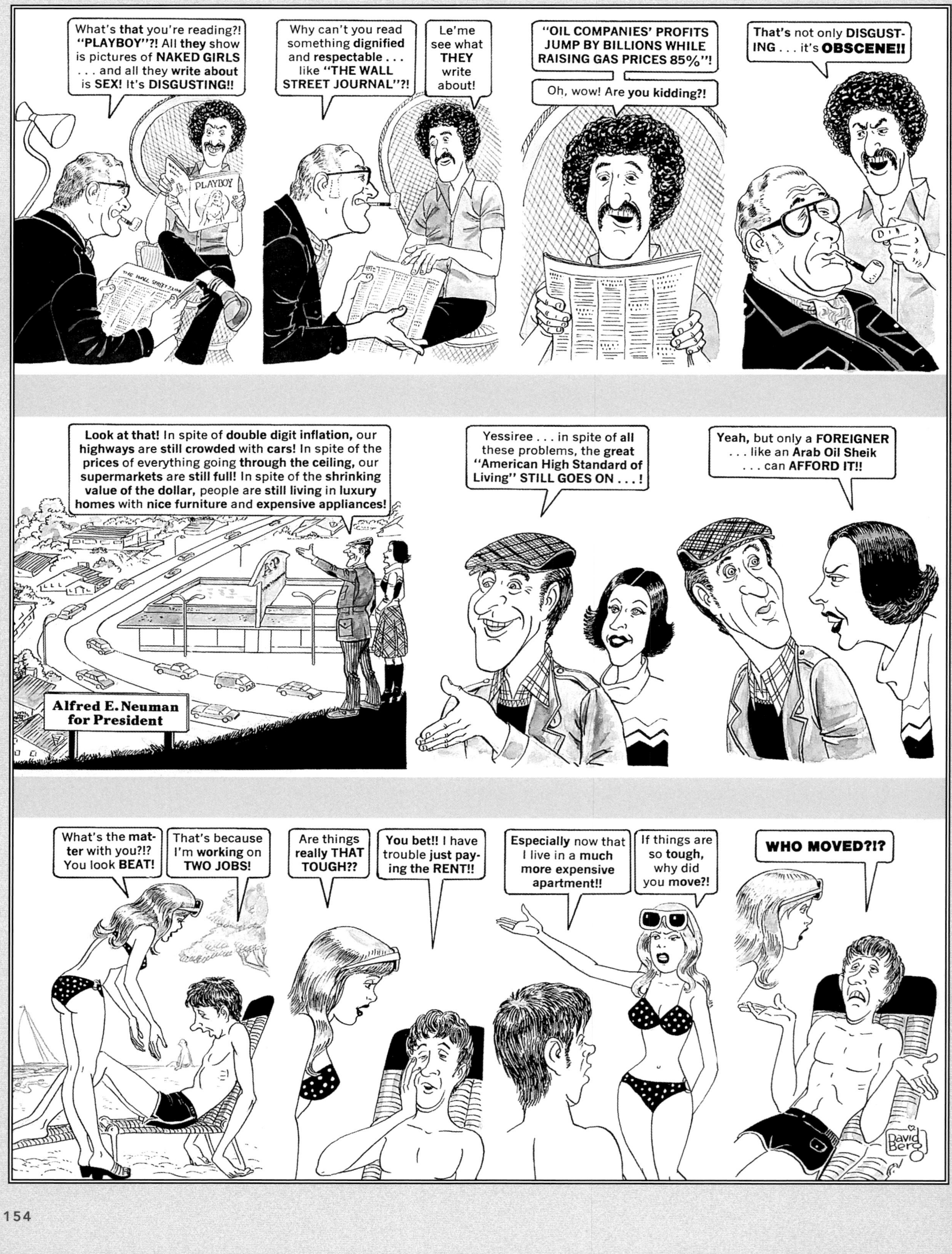
What's that you're reading?! "PLAYBOY"?! All they show is pictures of NAKED GIRLS . . . and all they write about is SEX! It's DISGUSTING!!
PLAYBOY
THE WALL STREET JOURNAL
Why can't you read something dignified and respectable . . . like "THE WALL STREET JOURNAL"?!
Le'me see what THEY write about!
"OIL COMPANIES' PROFITS JUMP BY BILLIONS WHILE RAISING GAS PRICES 85%"!
Oh, wow! Are you kidding?!
That's not only DISGUSTING . . . it's OBSCENE!!
Look at that! In spite of double digit inflation, our highways are still crowded with cars! In spite of the prices of everything going through the ceiling, our supermarkets are still full! In spite of the shrinking value of the dollar, people are still living in luxury homes with nice furniture and expensive appliances!
A&P
Alfred E. Neuman for President
Yessiree . . . in spite of all these problems, the great "American High Standard of Living" STILL GOES ON . . . !
Yeah, but only a FOREIGNER . . . like an Arab Oil Sheik . . . can AFFORD IT!!
What's the matter with you?!? You look BEAT!
That's because I'm working on TWO JOBS!
Are things really THAT TOUGH??
You bet!! I have trouble just paying the RENT!!
Especially now that I live in a much more expensive apartment!!
If things are so tough, why did you move?!
WHO MOVED?!?
David Berg

Dave Berg, A Man and His Pipe

Photos from the Berg Family Collection

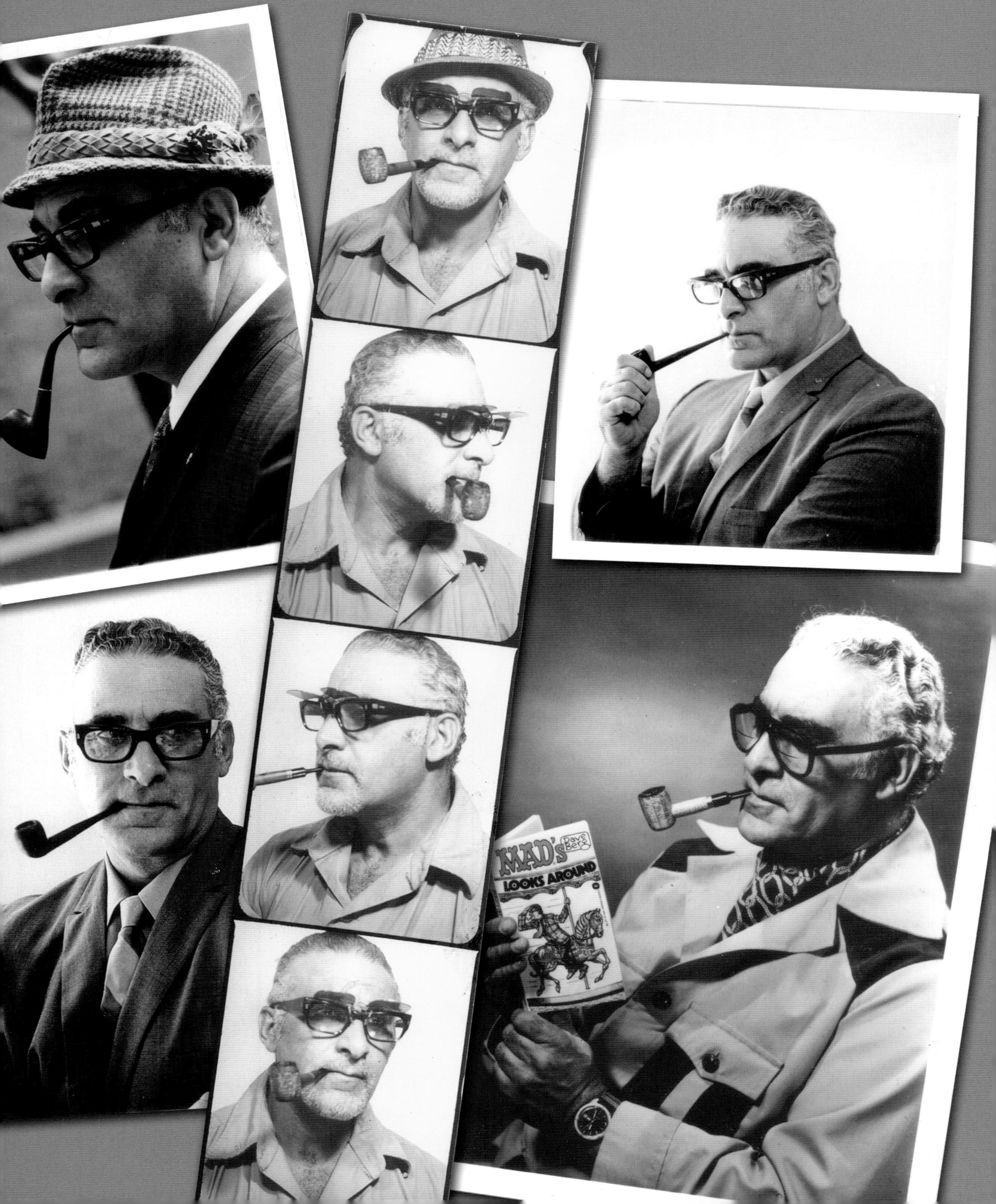
MAD's
Dave Berg
LOOKS AROUND

SCHOOL

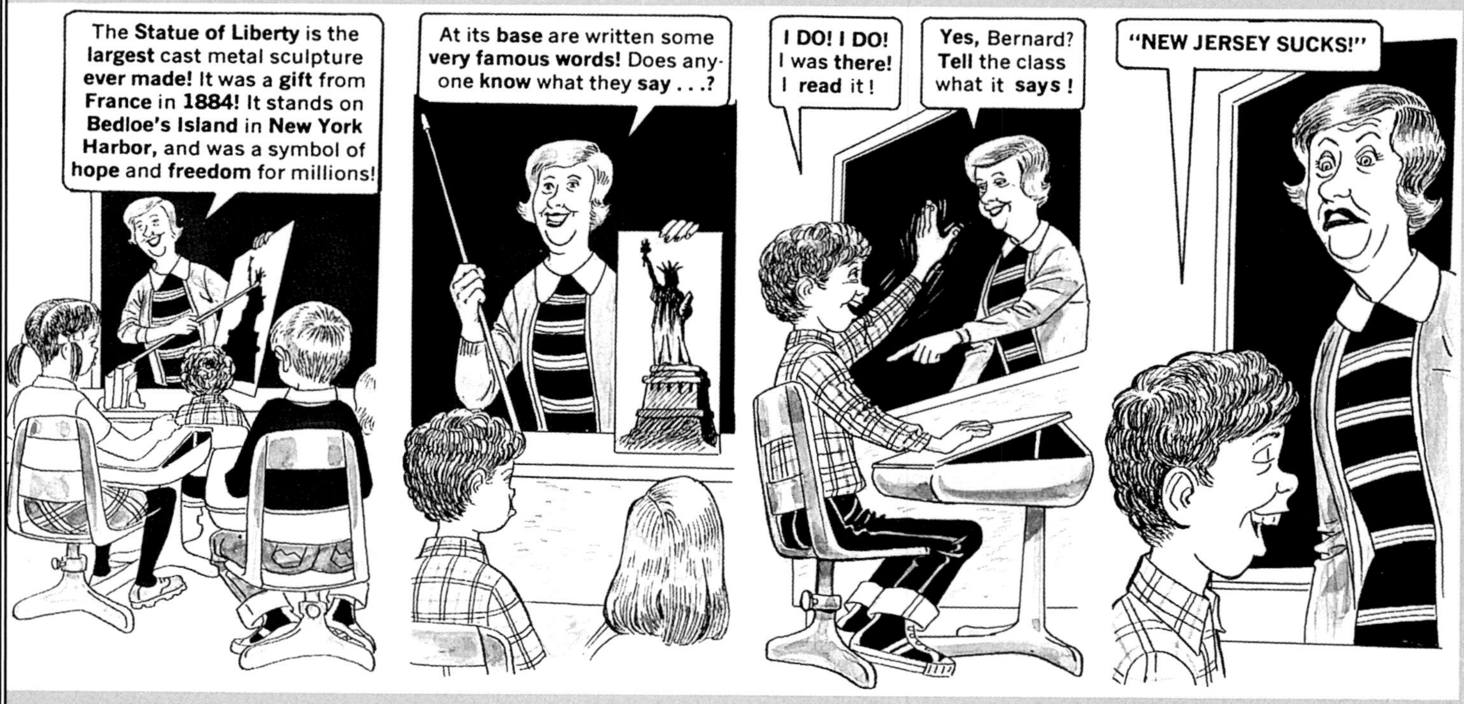
The Statue of Liberty is the largest cast metal sculpture ever made! It was a gift from France in 1884! It stands on Bedloe's Island in New York Harbor, and was a symbol of hope and freedom for millions!
At its base are written some very famous words! Does anyone know what they say . . .?
I DO! I DO! I was there! I read it!
Yes, Bernard? Tell the class what it says!
"NEW JERSEY SUCKS!"

BERG'S-EYE VIEW DEPT.

THE LIGHTE

TRAVEL

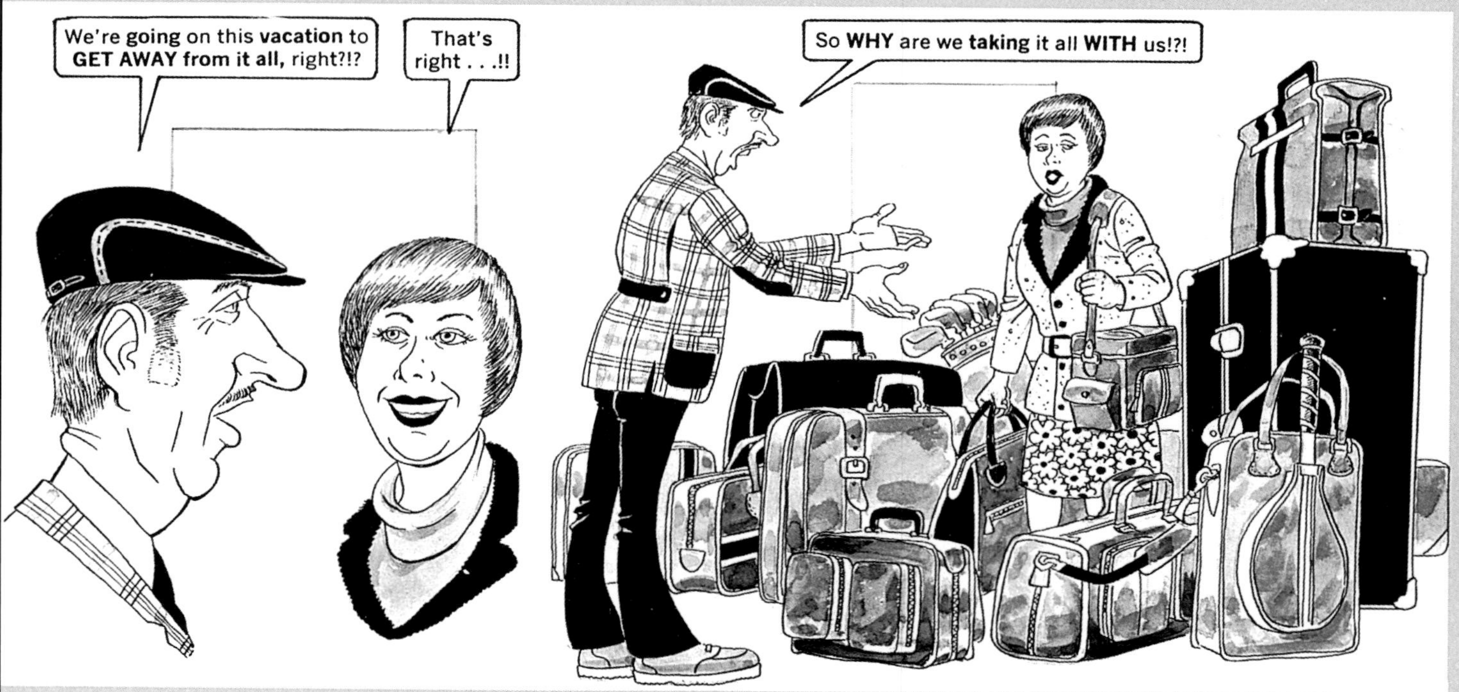
We're going on this vacation to GET AWAY from it all, right?!?
That's right . . .!!
So WHY are we taking it all WITH us!?!

After writing 148 "single topic" editions of "The Lighter Side of...," Dave transitioned to multi-topic installments beginning with MAD #218, October 1980

DIVORCE

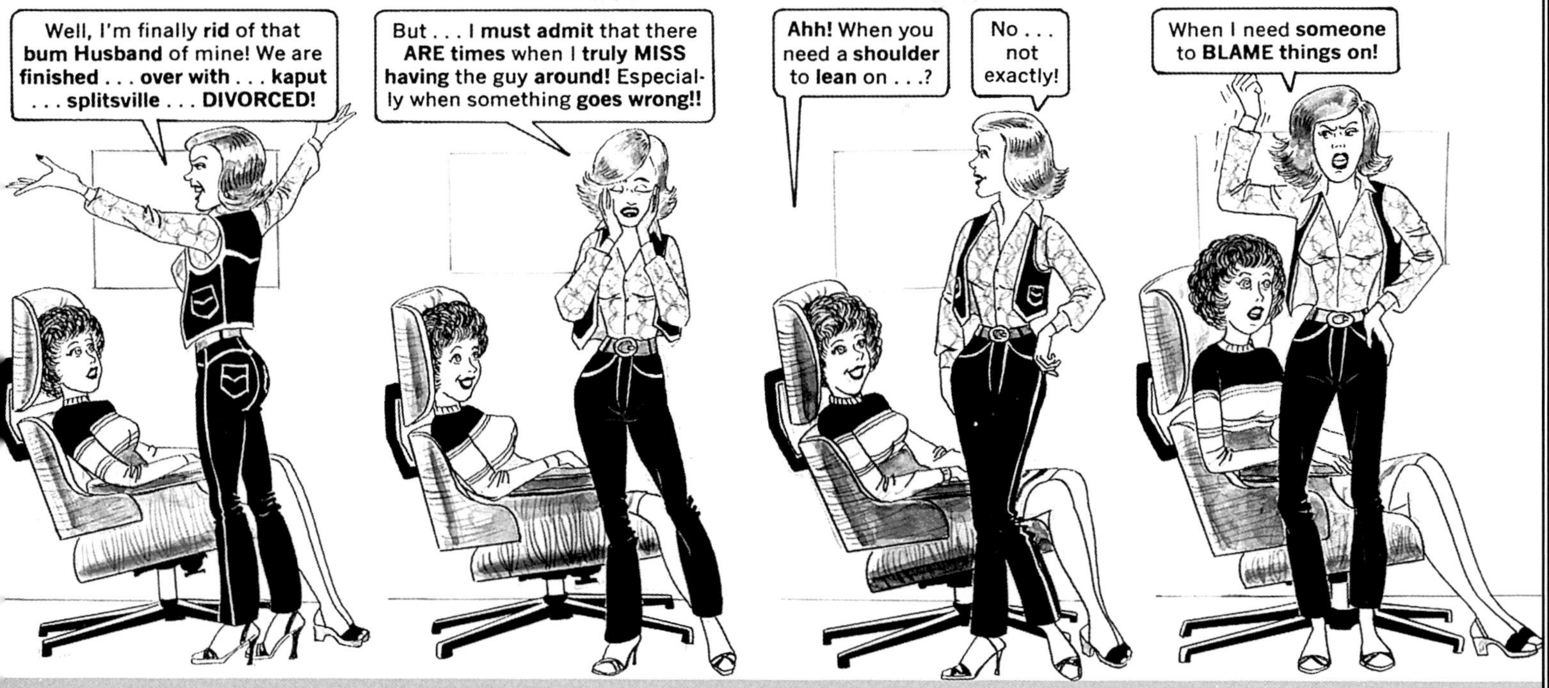
Well, I'm finally rid of that bum Husband of mine! We are finished . . . over with . . . kaput . . . splitsville . . . DIVORCED!
But . . . I must admit that there ARE times when I truly MISS having the guy around! Especially when something goes wrong!!
Ahh! When you need a shoulder to lean on . . .?
No . . . not exactly!
When I need someone to BLAME things on!

R SIDE OF...

ARTIST & WRITER:
DAVE BERG

SPORTS

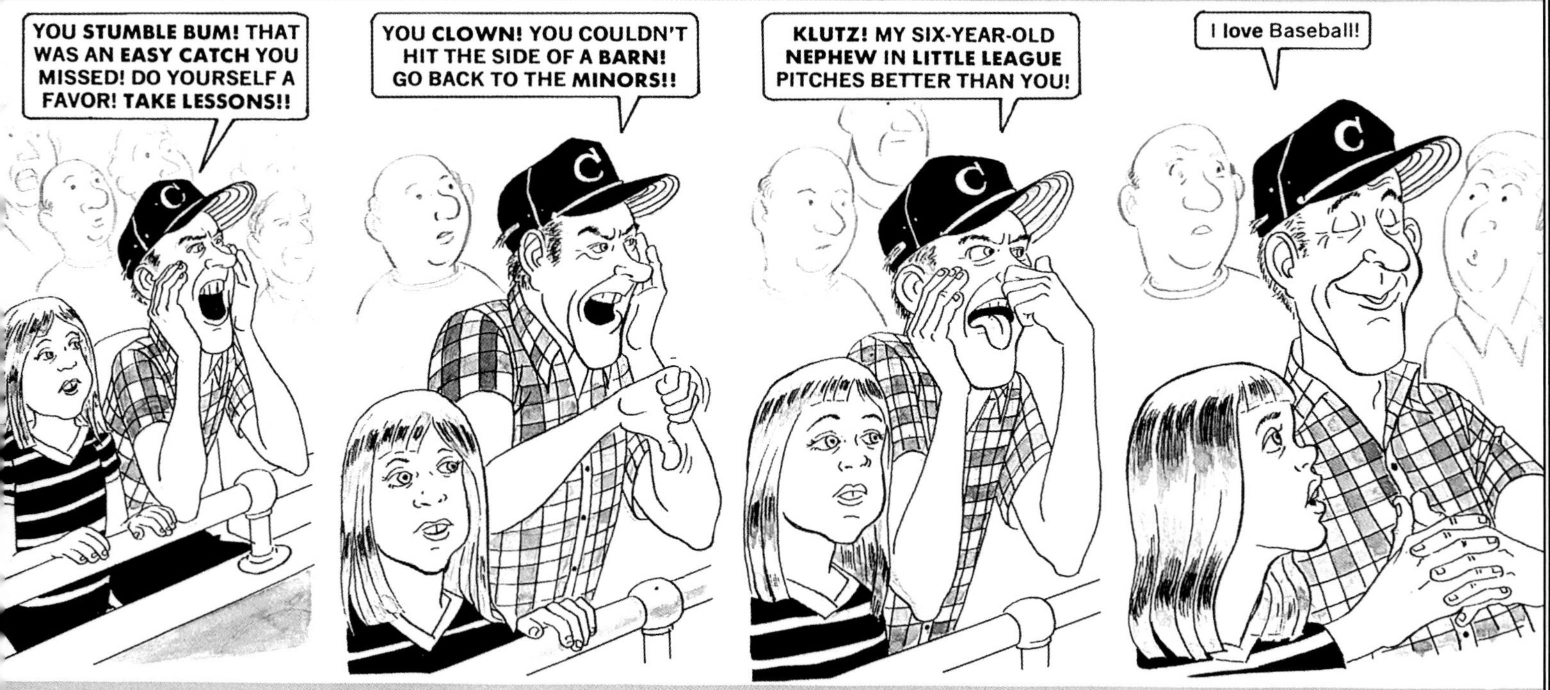
YOU STUMBLE BUM! THAT WAS AN EASY CATCH YOU MISSED! DO YOURSELF A FAVOR! TAKE LESSONS!!
YOU CLOWN! YOU COULDN'T HIT THE SIDE OF A BARN! GO BACK TO THE MINORS!!
KLUTZ! MY SIX-YEAR-OLD NEPHEW IN LITTLE LEAGUE PITCHES BETTER THAN YOU!
I love Baseball!

MARRIAGE

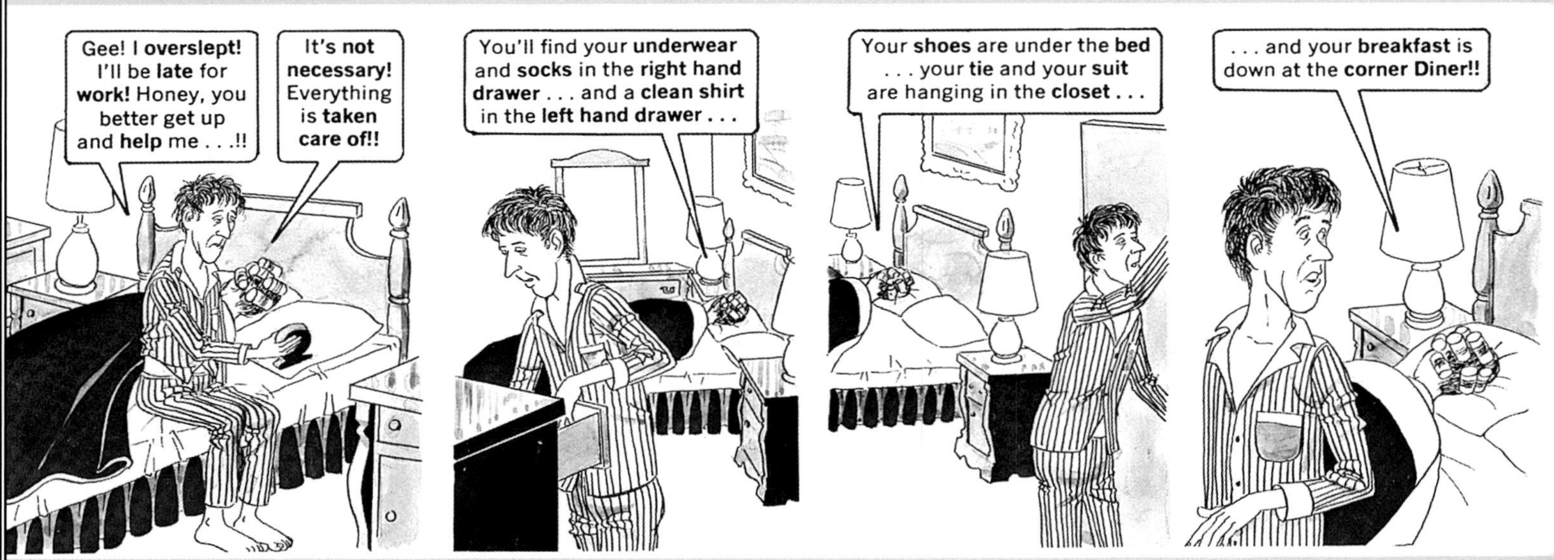
Gee! I overslept! I'll be late for work! Honey, you better get up and help me . . .!!
It's not necessary! Everything is taken care of!!
You'll find your underwear and socks in the right hand drawer . . . and a clean shirt in the left hand drawer . . .
Your shoes are under the bed . . . your tie and your suit are hanging in the closet . . .
. . . and your breakfast is down at the corner Diner!!

OLD AGE

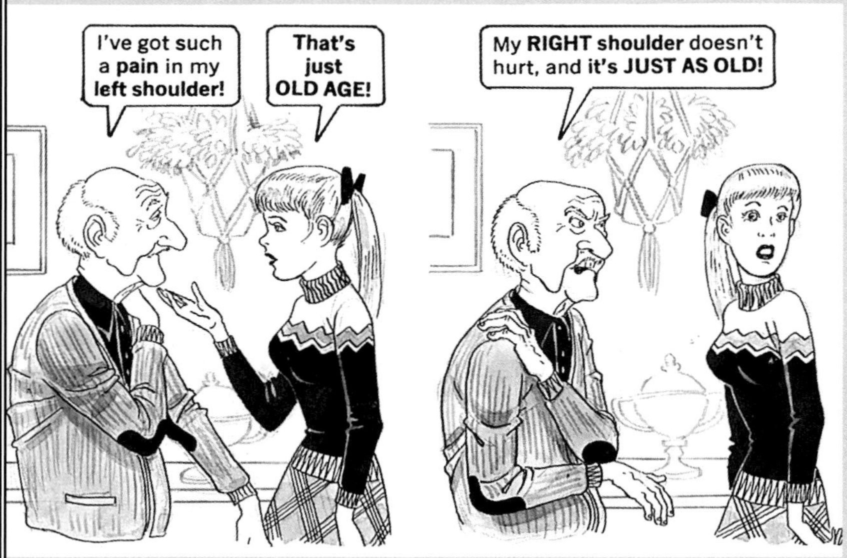
I've got such a pain in my left shoulder!
That's just OLD AGE!
My RIGHT shoulder doesn't hurt, and it's JUST AS OLD!

WEDDINGS

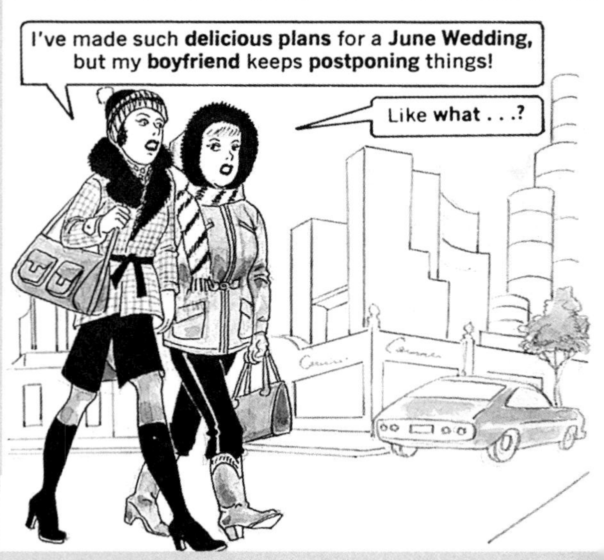
I've made such delicious plans for a June Wedding, but my boyfriend keeps postponing things!
Like what . . .?

MOTHERS

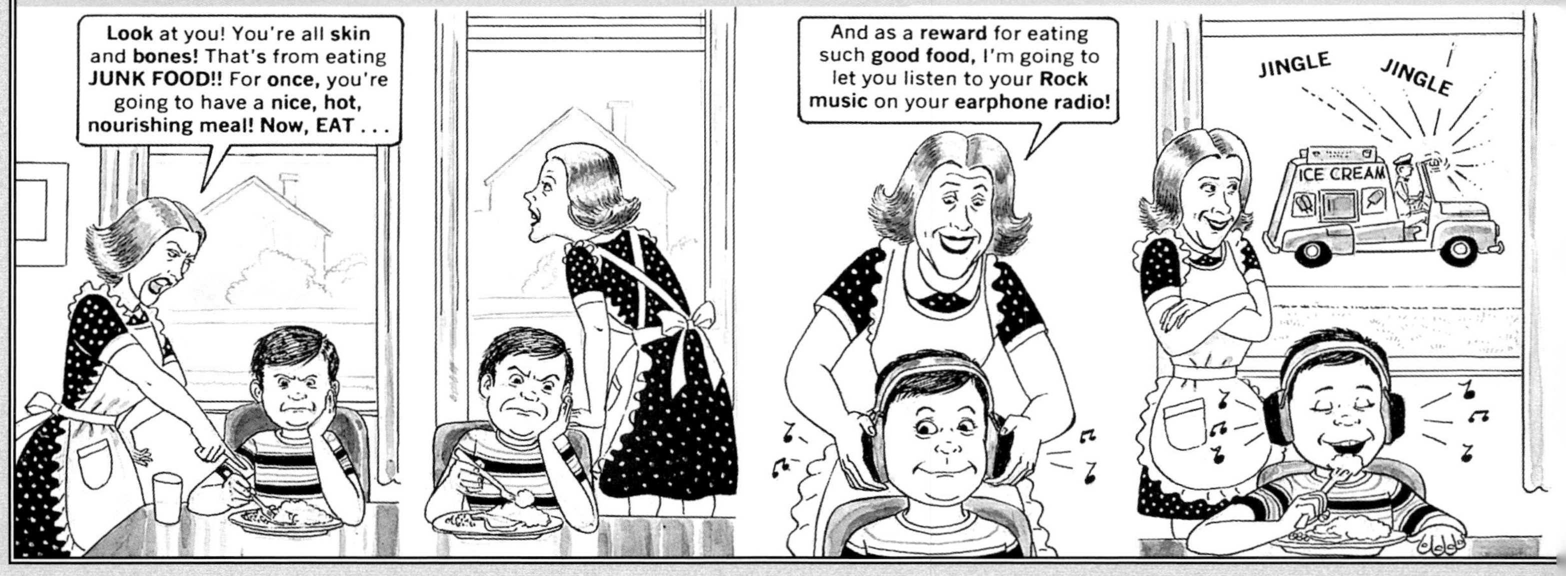
Look at you! You're all skin and bones! That's from eating JUNK FOOD!! For once, you're going to have a nice, hot, nourishing meal! Now, EAT . . .
And as a reward for eating such good food, I'm going to let you listen to your Rock music on your earphone radio!
JINGLE
JINGLE
ICE CREAM

MEDICINE

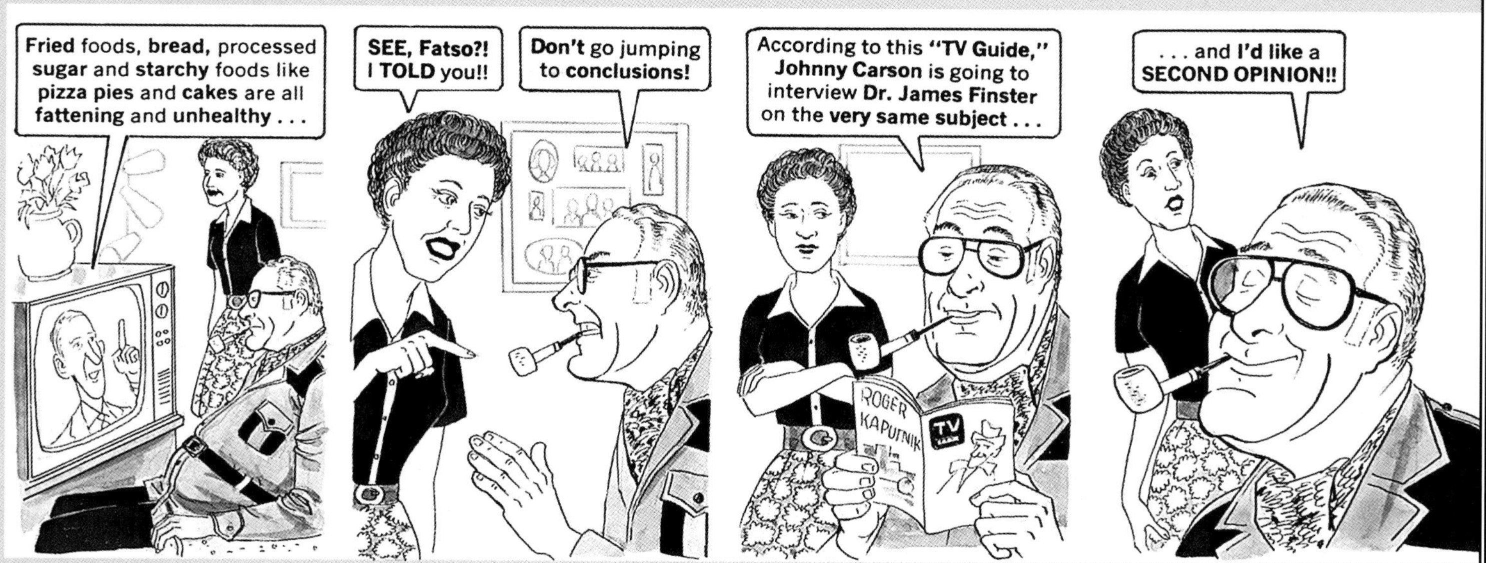
Fried foods, bread, processed sugar and starchy foods like pizza pies and cakes are all fattening and unhealthy . . .
SEE, Fatso?! I TOLD you!!
Don't go jumping to conclusions!
According to this "TV Guide," Johnny Carson is going to interview Dr. James Finster on the very same subject . . .
ROGER KAPUTNIK
TV
. . . and I'd like a SECOND OPINION!!

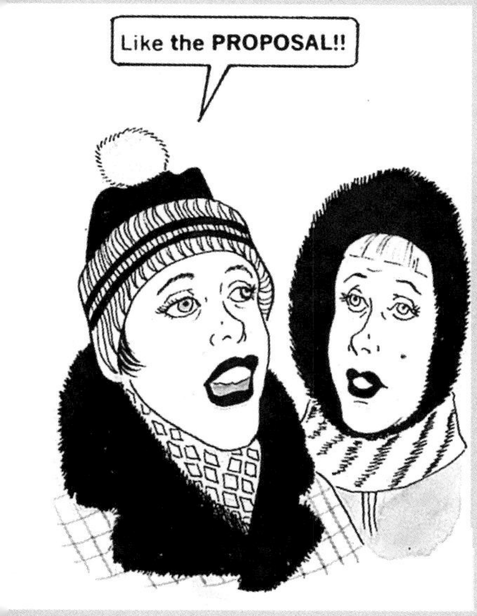
Like the PROPOSAL!!

CONVENTIONS

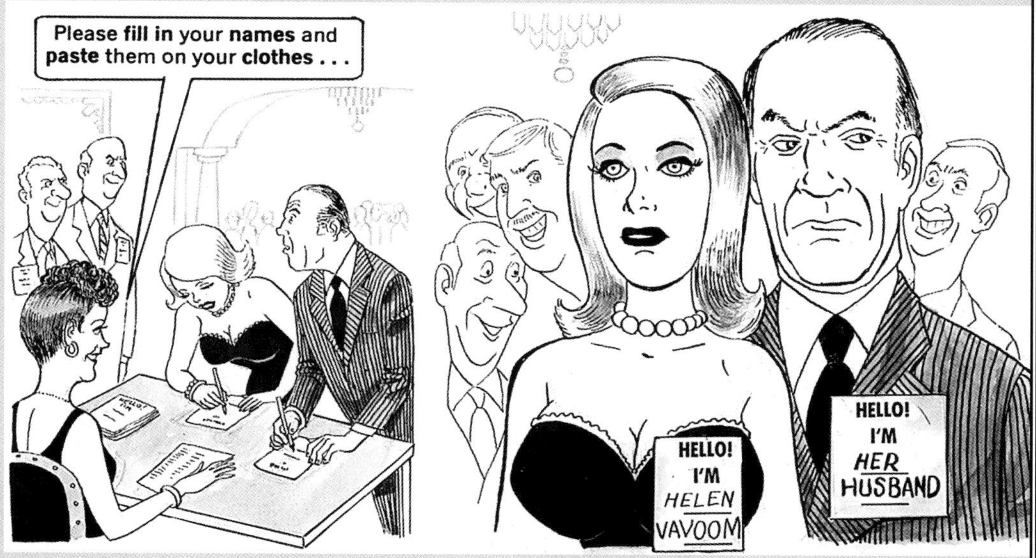
Please fill in your names and paste them on your clothes . . .
HELLO! I'M HELEN VAVOOM
HELLO! I'M HER HUSBAND

FAMILY

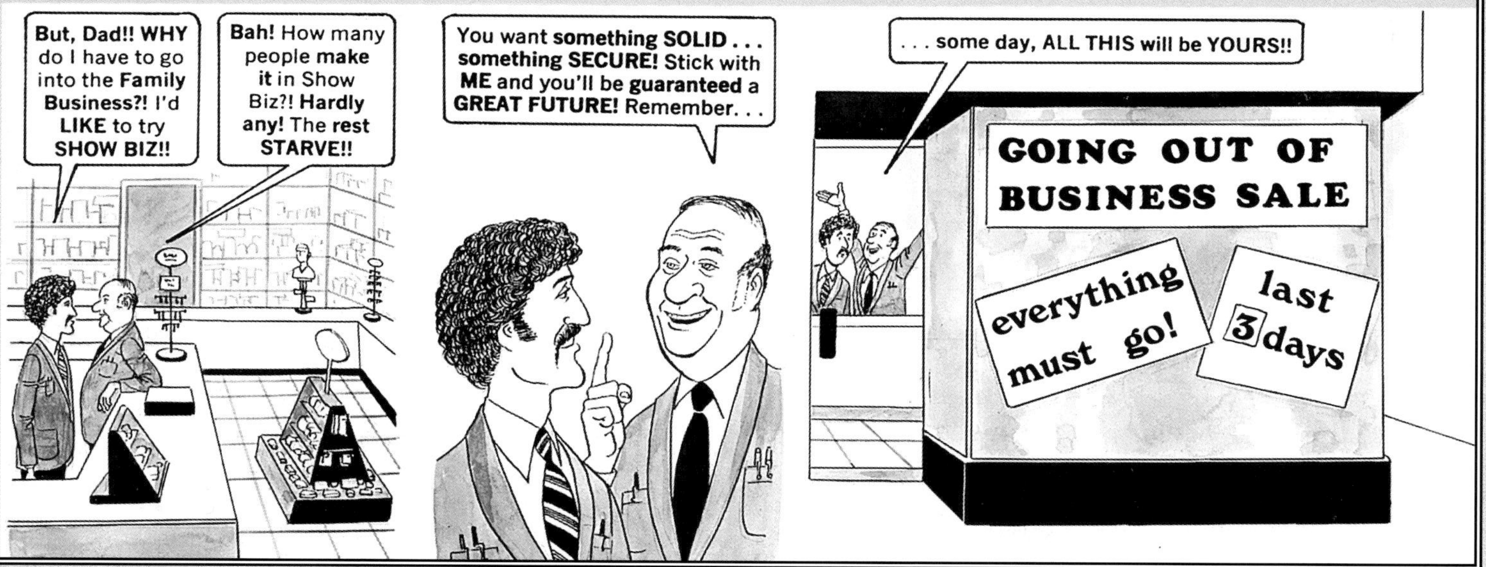
But, Dad!! WHY do I have to go into the Family Business?! I'd LIKE to try SHOW BIZ!!
Bah! How many people make it in Show Biz?! Hardly any! The rest STARVE!!
You want something SOLID . . . something SECURE! Stick with ME and you'll be guaranteed a GREAT FUTURE! Remember. . .
. . . some day, ALL THIS will be YOURS!!
GOING OUT OF BUSINESS SALE
everything must go!
last 3 days

PHONE CALLS

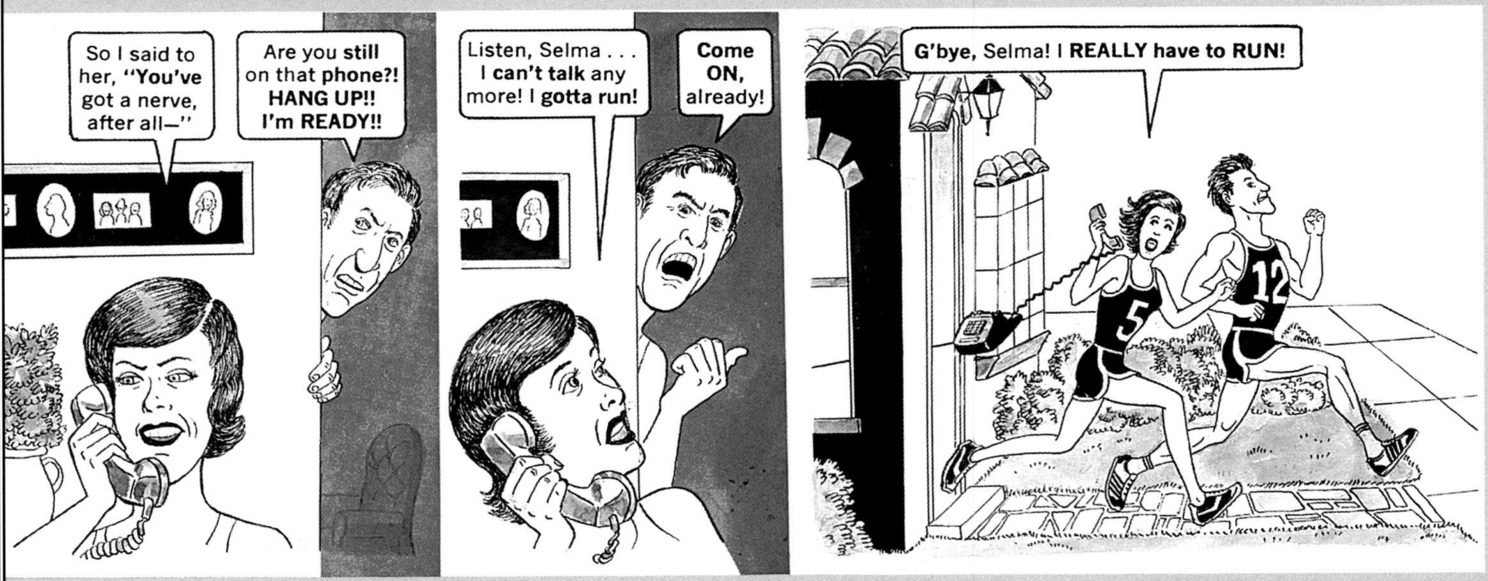
So I said to her, "You've got a nerve, after all—"
Are you still on that phone?! HANG UP!! I'm READY!!
Listen, Selma . . . I can't talk any more! I gotta run!
Come ON, already!
G'bye, Selma! I REALLY have to RUN!
5
12

CHILDREN

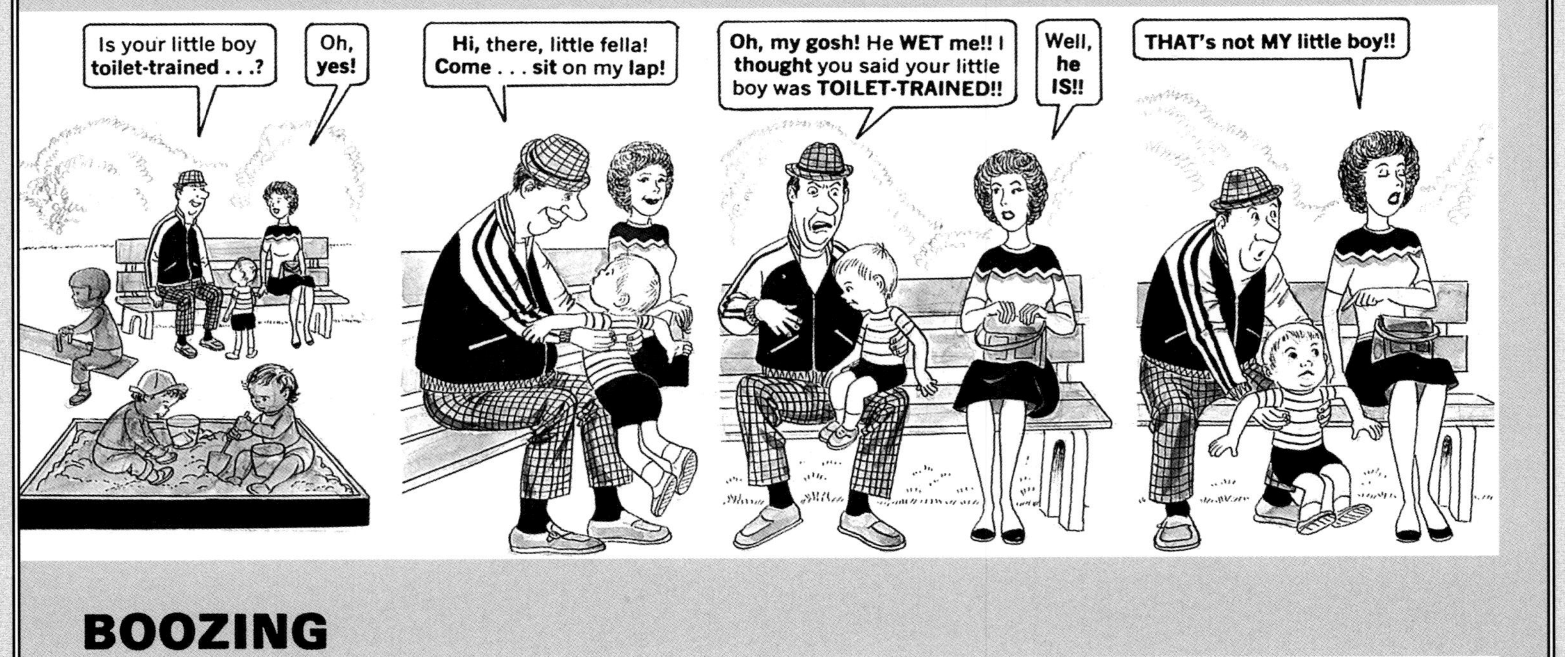
Is your little boy toilet-trained . . .?
Oh, yes!
Hi, there, little fella! Come . . . sit on my lap!
Oh, my gosh! He WET me!! I thought you said your little boy was TOILET-TRAINED!!
Well, he IS!!
THAT's not MY little boy!!

BOOZING

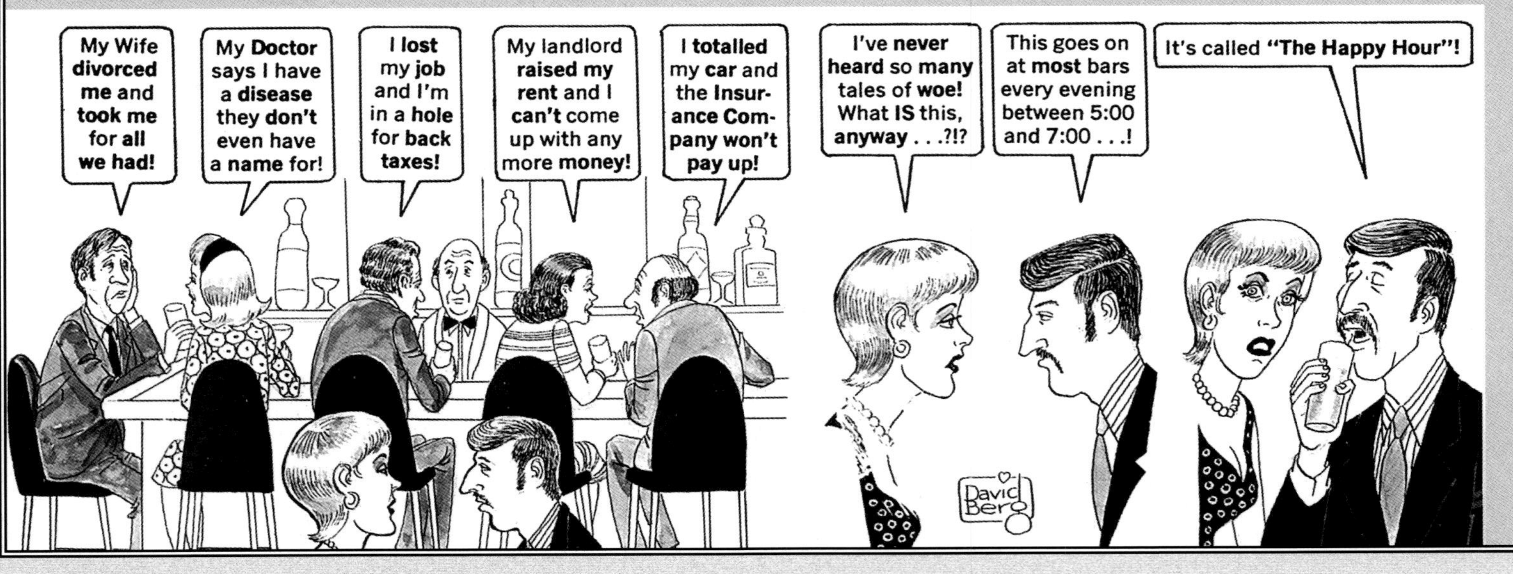
My Wife divorced me and took me for all we had!
My Doctor says I have a disease they don't even have a name for!
I lost my job and I'm in a hole for back taxes!
My landlord raised my rent and I can't come up with any more money!
I totalled my car and the Insurance Company won't pay up!
I've never heard so many tales of woe! What IS this, anyway . . .?!?
This goes on at most bars every evening between 5:00 and 7:00 . . .!
It's called "The Happy Hour"!
David Berg

Roughs and Finishes

More examples of Dave's initial rough sketches, with added editor's marks and how the final strips appeared in the pages of MAD.

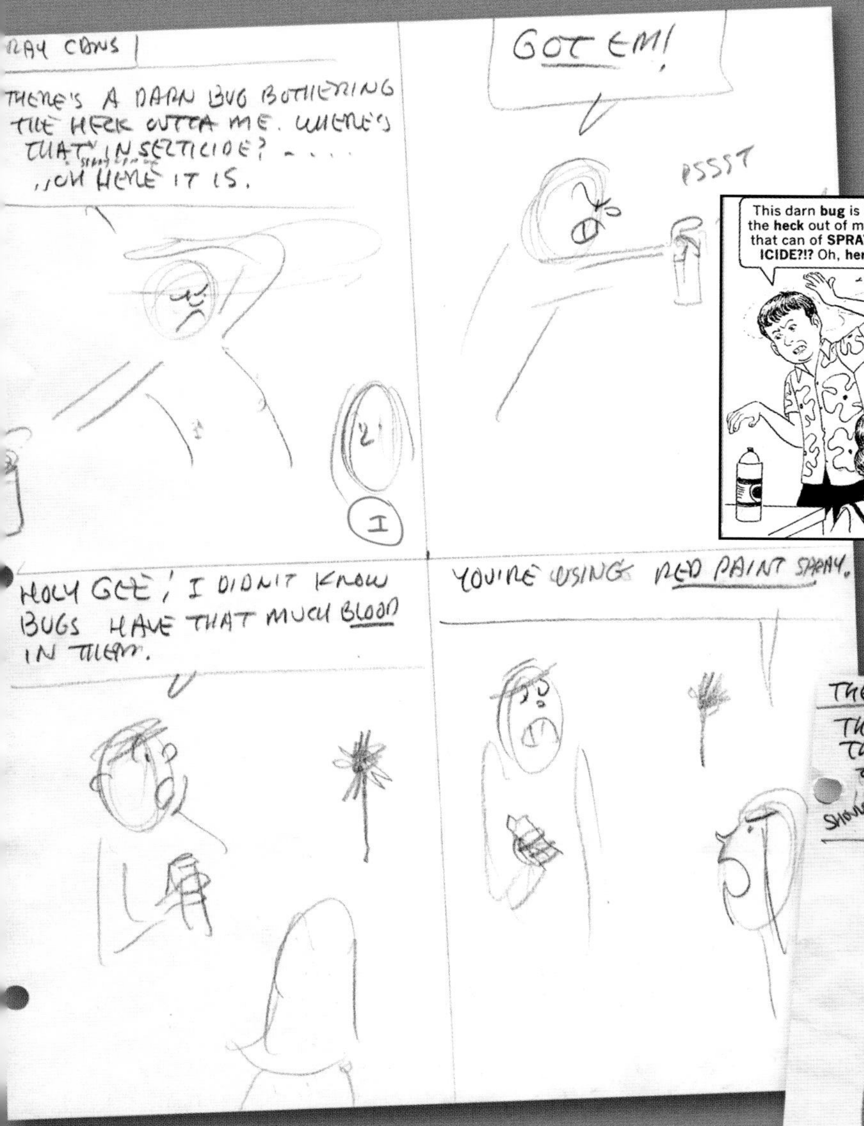
THERE'S A DARN BUG BOTHERING THE HECK OUTTA ME. WHERE'S THAT INSECTICIDE? .... OH HERE IT IS.
GOT EM!
PSSST
HOLY GEE, I DIDN'T KNOW BUGS HAVE THAT MUCH BLOOD IN THEM.
YOU'RE USING RED PAINT SPRAY.

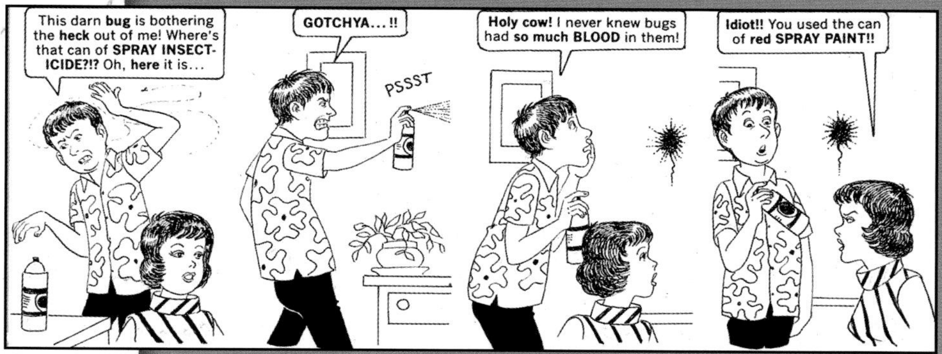
This darn **bug** is bothering the **heck** out of me! Where's that can of **SPRAY INSECT-ICIDE?!?** Oh, **here** it is...
GOTCHYA...!!
PSSST
Holy cow! I never knew bugs had **so much BLOOD** in them!
Idiot!! You used the can of **red SPRAY PAINT!!**

The Lighter Side of... MAD #236, January 1983

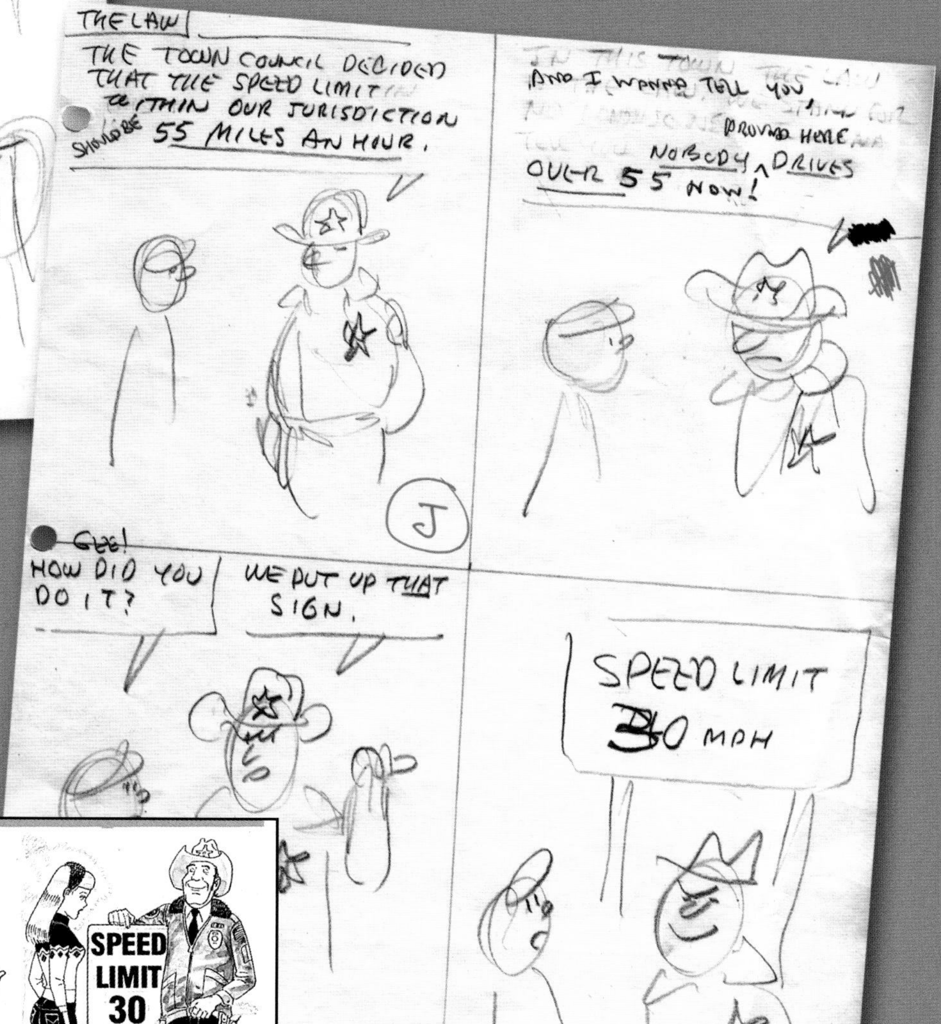
THE LAW
THE TOWN COUNCIL DECIDED THAT THE SPEED LIMIT WITHIN OUR JURISDICTION SHOULD BE 55 MILES AN HOUR.
NOBODY DRIVES OVER 55 NOW!
HOW DID YOU DO IT?
WE PUT UP THAT SIGN.
SPEED LIMIT
MPH

The Lighter Side of... MAD #247, June 1984

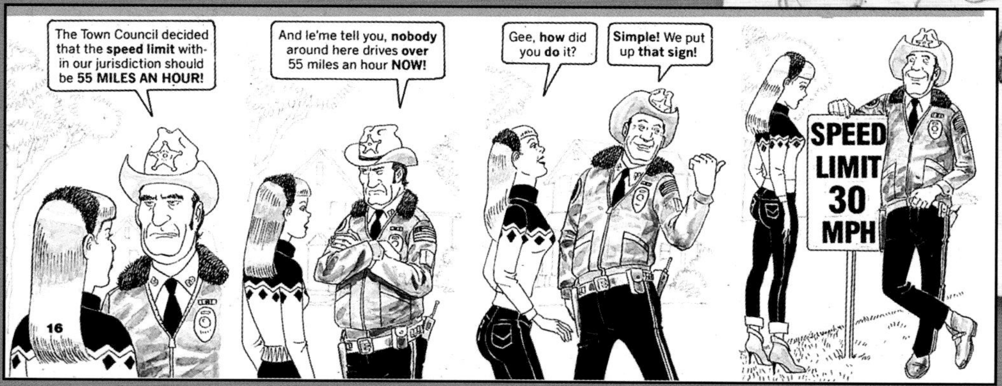
The Town Council decided that the **speed limit** with-in our jurisdiction should be **55 MILES AN HOUR!**
And le'me tell you, **nobody** around here drives **over** 55 miles an hour **NOW!**
Gee, **how** did you **do** it?
Simple! We put up **that sign!**
SPEED LIMIT 30 MPH
16

DRUGS

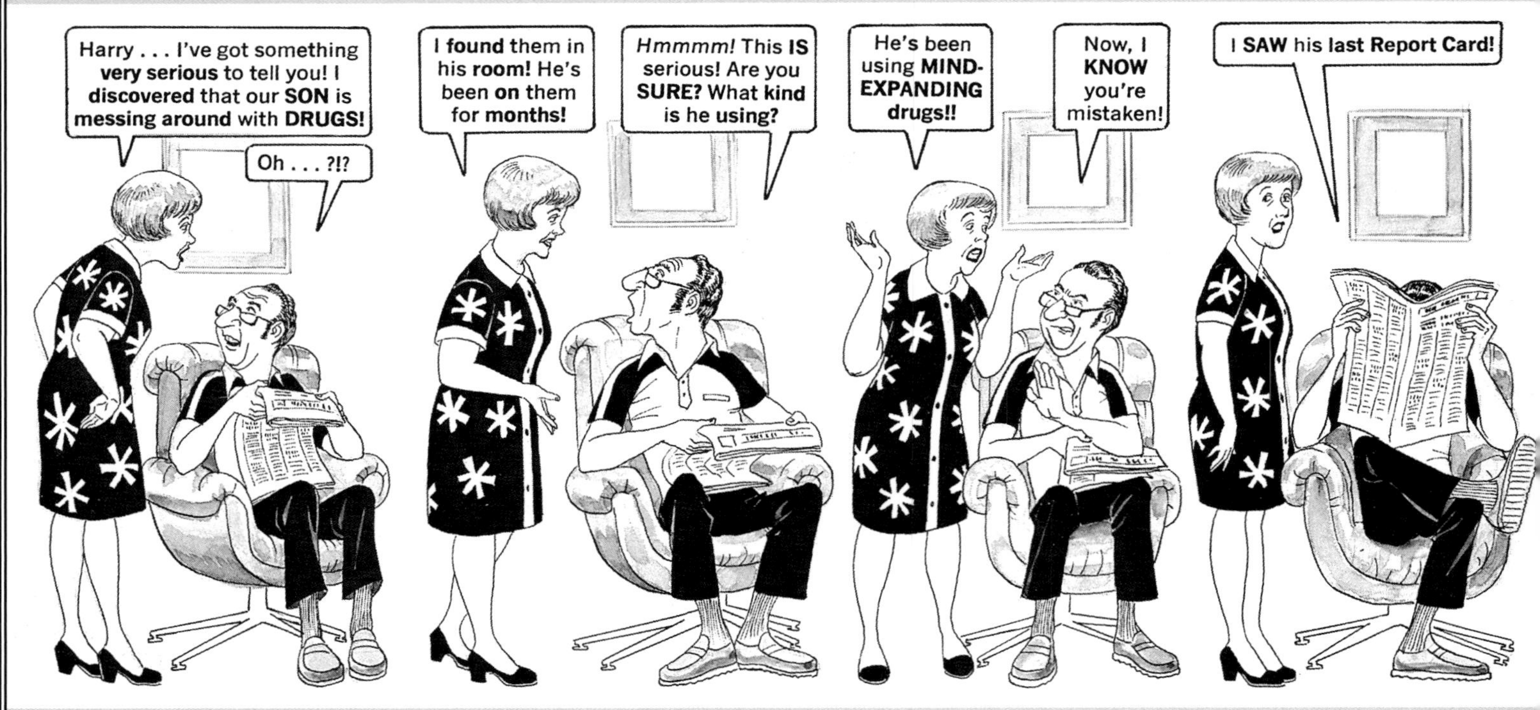
Harry . . . I've got something very serious to tell you! I discovered that our SON is messing around with DRUGS!
Oh . . . ?!?
I found them in his room! He's been on them for months!
Hmmmm! This IS serious! Are you SURE? What kind is he using?
He's been using MIND-EXPANDING drugs!!
Now, I KNOW you're mistaken!
I SAW his last Report Card!

BERG'S-EYE VIEW DEPT.

THE LIGHTE

SOCIAL CALLS

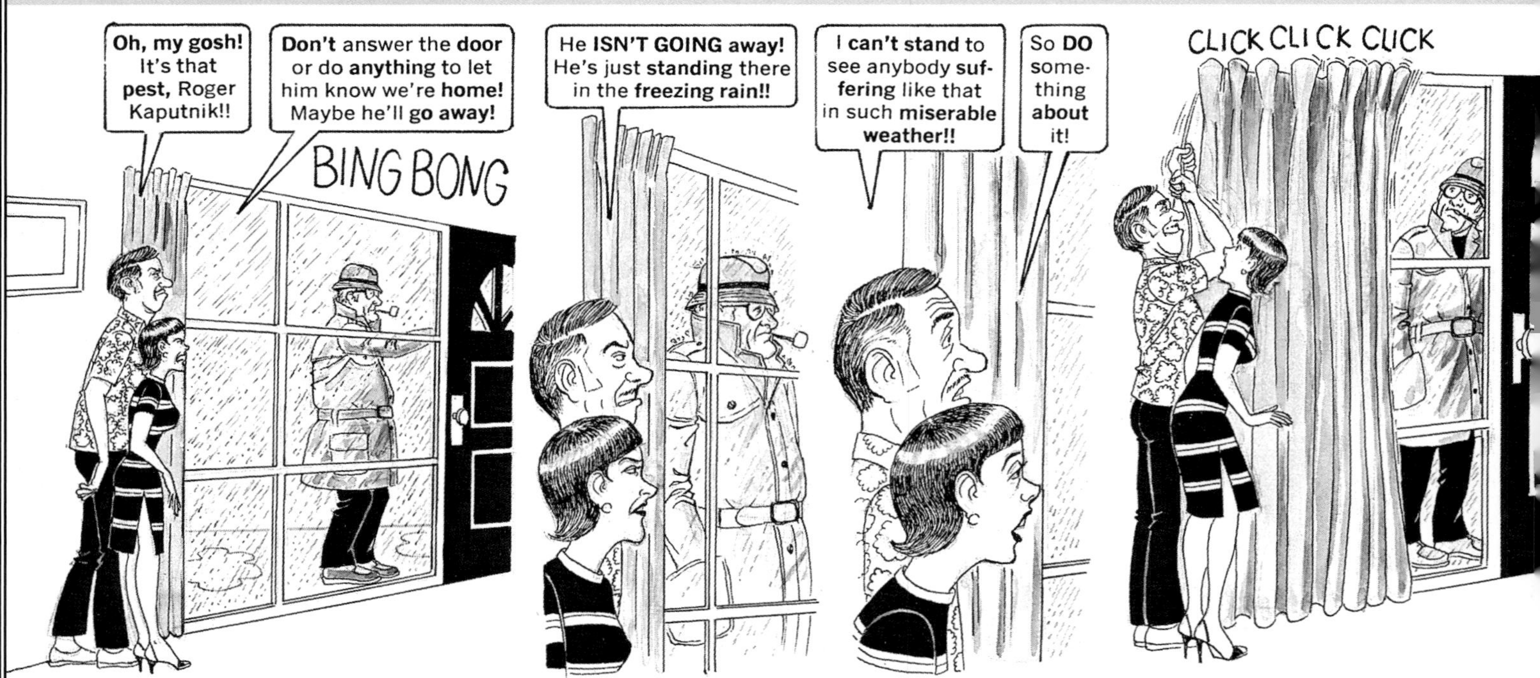
Oh, my gosh! It's that pest, Roger Kaputnik!!
Don't answer the door or do anything to let him know we're home! Maybe he'll go away!
BING BONG
He ISN'T GOING away! He's just standing there in the freezing rain!!
I can't stand to see anybody suffering like that in such miserable weather!!
So DO something about it!
CLICK CLICK CLICK

CHILDPLAY

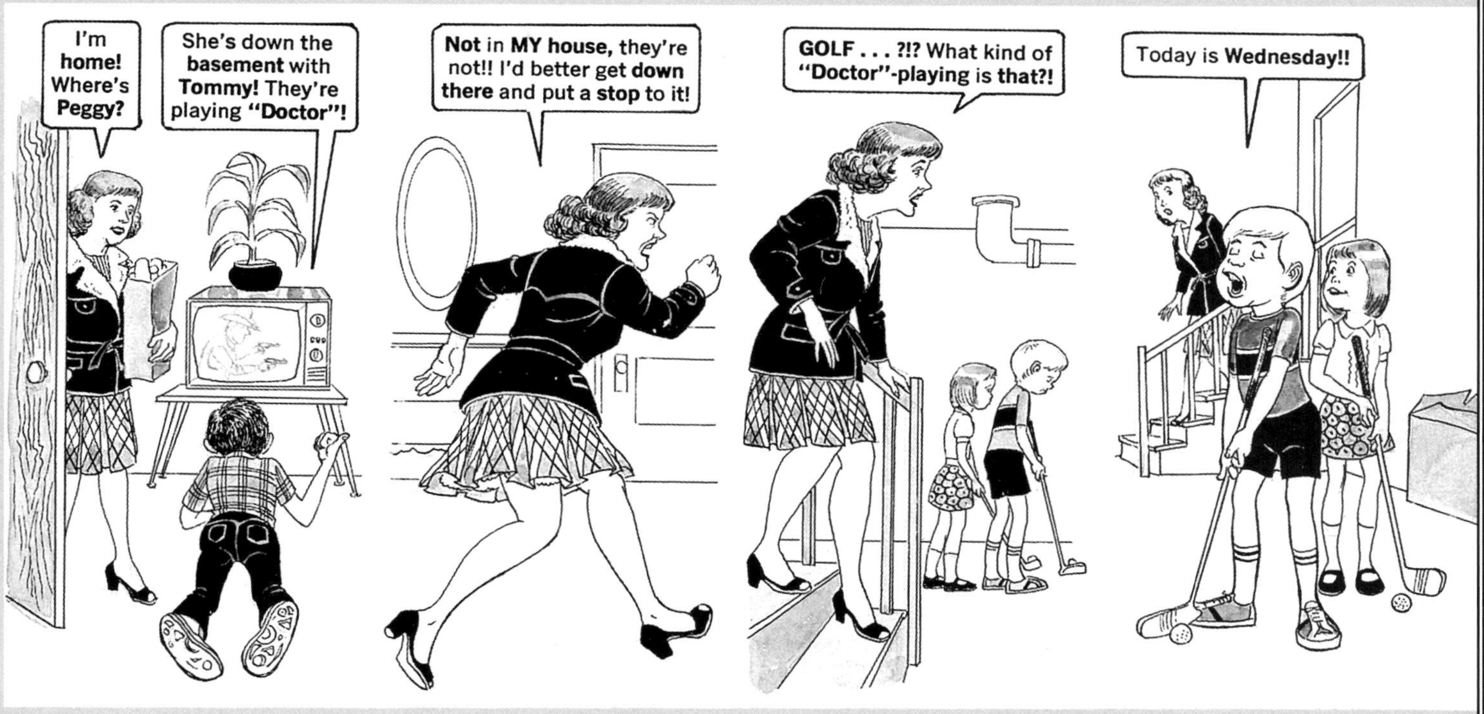
I'm home! Where's Peggy?
She's down the basement with Tommy! They're playing "Doctor"!
Not in MY house, they're not!! I'd better get down there and put a stop to it!
GOLF . . . ?!? What kind of "Doctor"-playing is that?!
Today is Wednesday!!

R SIDE OF...

ARTIST & WRITER: DAVE BERG

MEDICINE

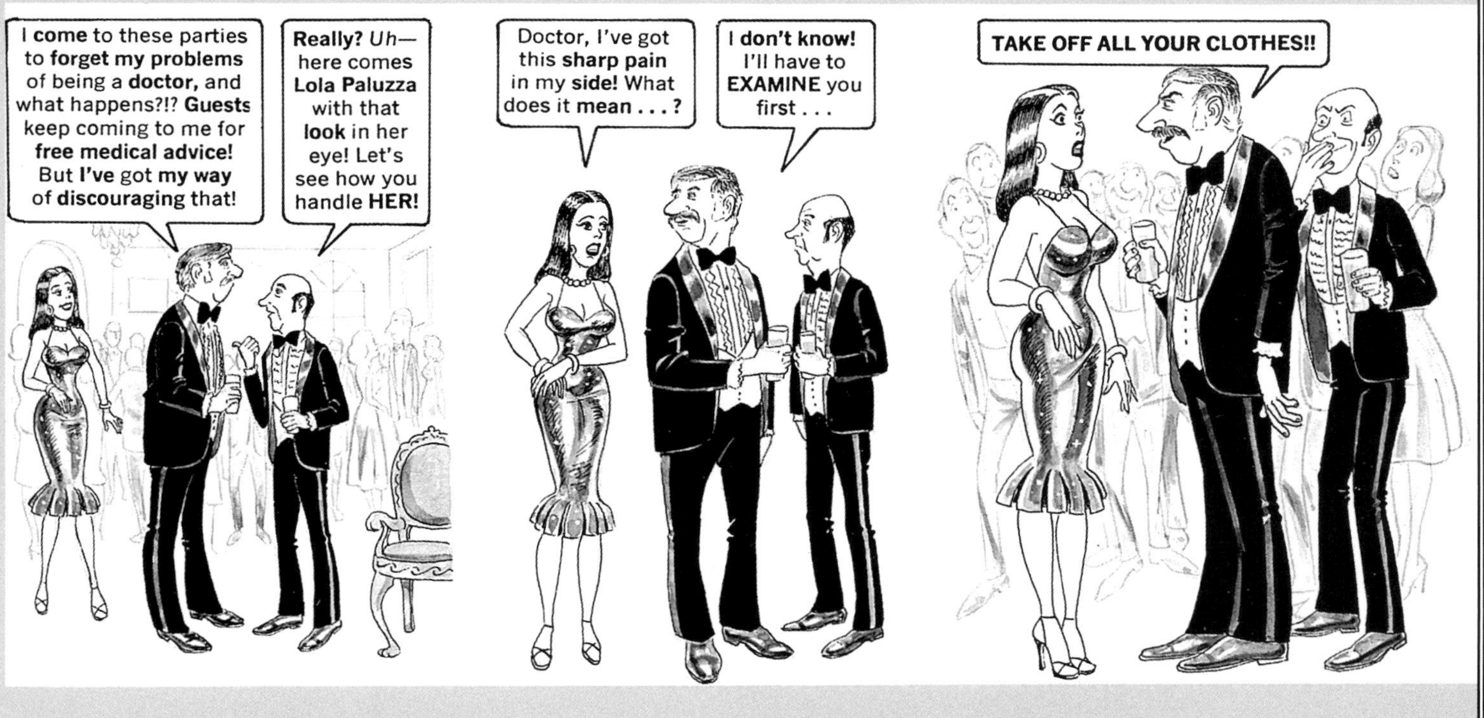
I come to these parties to forget my problems of being a doctor, and what happens?!? Guests keep coming to me for free medical advice! But I've got my way of discouraging that!
Really? Uh— here comes Lola Paluzza with that look in her eye! Let's see how you handle HER!
Doctor, I've got this sharp pain in my side! What does it mean . . . ?
I don't know! I'll have to EXAMINE you first . . .
TAKE OFF ALL YOUR CLOTHES!!

INFLATION

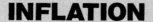

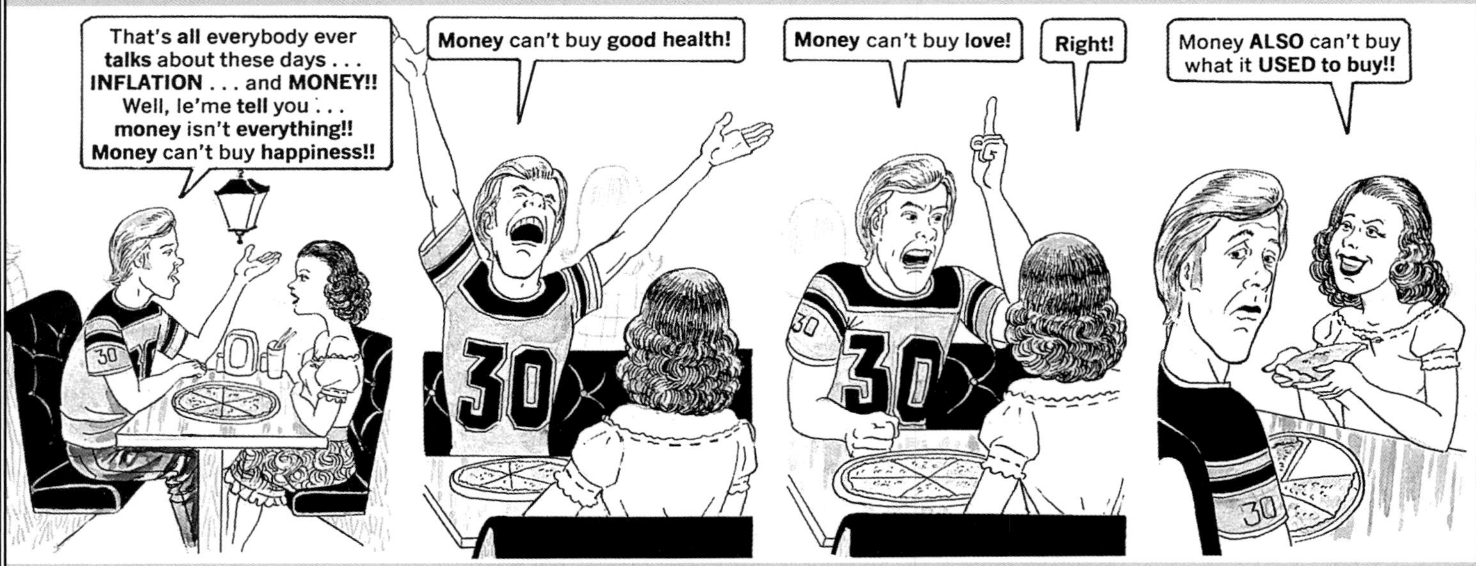
That's all everybody ever talks about these days . . . INFLATION . . . and MONEY!! Well, le'me tell you . . . money isn't everything!! Money can't buy happiness!!
Money can't buy good health!
Money can't buy love!
Right!
Money ALSO can't buy what it USED to buy!!

ON THE JOB

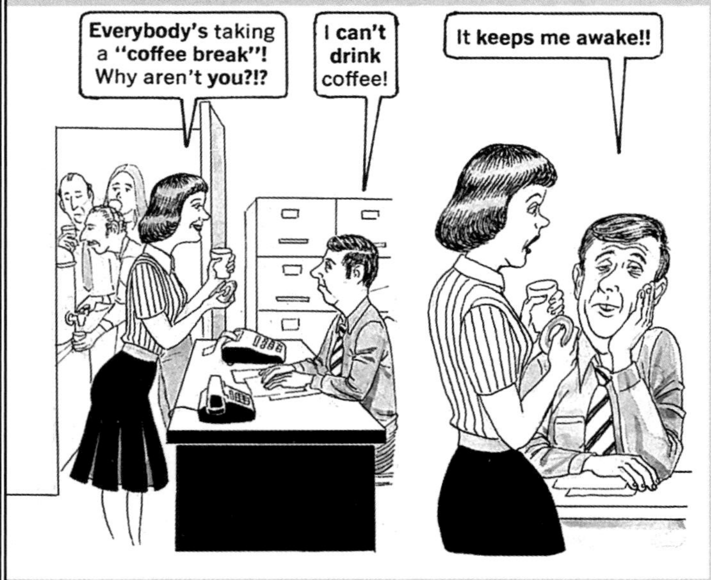
Everybody's taking a "coffee break"! Why aren't you?!?
I can't drink coffee!
It keeps me awake!!

DRESSING UP

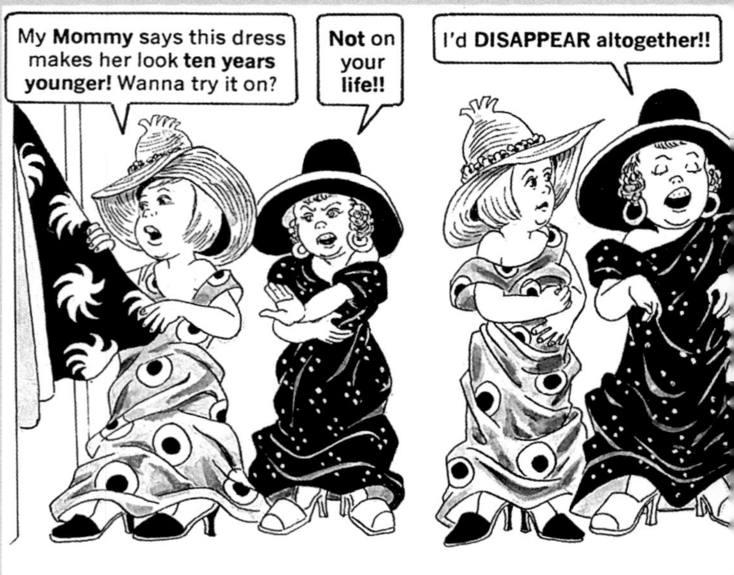
My Mommy says this dress makes her look ten years younger! Wanna try it on?
Not on your life!!
I'd DISAPPEAR altogether!!

STYLES

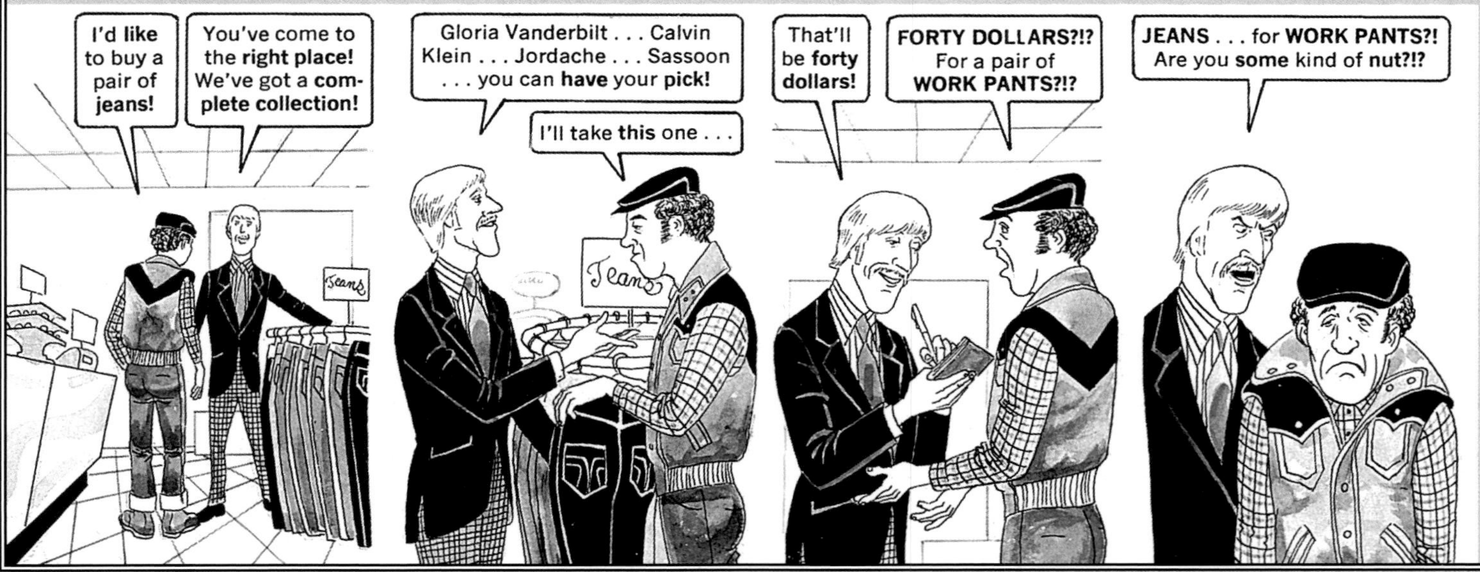
I'd like to buy a pair of jeans!
You've come to the right place! We've got a complete collection!
Gloria Vanderbilt . . . Calvin Klein . . . Jordache . . . Sassoon . . . you can have your pick!
I'll take this one . . .
That'll be forty dollars!
FORTY DOLLARS?!? For a pair of WORK PANTS?!?
JEANS . . . for WORK PANTS?! Are you some kind of nut?!?

GIFTS

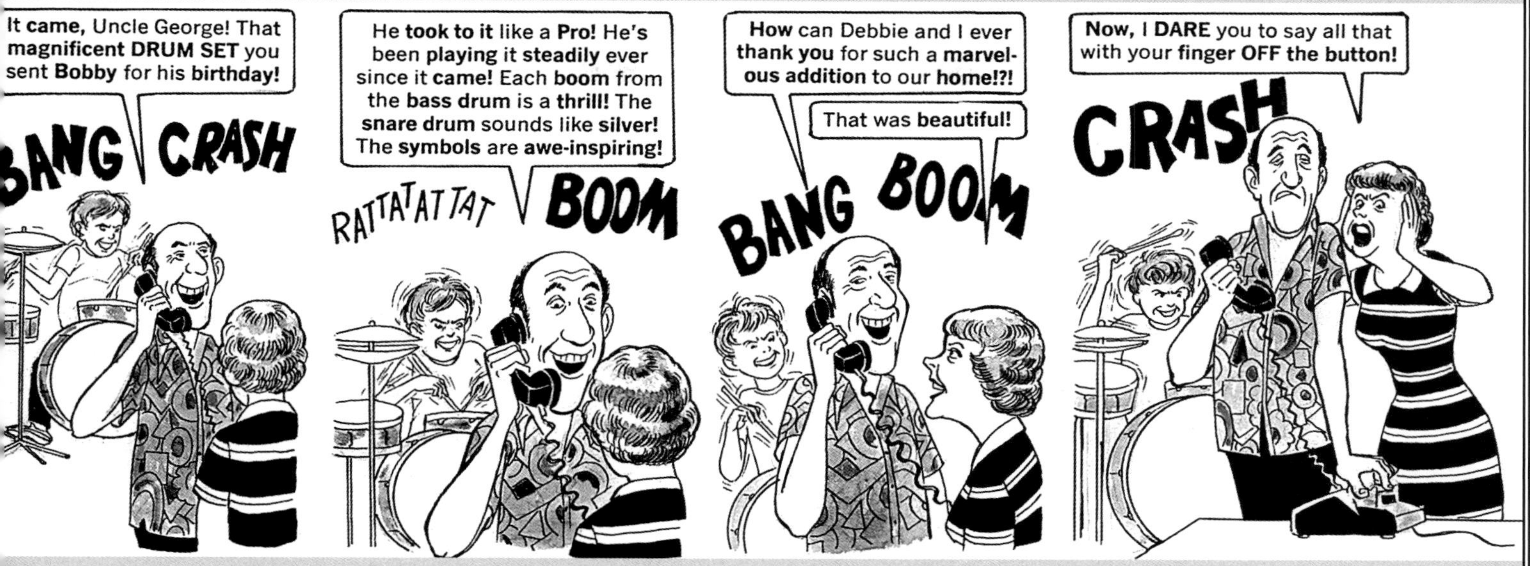
It came, Uncle George! That magnificent DRUM SET you sent Bobby for his birthday!
BANG CRASH
He took to it like a Pro! He's been playing it steadily ever since it came! Each boom from the bass drum is a thrill! The snare drum sounds like silver! The symbols are awe-inspiring!
RATTATATTAT TAT BOOM
How can Debbie and I ever thank you for such a marvel- ous addition to our home!?!
That was beautiful!
BANG BOOM
Now, I DARE you to say all that with your finger OFF the button!
CRASH

ACTIVISTS

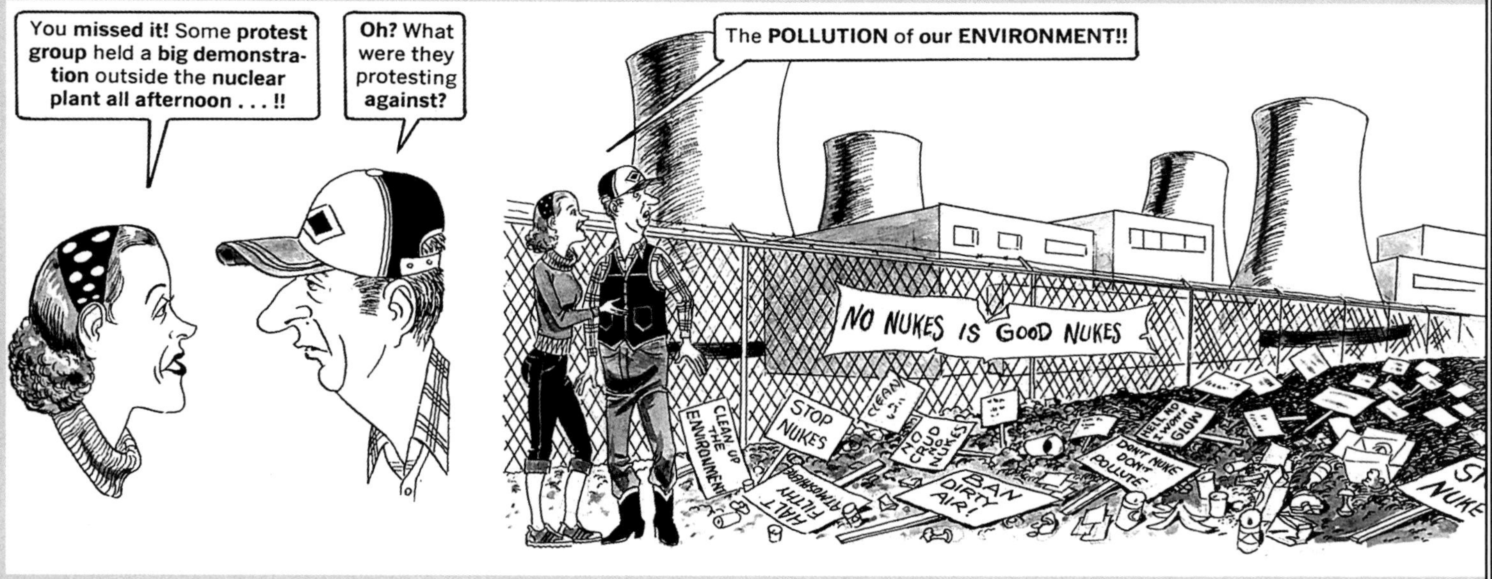
You missed it! Some protest group held a big demonstra- tion outside the nuclear plant all afternoon . . . !!
Oh? What were they protesting against?
The POLLUTION of our ENVIRONMENT!!
NO NUKES IS GOOD NUKES
STOP NUKES
CLEAN UP THE ENVIRONMENT
BAN DIRTY AIR!
DON'T NUKE DON'T POLLUTE

SHOPPING

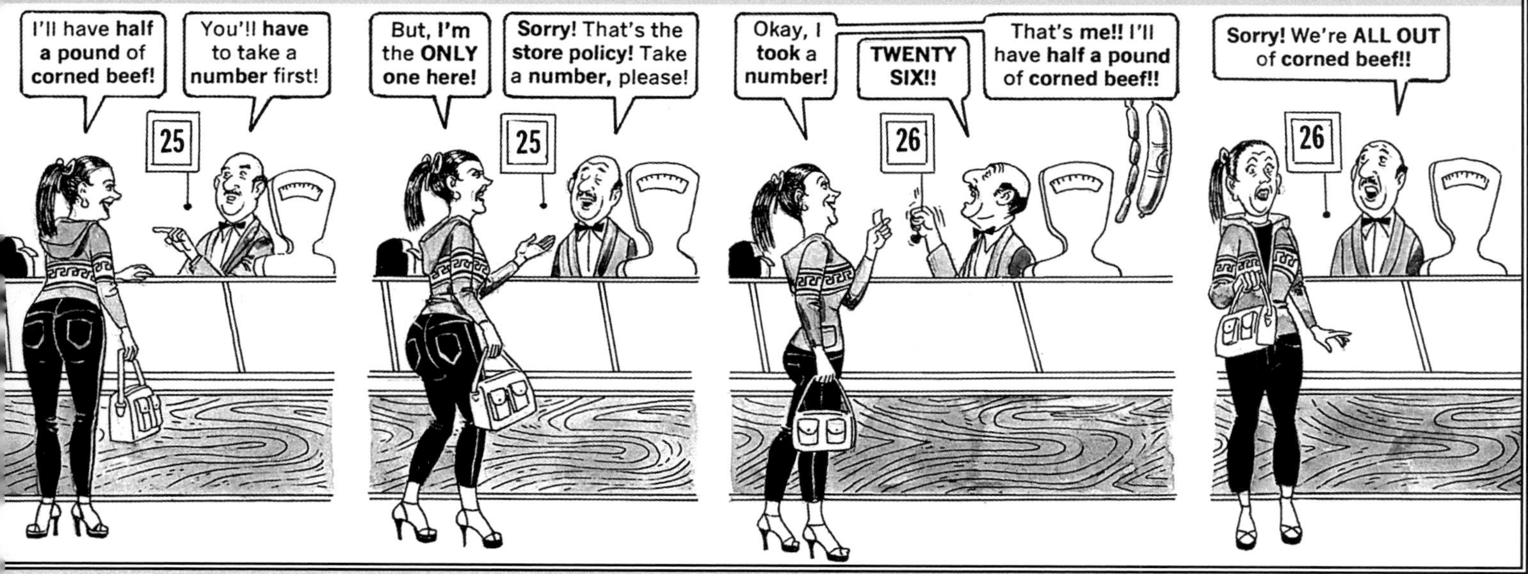
I'll have half a pound of corned beef!
You'll have to take a number first!
25
But, I'm the ONLY one here!
Sorry! That's the store policy! Take a number, please!
25
Okay, I took a number!
TWENTY SIX!!
That's me!! I'll have half a pound of corned beef!!
26
Sorry! We're ALL OUT of corned beef!!
26

THE CAR

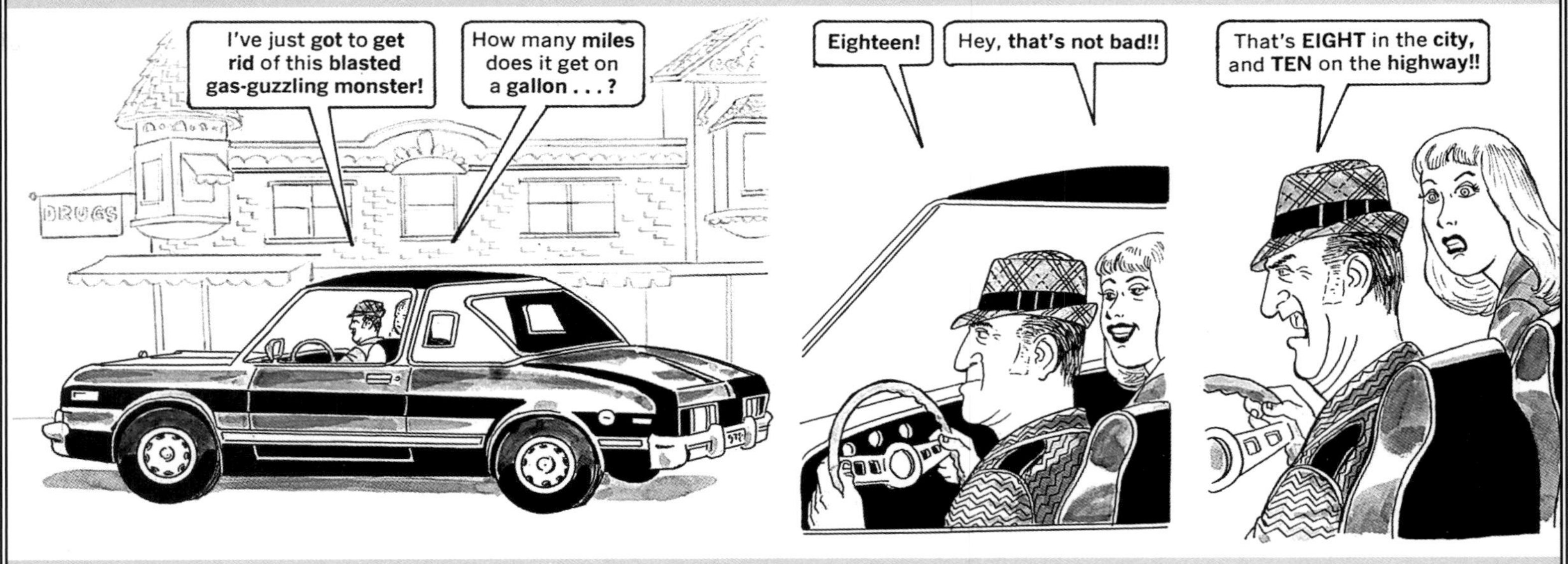
I've just got to get rid of this blasted gas-guzzling monster!
How many miles does it get on a gallon . . . ?
DRUGS
Eighteen!
Hey, that's not bad!!
That's EIGHT in the city, and TEN on the highway!!

EATING

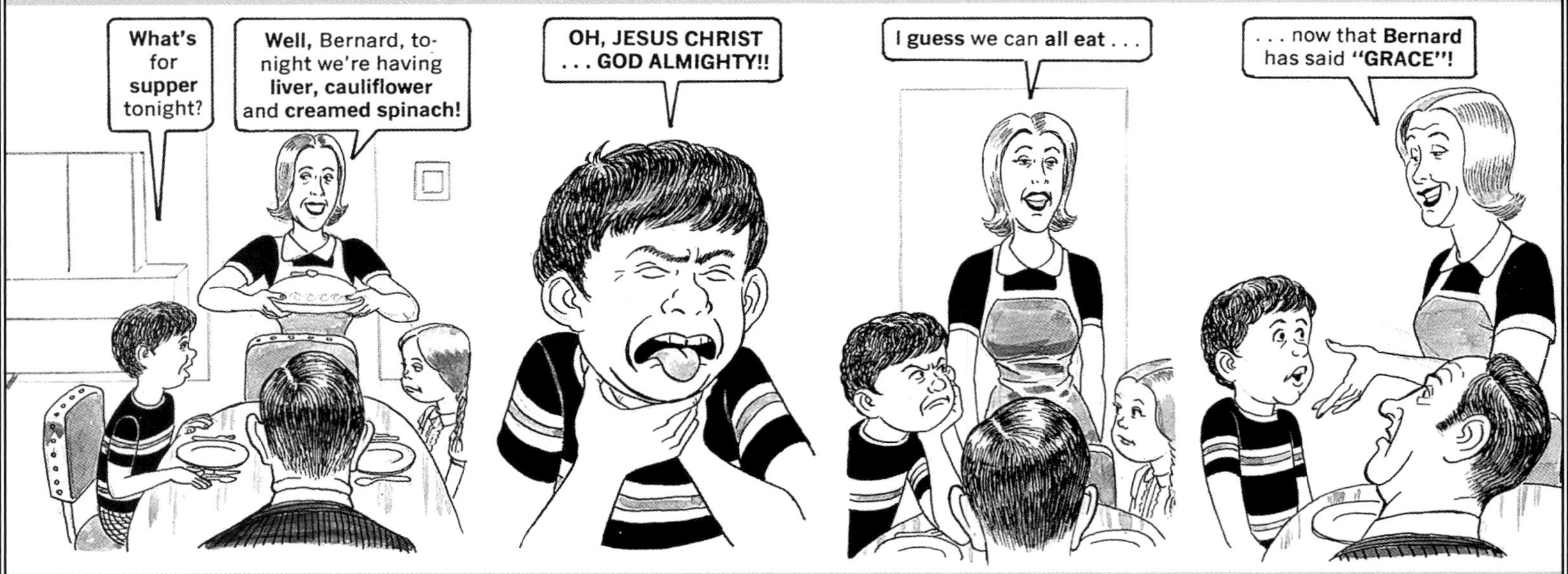
What's for supper tonight?
Well, Bernard, tonight we're having liver, cauliflower and creamed spinach!
OH, JESUS CHRIST . . . GOD ALMIGHTY!!
I guess we can all eat . . .
. . . now that Bernard has said "GRACE"!

MARRIAGE

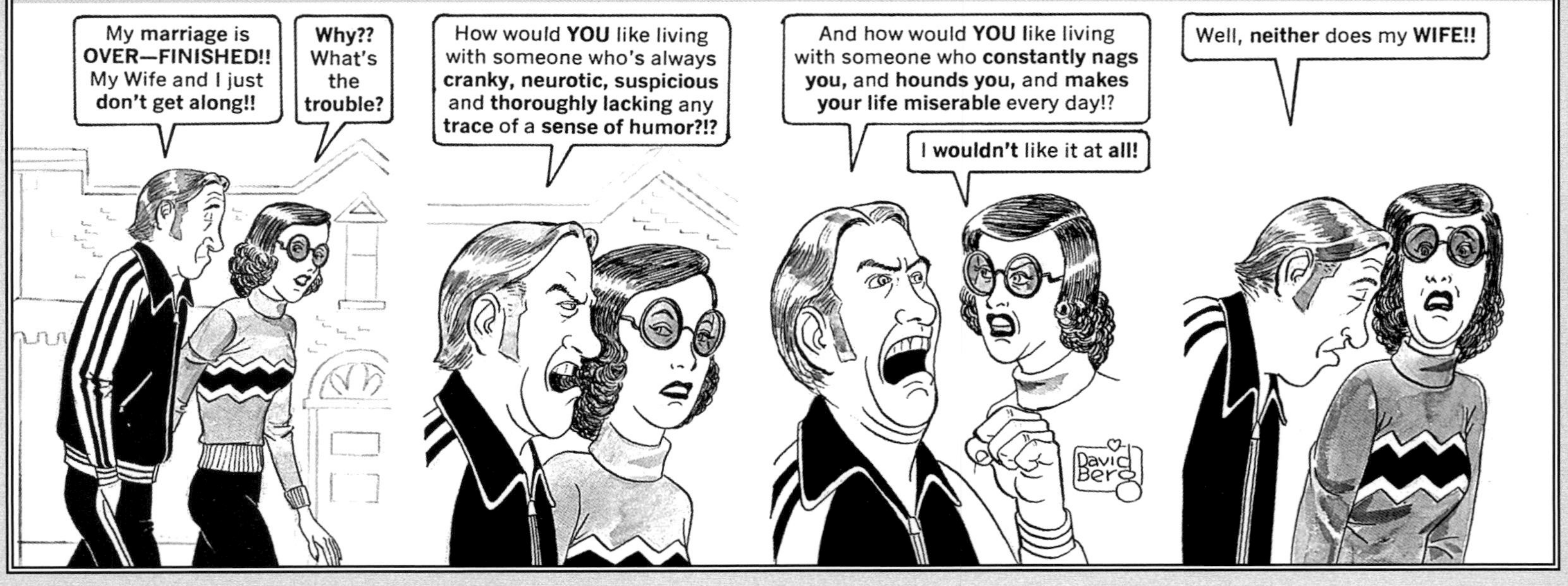
My marriage is OVER—FINISHED!! My Wife and I just don't get along!!
Why?? What's the trouble?
How would YOU like living with someone who's always cranky, neurotic, suspicious and thoroughly lacking any trace of a sense of humor?!?
And how would YOU like living with someone who constantly nags you, and hounds you, and makes your life miserable every day!?
I wouldn't like it at all!
Well, neither does my WIFE!!
David Berg

MAD Kids: Little Roger Kaputnik

From 2005 to 2009, MAD also published MAD Kids, a magazine for younger readers presenting new and classic features. Several strips were created using Dave Berg's vast archive of comic scripts, re-imagined by artists in color. As a salute to Dave, one of the comics spotlighted a young man named Little Roger Kaputnik, as drawn by Doug Holgate.

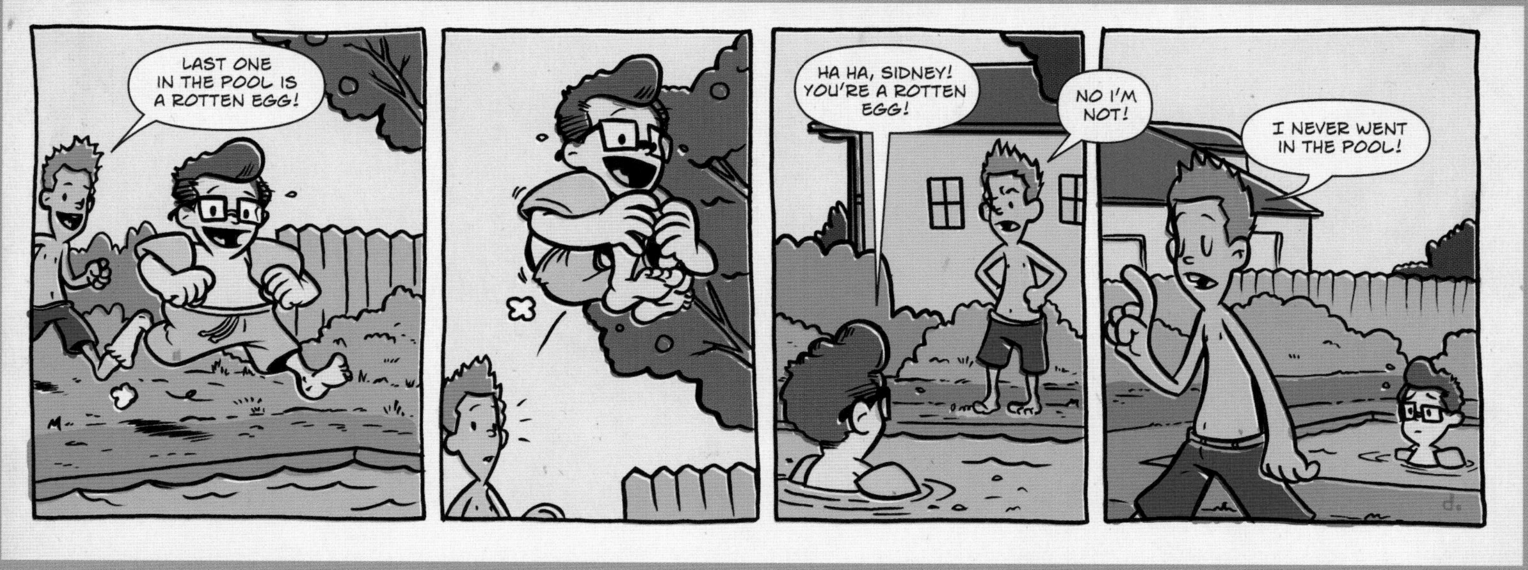
LAST ONE IN THE POOL IS A ROTTEN EGG!
HA HA, SIDNEY! YOU'RE A ROTTEN EGG!
NO I'M NOT!
I NEVER WENT IN THE POOL!

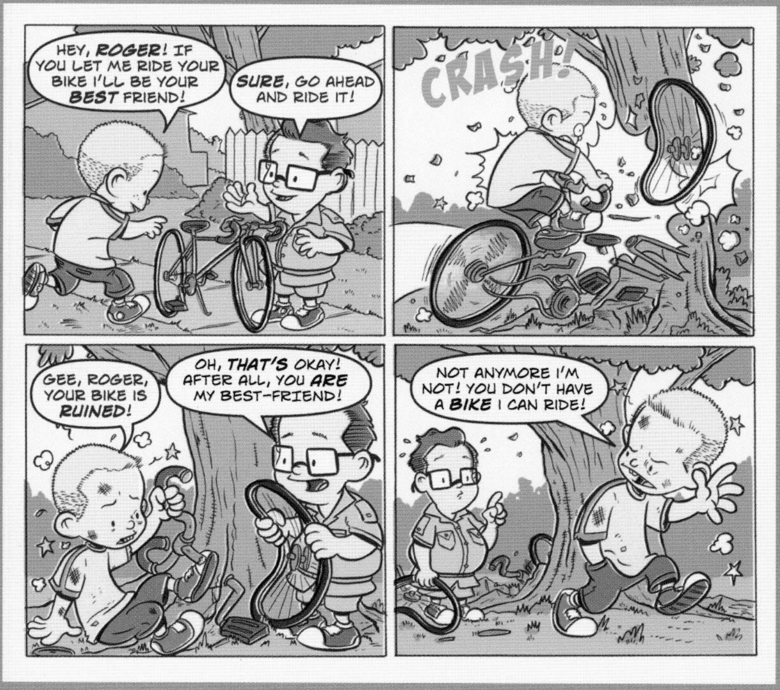
HEY, ROGER! IF YOU LET ME RIDE YOUR BIKE I'LL BE YOUR BEST FRIEND!
SURE, GO AHEAD AND RIDE IT!
CRASH!
GEE, ROGER, YOUR BIKE IS RUINED!
OH, THAT'S OKAY! AFTER ALL, YOU ARE MY BEST-FRIEND!
NOT ANYMORE I'M NOT! YOU DON'T HAVE A BIKE I CAN RIDE!

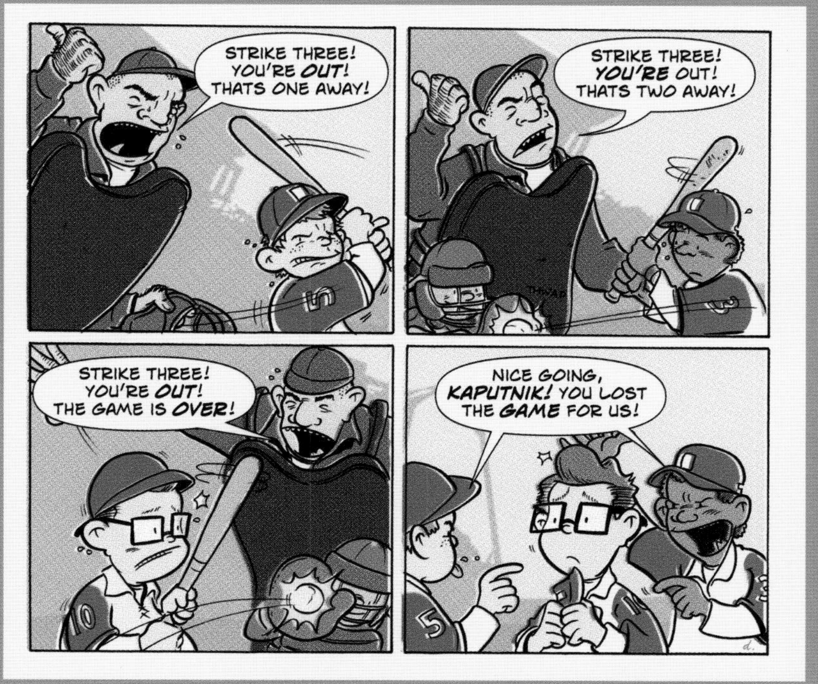
STRIKE THREE! YOU'RE OUT! THATS ONE AWAY!
STRIKE THREE! YOU'RE OUT! THATS TWO AWAY!
STRIKE THREE! YOU'RE OUT! THE GAME IS OVER!
NICE GOING, KAPUTNIK! YOU LOST THE GAME FOR US!

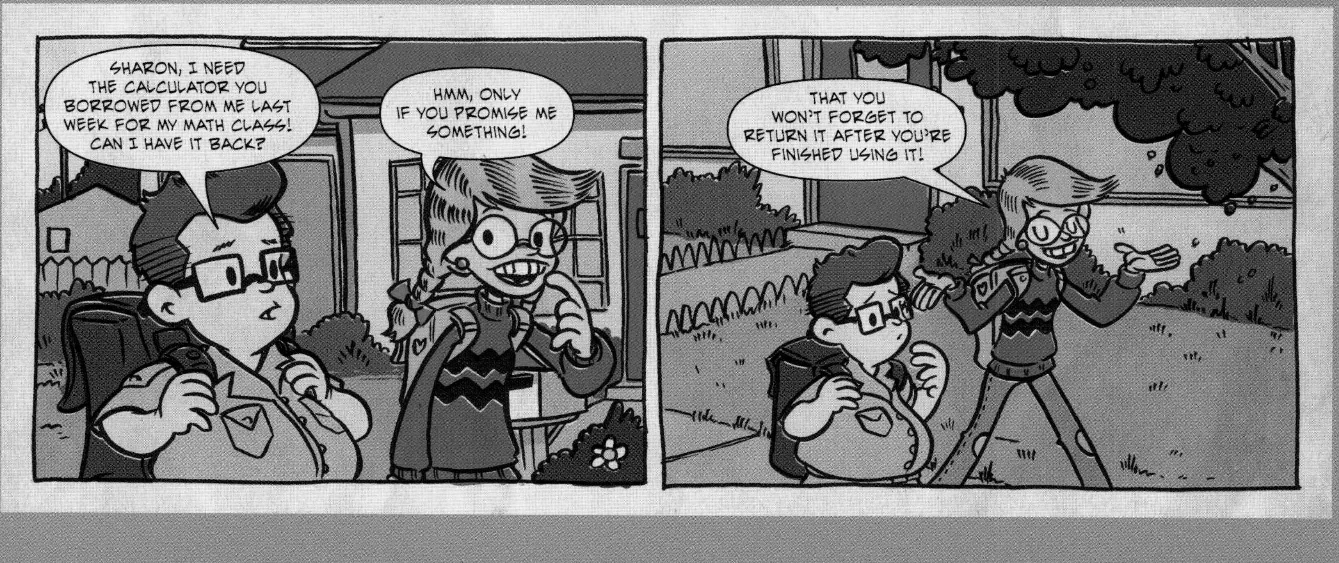
SHARON, I NEED THE CALCULATOR YOU BORROWED FROM ME LAST WEEK FOR MY MATH CLASS! CAN I HAVE IT BACK?
HMM, ONLY IF YOU PROMISE ME SOMETHING!
THAT YOU WON'T FORGET TO RETURN IT AFTER YOU'RE FINISHED USING IT!

COMPARISONS

Are you playing with that **video game** again? What about **studying?!** What about **homework?!**

Ahhhh, school is such a **bore!**

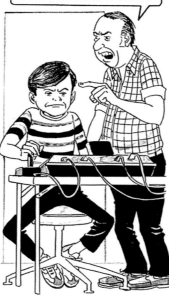

Listen, bum! When **Abraham Lincoln** was your age, he **walked ten miles** to school!

When **Abraham Lincoln** was your age, he did his **homework** by **fire-light!!**

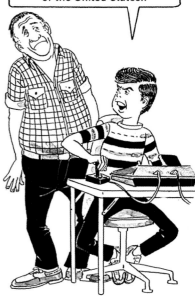

And when **Abraham Lincoln** was YOUR age, he was **President of the United States!!**

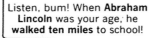

BERG'S-EYE VIEW DEPT.

THE LIGHTE

EMERGENCIES

Mmmmmm! That was one heck of a **delicious barbecue!!**

Oh, my gosh...! I think I swallowed a **TOOTHPICK!**

Better call a **DOCTOR!**

That **won't** be **necessary!!**

We have **lots more toothpicks!**

BABY SITTERS

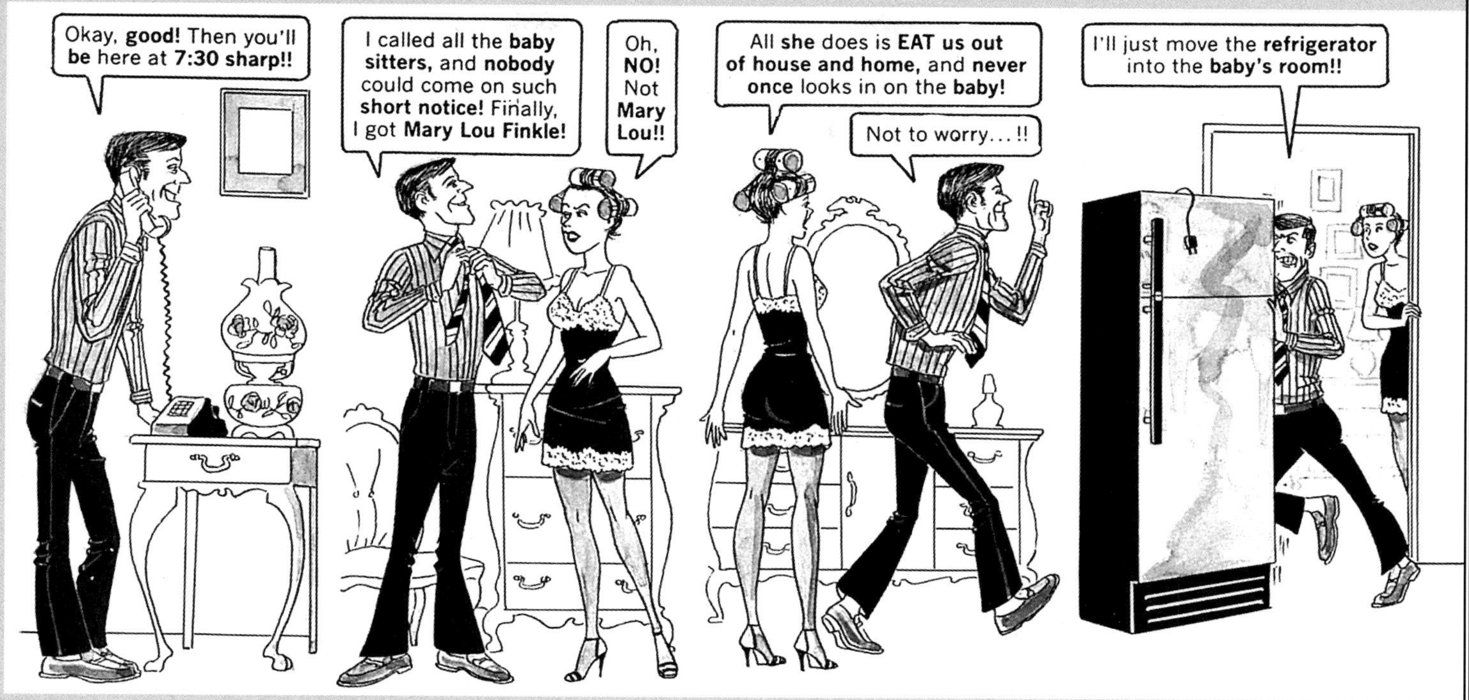
Okay, good! Then you'll be here at 7:30 sharp!!
I called all the baby sitters, and nobody could come on such short notice! Finally, I got Mary Lou Finkle!
Oh, NO! Not Mary Lou!!
All she does is EAT us out of house and home, and never once looks in on the baby!
Not to worry...!!
I'll just move the refrigerator into the baby's room!!

R SIDE OF...

ARTIST & WRITER:
DAVE BERG

GUILT

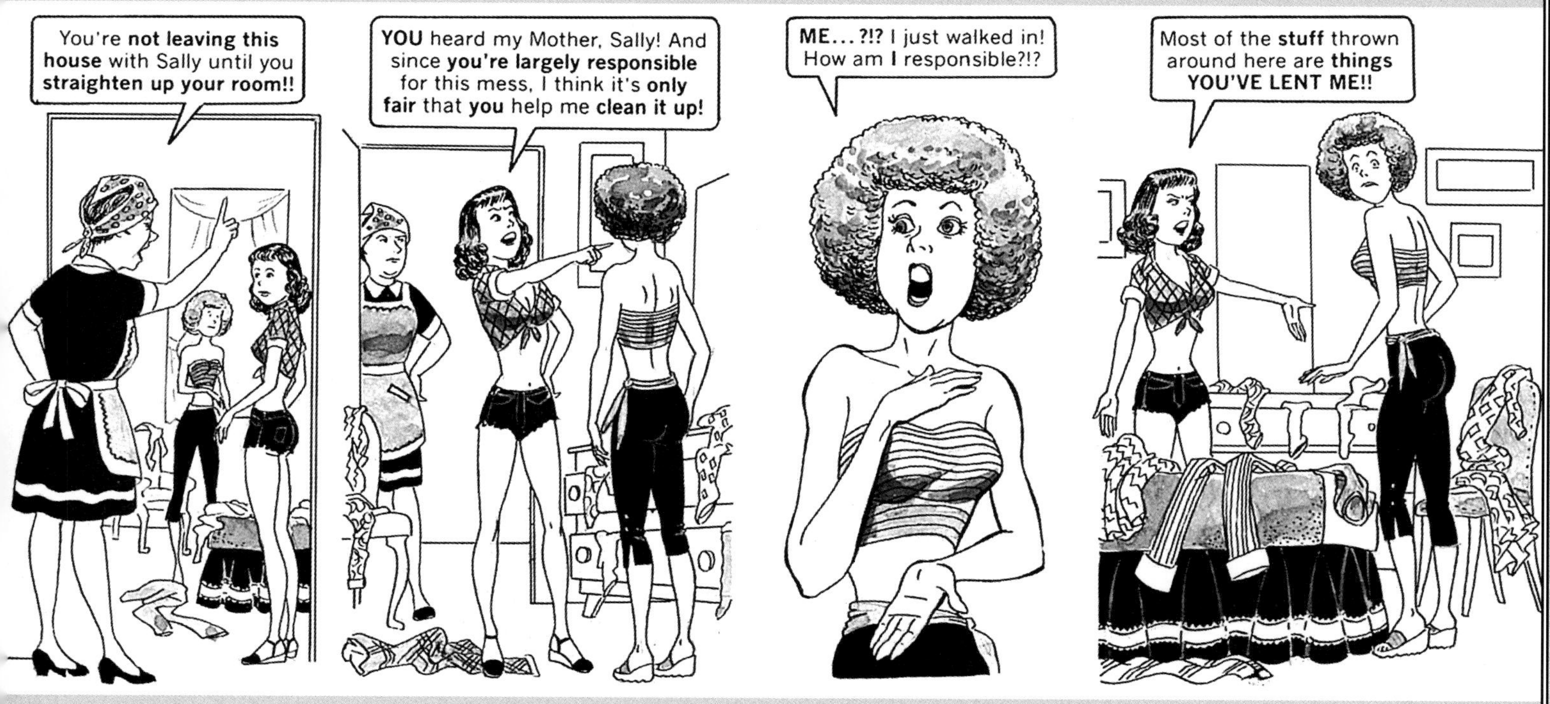
You're not leaving this house with Sally until you straighten up your room!!
YOU heard my Mother, Sally! And since you're largely responsible for this mess, I think it's only fair that you help me clean it up!
ME...?!? I just walked in! How am I responsible?!?
Most of the stuff thrown around here are things YOU'VE LENT ME!!

SPLITSVILLE

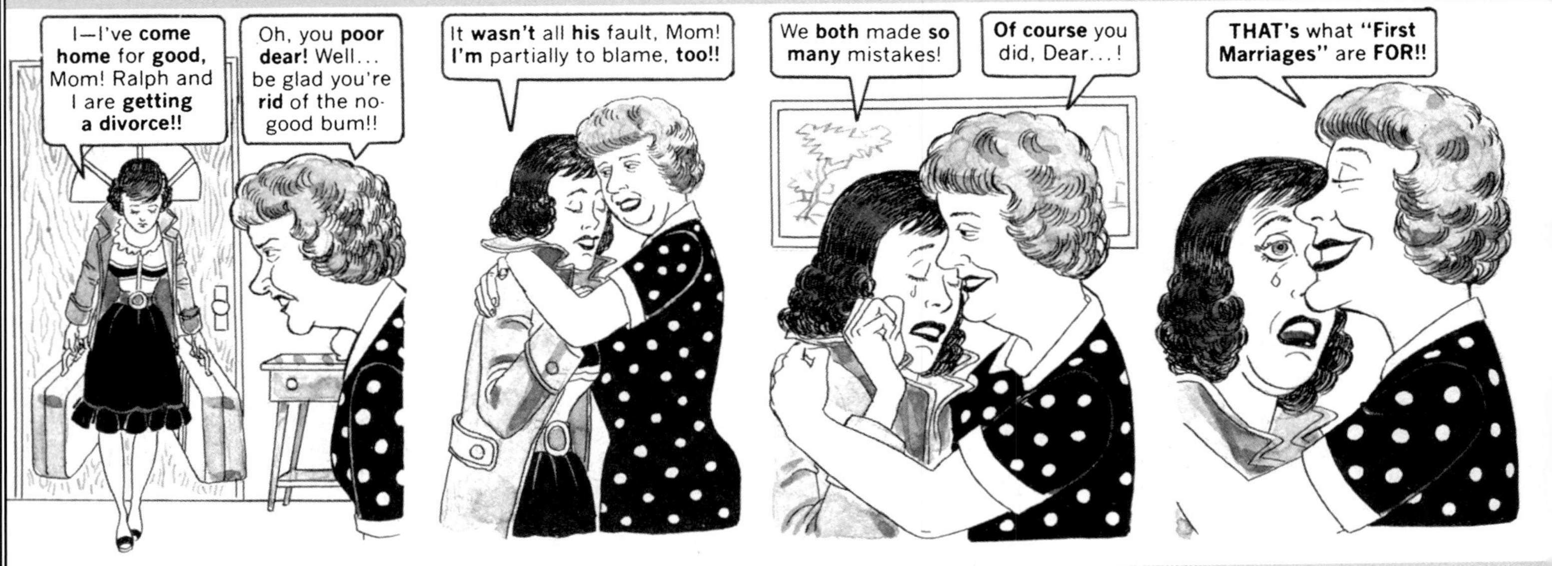
I—I've **come home** for **good,** Mom! Ralph and I are **getting a divorce!!**
Oh, you **poor dear!** Well... be glad you're **rid** of the no-good bum!!
It **wasn't** all **his** fault, Mom! **I'm** partially to blame, **too!!**
We **both** made **so many** mistakes!
Of course you did, Dear...!
THAT's what **"First Marriages"** are **FOR!!**

OLD AGE

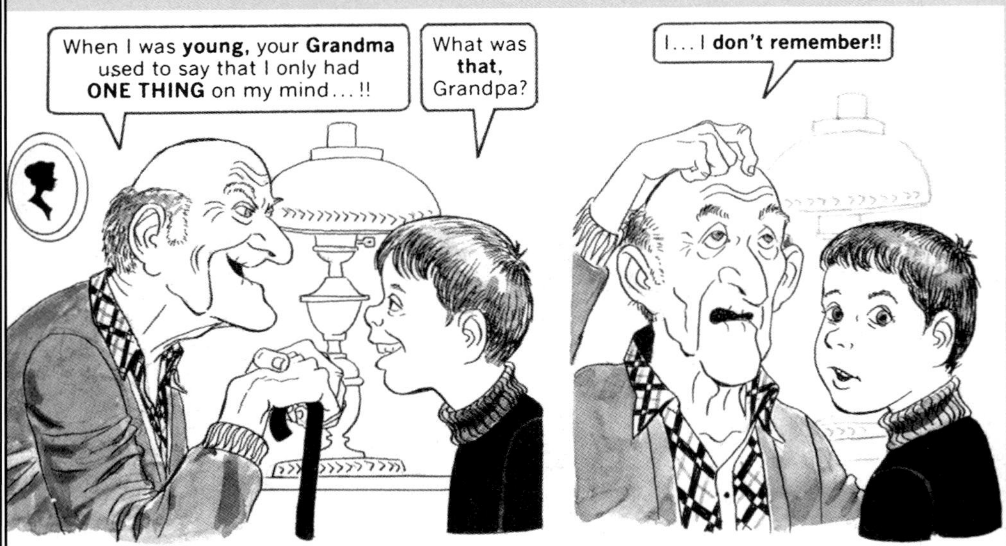
When I was **young,** your **Grandma** used to say that I only had **ONE THING** on my mind...!!
What was **that,** Grandpa?
I... I **don't remember!!**

TRAVELING

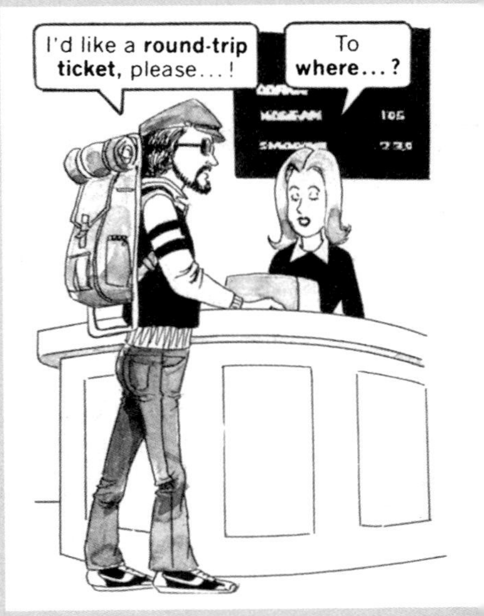
I'd like a **round-trip ticket,** please...!
To **where...?**

EATING OUT

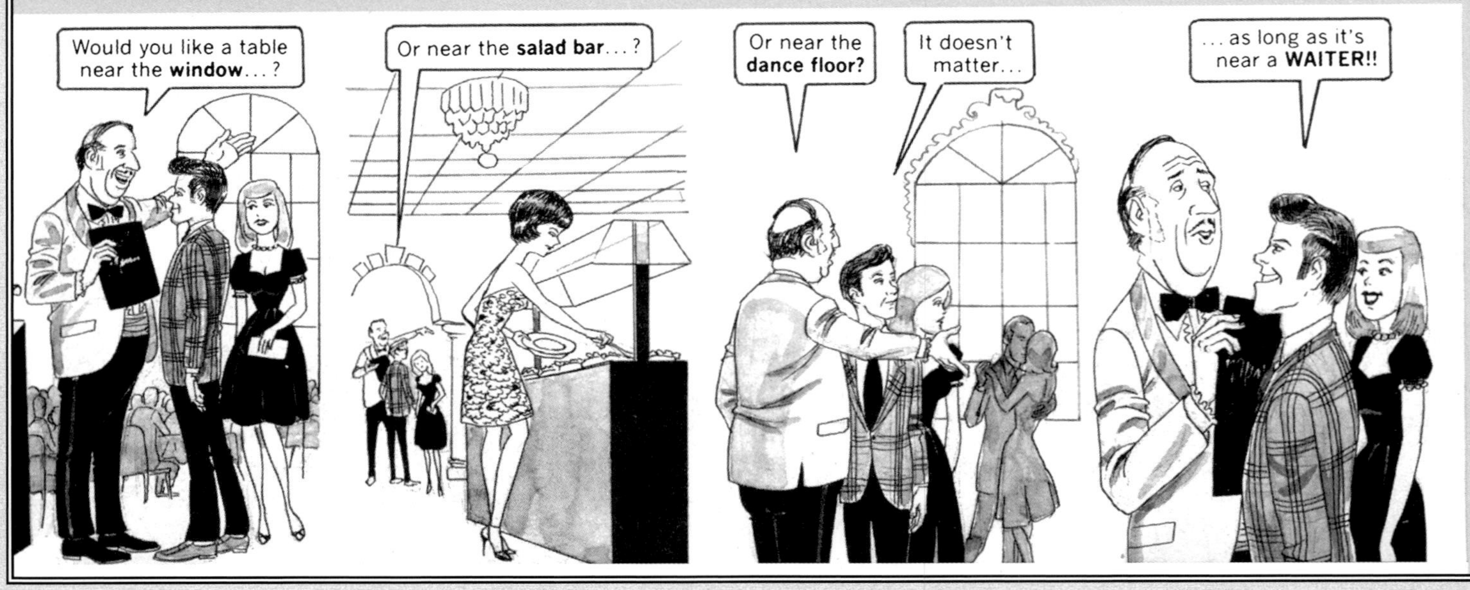
Would you like a table near the **window**...?
Or near the **salad bar**...?
Or near the **dance floor?**
It doesn't matter...
...as long as it's near a **WAITER!!**

ANSWERS

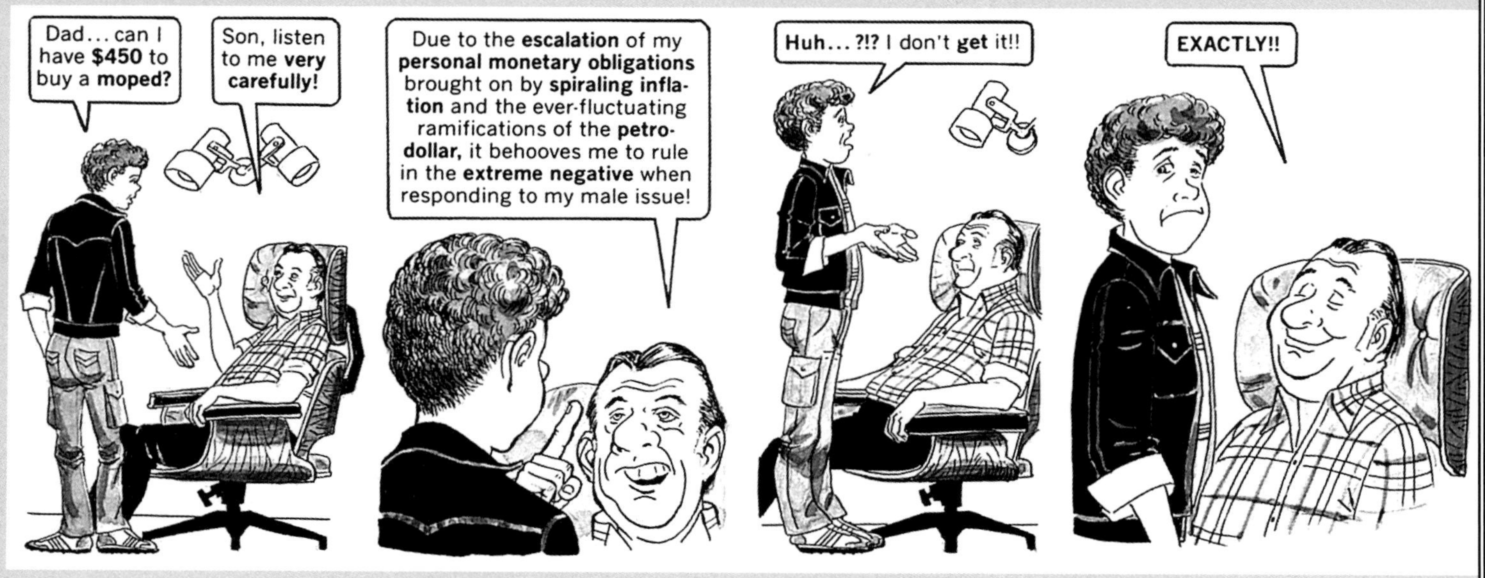
Dad... can I have $450 to buy a moped?
Son, listen to me very carefully!
Due to the escalation of my personal monetary obligations brought on by spiraling inflation and the ever-fluctuating ramifications of the petro-dollar, it behooves me to rule in the extreme negative when responding to my male issue!
Huh... ?!? I don't get it!!
EXACTLY!!

FAST FOOD JOINTS

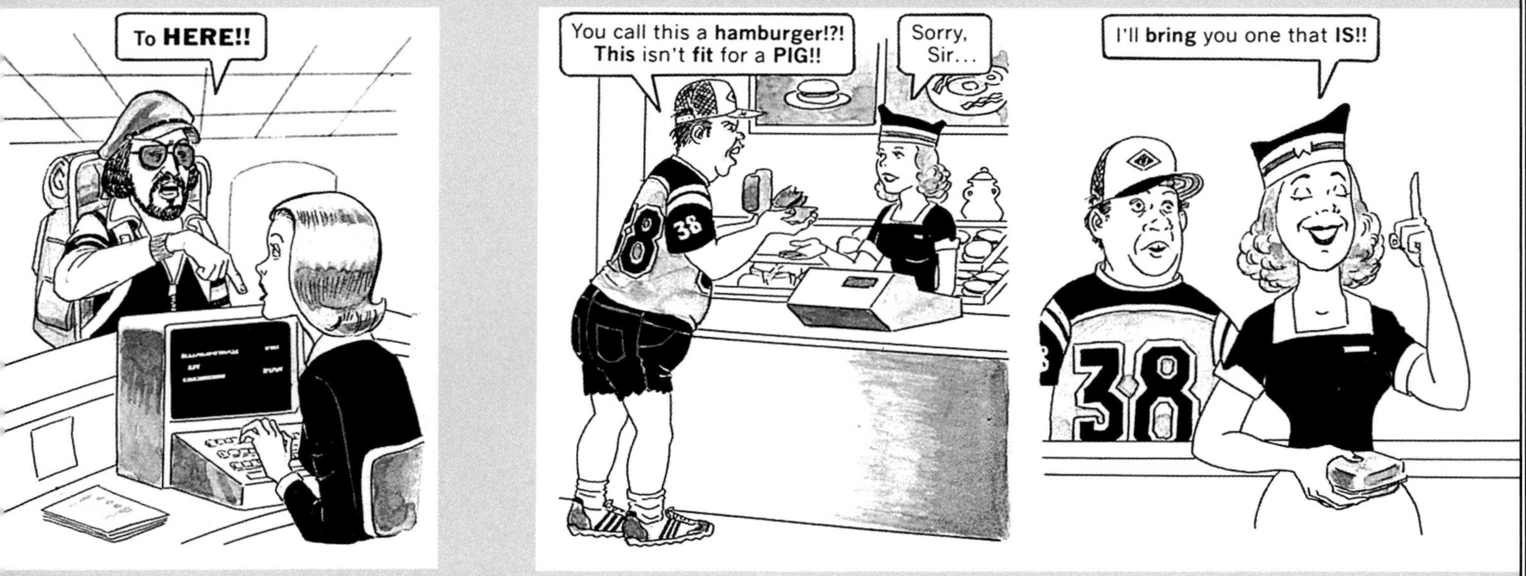
To HERE!!
You call this a hamburger!?! This isn't fit for a PIG!!
Sorry, Sir...
I'll bring you one that IS!!

NEIGHBORS

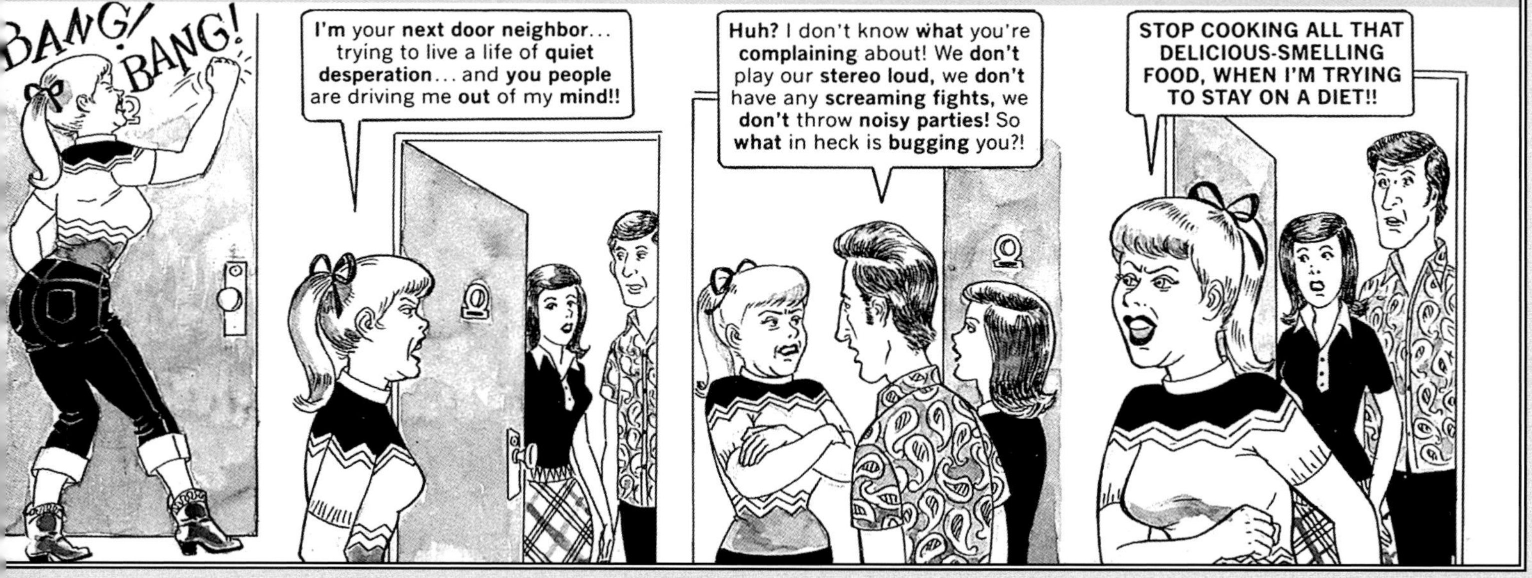
BANG! BANG!
I'm your next door neighbor... trying to live a life of quiet desperation... and you people are driving me out of my mind!!
Huh? I don't know what you're complaining about! We don't play our stereo loud, we don't have any screaming fights, we don't throw noisy parties! So what in heck is bugging you?!
STOP COOKING ALL THAT DELICIOUS-SMELLING FOOD, WHEN I'M TRYING TO STAY ON A DIET!!

HANDGUNS

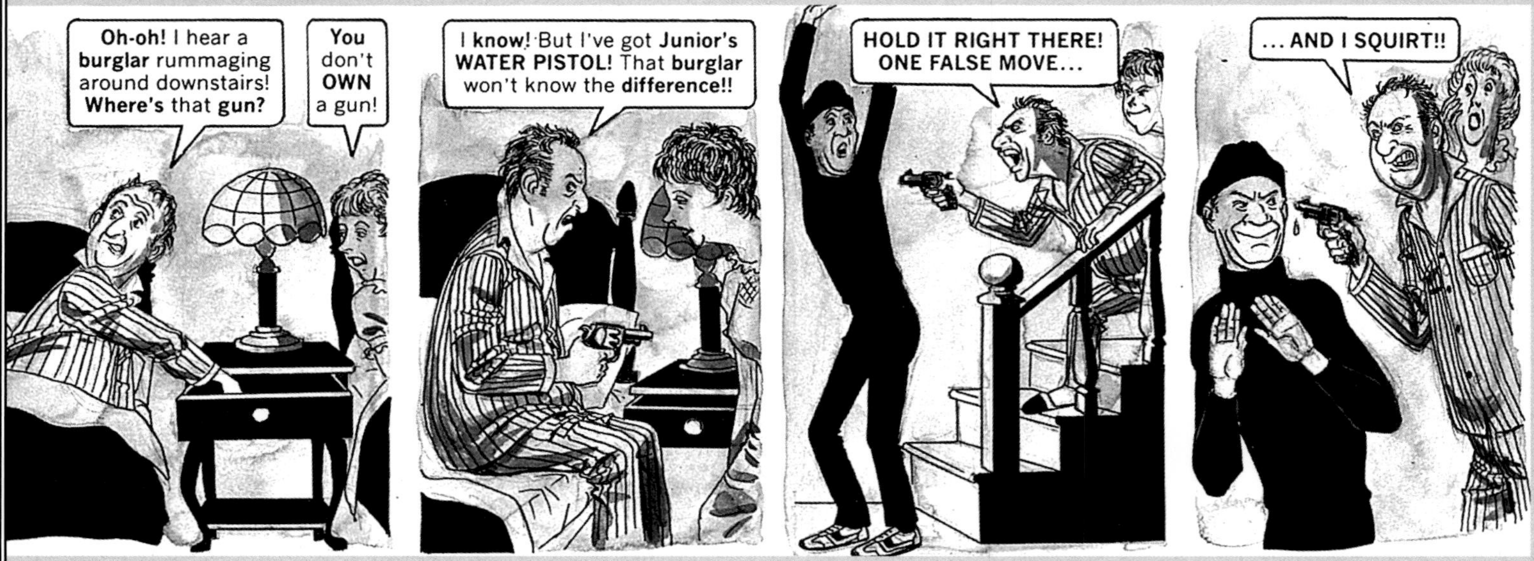
Oh-oh! I hear a burglar rummaging around downstairs! Where's that gun?
You don't OWN a gun!
I know! But I've got Junior's WATER PISTOL! That burglar won't know the difference!!
HOLD IT RIGHT THERE! ONE FALSE MOVE...
...AND I SQUIRT!!

EXAMS

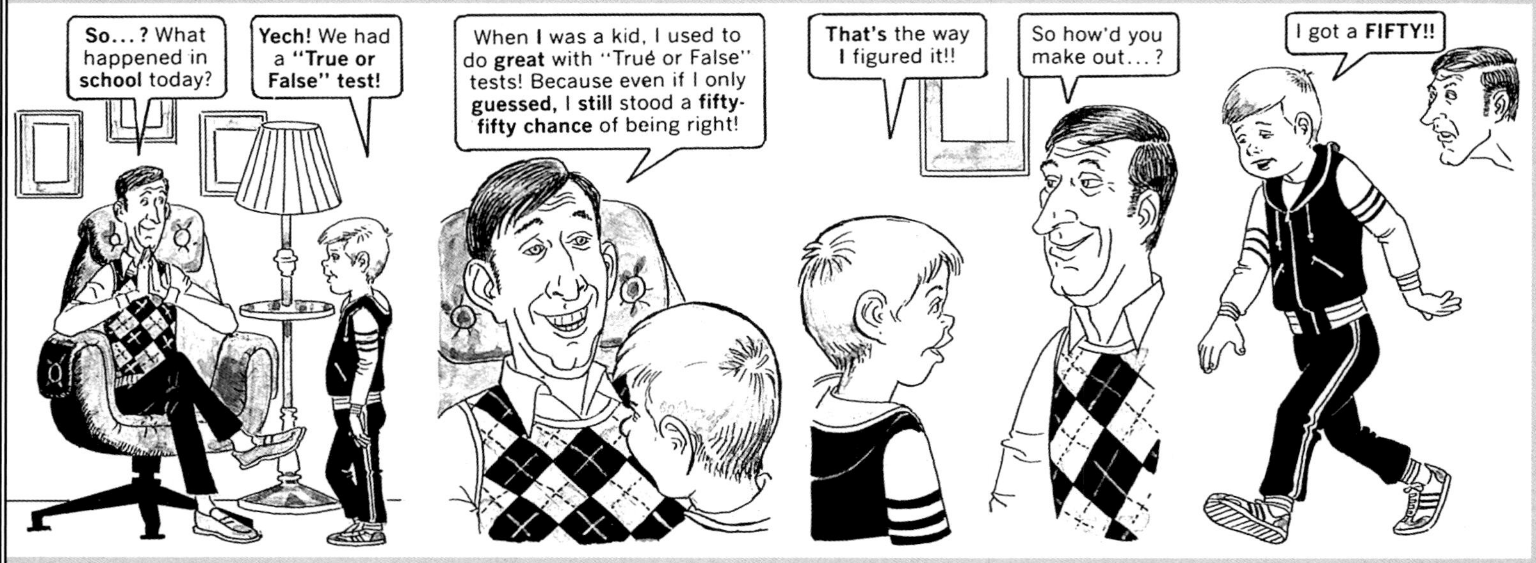
So...? What happened in school today?
Yech! We had a "True or False" test!
When I was a kid, I used to do great with "True or False" tests! Because even if I only guessed, I still stood a fifty-fifty chance of being right!
That's the way I figured it!!
So how'd you make out...?
I got a FIFTY!!

RUNNING

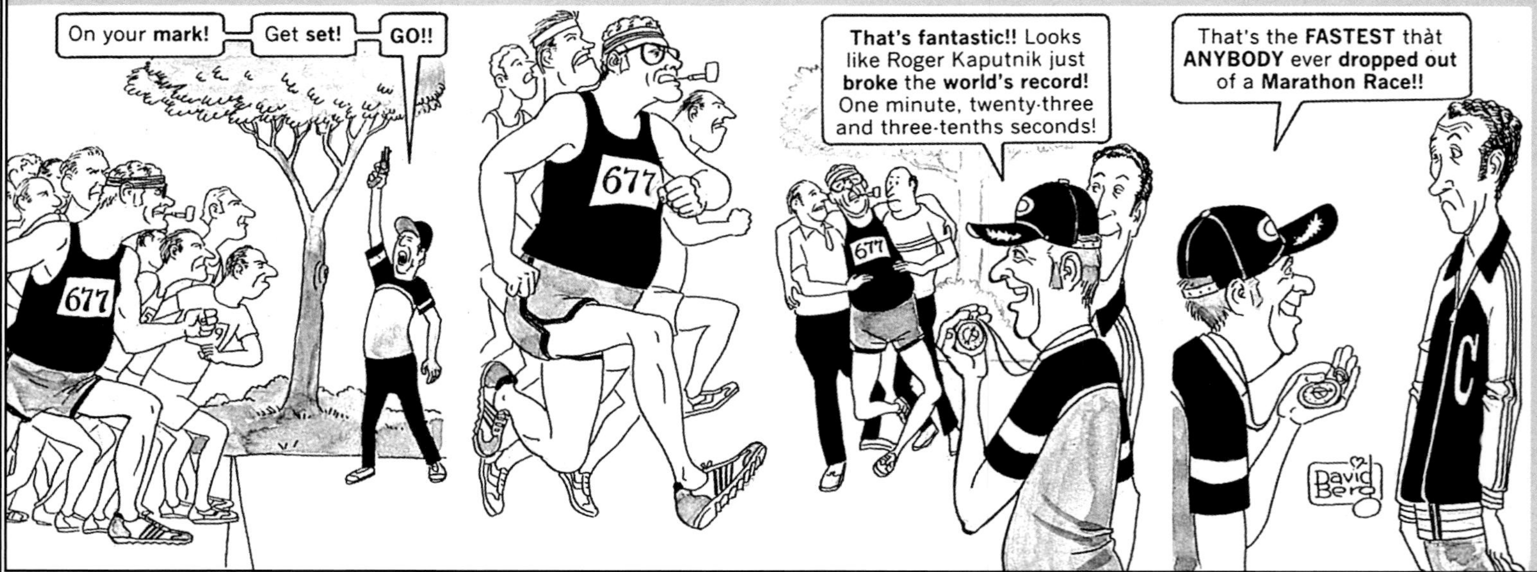
On your mark!
Get set!
GO!!
677
That's fantastic!! Looks like Roger Kaputnik just broke the world's record! One minute, twenty-three and three-tenths seconds!
That's the FASTEST that ANYBODY ever dropped out of a Marathon Race!!
David Berg

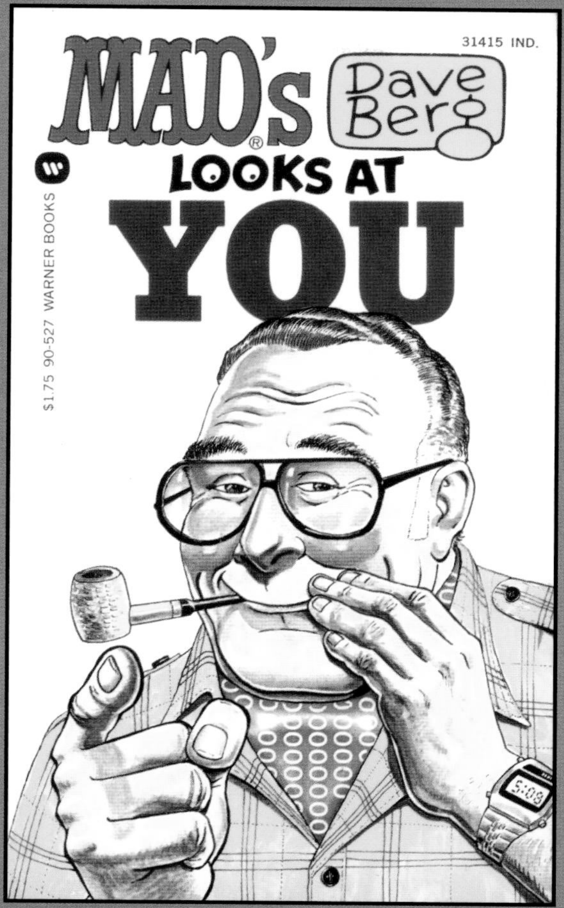
31415 IND.
MAD's
Dave Berg
LOOKS AT
YOU
$1.75 90-527 WARNER BOOKS

1982

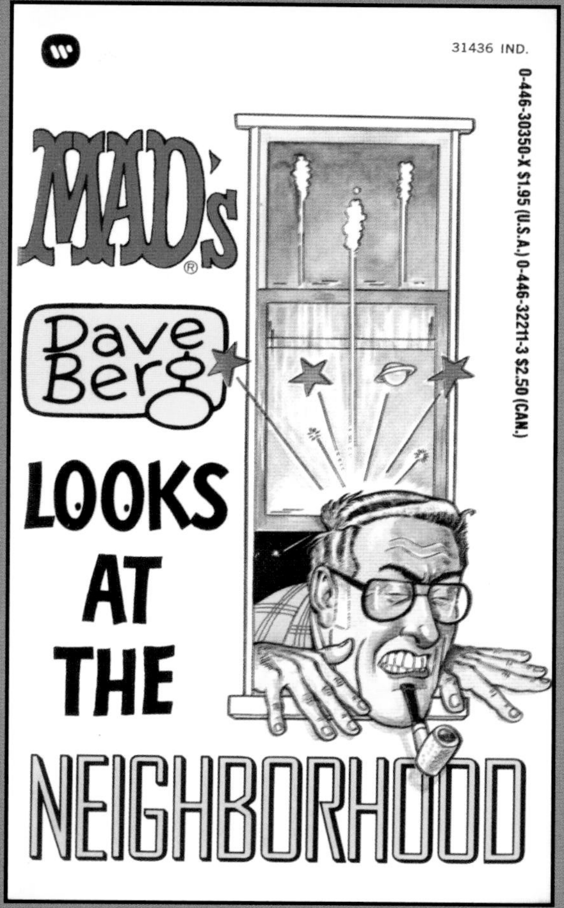
31436 IND.
0-446-30350-X $1.95 (U.S.A.) 0-446-32211-3 $2.50 (CAN.)
MAD's
Dave Berg
LOOKS
AT
THE
NEIGHBORHOOD

1984

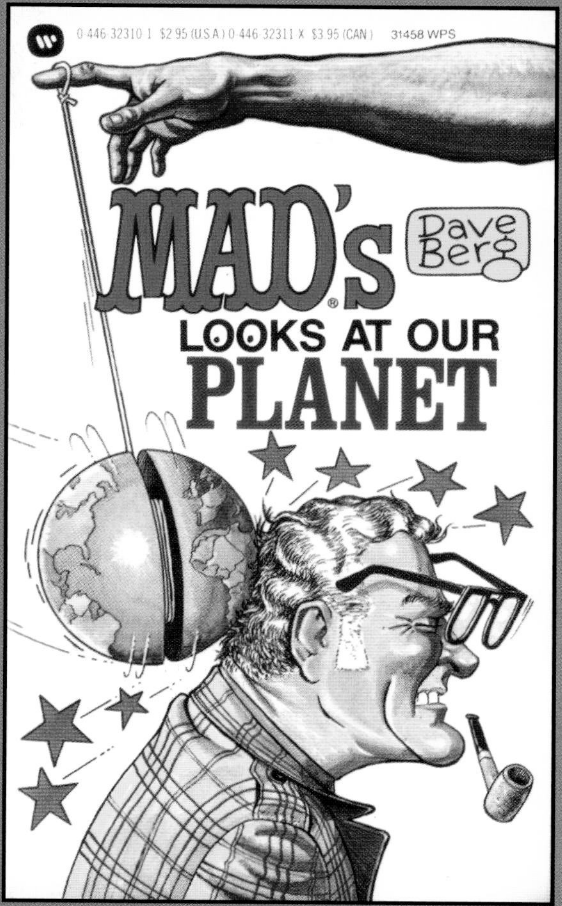
0-446-32310-1 $2.95 (U.S.A.) 0-446-32311-X $3.95 (CAN.) 31458 WPS
MAD's
Dave Berg
LOOKS AT OUR
PLANET

1986

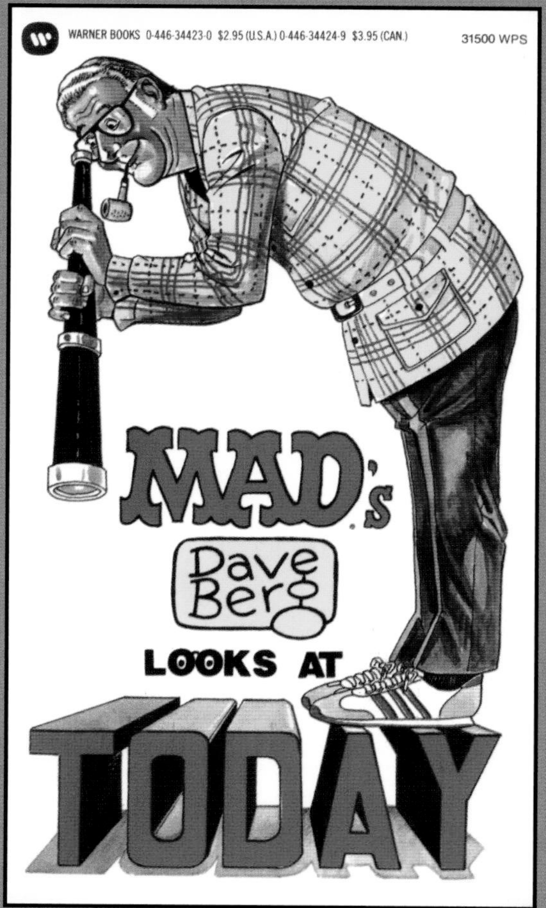
WARNER BOOKS 0-446-34423-0 $2.95 (U.S.A.) 0-446-34424-9 $3.95 (CAN.)
31500 WPS
MAD's
Dave Berg
LOOKS AT
TODAY

1987

The Lighter Side of . . . Spoofs

MAD's policy has always been to spoof anyone and anything, including itself. Over the years, Dave has done his part, illustrating takeoffs of his signature feature.

From "The Book of MAD," written by Lou Silverstone, MAD #243, December 1983

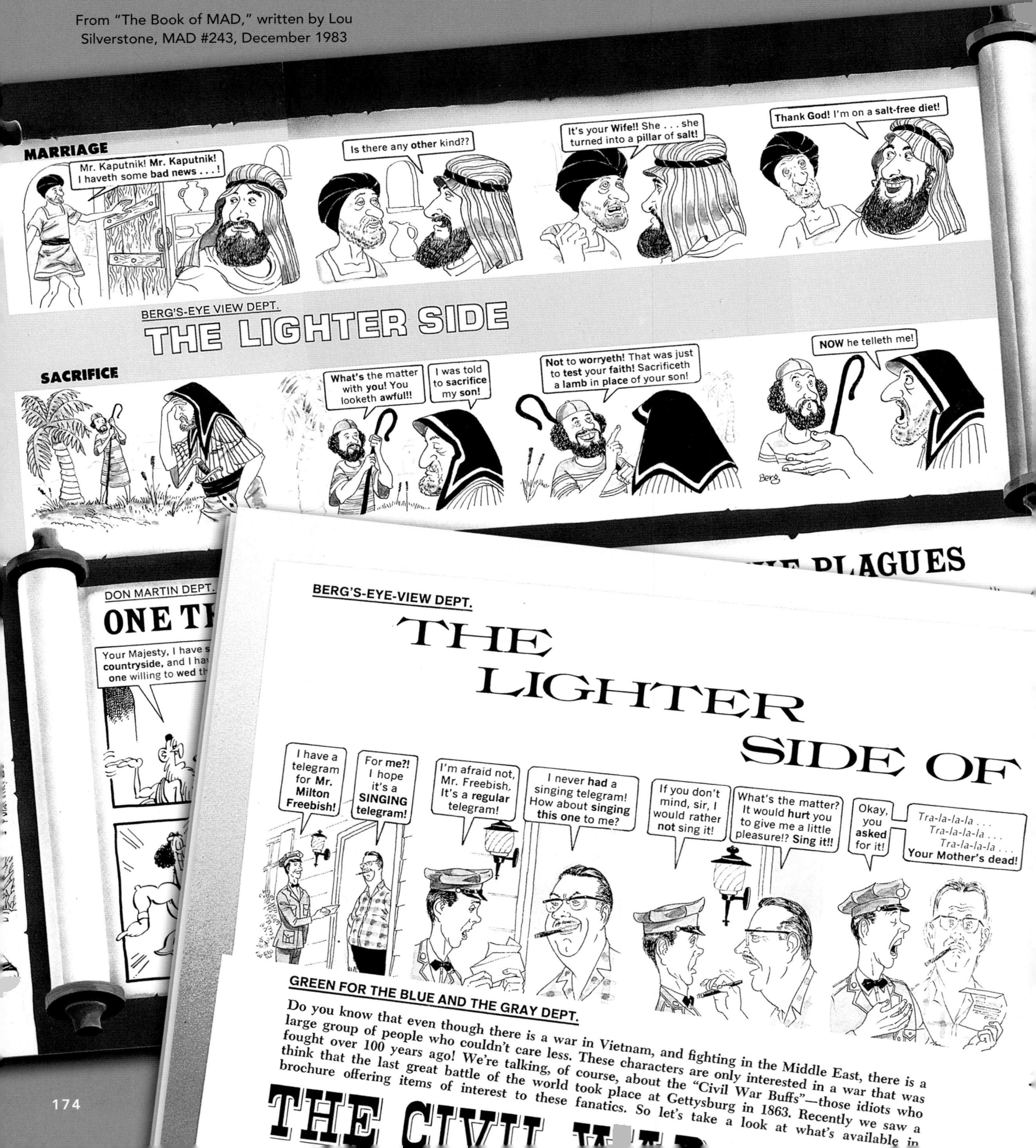

BERG'S-EYE VIEW DEPT.
THE LIGHTER SIDE
MARRIAGE
Mr. Kaputnik! Mr. Kaputnik! I haveth some bad news . . . !
Is there any other kind??
It's your Wife!! She . . . she turned into a pillar of salt!
Thank God! I'm on a salt-free diet!
SACRIFICE
What's the matter with you! You looketh awful!!
I was told to sacrifice my son!
Not to worryeth! That was just to test your faith! Sacrificeth a lamb in place of your son!
NOW he telleth me!
Berg
DON MARTIN DEPT.
ONE T
Your Majesty, I have s
countryside, and I ha
one willing to wed th
PLAGUES
BERG'S-EYE-VIEW DEPT.
THE LIGHTER SIDE OF
I have a telegram for Mr. Milton Freebish!
For me?! I hope it's a SINGING telegram!
I'm afraid not, Mr. Freebish. It's a regular telegram!
I never had a singing telegram! How about singing this one to me?
If you don't mind, sir, I would rather not sing it!
What's the matter? It would hurt you to give me a little pleasure!? Sing it!!
Okay, you asked for it!
Tra-la-la-la . . . Tra-la-la-la . . . Tra-la-la-la . . . Your Mother's dead!
GREEN FOR THE BLUE AND THE GRAY DEPT.
Do you know that even though there is a war in Vietnam, and fighting in the Middle East, there is a large group of people who couldn't care less. These characters are only interested in a war that was fought over 100 years ago! We're talking, of course, about the "Civil War Buffs"—those idiots who think that the last great battle of the world took place at Gettysburg in 1863. Recently we saw a brochure offering items of interest to these fanatics. So let's take a look at what's available in
THE CIVIL

From "MAD in the Year 2038," written by Desmond Devlin, MAD #355, March 1997

PREPAREDNESS
1980s
I knew this bomb shelter would come in handy! While they incinerate the Earth up there, we've got canned meat, canned vegetables, canned soup and canned drinks! I remembered everything we need to survive the apocalypse!
Yeah, everything except the can opener!
MEAT
SOUP
THE LIGHTER SIDE OF...
CONVENIENCES
Boy, did my folks lay down the law! They told me that unless I passed all my classes and did all my chores, I couldn't go out with Marcie on the weekends!
Wow, that's rough! So what did you do?
I bought one of those home cyborgs! He did all my homework, and I got straight A's! Then he cleaned the house so well, Dad gave me a bonus in my allowance! He does everything better than I ever could!
Cool! He sounds abso-lutley fantastic! Let me see him!
You can't! He's out with Marcie!
DOCTORS
You know, Doctor, even though I'm nothing more than a head attached to some machinery, I feel pretty good!
It's true, Kaputnik-XF7, you're in excellent shape! However, there is bad news to report...
...you have head lice!
Oh no!

DEATH
rgeant, we just received d that Roger Kaputnik's ife died. I want you to ak the news to him . . . t do it gently, please!
Yes, sir! I'll do it real gentle, sir!
All right, men! Fall in . . . on the double . . .
At ease! Now I got an announcement to make . . .
But before I do, I want all you married men to step forward—
Not so fast there, Kaputnik!
HIELD VIPERS DEPT.

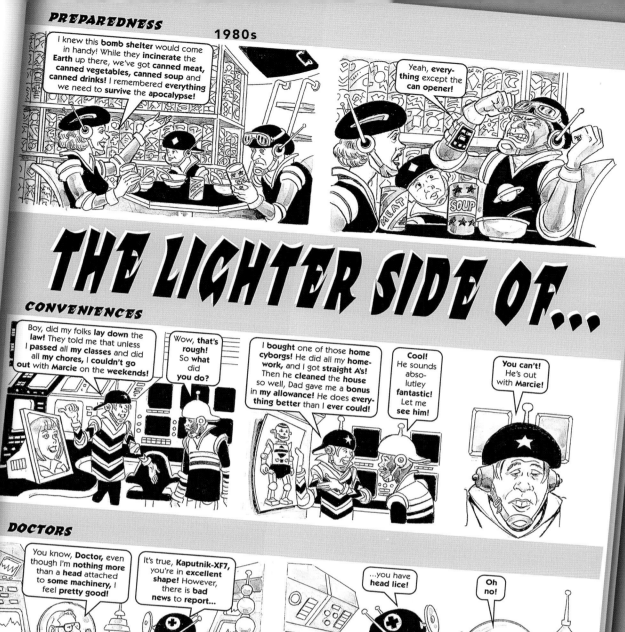

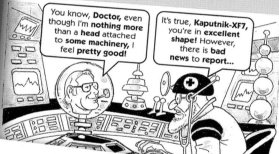

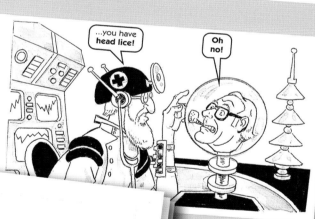

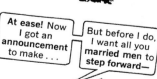

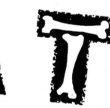

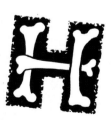

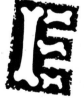

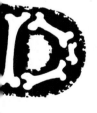

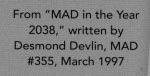

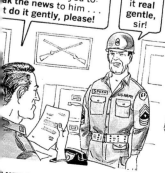

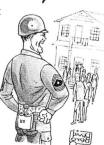

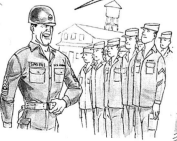

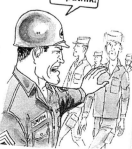

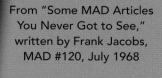

From "Some MAD Articles You Never Got to See," written by Frank Jacobs, MAD #120, July 1968

SQUABBLING

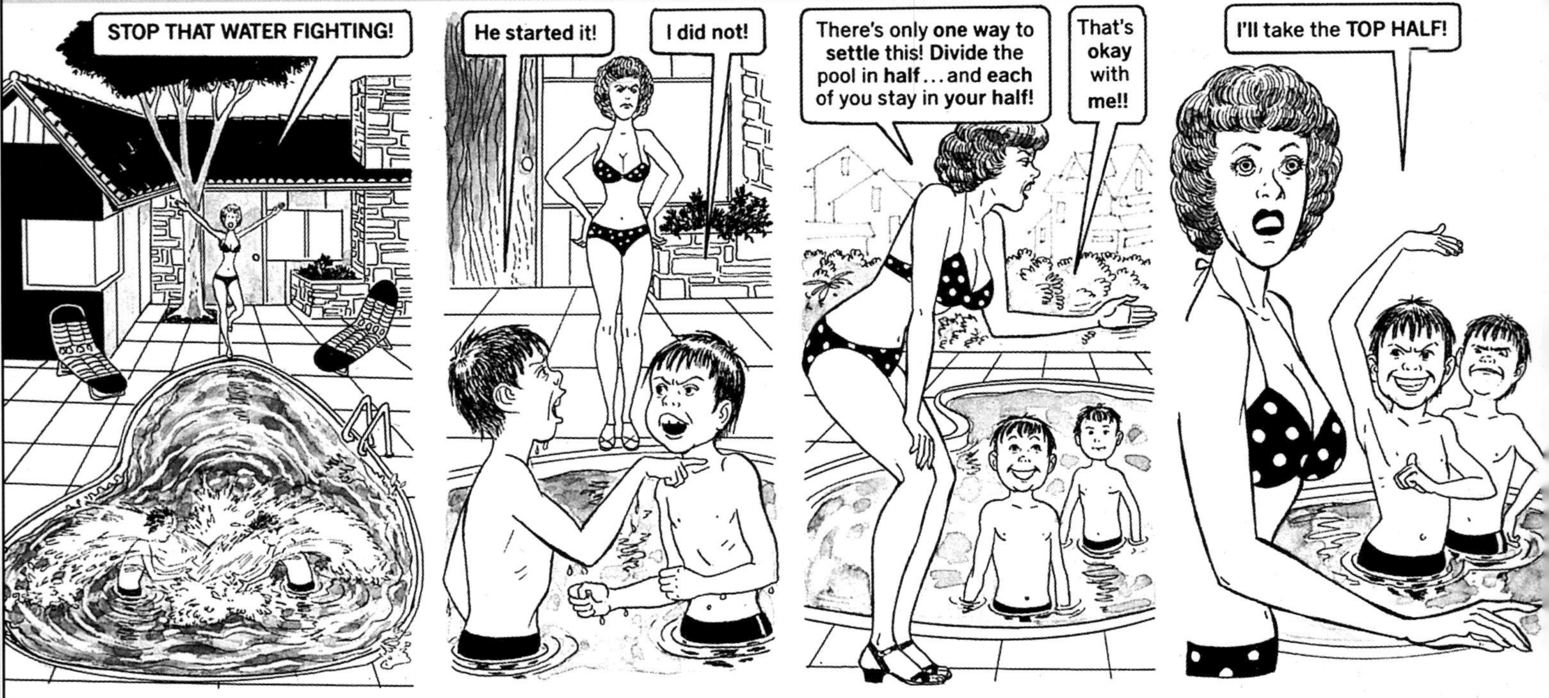
STOP THAT WATER FIGHTING!
He started it!
I did not!
There's only one way to settle this! Divide the pool in half... and each of you stay in your half!
That's okay with me!!
I'll take the TOP HALF!

BERG'S-EYE VIEW DEPT.

THE LIGHTE

AUTOMOBILE REPAIRS

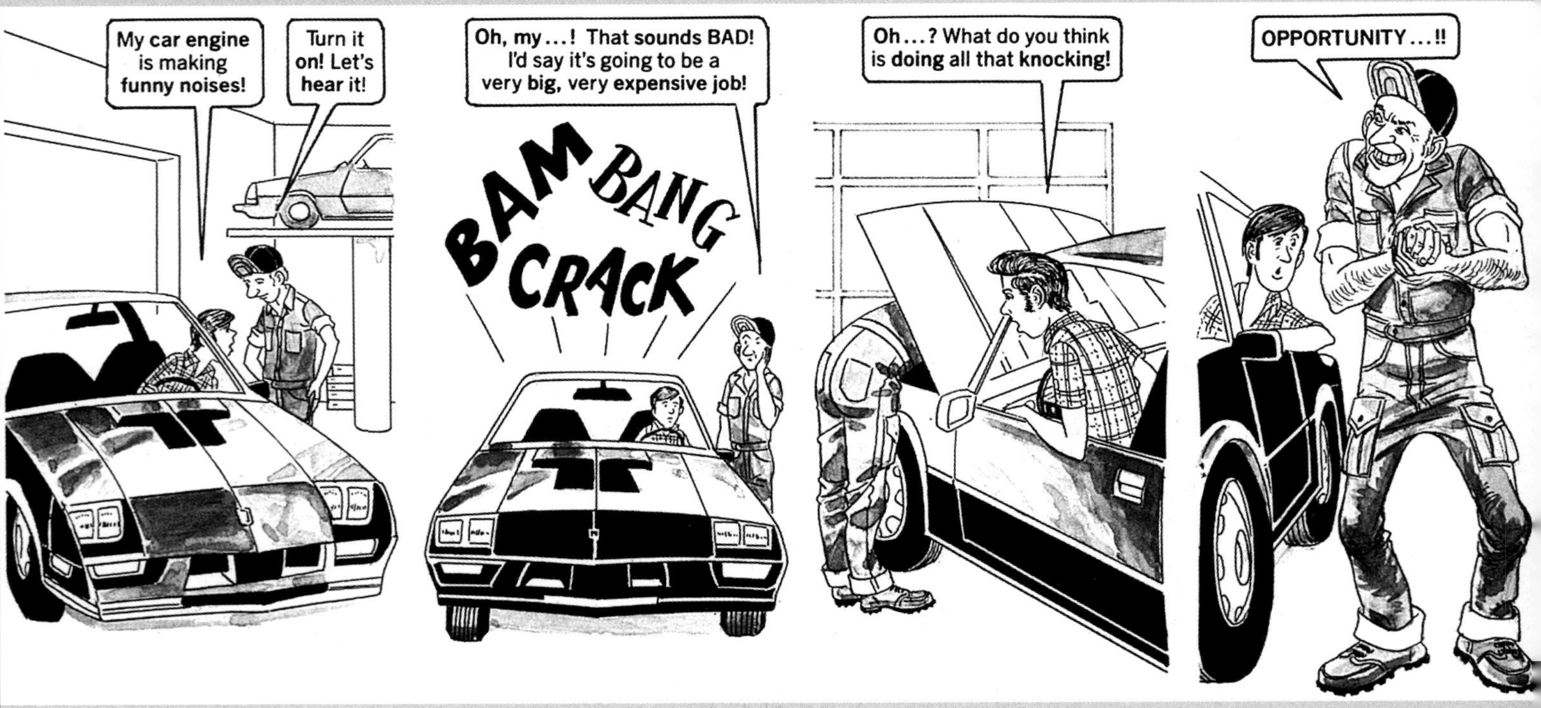
My car engine is making funny noises!
Turn it on! Let's hear it!
Oh, my...! That sounds BAD! I'd say it's going to be a very big, very expensive job!
BAM BANG CRACK
Oh...? What do you think is doing all that knocking!
OPPORTUNITY...!!

ECONOMIZING

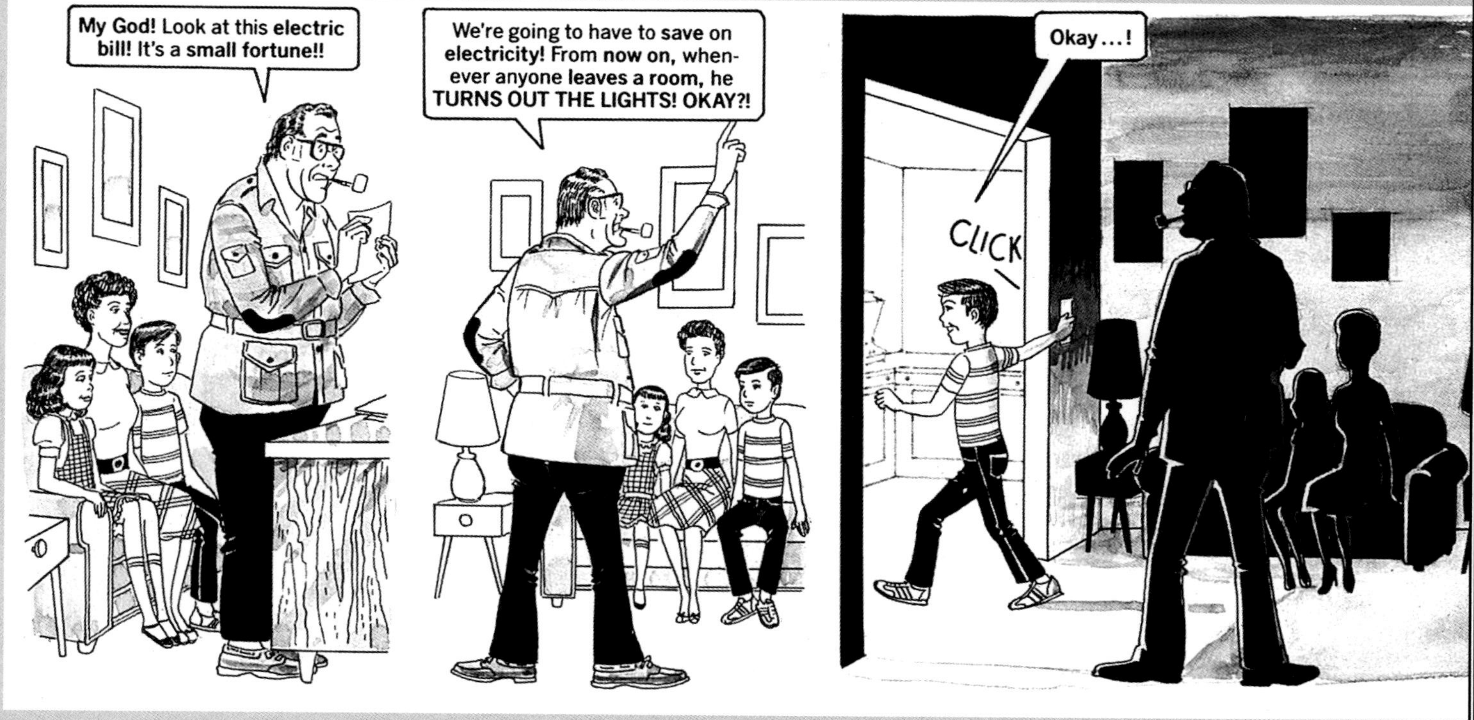
My God! Look at this electric bill! It's a small fortune!!
We're going to have to save on electricity! From now on, whenever anyone leaves a room, he TURNS OUT THE LIGHTS! OKAY?!
Okay...!
CLICK

R SIDE OF...

ARTIST & WRITER:
DAVE BERG

PETS

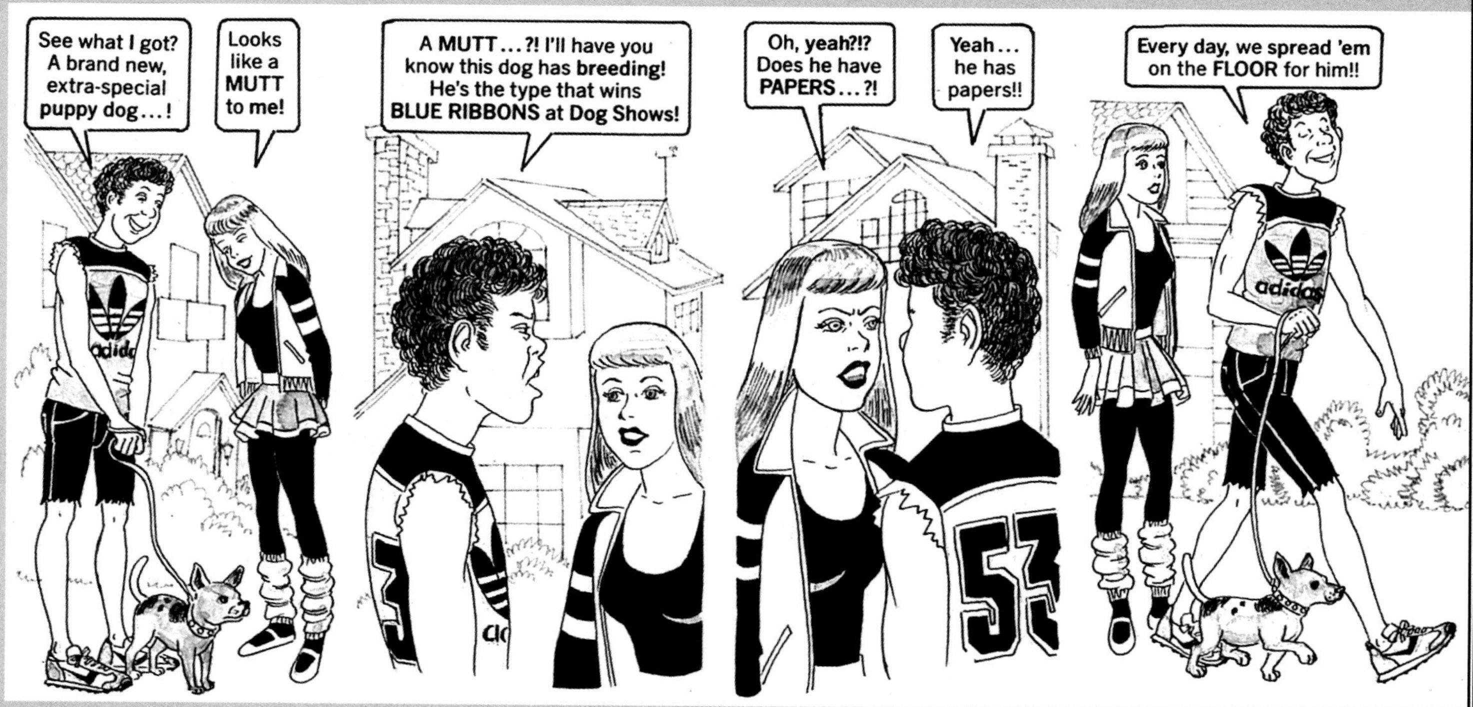
See what I got? A brand new, extra-special puppy dog...!
Looks like a MUTT to me!
A MUTT...?! I'll have you know this dog has breeding! He's the type that wins BLUE RIBBONS at Dog Shows!
Oh, yeah?!? Does he have PAPERS...?!
Yeah... he has papers!!
Every day, we spread 'em on the FLOOR for him!!

PROPER NAMES

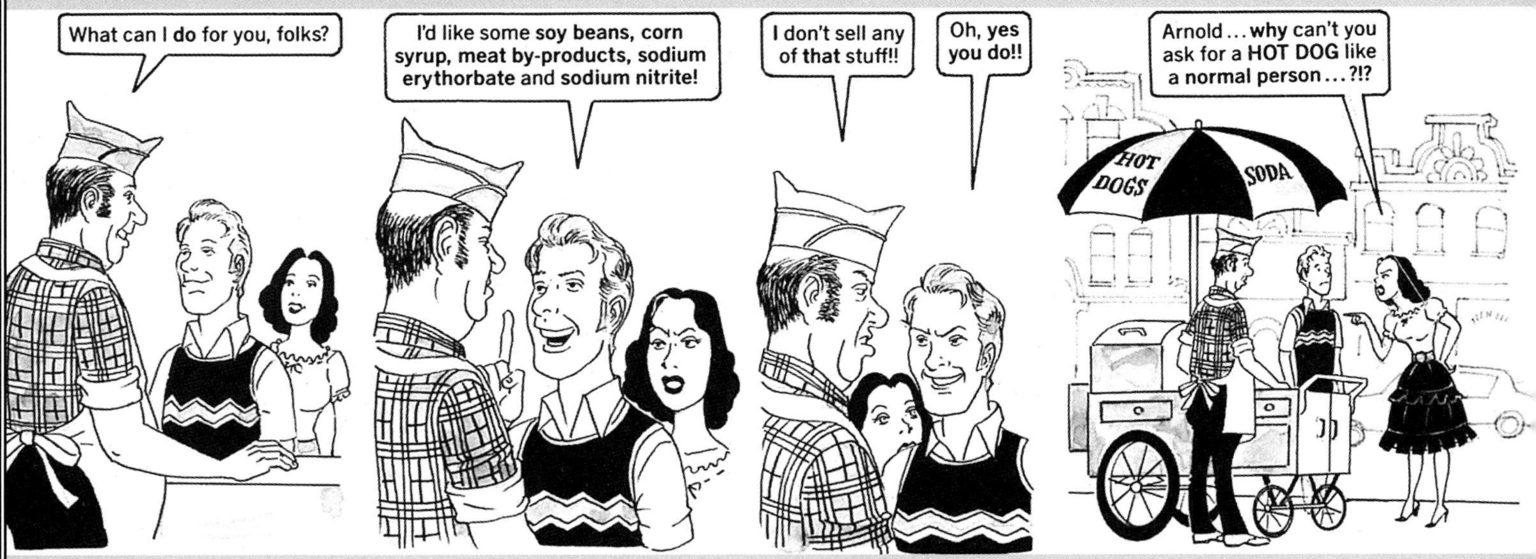
What can I do for you, folks?
I'd like some soy beans, corn syrup, meat by-products, sodium erythorbate and sodium nitrite!
I don't sell any of that stuff!!
Oh, yes you do!!
Arnold... why can't you ask for a HOT DOG like a normal person...?!?
HOT DOGS
SODA

HOBBIES

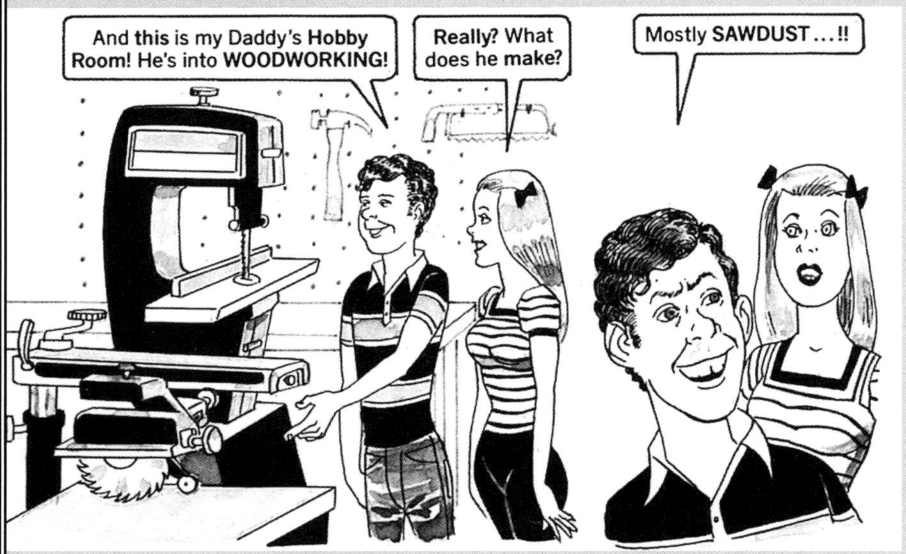
And this is my Daddy's Hobby Room! He's into WOODWORKING!
Really? What does he make?
Mostly SAWDUST...!!

FLORISTS

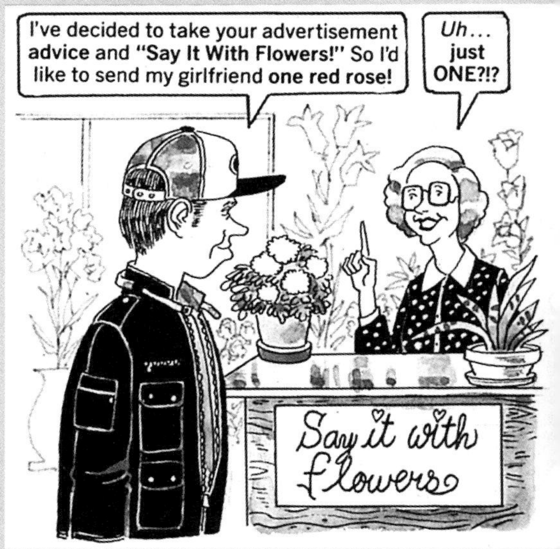
I've decided to take your advertisement advice and "Say It With Flowers!" So I'd like to send my girlfriend one red rose!
Uh... just ONE?!?
Say it with flowers

DINING OUT

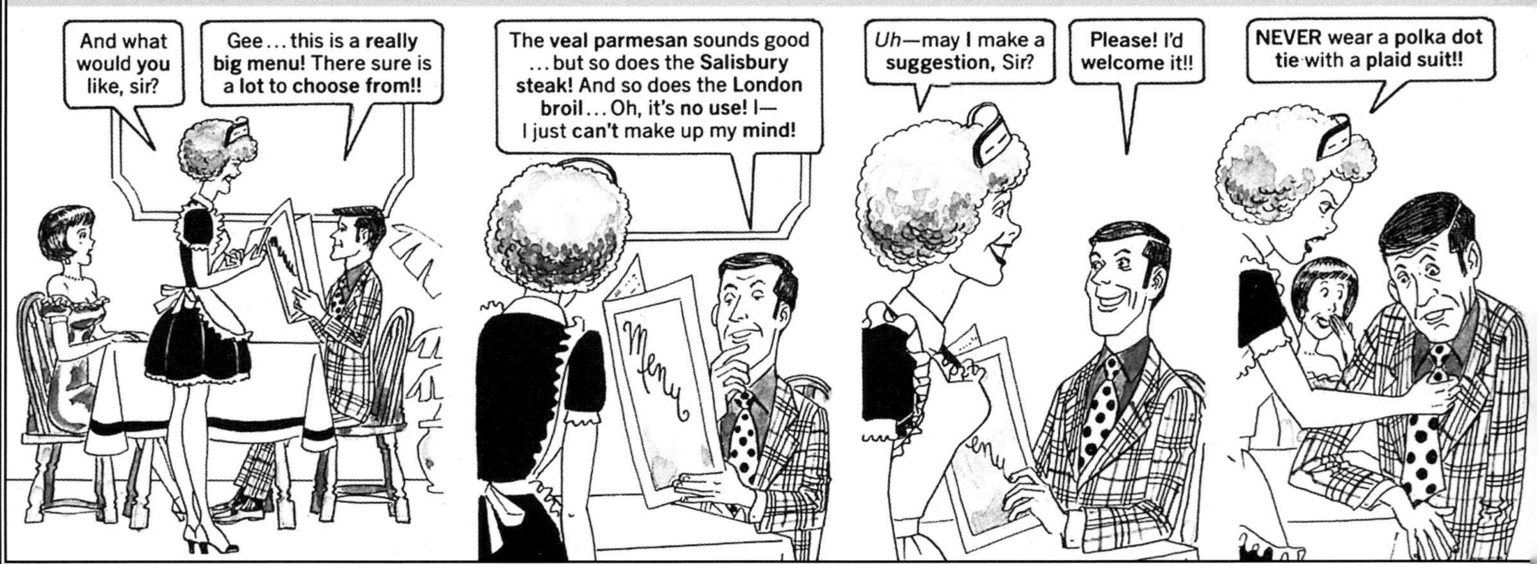
And what would you like, sir?
Gee... this is a really big menu! There sure is a lot to choose from!!
The veal parmesan sounds good ...but so does the Salisbury steak! And so does the London broil... Oh, it's no use! I— I just can't make up my mind!
Menu
Uh—may I make a suggestion, Sir?
Please! I'd welcome it!!
NEVER wear a polka dot tie with a plaid suit!!

CHORES

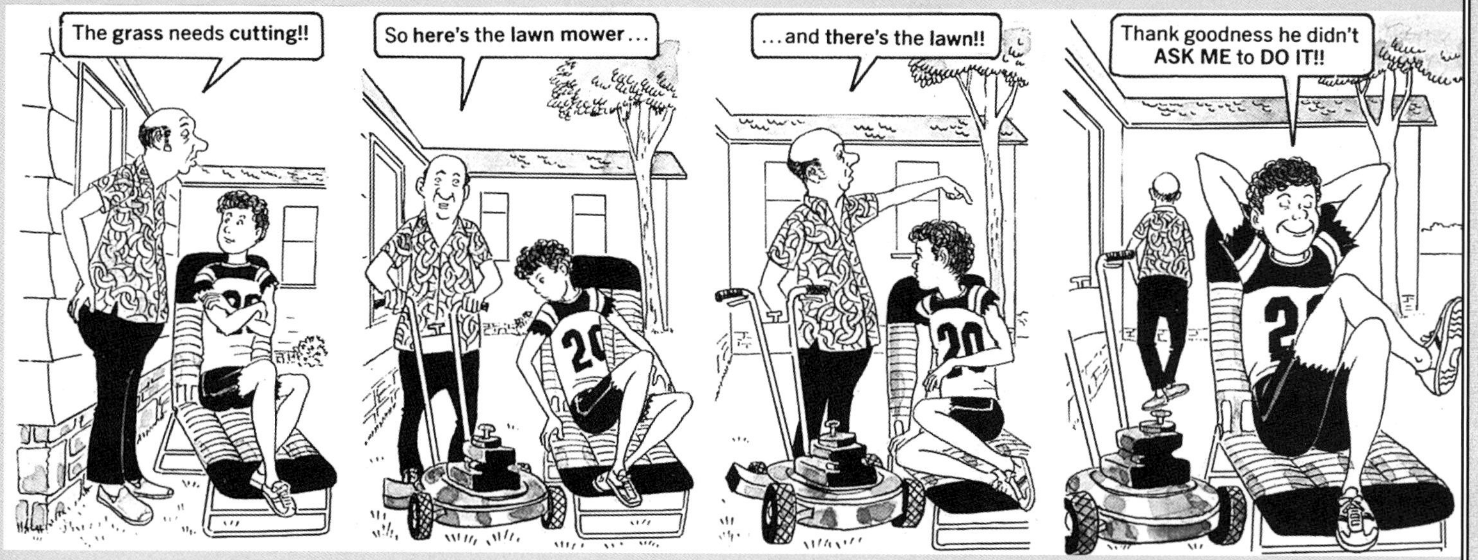
The grass needs cutting!!
So here's the lawn mower...
...and there's the lawn!!
Thank goodness he didn't ASK ME to DO IT!!

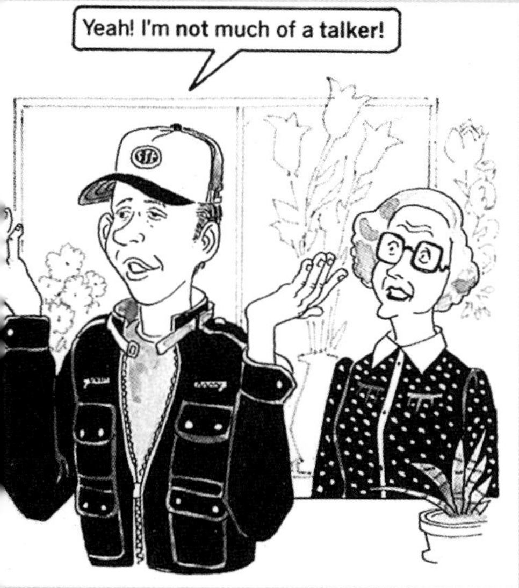
Yeah! I'm not much of a talker!

FEAR

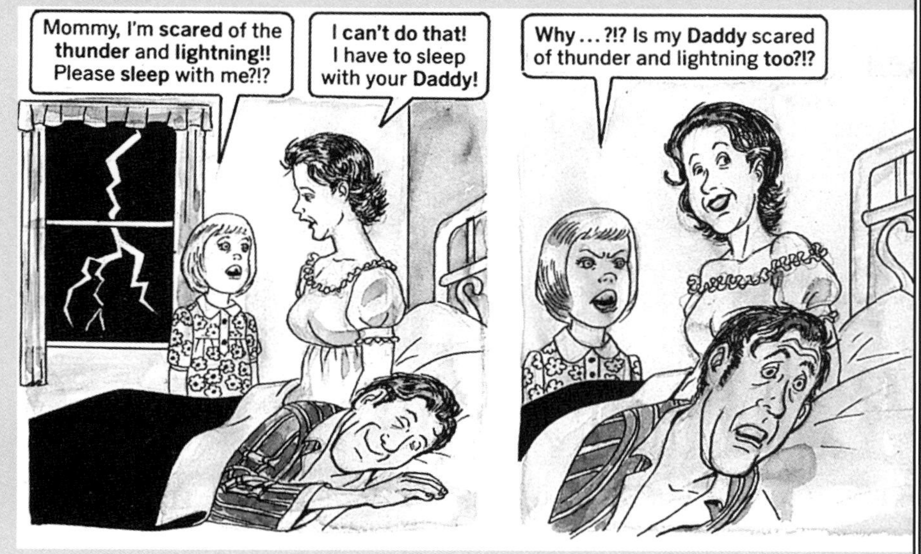
Mommy, I'm scared of the thunder and lightning!! Please sleep with me?!?
I can't do that! I have to sleep with your Daddy!
Why...?!? Is my Daddy scared of thunder and lightning too?!?

INHERITANCES

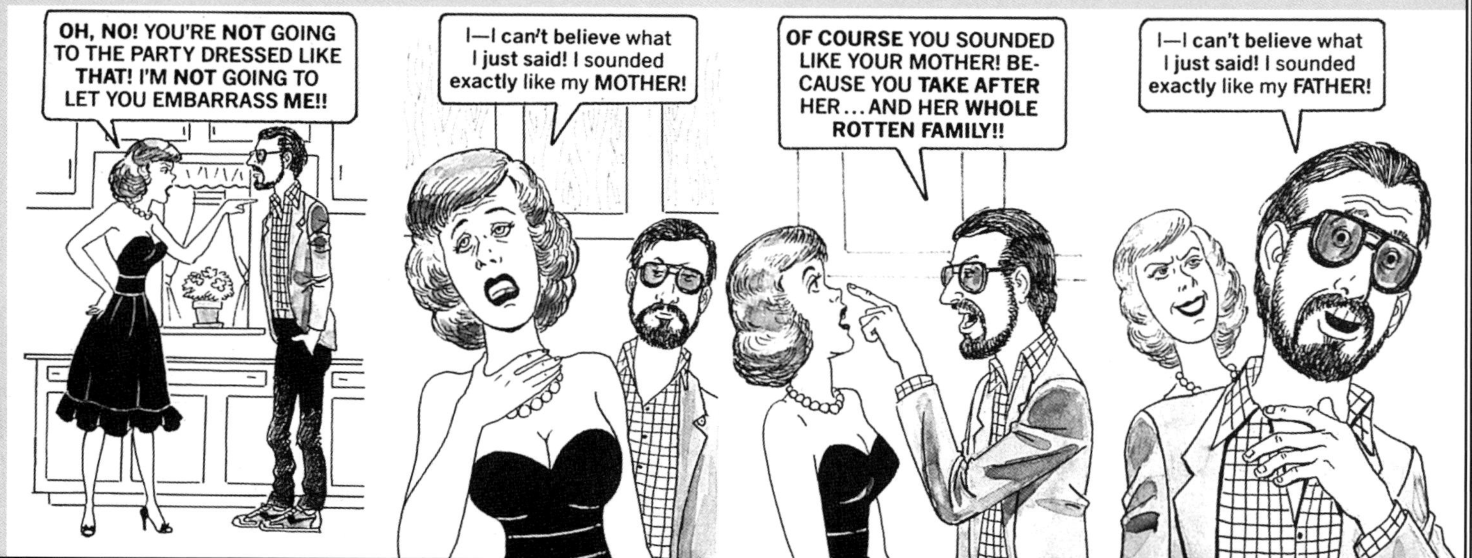
OH, NO! YOU'RE NOT GOING TO THE PARTY DRESSED LIKE THAT! I'M NOT GOING TO LET YOU EMBARRASS ME!!
I—I can't believe what I just said! I sounded exactly like my MOTHER!
OF COURSE YOU SOUNDED LIKE YOUR MOTHER! BE-CAUSE YOU TAKE AFTER HER...AND HER WHOLE ROTTEN FAMILY!!
I—I can't believe what I just said! I sounded exactly like my FATHER!

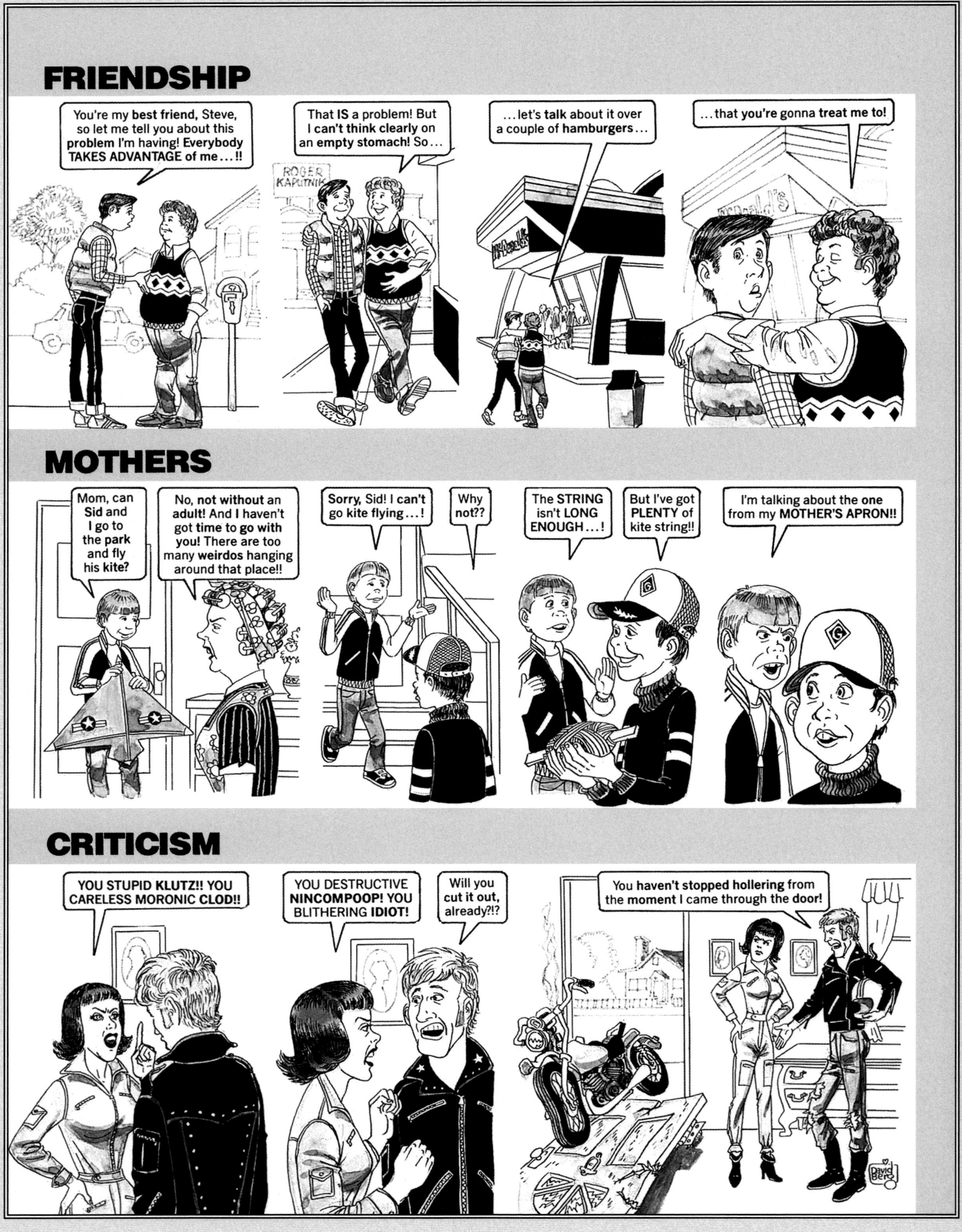
FRIENDSHIP
You're my best friend, Steve, so let me tell you about this problem I'm having! Everybody TAKES ADVANTAGE of me...!!
That IS a problem! But I can't think clearly on an empty stomach! So...
...let's talk about it over a couple of hamburgers...
...that you're gonna treat me to!
MOTHERS
Mom, can Sid and I go to the park and fly his kite?
No, not without an adult! And I haven't got time to go with you! There are too many weirdos hanging around that place!!
Sorry, Sid! I can't go kite flying...!
Why not??
The STRING isn't LONG ENOUGH...!
But I've got PLENTY of kite string!!
I'm talking about the one from my MOTHER'S APRON!!
CRITICISM
YOU STUPID KLUTZ!! YOU CARELESS MORONIC CLOD!!
YOU DESTRUCTIVE NINCOMPOOP! YOU BLITHERING IDIOT!
Will you cut it out, already?!?
You haven't stopped hollering from the moment I came through the door!

MAD Kids: Family Funnies and Motor Mutts

Additional examples of "The Lighter Side of..." scripts used in MAD Kids magazine

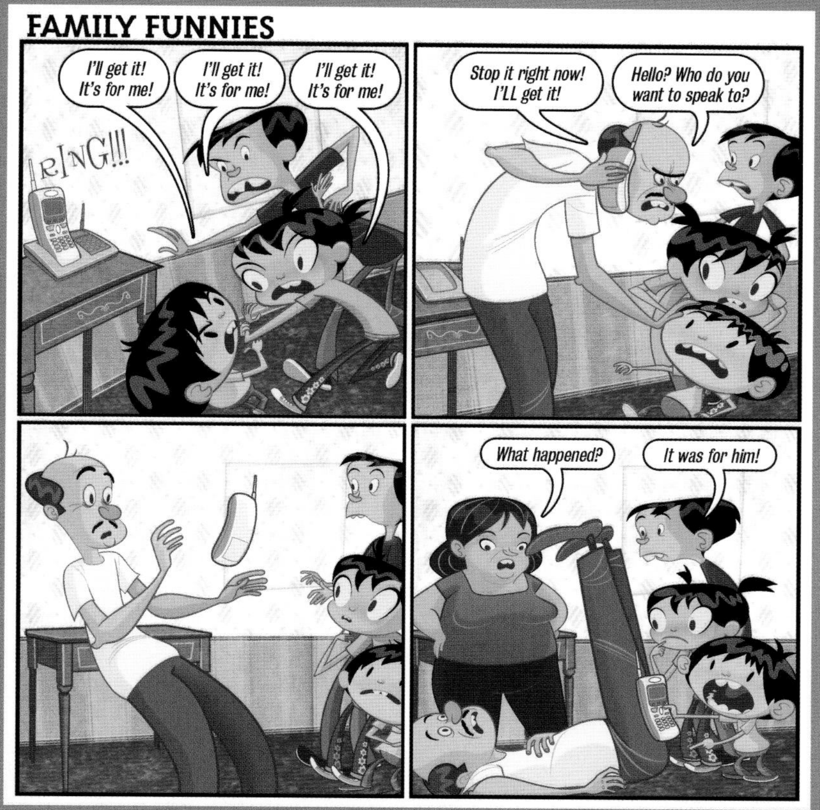
FAMILY FUNNIES
I'll get it! It's for me!
I'll get it! It's for me!
I'll get it! It's for me!
RING!!!
Stop it right now! I'LL get it!
Hello? Who do you want to speak to?
What happened?
It was for him!

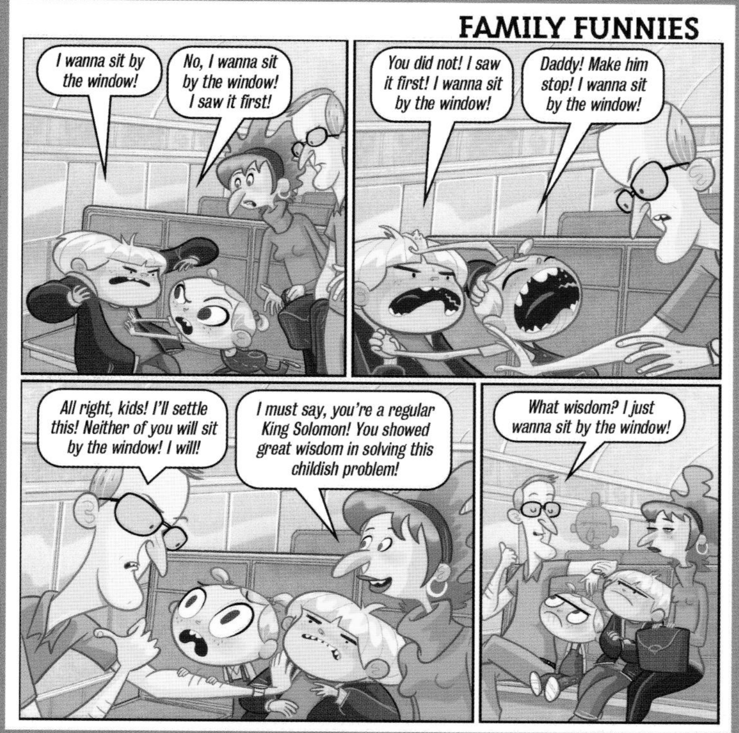
FAMILY FUNNIES
I wanna sit by the window!
No, I wanna sit by the window! I saw it first!
You did not! I saw it first! I wanna sit by the window!
Daddy! Make him stop! I wanna sit by the window!
All right, kids! I'll settle this! Neither of you will sit by the window! I will!
I must say, you're a regular King Solomon! You showed great wisdom in solving this childish problem!
What wisdom? I just wanna sit by the window!

Family Funnies drawn by Jose Garibaldi

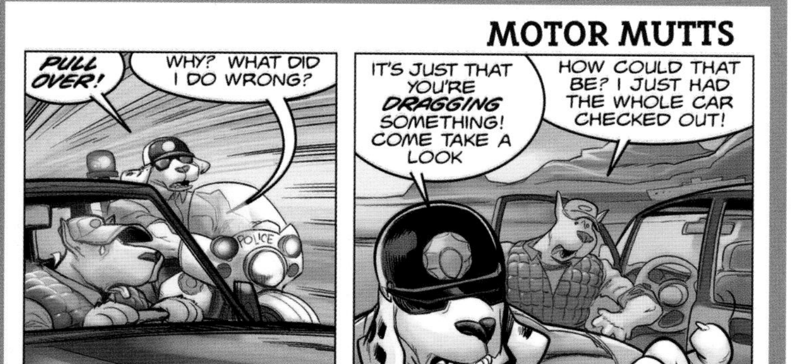
MOTOR MUTTS
PULL OVER!
WHY? WHAT DID I DO WRONG?
IT'S JUST THAT YOU'RE DRAGGING SOMETHING! COME TAKE A LOOK
HOW COULD THAT BE? I JUST HAD THE WHOLE CAR CHECKED OUT!
IT'S NOTHING SERIOUS! IT LOOKS LIKE YOUR TRAILER HITCH IS...
HOW CAN YOU SAY IT'S NOTHING SERIOUS?! IT'S VERY SERIOUS!!
WHERE'S THE BOAT I WAS HAULING?!?

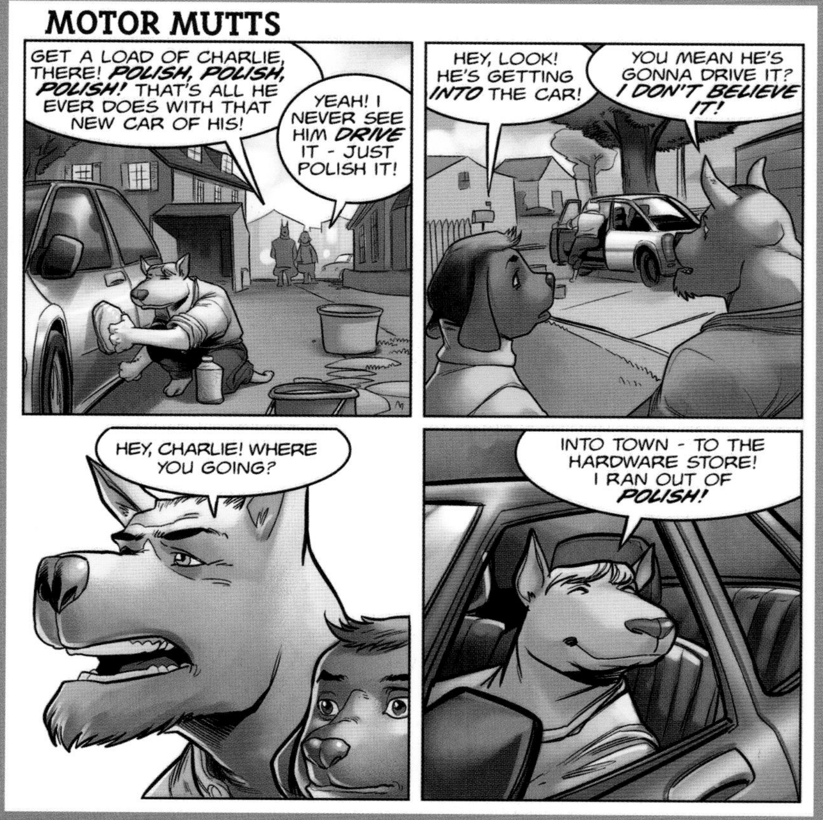
MOTOR MUTTS
GET A LOAD OF CHARLIE, THERE! POLISH, POLISH, POLISH! THAT'S ALL HE EVER DOES WITH THAT NEW CAR OF HIS!
YEAH! I NEVER SEE HIM DRIVE IT - JUST POLISH IT!
HEY, LOOK! HE'S GETTING INTO THE CAR!
YOU MEAN HE'S GONNA DRIVE IT? I DON'T BELIEVE IT!
HEY, CHARLIE! WHERE YOU GOING?
INTO TOWN - TO THE HARDWARE STORE! I RAN OUT OF POLISH!

Motor Mutts drawn by Bachan

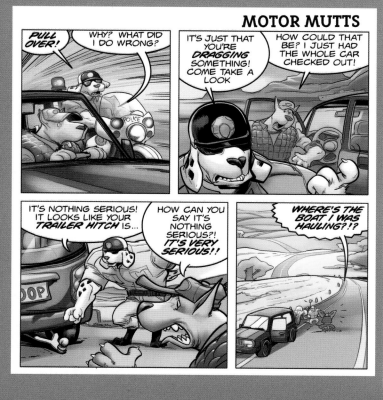

INVESTMENTS

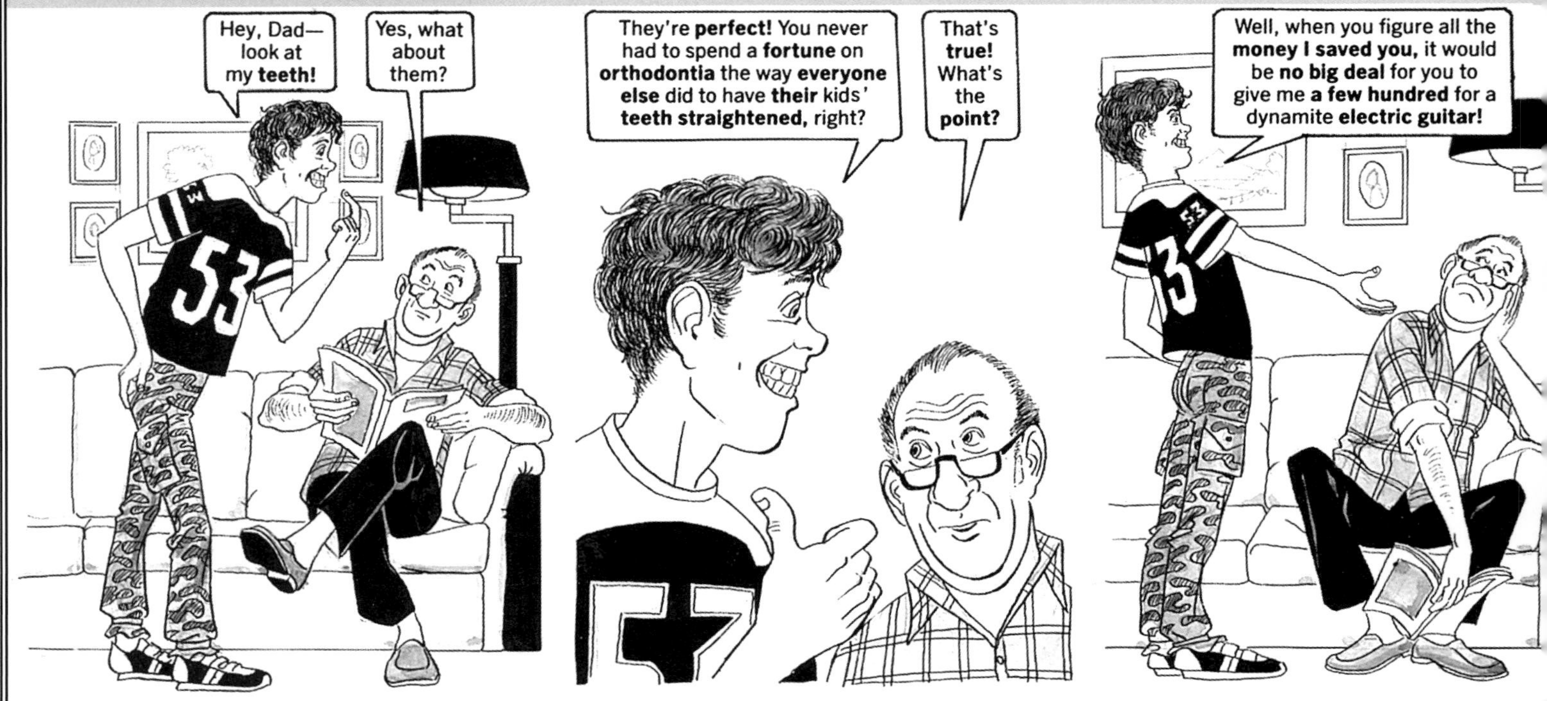
Hey, Dad—look at my teeth!
Yes, what about them?
They're perfect! You never had to spend a fortune on orthodontia the way everyone else did to have their kids' teeth straightened, right?
That's true! What's the point?
Well, when you figure all the money I saved you, it would be no big deal for you to give me a few hundred for a dynamite electric guitar!

BERG'S-EYE VIEW DEPT.

THE LIGHTE

MODERN TECHNOLOGY

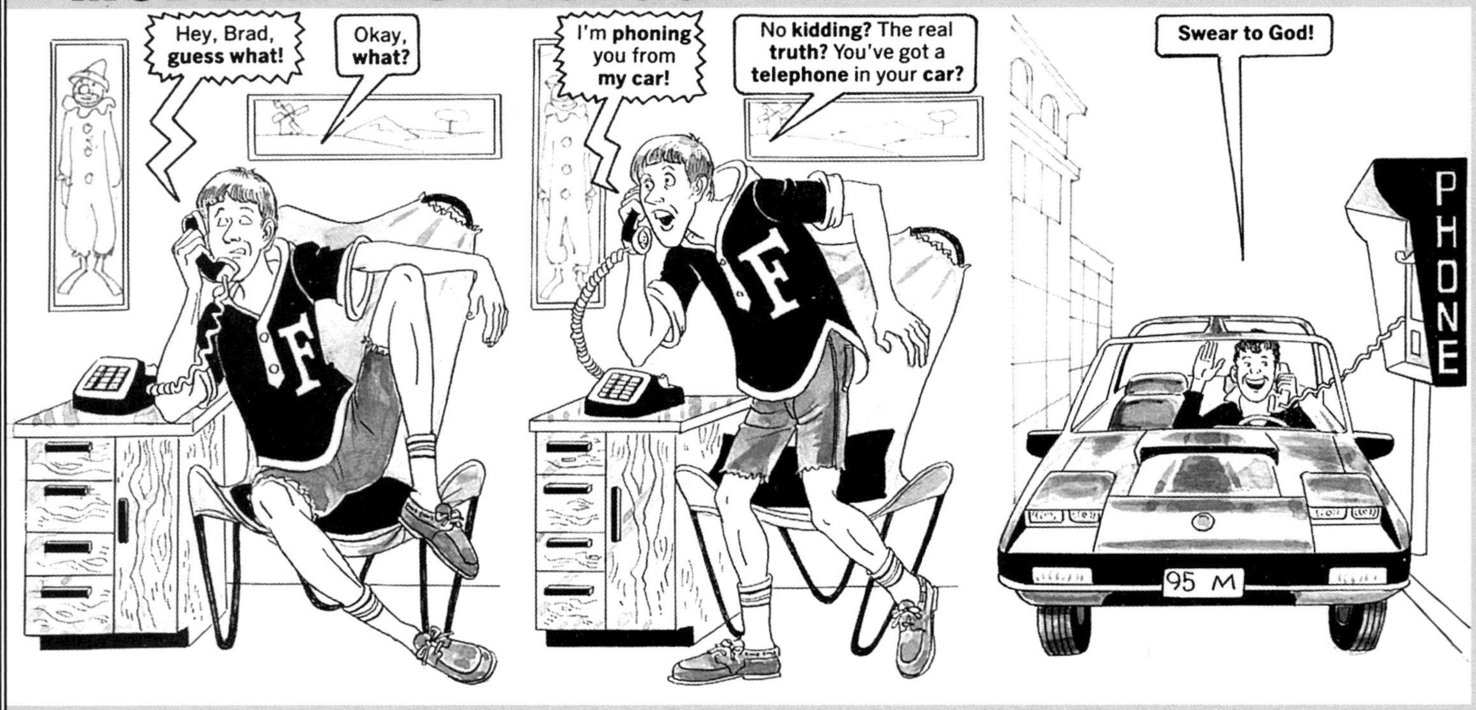
Hey, Brad, guess what!
Okay, what?
I'm phoning you from my car!
No kidding? The real truth? You've got a telephone in your car?
Swear to God!
PHONE
95 M

LOGIC

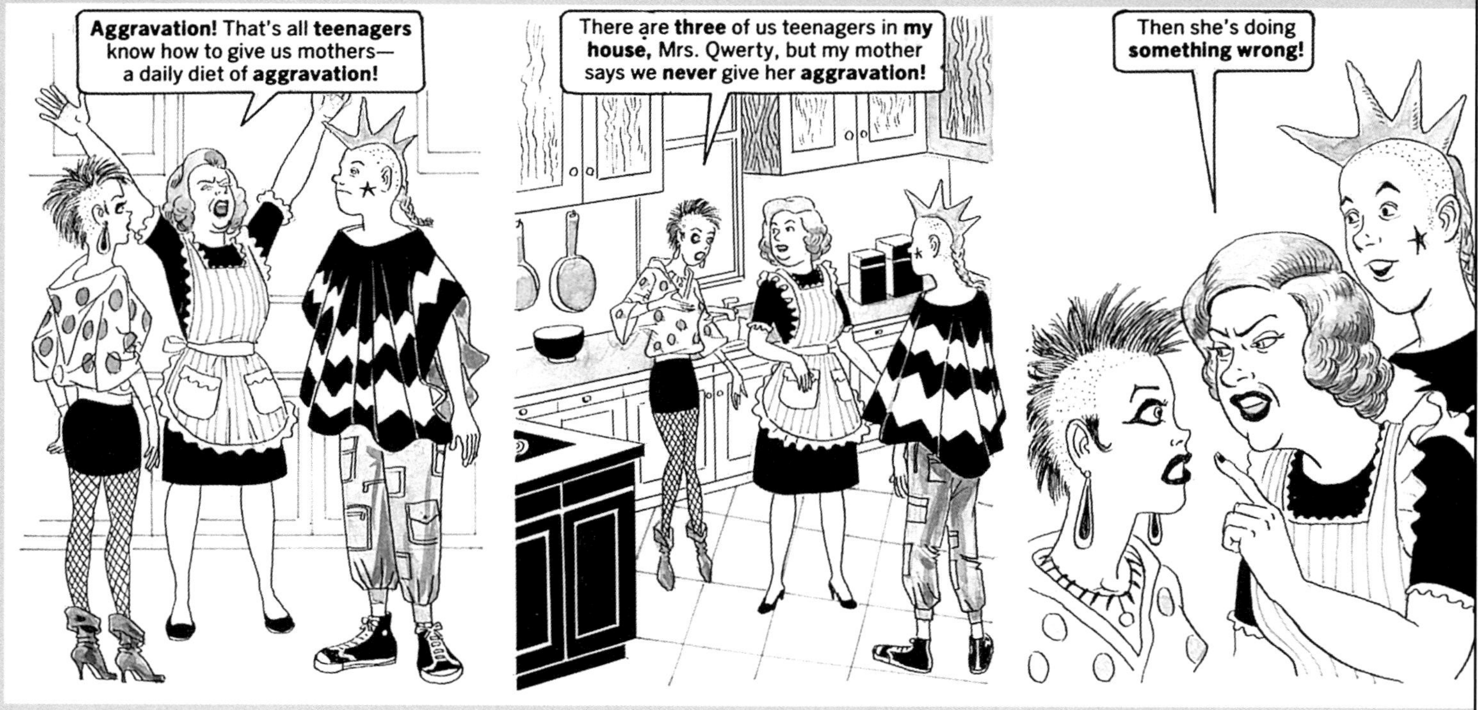
Aggravation! That's all teenagers know how to give us mothers— a daily diet of aggravation!
There are three of us teenagers in my house, Mrs. Qwerty, but my mother says we never give her aggravation!
Then she's doing something wrong!

R SIDE OF...

ARTIST & WRITER:
DAVE BERG

PETS

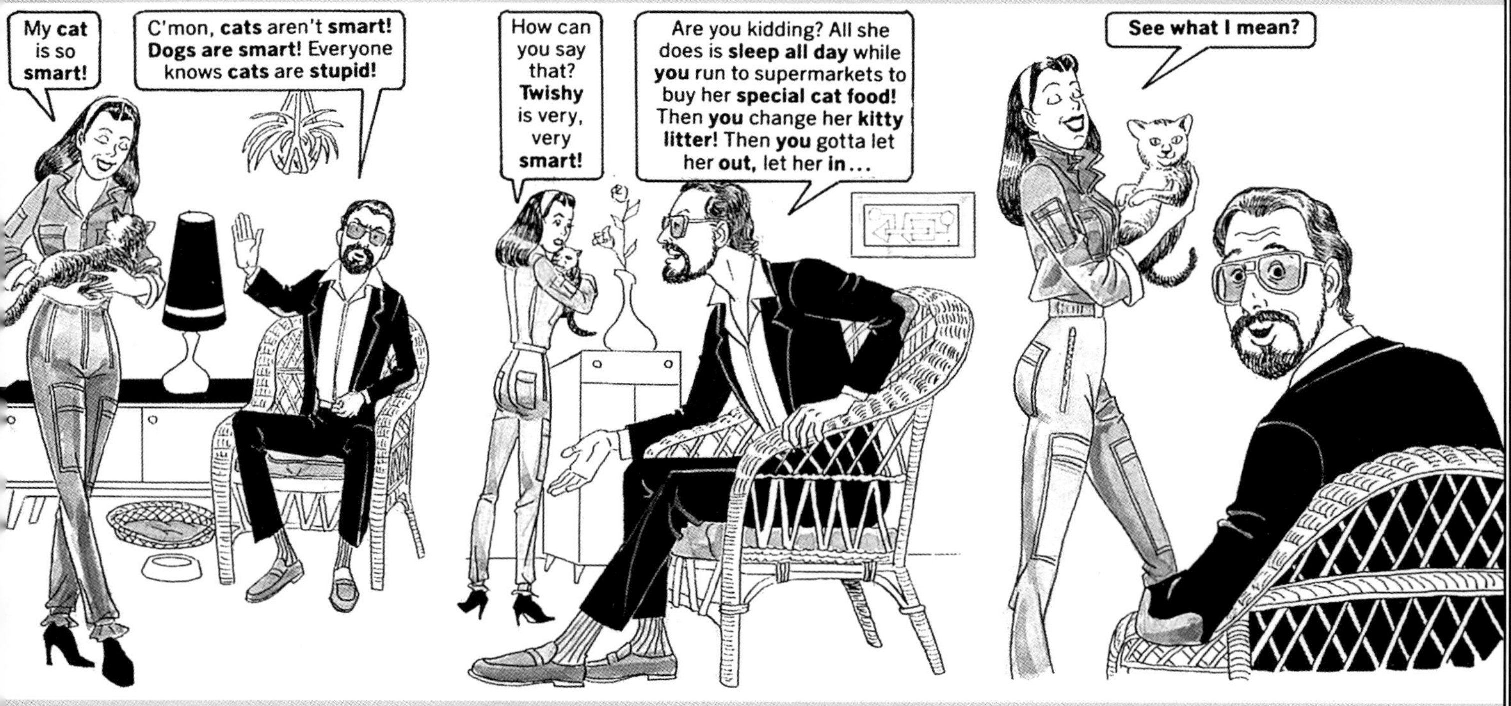
My cat is so smart!
C'mon, cats aren't smart! Dogs are smart! Everyone knows cats are stupid!
How can you say that? Twishy is very, very smart!
Are you kidding? All she does is sleep all day while you run to supermarkets to buy her special cat food! Then you change her kitty litter! Then you gotta let her out, let her in...
See what I mean?

NEW CARS

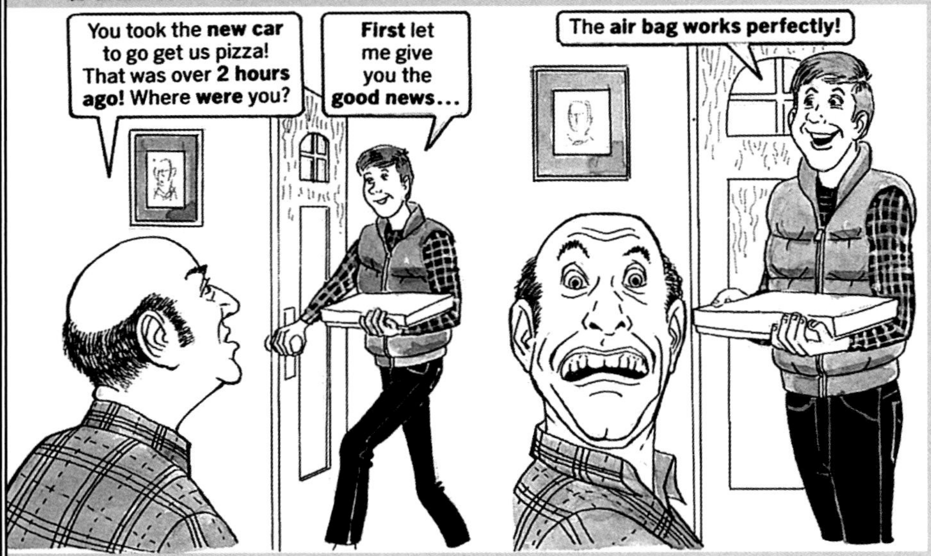
You took the new car to go get us pizza! That was over 2 hours ago! Where were you?
First let me give you the good news...
The air bag works perfectly!

CHEMISTRY

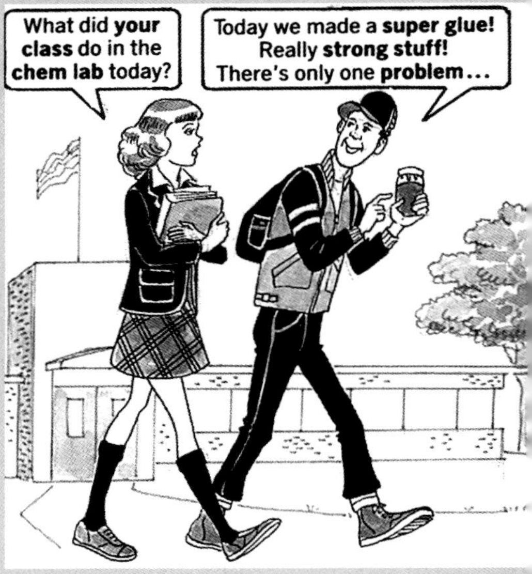
What did your class do in the chem lab today?
Today we made a super glue! Really strong stuff! There's only one problem...

CRIME

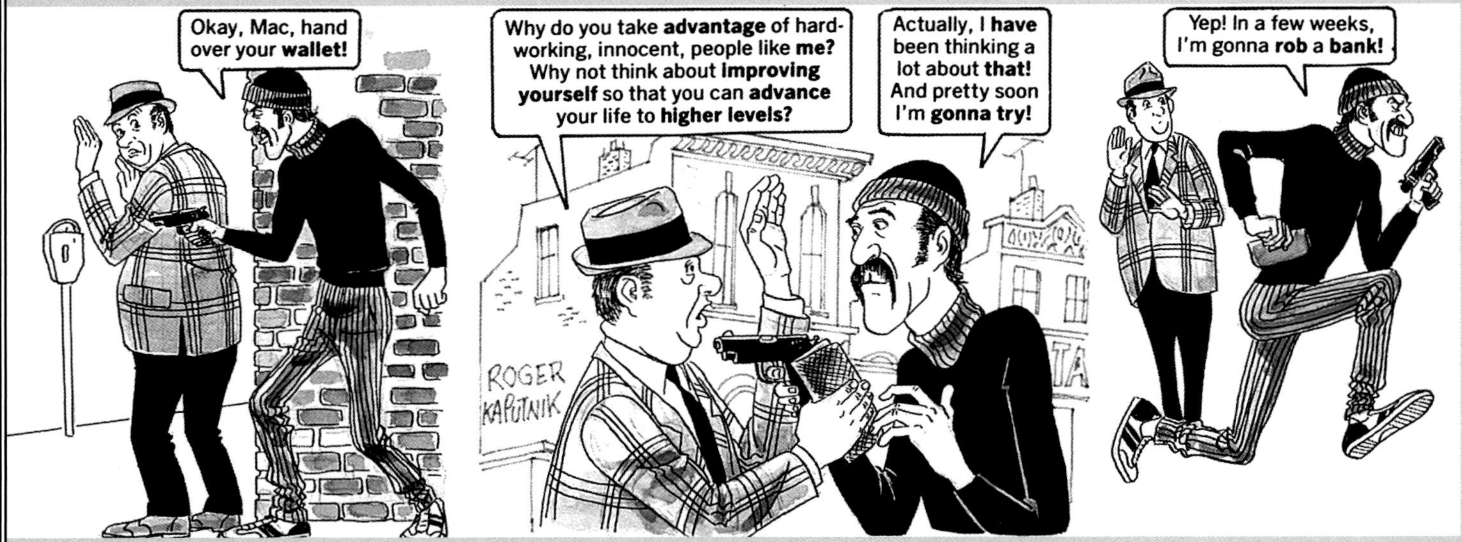
Okay, Mac, hand over your wallet!
Why do you take advantage of hard-working, innocent, people like me? Why not think about improving yourself so that you can advance your life to higher levels?
Actually, I have been thinking a lot about that! And pretty soon I'm gonna try!
ROGER KAPUTNIK
Yep! In a few weeks, I'm gonna rob a bank!

COMPLIMENTS

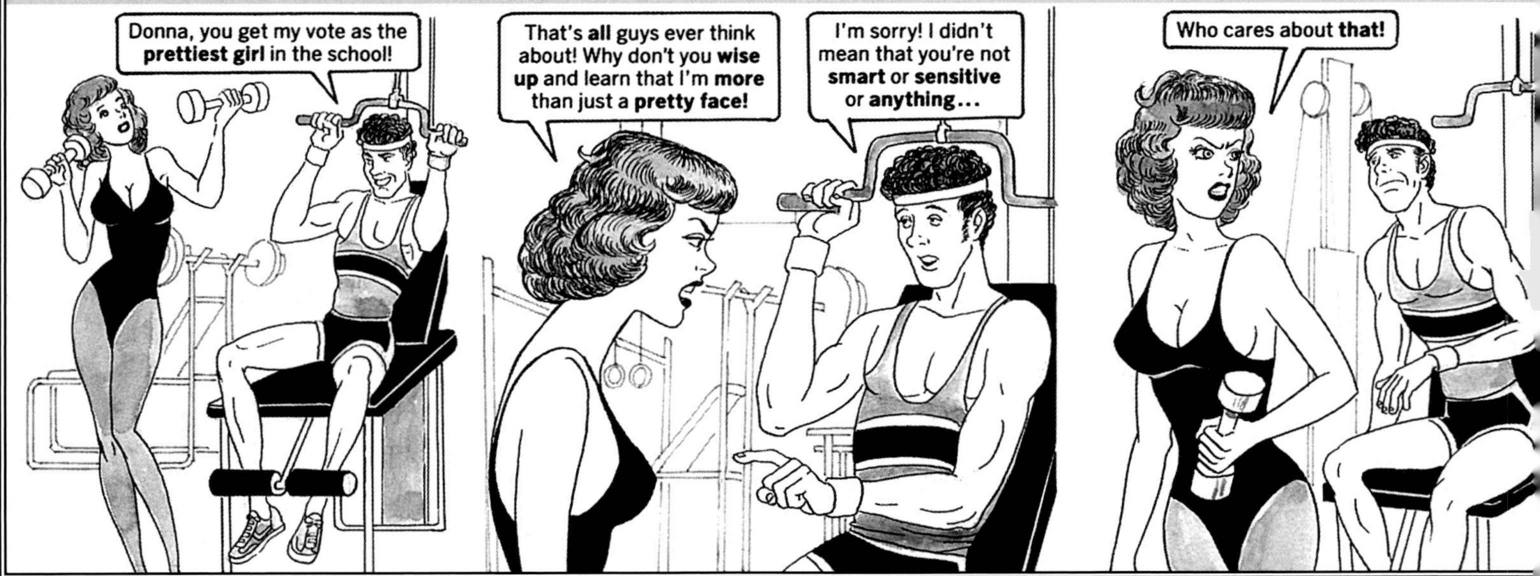
Donna, you get my vote as the prettiest girl in the school!
That's all guys ever think about! Why don't you wise up and learn that I'm more than just a pretty face!
I'm sorry! I didn't mean that you're not smart or sensitive or anything...
Who cares about that!

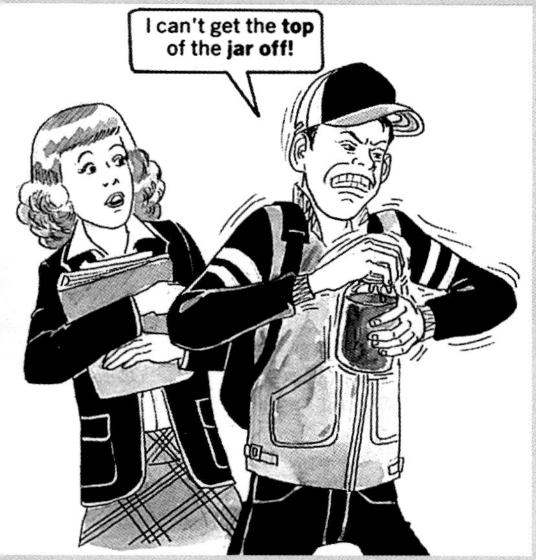
I can't get the top of the jar off!

TOYS

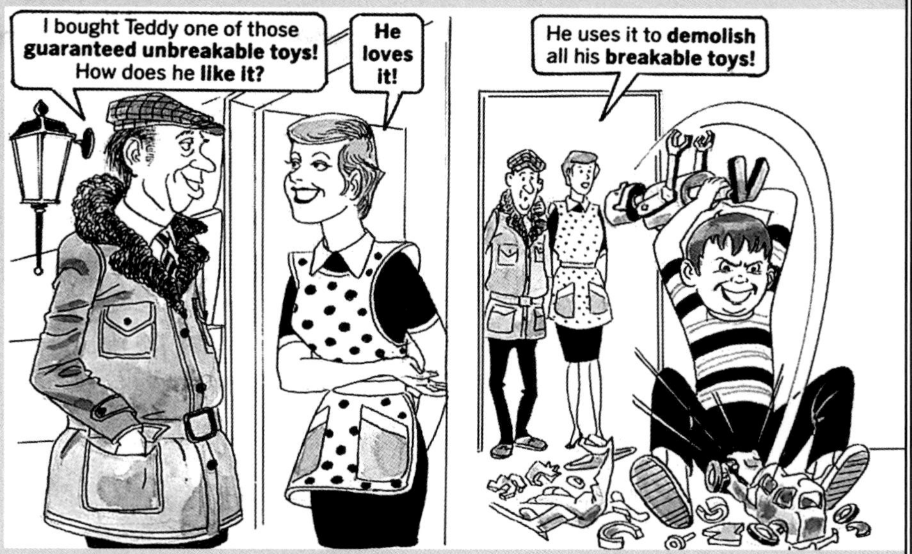
I bought Teddy one of those guaranteed unbreakable toys! How does he like it?
He loves it!
He uses it to demolish all his breakable toys!

DATING

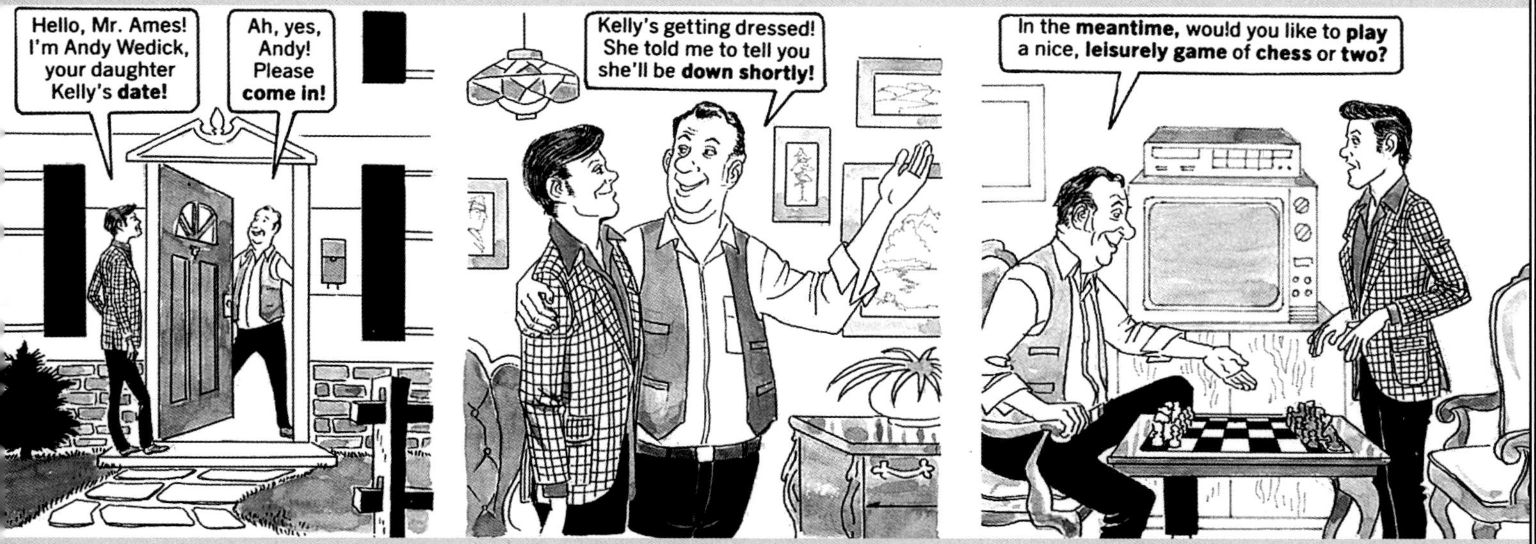
Hello, Mr. Ames! I'm Andy Wedick, your daughter Kelly's date!
Ah, yes, Andy! Please come in!
Kelly's getting dressed! She told me to tell you she'll be down shortly!
In the meantime, would you like to play a nice, leisurely game of chess or two?

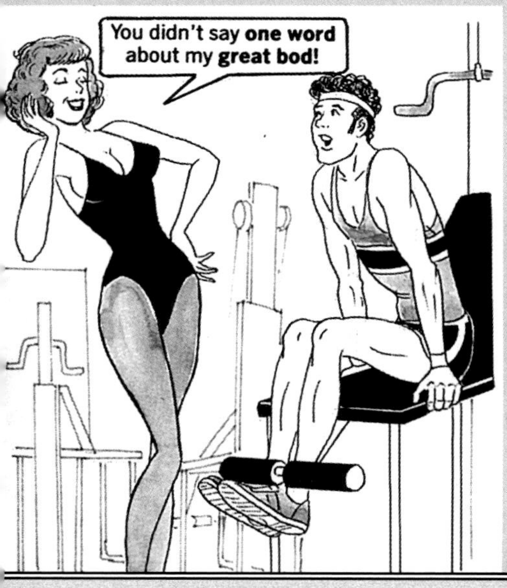
You didn't say one word about my great bod!

DOCTORS

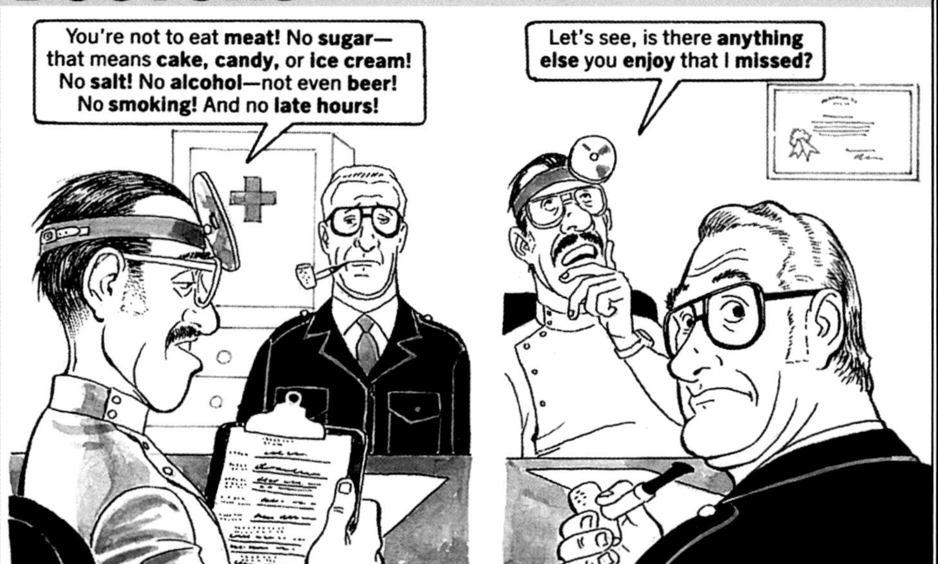
You're not to eat meat! No sugar—that means cake, candy, or ice cream! No salt! No alcohol—not even beer! No smoking! And no late hours!
Let's see, is there anything else you enjoy that I missed?

HIGHER EDUCATION

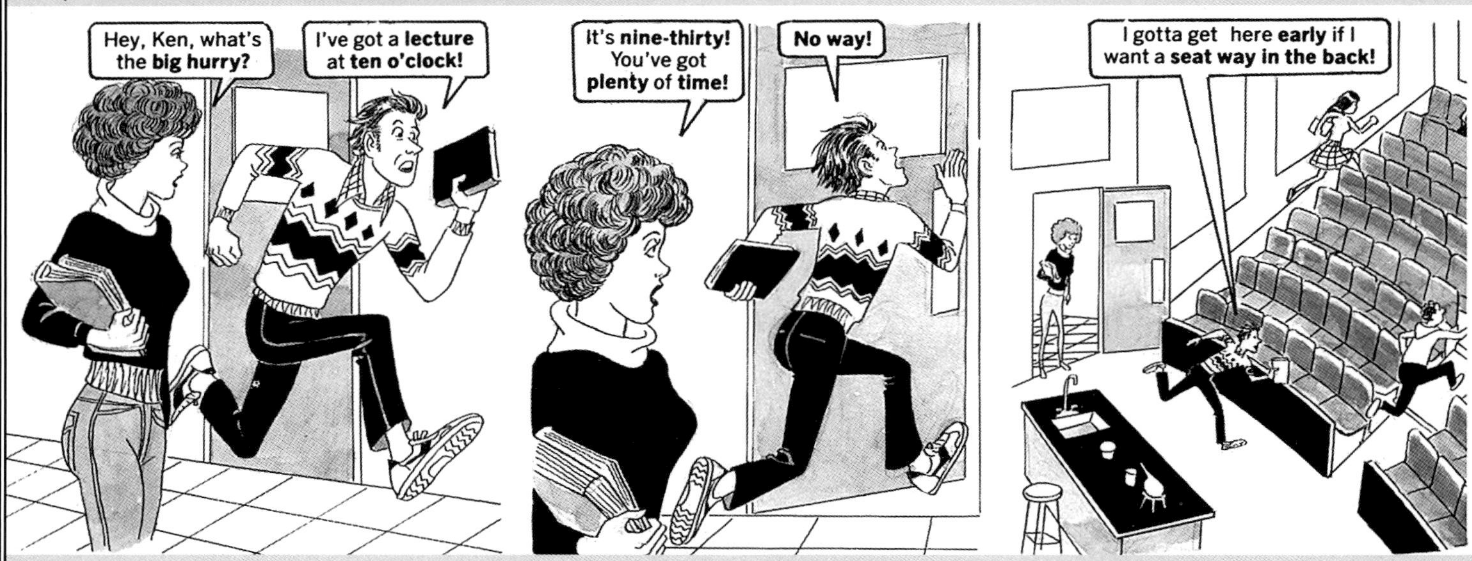
Hey, Ken, what's the big hurry?
I've got a lecture at ten o'clock!
It's nine-thirty! You've got plenty of time!
No way!
I gotta get here early if I want a seat way in the back!

COMMUNICATION

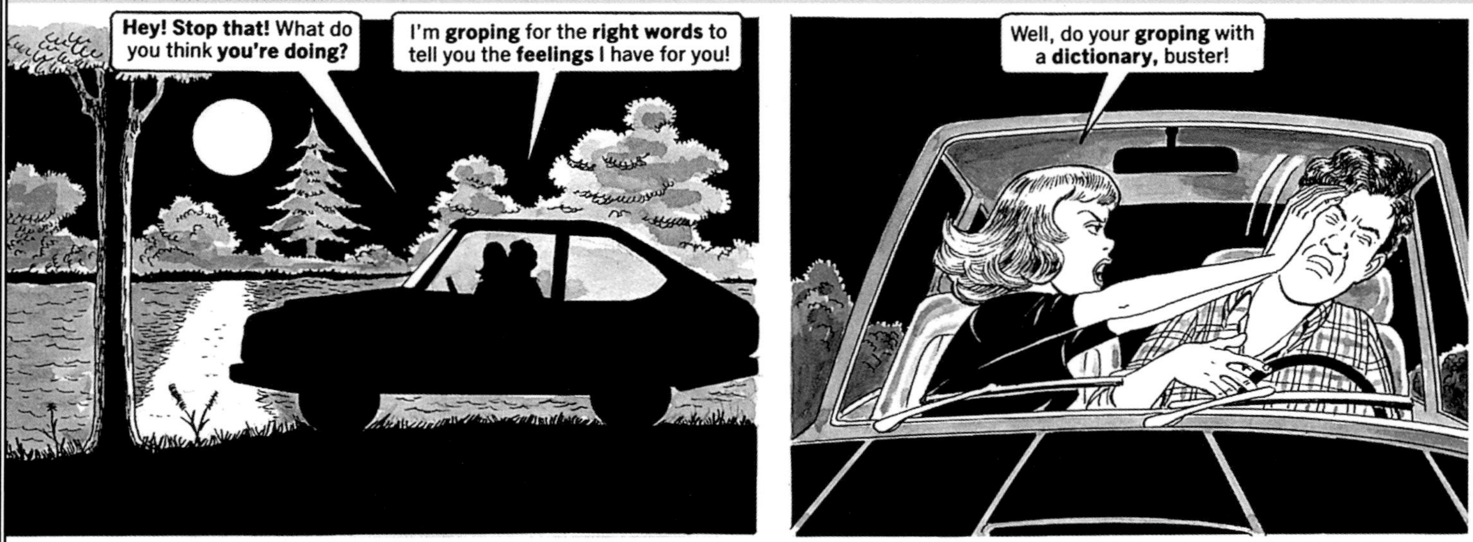
Hey! Stop that! What do you think you're doing?
I'm groping for the right words to tell you the feelings I have for you!
Well, do your groping with a dictionary, buster!

LOWER EDUCATION

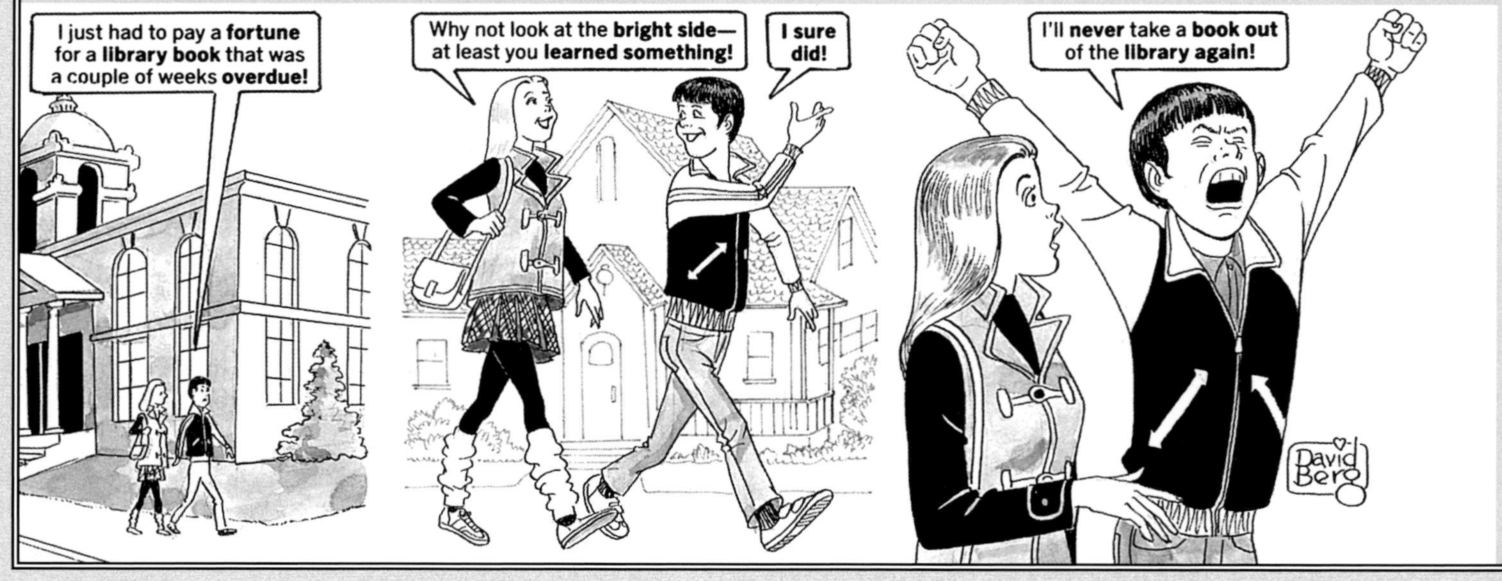
I just had to pay a fortune for a library book that was a couple of weeks overdue!
Why not look at the bright side—at least you learned something!
I sure did!
I'll never take a book out of the library again!
David Berg

Dave's Celebrity Snaps

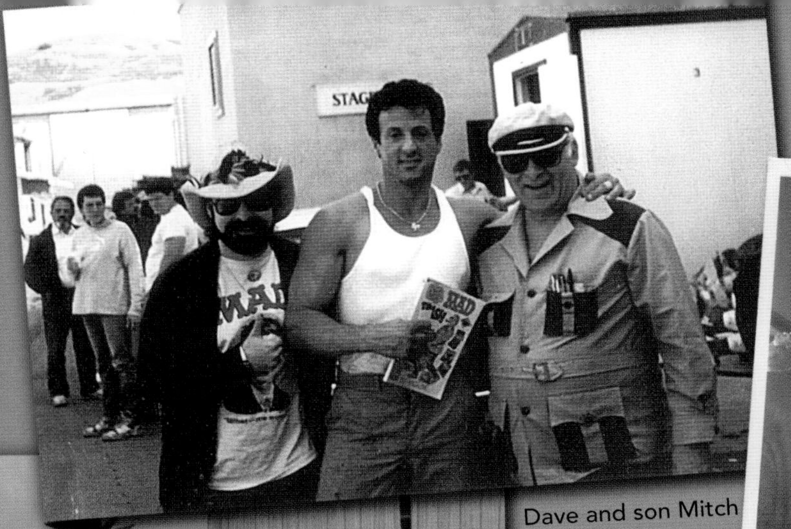
STAGE
MAD

Dave and son Mitch pay a call on Sylvester Stallone

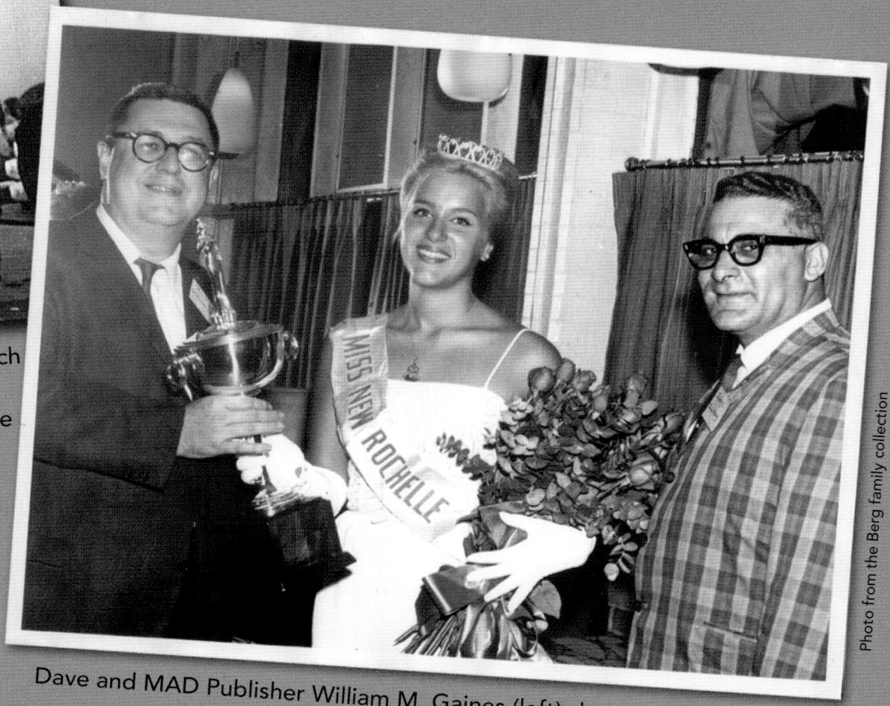
MISS NEW ROCHELLE

Dave and MAD Publisher William M. Gaines (left) share a photo op with Miss New Rochelle, Yolanda Stene

Photo from the Berg family collection

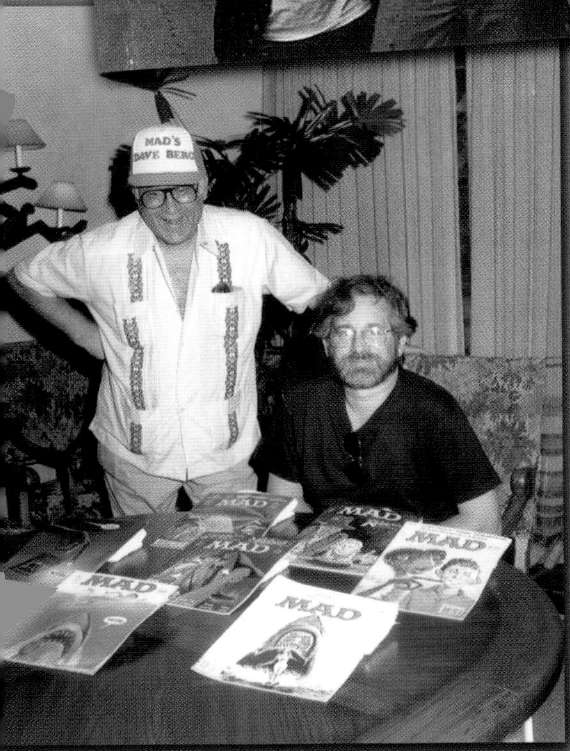
MAD'S
DAVE BERG
MAD

Dave visits Steven Spielberg

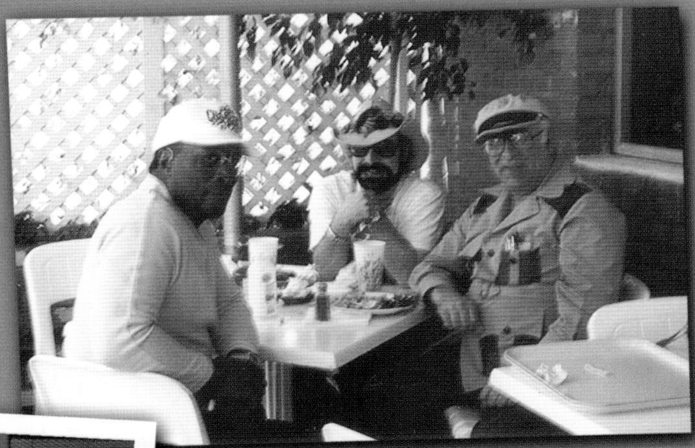

Dave and Mitch relaxing with John Amos

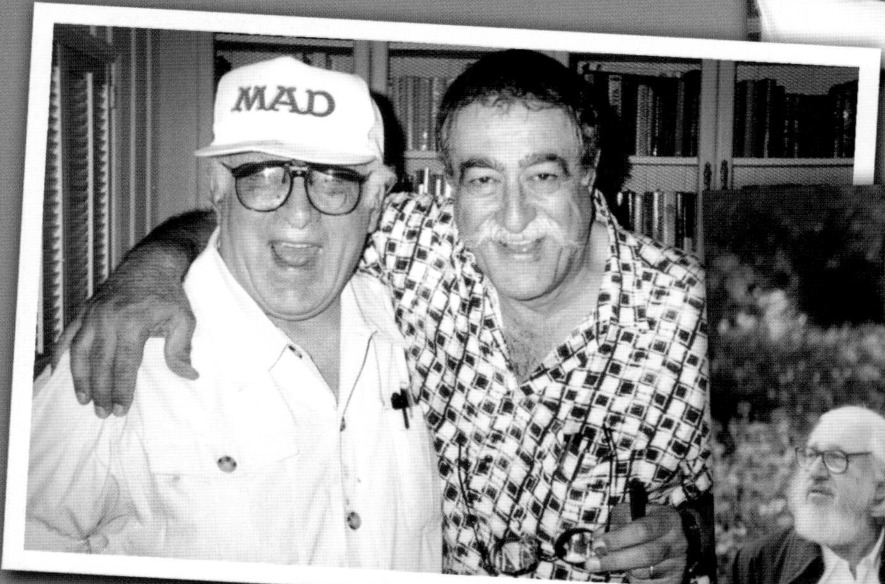
MAD

Dave and MAD's Sergio Aragonés

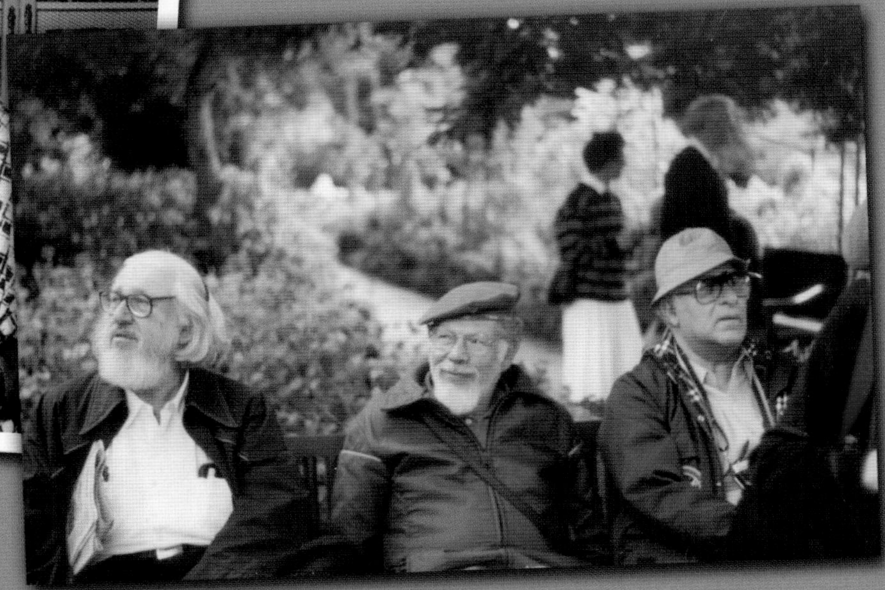

At Monet's Garden in Giverny, France (left to right):
William M. Gaines, Al Jaffee, and Dave Berg ponder life and art

Photo from the personal collection of Charlie Kadau

PUMPING IRON

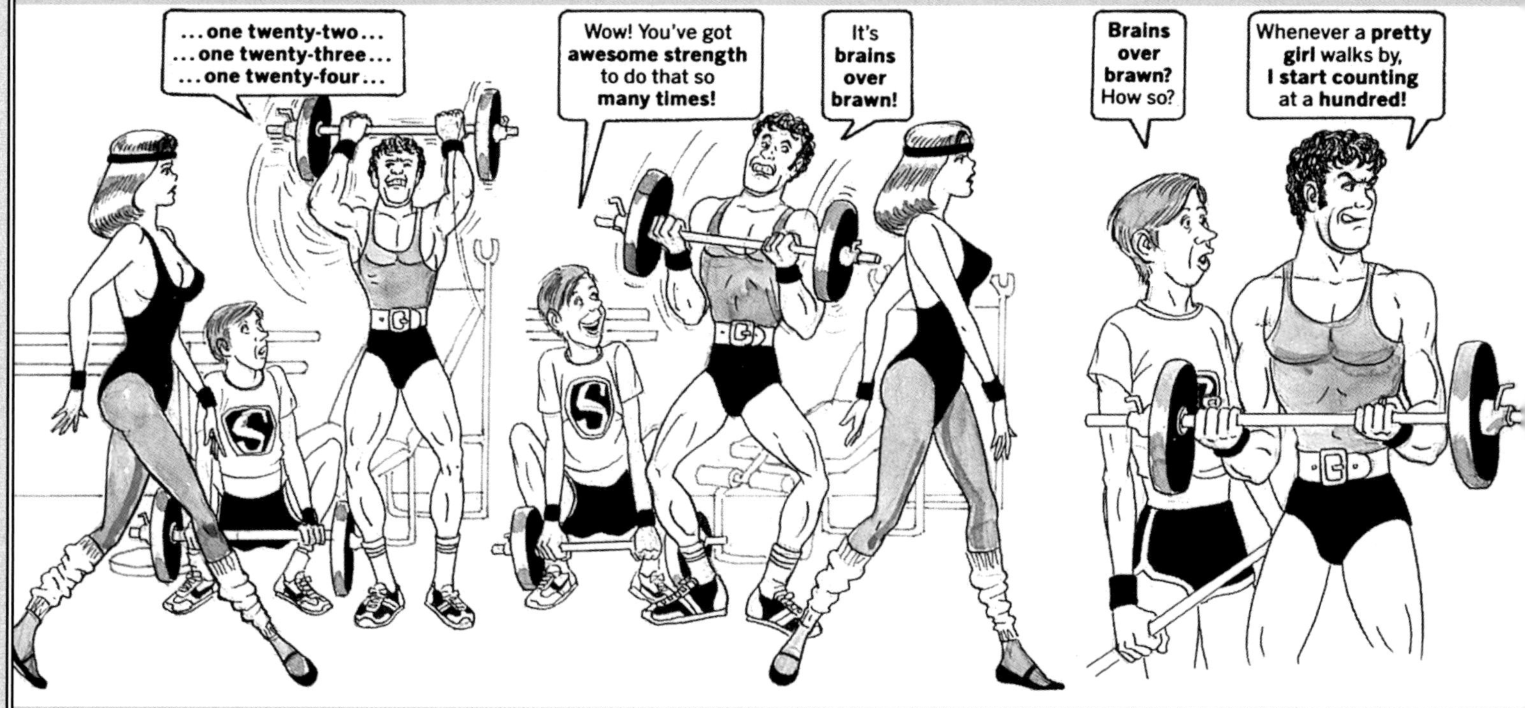
...one twenty-two...
...one twenty-three...
...one twenty-four...
Wow! You've got awesome strength to do that so many times!
It's brains over brawn!
Brains over brawn? How so?
Whenever a pretty girl walks by, I start counting at a hundred!

BERG'S-EYE VIEW DEPT.

THE LIGHTE

CLOTHES

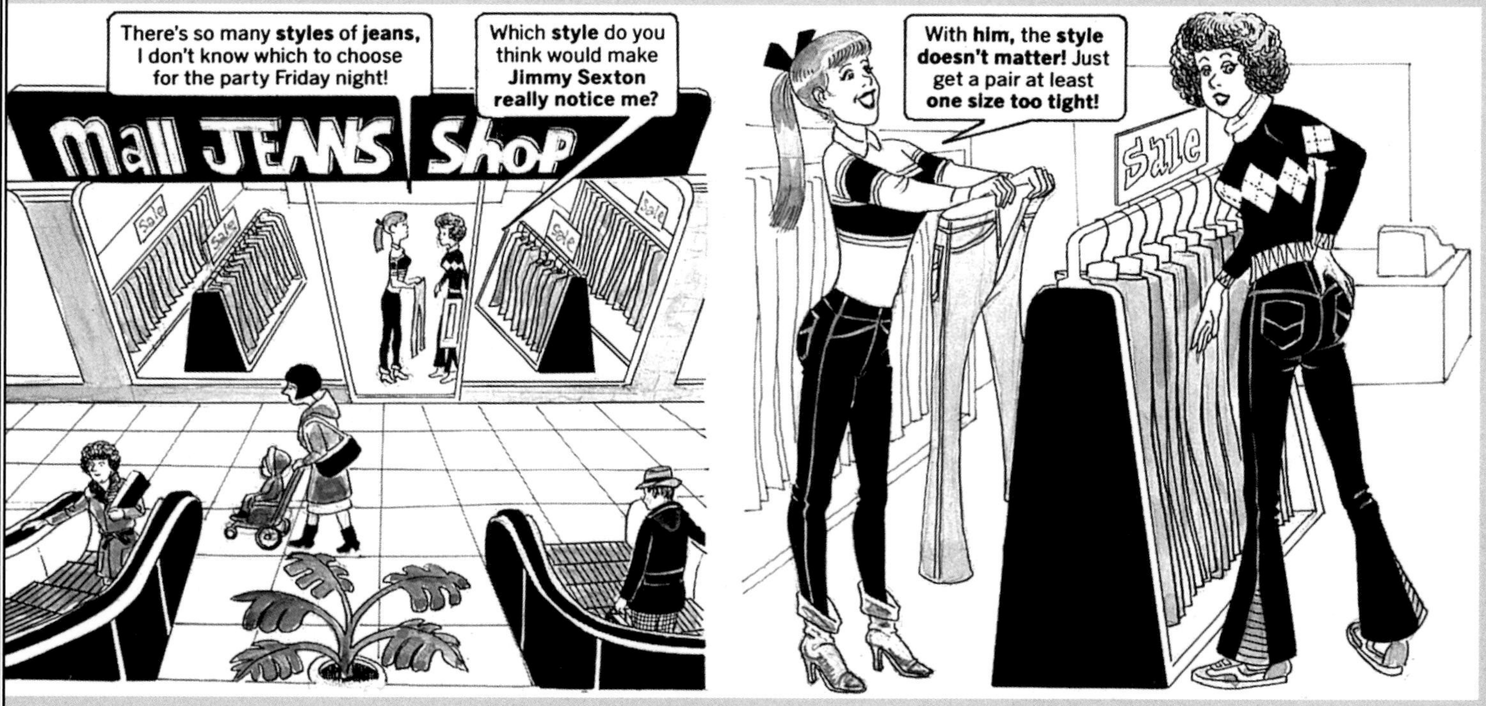
There's so many styles of jeans, I don't know which to choose for the party Friday night!
Which style do you think would make Jimmy Sexton really notice me?
mall JEANS Shop
Sale
With him, the style doesn't matter! Just get a pair at least one size too tight!
Sale

DRIVING

Seat belts are the greatest **safety factor** they've come up with in years!

That's true, but I don't see you **wearing yours!**

No, I **sit on** the **buckle!**

How is **that** a **"safety factor?"**

It's so **uncomfortable**, it keeps me from **falling asleep** at the **wheel!**

R SIDE OF...

ARTIST & WRITER:
DAVE BERG

EXAMS

I think I got a **100%** on today's biology exam!

How do you figure? It was a **killer**, and you didn't even study **10 minutes** for it!

Yeah, but I was able to **copy** all the answers from "Boom Boom" Wayne!

Are you kidding? "Boom Boom's" the **dumbest** kid in the class!

True, but "Boom Boom" **copied every answer** from Meg Bongiovanni! She **always** gets **100%!**

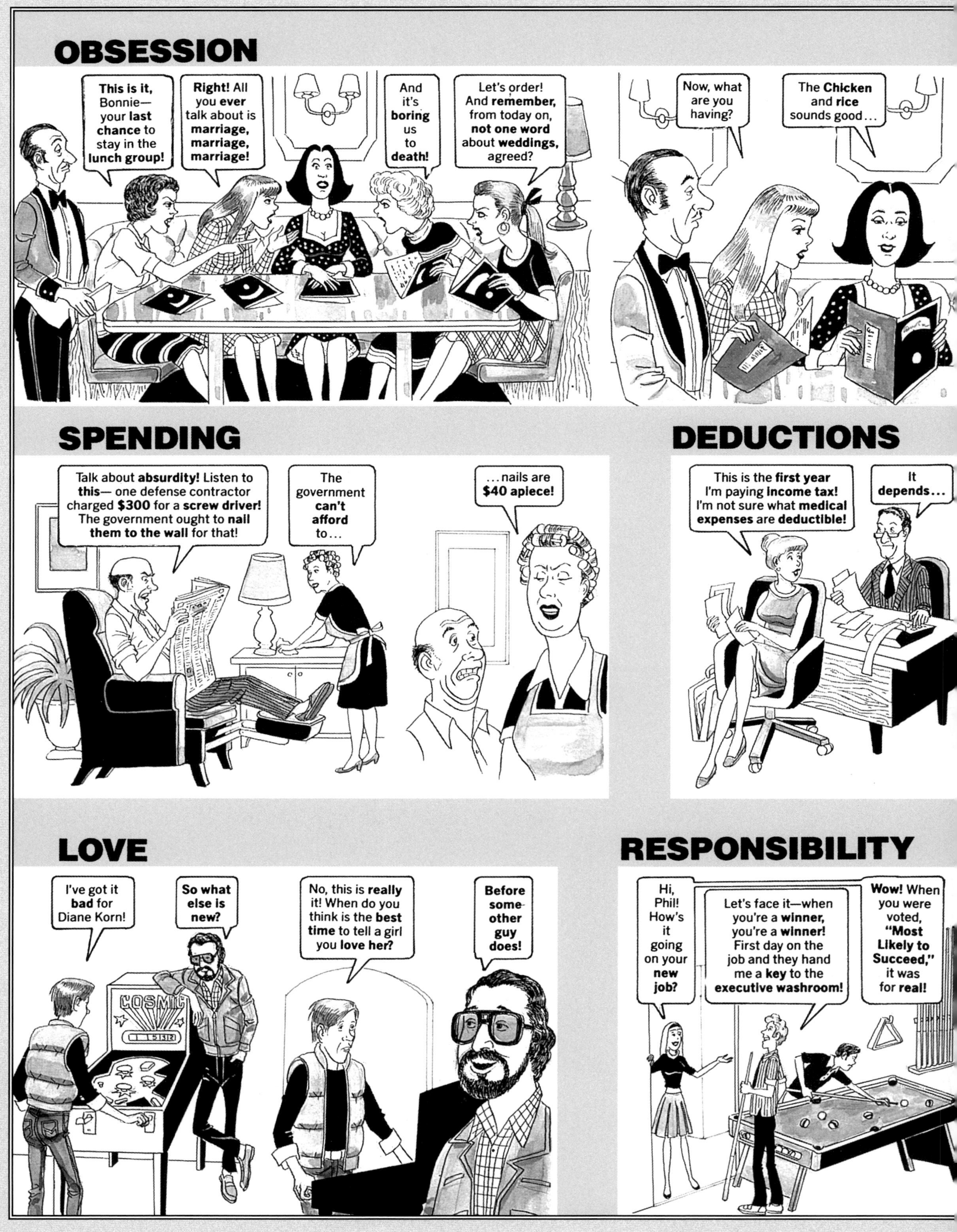
OBSESSION
This is it, Bonnie— your last chance to stay in the lunch group!
Right! All you ever talk about is marriage, marriage, marriage!
And it's boring us to death!
Let's order! And remember, from today on, not one word about weddings, agreed?
Now, what are you having?
The Chicken and rice sounds good...
SPENDING
Talk about absurdity! Listen to this— one defense contractor charged $300 for a screw driver! The government ought to nail them to the wall for that!
The government can't afford to...
...nails are $40 apiece!
DEDUCTIONS
This is the first year I'm paying income tax! I'm not sure what medical expenses are deductible!
It depends...
LOVE
I've got it bad for Diane Korn!
So what else is new?
No, this is really it! When do you think is the best time to tell a girl you love her?
Before some-other guy does!
RESPONSIBILITY
Hi, Phil! How's it going on your new job?
Let's face it—when you're a winner, you're a winner! First day on the job and they hand me a key to the executive washroom!
Wow! When you were voted, "Most Likely to Succeed," it was for real!

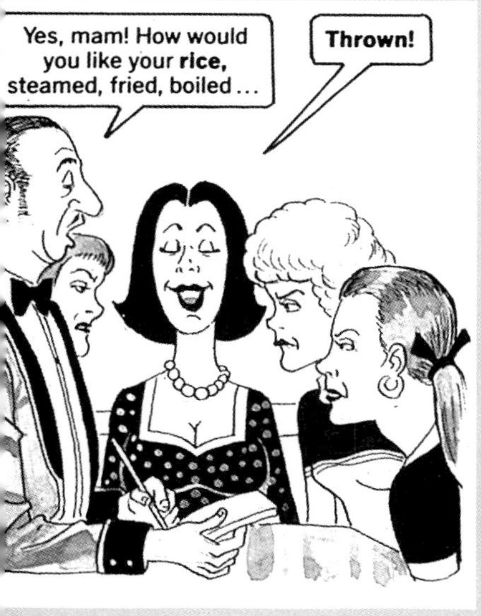
Yes, mam! How would you like your **rice,** steamed, fried, boiled . . .
Thrown!

TELEVISION

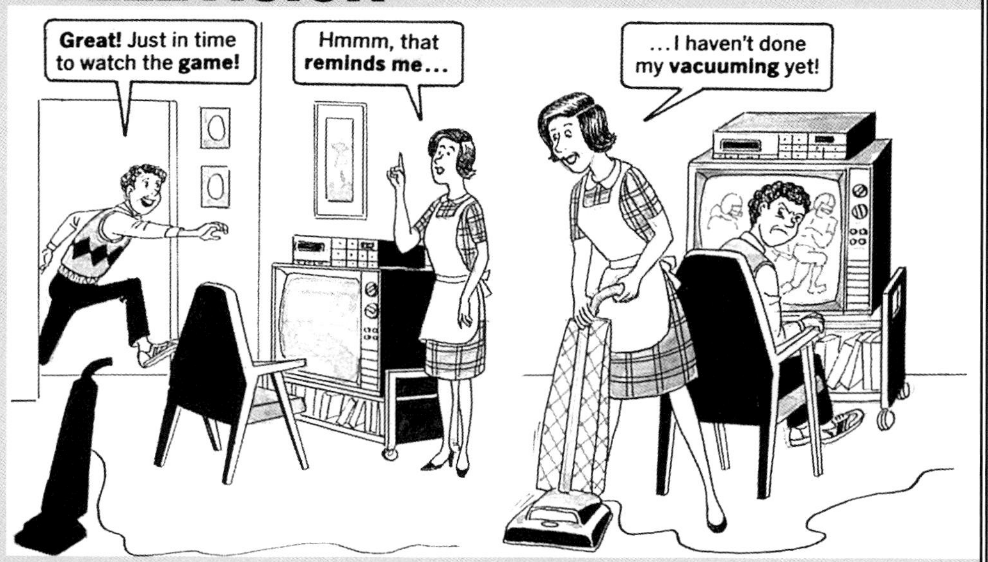
Great! Just in time to watch the **game!**
Hmmm, that **reminds me . . .**
. . . I haven't done my **vacuuming** yet!

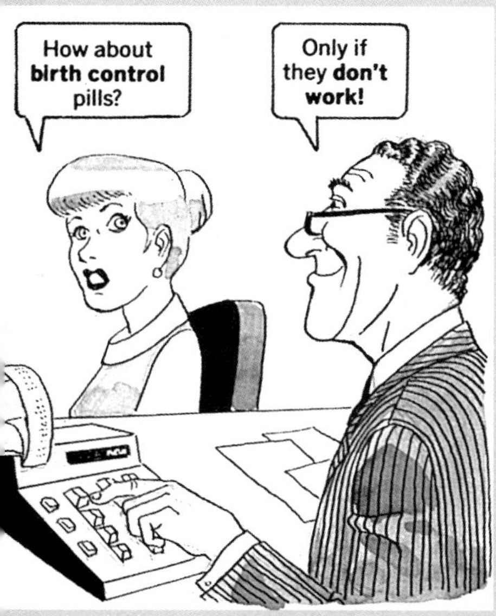
How about **birth control** pills?
Only if they **don't work!**

SELF-EFFACEMENT

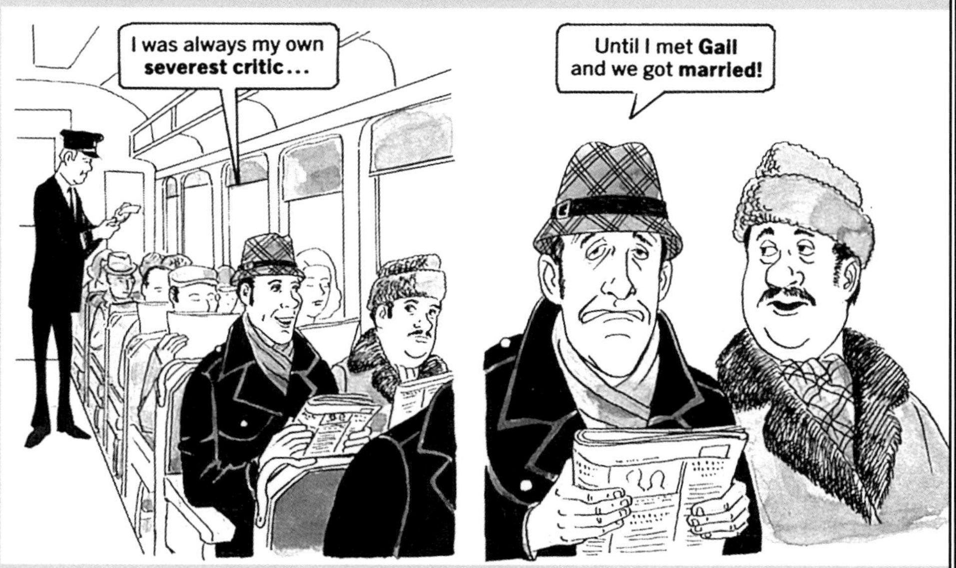
I was always my own **severest critic . . .**
Until I met **Gail** and we got **married!**

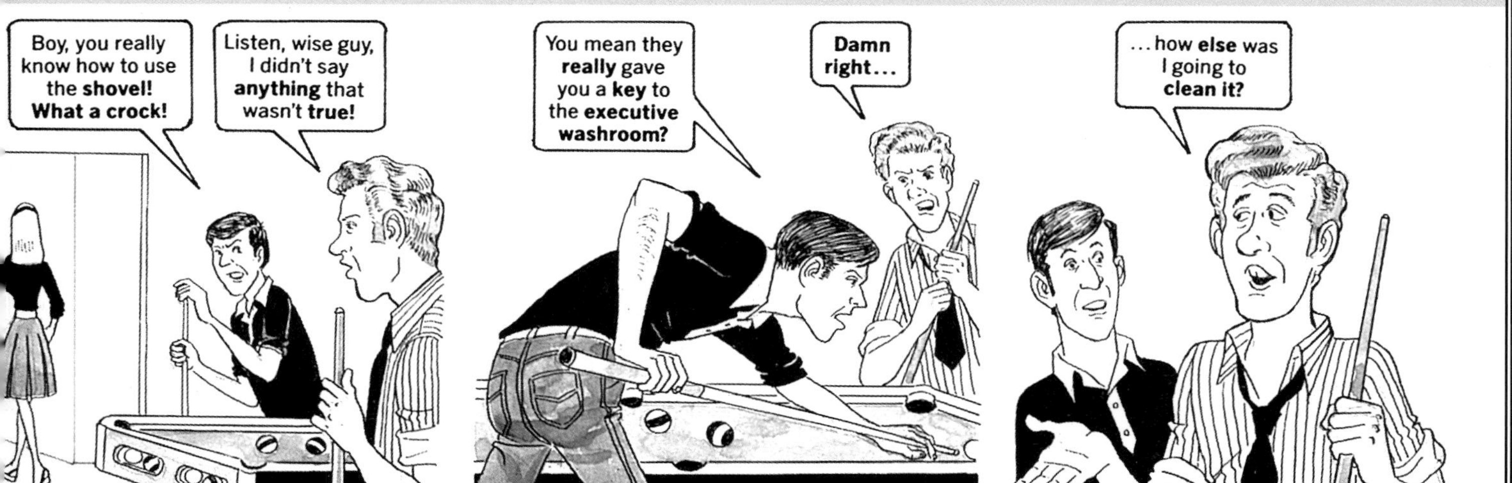
Boy, you really know how to use the **shovel! What a crock!**
Listen, wise guy, I didn't say **anything** that wasn't **true!**
You mean they **really** gave you a **key** to the **executive washroom?**
Damn right . . .
. . . how **else** was I going to **clean it?**

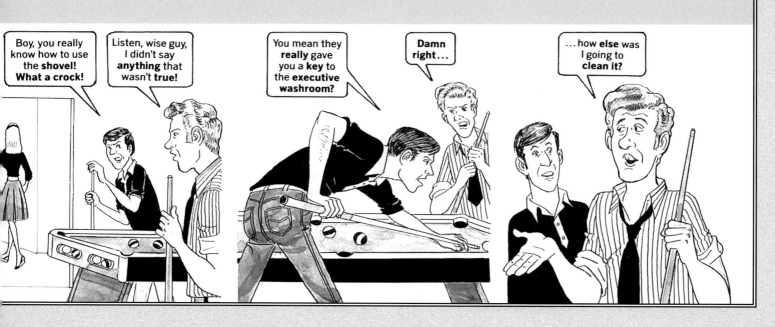

GOLF

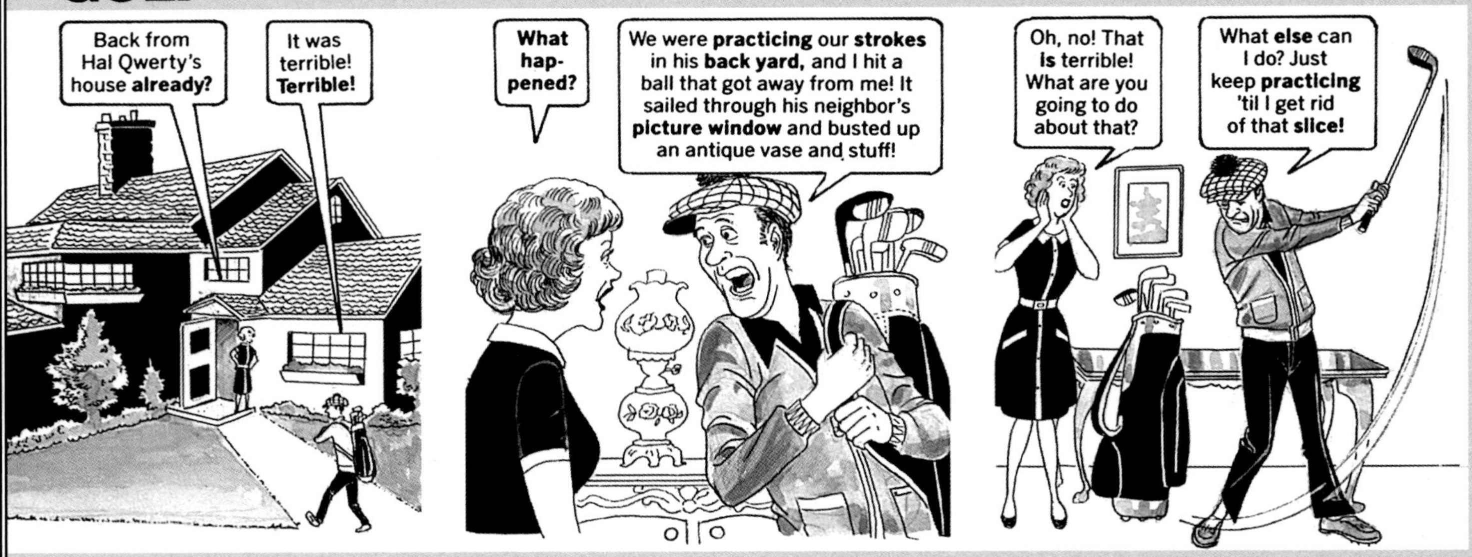
Back from Hal Qwerty's house **already?**
It was terrible! **Terrible!**
What hap-pened?
We were **practicing** our **strokes** in his **back yard,** and I hit a ball that got away from me! It sailed through his neighbor's **picture window** and busted up an antique vase and stuff!
Oh, no! That **is** terrible! What are you going to do about that?
What **else** can I do? Just keep **practicing** 'til I get rid of that **slice!**

HABITS

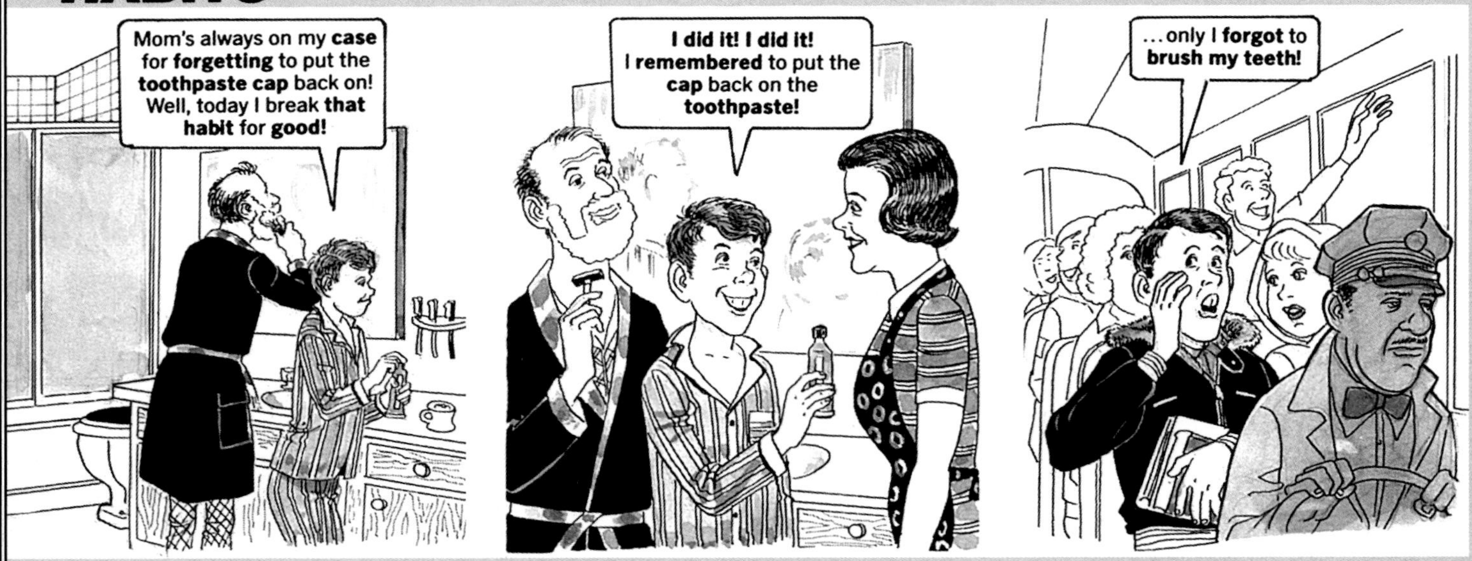
Mom's always on my **case** for **forgetting** to put the **toothpaste cap** back on! Well, today I break **that habit** for **good!**
I did it! I did it! I **remembered** to put the **cap** back on the **toothpaste!**
...only I **forgot** to **brush my teeth!**

DOCTORS

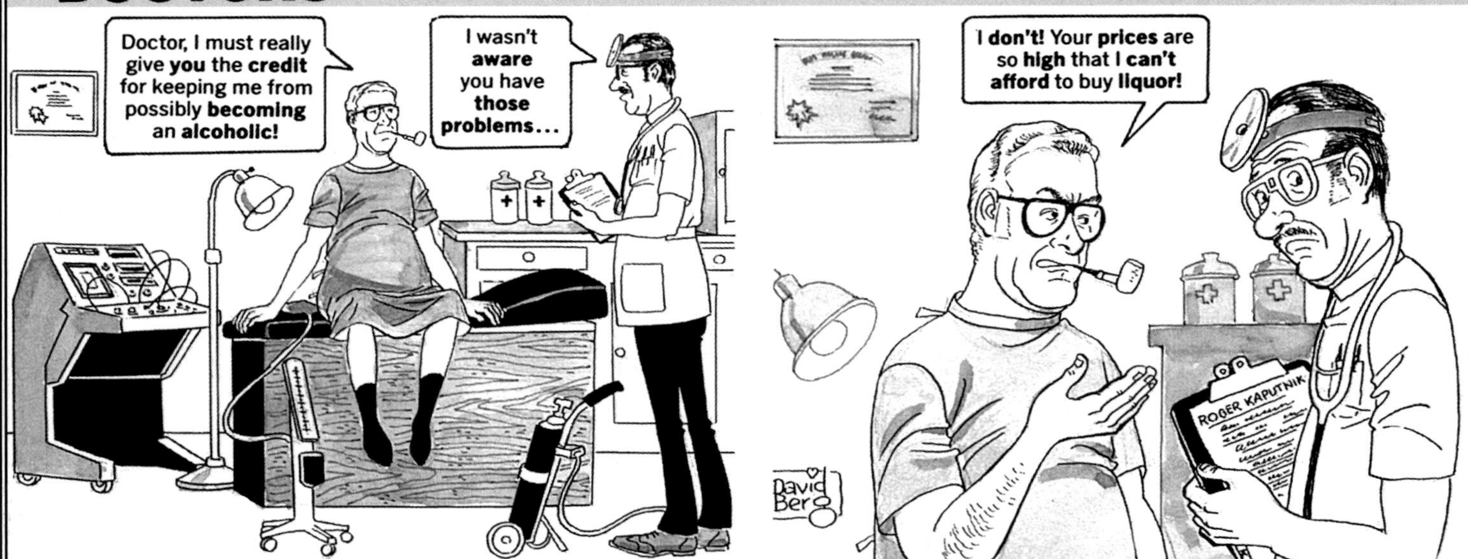
Doctor, I must really give **you** the **credit** for keeping me from possibly **becoming** an **alcoholic!**
I wasn't **aware** you have **those problems...**
I don't! Your **prices** are so **high** that I **can't afford** to buy **liquor!**
ROGER KAPUTNIK
David Berg

MAD Kids: Brothers & Sisters and Hidden Parent Cam

Additional examples of "The Lighter Side of..." scripts used in MAD Kids magazine

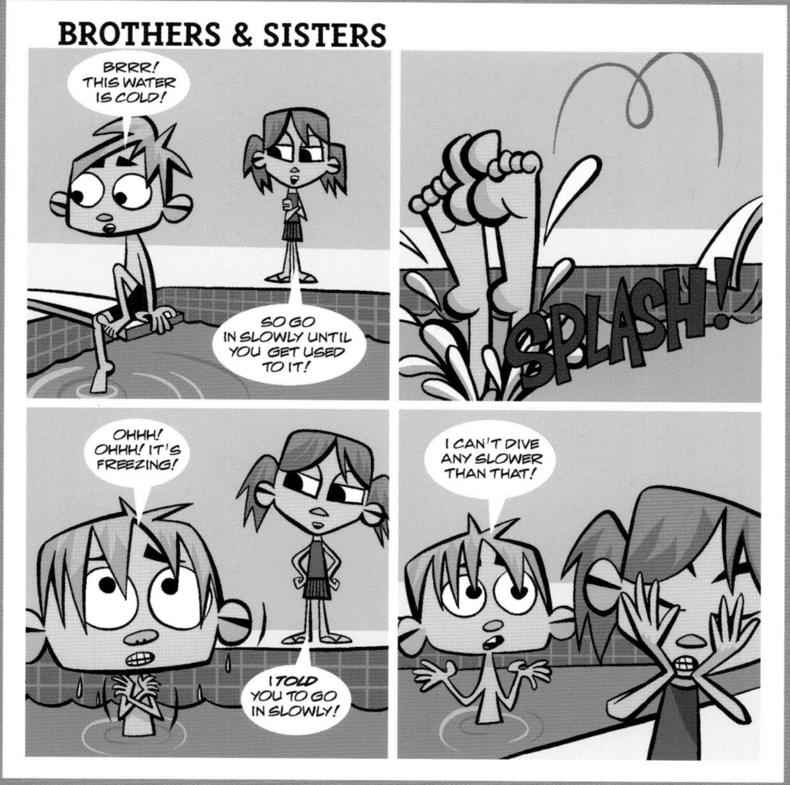
BROTHERS & SISTERS
BRRR! THIS WATER IS COLD!
SO GO IN SLOWLY UNTIL YOU GET USED TO IT!
SPLASH!
OHHH! OHHH! IT'S FREEZING!
I TOLD YOU TO GO IN SLOWLY!
I CAN'T DIVE ANY SLOWER THAN THAT!

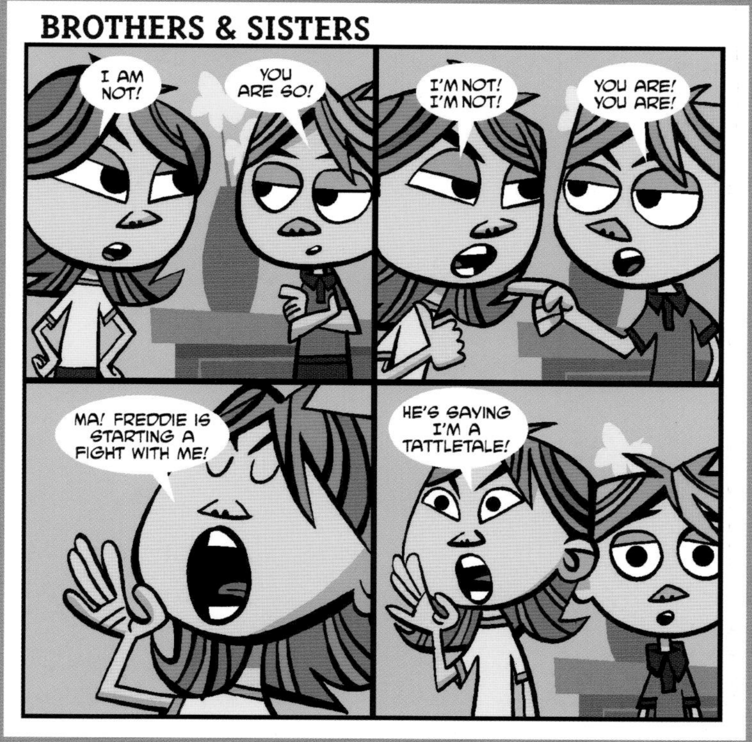
BROTHERS & SISTERS
I AM NOT!
YOU ARE SO!
I'M NOT! I'M NOT!
YOU ARE! YOU ARE!
MA! FREDDIE IS STARTING A FIGHT WITH ME!
HE'S SAYING I'M A TATTLETALE!

Brothers and Sisters drawn by Jonathan Edwards

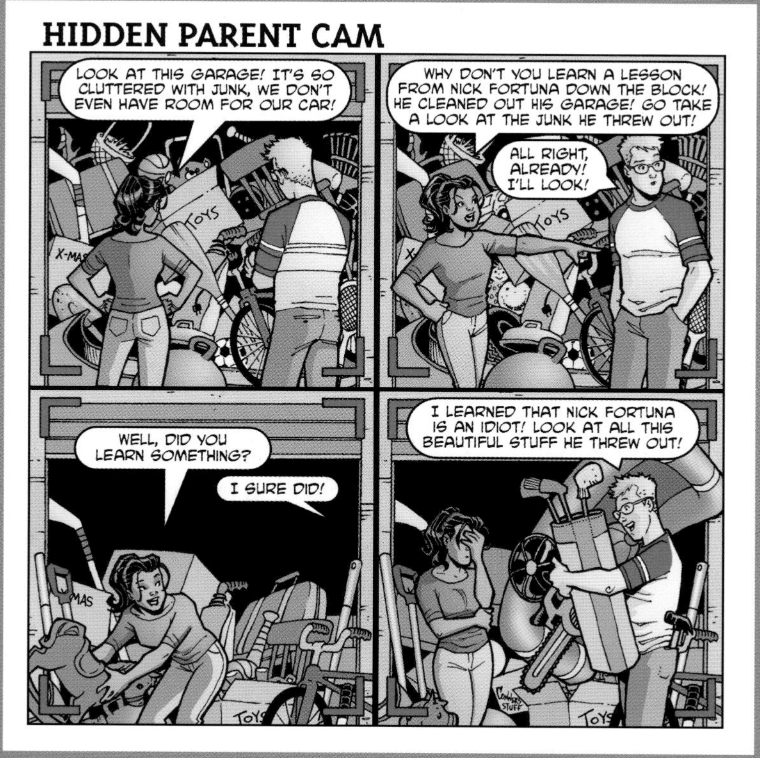
HIDDEN PARENT CAM
LOOK AT THIS GARAGE! IT'S SO CLUTTERED WITH JUNK, WE DON'T EVEN HAVE ROOM FOR OUR CAR!
WHY DON'T YOU LEARN A LESSON FROM NICK FORTUNA DOWN THE BLOCK! HE CLEANED OUT HIS GARAGE! GO TAKE A LOOK AT THE JUNK HE THREW OUT!
ALL RIGHT, ALREADY! I'LL LOOK!
WELL, DID YOU LEARN SOMETHING?
I SURE DID!
I LEARNED THAT NICK FORTUNA IS AN IDIOT! LOOK AT ALL THIS BEAUTIFUL STUFF HE THREW OUT!

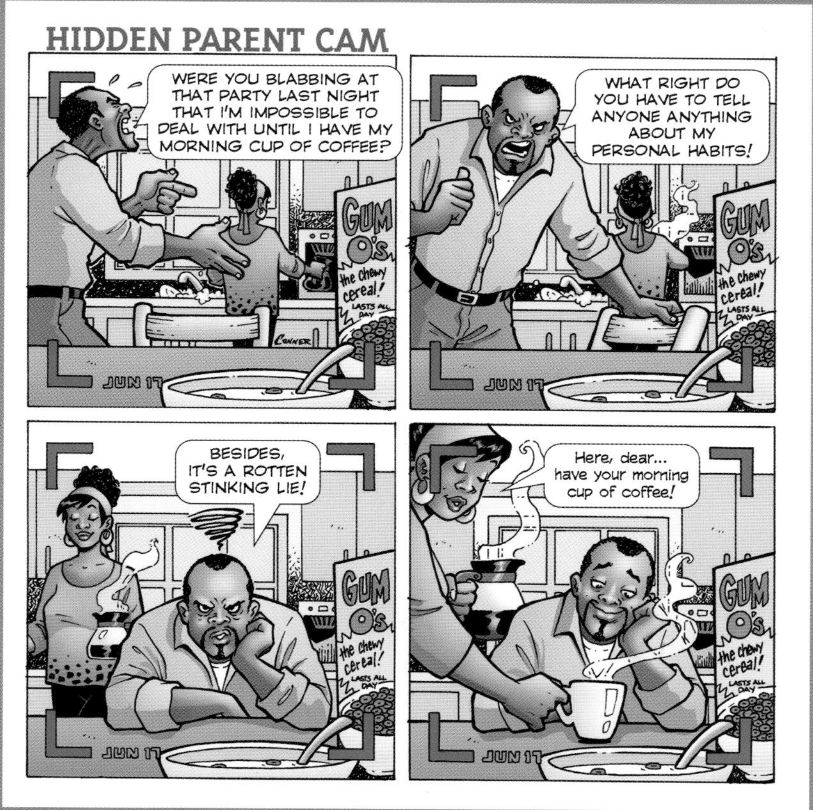
HIDDEN PARENT CAM
WERE YOU BLABBING AT THAT PARTY LAST NIGHT THAT I'M IMPOSSIBLE TO DEAL WITH UNTIL I HAVE MY MORNING CUP OF COFFEE?
WHAT RIGHT DO YOU HAVE TO TELL ANYONE ANYTHING ABOUT MY PERSONAL HABITS!
BESIDES, IT'S A ROTTEN STINKING LIE!
Here, dear... have your morning cup of coffee!
GUM O's the chewy cereal!
JUN 17

Hidden Parent Cam drawn by Amanda Conner

SPEEDING TICKETS

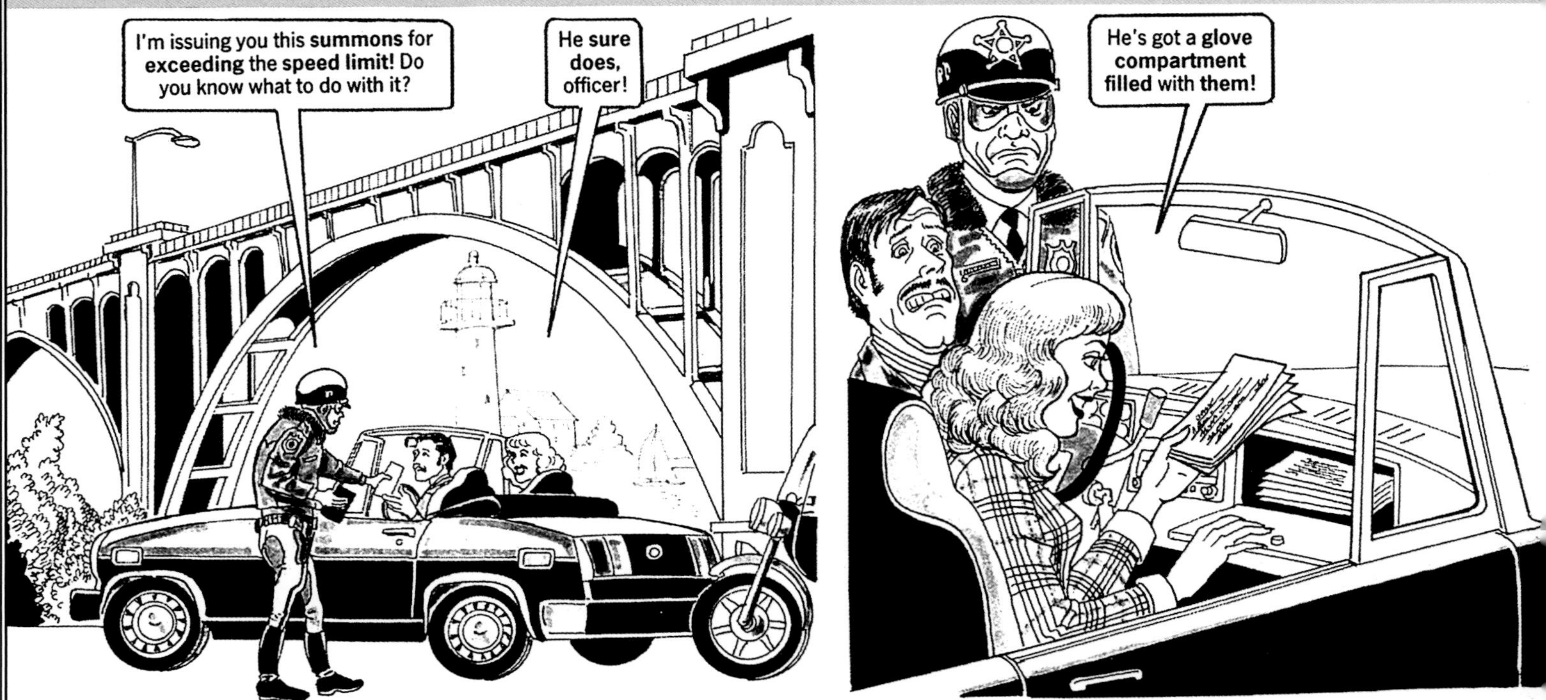
I'm issuing you this summons for exceeding the speed limit! Do you know what to do with it?
He sure does, officer!
He's got a glove compartment filled with them!

BERG'S-EYE VIEW DEPT.

THE LIGHTE

ATTRACTION

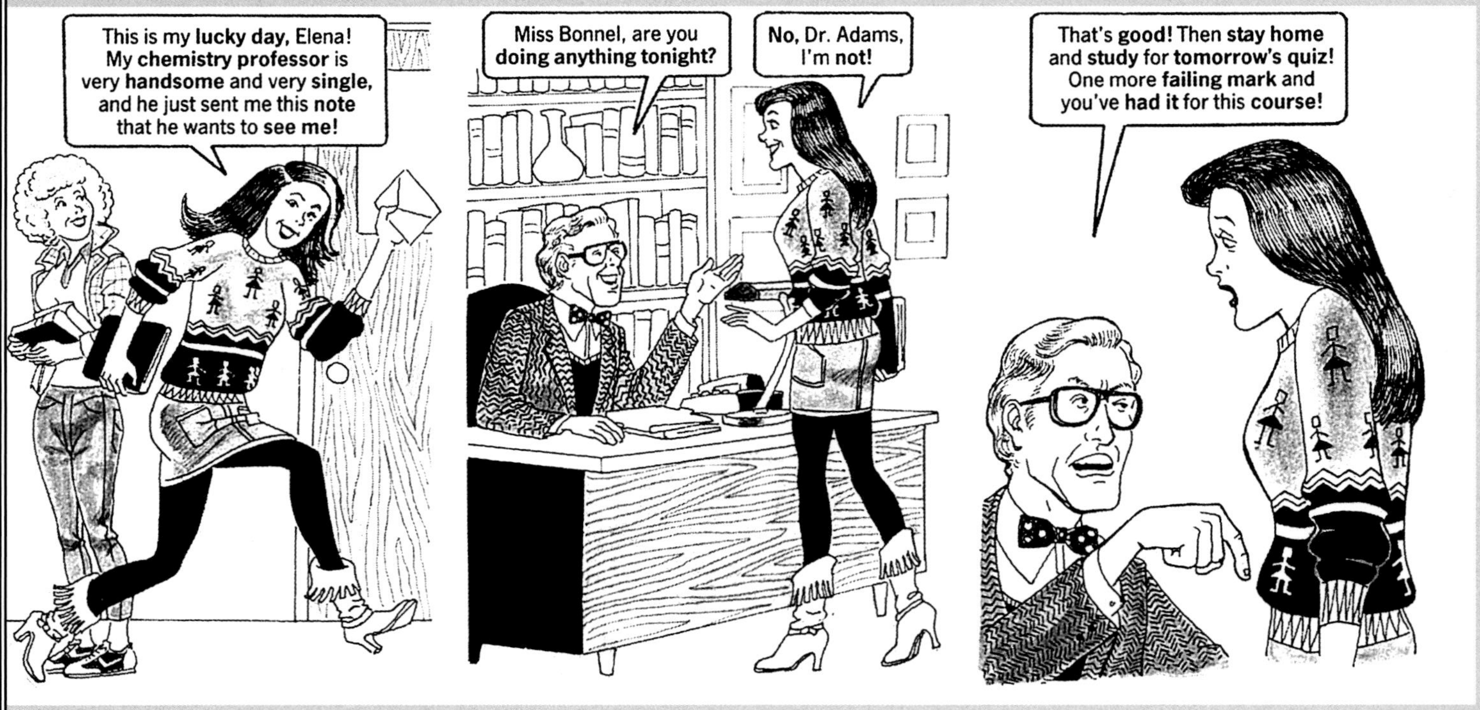
This is my lucky day, Elena! My chemistry professor is very handsome and very single, and he just sent me this note that he wants to see me!
Miss Bonnel, are you doing anything tonight?
No, Dr. Adams, I'm not!
That's good! Then stay home and study for tomorrow's quiz! One more failing mark and you've had it for this course!

REPAIRS

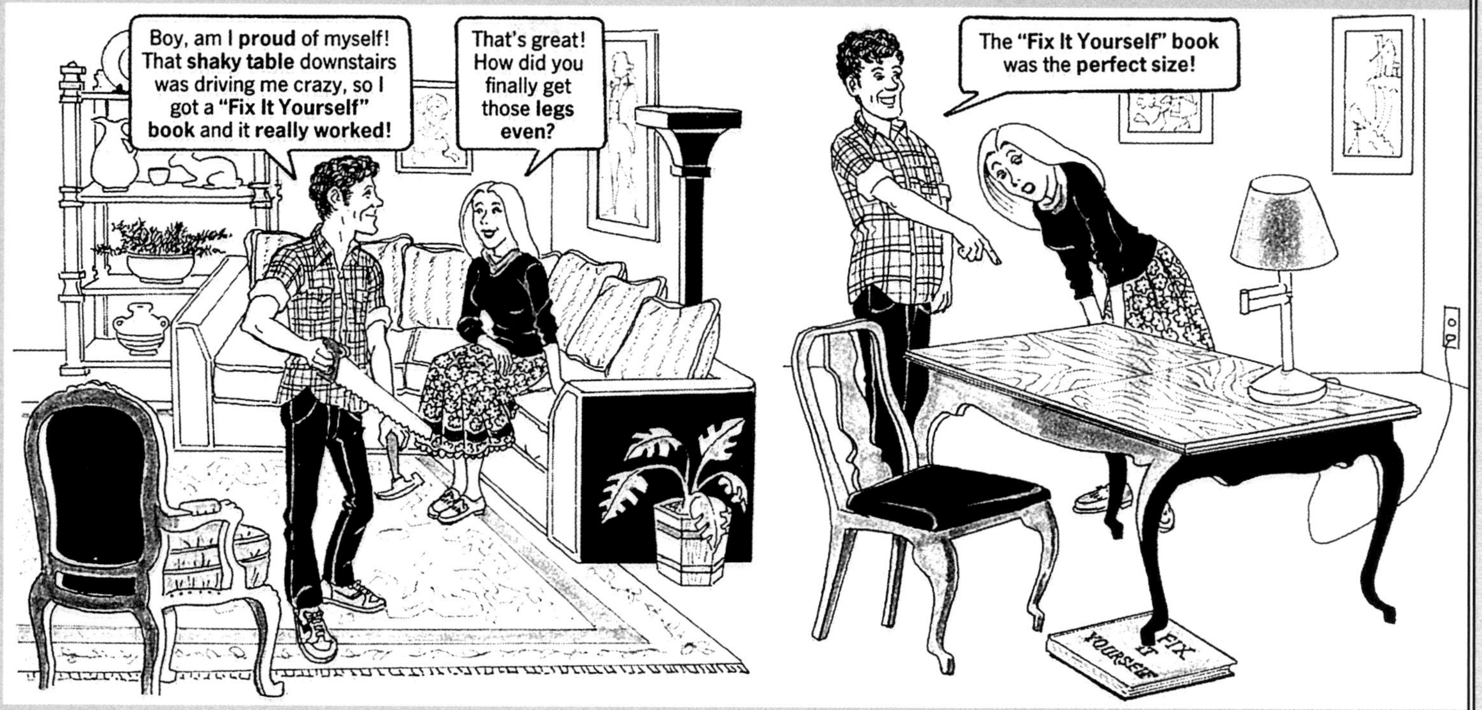
Boy, am I proud of myself! That shaky table downstairs was driving me crazy, so I got a "Fix It Yourself" book and it really worked!
That's great! How did you finally get those legs even?
The "Fix It Yourself" book was the perfect size!

R SIDE OF...

ARTIST & WRITER:
DAVE BERG

PHYSICAL FITNESS

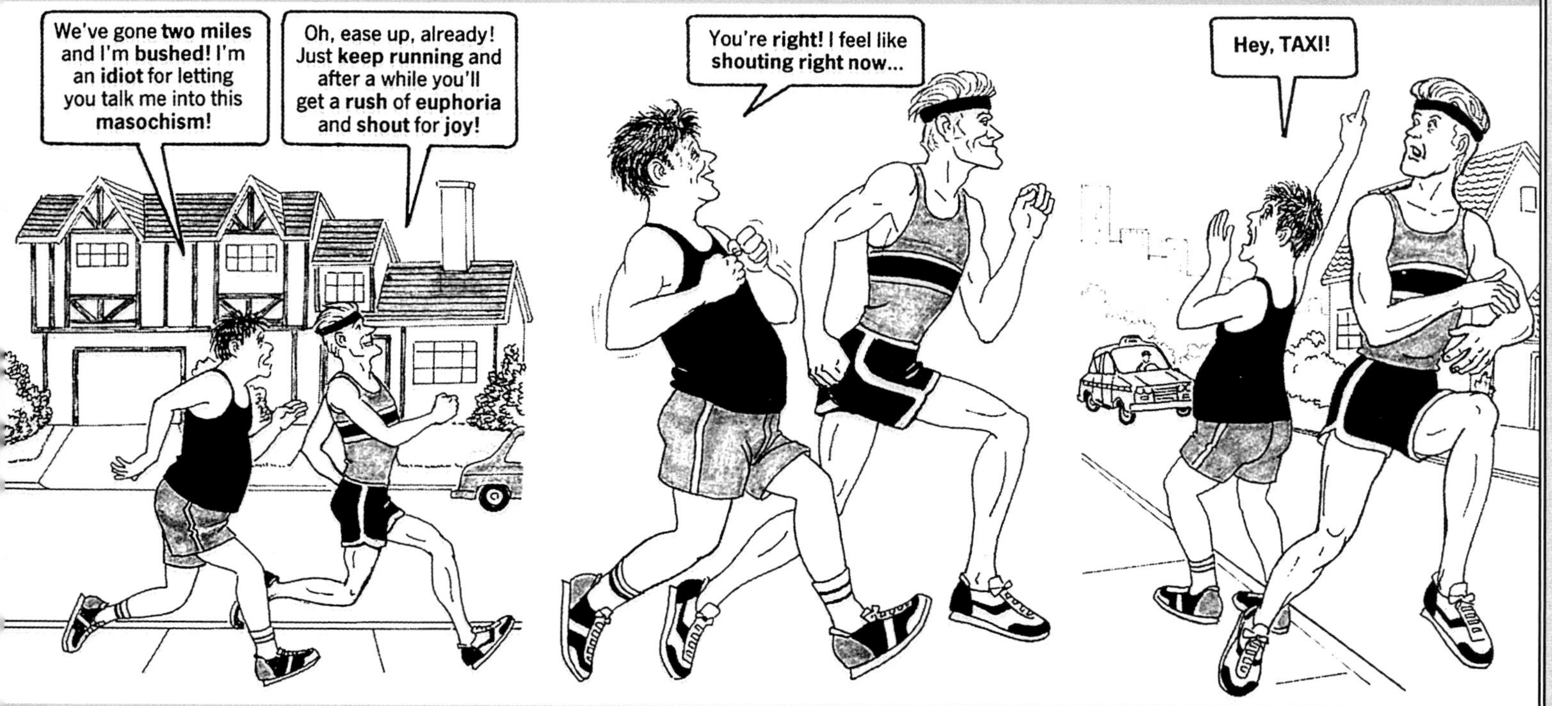
We've gone two miles and I'm bushed! I'm an idiot for letting you talk me into this masochism!
Oh, ease up, already! Just keep running and after a while you'll get a rush of euphoria and shout for joy!
You're right! I feel like shouting right now...
Hey, TAXI!

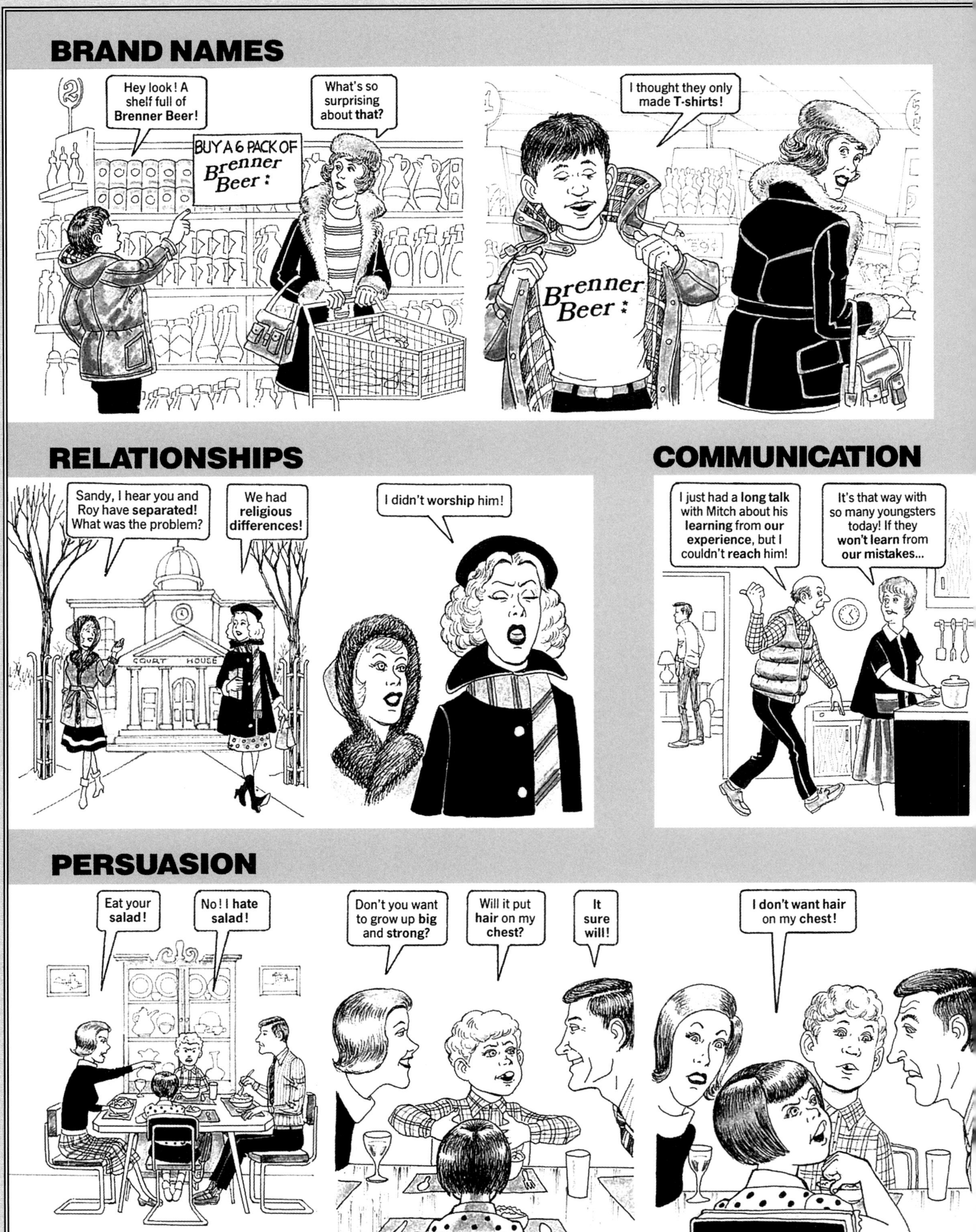
BRAND NAMES
Hey look! A shelf full of Brenner Beer!
BUY A 6 PACK OF Brenner Beer
What's so surprising about that?
I thought they only made T-shirts!
Brenner Beer
RELATIONSHIPS
Sandy, I hear you and Roy have separated! What was the problem?
We had religious differences!
COURT HOUSE
I didn't worship him!
COMMUNICATION
I just had a long talk with Mitch about his learning from our experience, but I couldn't reach him!
It's that way with so many youngsters today! If they won't learn from our mistakes...
PERSUASION
Eat your salad!
No! I hate salad!
Don't you want to grow up big and strong?
Will it put hair on my chest?
It sure will!
I don't want hair on my chest!

HOME DECORATION

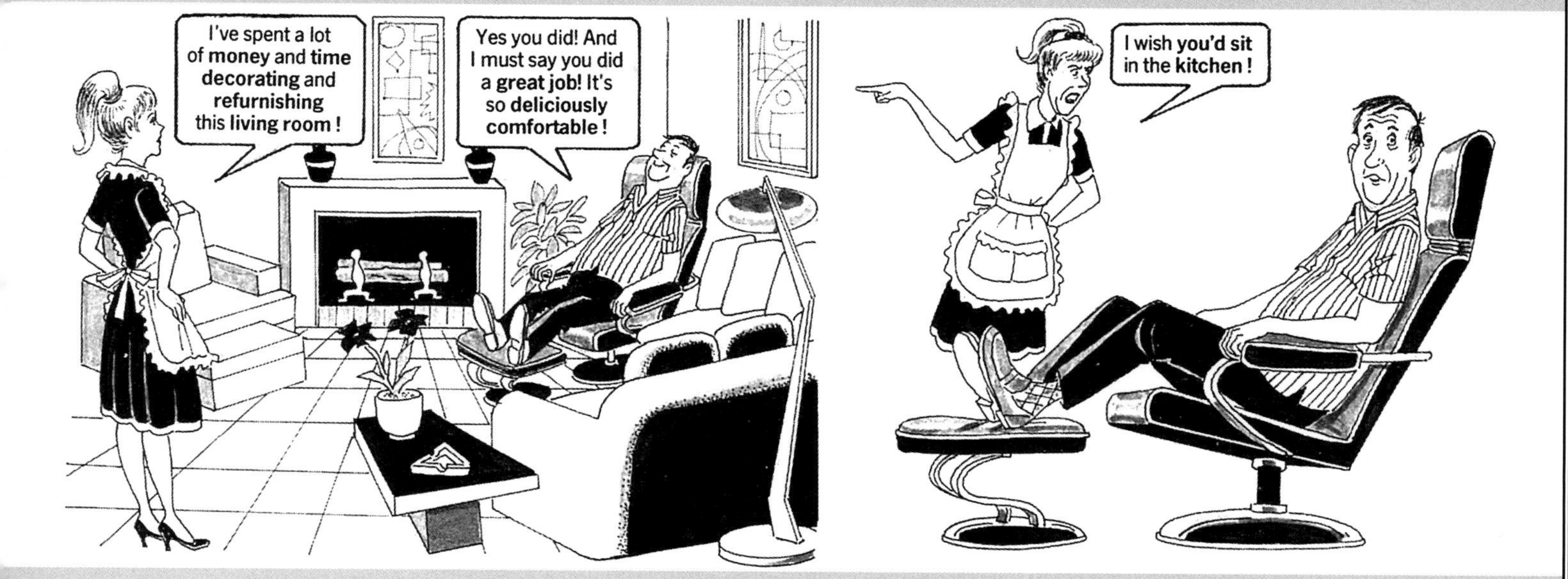
I've spent a lot of money and time decorating and refurnishing this living room!
Yes you did! And I must say you did a great job! It's so deliciously comfortable!
I wish you'd sit in the kitchen!

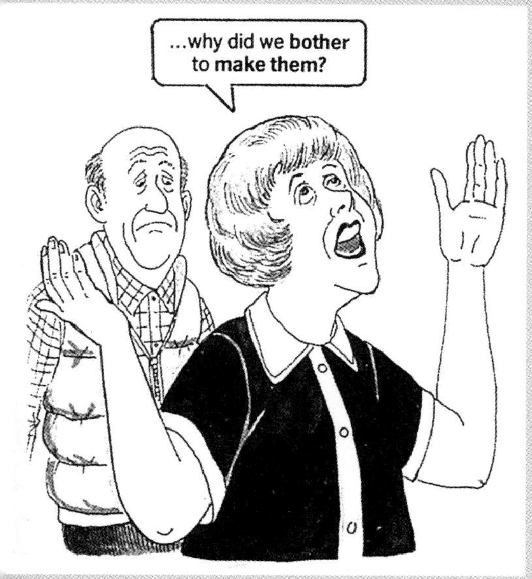
...why did we bother to make them?

SHOPPING

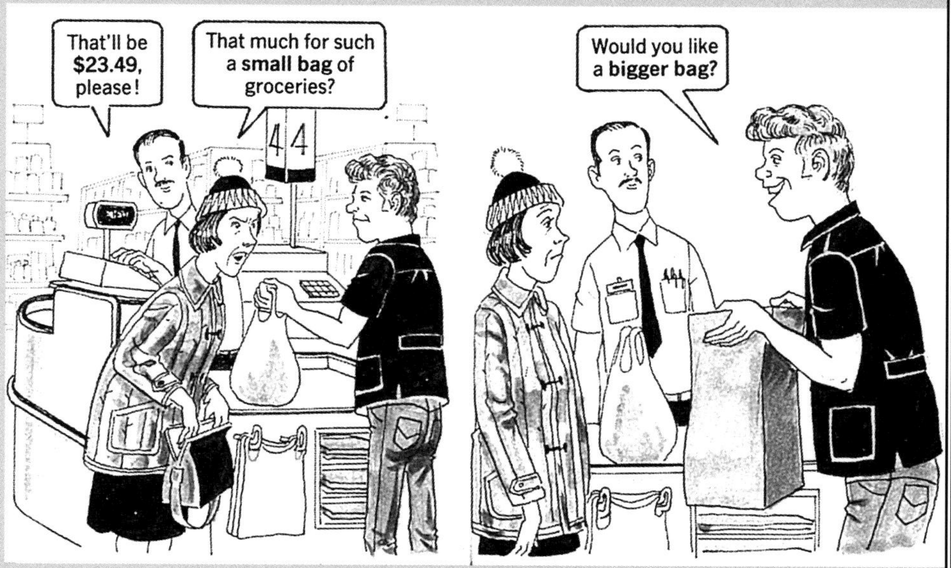
That'll be $23.49, please!
That much for such a small bag of groceries?
Would you like a bigger bag?

PARTIES

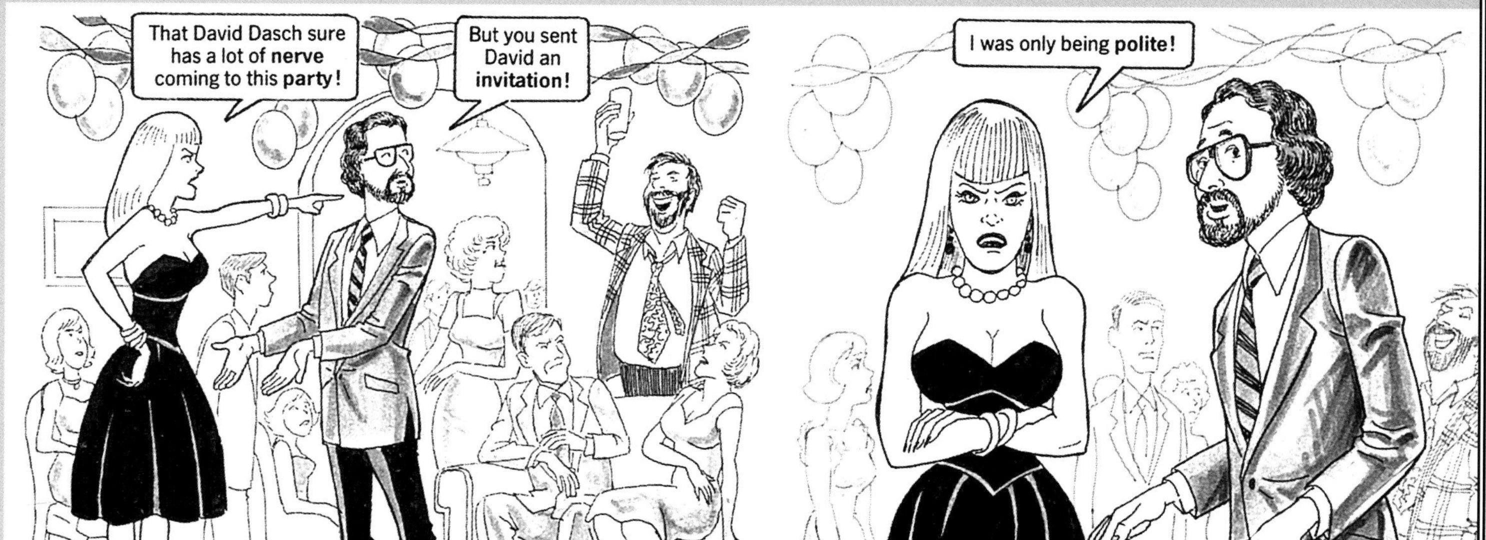
That David Dasch sure has a lot of nerve coming to this party!
But you sent David an invitation!
I was only being polite!

INVESTMENTS

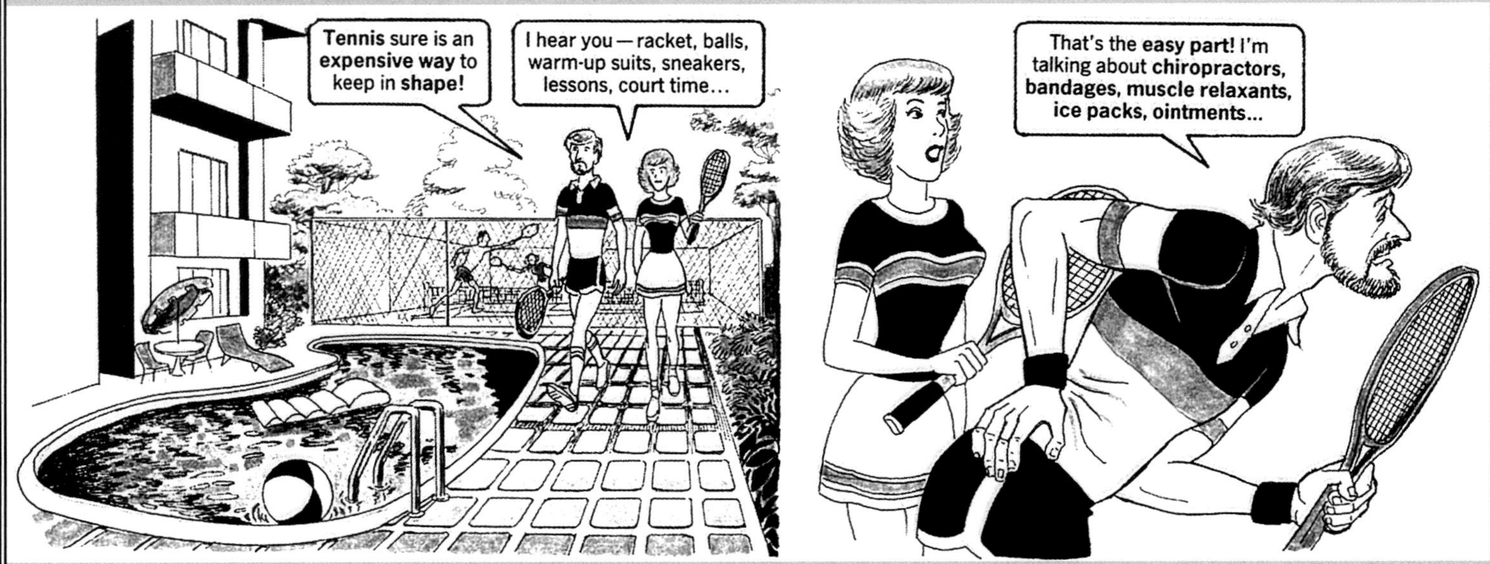
Tennis sure is an expensive way to keep in shape!
I hear you — racket, balls, warm-up suits, sneakers, lessons, court time…
That's the easy part! I'm talking about chiropractors, bandages, muscle relaxants, ice packs, ointments...

CREATIVITY

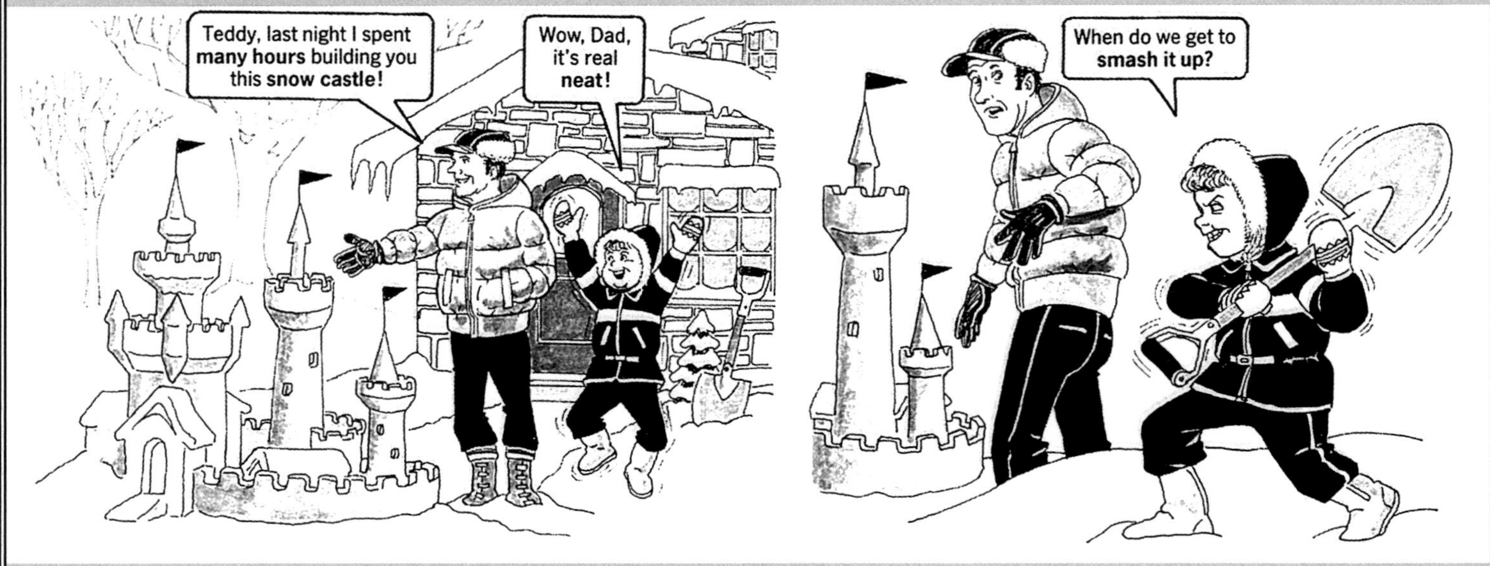
Teddy, last night I spent many hours building you this snow castle!
Wow, Dad, it's real neat!
When do we get to smash it up?

DOCTORS

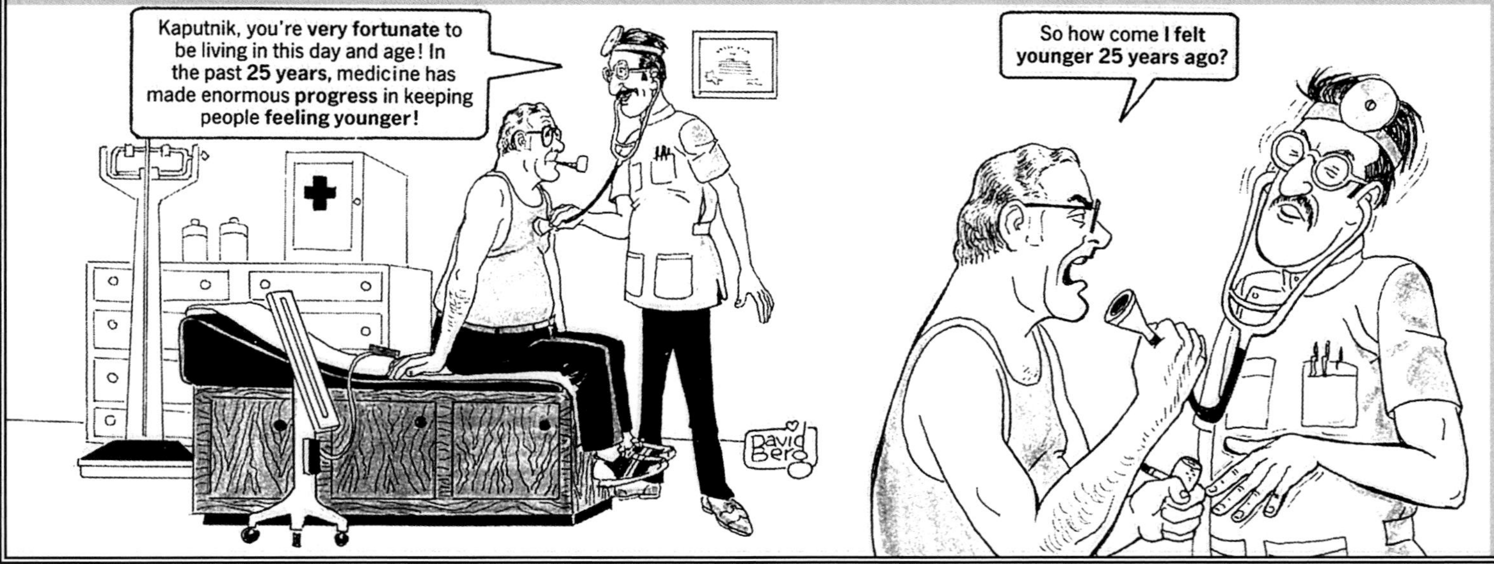
Kaputnik, you're very fortunate to be living in this day and age! In the past 25 years, medicine has made enormous progress in keeping people feeling younger!
David Berg
So how come I felt younger 25 years ago?

The 1990s

• •

COMMUNICATION

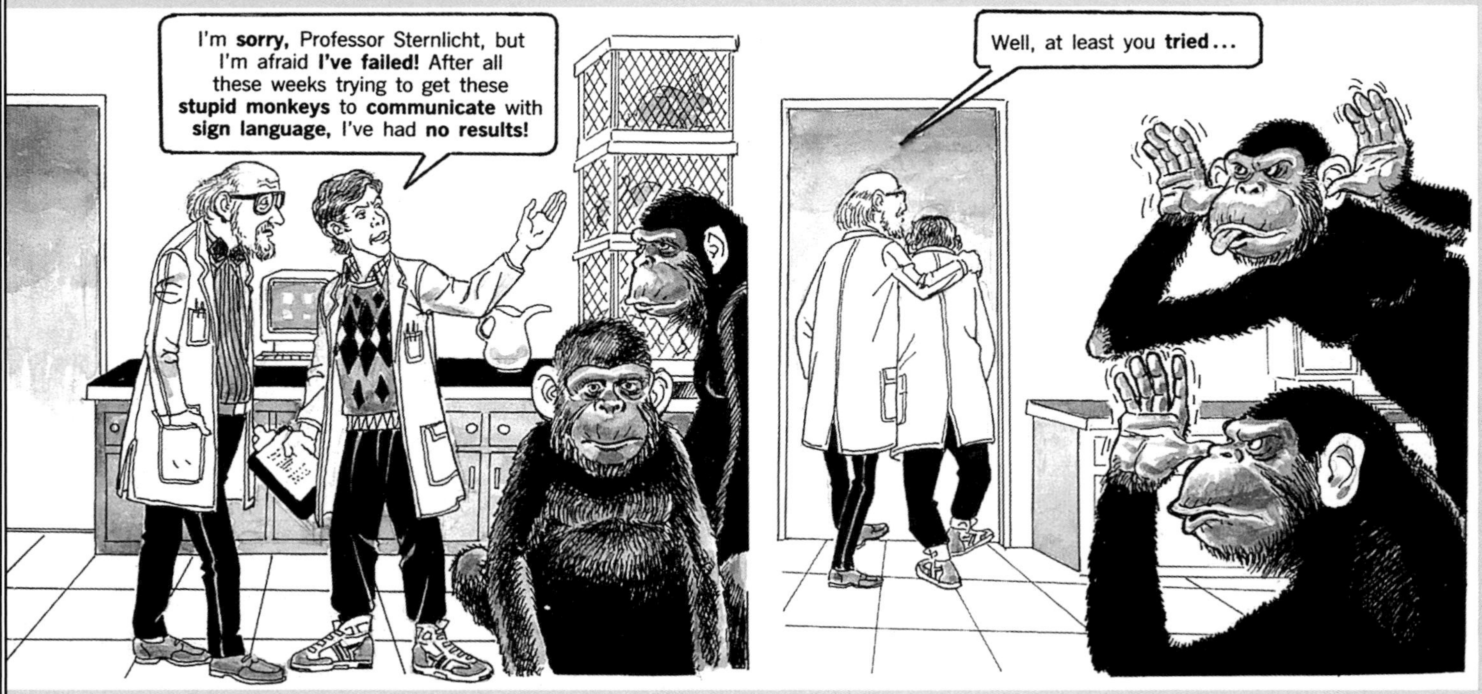
I'm sorry, Professor Sternlicht, but I'm afraid I've failed! After all these weeks trying to get these stupid monkeys to communicate with sign language, I've had no results!
Well, at least you tried...

BERG'S-EYE VIEW DEPT.

THE LIGHTE

MATHEMATICS

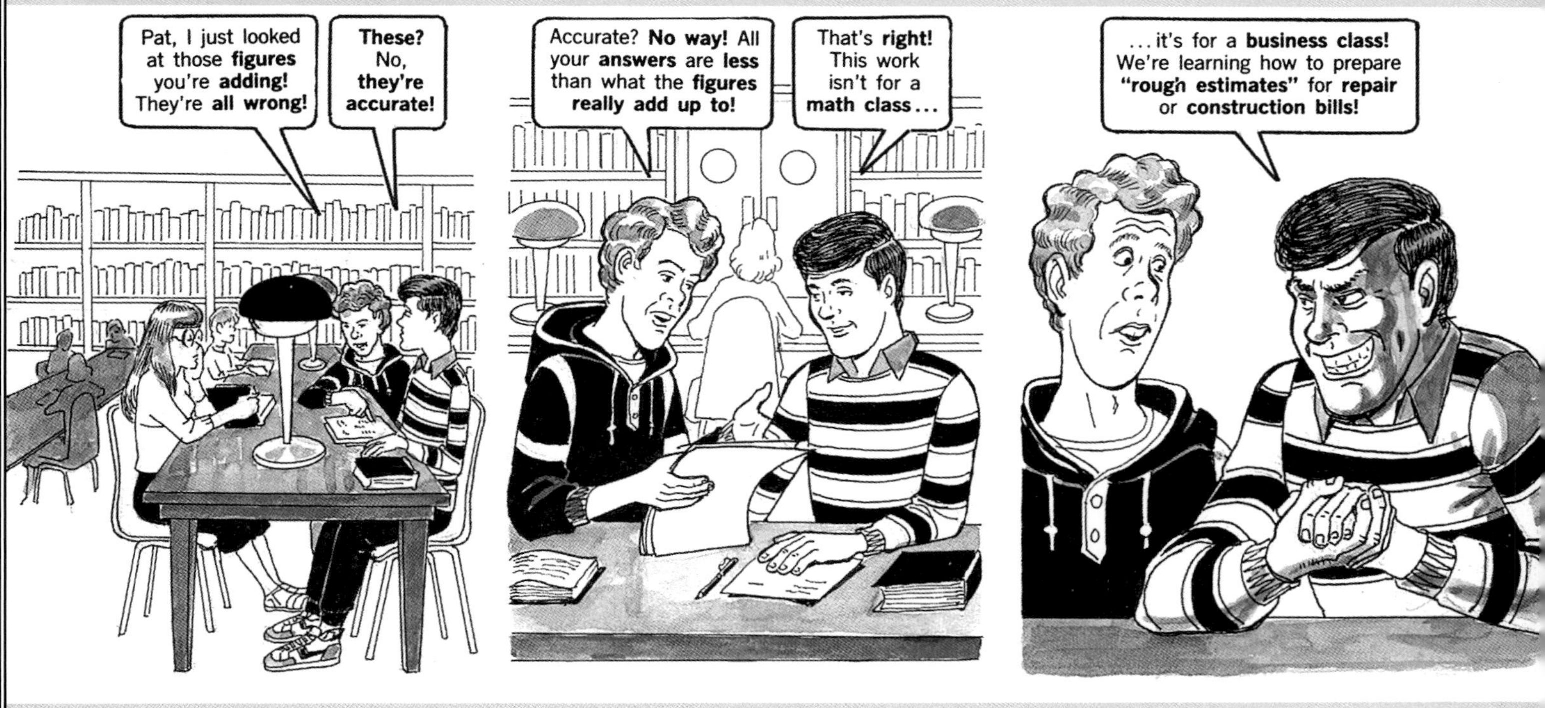
Pat, I just looked at those figures you're adding! They're all wrong!
These? No, they're accurate!
Accurate? No way! All your answers are less than what the figures really add up to!
That's right! This work isn't for a math class...
...it's for a business class! We're learning how to prepare "rough estimates" for repair or construction bills!

BUREAUCRACY

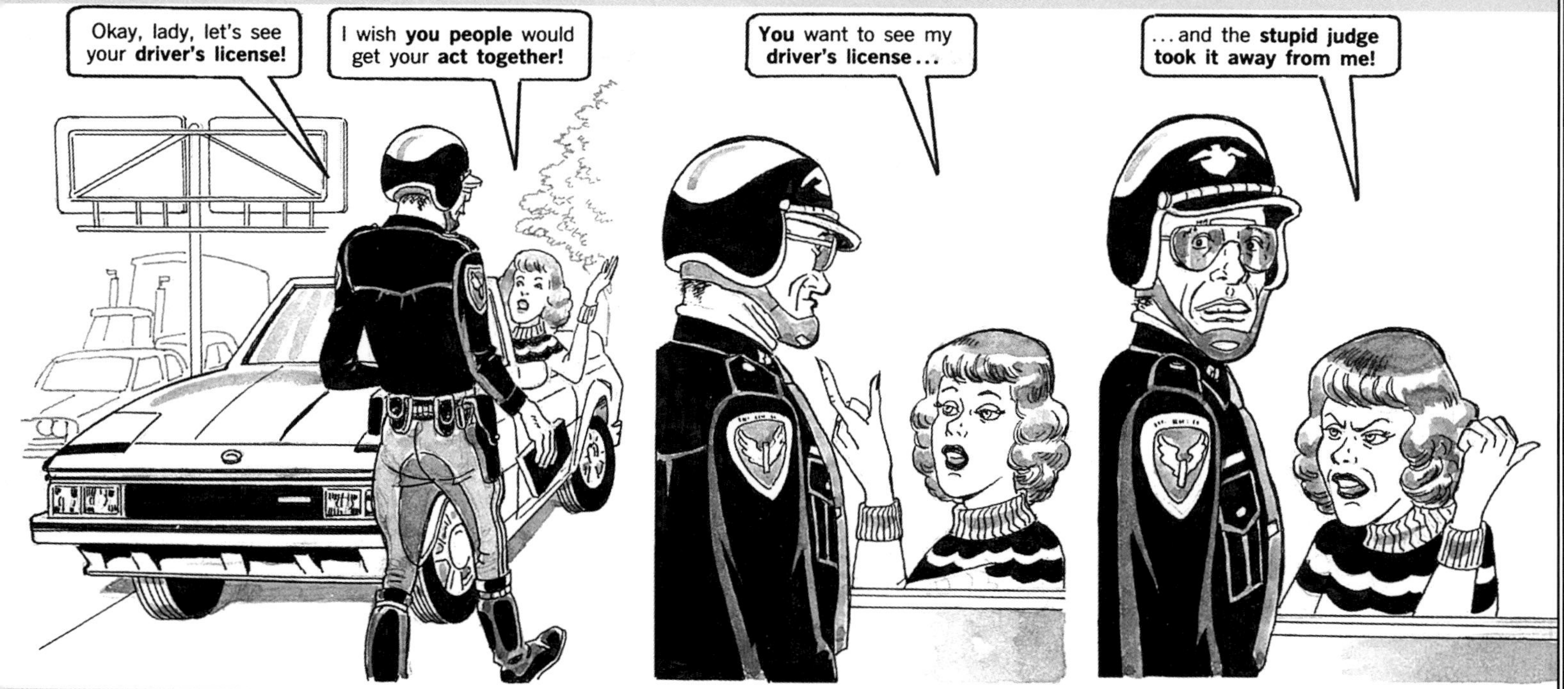
Okay, lady, let's see your **driver's license!**
I wish **you people** would get your **act together!**
You want to see my **driver's license...**
...and the **stupid judge took it away from me!**

R SIDE OF...

ARTIST & WRITER:
DAVE BERG

COUCH POTATOES

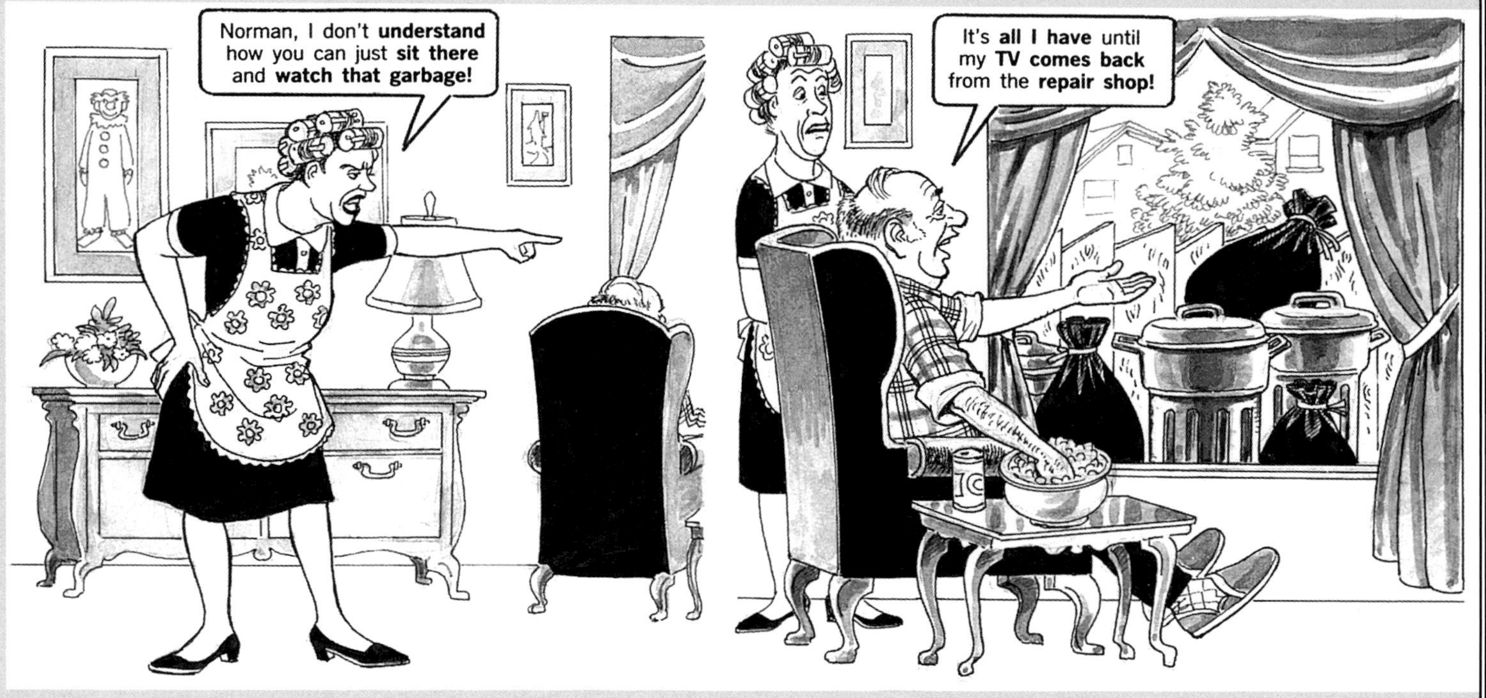
Norman, I don't **understand** how you can just **sit there** and **watch that garbage!**
It's **all I have** until my **TV comes back** from the **repair shop!**

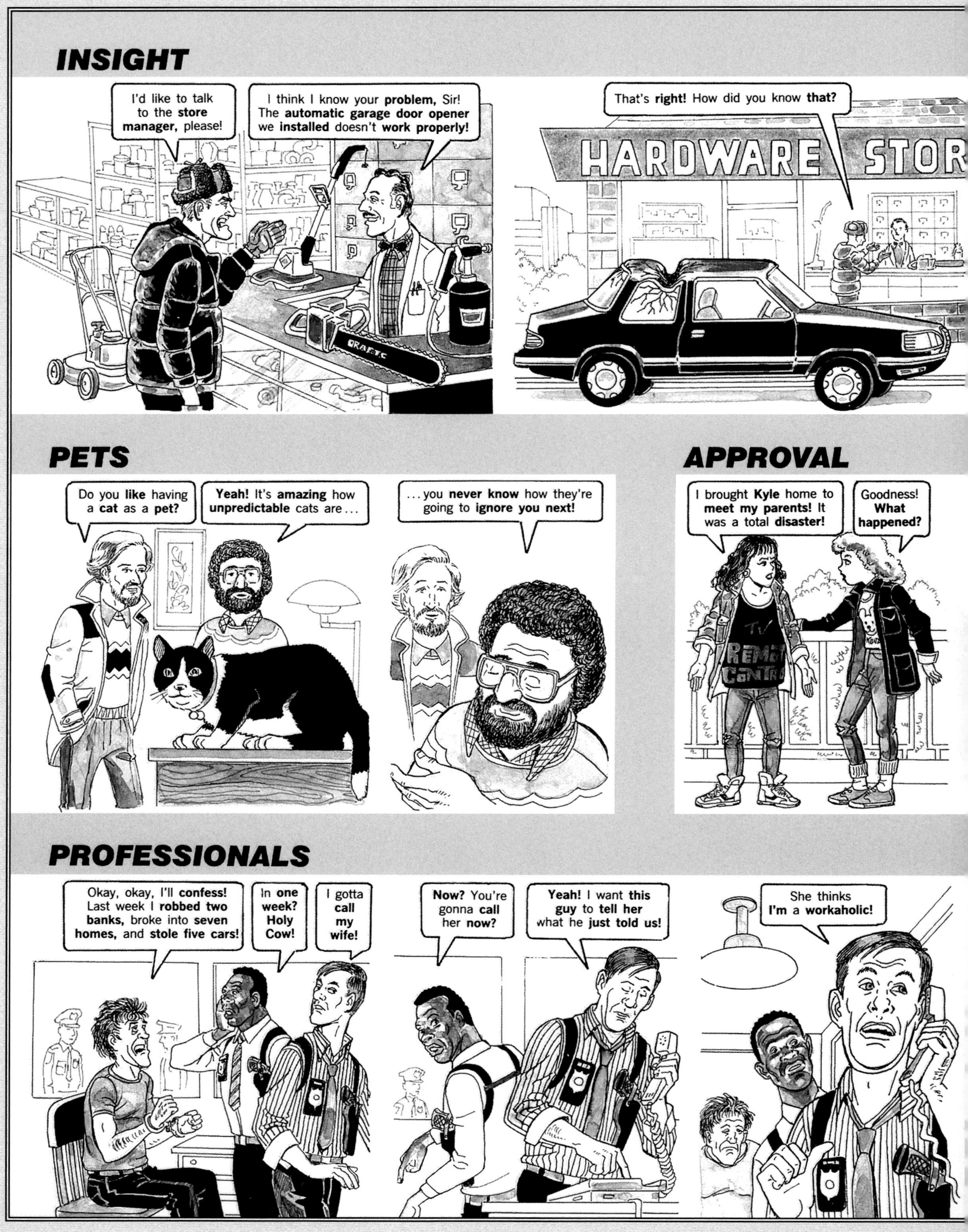
INSIGHT
I'd like to talk to the store manager, please!
I think I know your problem, Sir! The automatic garage door opener we installed doesn't work properly!
That's right! How did you know that?
HARDWARE STOR
PETS
Do you like having a cat as a pet?
Yeah! It's amazing how unpredictable cats are...
...you never know how they're going to ignore you next!
APPROVAL
I brought Kyle home to meet my parents! It was a total disaster!
Goodness! What happened?
PROFESSIONALS
Okay, okay, I'll confess! Last week I robbed two banks, broke into seven homes, and stole five cars!
In one week? Holy Cow!
I gotta call my wife!
Now? You're gonna call her now?
Yeah! I want this guy to tell her what he just told us!
She thinks I'm a workaholic!

POLITICS

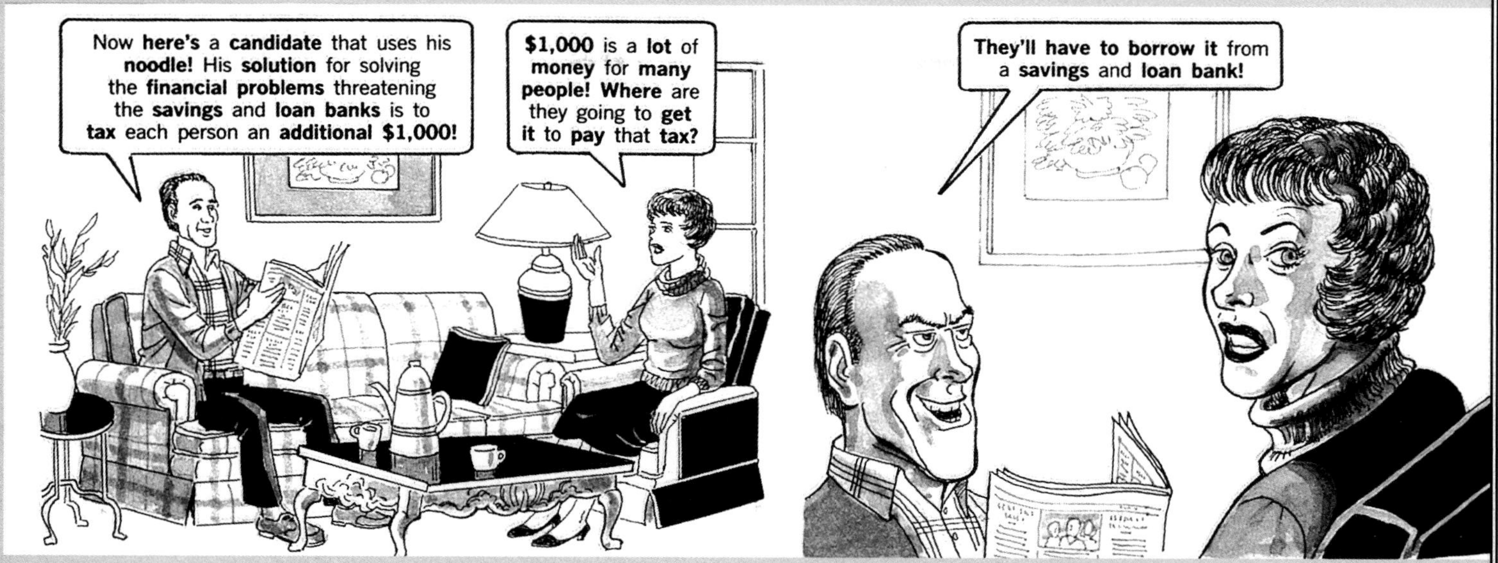
Now here's a candidate that uses his noodle! His solution for solving the financial problems threatening the savings and loan banks is to tax each person an additional $1,000!
$1,000 is a lot of money for many people! Where are they going to get it to pay that tax?
They'll have to borrow it from a savings and loan bank!

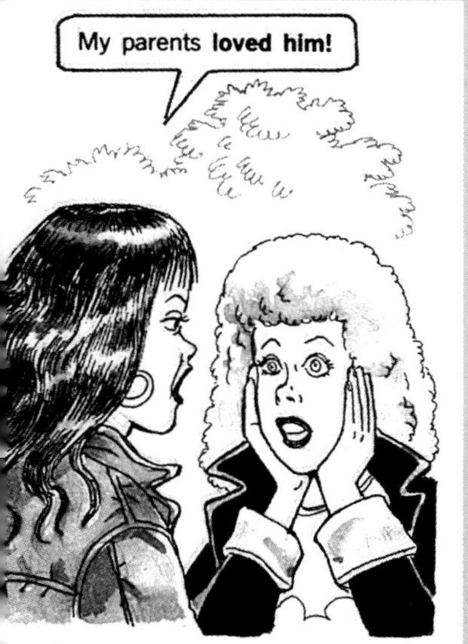
My parents loved him!

COMPUTERS

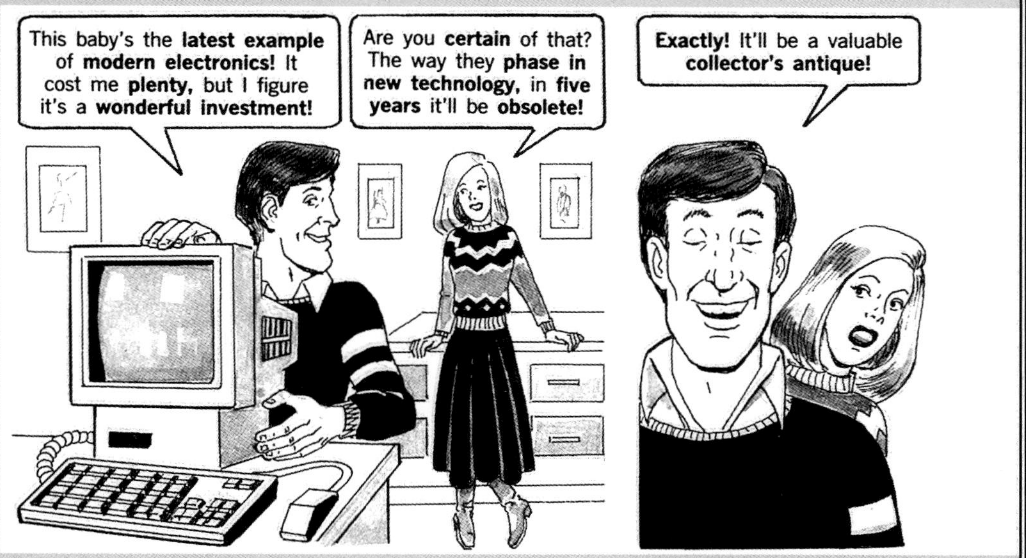
This baby's the latest example of modern electronics! It cost me plenty, but I figure it's a wonderful investment!
Are you certain of that? The way they phase in new technology, in five years it'll be obsolete!
Exactly! It'll be a valuable collector's antique!

COMMITMENT

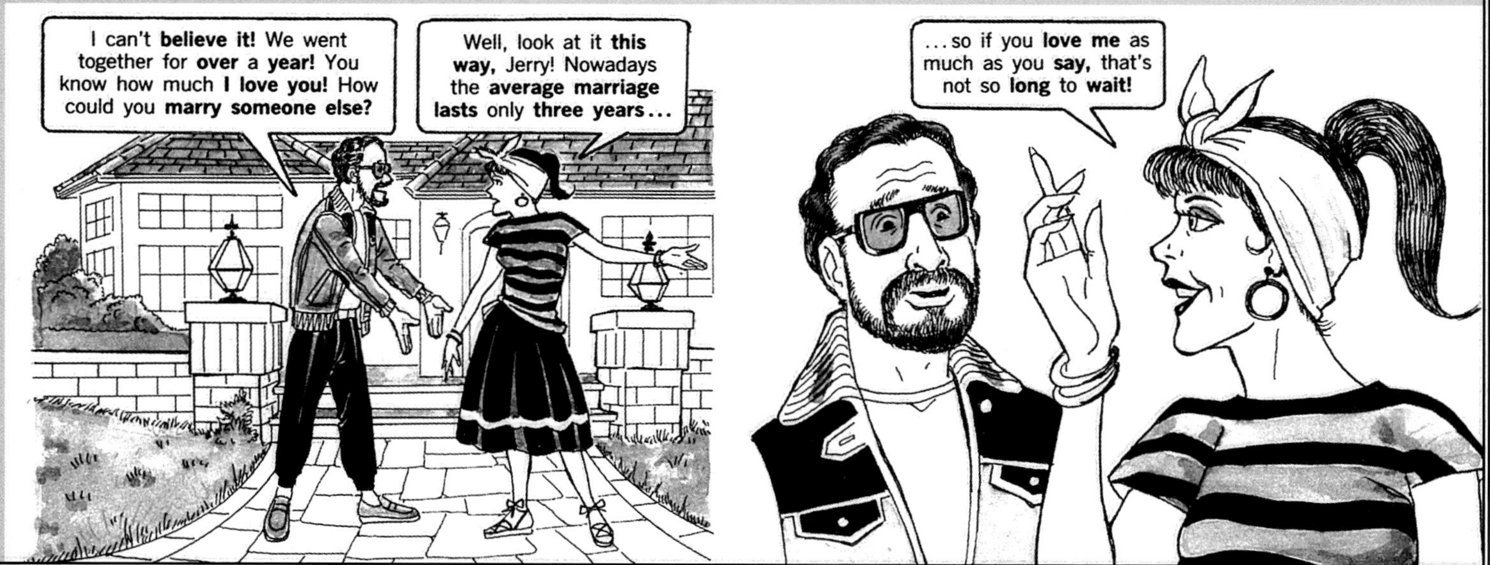
I can't believe it! We went together for over a year! You know how much I love you! How could you marry someone else?
Well, look at it this way, Jerry! Nowadays the average marriage lasts only three years...
...so if you love me as much as you say, that's not so long to wait!

THE OFFICE

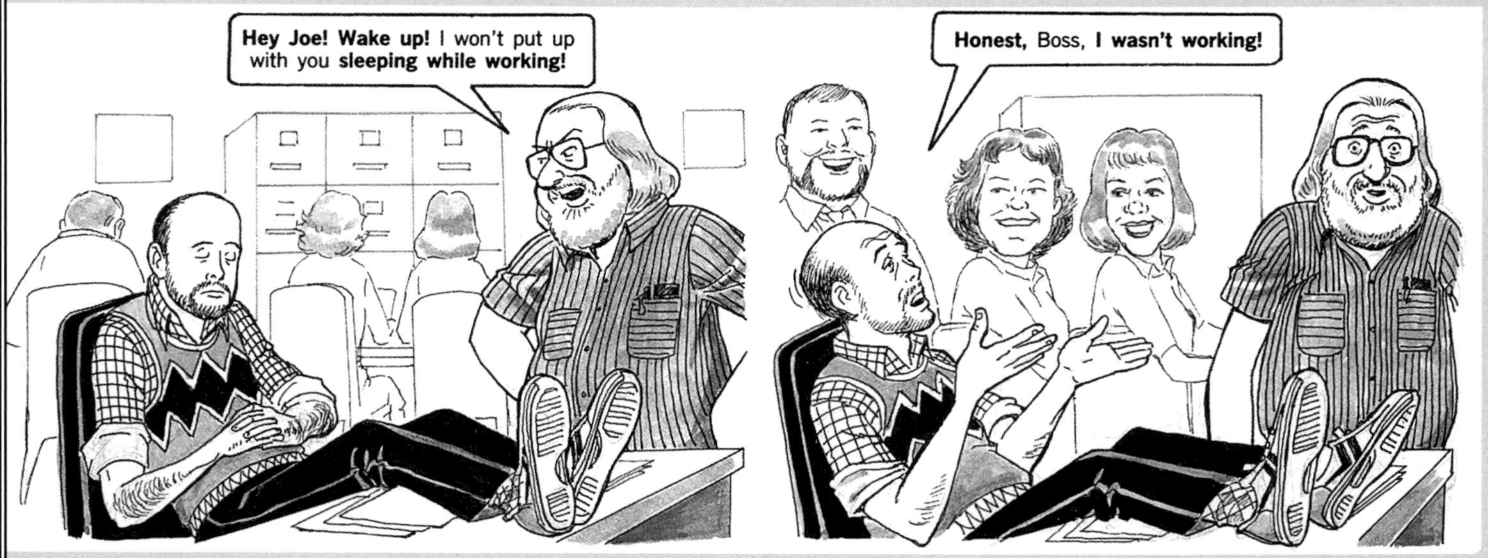
Hey Joe! Wake up! I won't put up with you sleeping while working!
Honest, Boss, I wasn't working!

CRIME AND PUNISHMENT

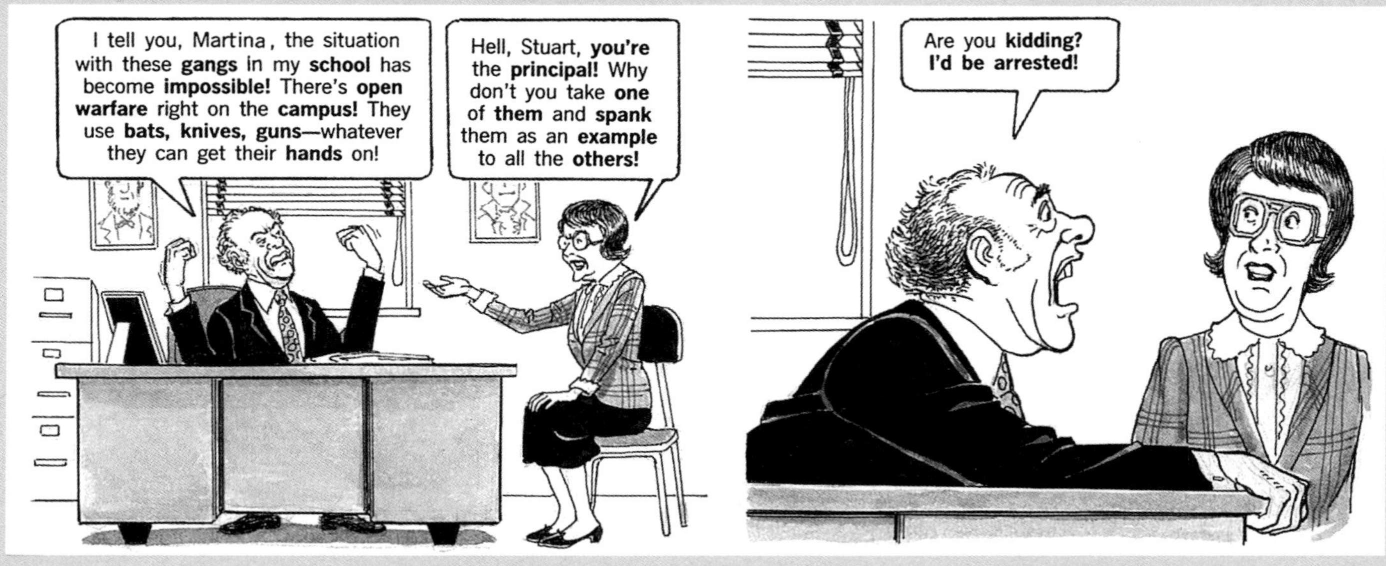
I tell you, Martina, the situation with these gangs in my school has become impossible! There's open warfare right on the campus! They use bats, knives, guns—whatever they can get their hands on!
Hell, Stuart, you're the principal! Why don't you take one of them and spank them as an example to all the others!
Are you kidding? I'd be arrested!

DOCTORS

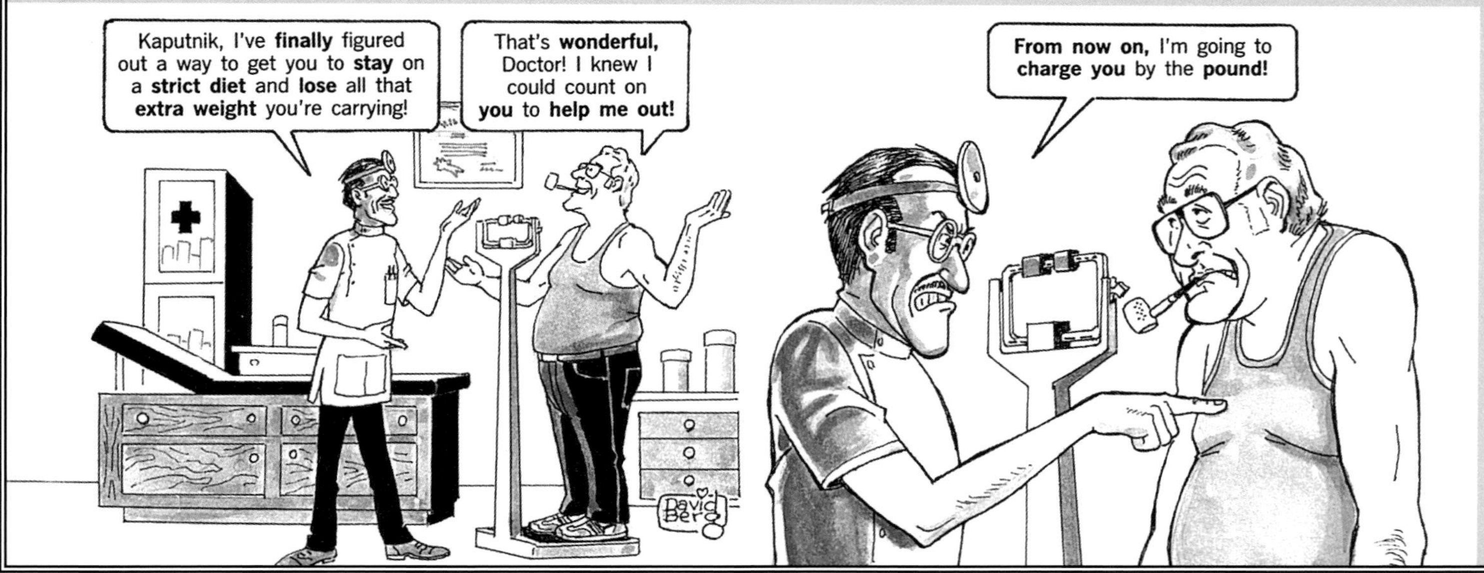
Kaputnik, I've finally figured out a way to get you to stay on a strict diet and lose all that extra weight you're carrying!
That's wonderful, Doctor! I knew I could count on you to help me out!
From now on, I'm going to charge you by the pound!

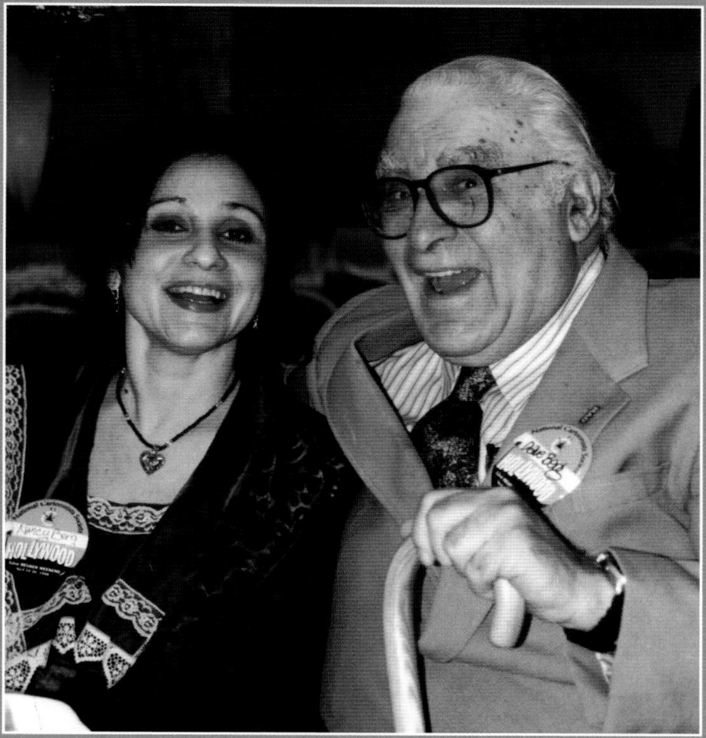

Photo from the Berg family collection

Nancy Berg and her dad, Dave Berg

My Dad, Dave Berg

by Nancy Berg

When my father entered art school at Cooper Union, he knew he needed something, but had no idea what until he walked into class one day and met Vivian Lipman, a first-generation American like him, a kind and lovely young woman with a ready laugh who seemed mysteriously lit from within. *Could this be my complementary fershimmeled one, always with the drawing and the scribbling like me? Is there truly, as they say, a lid for every pot?* Apparently, at least in this case, it was true. But the U.S. was about to enter World War II, and it wasn't long before the two were separated. Sergeant David Berg found himself in the South Pacific, painting voluptuous images of Vivian on the nosecones of P-47 Thunderbolt fighter planes, inscribing her name in cheerful, stylized letters on his weapons carrier. He'd mail her hand-drawn, wordless cartoon postcards featuring his own uniformed countenance besotted with love, seated in the crook of the crescent moon and filling all the dark sky with bright rays of affection. Back in New York and missing her soldier, Vivian Lipman, age 19, became an editor at *Archie Comics*. Both before and after she married Dave Berg, she would go on to work as an artist, writer, or letterer for *Classics Illustrated*, *Tales of Suspense*, *Adventure Comics*, *Mighty Mouse*, *Superboy*, *The Invincible Iron Man*, and more.

These two outlandish, nocturnal cartoonists are my parents. My dad started at MAD not long after I was born, so I literally grew up as a cartoon character, publicly growing a little older and more rebellious each year on the pages of MAD magazine. Is it any surprise that I speak in visible dialogue balloons and walk through the world fervently wishing inanimate objects would burst into song? (It's not exactly a shocker that I named my poetry book *Oracles for Night-Blooming Eccentrics*.)

People seem to have the impression that my dad sort of blinked into existence at the MAD office one day, a tabula rasa with no fingerprints or previous body of work. It's true that he genuinely loved being a MAD man and was more than happy to be solely identified that way for 47 years of his life. But in truth, he also created a huge portfolio throughout the Golden Age of comics, and well into the Silver Age, drawing and writing, credited or uncredited, for an enormous range of both classic and obscure comic books. He was a

Titles Featuring the Work of Dave Berg

Sci-fi, Fantasy, and Horror Comic Books

Amazing Fantasy
Astonishing Tales
Dead of Night
Ibis the Invincible
Journey into Mystery
Journey into Unknown Worlds
Mystery
Mystery Tales
Strange Tales
Uncanny Tales

Comic Books for Younger Kids

Alice (New Adventures in Wonderland)
Dolly
Fairy Tales
Krazy Comics (With Bunny the Junior G-Man)
Nancy and Sluggo
Nursery Rhymes Comics
Strange Tales of Super Duck

Teenage Comic Books

Archie Comics
Archie's Girls: Betty and Veronica
Archie's Pal: Jughead
Cindy
Frankie
Georgie
Hedy DeVine
Jeannie (Queen of the Teens)
Joe College
Junior Hopp
Kit Karter
Lana
Laugh
Leroy
Margy
Meet Merton
Millie the Model
Mitzi's Boyfriend
Oscar
Patsy Walker
Pep Comics
Ponytail
Rusty
Suzie
Teen
Teen Timers
Tessie the Typist
Wilbur
Willie

Girlie/Cheesecake Cartoons

Breezy
Gee-Whiz
Snappy

consummate freelance genre surfer, effortlessly shape-shifting among the categories. Looking through the remaining file copies of his work is like entering a fascinating parallel universe in which a bewildering number of entities go by strangely similar names. Check out the sidebar list of some of the titles he contributed to—they only represent the ones I could find—he definitely contributed to other titles as well. The man had a formidable work ethic.

In a good mood, or even a neutral one, my father was almost preternaturally friendly. Some guy would call me long distance, and my dad would answer and greet him as if he were a disappeared compatriot, long-presumed dead. He'd converse enthusiastically for a couple of hours or so, then remember to say, "By the way, Nancy isn't here. Who is this?"

We lived in New Rochelle, in a relatively funky apartment which bore little resemblance to the split-level confections depicted in "The Lighter Side of..." (although those were plentiful a block or two away). I guess, as a child of immigrants, my father instinctively carried a vivid understanding of the primal American dreamscape. (All those suburban homeowner cartoons may well have been at least partially aspirational.) He was tremendously popular in town, where he shared celebrity status with the fictional address of *The Dick Van Dyke Show*. He seemed to know all kinds of people, and called a vast array of male acquaintances "Brother."

As a teenager, of course, I doubted the sincerity of all his warmth. My father was at least as complicated as the rest of us, and you only have to look at all those capitalized, bold-faced shouting matches in his work to sense there might have been some free-floating anger involved. But I've come to see that the ever-gregarious love was more authentic than the other stuff. On the last page of his book, *MAD's Dave Berg Look at Our Sick World*, you'll find, in great big letters: "In this sick world we are all rotten to the core . . . but the core can be beautiful." You could say that sort of summed up his philosophy.

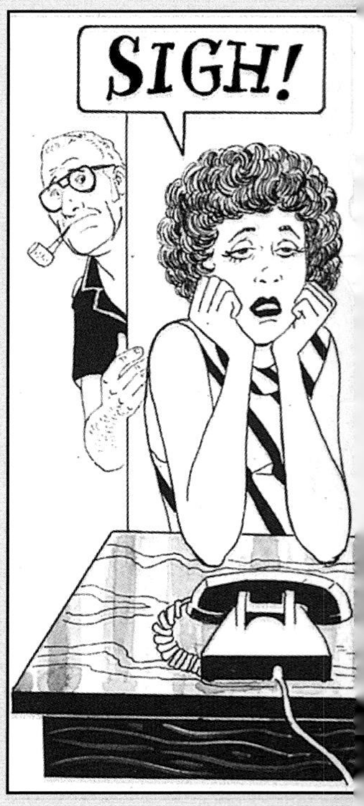
SIGH!

At 21, on my way to an extended meditation course in Switzerland, I took a long, vertiginous train ride to a small, relatively isolated town, very high up in the Alps. I was teaching in London at the time, living far away from home for close to a year. As I got off that train in the Swiss Alps, I glanced up at the tiny station's outdoor vending area, and the very first thing I saw was a brightly-colored copy of *MAD's Dave Berg Takes a Loving Look*.

I can't remember whether the book was in German or French or Italian or English—I only remember being completely blown away. There, on the cover, was my dad in heart-shaped glasses, blowing heart-shaped smoke rings out of that ubiquitous pipe. On the last page was his trademark tree with heart and arrow. Inside was carved (in a slight departure from the early books), "D.B. LOVES ______ (FILL IN YOUR NAME)." And I think, when it came to every abstract reader, he absolutely meant that, regardless of any human complexities and personal grudges that may have plagued him. That message somehow made it across all those time zones to wave at me in Switzerland, and that book's painted original cover is one I'll never sell.

Now, disembodied or otherwise, Roger Kaputnik is anything but Kaput. I occasionally receive emails from his fans in Norway, Lebanon, Finland, Pakistan, India—you name it. They tell me how deeply my father's work touched their lives, somehow transcending all cultural barriers. I hear all kinds of incredible stories like that when I now and then sell his original art at comic book conventions. Dave Berg may have sometimes felt frustrated about rarely being given the leeway to write cartoons about edgier subjects, but clearly his influence was real.

We held my father's ash-scattering at sea, and at one point, the skipper pulled me aside to express how honored he felt to pilot the ship for Dave Berg's send-off. He explained that his own father had been a Holocaust survivor who carried a deep, lifelong sorrow. The Skipper only heard that man laugh twice in his life—once, oddly enough, from the other side of the bathroom door. When the door opened and the boy had a chance to investigate what on earth could have been the source of this singularly rare laughter, he saw that his dad had been reading the "Berg's Eye View Department" in MAD.

—Nancy Berg

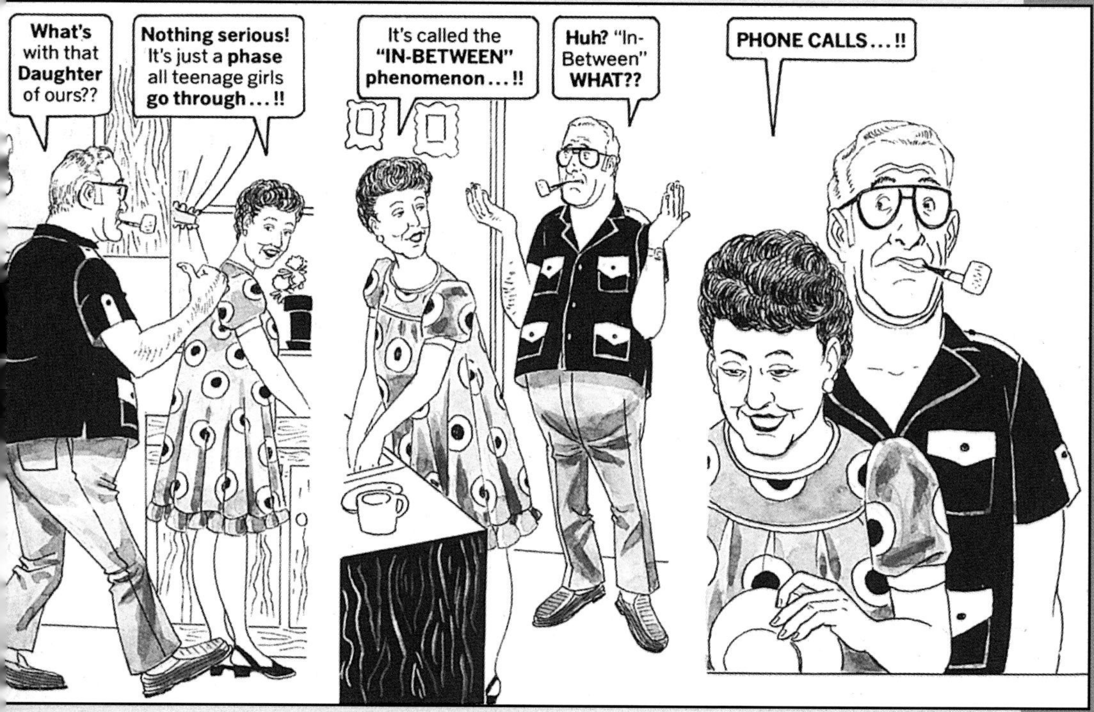

What's with that Daughter of ours??
Nothing serious! It's just a phase all teenage girls go through...!!
It's called the "IN-BETWEEN" phenomenon...!!
Huh? "In-Between" WHAT??
PHONE CALLS...!!

Dave and his wife, Vivian, discuss daughter Nancy's behavior in "The Lighter Side of...Teenage Phases," MAD #248, July 1984

Titles Featuring the Work of Dave Berg

Satirical Comic Books
MAD
Wild
Whack!
3-D Comics
Man! Dig This Crazy Little Mixed-Up Mag!

Detective Comic Books
Crime Detective
Detective
Don Fortune
Real Clue
The Spirit

Superhero Comic Books
Adventure Comics
Bulletman
Captain Marvel
National Comics
Uncle Sam Quarterly
Wow Comics

War Comic Books
Battle
Battle Action
Battlefield
Battlefront
Combat Kelly
Frontline Comics
Man Comics
Marines in Action
Men's Adventures
Military Comics
Nave Action
Navy Combat
Spy Smasher
War
War Action
War Combat
Young Men on the Battlefield!

Comic Books with a TV Connection
Ensign O'Toole
McHale's Navy
My Friend Irma
The Bullwinkle Mother Moose

Western Comic Books
Arizona Kid
Kid Cowboy
Ringo Kid
The Outlaw Kid
True Western
Western Fighters
Wild Western
Wyatt Earp

SPORTS

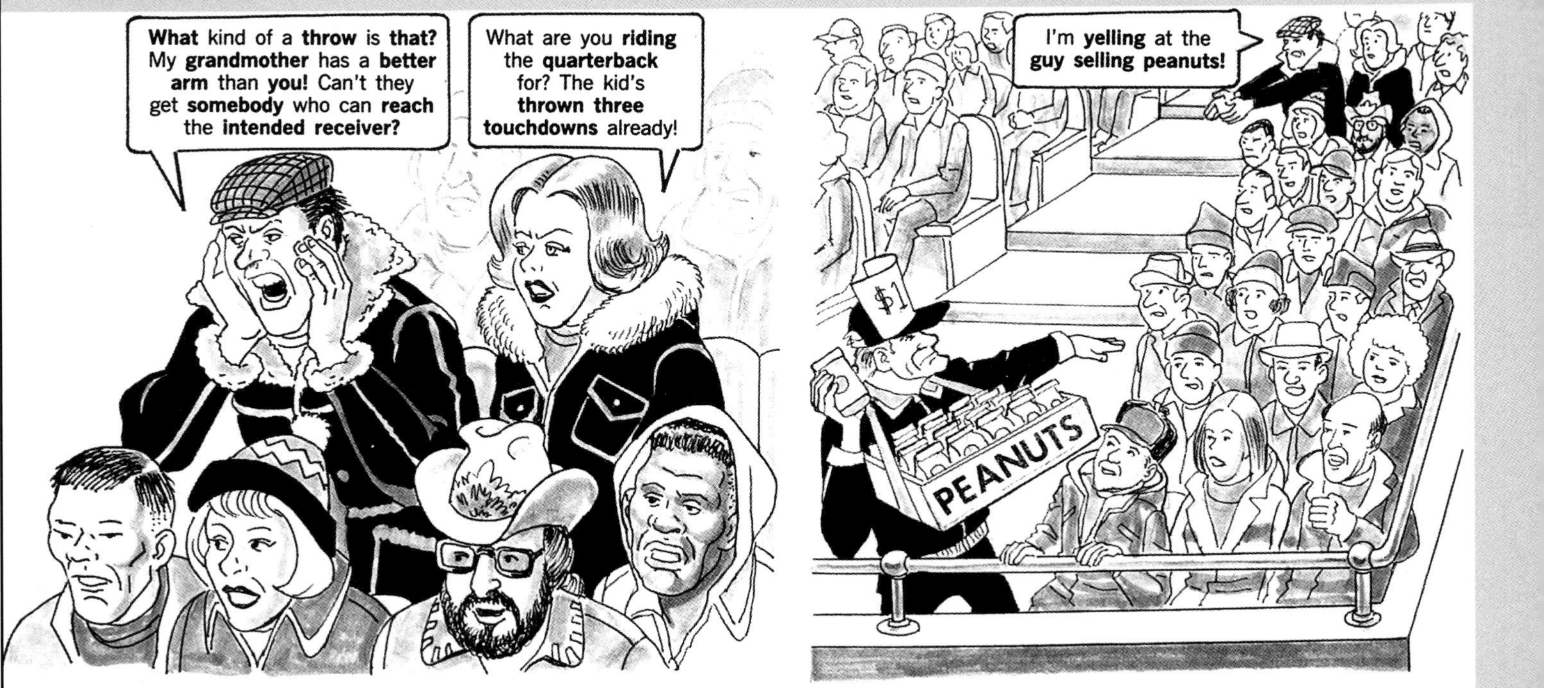
What kind of a throw is that? My grandmother has a better arm than you! Can't they get somebody who can reach the intended receiver?
What are you riding the quarterback for? The kid's thrown three touchdowns already!
I'm yelling at the guy selling peanuts!
$1
PEANUTS

BERG'S-EYE VIEW DEPT.

THE LIGHTE

CORPORATE IMAGE

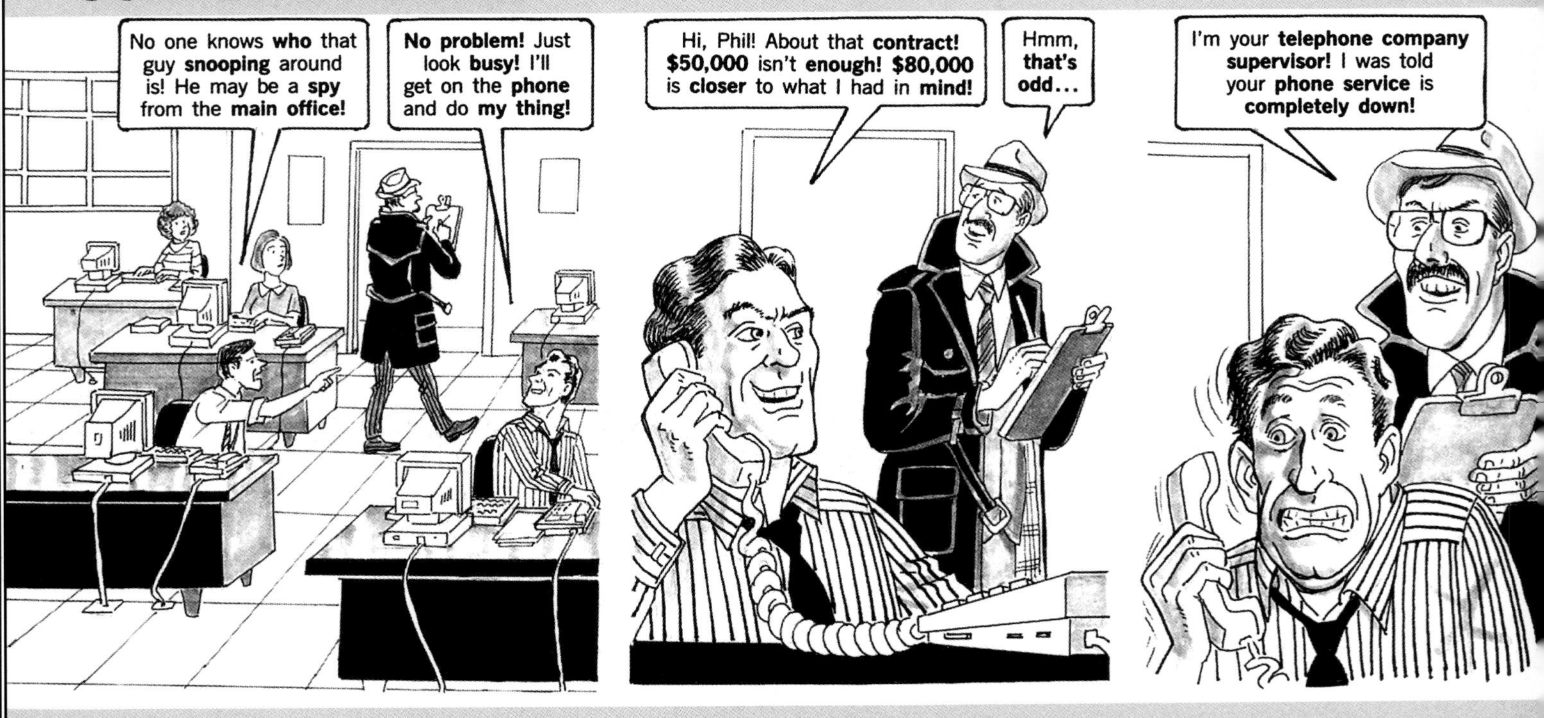
No one knows who that guy snooping around is! He may be a spy from the main office!
No problem! Just look busy! I'll get on the phone and do my thing!
Hi, Phil! About that contract! $50,000 isn't enough! $80,000 is closer to what I had in mind!
Hmm, that's odd...
I'm your telephone company supervisor! I was told your phone service is completely down!

NEGOTIATION

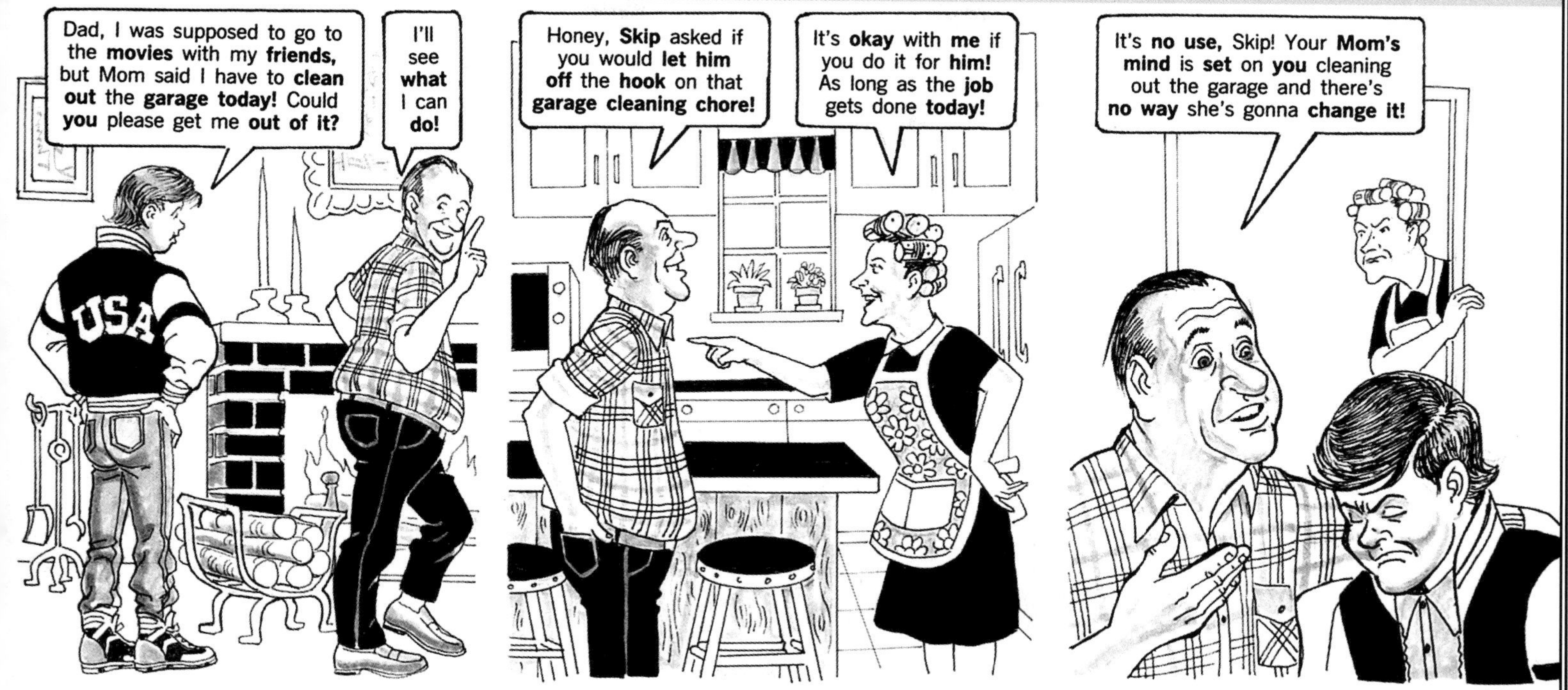
Dad, I was supposed to go to the movies with my friends, but Mom said I have to clean out the garage today! Could you please get me out of it?
I'll see what I can do!
USA
Honey, Skip asked if you would let him off the hook on that garage cleaning chore!
It's okay with me if you do it for him! As long as the job gets done today!
It's no use, Skip! Your Mom's mind is set on you cleaning out the garage and there's no way she's gonna change it!

R SIDE OF...

ARTIST & WRITER:
DAVE BERG

PRIDE

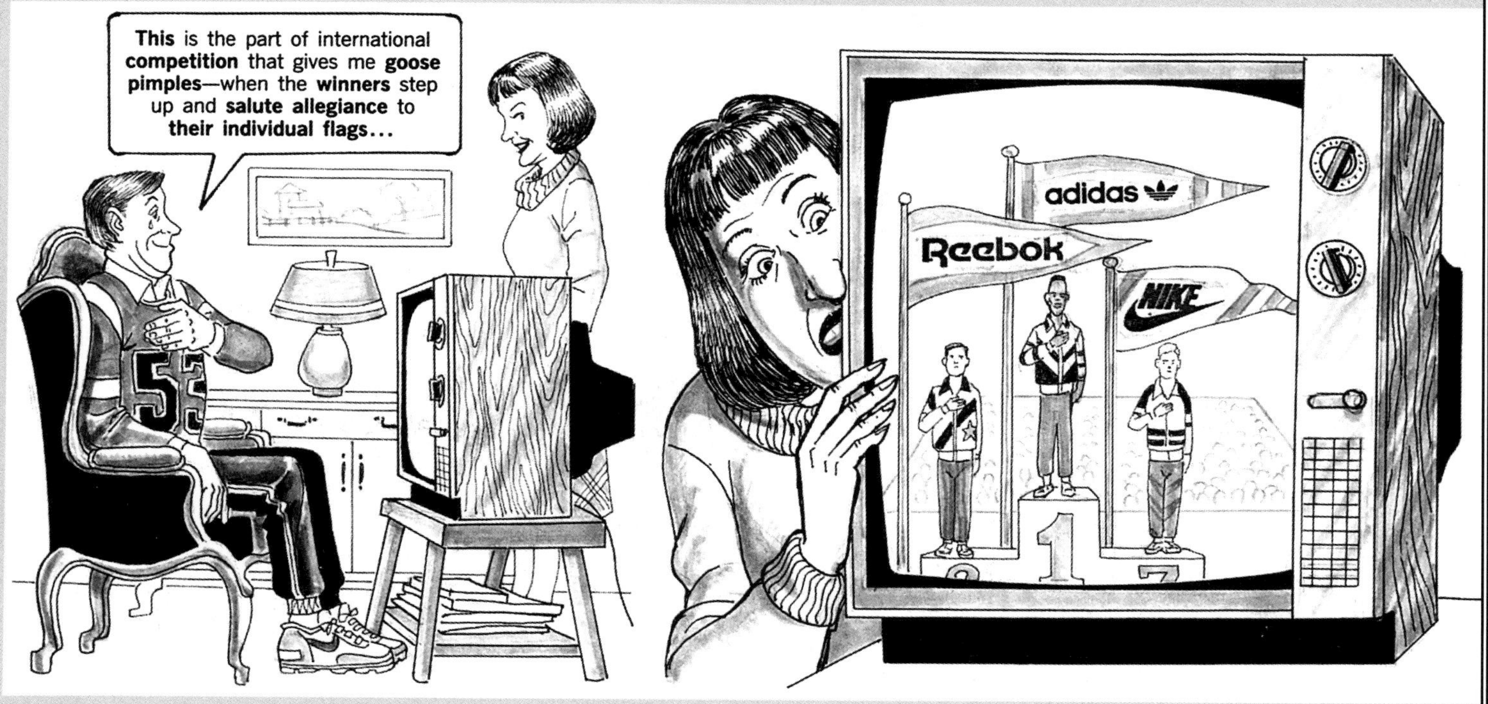
This is the part of international competition that gives me goose pimples—when the winners step up and salute allegiance to their individual flags...
55
adidas
Reebok
NIKE
1

RESEARCH

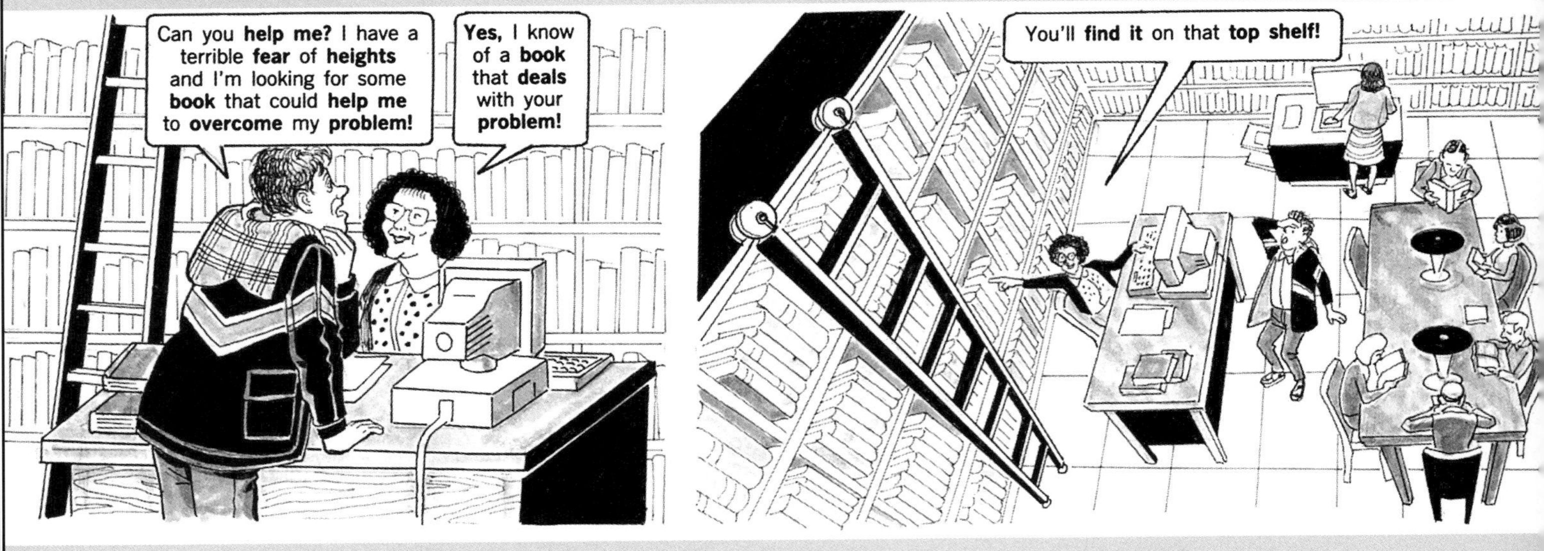
Can you **help me?** I have a terrible **fear** of **heights** and I'm looking for some **book** that could **help me** to **overcome** my **problem!**
Yes, I know of a **book** that **deals** with your **problem!**
You'll **find it** on that **top shelf!**

COUNSELING

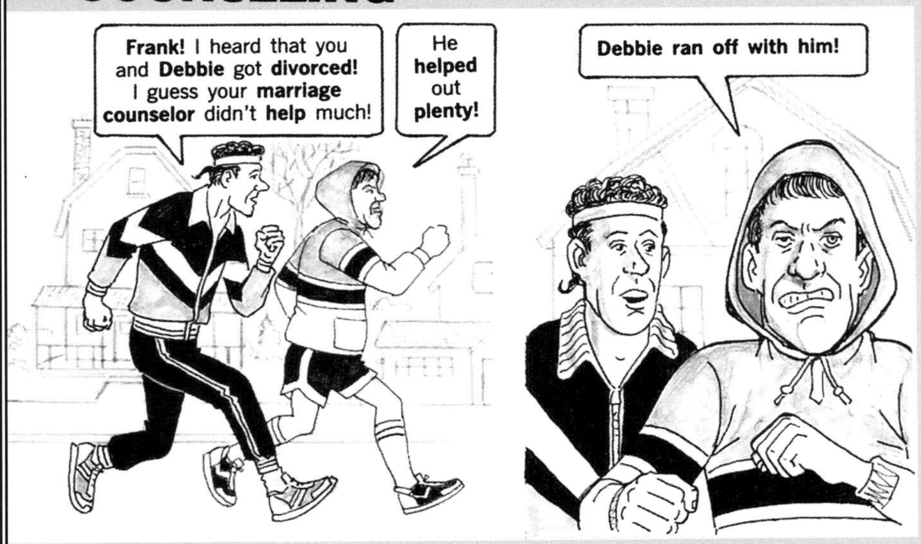
Frank! I heard that you and **Debbie** got **divorced!** I guess your **marriage counselor** didn't **help** much!
He **helped** out **plenty!**
Debbie ran off with him!

DANCING

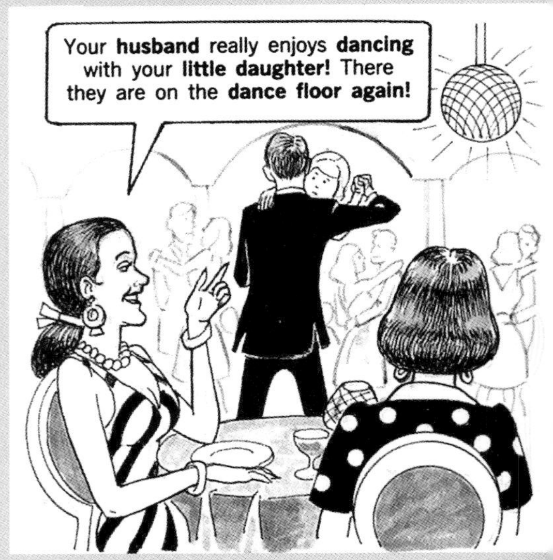
Your **husband** really enjoys **dancing** with your **little daughter!** There they are on the **dance floor again!**

MUSIC

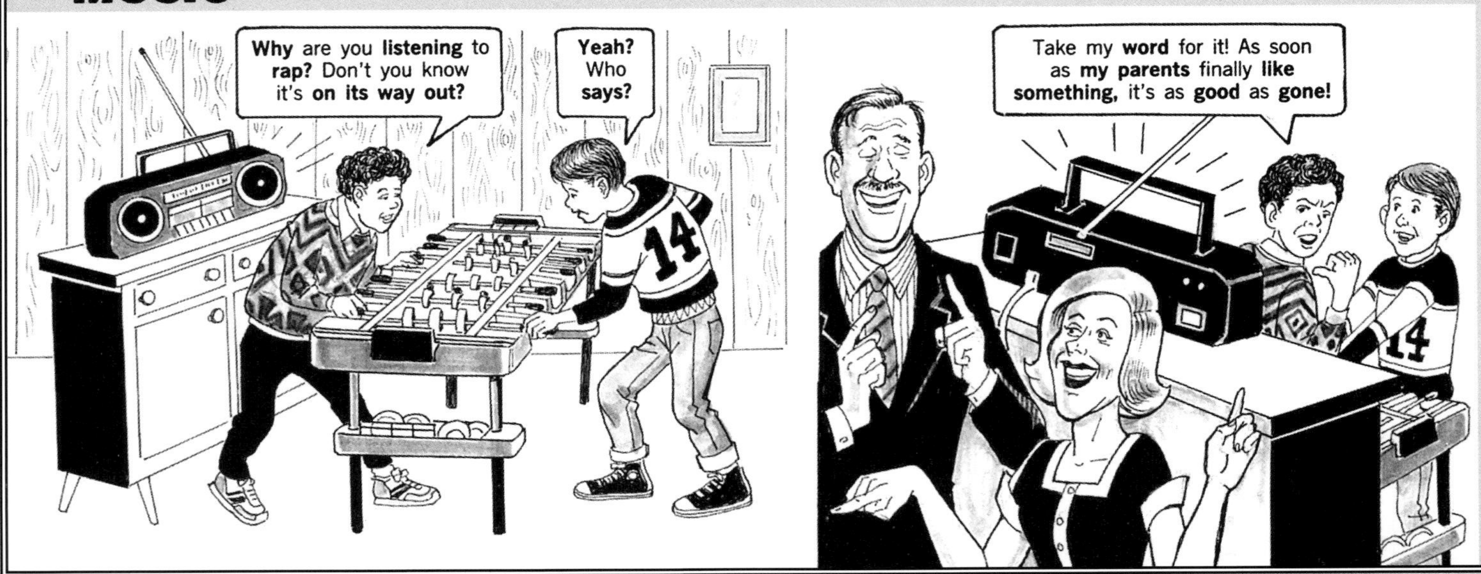
Why are you **listening** to **rap?** Don't you know it's **on its way out?**
Yeah? Who **says?**
Take my **word** for it! As soon as **my parents** finally **like something,** it's as **good** as **gone!**

GUNS

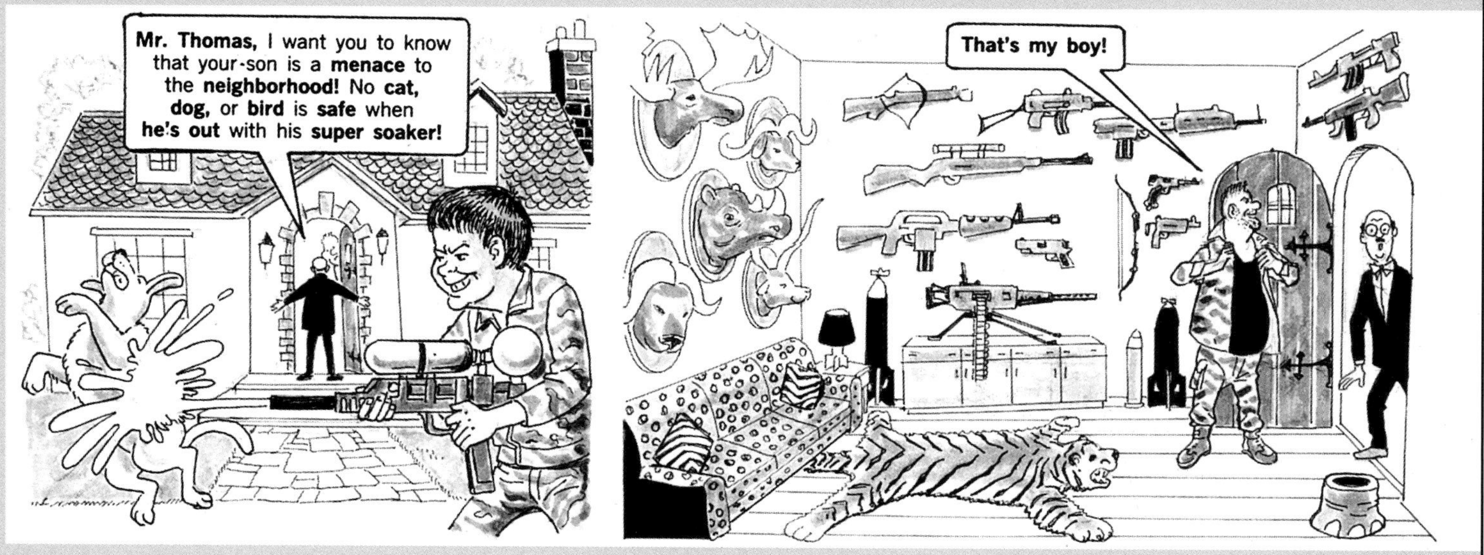
Mr. Thomas, I want you to know that your-son is a menace to the neighborhood! No cat, dog, or bird is safe when he's out with his super soaker!
That's my boy!

FINANCES

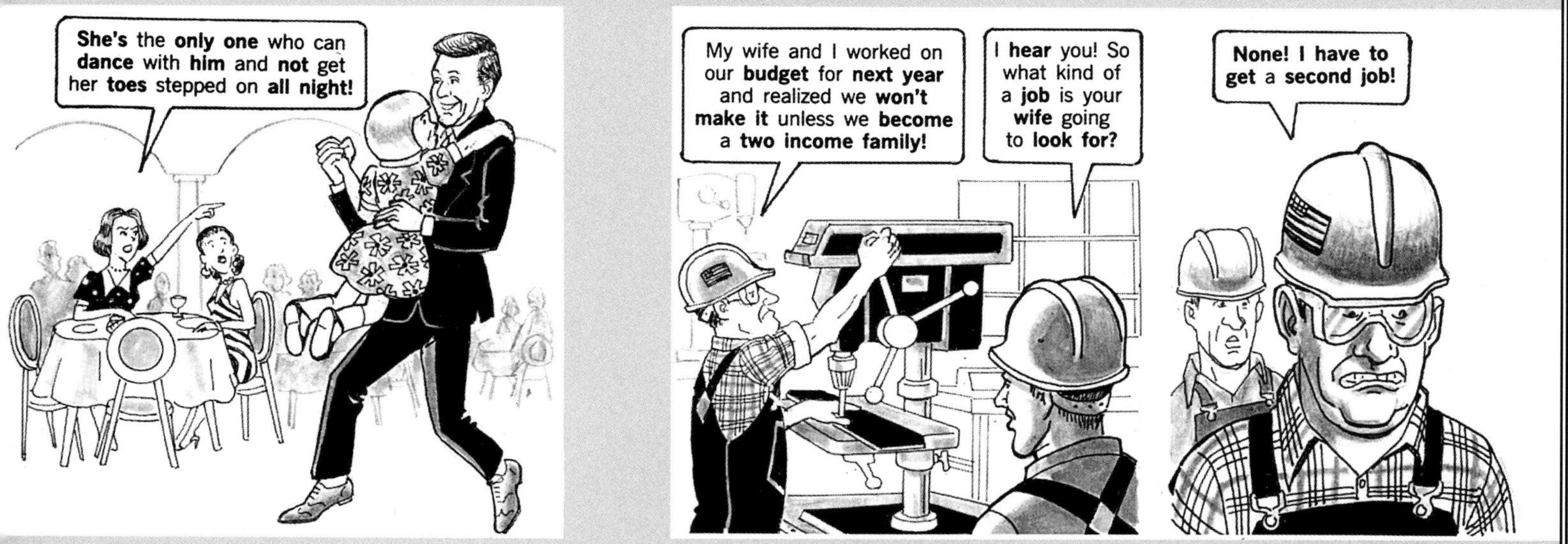
She's the only one who can dance with him and not get her toes stepped on all night!
My wife and I worked on our budget for next year and realized we won't make it unless we become a two income family!
I hear you! So what kind of a job is your wife going to look for?
None! I have to get a second job!

PANIC

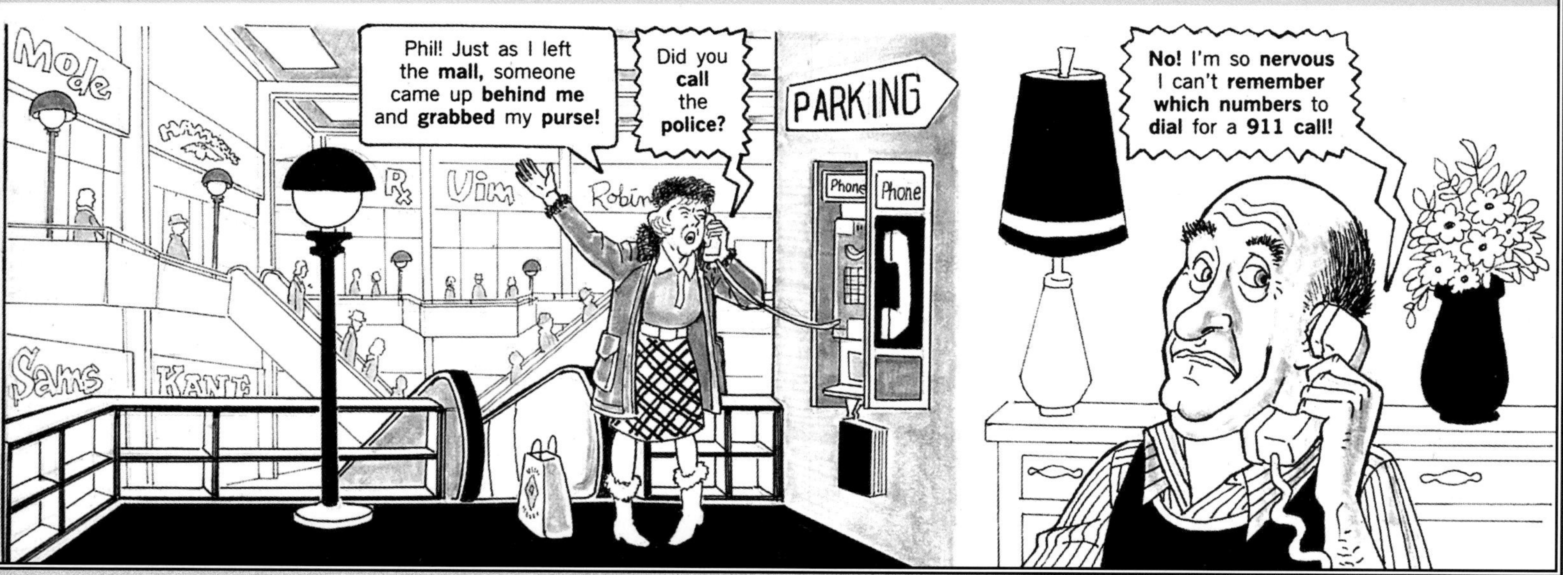
Mode
Sams
Vim
Phil! Just as I left the mall, someone came up behind me and grabbed my purse!
Did you call the police?
PARKING
Phone
Phone
No! I'm so nervous I can't remember which numbers to dial for a 911 call!

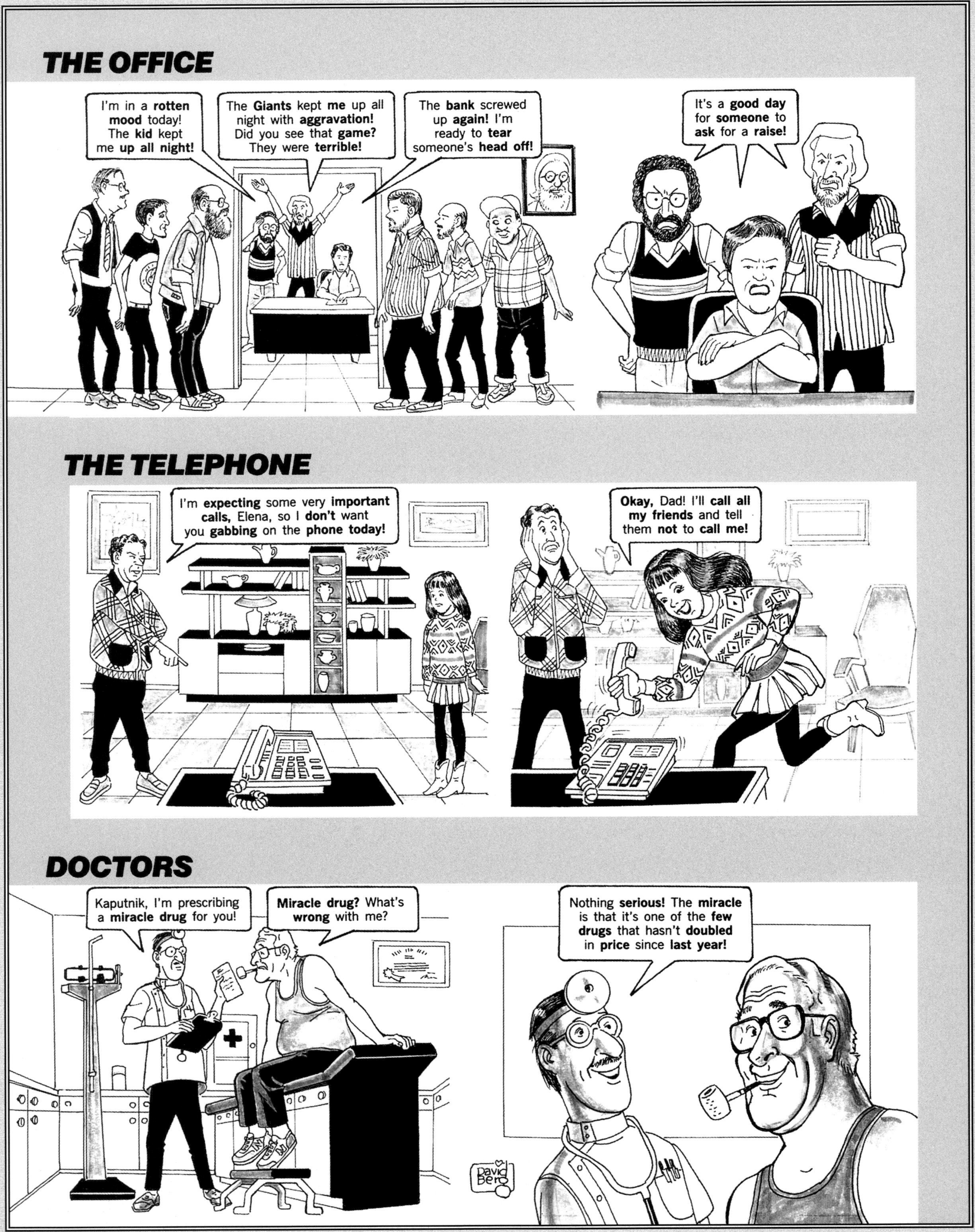
THE OFFICE
I'm in a rotten mood today! The kid kept me up all night!
The Giants kept me up all night with aggravation! Did you see that game? They were terrible!
The bank screwed up again! I'm ready to tear someone's head off!
It's a good day for someone to ask for a raise!
THE TELEPHONE
I'm expecting some very important calls, Elena, so I don't want you gabbing on the phone today!
Okay, Dad! I'll call all my friends and tell them not to call me!
DOCTORS
Kaputnik, I'm prescribing a miracle drug for you!
Miracle drug? What's wrong with me?
Nothing serious! The miracle is that it's one of the few drugs that hasn't doubled in price since last year!
David Berg

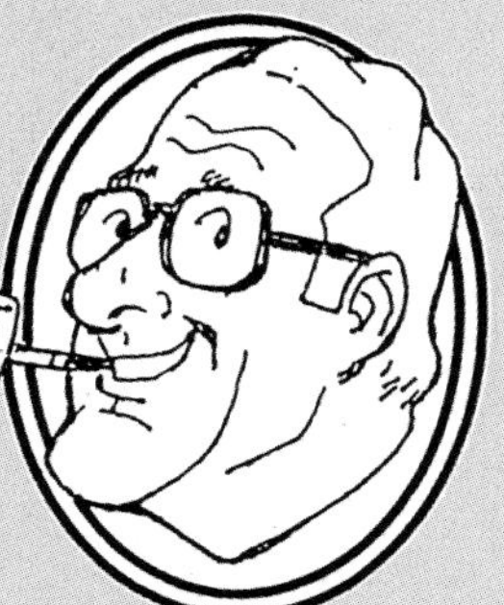

BERG'S-EYE VIEW DEPT.

The Lighter Side Of...

ARTIST AND WRITER: DAVE BERG

PREPAREDNESS

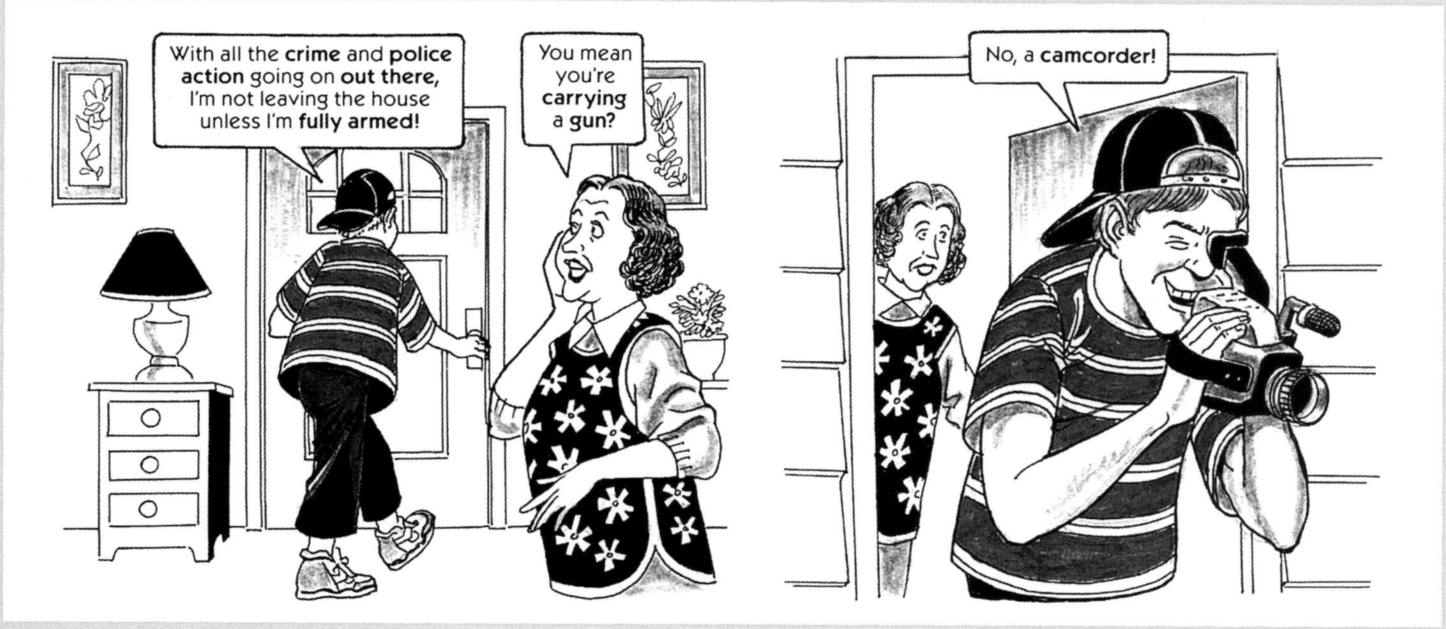
With all the crime and police action going on out there, I'm not leaving the house unless I'm fully armed!
You mean you're carrying a gun?
No, a camcorder!

COMPROMISE

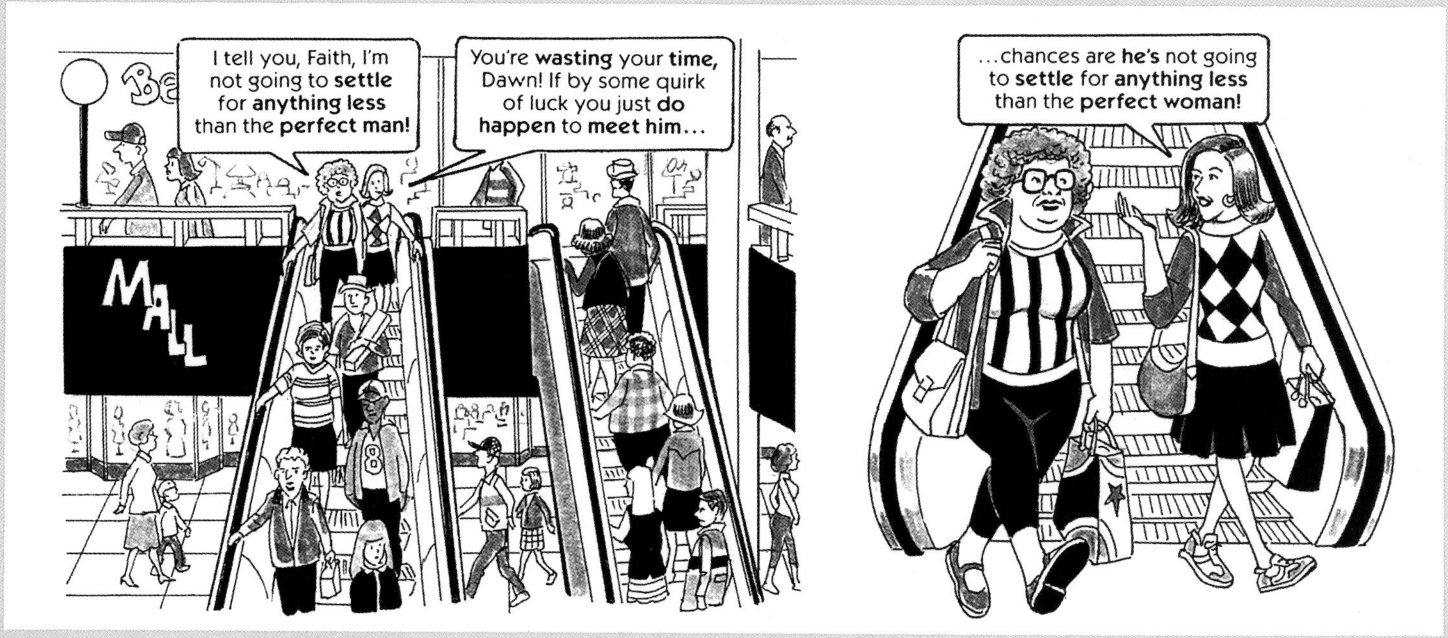
I tell you, Faith, I'm not going to settle for anything less than the perfect man!
You're wasting your time, Dawn! If by some quirk of luck you just do happen to meet him...
MALL
...chances are he's not going to settle for anything less than the perfect woman!

INTELLIGENCE

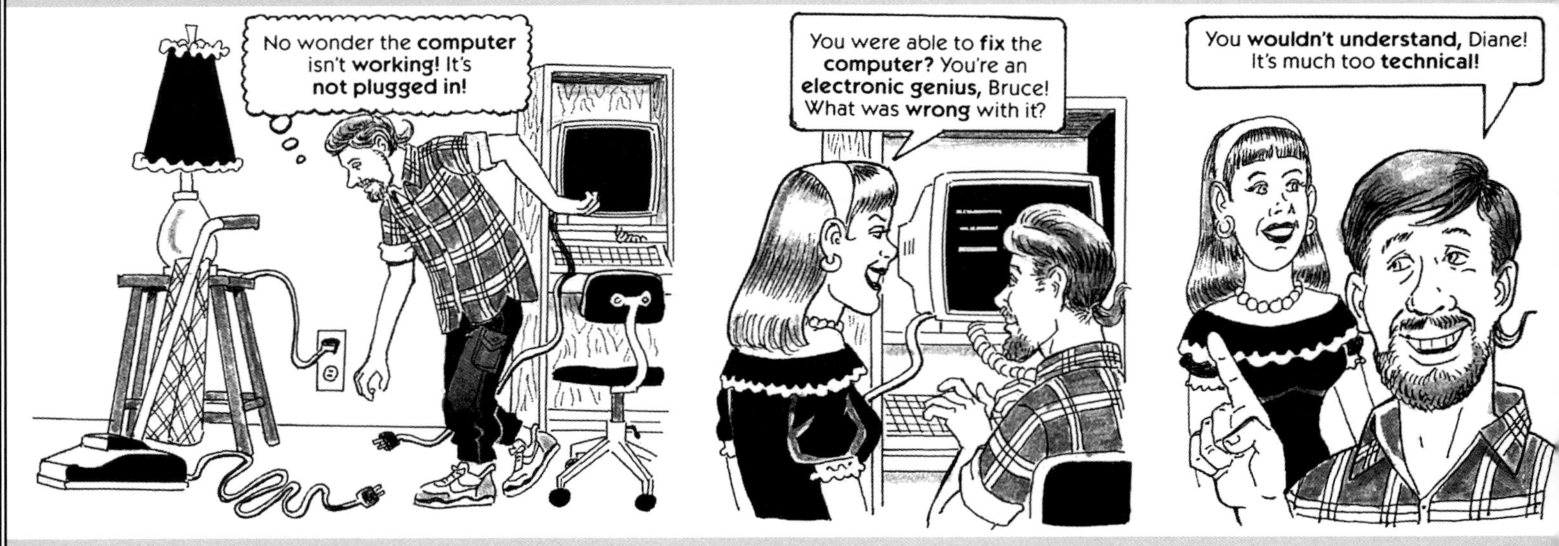
No wonder the computer isn't working! It's not plugged in!
You were able to fix the computer? You're an electronic genius, Bruce! What was wrong with it?
You wouldn't understand, Diane! It's much too technical!

RELATIONSHIPS

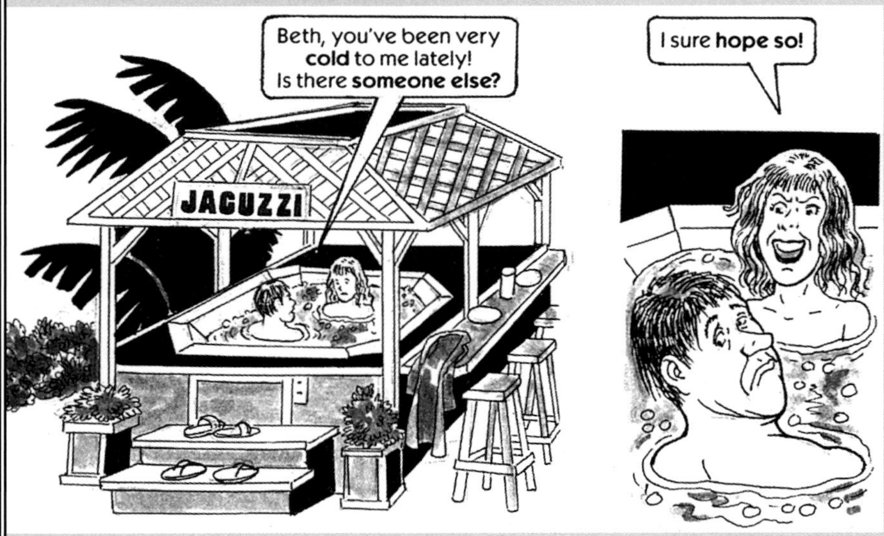
JACUZZI
Beth, you've been very cold to me lately! Is there someone else?
I sure hope so!

POLITICS

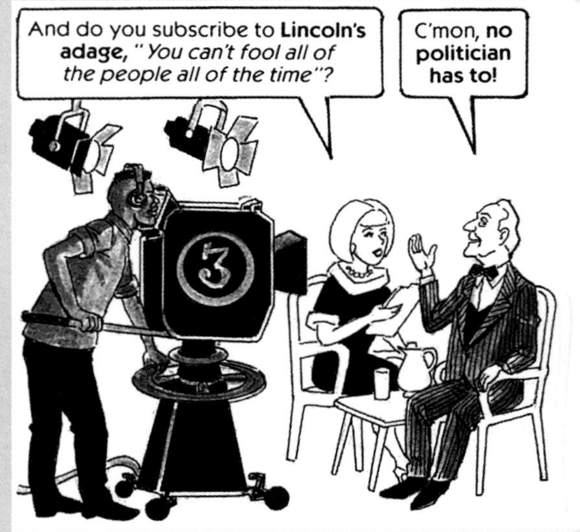
And do you subscribe to Lincoln's adage, "You can't fool all of the people all of the time"?
C'mon, no politician has to!

POWER

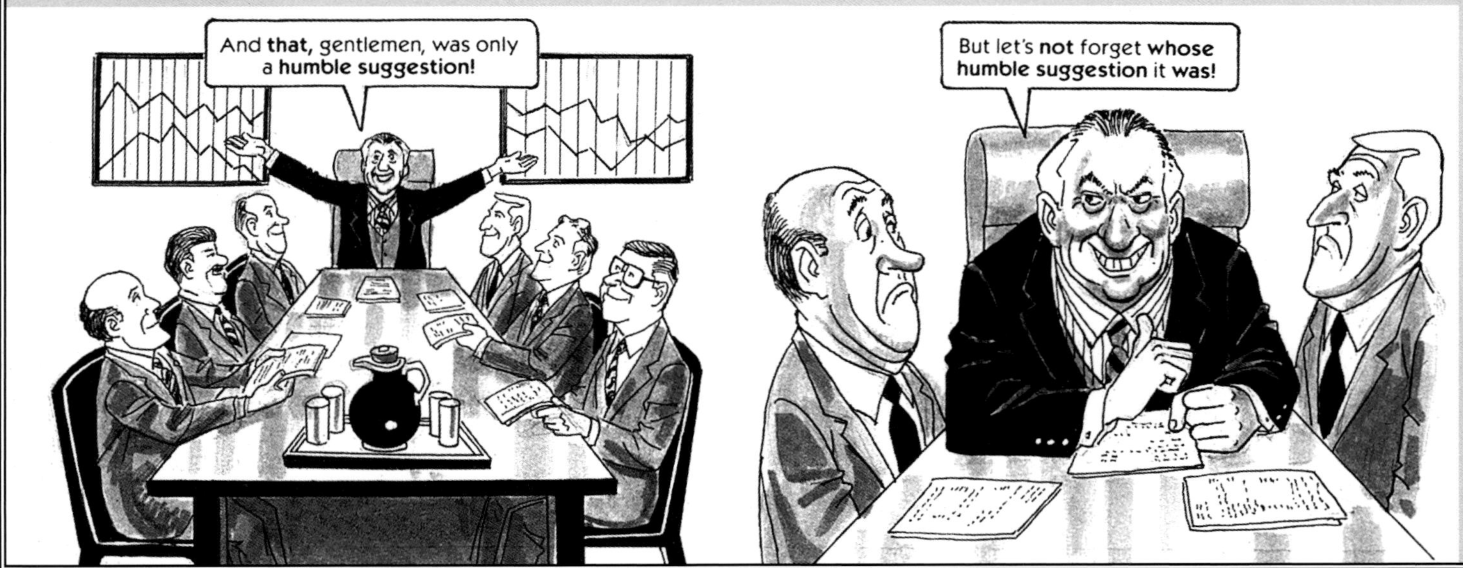
And that, gentlemen, was only a humble suggestion!
But let's not forget whose humble suggestion it was!

REPAIRS

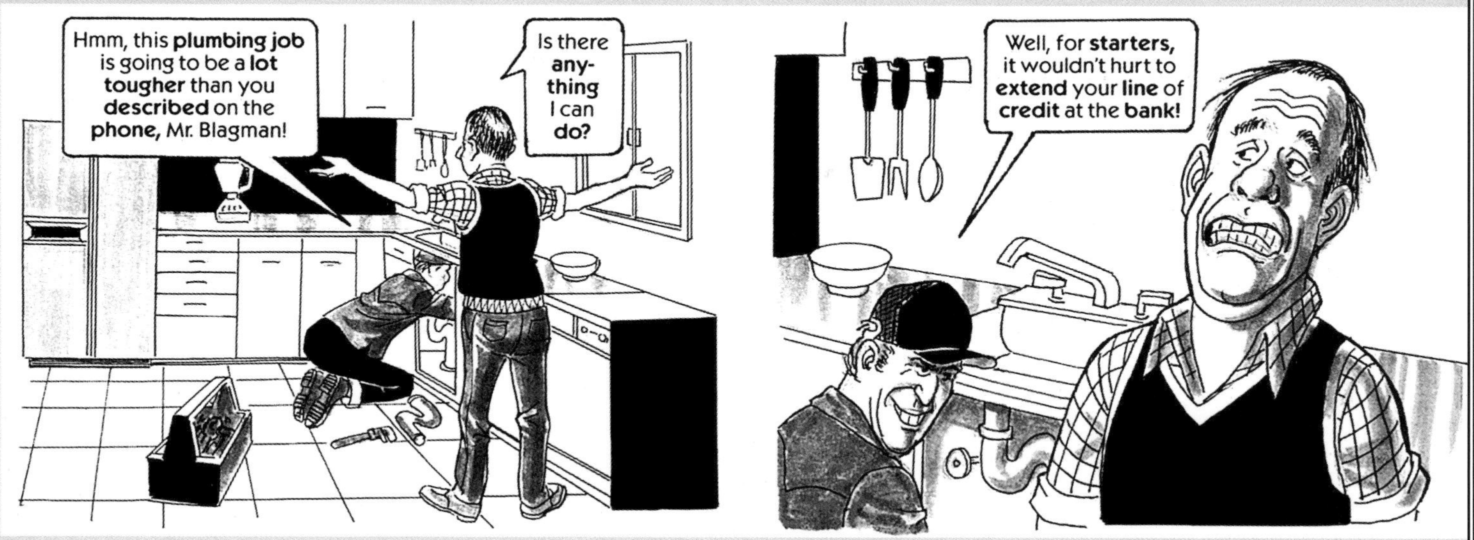
Hmm, this plumbing job is going to be a lot tougher than you described on the phone, Mr. Blagman!
Is there any-thing I can do?
Well, for starters, it wouldn't hurt to extend your line of credit at the bank!

RESPONSIBILITIES

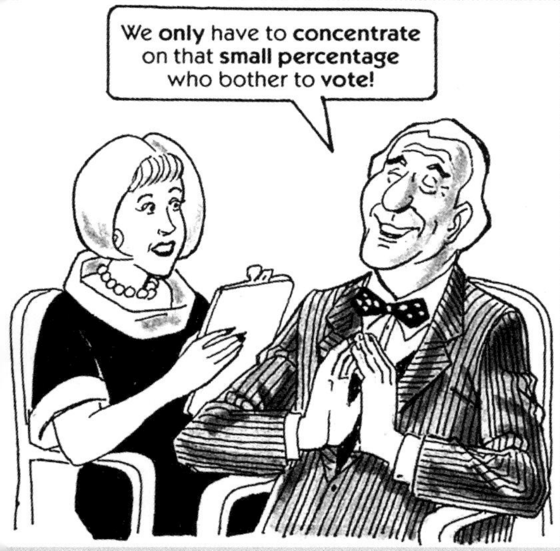
We only have to concentrate on that small percentage who bother to vote!

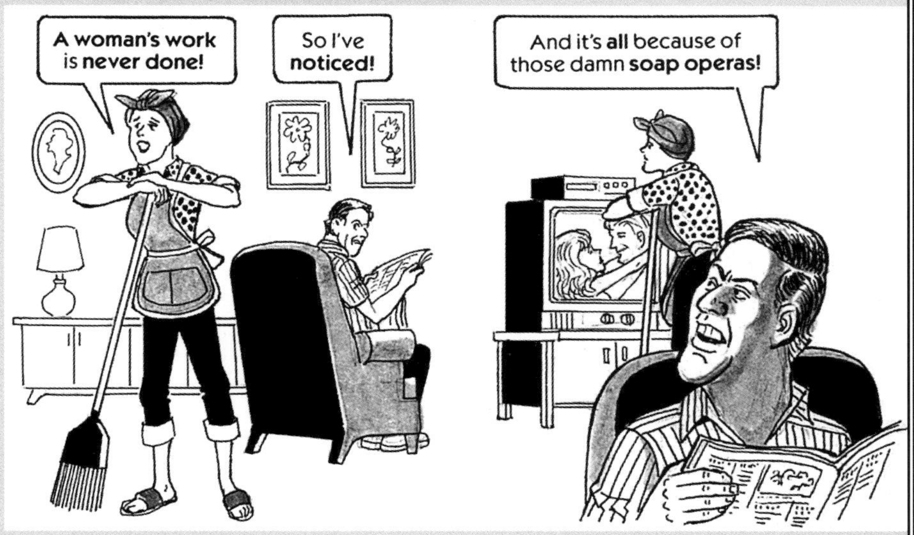
A woman's work is never done!
So I've noticed!
And it's all because of those damn soap operas!

REAL ESTATE

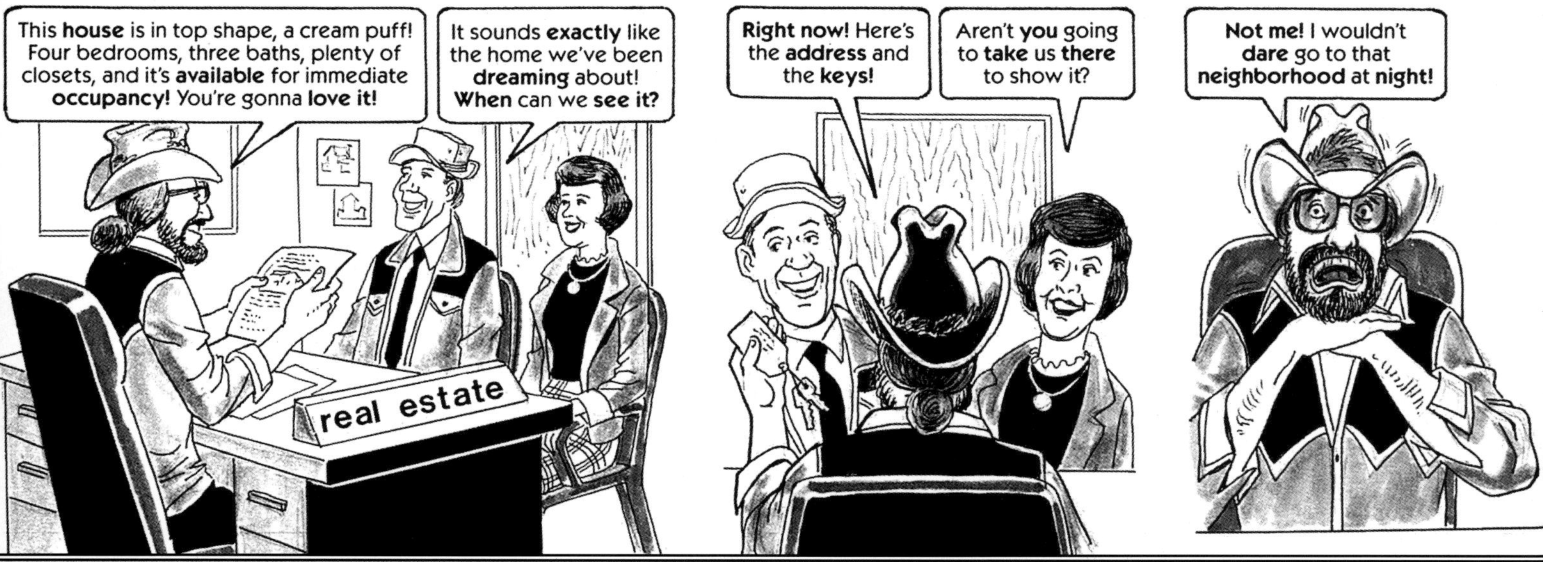
This house is in top shape, a cream puff! Four bedrooms, three baths, plenty of closets, and it's available for immediate occupancy! You're gonna love it!
It sounds exactly like the home we've been dreaming about! When can we see it?
real estate
Right now! Here's the address and the keys!
Aren't you going to take us there to show it?
Not me! I wouldn't dare go to that neighborhood at night!

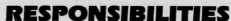

THE OFFICE

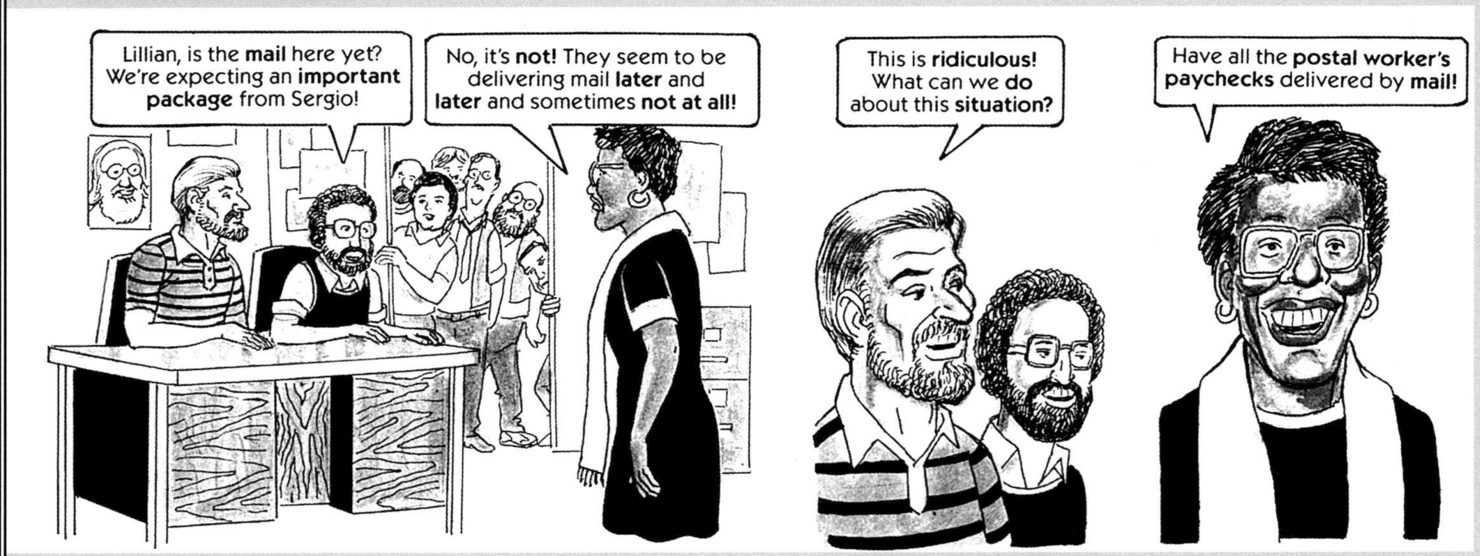
Lillian, is the **mail** here yet? We're expecting an **important package** from Sergio!
No, it's **not!** They seem to be delivering mail **later** and **later** and sometimes **not at all!**
This is **ridiculous!** What can we **do** about this **situation?**
Have all the **postal worker's paychecks** delivered by **mail!**

IMPORTANCE

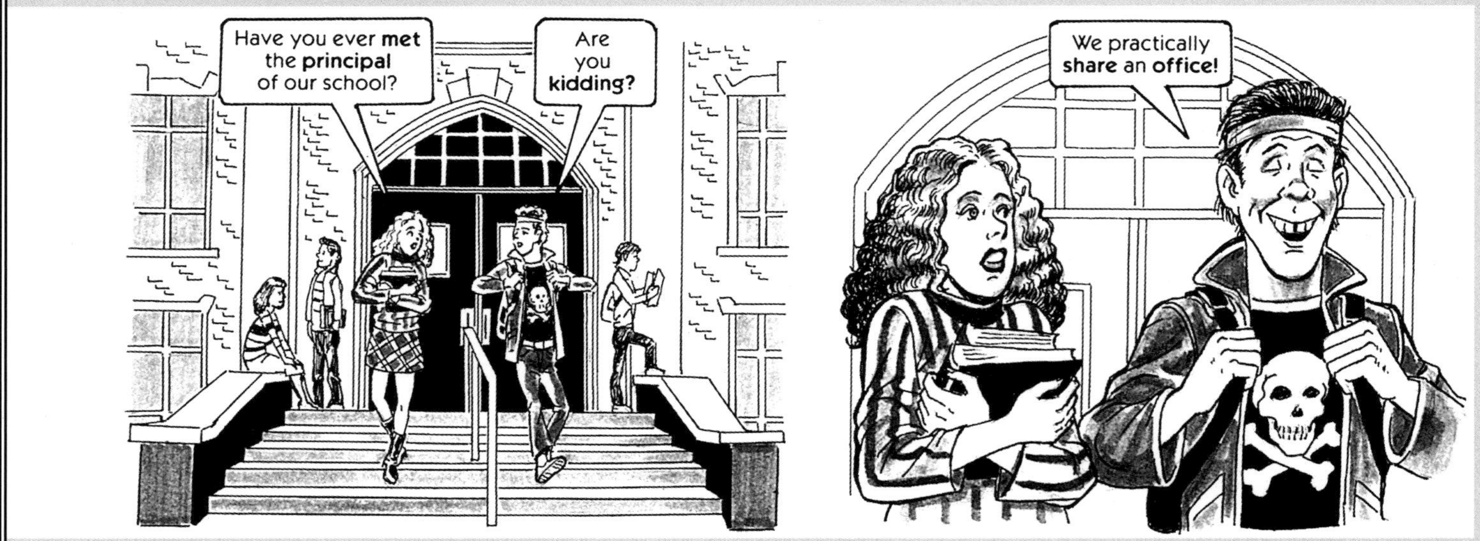
Have you ever **met** the **principal** of our school?
Are you **kidding?**
We practically **share** an **office!**

DOCTORS

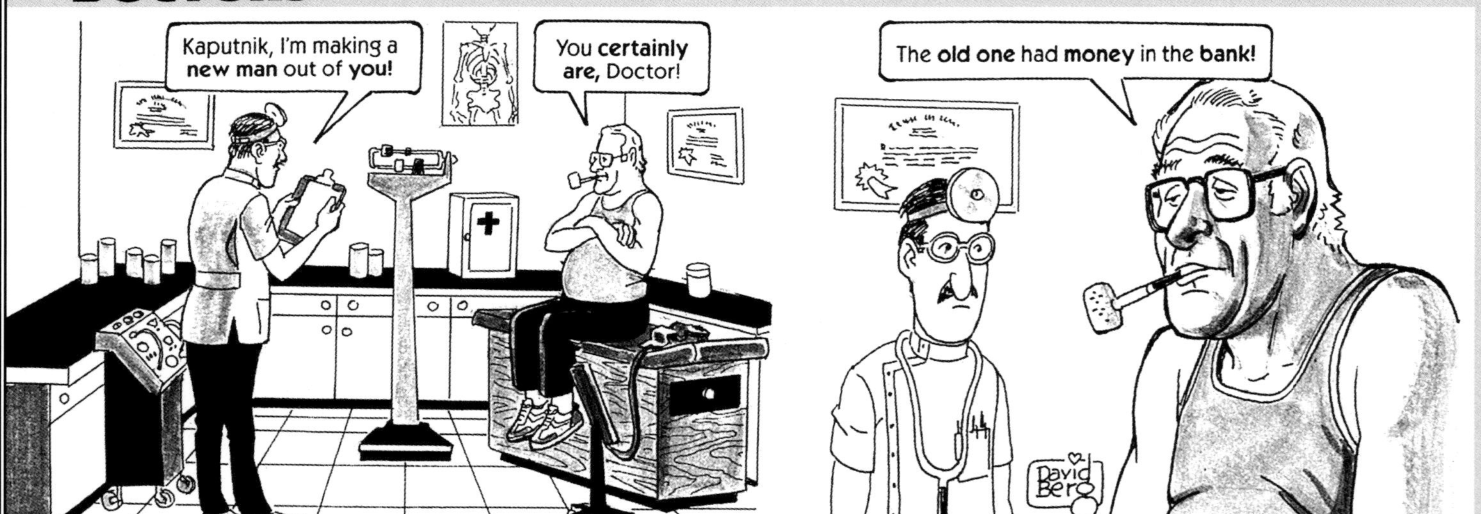
Kaputnik, I'm making a **new man** out of **you!**
You **certainly are,** Doctor!
The **old one** had **money** in the **bank!**
David Berg

Front Cover MAD Super Special #95

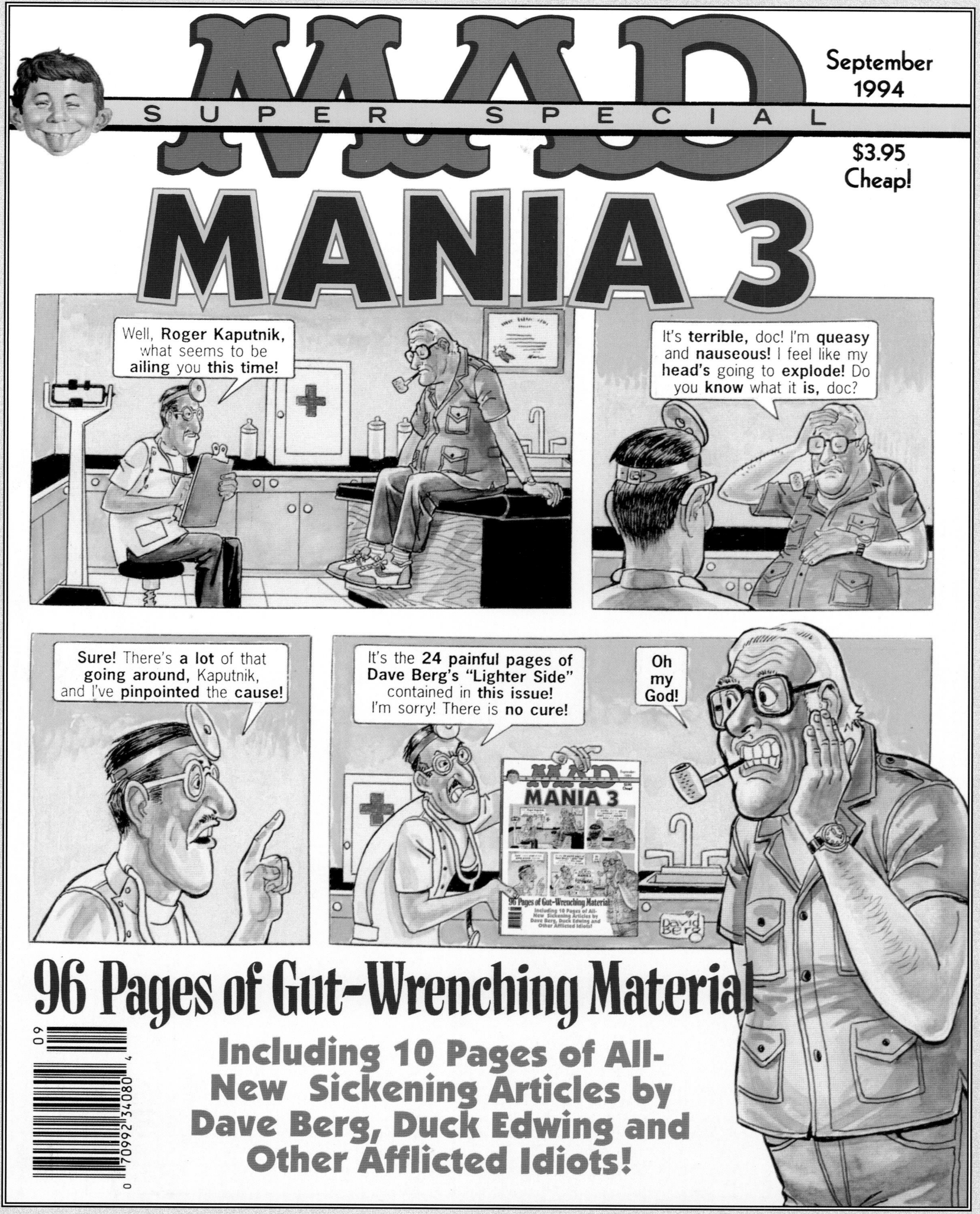
MAD
SUPER SPECIAL
September 1994
$3.95 Cheap!
MANIA 3
Well, Roger Kaputnik, what seems to be ailing you this time!
It's terrible, doc! I'm queasy and nauseous! I feel like my head's going to explode! Do you know what it is, doc?
Sure! There's a lot of that going around, Kaputnik, and I've pinpointed the cause!
It's the 24 painful pages of Dave Berg's "Lighter Side" contained in this issue! I'm sorry! There is no cure!
Oh my God!
David Berg
96 Pages of Gut-Wrenching Material
Including 10 Pages of All-New Sickening Articles by Dave Berg, Duck Edwing and Other Afflicted Idiots!

The only MAD cover illustrated by Berg, for a Special spotlighting "The Lighter Side of..."

BERG'S-EYE VIEW DEPT.

THE LIGHTER SIDE OF...

ARTIST AND WRITER: DAVE BERG

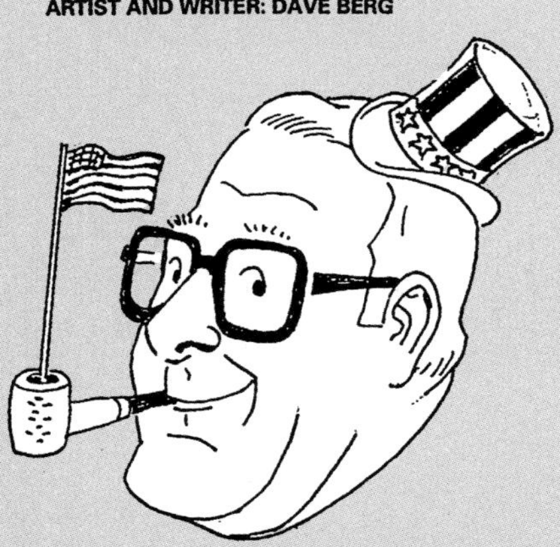

THE MALE EGO

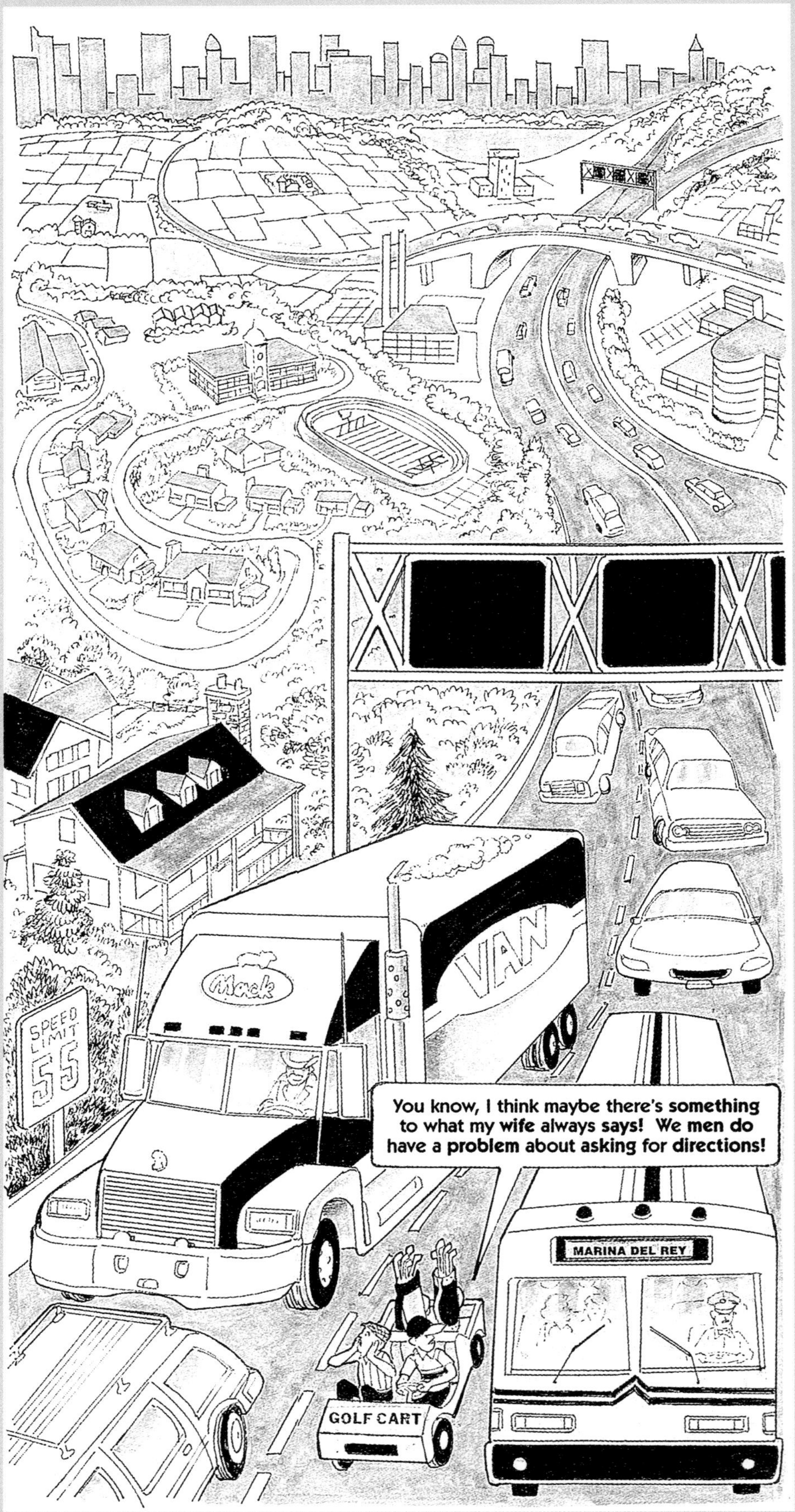
SPEED LIMIT 55
Mack
VAN
You know, I think maybe there's something to what my wife always says! We men do have a problem about asking for directions!
MARINA DEL REY
GOLF CART

CRIME

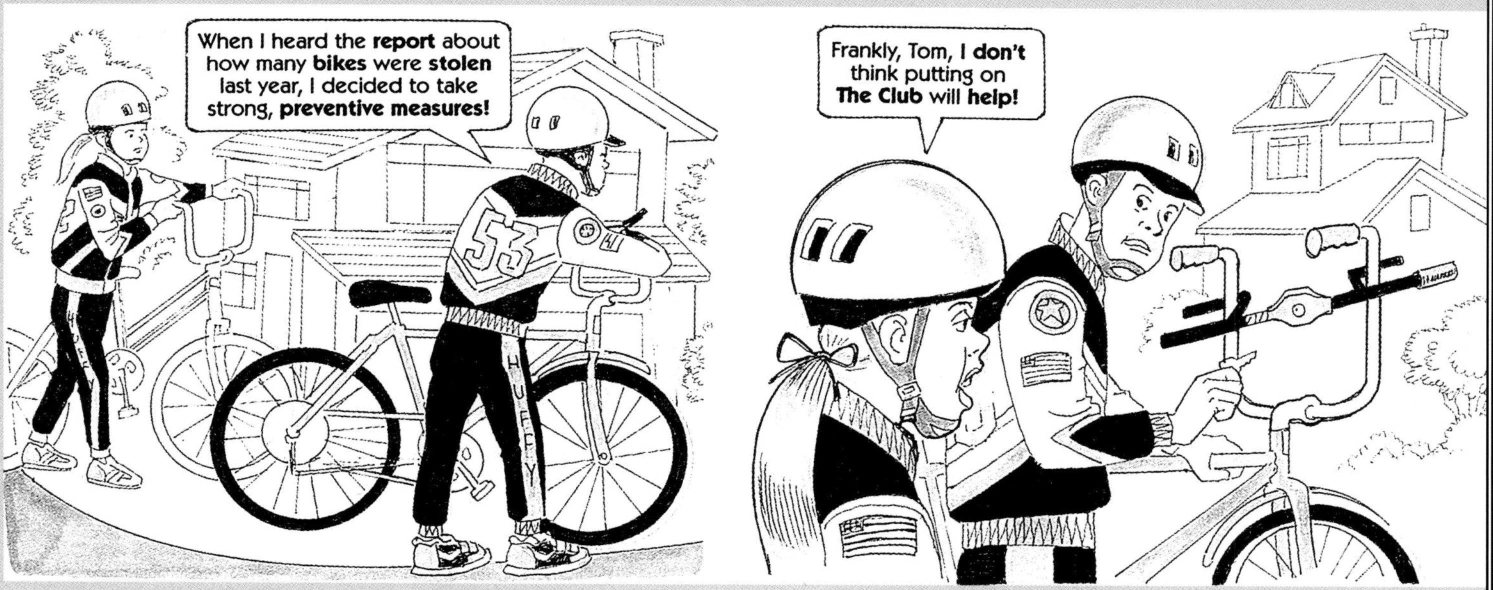
When I heard the **report** about how many **bikes** were **stolen** last year, I decided to take strong, **preventive measures!**
HUFFY
53
Frankly, Tom, **I don't** think putting on **The Club** will **help!**

GIFTS

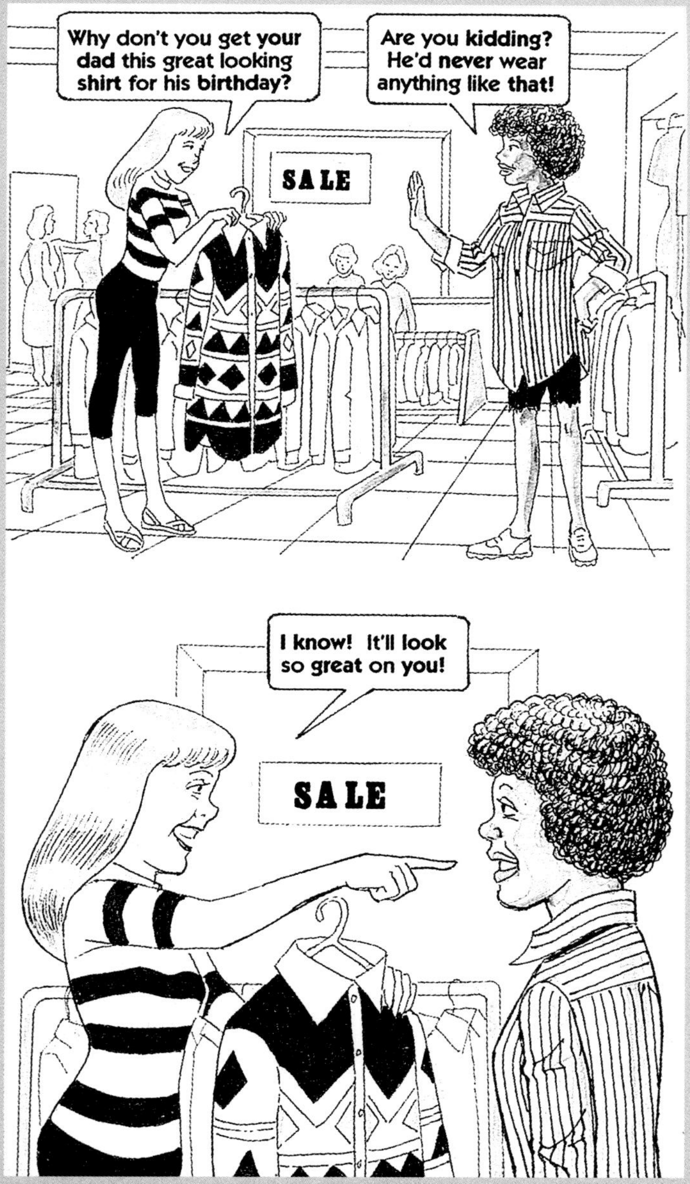
Why don't you get your **dad this great looking shirt for his birthday?**
Are you **kidding?** He'd **never** wear **anything like that!**
SALE
I know! It'll look so great on you!
SALE

DISASTER

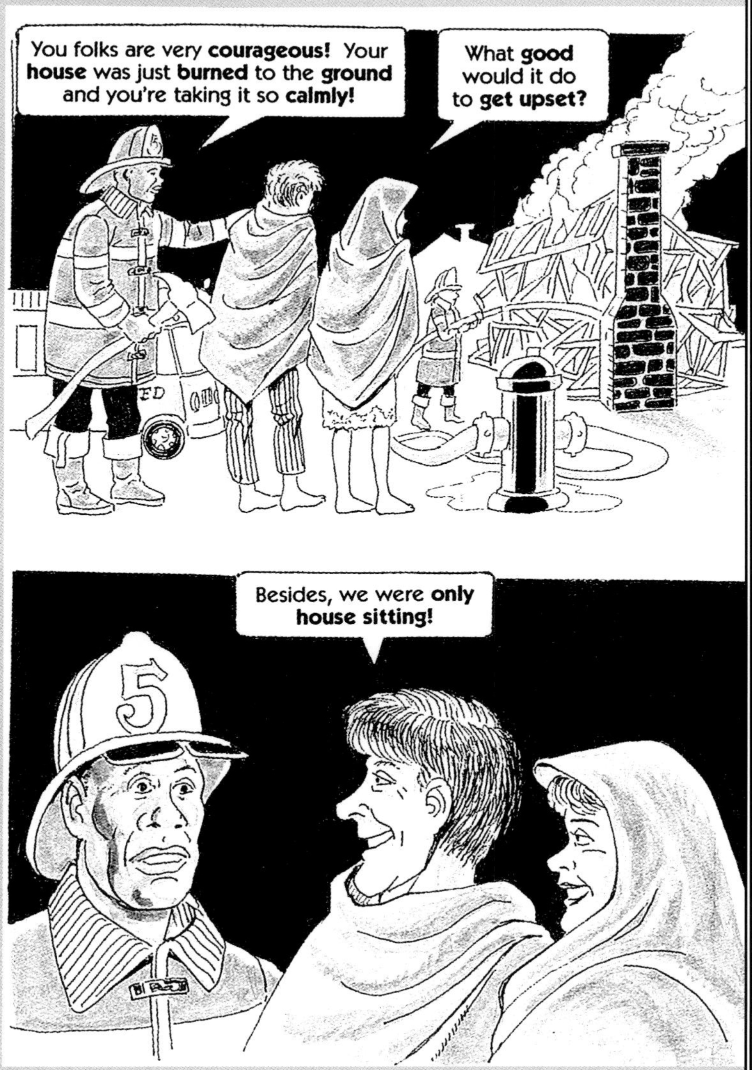
You folks are very **courageous!** Your **house** was just **burned** to the **ground** and you're taking it so **calmly!**
What **good** would it do to **get upset?**
Besides, we were **only house sitting!**
5

SCHOOL

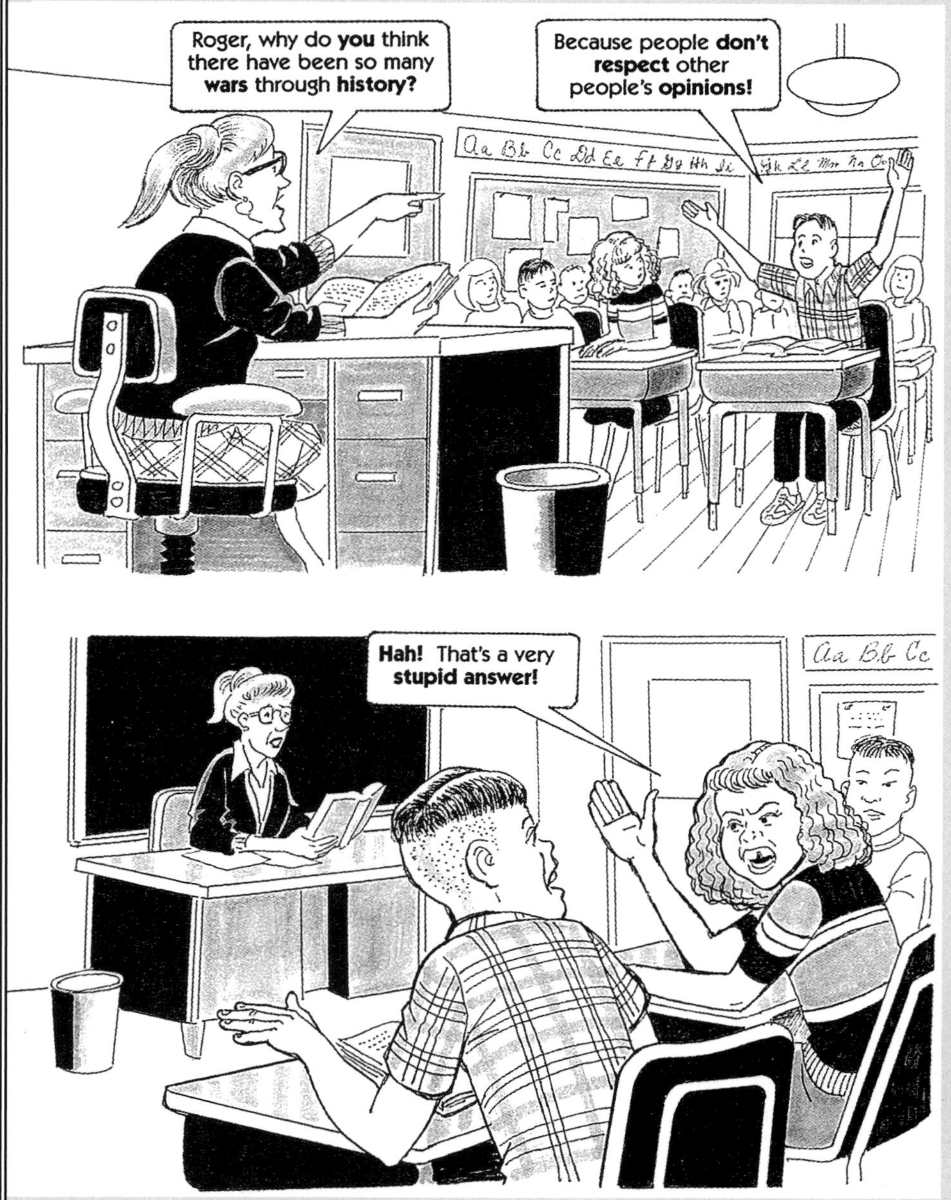
Roger, why do **you** think there have been so many **wars** through **history?**
Because people **don't respect** other people's **opinions!**
Aa Bb Cc Dd Ee Ff Gg Hh Ii
Aa Bb Cc
Hah! That's a very **stupid answer!**

VIEWING

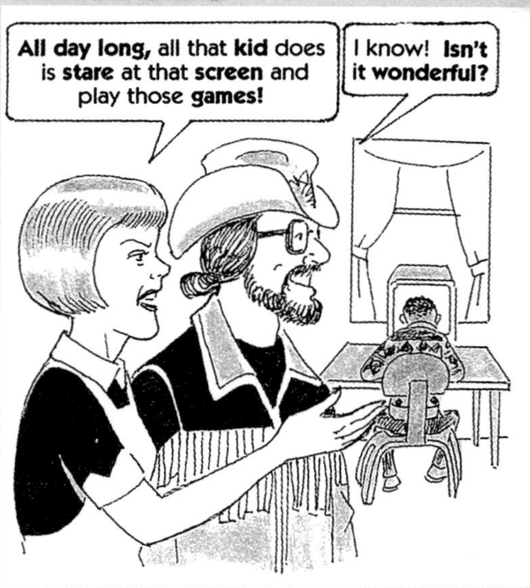
All day long, all that **kid** does is **stare** at that **screen** and play those **games!**
I know! **Isn't it wonderful?**

THERAPY

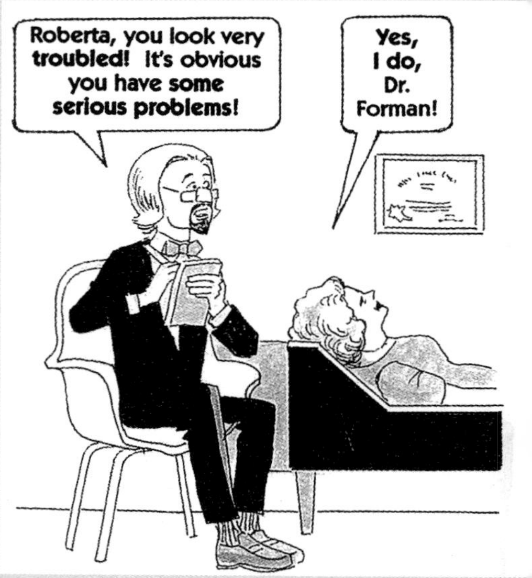
Roberta, you look very troubled! It's obvious you have some serious problems!
Yes, I do, Dr. Forman!

PLEASURE

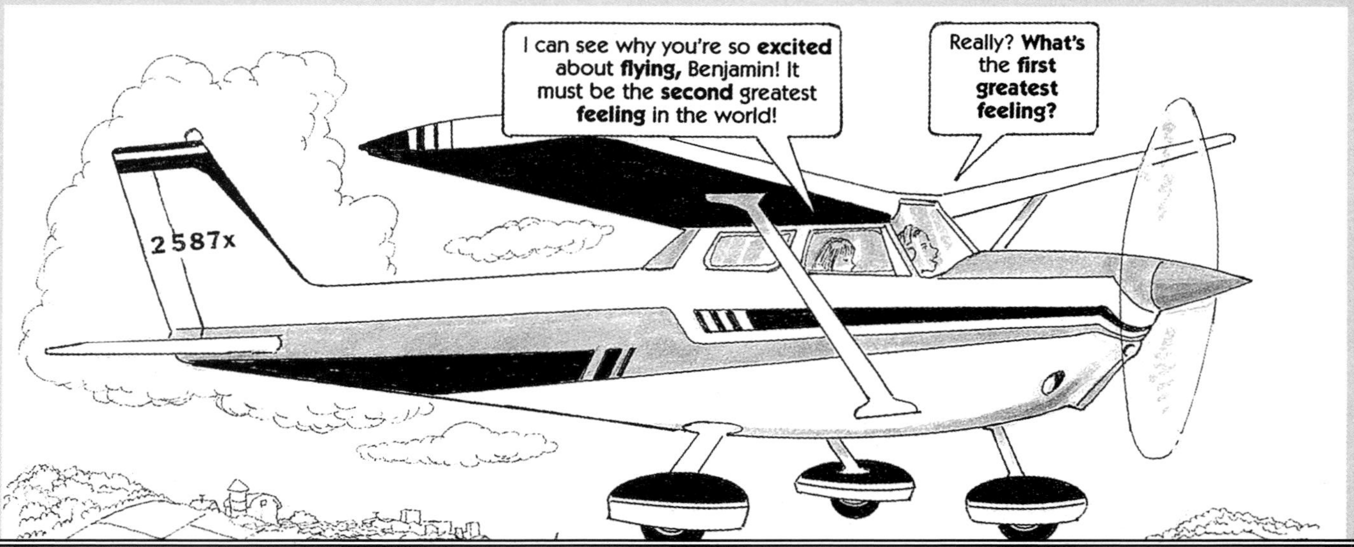
I can see why you're so **excited** about **flying,** Benjamin! It must be the **second** greatest **feeling** in the world!
Really? **What's** the **first greatest feeling?**
2587x

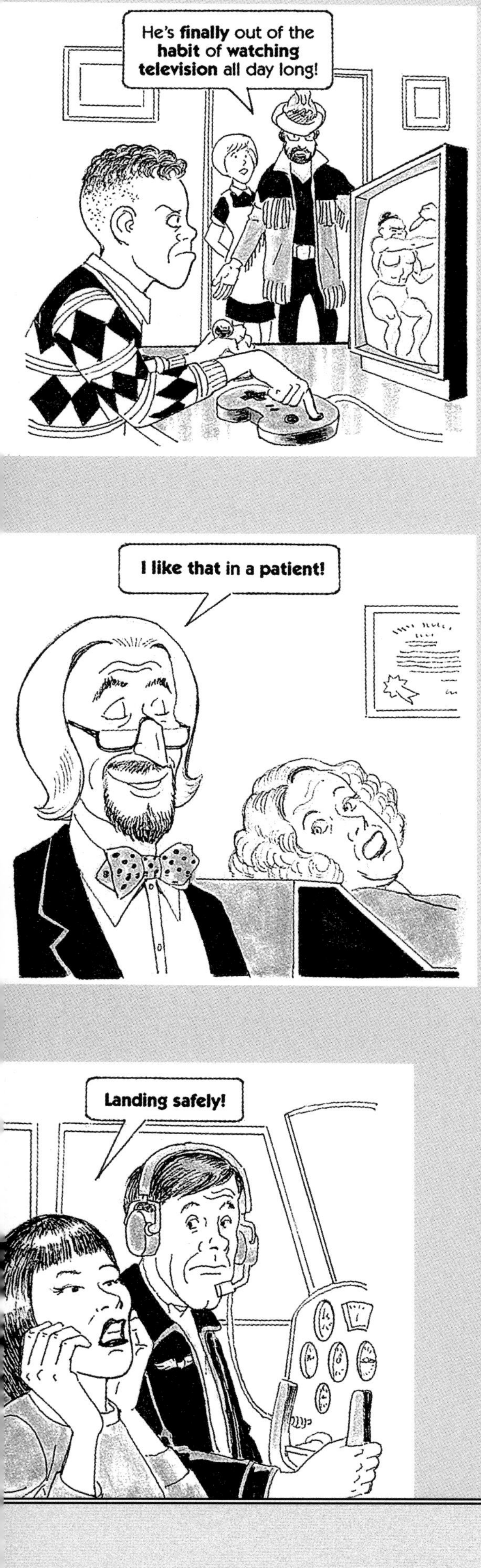
He's finally out of the habit of watching television all day long!
I like that in a patient!
Landing safely!

REVENGE

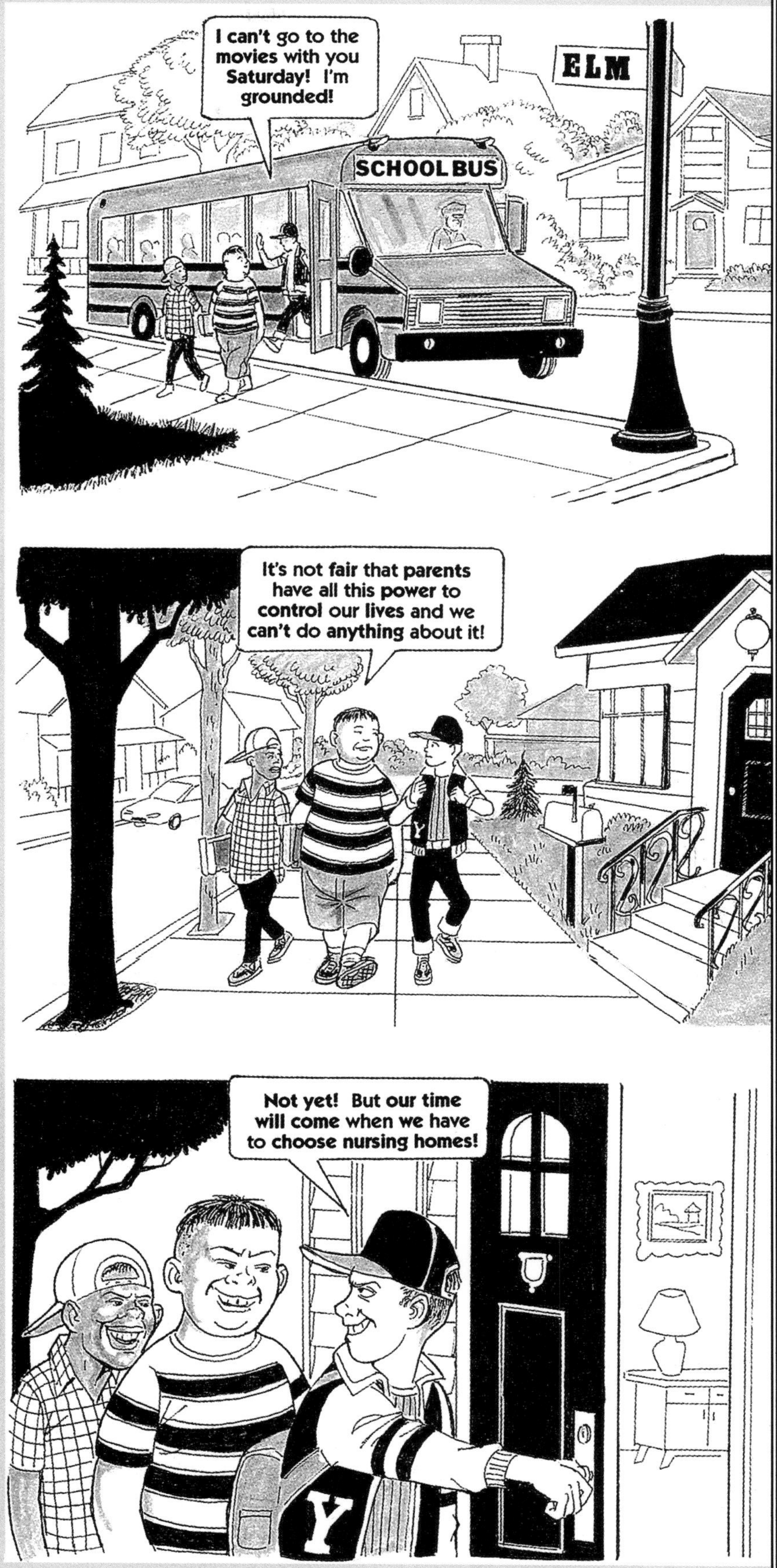
ELM
SCHOOL BUS
I can't go to the movies with you Saturday! I'm grounded!
It's not fair that parents have all this power to control our lives and we can't do anything about it!
Not yet! But our time will come when we have to choose nursing homes!
Y

THE OFFICE

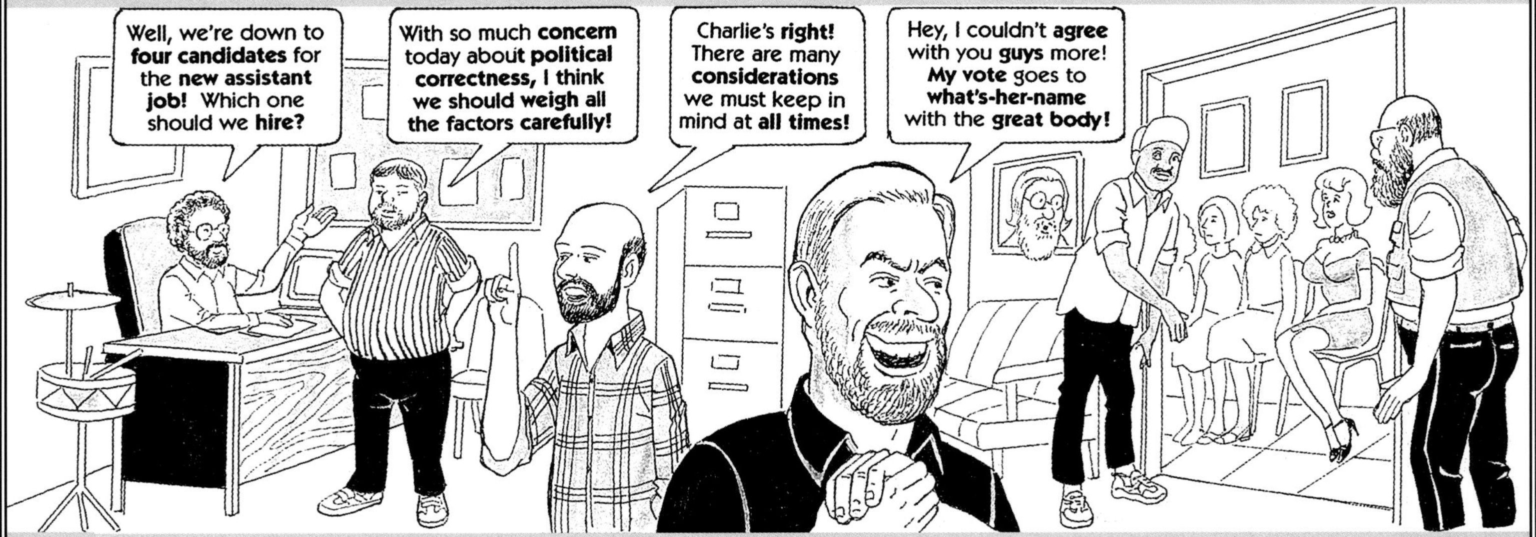
Well, we're down to four candidates for the new assistant job! Which one should we hire?
With so much concern today about political correctness, I think we should weigh all the factors carefully!
Charlie's right! There are many considerations we must keep in mind at all times!
Hey, I couldn't agree with you guys more! My vote goes to what's-her-name with the great body!

LOGIC

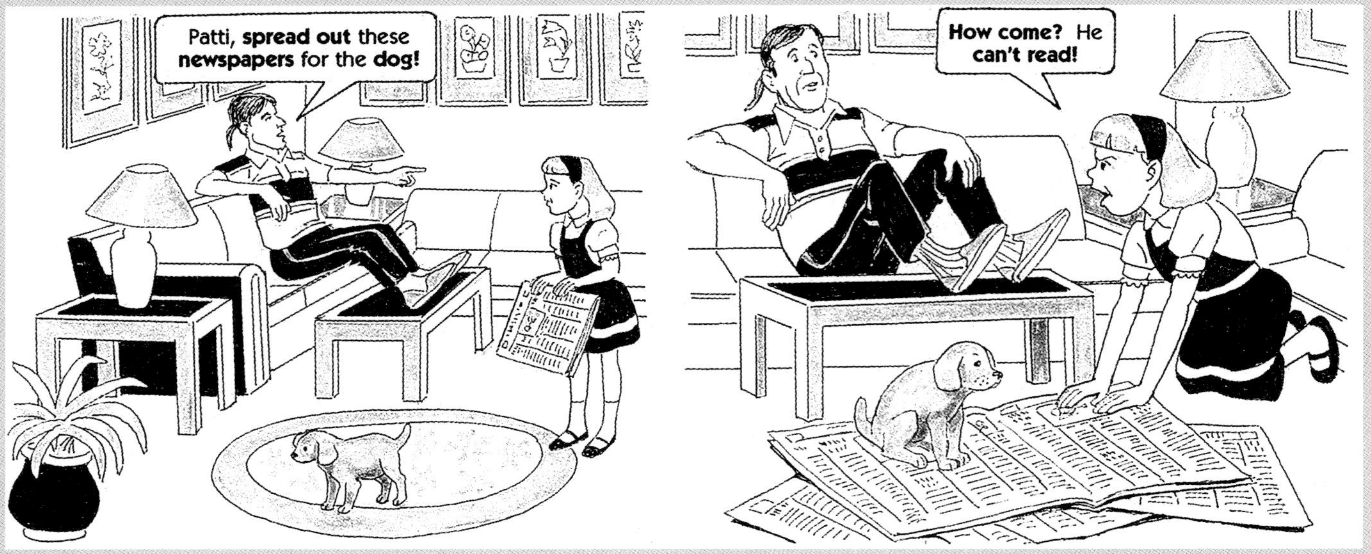
Patti, spread out these newspapers for the dog!
How come? He can't read!

DOCTORS

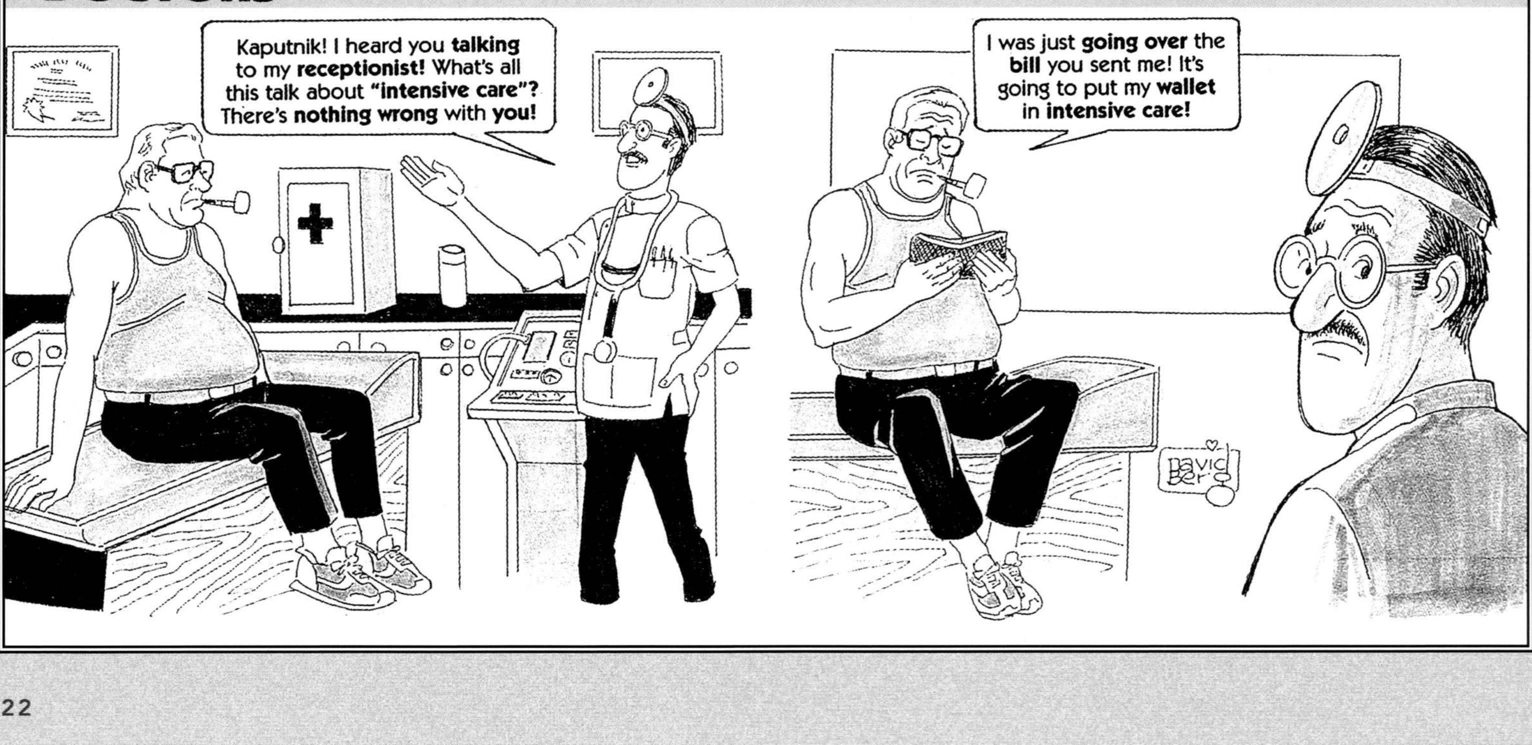
Kaputnik! I heard you talking to my receptionist! What's all this talk about "intensive care"? There's nothing wrong with you!
I was just going over the bill you sent me! It's going to put my wallet in intensive care!
David Berg

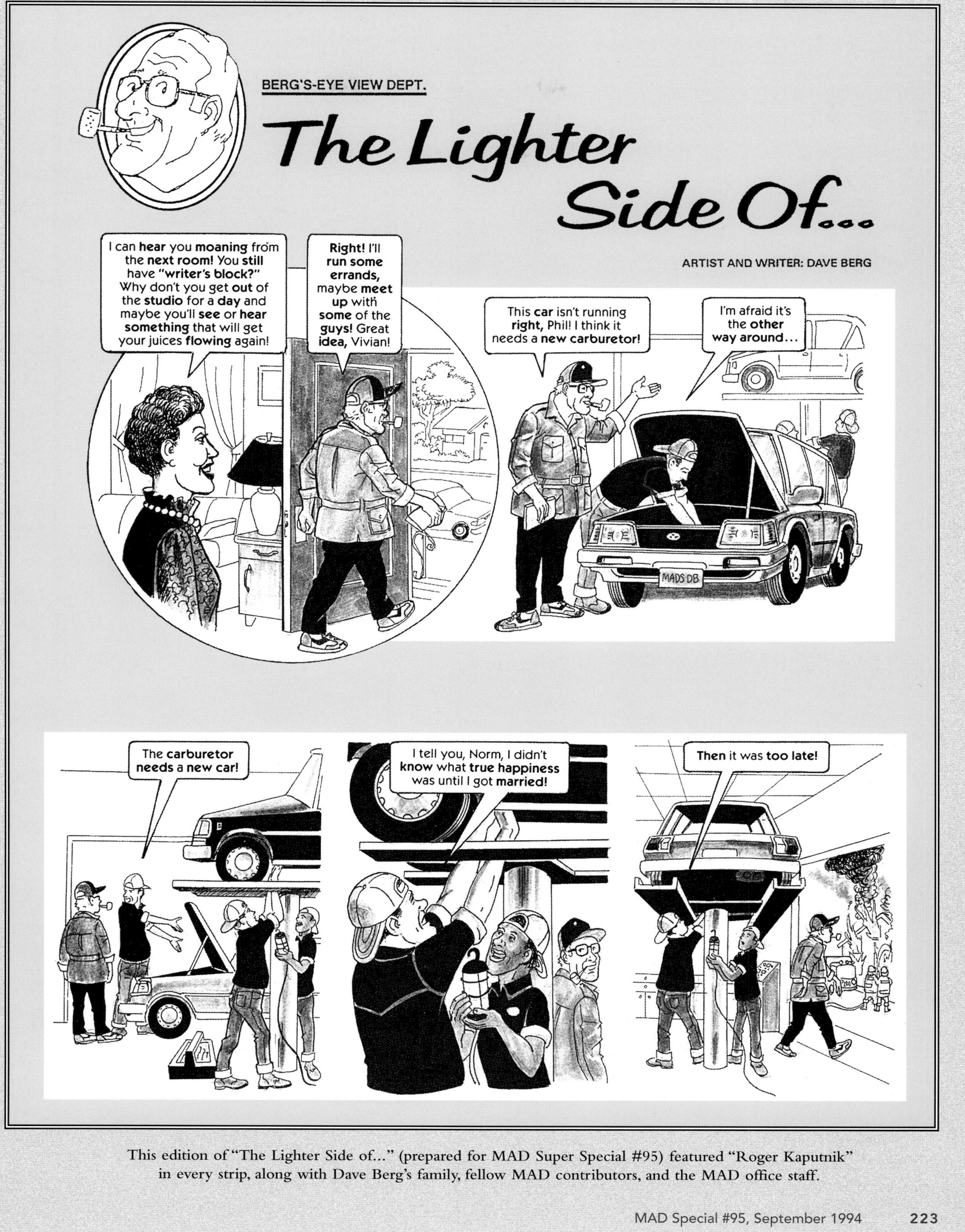
BERG'S-EYE VIEW DEPT.
The Lighter Side Of...
ARTIST AND WRITER: DAVE BERG
I can hear you moaning from the next room! You still have "writer's block?" Why don't you get out of the studio for a day and maybe you'll see or hear something that will get your juices flowing again!
Right! I'll run some errands, maybe meet up with some of the guys! Great idea, Vivian!
This car isn't running right, Phil! I think it needs a new carburetor!
I'm afraid it's the other way around...
MADS DB
The carburetor needs a new car!
I tell you, Norm, I didn't know what true happiness was until I got married!
Then it was too late!

This edition of "The Lighter Side of..." (prepared for MAD Super Special #95) featured "Roger Kaputnik" in every strip, along with Dave Berg's family, fellow MAD contributors, and the MAD office staff.

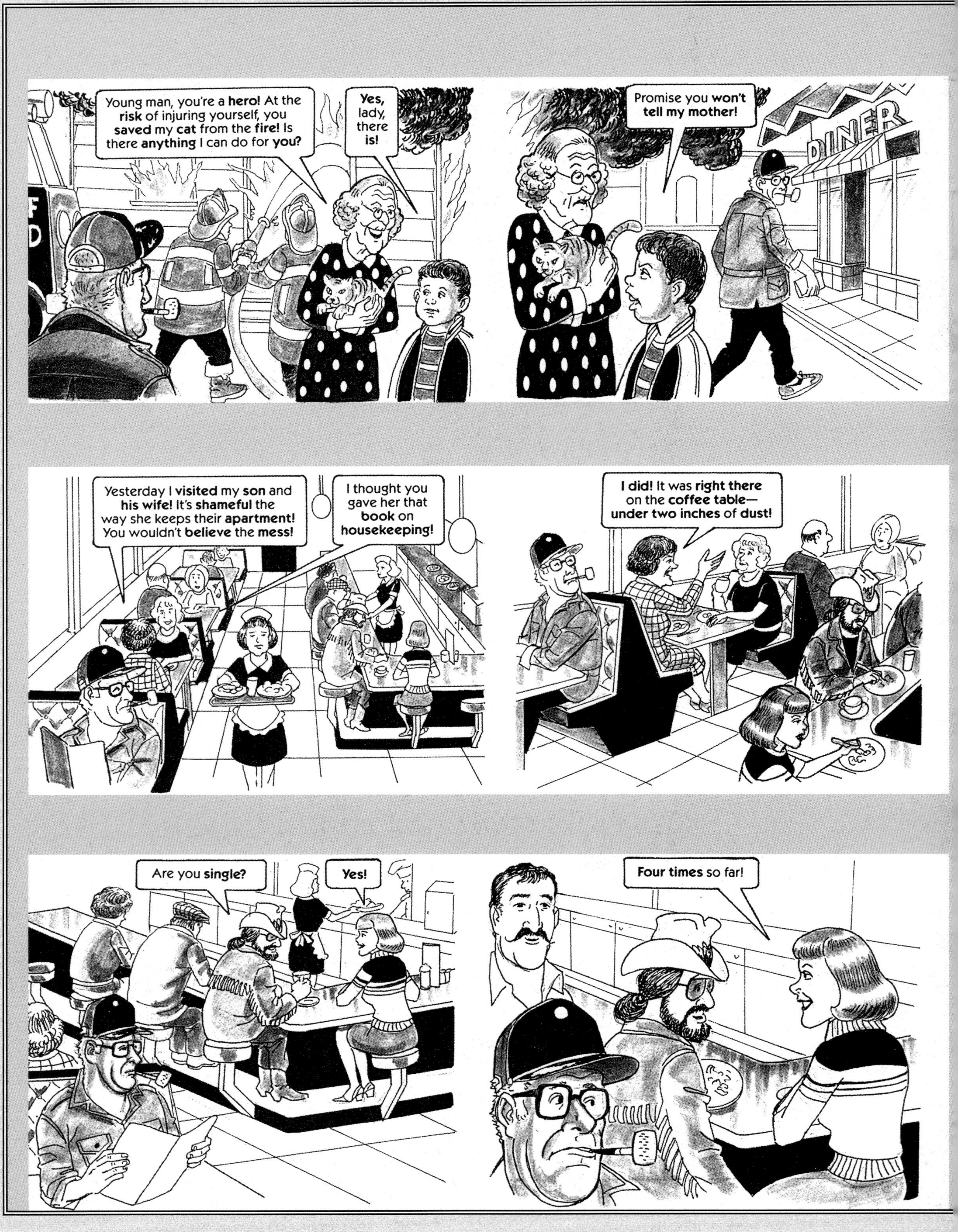
Young man, you're a **hero!** At the **risk** of injuring yourself, you **saved** my **cat** from the **fire!** Is there **anything** I can do for **you?**
Yes, lady, there **is!**
Promise you **won't tell my mother!**
DINER
Yesterday I **visited** my **son** and **his wife!** It's **shameful** the way she keeps their **apartment!** You wouldn't **believe** the **mess!**
I thought you gave her that **book** on **housekeeping!**
I did! It was **right there** on the **coffee table—under two inches of dust!**
Are you **single?**
Yes!
Four times so far!

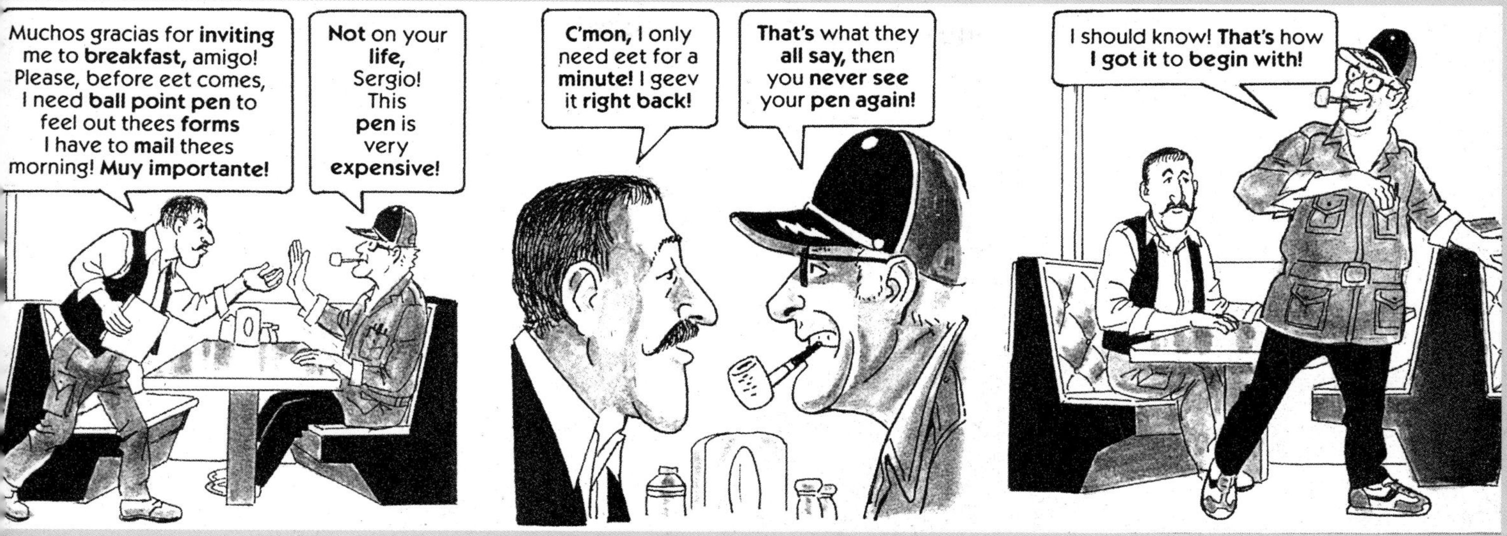
Muchos gracias for **inviting** me to **breakfast,** amigo! Please, before eet comes, I need **ball point pen** to feel out thees **forms** I have to **mail** thees morning! **Muy importante!**
Not on your **life,** Sergio! This **pen** is very **expensive!**
C'mon, I only need eet for a **minute!** I geev it **right back!**
That's what they **all say,** then you **never see** your **pen again!**
I should know! **That's** how **I got it to begin with!**

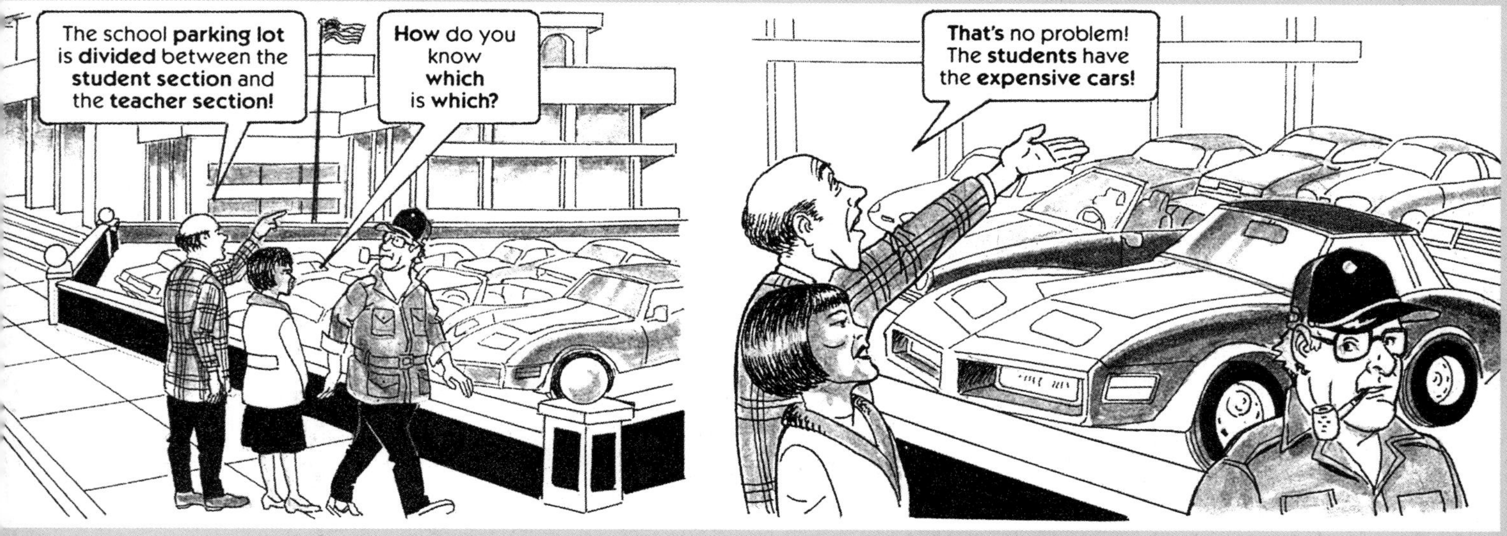
The school **parking lot** is **divided** between the **student section** and the **teacher section!**
How do you know **which** is **which?**
That's no problem! The **students** have the **expensive cars!**

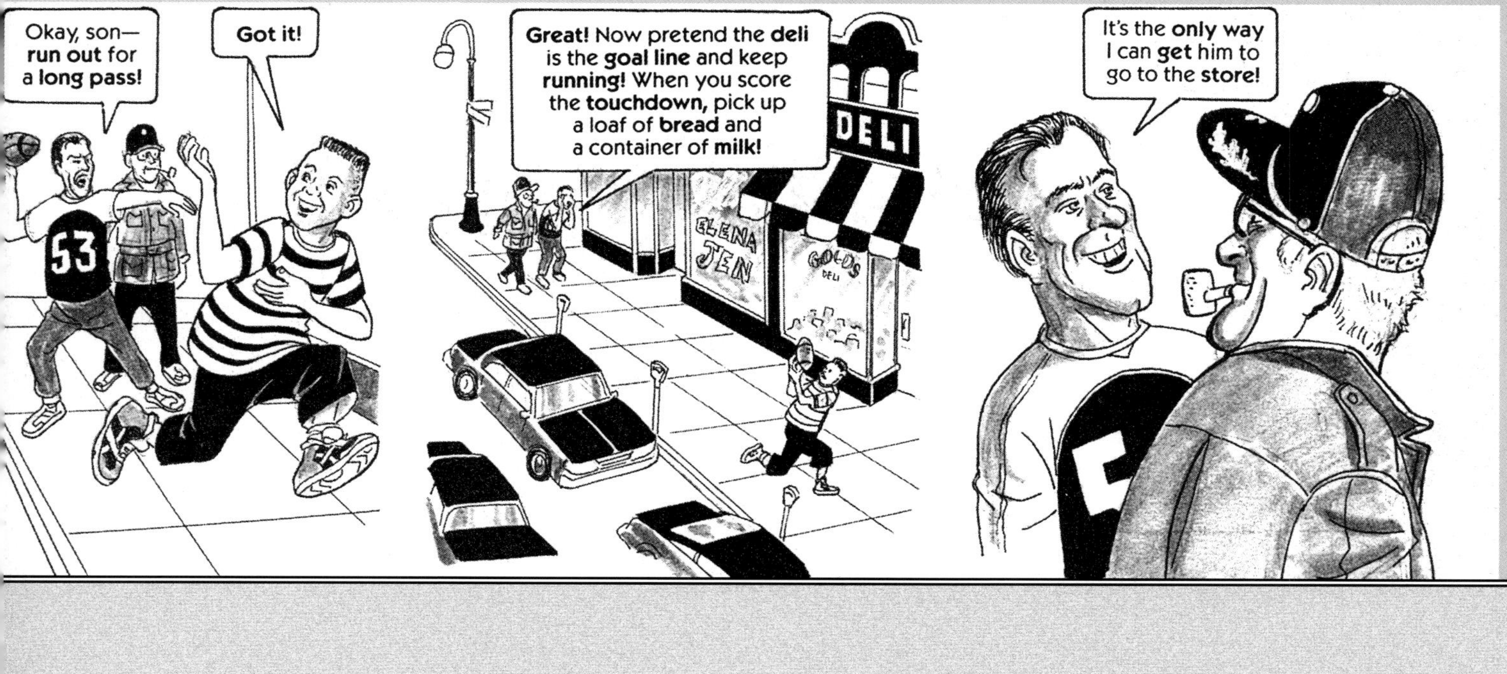
Okay, son— **run out** for a **long pass!**
Got it!
Great! Now pretend the **deli** is the **goal line** and keep **running!** When you score the **touchdown,** pick up a loaf of **bread** and a container of **milk!**
DELI
It's the **only way** I can **get** him to go to the **store!**

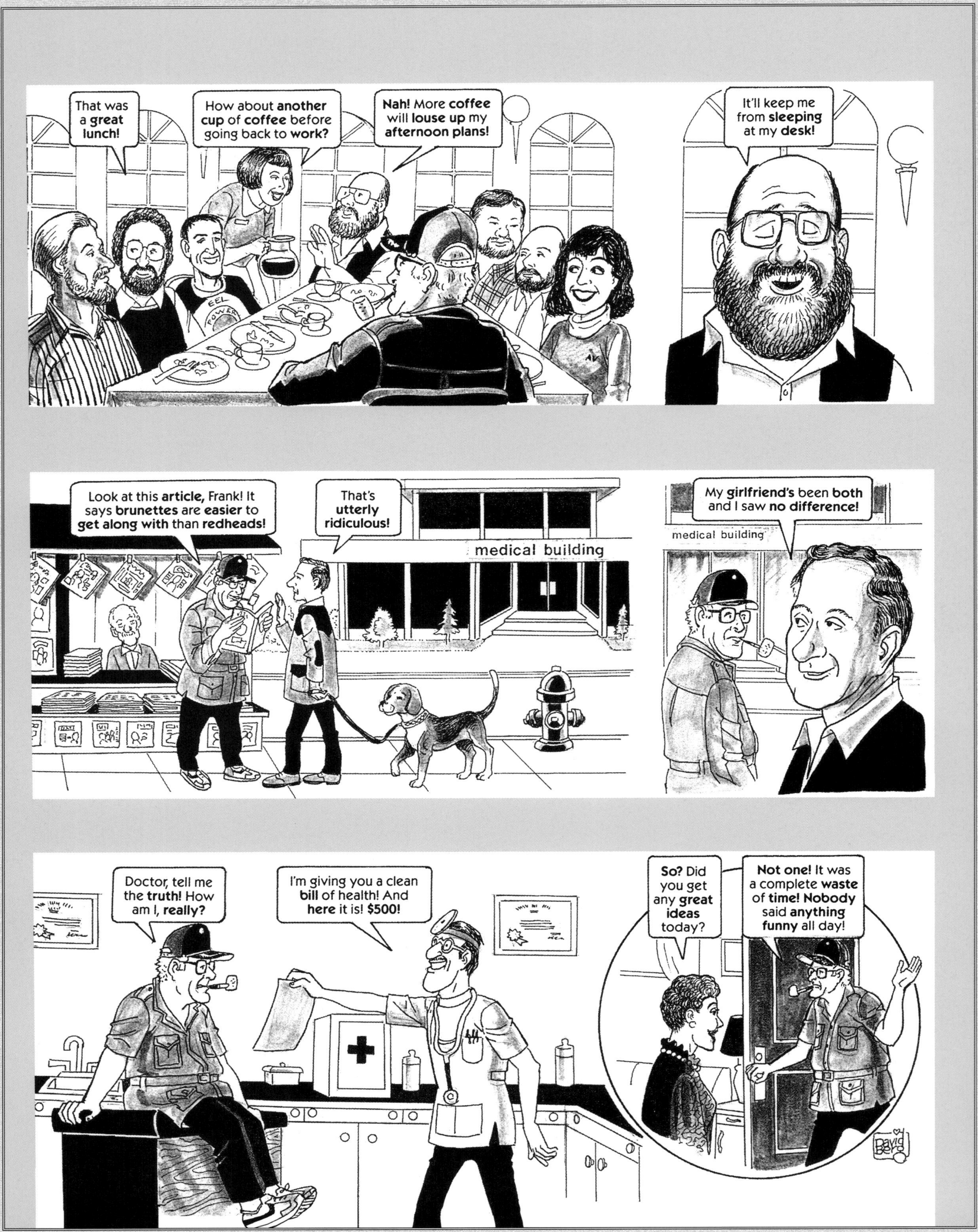
That was a great lunch!
How about another cup of coffee before going back to work?
Nah! More coffee will louse up my afternoon plans!
It'll keep me from sleeping at my desk!
Look at this article, Frank! It says brunettes are easier to get along with than redheads!
That's utterly ridiculous!
medical building
My girlfriend's been both and I saw no difference!
medical building
Doctor, tell me the truth! How am I, really?
I'm giving you a clean bill of health! And here it is! $500!
So? Did you get any great ideas today?
Not one! It was a complete waste of time! Nobody said anything funny all day!
David Berg

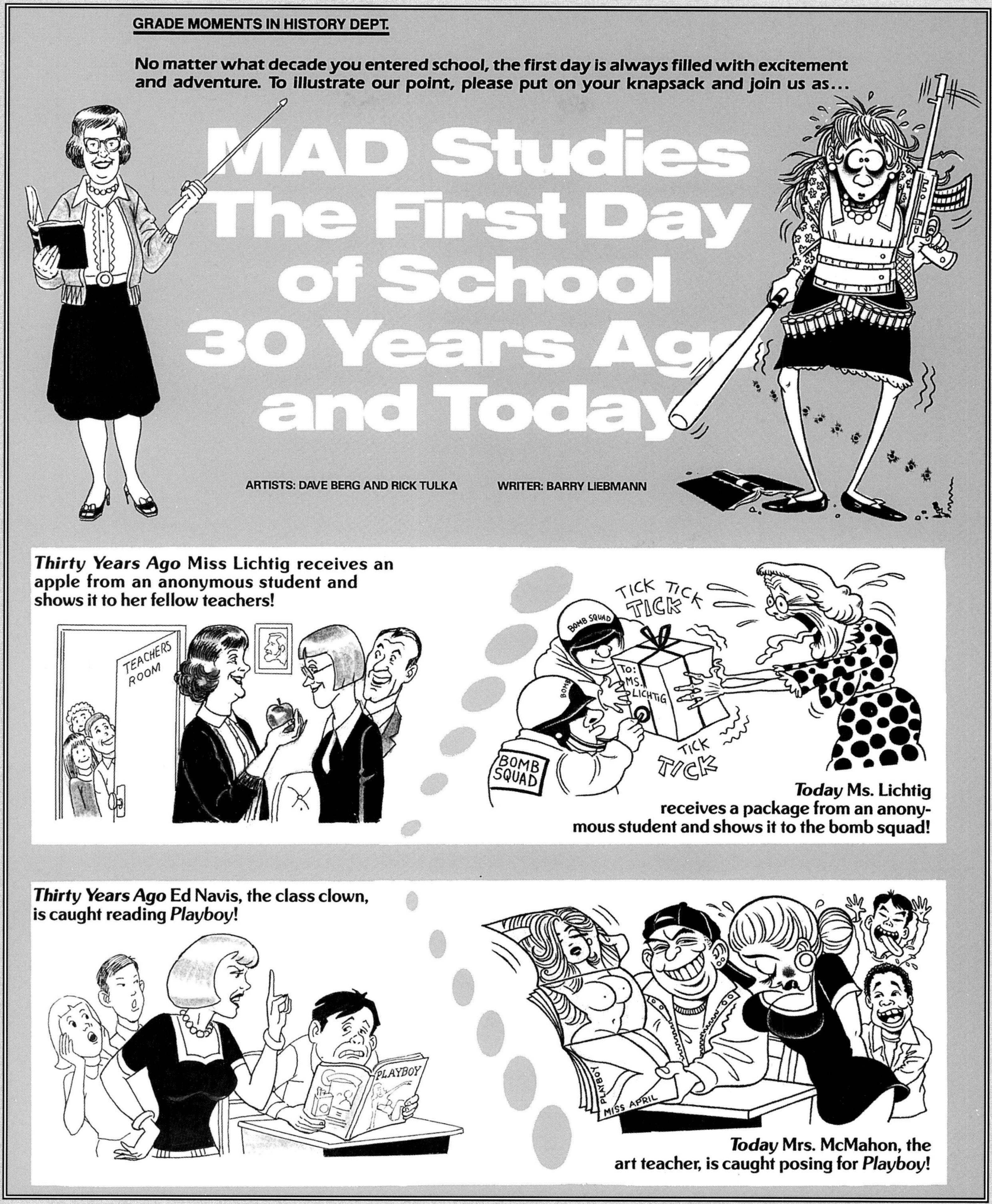
GRADE MOMENTS IN HISTORY DEPT.
No matter what decade you entered school, the first day is always filled with excitement and adventure. To illustrate our point, please put on your knapsack and join us as...
MAD Studies The First Day of School 30 Years Ago and Today
ARTISTS: DAVE BERG AND RICK TULKA
WRITER: BARRY LIEBMANN
Thirty Years Ago Miss Lichtig receives an apple from an anonymous student and shows it to her fellow teachers!
TEACHERS ROOM
TICK TICK TICK
BOMB SQUAD
TO: MS. LICHTIG
BOMB SQUAD
TICK TICK
Today Ms. Lichtig receives a package from an anonymous student and shows it to the bomb squad!
Thirty Years Ago Ed Navis, the class clown, is caught reading Playboy!
PLAYBOY
PLAYBOY
MISS APRIL
Today Mrs. McMahon, the art teacher, is caught posing for Playboy!

In a departure, Dave shared the artist duties with Rick Tulka for this comparison of schools in years gone by with the harsh realities of today. (Guess which era Dave drew?)

Thirty Years Ago **his entire first-grade class groans when Melvin asks the teacher "Didn't you forget to give us homework?"**

DICK DOES JANE

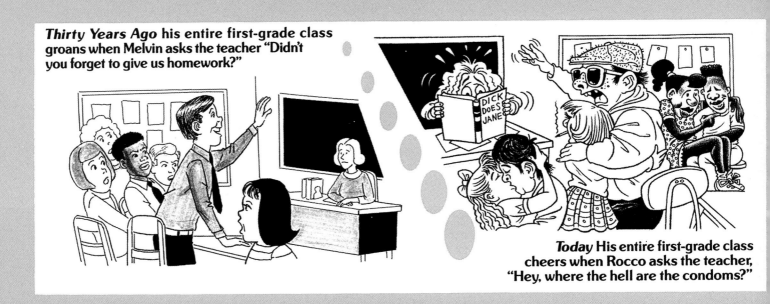

Today **His entire first-grade class cheers when Rocco asks the teacher, "Hey, where the hell are the condoms?"**

Thirty Years Ago **Nurse Dweezel treats the fifth grade's first case of whooping cough!**

FACTS ON BIRTH CONTROL

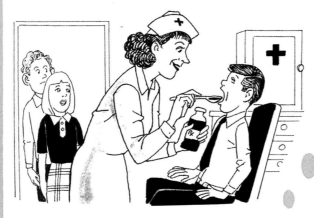

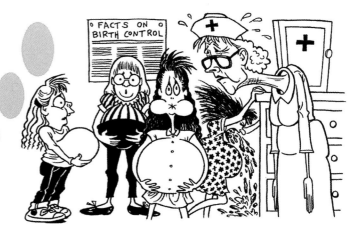

Today **Nurse Dweezel treats the fifth grade's first case of morning sickness!**

Thirty Years Ago **students find mercury, lead, and cobalt on the periodic table!**

Actinium Ac [227] 89
Aluminum Al 26.9815 13
Americium Am [243] 95
Antimony Sb 121.75
Argon Ar 39.948 18
Arsenic As
Astatine At
Barium Ba
Berkelium Bk

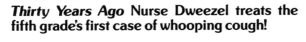

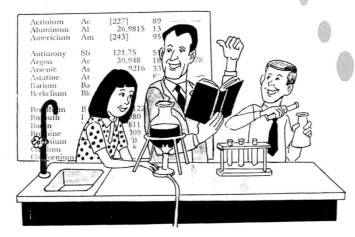

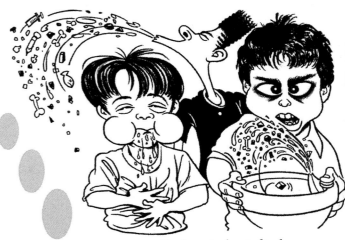

Today **students find mercury, lead, and cobalt in the drinking water!**

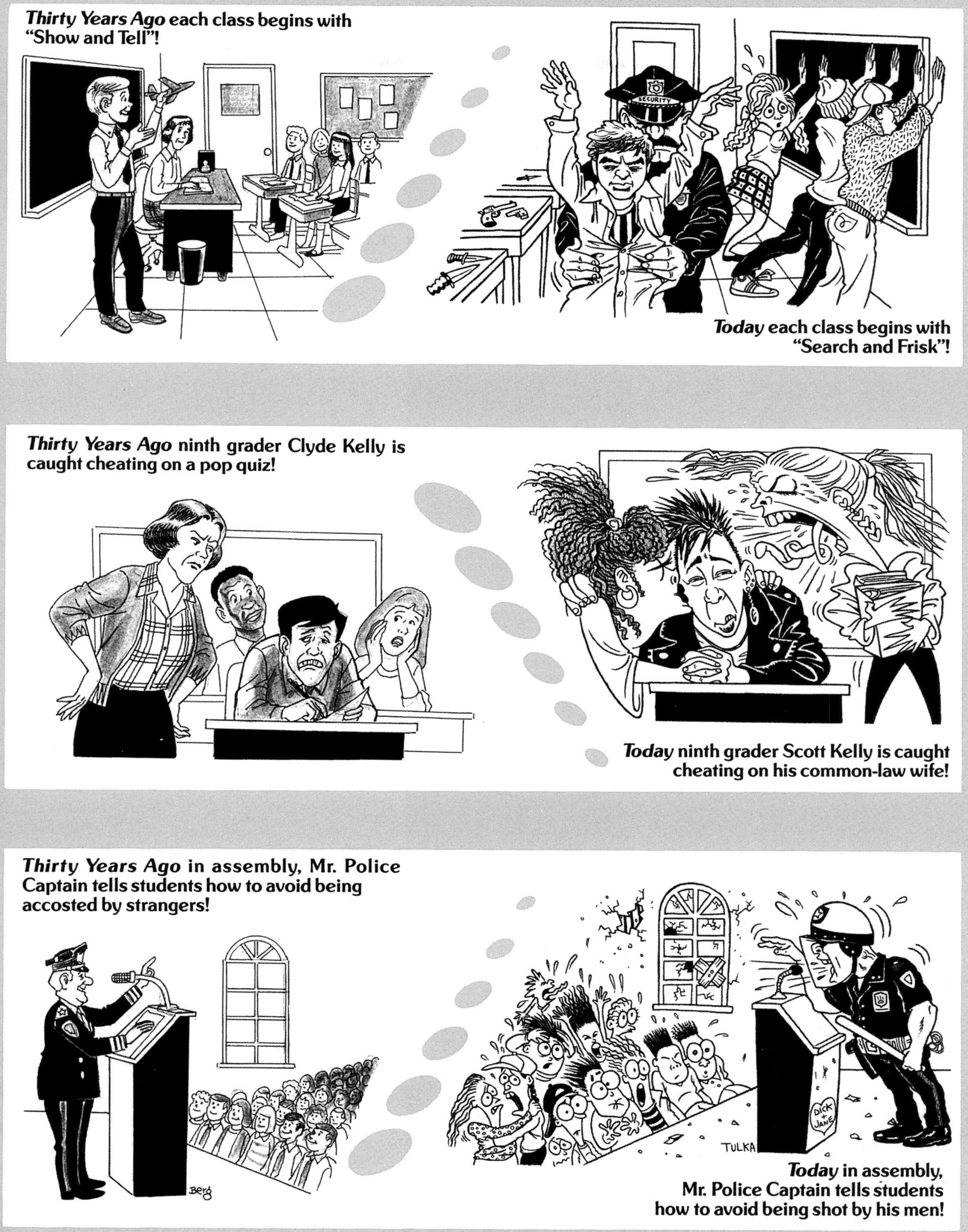
Thirty Years Ago each class begins with "Show and Tell"!
SECURITY
Today each class begins with "Search and Frisk"!
Thirty Years Ago ninth grader Clyde Kelly is caught cheating on a pop quiz!
Today ninth grader Scott Kelly is caught cheating on his common-law wife!
Thirty Years Ago in assembly, Mr. Police Captain tells students how to avoid being accosted by strangers!
Berg
DICK + JANE
TULKA
Today in assembly, Mr. Police Captain tells students how to avoid being shot by his men!

THE UNIVERSE

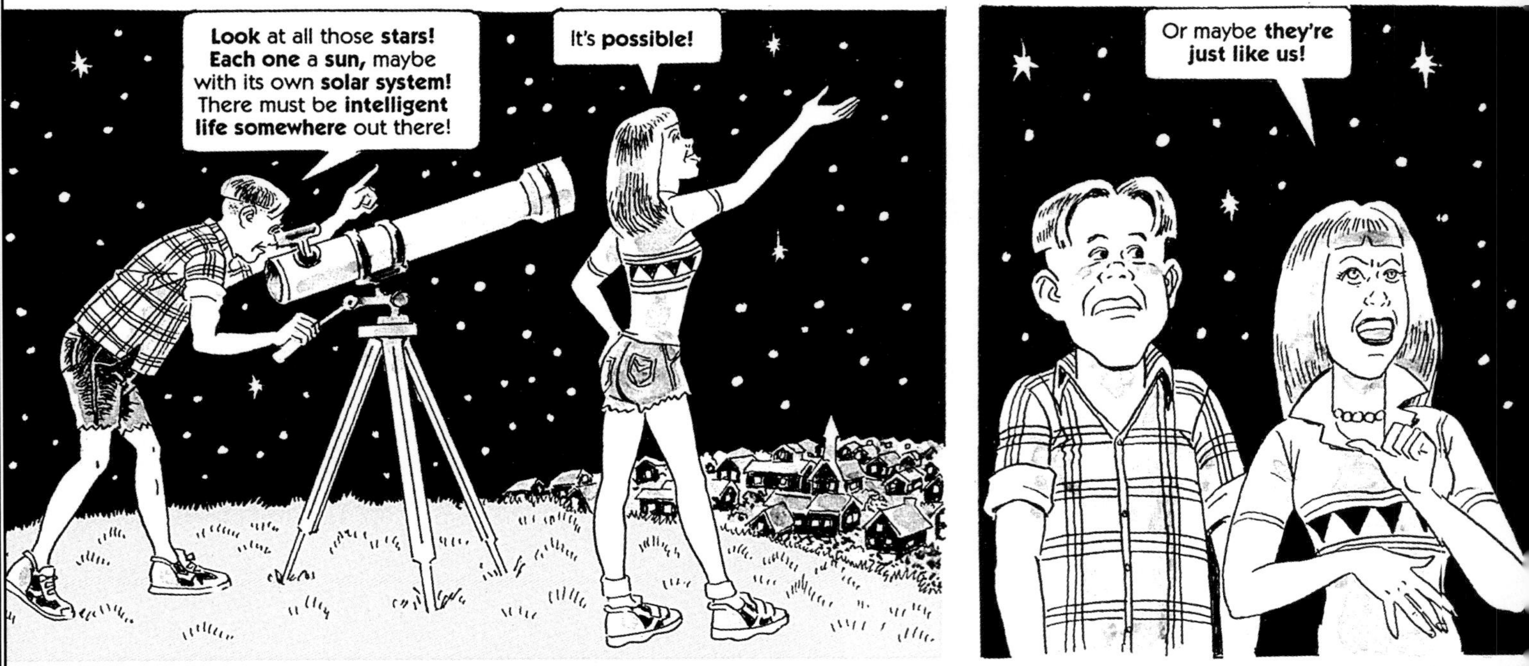
Look at all those stars! Each one a sun, maybe with its own solar system! There must be intelligent life somewhere out there!
It's possible!
Or maybe they're just like us!

BERG'S-EYE VIEW DEPT.

THE LIGHTE

HARMONY

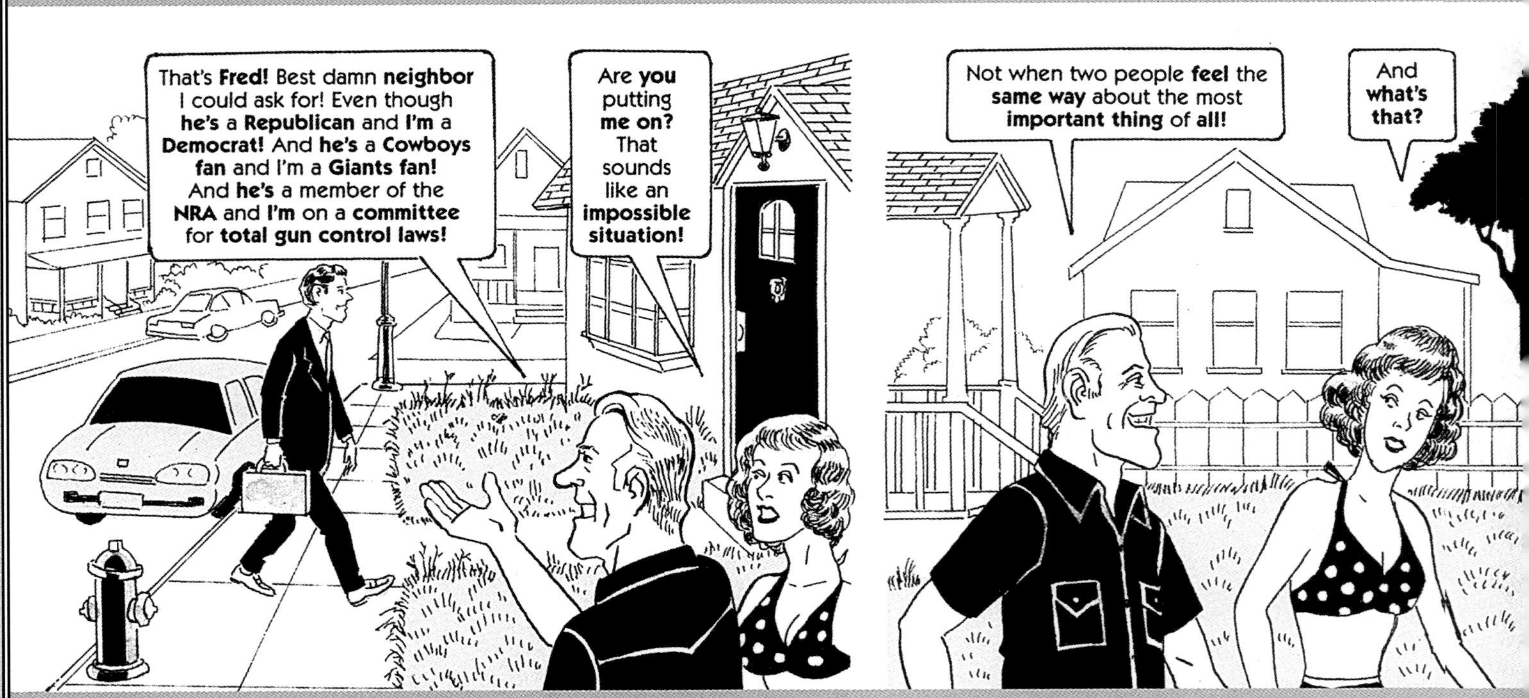
That's Fred! Best damn neighbor I could ask for! Even though he's a Republican and I'm a Democrat! And he's a Cowboys fan and I'm a Giants fan! And he's a member of the NRA and I'm on a committee for total gun control laws!
Are you putting me on? That sounds like an impossible situation!
Not when two people feel the same way about the most important thing of all!
And what's that?

CONCERN

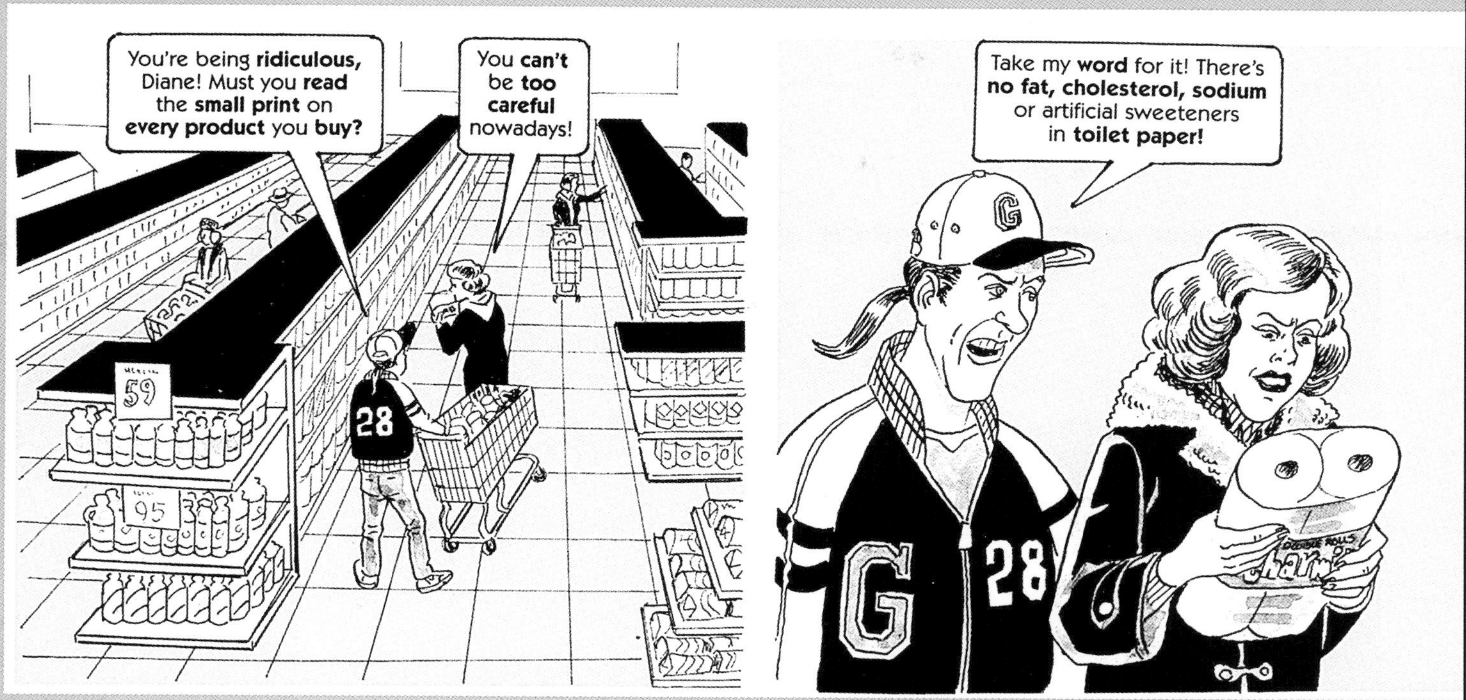
You're being ridiculous, Diane! Must you read the small print on every product you buy?
You can't be too careful nowadays!
Take my word for it! There's no fat, cholesterol, sodium or artificial sweeteners in toilet paper!

R SIDE OF...

ARTIST AND WRITER: DAVE BERG

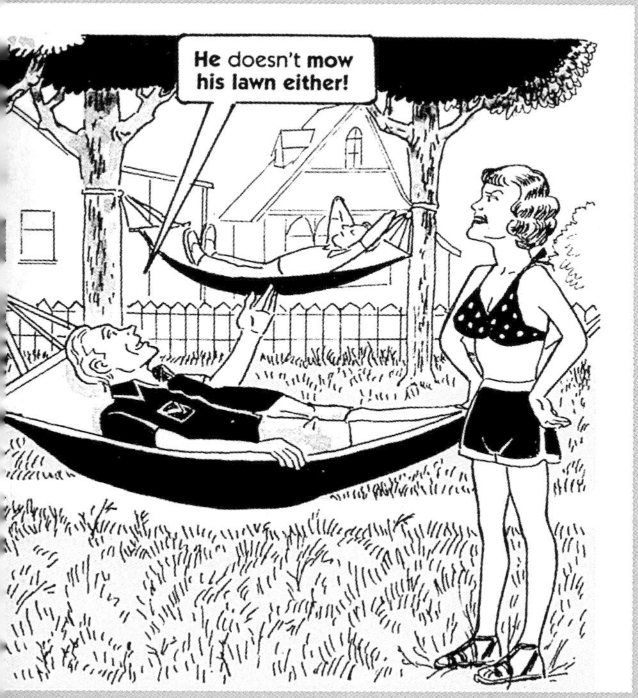
He doesn't mow his lawn either!

INNER PEACE

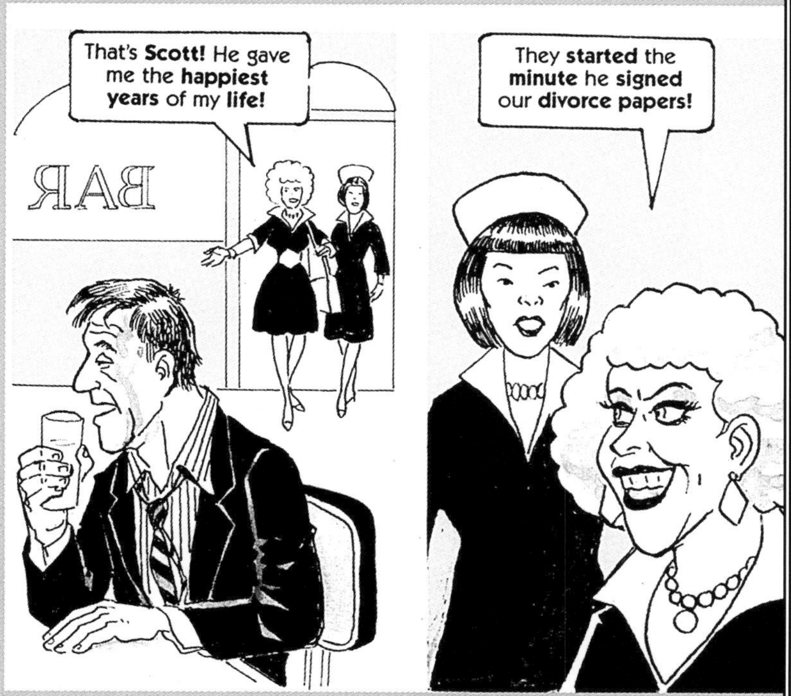
That's Scott! He gave me the happiest years of my life!
They started the minute he signed our divorce papers!

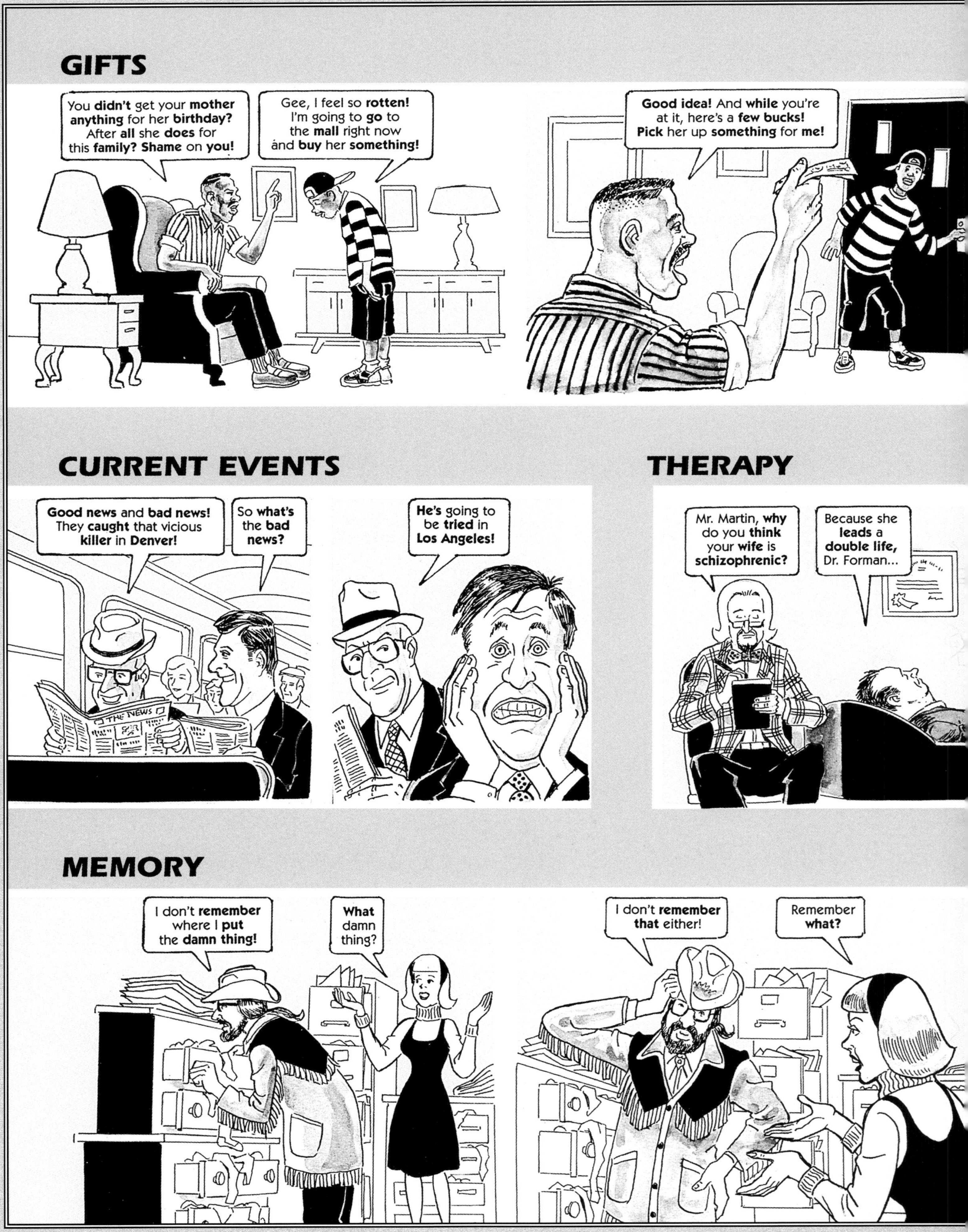
GIFTS
You didn't get your mother anything for her birthday? After all she does for this family? Shame on you!
Gee, I feel so rotten! I'm going to go to the mall right now and buy her something!
Good idea! And while you're at it, here's a few bucks! Pick her up something for me!
CURRENT EVENTS
Good news and bad news! They caught that vicious killer in Denver!
So what's the bad news?
He's going to be tried in Los Angeles!
THE NEWS
THERAPY
Mr. Martin, why do you think your wife is schizophrenic?
Because she leads a double life, Dr. Forman...
MEMORY
I don't remember where I put the damn thing!
What damn thing?
I don't remember that either!
Remember what?

TECHNOLOGY

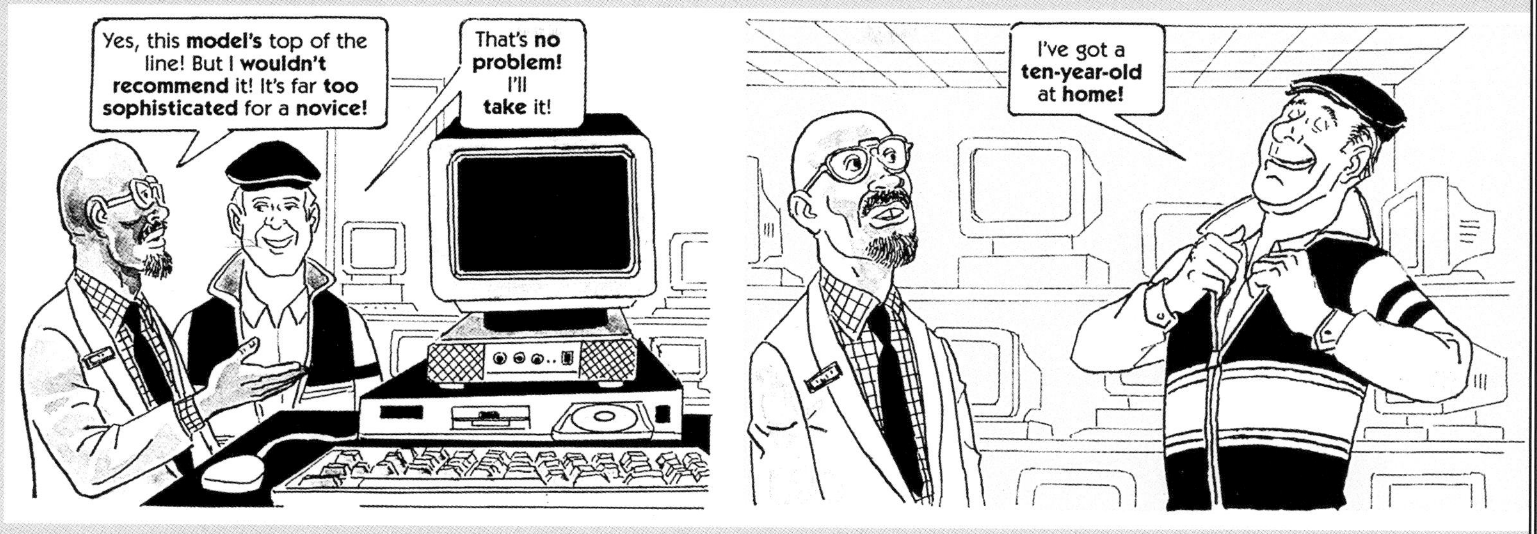
Yes, this model's top of the line! But I wouldn't recommend it! It's far too sophisticated for a novice!
That's no problem! I'll take it!
I've got a ten-year-old at home!

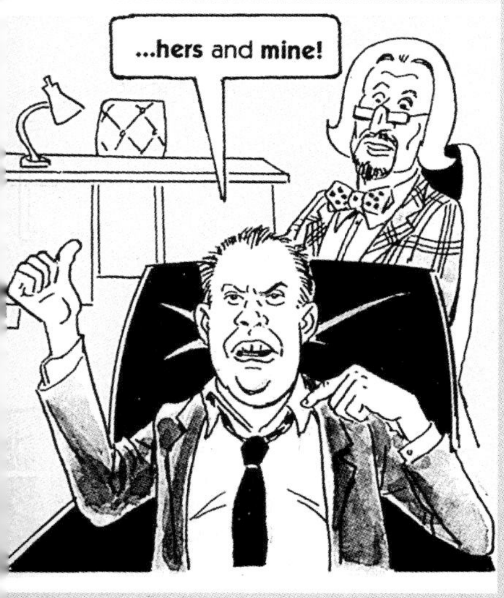
...hers and mine!

ADVANTAGES

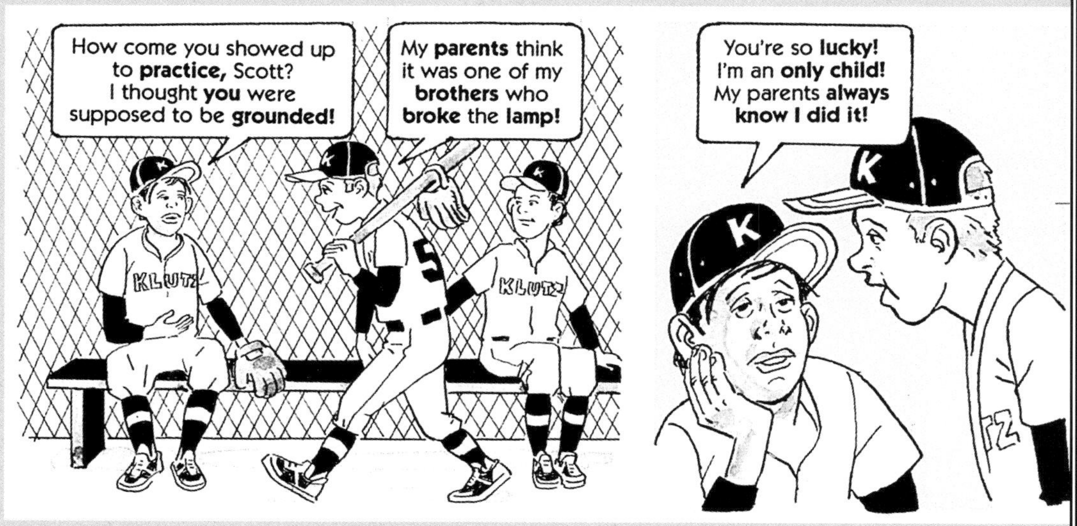
How come you showed up to practice, Scott? I thought you were supposed to be grounded!
My parents think it was one of my brothers who broke the lamp!
KLUTZ
KLUTZ
You're so lucky! I'm an only child! My parents always know I did it!

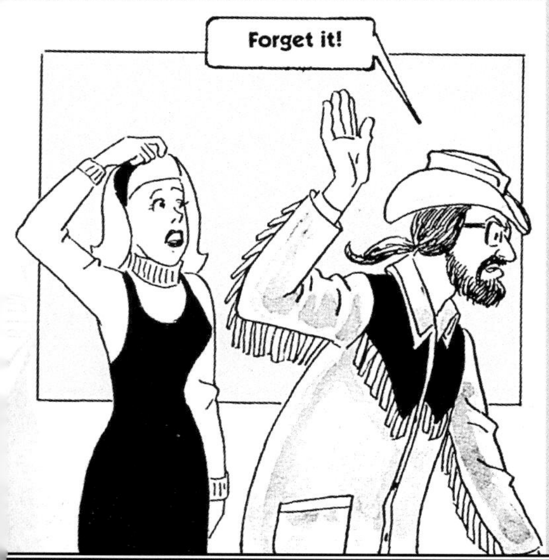
Forget it!

CHILD CARE

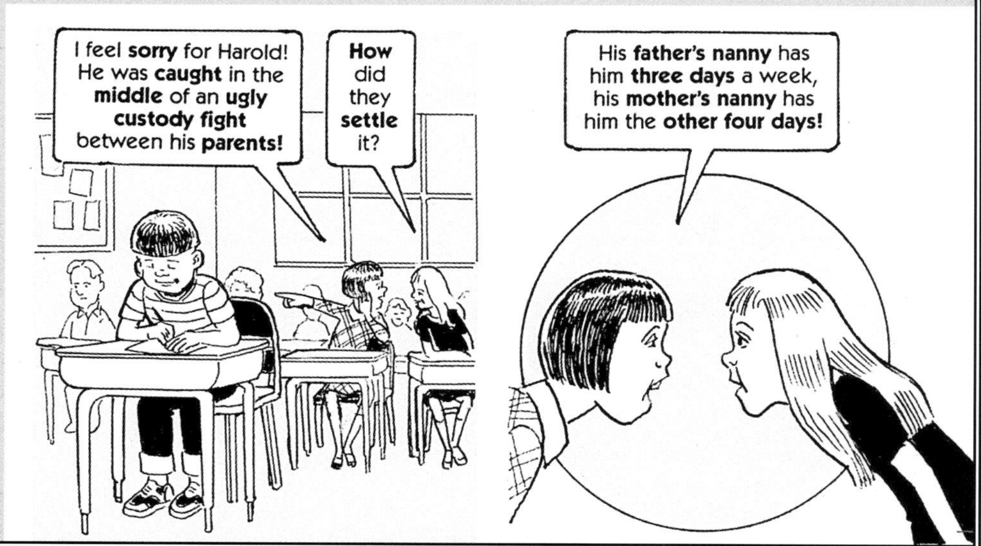
I feel sorry for Harold! He was caught in the middle of an ugly custody fight between his parents!
How did they settle it?
His father's nanny has him three days a week, his mother's nanny has him the other four days!

THE OFFICE

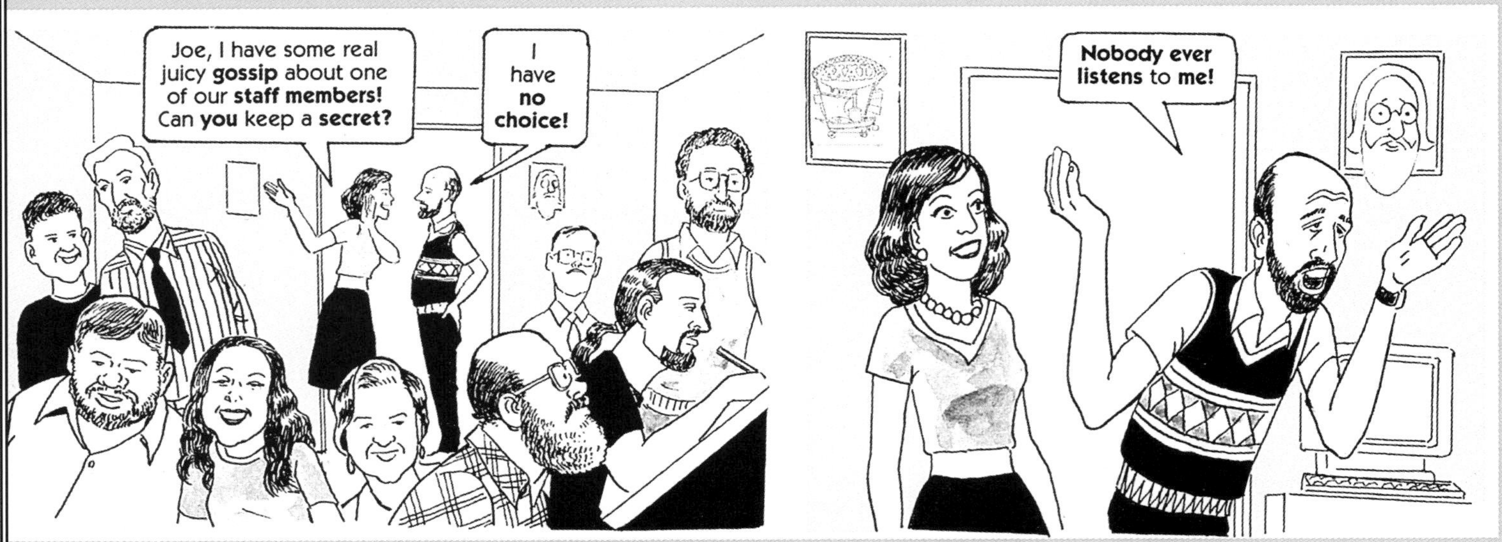
Joe, I have some real juicy **gossip** about one of our **staff members!** Can **you** keep a **secret?**
I have **no choice!**
Nobody ever listens to **me!**

CHEER

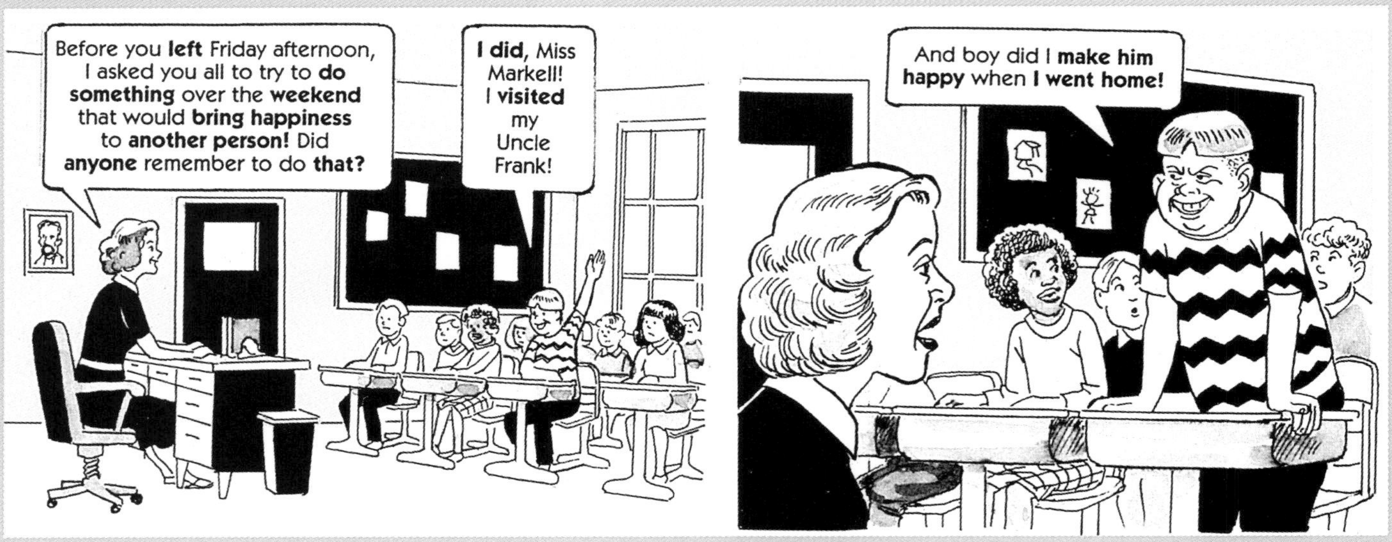
Before you **left** Friday afternoon, I asked you all to try to **do something** over the **weekend** that would **bring happiness** to **another person!** Did **anyone** remember to do **that?**
I did, Miss Markell! I **visited** my Uncle Frank!
And boy did I **make him happy** when **I went home!**

DOCTORS

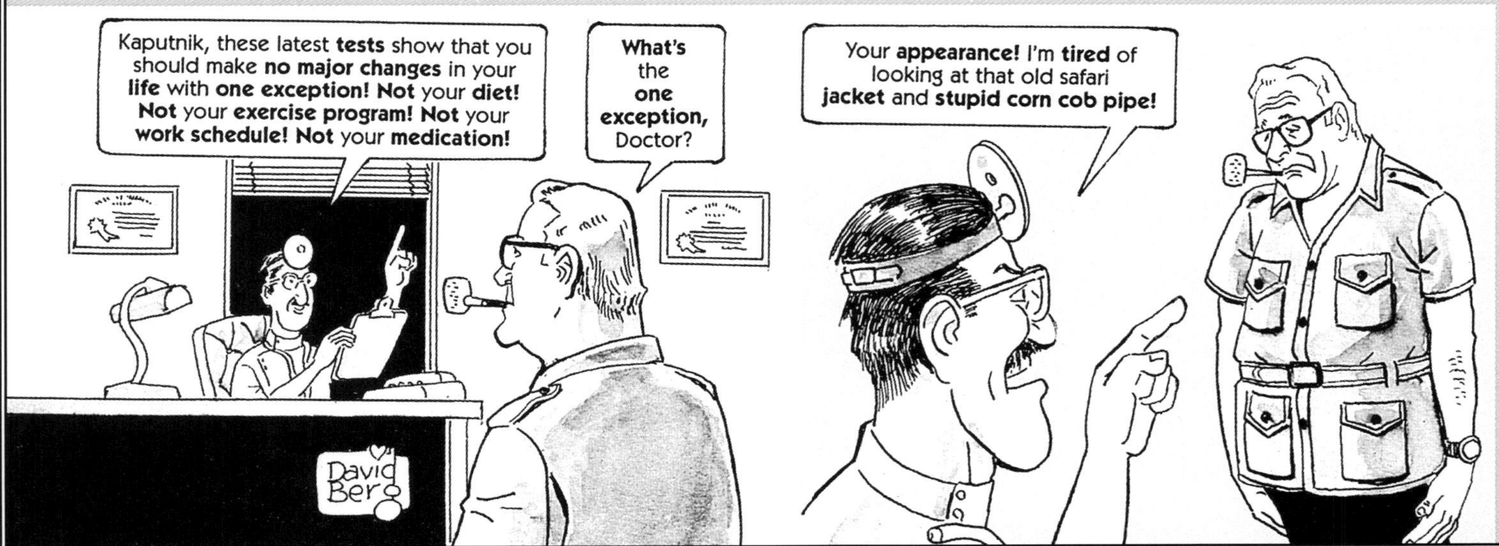
Kaputnik, these latest **tests** show that you should make **no major changes** in your **life** with **one exception! Not** your **diet! Not** your **exercise program! Not** your **work schedule! Not** your **medication!**
What's the **one exception,** Doctor?
Your **appearance!** I'm **tired** of looking at that old safari **jacket** and **stupid corn cob pipe!**
David Berg

BERG'S-EYE VIEW DEPT.

THE LIGHTER SIDE OF...

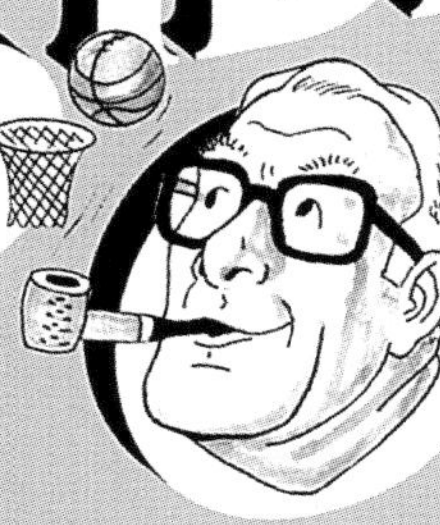

DIFFICULTIES

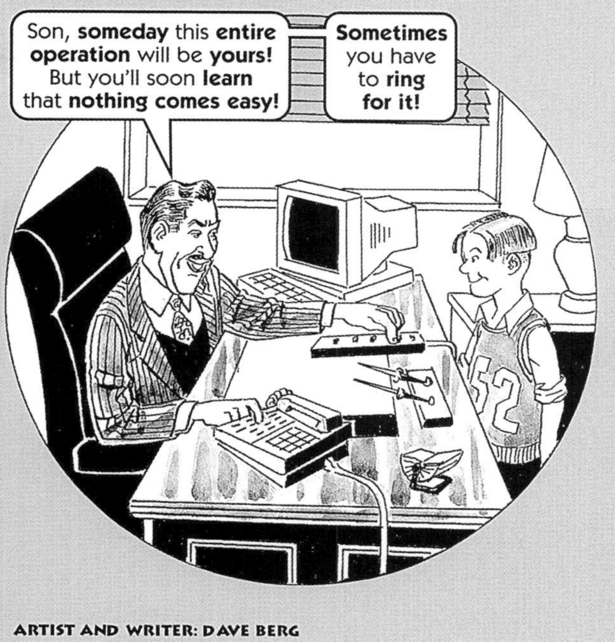
Son, someday this entire operation will be yours! But you'll soon learn that nothing comes easy!
Sometimes you have to ring for it!

ARTIST AND WRITER: DAVE BERG

MUSIC

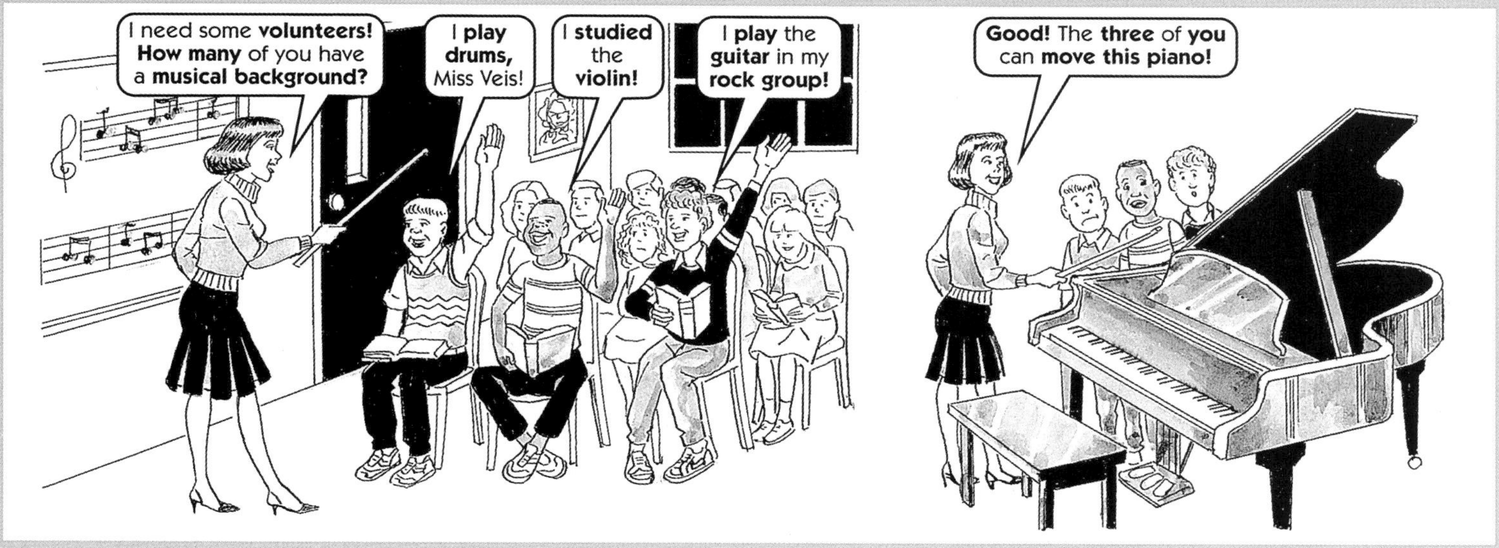
I need some volunteers! How many of you have a musical background?
I play drums, Miss Veis!
I studied the violin!
I play the guitar in my rock group!
Good! The three of you can move this piano!

NEWS

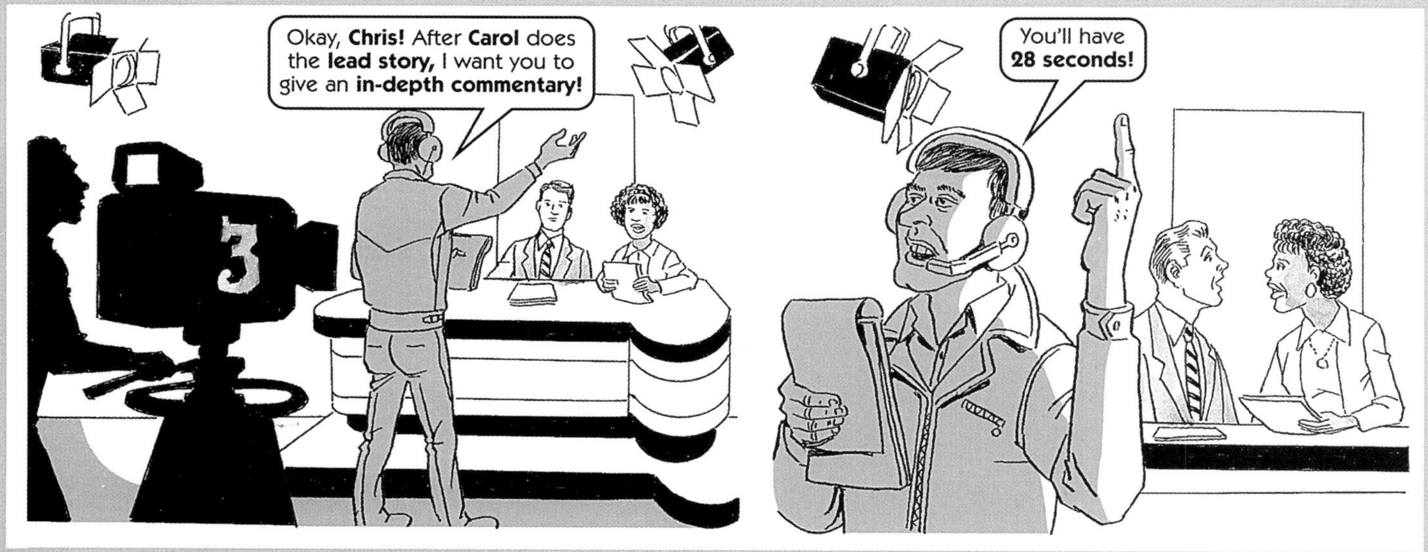
Okay, Chris! After Carol does the lead story, I want you to give an in-depth commentary!
3
You'll have 28 seconds!

MOVING

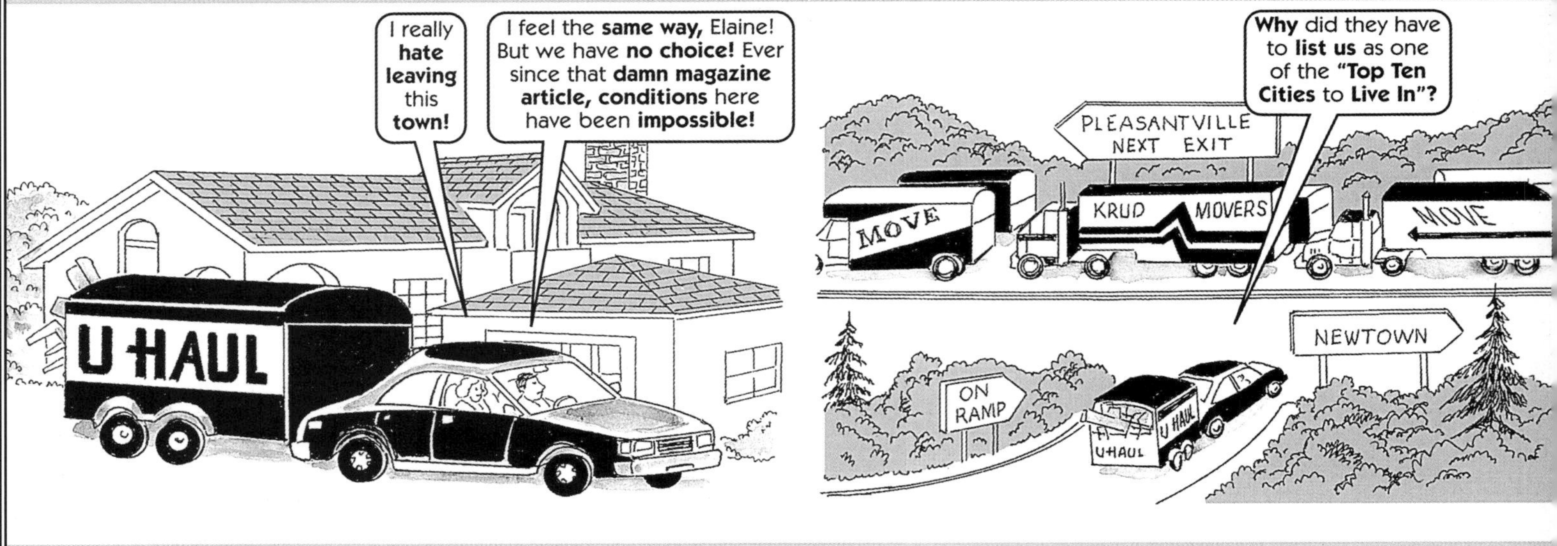
I really hate leaving this town!
I feel the same way, Elaine! But we have no choice! Ever since that damn magazine article, conditions here have been impossible!
U-HAUL
Why did they have to list us as one of the "Top Ten Cities to Live In"?
PLEASANTVILLE NEXT EXIT
MOVE
KRUD MOVERS
MOVE
NEWTOWN
ON RAMP
U-HAUL

RELATIONSHIPS

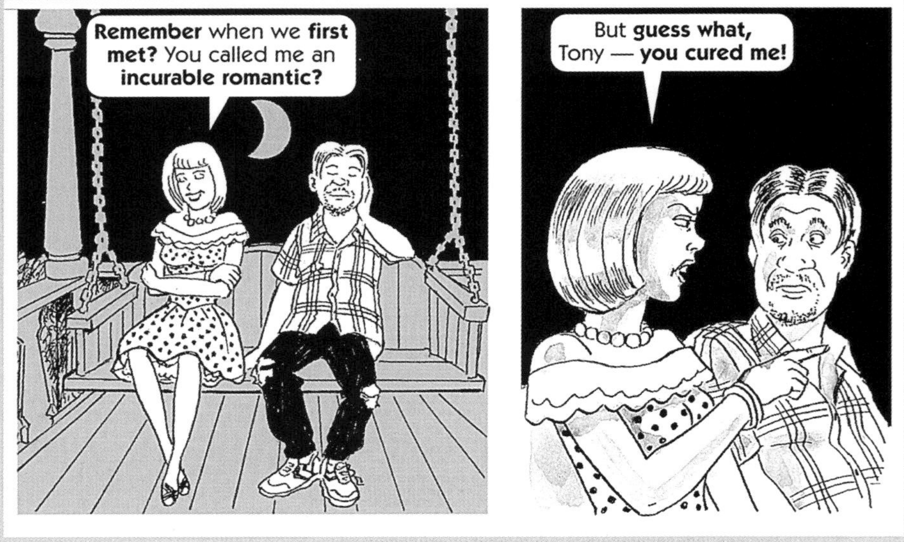
Remember when we first met? You called me an incurable romantic?
But guess what, Tony — you cured me!

SUPPORT

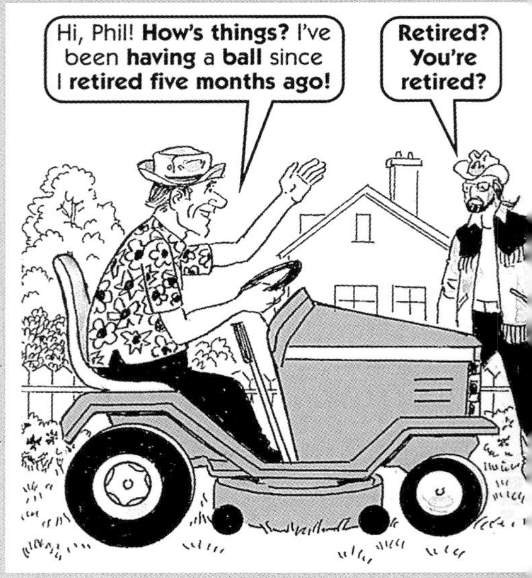
Hi, Phil! How's things? I've been having a ball since I retired five months ago!
Retired? You're retired?

DINNER

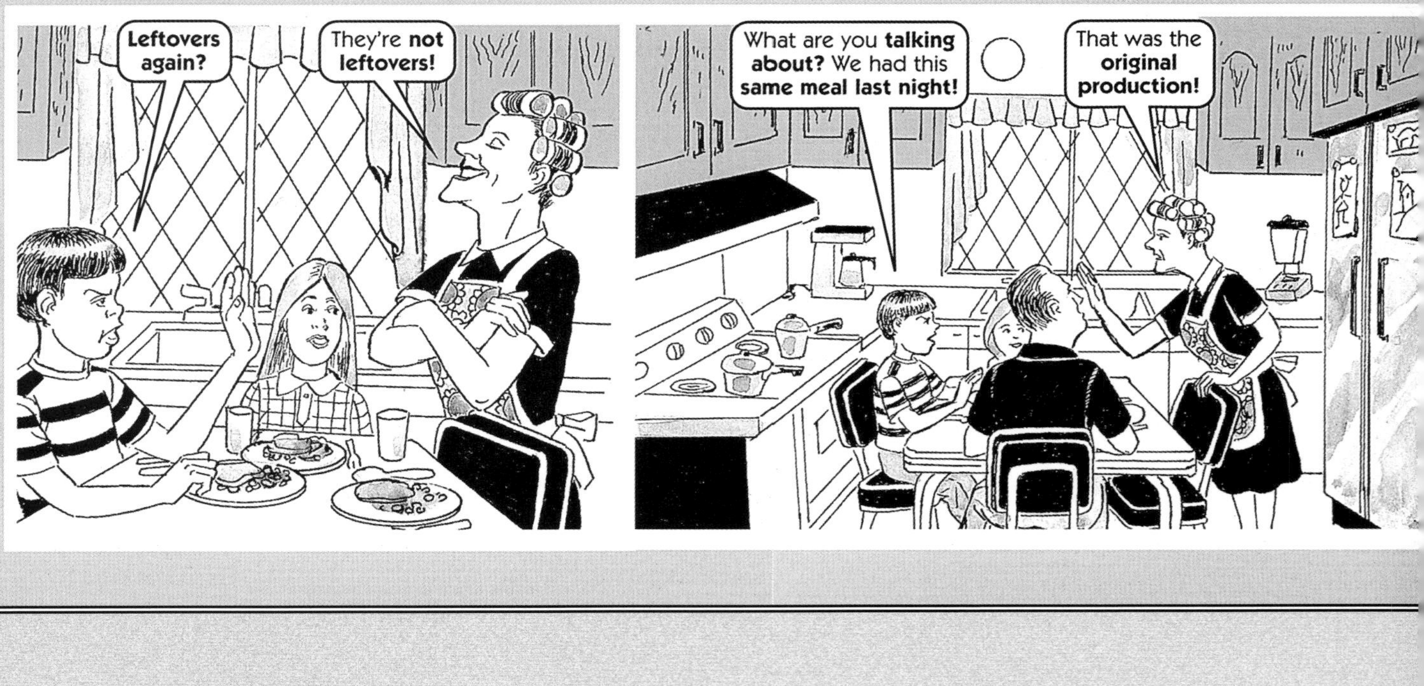
Leftovers again?
They're not leftovers!
What are you talking about? We had this same meal last night!
That was the original production!

ACHIEVEMENT

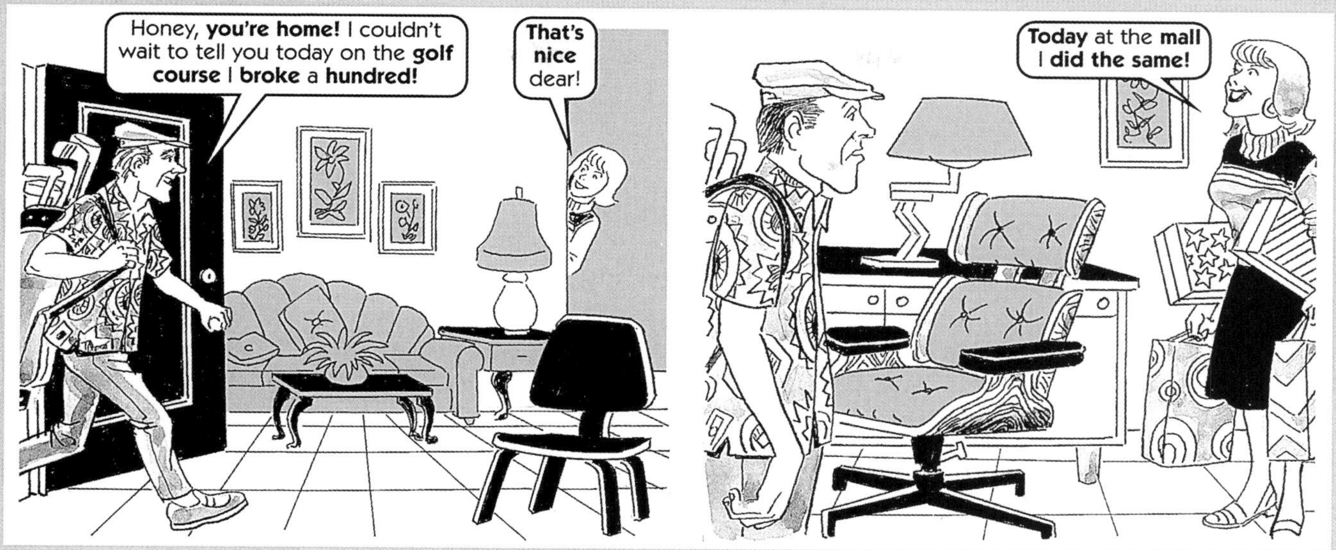
Honey, **you're home!** I couldn't wait to tell you today on the **golf course** I **broke** a **hundred!**
That's nice dear!
Today at the **mall** I **did the same!**

THERAPY

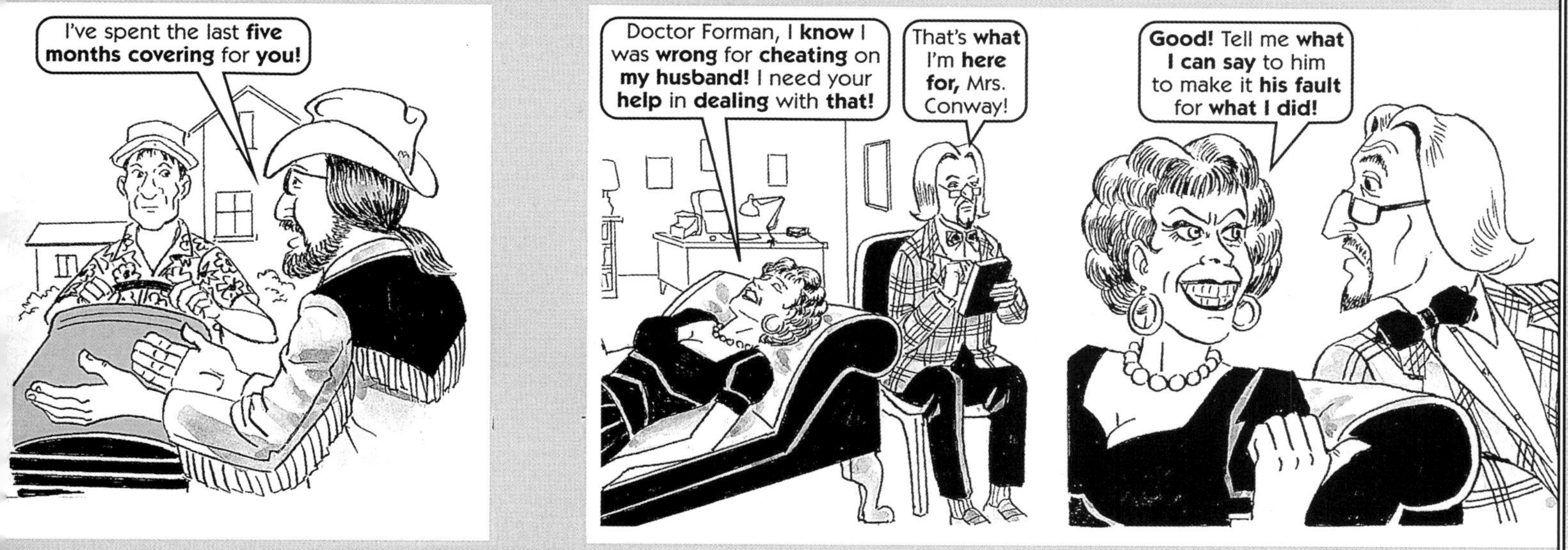
I've spent the last **five months covering** for **you!**
Doctor Forman, I **know** I was **wrong** for **cheating** on **my husband!** I need your **help** in **dealing** with **that!**
That's **what** I'm **here for,** Mrs. Conway!
Good! Tell me **what I can say** to him to make it **his fault** for **what I did!**

GIFTS

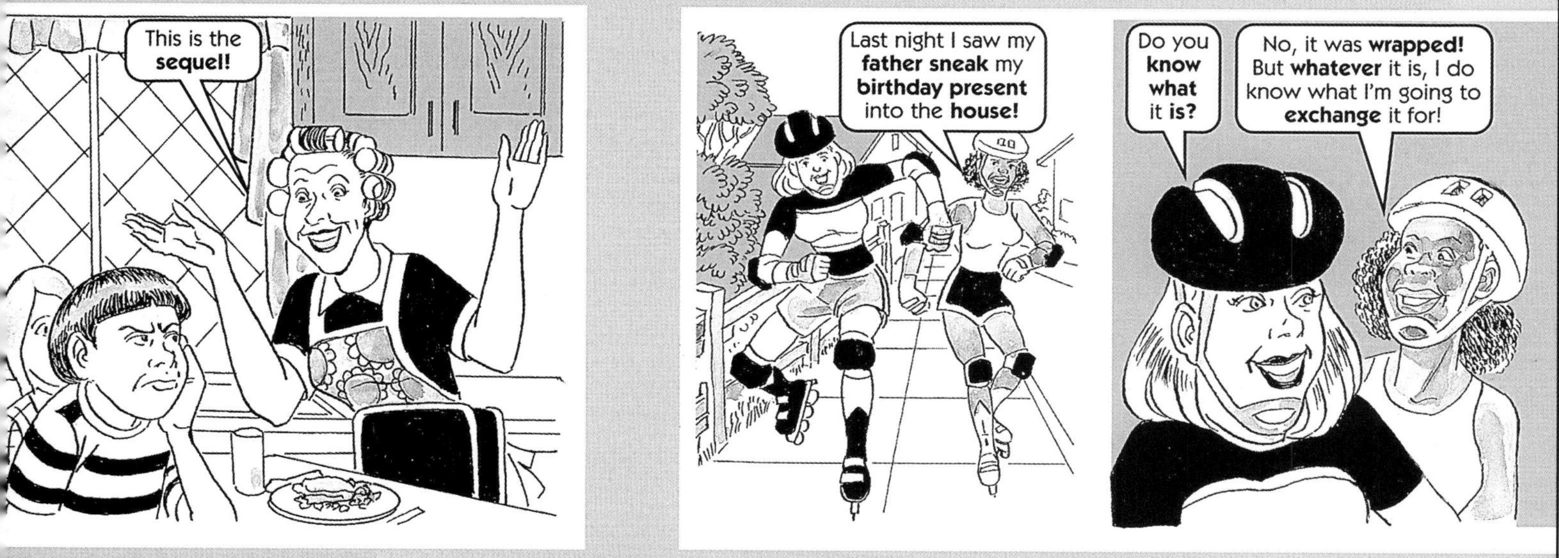
This is the **sequel!**
Last night I saw my **father sneak** my **birthday present** into the **house!**
Do you **know what** it **is?**
No, it was **wrapped!** But **whatever** it is, I do know what I'm going to **exchange** it for!

THE OFFICE

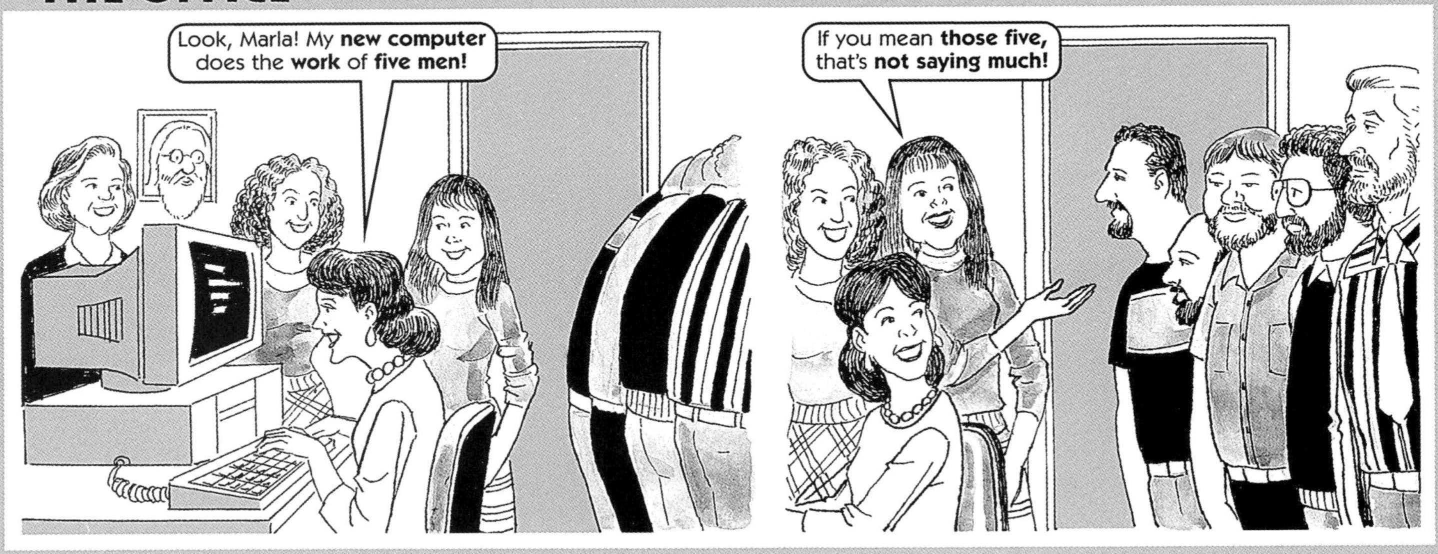
Look, Marla! My new computer does the work of five men!
If you mean those five, that's not saying much!

MATURITY

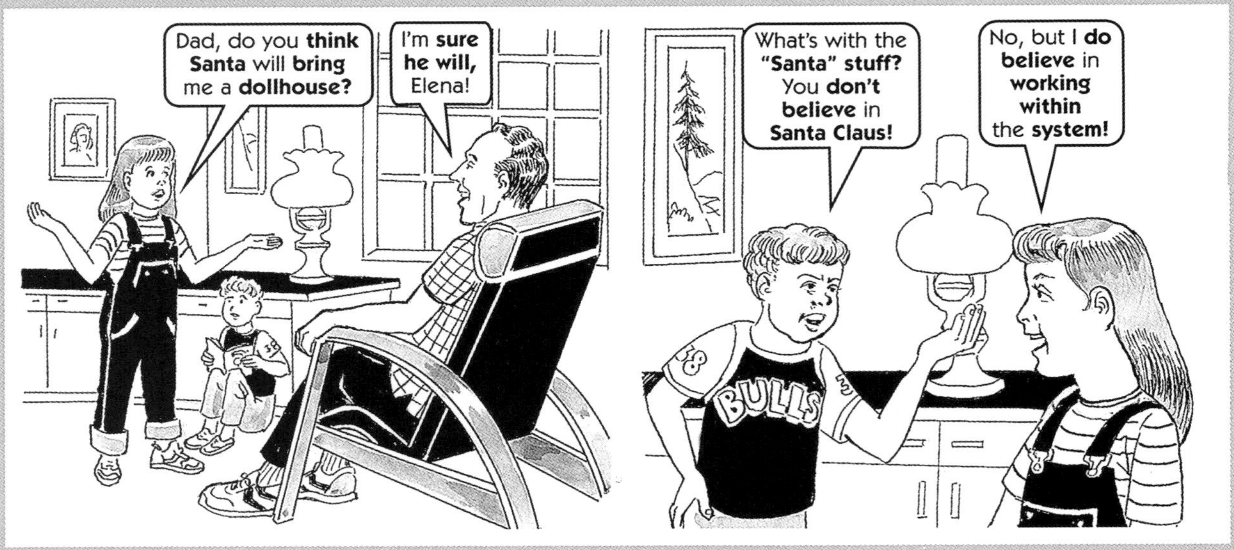
Dad, do you think Santa will bring me a dollhouse?
I'm sure he will, Elena!
BULLS
What's with the "Santa" stuff? You don't believe in Santa Claus!
No, but I do believe in working within the system!

DOCTORS

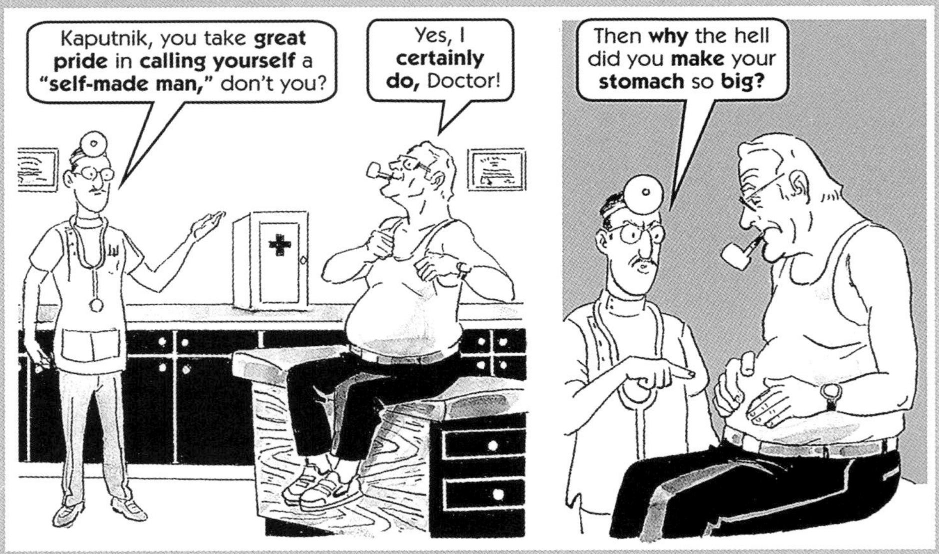
Kaputnik, you take great pride in calling yourself a "self-made man," don't you?
Yes, I certainly do, Doctor!
Then why the hell did you make your stomach so big?

POLITICS

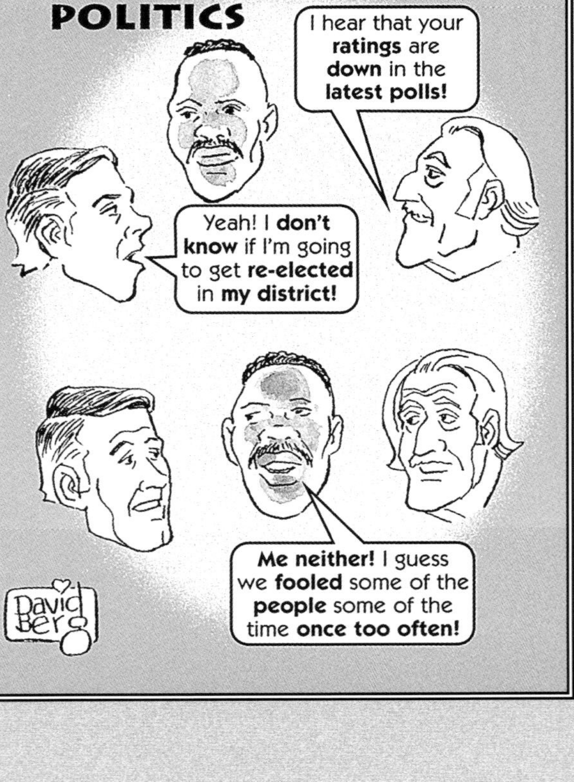
I hear that your ratings are down in the latest polls!
Yeah! I don't know if I'm going to get re-elected in my district!
Me neither! I guess we fooled some of the people some of the time once too often!
David Berg

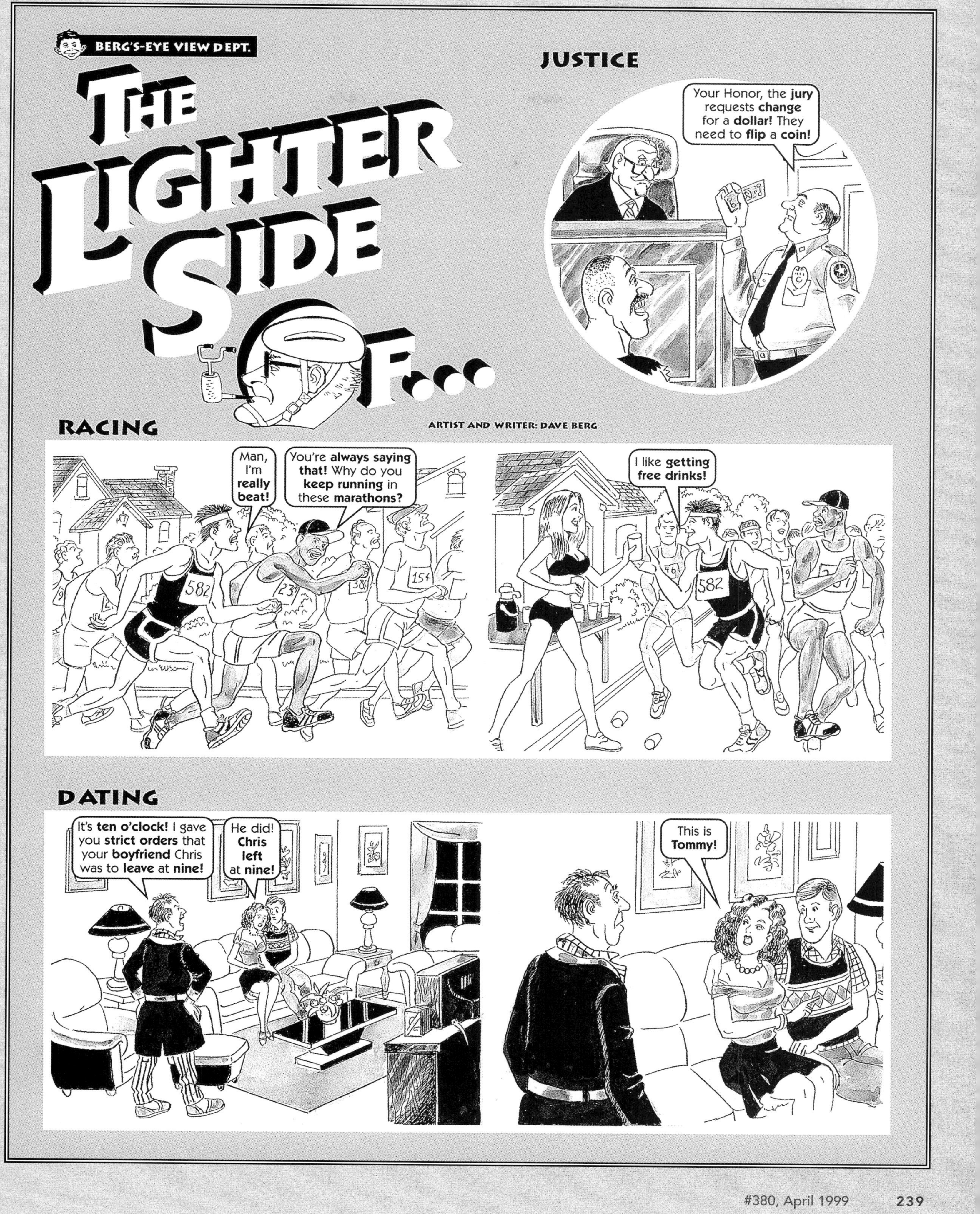
BERG'S-EYE VIEW DEPT.
THE LIGHTER SIDE OF...
JUSTICE
Your Honor, the jury requests change for a dollar! They need to flip a coin!
RACING
ARTIST AND WRITER: DAVE BERG
Man, I'm really beat!
You're always saying that! Why do you keep running in these marathons?
I like getting free drinks!
DATING
It's ten o'clock! I gave you strict orders that your boyfriend Chris was to leave at nine!
He did! Chris left at nine!
This is Tommy!

PRAYERS

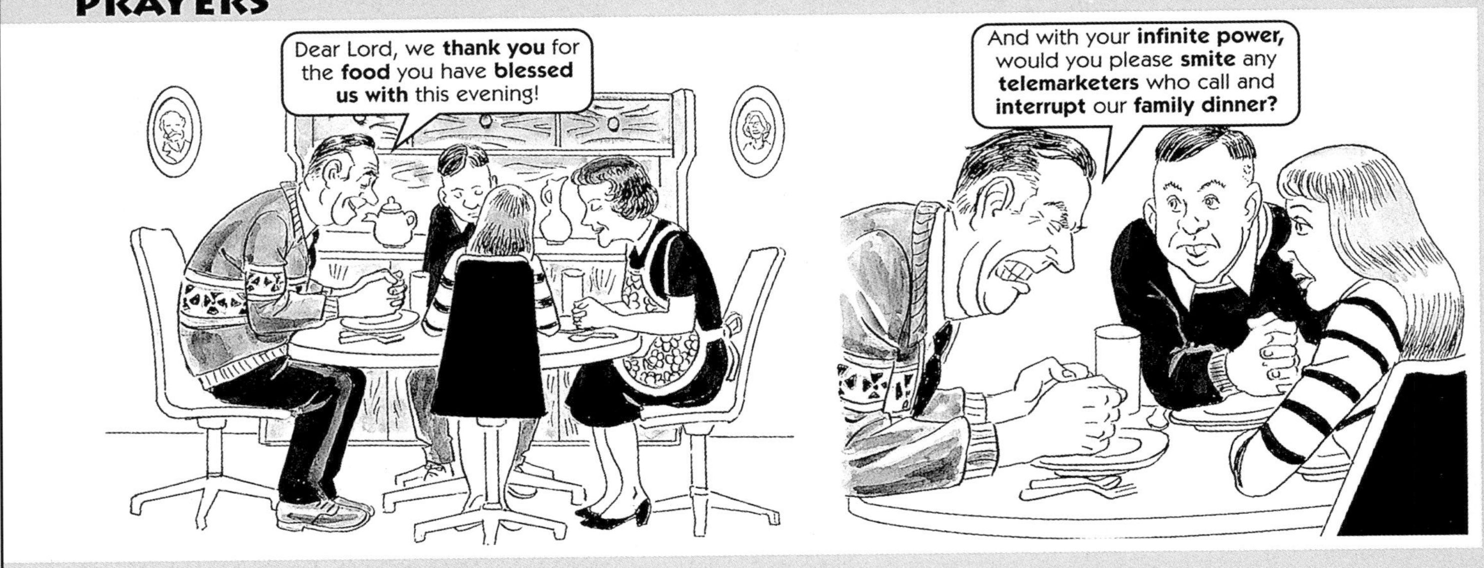
Dear Lord, we thank you for the food you have blessed us with this evening!
And with your infinite power, would you please smite any telemarketers who call and interrupt our family dinner?

THERAPY

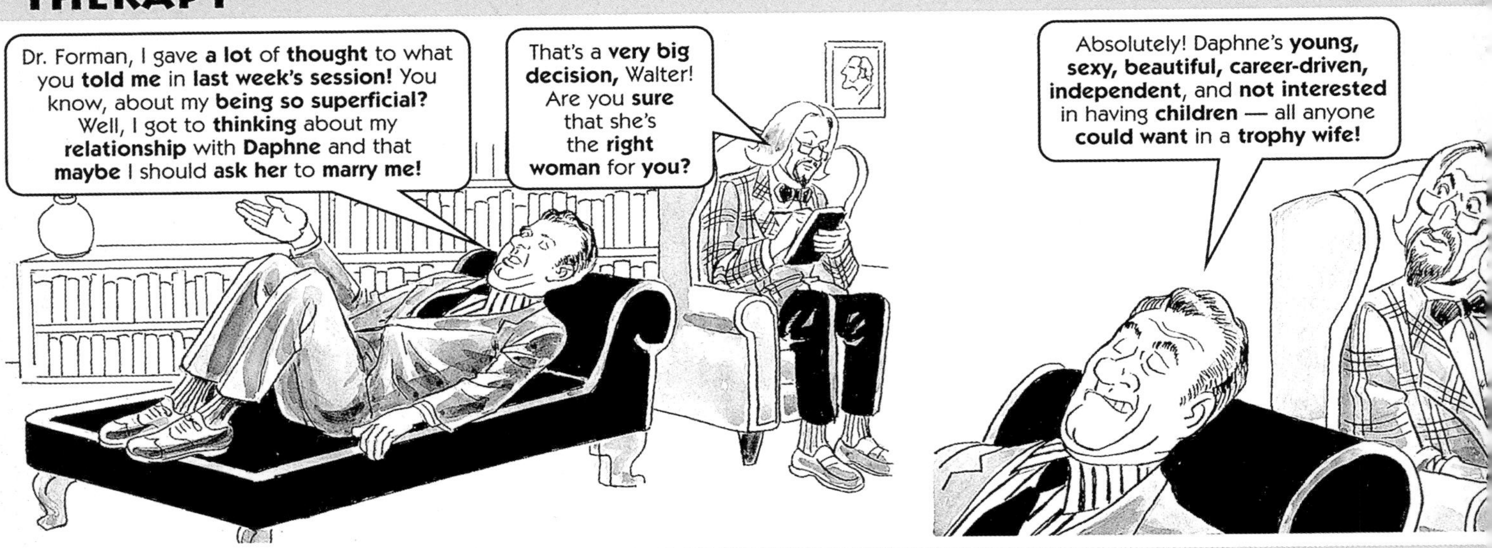
Dr. Forman, I gave a lot of thought to what you told me in last week's session! You know, about my being so superficial? Well, I got to thinking about my relationship with Daphne and that maybe I should ask her to marry me!
That's a very big decision, Walter! Are you sure that she's the right woman for you?
Absolutely! Daphne's young, sexy, beautiful, career-driven, independent, and not interested in having children — all anyone could want in a trophy wife!

FLYING

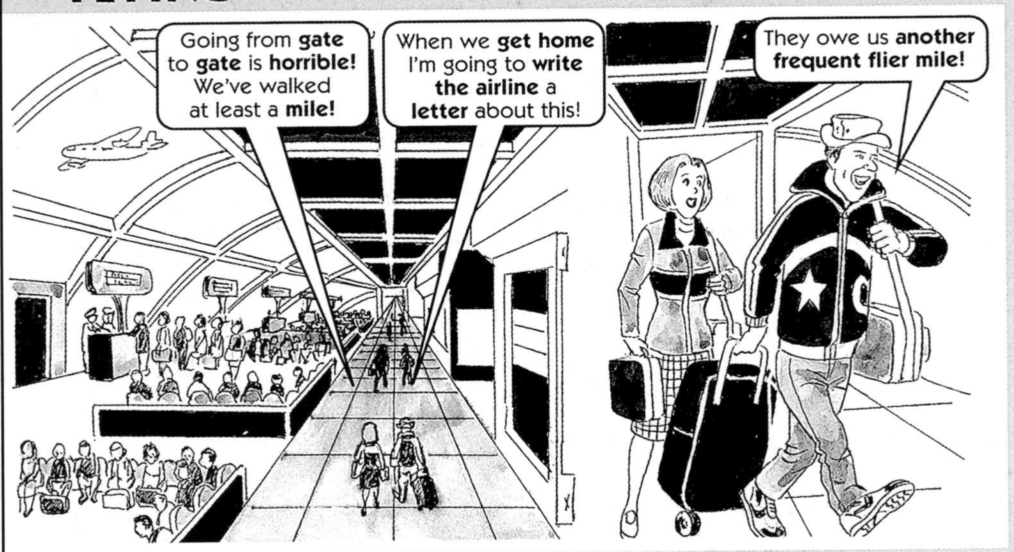
Going from gate to gate is horrible! We've walked at least a mile!
When we get home I'm going to write the airline a letter about this!
They owe us another frequent flier mile!

CREATIVITY

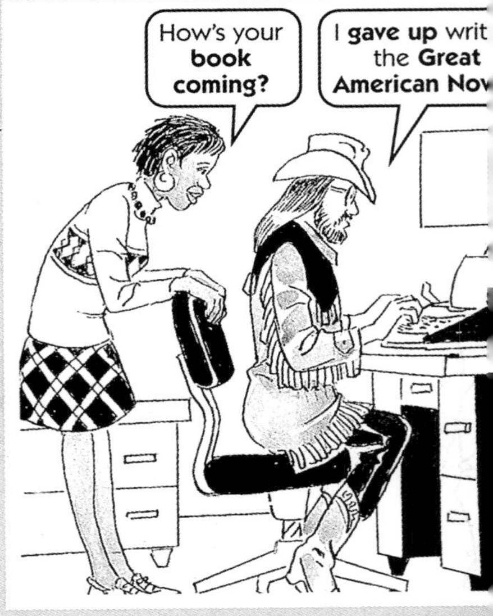
How's your book coming?

SPORTS

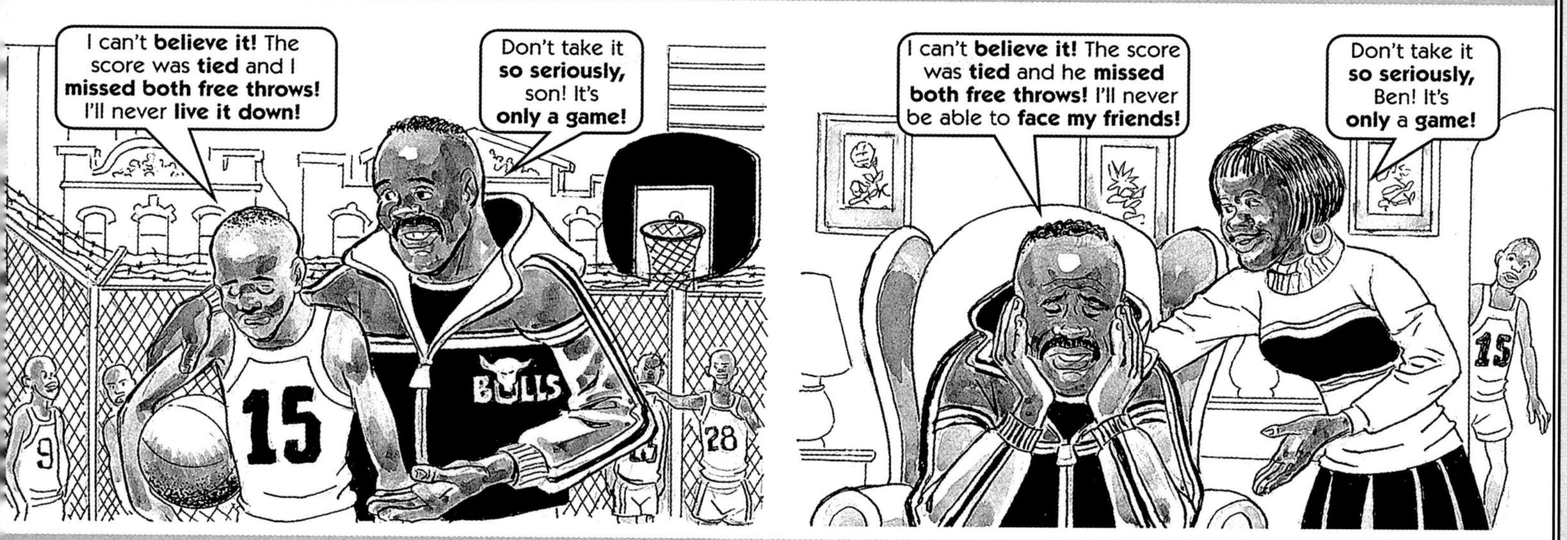
I can't believe it! The score was tied and I missed both free throws! I'll never live it down!
Don't take it so seriously, son! It's only a game!
BULLS
15
9
28
I can't believe it! The score was tied and he missed both free throws! I'll never be able to face my friends!
Don't take it so seriously, Ben! It's only a game!
15

RELATIONSHIPS

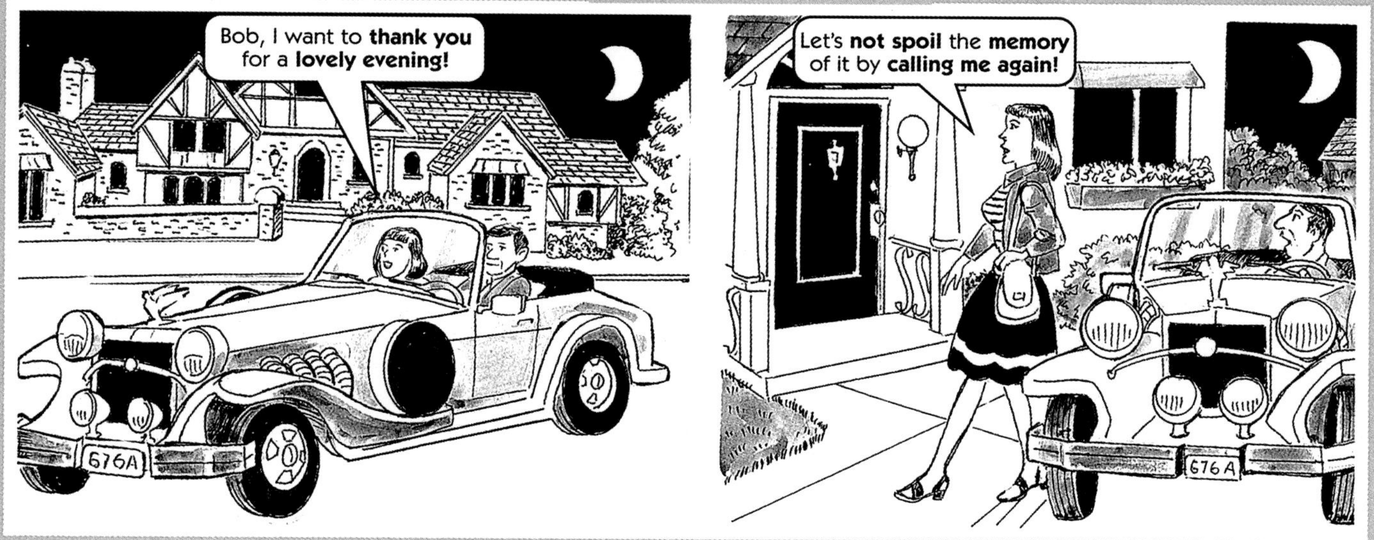
Bob, I want to thank you for a lovely evening!
676A
Let's not spoil the memory of it by calling me again!
676 A

ENLIGHTENMENT

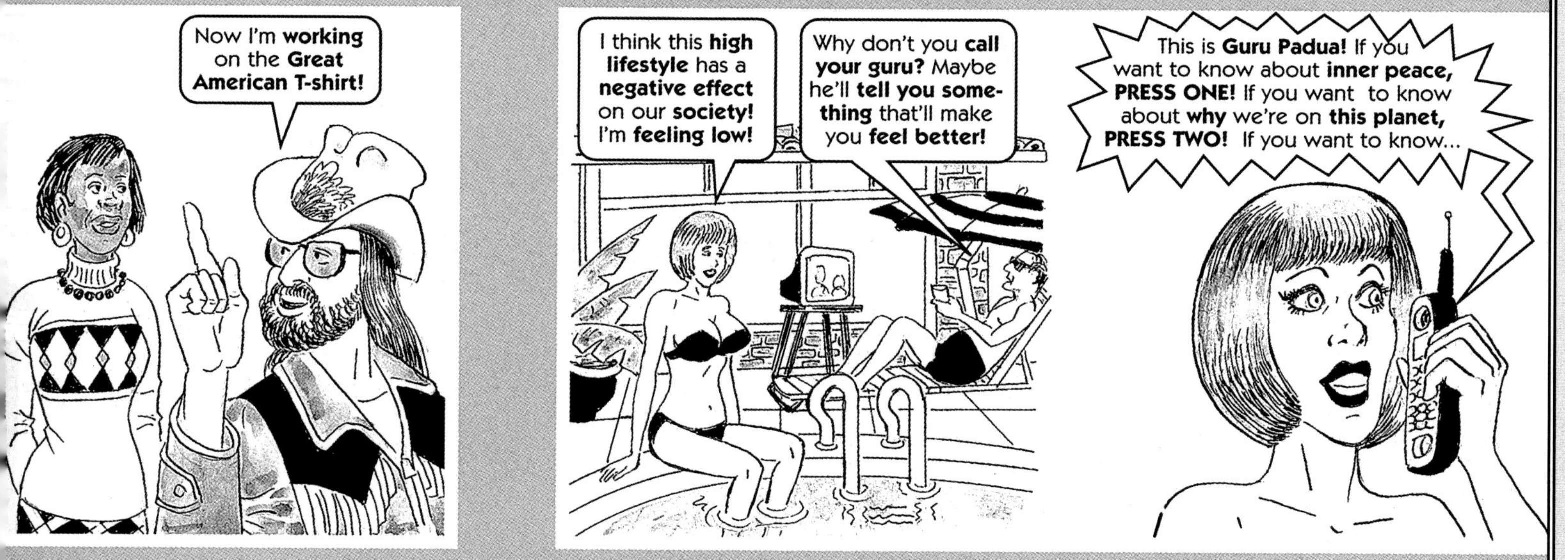
Now I'm working on the Great American T-shirt!
I think this high lifestyle has a negative effect on our society! I'm feeling low!
Why don't you call your guru? Maybe he'll tell you something that'll make you feel better!
This is Guru Padua! If you want to know about inner peace, PRESS ONE! If you want to know about why we're on this planet, PRESS TWO! If you want to know...

THE OFFICE

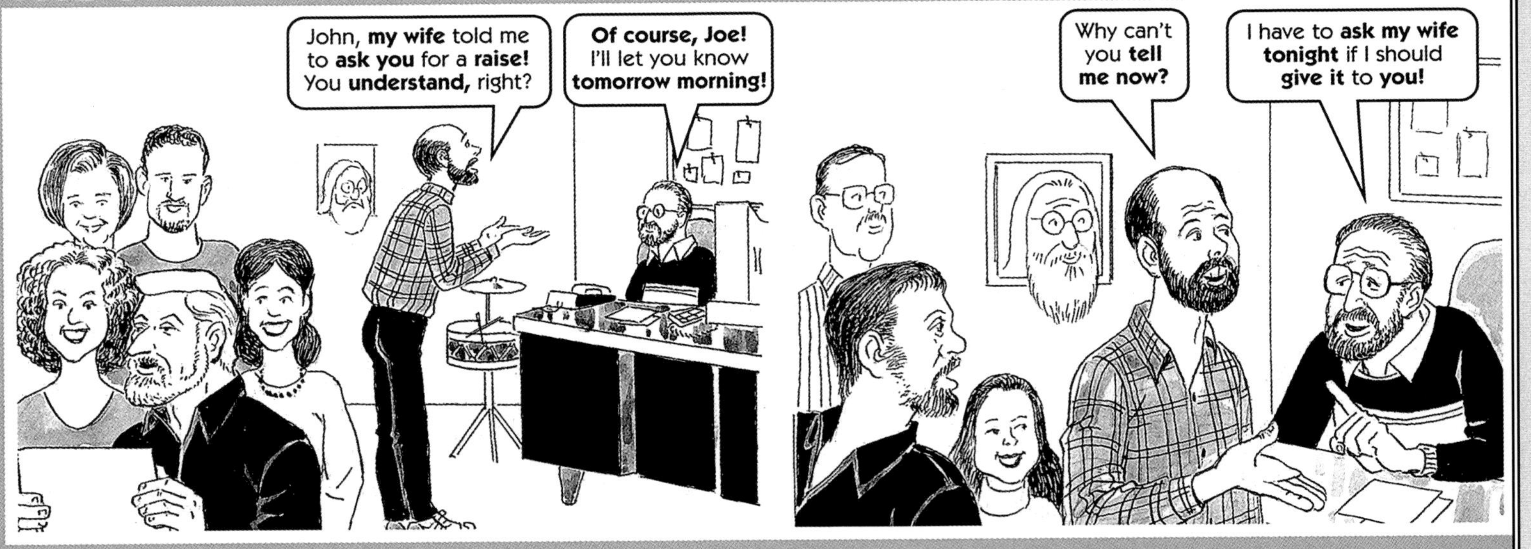
John, my wife told me to ask you for a raise! You understand, right?
Of course, Joe! I'll let you know tomorrow morning!
Why can't you tell me now?
I have to ask my wife tonight if I should give it to you!

FASHION

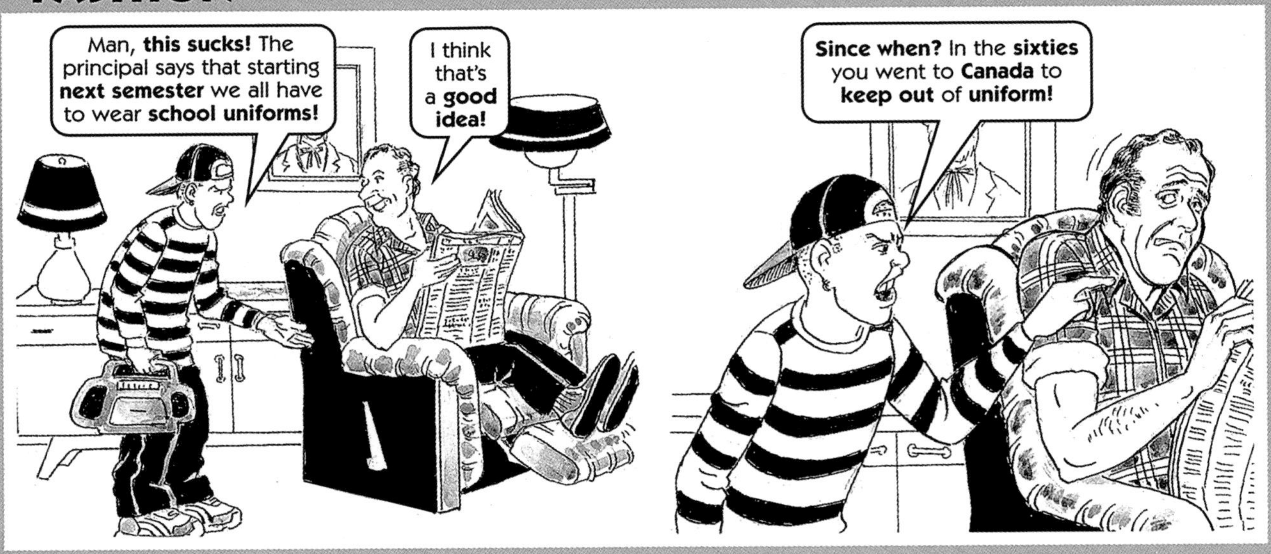
Man, this sucks! The principal says that starting next semester we all have to wear school uniforms!
I think that's a good idea!
Since when? In the sixties you went to Canada to keep out of uniform!

DOCTORS

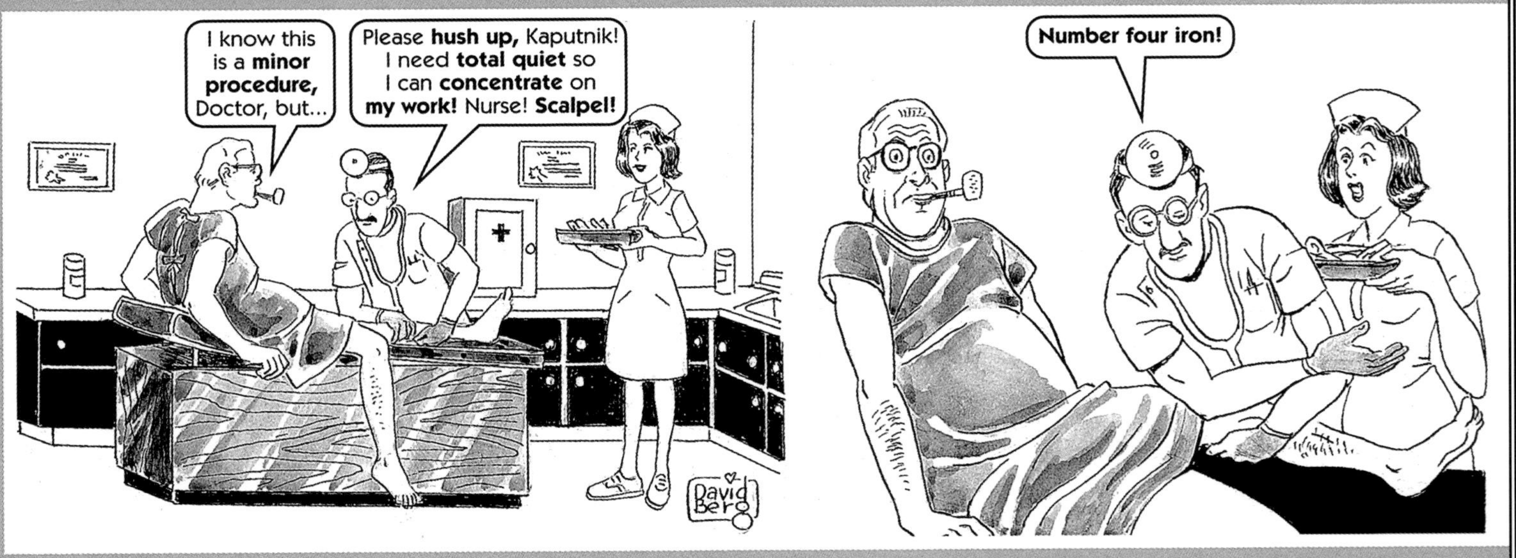
I know this is a minor procedure, Doctor, but...
Please hush up, Kaputnik! I need total quiet so I can concentrate on my work! Nurse! Scalpel!
David Berg
Number four iron!

The 2000s

Dave Berg in Japanese

MAD magazines and books are available across the globe, though in this Asian version we don't know if "The Lighter Side of..." is being presented for purely entertaining purposes or is part of an "English as a second corny language" program.

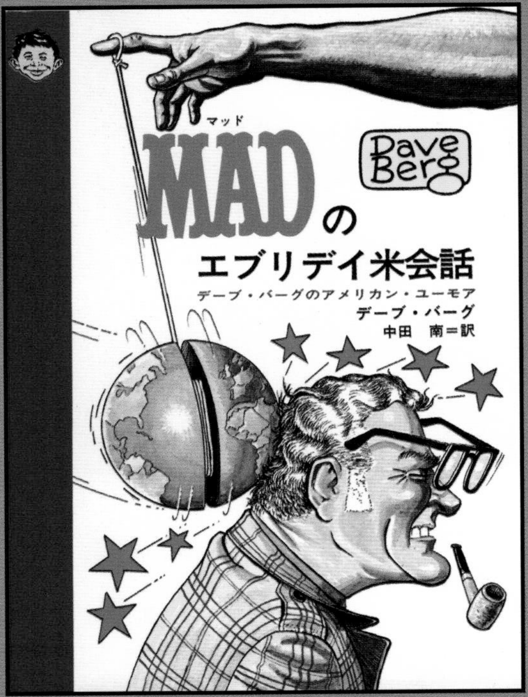

マッド
MAD
Dave Berg
の
エブリデイ米会話
デーブ・バーグのアメリカン・ユーモア
デーブ・バーグ
中田　南＝訳

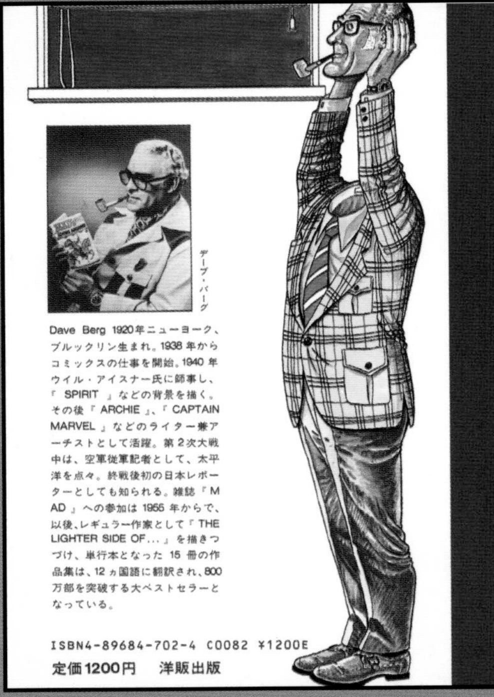

デーブ・バーグ
Dave Berg 1920年ニューヨーク、ブルックリン生まれ。1938年からコミックスの仕事を開始。1940年ウイル・アイスナー氏に師事し、『SPIRIT』などの背景を描く。その後『ARCHIE』、『CAPTAIN MARVEL』などのライター兼アーチストとして活躍。第2次大戦中は、空軍従軍記者として、太平洋を点々。終戦後初の日本レポーターとしても知られる。雑誌『MAD』への参加は1955年からで、以後、レギュラー作家として『THE LIGHTER SIDE OF...』を描きつづけ、単行本となった15冊の作品集は、12ヵ国語に翻訳され、800万部を突破する大ベストセラーとなっている。
ISBN4-89684-702-4 C0082 ¥1200E
定価1200円　洋販出版

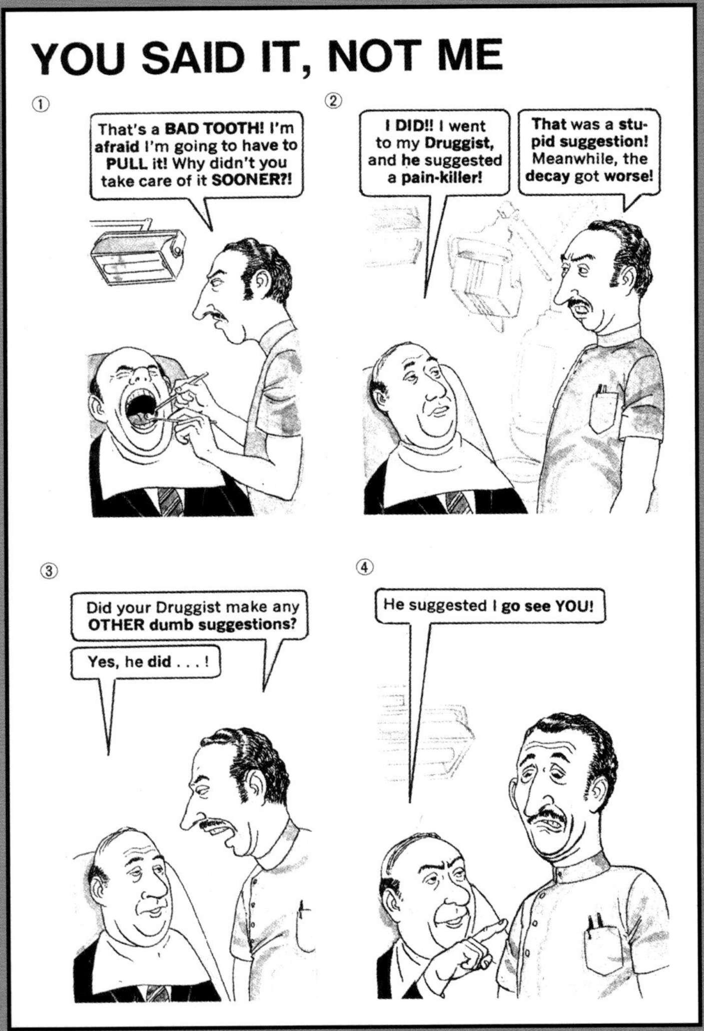

YOU SAID IT, NOT ME
①
That's a BAD TOOTH! I'm afraid I'm going to have to PULL it! Why didn't you take care of it SOONER?!
②
I DID!! I went to my Druggist, and he suggested a pain-killer!
That was a stupid suggestion! Meanwhile, the decay got worse!
③
Did your Druggist make any OTHER dumb suggestions?
Yes, he did . . . !
④
He suggested I go see YOU!

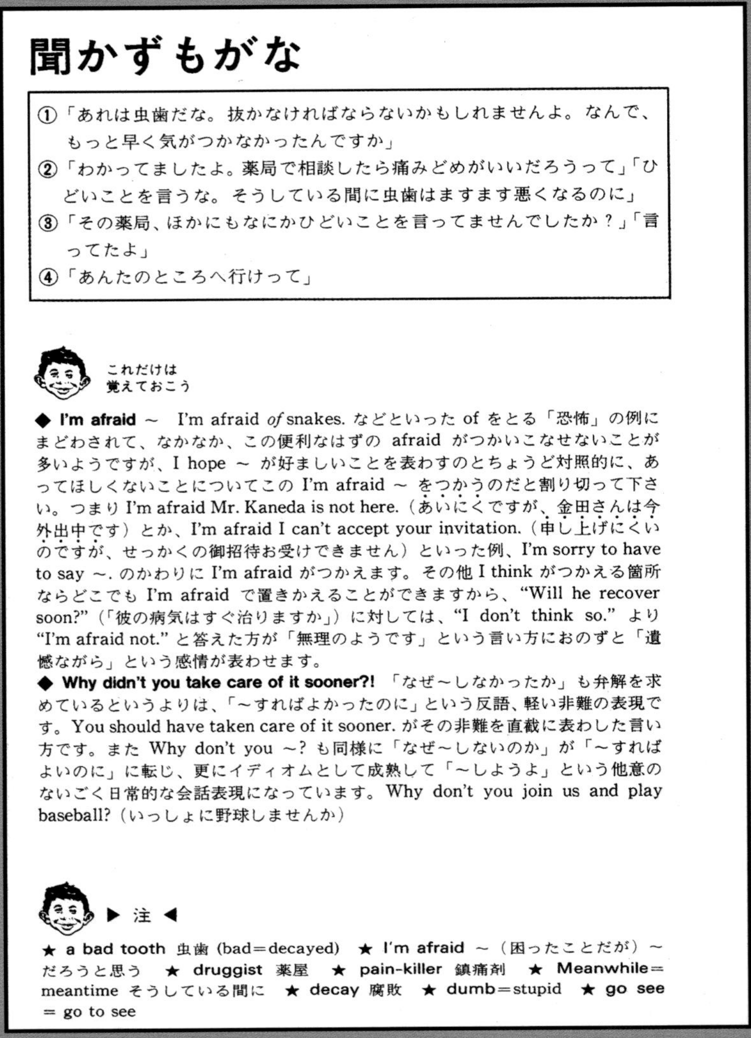

聞かずもがな

①「あれは虫歯だな。抜かなければならないかもしれませんよ。なんで、もっと早く気がつかなかったんですか」
②「わかってましたよ。薬局で相談したら痛みどめがいいだろうって」「ひどいことを言うな。そうしている間に虫歯はますます悪くなるのに」
③「その薬局、ほかにもなにかひどいことを言ってませんでしたか？」「言ってたよ」
④「あんたのところへ行けって」

これだけは
覚えておこう

◆ **I'm afraid ～**　I'm afraid *of* snakes. などといった of をとる「恐怖」の例にまどわされて、なかなか、この便利なはずの afraid がつかいこなせないことが多いようですが、I hope ～ が好ましいことを表わすのとちょうど対照的に、あってほしくないことについてこの I'm afraid ～ をつかうのだと割り切って下さい。つまり I'm afraid Mr. Kaneda is not here.（あいにくですが、金田さんは今外出中です）とか、I'm afraid I can't accept your invitation.（申し上げにくいのですが、せっかくの御招待お受けできません）といった例、I'm sorry to have to say ～. のかわりに I'm afraid がつかえます。その他 I think がつかえる箇所ならどこでも I'm afraid で置きかえることができますから、"Will he recover soon?"（「彼の病気はすぐ治りますか」）に対しては、"I don't think so." より "I'm afraid not." と答えた方が「無理のようです」という言い方におのずと「遺憾ながら」という感情が表わせます。

◆ **Why didn't you take care of it sooner?!** 「なぜ～しなかったか」も弁解を求めているというよりは、「～すればよかったのに」という反語、軽い非難の表現です。You should have taken care of it sooner. がその非難を直截に表わした言い方です。また Why don't you ～? も同様に「なぜ～しないのか」が「～すればよいのに」に転じ、更にイディオムとして成熟して「～しようよ」という他意のないごく日常的な会話表現になっています。Why don't you join us and play baseball?（いっしょに野球しませんか）

▶ 注 ◀

★ **a bad tooth** 虫歯 (bad＝decayed)　★ **I'm afraid** ～（困ったことだが）～だろうと思う　★ **druggist** 薬屋　★ **pain-killer** 鎮痛剤　★ **Meanwhile**＝meantime そうしている間に　★ **decay** 腐敗　★ **dumb**＝stupid　★ **go see**＝go to see

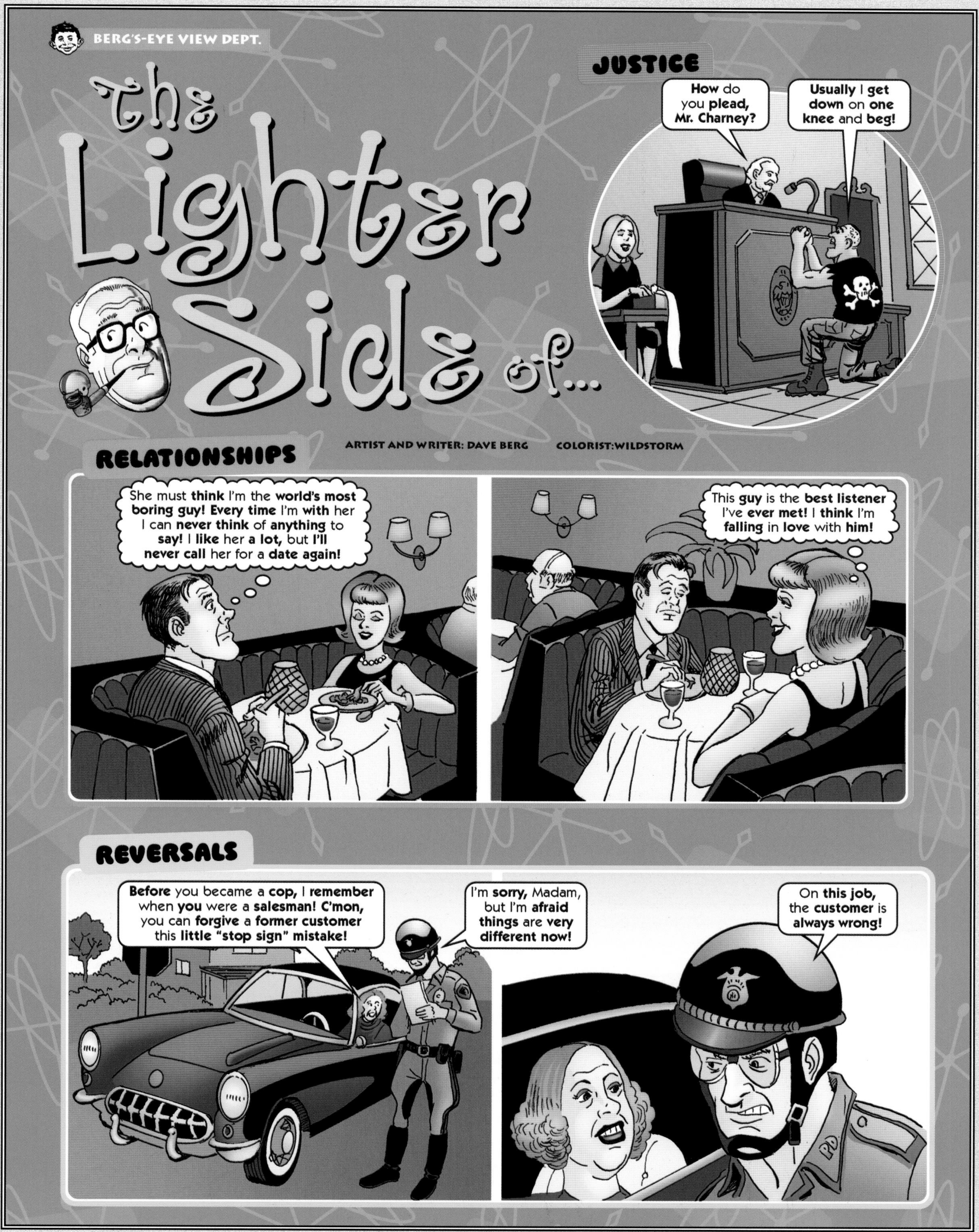
BERG'S-EYE VIEW DEPT.
The Lighter Side of...
JUSTICE
How do you plead, Mr. Charney?
Usually I get down on one knee and beg!
ARTIST AND WRITER: DAVE BERG
COLORIST: WILDSTORM
RELATIONSHIPS
She must think I'm the world's most boring guy! Every time I'm with her I can never think of anything to say! I like her a lot, but I'll never call her for a date again!
This guy is the best listener I've ever met! I think I'm falling in love with him!
REVERSALS
Before you became a cop, I remember when you were a salesman! C'mon, you can forgive a former customer this little "stop sign" mistake!
I'm sorry, Madam, but I'm afraid things are very different now!
On this job, the customer is always wrong!

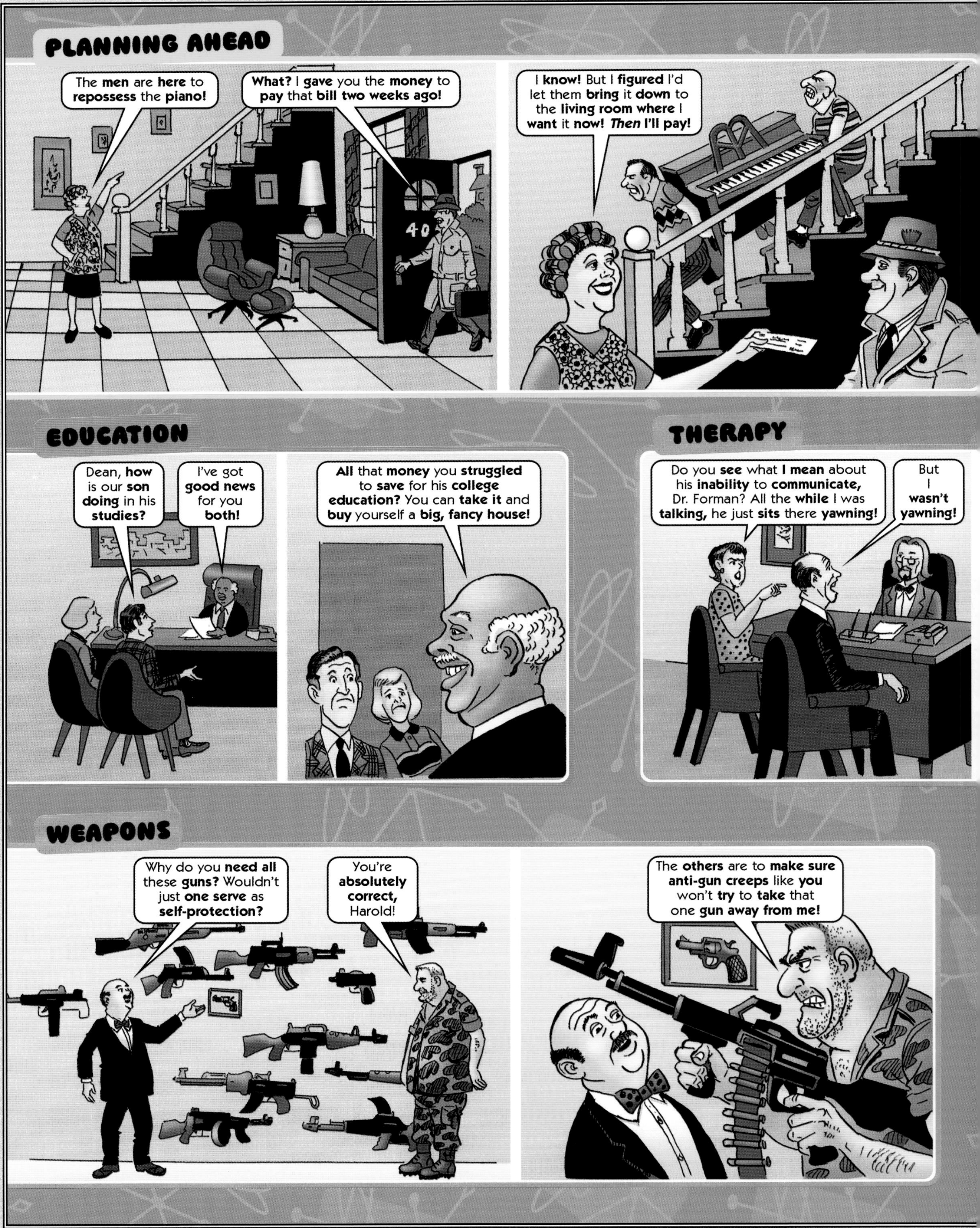
PLANNING AHEAD
The men are here to repossess the piano!
What? I gave you the money to pay that bill two weeks ago!
I know! But I figured I'd let them bring it down to the living room where I want it now! Then I'll pay!
EDUCATION
Dean, how is our son doing in his studies?
I've got good news for you both!
All that money you struggled to save for his college education? You can take it and buy yourself a big, fancy house!
THERAPY
Do you see what I mean about his inability to communicate, Dr. Forman? All the while I was talking, he just sits there yawning!
But I wasn't yawning!
WEAPONS
Why do you need all these guns? Wouldn't just one serve as self-protection?
You're absolutely correct, Harold!
The others are to make sure anti-gun creeps like you won't try to take that one gun away from me!

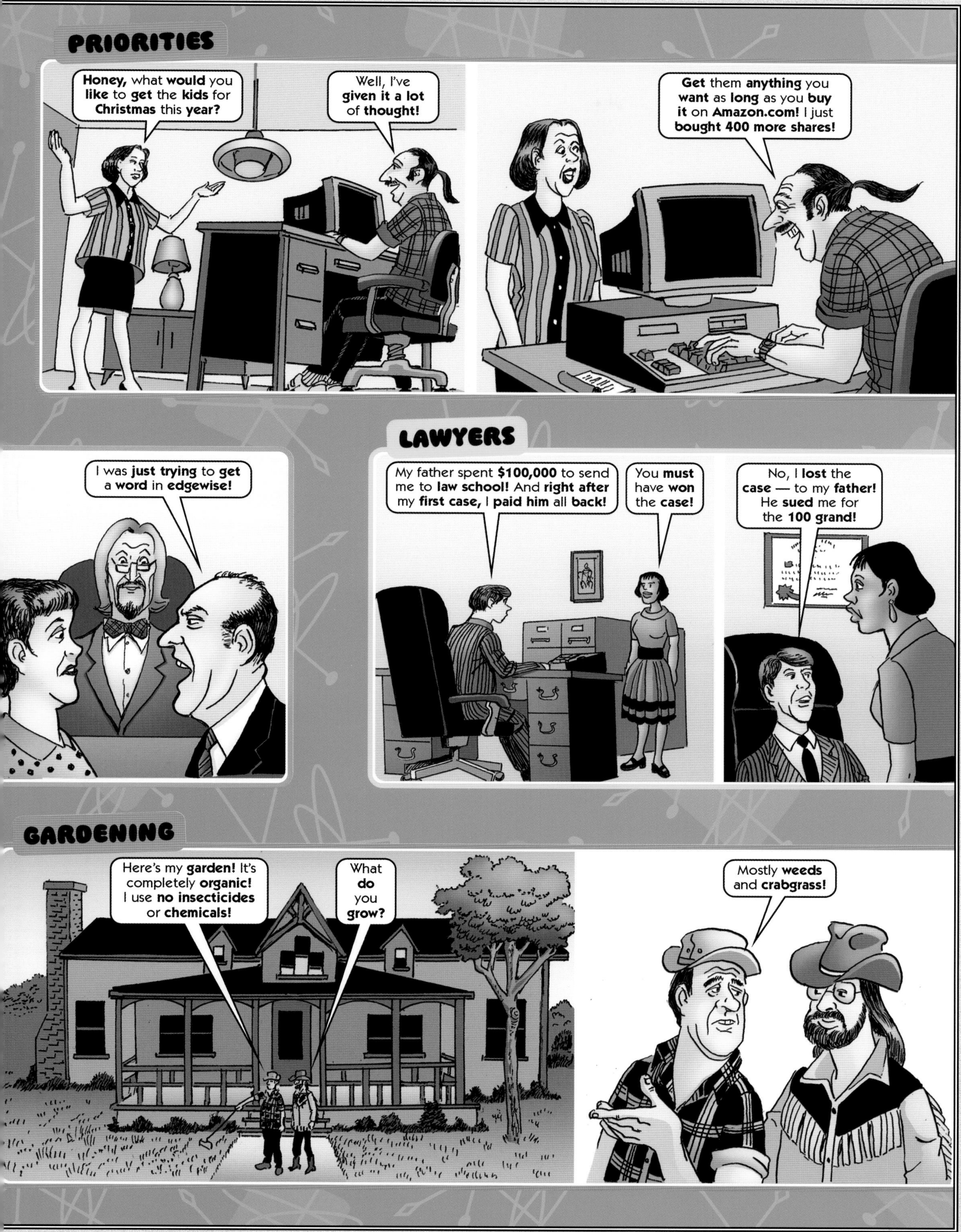
PRIORITIES
Honey, what would you like to get the kids for Christmas this year?
Well, I've given it a lot of thought!
Get them anything you want as long as you buy it on Amazon.com! I just bought 400 more shares!
I was just trying to get a word in edgewise!
LAWYERS
My father spent $100,000 to send me to law school! And right after my first case, I paid him all back!
You must have won the case!
No, I lost the case — to my father! He sued me for the 100 grand!
GARDENING
Here's my garden! It's completely organic! I use no insecticides or chemicals!
What do you grow?
Mostly weeds and crabgrass!

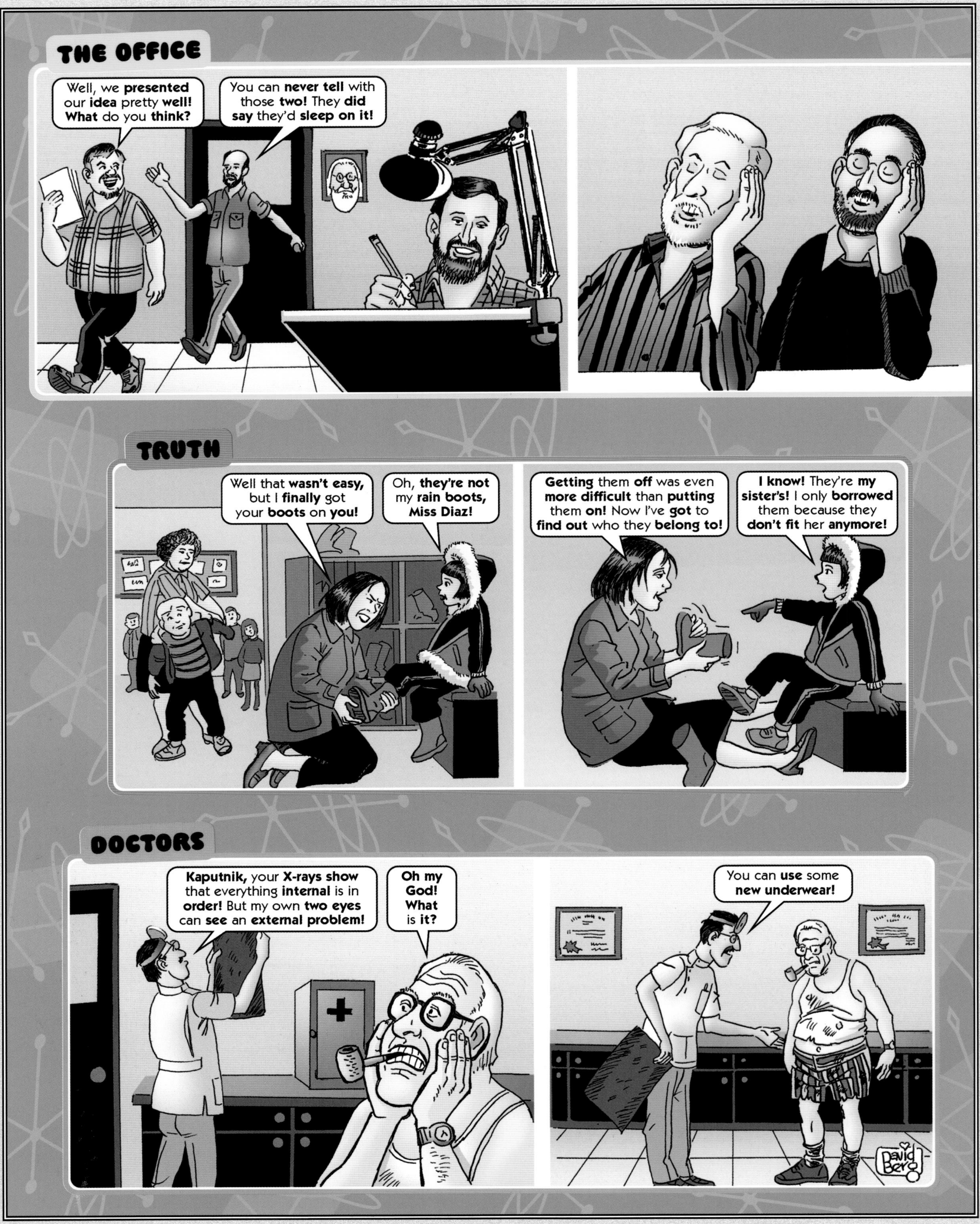
THE OFFICE
Well, we presented our idea pretty well! What do you think?
You can never tell with those two! They did say they'd sleep on it!
TRUTH
Well that wasn't easy, but I finally got your boots on you!
Oh, they're not my rain boots, Miss Diaz!
Getting them off was even more difficult than putting them on! Now I've got to find out who they belong to!
I know! They're my sister's! I only borrowed them because they don't fit her anymore!
DOCTORS
Kaputnik, your X-rays show that everything internal is in order! But my own two eyes can see an external problem!
Oh my God! What is it?
You can use some new underwear!
David Berg

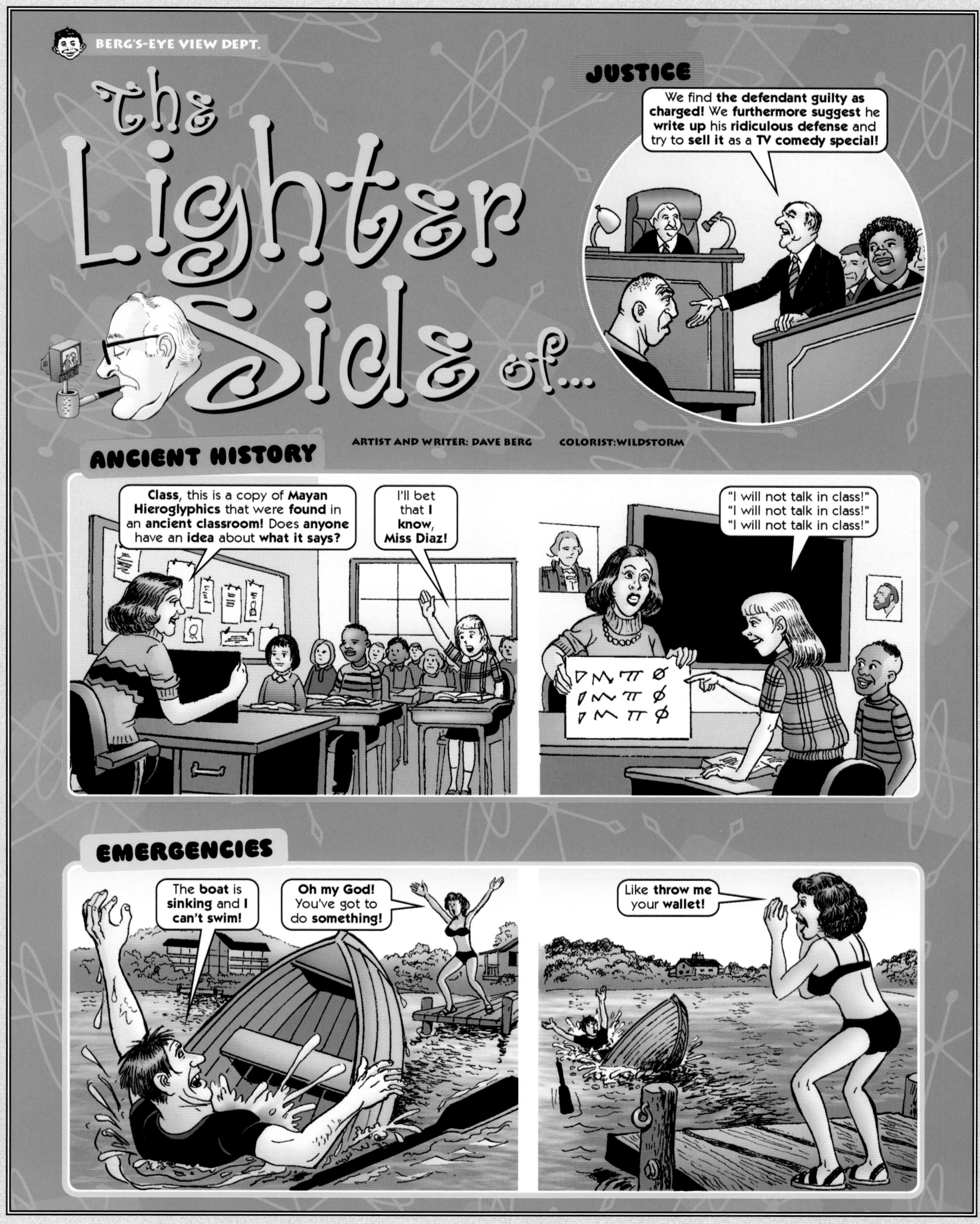
BERG'S-EYE VIEW DEPT.
The Lighter Side of...
JUSTICE
We find the defendant guilty as charged! We furthermore suggest he write up his ridiculous defense and try to sell it as a TV comedy special!
ARTIST AND WRITER: DAVE BERG
COLORIST: WILDSTORM
ANCIENT HISTORY
Class, this is a copy of Mayan Hieroglyphics that were found in an ancient classroom! Does anyone have an idea about what it says?
I'll bet that I know, Miss Diaz!
"I will not talk in class!" "I will not talk in class!" "I will not talk in class!"
EMERGENCIES
The boat is sinking and I can't swim!
Oh my God! You've got to do something!
Like throw me your wallet!

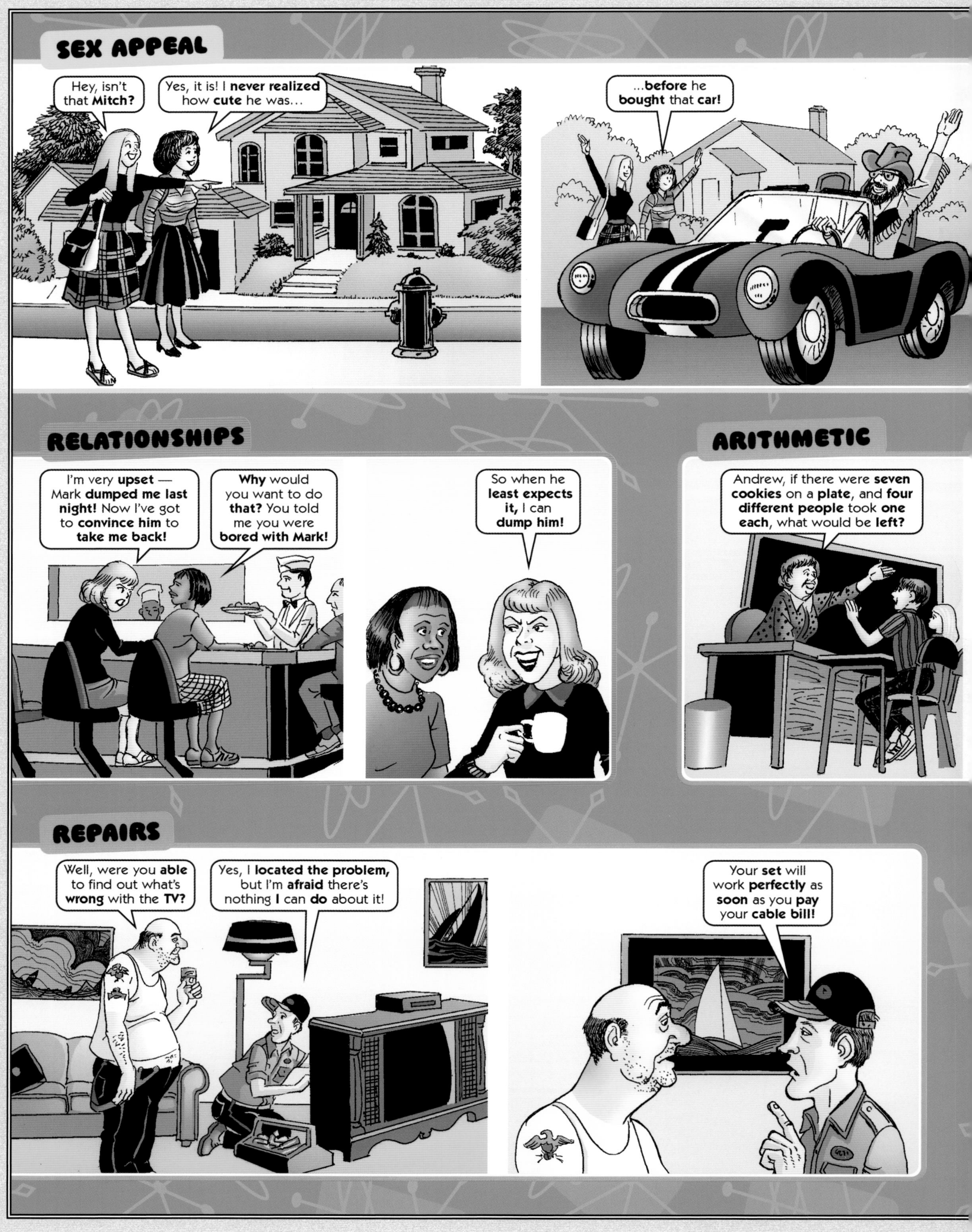
SEX APPEAL
Hey, isn't that Mitch?
Yes, it is! I never realized how cute he was...
...before he bought that car!
RELATIONSHIPS
I'm very upset — Mark dumped me last night! Now I've got to convince him to take me back!
Why would you want to do that? You told me you were bored with Mark!
So when he least expects it, I can dump him!
ARITHMETIC
Andrew, if there were seven cookies on a plate, and four different people took one each, what would be left?
REPAIRS
Well, were you able to find out what's wrong with the TV?
Yes, I located the problem, but I'm afraid there's nothing I can do about it!
Your set will work perfectly as soon as you pay your cable bill!

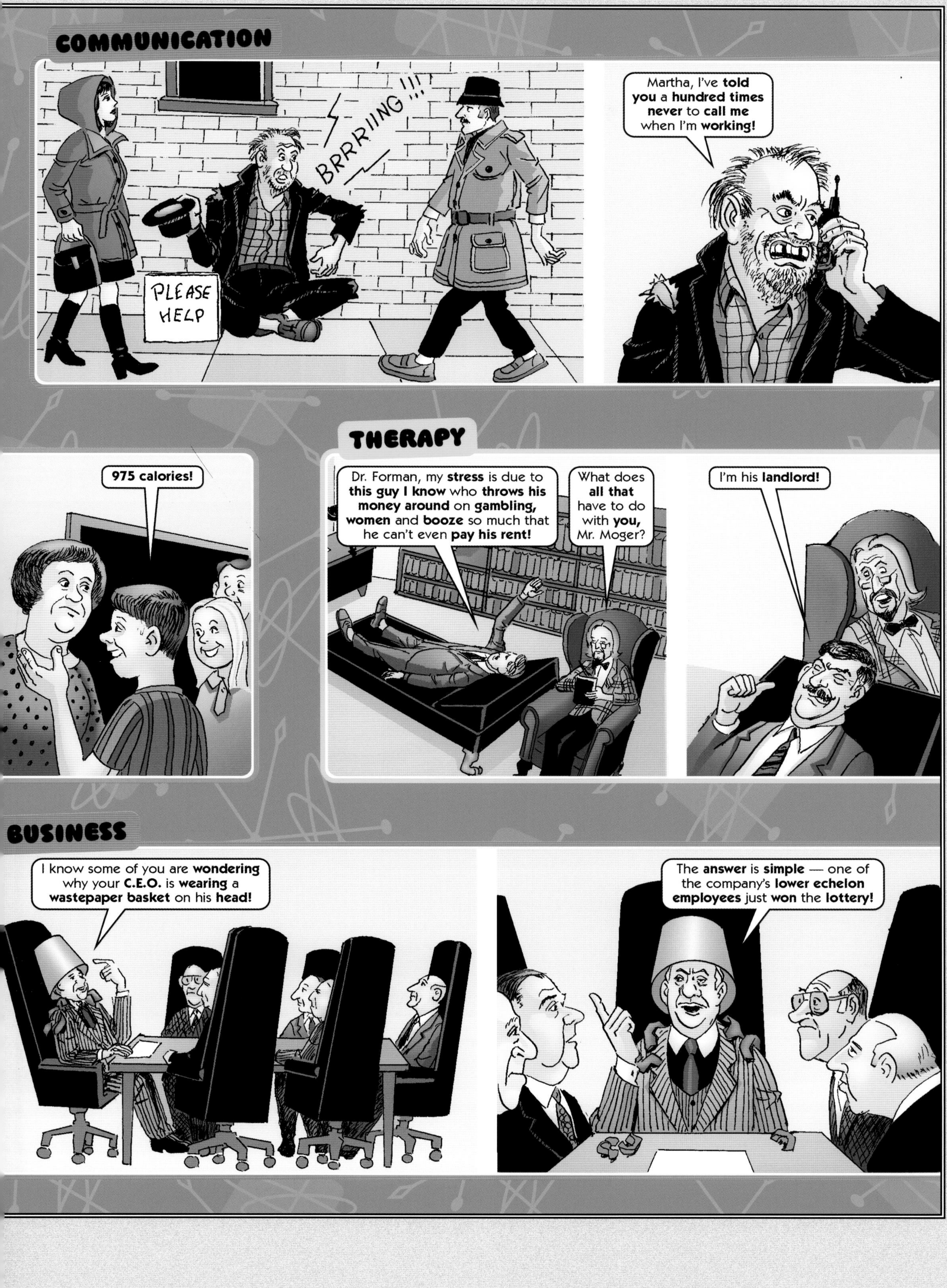
COMMUNICATION
PLEASE HELP
BRRRIING!!!
Martha, I've told you a hundred times never to call me when I'm working!
975 calories!
THERAPY
Dr. Forman, my stress is due to this guy I know who throws his money around on gambling, women and booze so much that he can't even pay his rent!
What does all that have to do with you, Mr. Moger?
I'm his landlord!
BUSINESS
I know some of you are wondering why your C.E.O. is wearing a wastepaper basket on his head!
The answer is simple — one of the company's lower echelon employees just won the lottery!

THE OFFICE

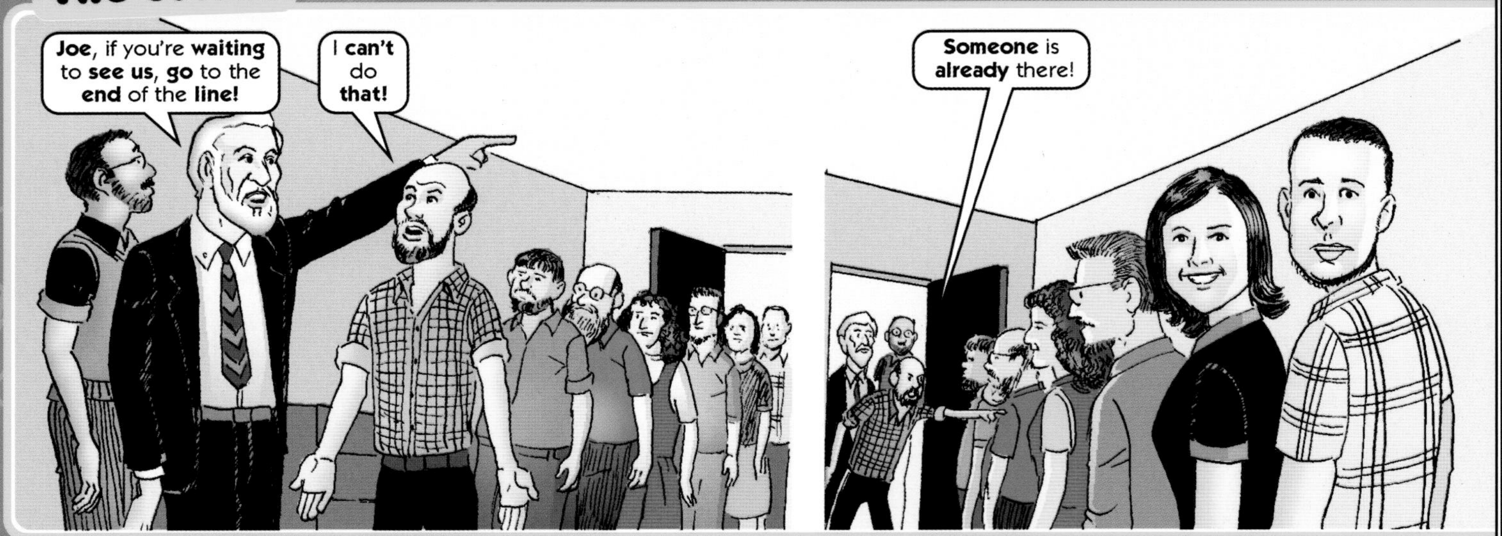
Joe, if you're waiting to see us, go to the end of the line!
I can't do that!
Someone is already there!

PRAYERS

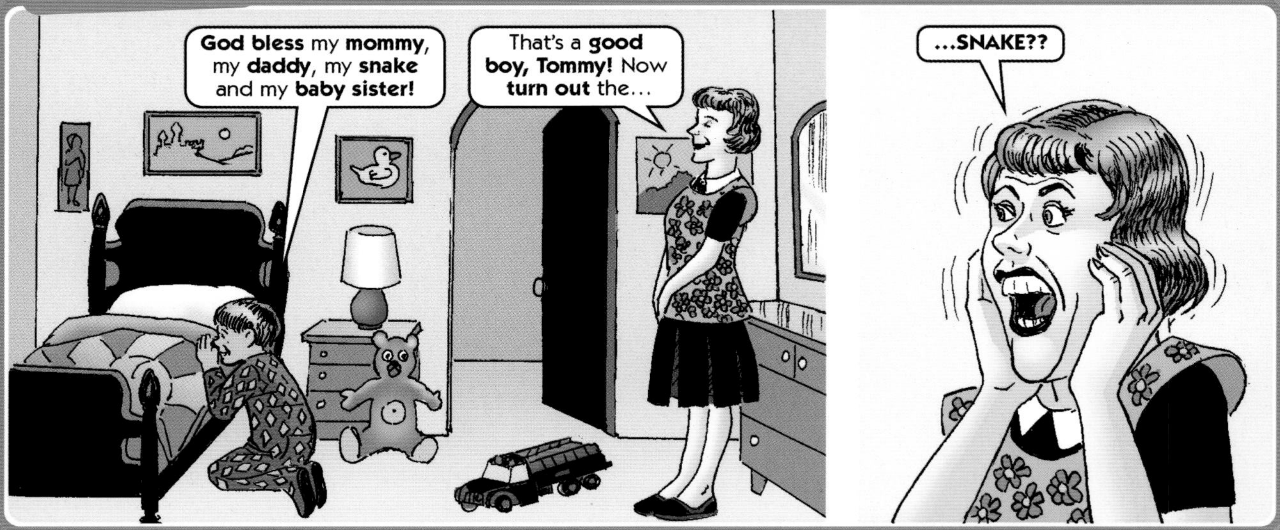
God bless my mommy, my daddy, my snake and my baby sister!
That's a good boy, Tommy! Now turn out the...
...SNAKE??

DOCTORS

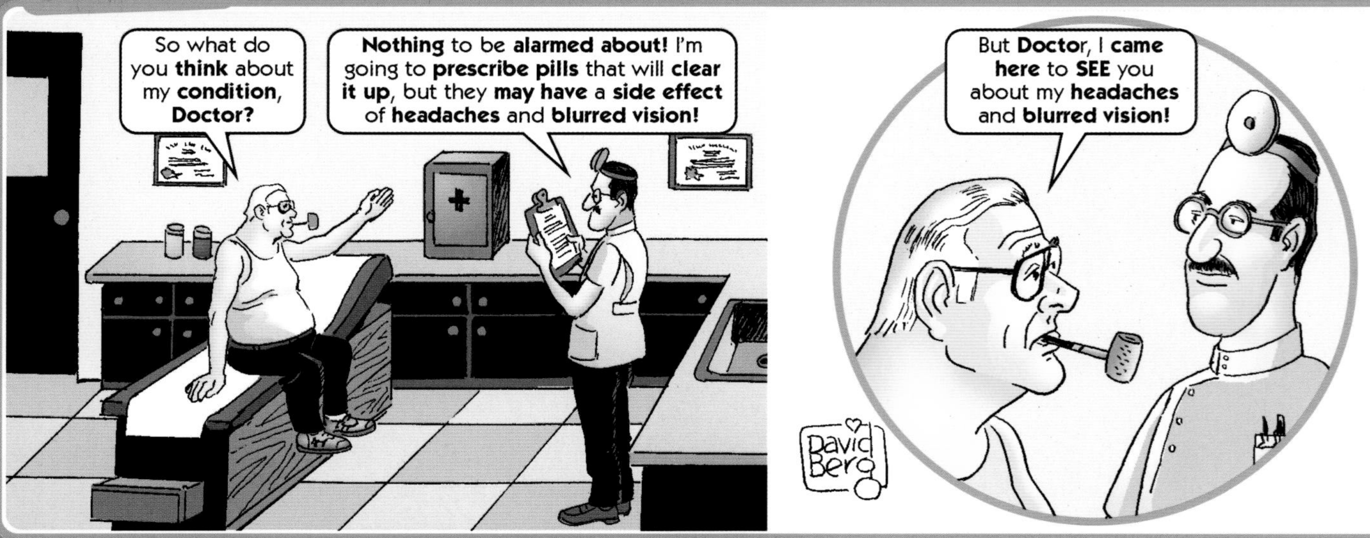
So what do you think about my condition, Doctor?
Nothing to be alarmed about! I'm going to prescribe pills that will clear it up, but they may have a side effect of headaches and blurred vision!
But Doctor, I came here to SEE you about my headaches and blurred vision!
David Berg

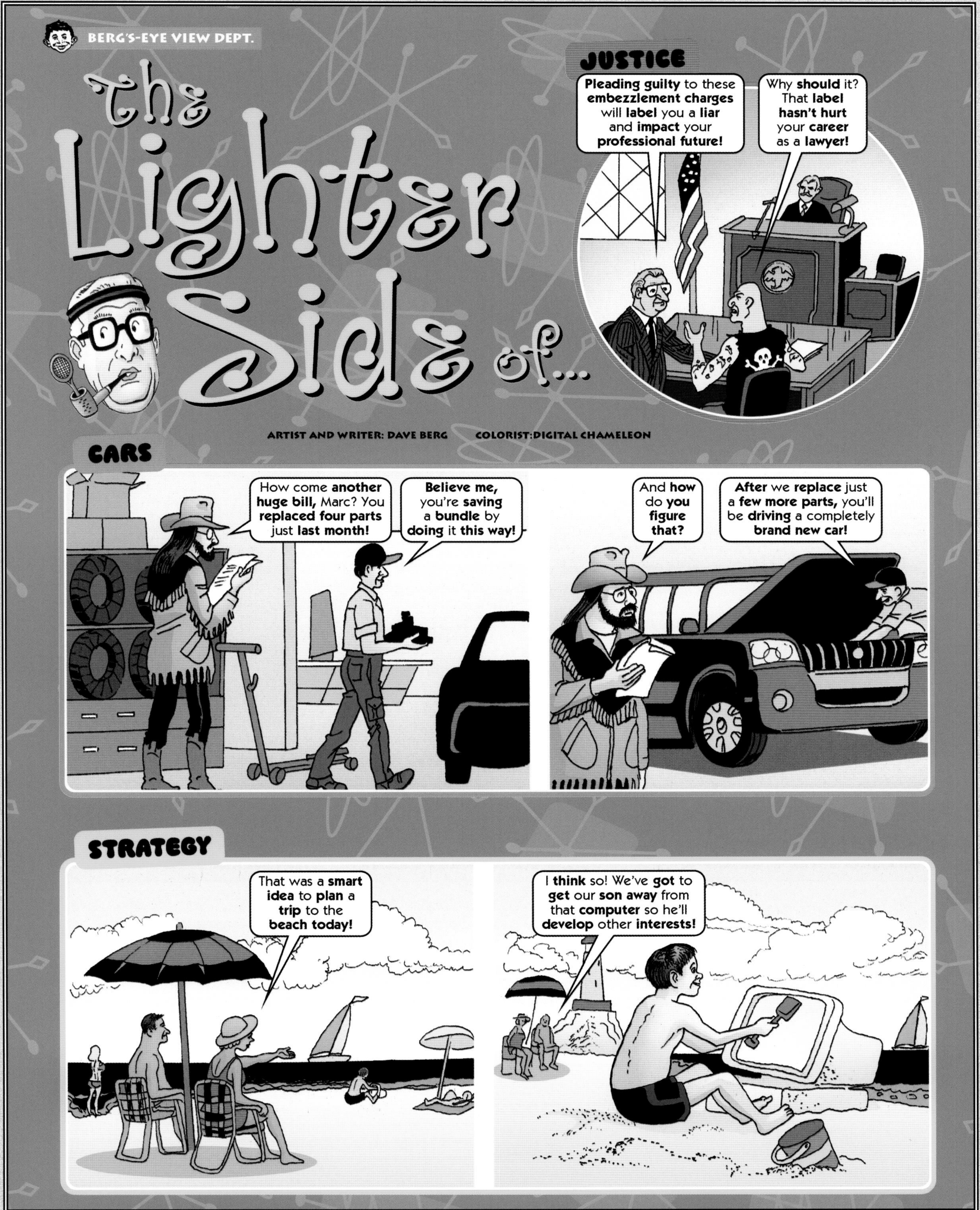
BERG'S-EYE VIEW DEPT.
The Lighter Side of...
JUSTICE
Pleading guilty to these embezzlement charges will label you a liar and impact your professional future!
Why should it? That label hasn't hurt your career as a lawyer!
ARTIST AND WRITER: DAVE BERG COLORIST: DIGITAL CHAMELEON
CARS
How come another huge bill, Marc? You replaced four parts just last month!
Believe me, you're saving a bundle by doing it this way!
And how do you figure that?
After we replace just a few more parts, you'll be driving a completely brand new car!
STRATEGY
That was a smart idea to plan a trip to the beach today!
I think so! We've got to get our son away from that computer so he'll develop other interests!

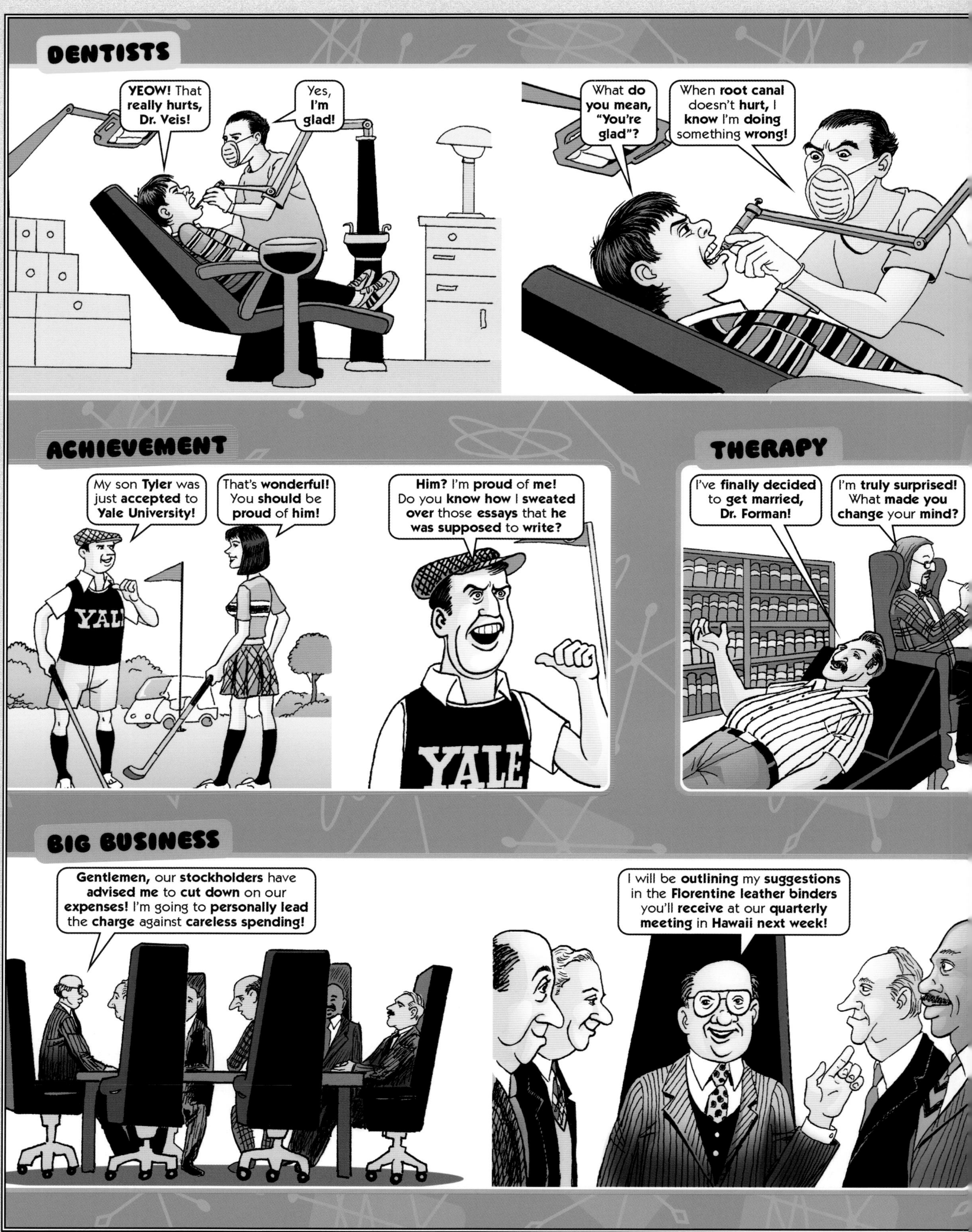
DENTISTS
YEOW! That really hurts, Dr. Veis!
Yes, I'm glad!
What do you mean, "You're glad"?
When root canal doesn't hurt, I know I'm doing something wrong!
ACHIEVEMENT
My son Tyler was just accepted to Yale University!
That's wonderful! You should be proud of him!
Him? I'm proud of me! Do you know how I sweated over those essays that he was supposed to write?
THERAPY
I've finally decided to get married, Dr. Forman!
I'm truly surprised! What made you change your mind?
BIG BUSINESS
Gentlemen, our stockholders have advised me to cut down on our expenses! I'm going to personally lead the charge against careless spending!
I will be outlining my suggestions in the Florentine leather binders you'll receive at our quarterly meeting in Hawaii next week!

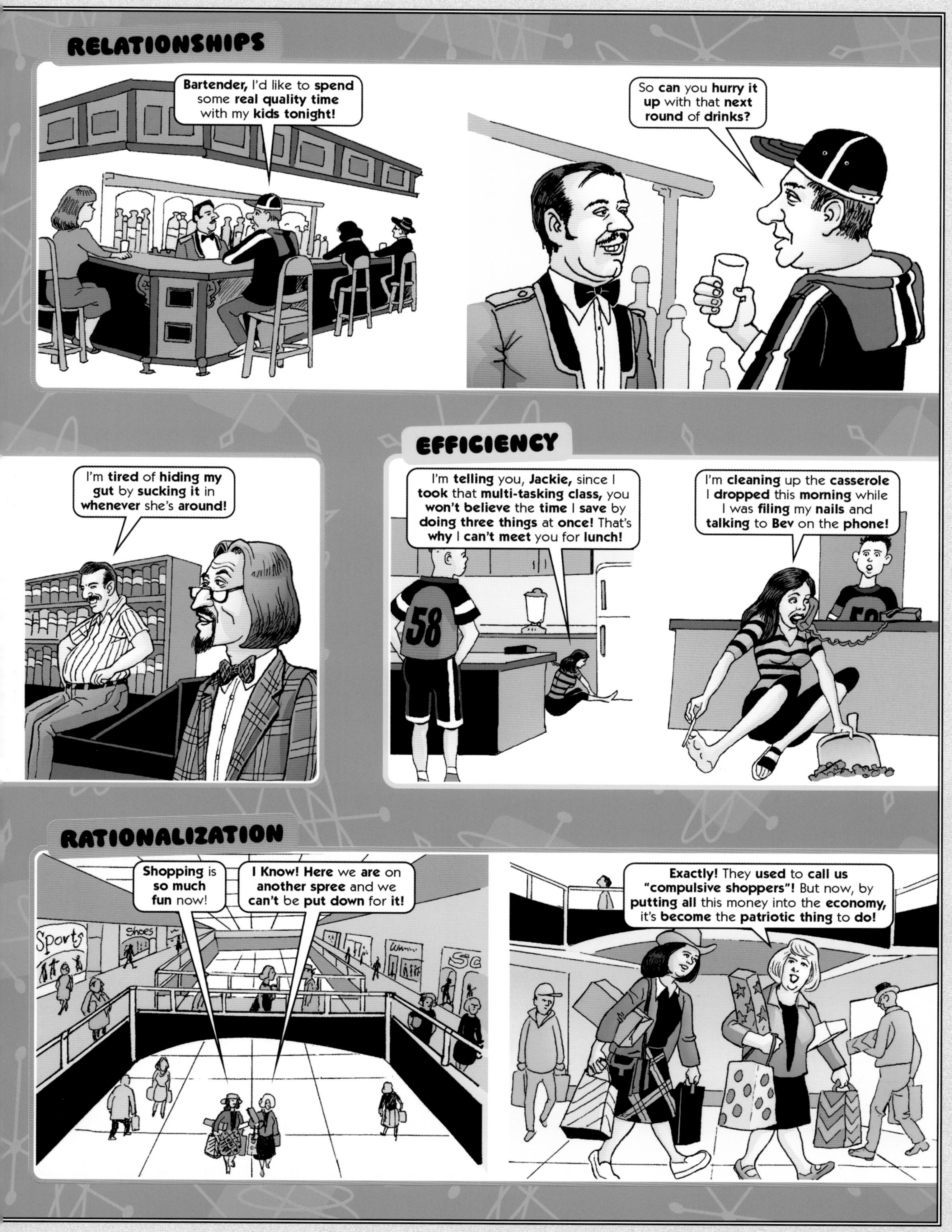
RELATIONSHIPS
Bartender, I'd like to spend some real quality time with my kids tonight!
So can you hurry it up with that next round of drinks?
I'm tired of hiding my gut by sucking it in whenever she's around!
EFFICIENCY
I'm telling you, Jackie, since I took that multi-tasking class, you won't believe the time I save by doing three things at once! That's why I can't meet you for lunch!
I'm cleaning up the casserole I dropped this morning while I was filing my nails and talking to Bev on the phone!
58
RATIONALIZATION
Shopping is so much fun now!
I Know! Here we are on another spree and we can't be put down for it!
Sports
Shoes
Exactly! They used to call us "compulsive shoppers"! But now, by putting all this money into the economy, it's become the patriotic thing to do!

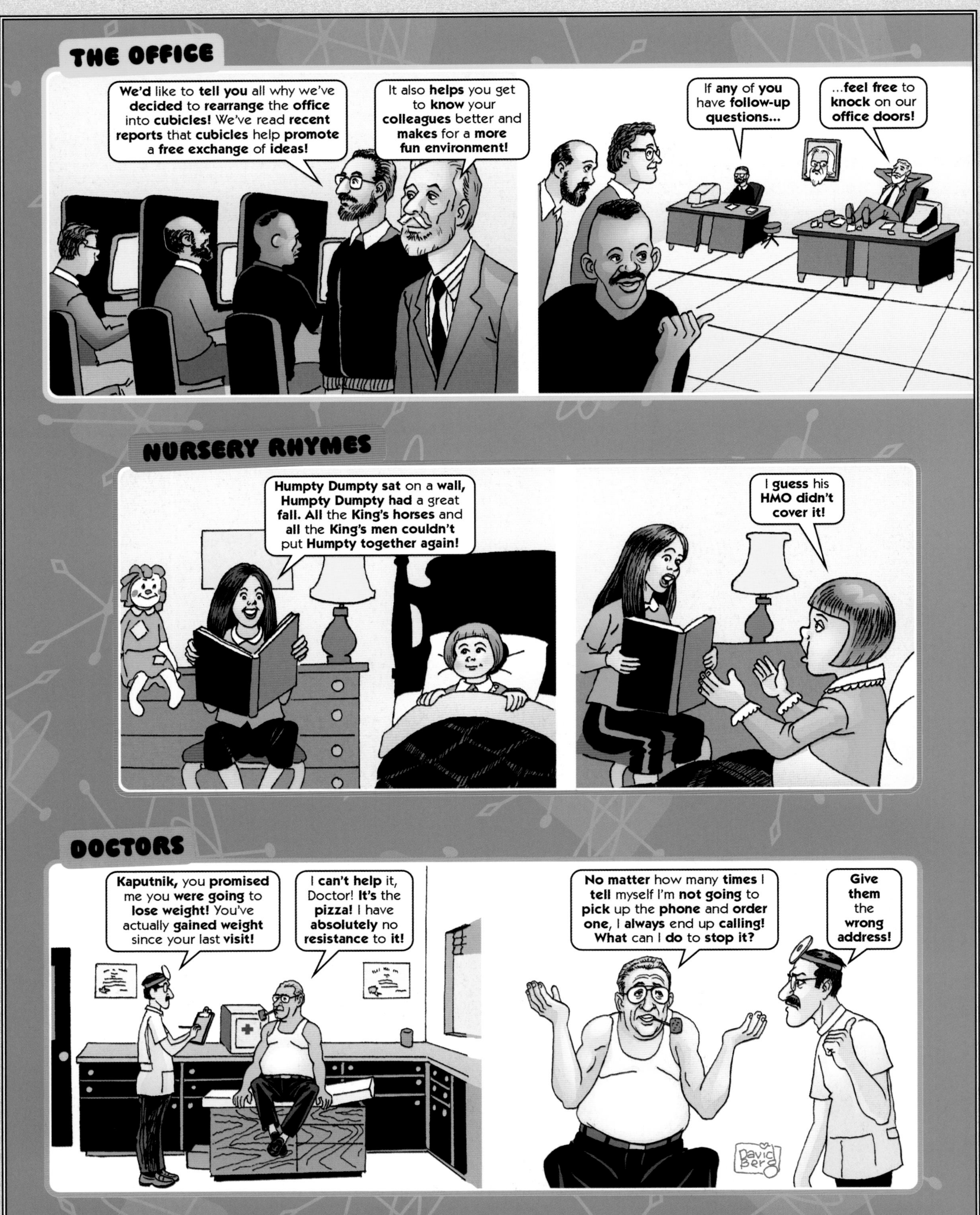
THE OFFICE
We'd like to tell you all why we've decided to rearrange the office into cubicles! We've read recent reports that cubicles help promote a free exchange of ideas!
It also helps you get to know your colleagues better and makes for a more fun environment!
If any of you have follow-up questions...
...feel free to knock on our office doors!
NURSERY RHYMES
Humpty Dumpty sat on a wall, Humpty Dumpty had a great fall. All the King's horses and all the King's men couldn't put Humpty together again!
I guess his HMO didn't cover it!
DOCTORS
Kaputnik, you promised me you were going to lose weight! You've actually gained weight since your last visit!
I can't help it, Doctor! It's the pizza! I have absolutely no resistance to it!
No matter how many times I tell myself I'm not going to pick up the phone and order one, I always end up calling! What can I do to stop it?
Give them the wrong address!
David Berg

MAD Kids: Class Dismissed

Additional examples of The Lighter Side of... scripts used in MAD *Kids* magazine

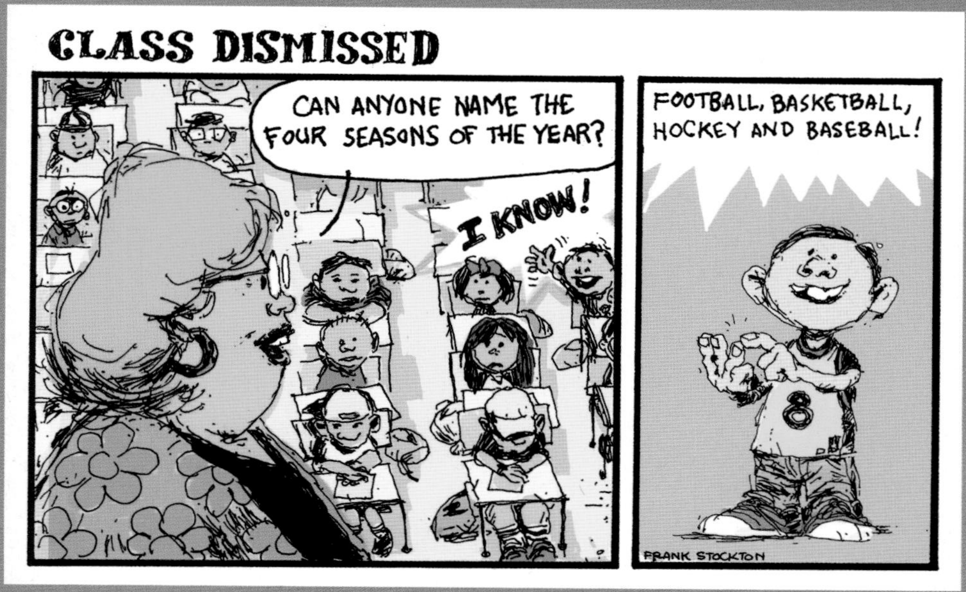

CLASS DISMISSED
CAN ANYONE NAME THE FOUR SEASONS OF THE YEAR?
I KNOW!
FOOTBALL, BASKETBALL, HOCKEY AND BASEBALL!
FRANK STOCKTON

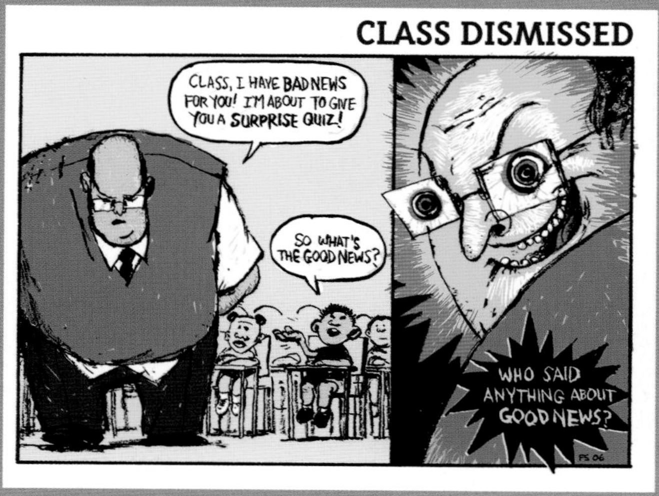

CLASS DISMISSED
CLASS, I HAVE BAD NEWS FOR YOU! I'M ABOUT TO GIVE YOU A SURPRISE QUIZ!
SO WHAT'S THE GOOD NEWS?
WHO SAID ANYTHING ABOUT GOOD NEWS?
PS 06

Class Dismissed drawn by Frank Stockton

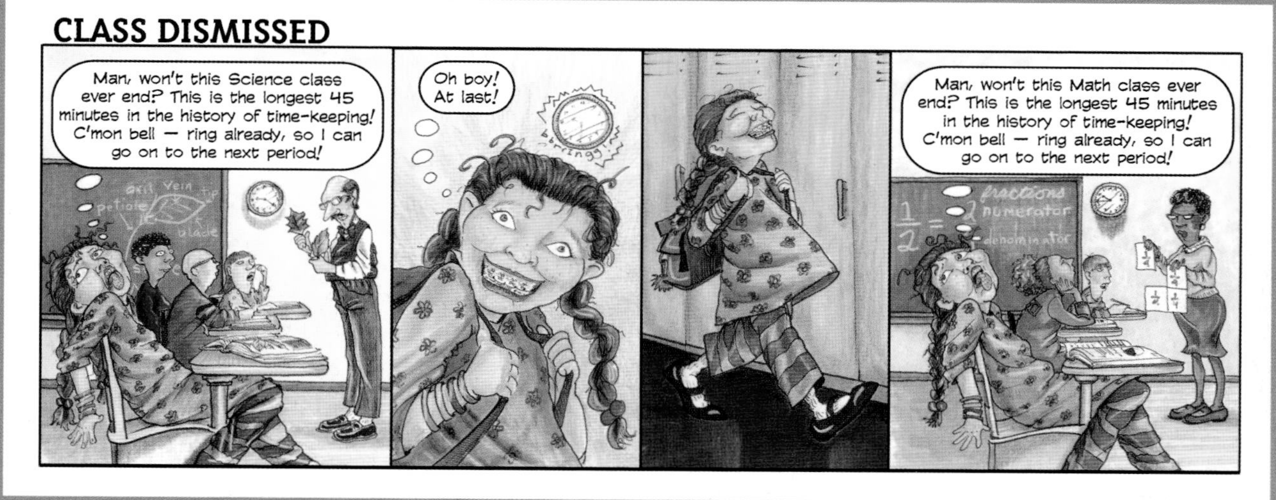

CLASS DISMISSED
Man, won't this Science class ever end? This is the longest 45 minutes in the history of time-keeping! C'mon bell — ring already, so I can go on to the next period!
Oh boy! At last!
Man, won't this Math class ever end? This is the longest 45 minutes in the history of time-keeping! C'mon bell — ring already, so I can go on to the next period!

Class Dismissed drawn by Teresa Burns Parkhurst

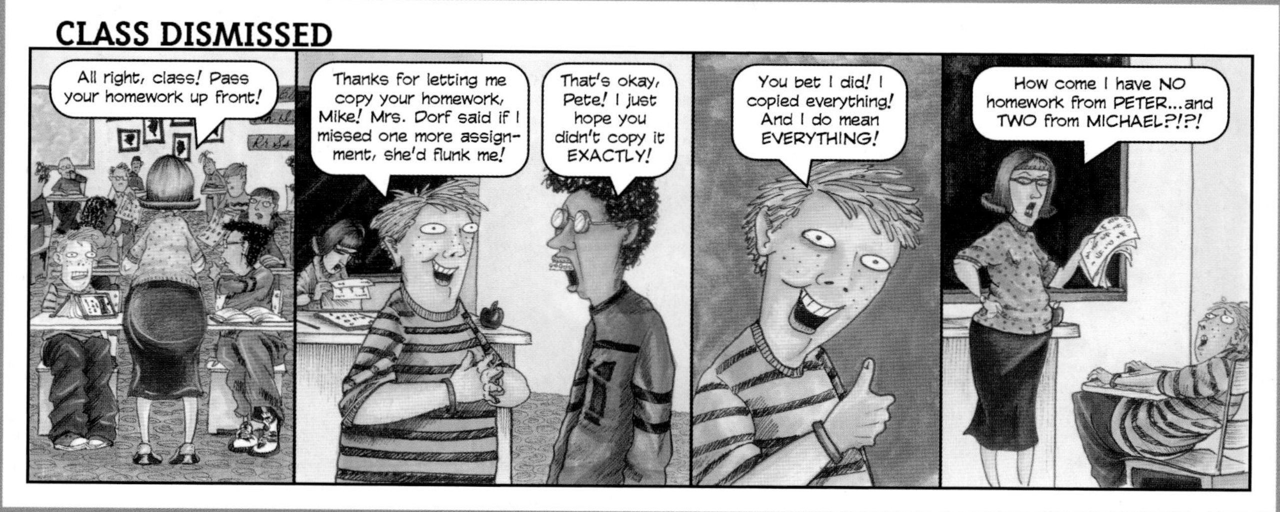

CLASS DISMISSED
All right, class! Pass your homework up front!
Thanks for letting me copy your homework, Mike! Mrs. Dorf said if I missed one more assignment, she'd flunk me!
That's okay, Pete! I just hope you didn't copy it EXACTLY!
You bet I did! I copied everything! And I do mean EVERYTHING!
How come I have NO homework from PETER...and TWO from MICHAEL?!?!

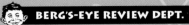

BERG'S-EYE REVIEW DEPT.

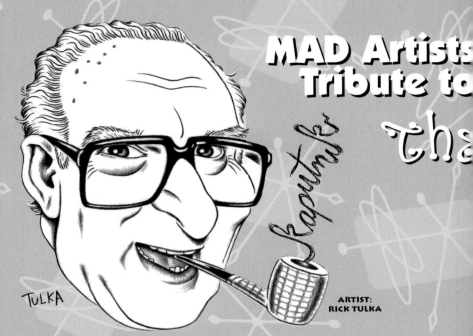

MAD Artists' Tribute to Tha

In our 50th Anniversary issue, we printed the final installment of "The Lighter Side," written and illustrated by the late Dave Berg. A legend of the magazine, Dave left behind countless fans, a giant body of work and, most startlingly, a script for the next issue that he had written, but not illustrated! Outraged by Dave's blatant disregard of his deadline, we had no choice but to divide his jokes among the MAD artists and let them illustrate Dave's words however they saw fit.

TULKA

ARTIST: RICK TULKA

ENTREPRENEURS

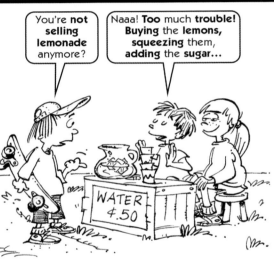

Get your water here!
Only 50 cents!
WATER ¢.50
You're not selling lemonade anymore?
Naaa! Too much trouble! Buying the lemons, squeezing them, adding the sugar...
WATER ¢.50
Besides, why bother when grownups are dumb enough to pay the same amount for plain water, anyway!

ARTIST: SERGIO ARAGONES

BUZZ

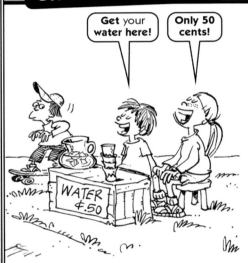

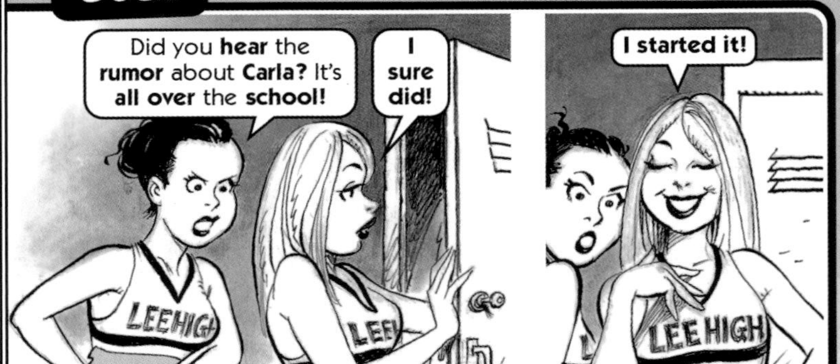

Did you hear the rumor about Carla? It's all over the school!
I sure did!
LEEHIGH
I started it!
LEE HIGH
DRUCKER

ARTIST: MORT DRUCKER

JOB INTERVIEWS

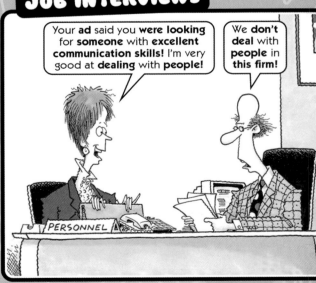

Your ad said you were looking for someone with excellent communication skills! I'm very good at dealing with people!
We don't deal with people in this firm!
PERSONNEL

ARTIST: JOHN CALDWELL

Pay Lighter Side of...

WRITER: DAVE BERG

JUSTICE

"Has the jury reached a decision?"

"Are you kidding? We can't agree who should have won this year's Oscar for Best Actor, let alone whether the defendant is guilty or not!"

ARTIST: PETER KUPER

HEALTH CLUBS

"How come you don't wear something on your feet around the locker room?"

"No reason to!"

"No reason? You're the only person I know who doesn't! Aren't you afraid of picking up some kind of foot fungus?"

"Not as long as everyone else wears protective footwear! That means the floor is perfectly safe!"

ARTIST: JACK DAVIS

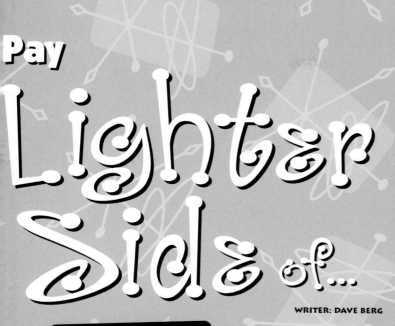

"Only lawyers!"

HOUSECLEANING

"I've vacuumed all of your downstairs carpeting with our latest model! You couldn't get cleaner results from a professional service! Shall I draw up the sales slip?"

"The rugs do look wonderful! But I'm still undecided!"

"Can you come back next week to demonstrate on the upstairs carpeting?"

ARTIST: GEORGE WOODBRIDGE

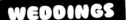

WEDDINGS

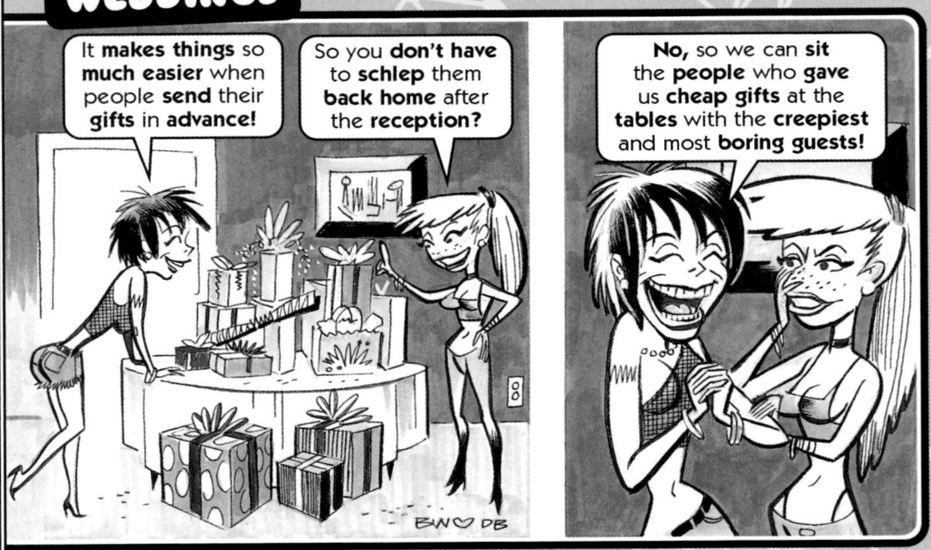
It makes things so much easier when people send their gifts in advance!
So you don't have to schlep them back home after the reception?
No, so we can sit the people who gave us cheap gifts at the tables with the creepiest and most boring guests!

ARTIST: BILL WRAY

FRIENDSHIP

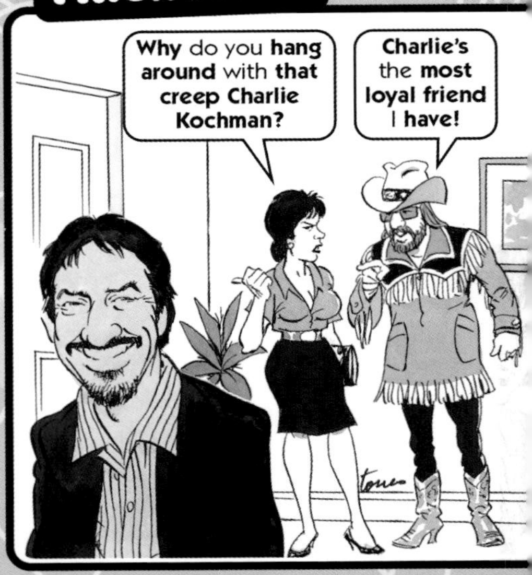
Why do you hang around with that creep Charlie Kochman?
Charlie's the most loyal friend I have!

ARTIST: ANGELO TORRES

RELATIONSHIPS

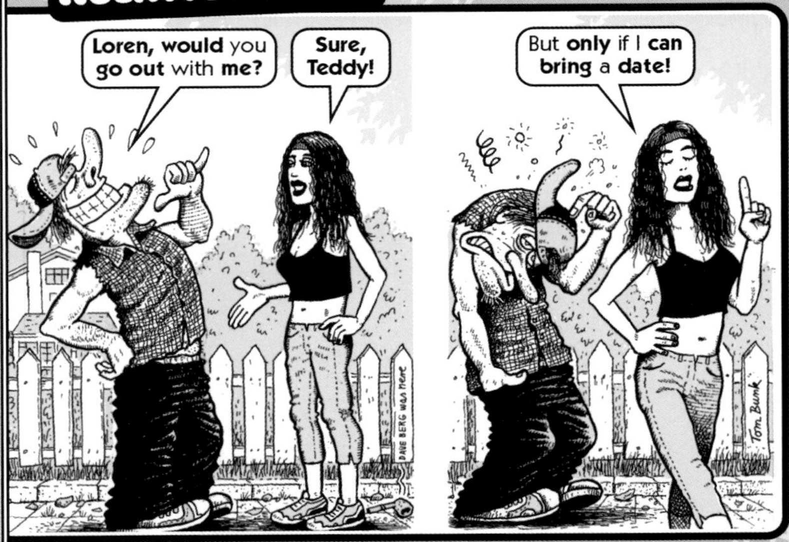
Loren, would you go out with me?
Sure, Teddy!
But only if I can bring a date!

ARTIST: TOM BUNK

THERAPY

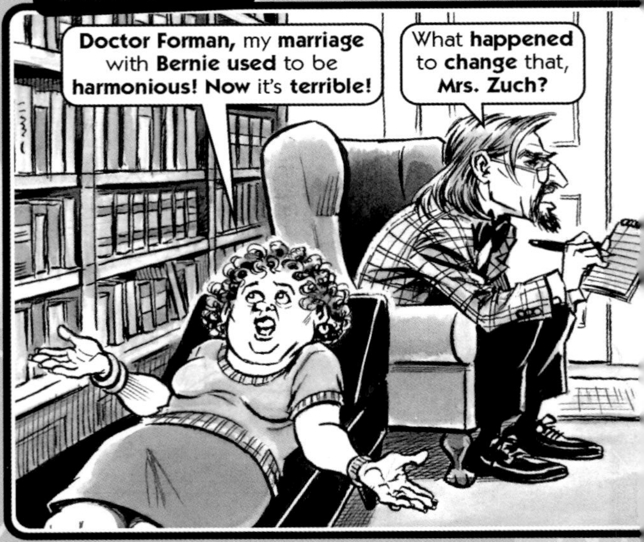
Doctor Forman, my marriage with Bernie used to be harmonious! Now it's terrible!
What happened to change that, Mrs. Zuch?

ARTIST: SAM VIVIANO

ATTACHMENTS

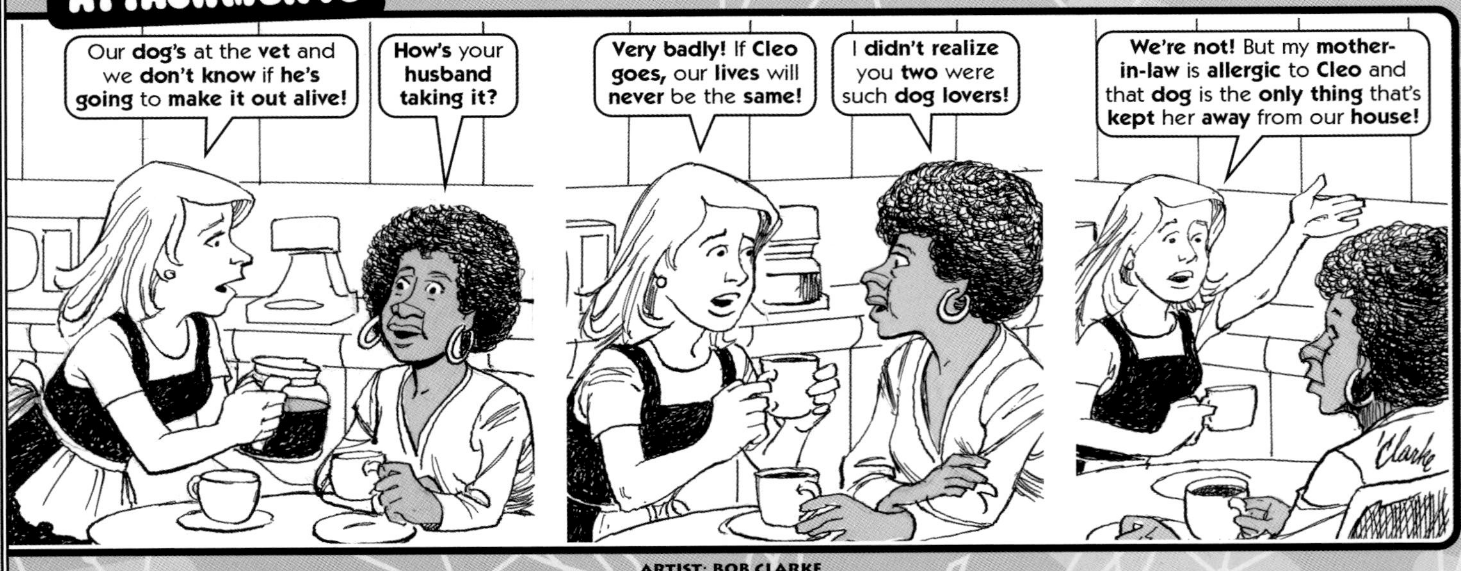
Our dog's at the vet and we don't know if he's going to make it out alive!
How's your husband taking it?
Very badly! If Cleo goes, our lives will never be the same!
I didn't realize you two were such dog lovers!
We're not! But my mother-in-law is allergic to Cleo and that dog is the only thing that's kept her away from our house!

ARTIST: BOB CLARKE

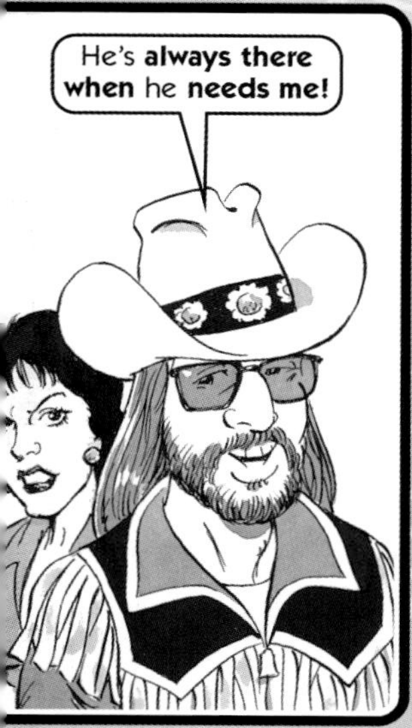
He's always there when he needs me!

ASSIGNMENTS

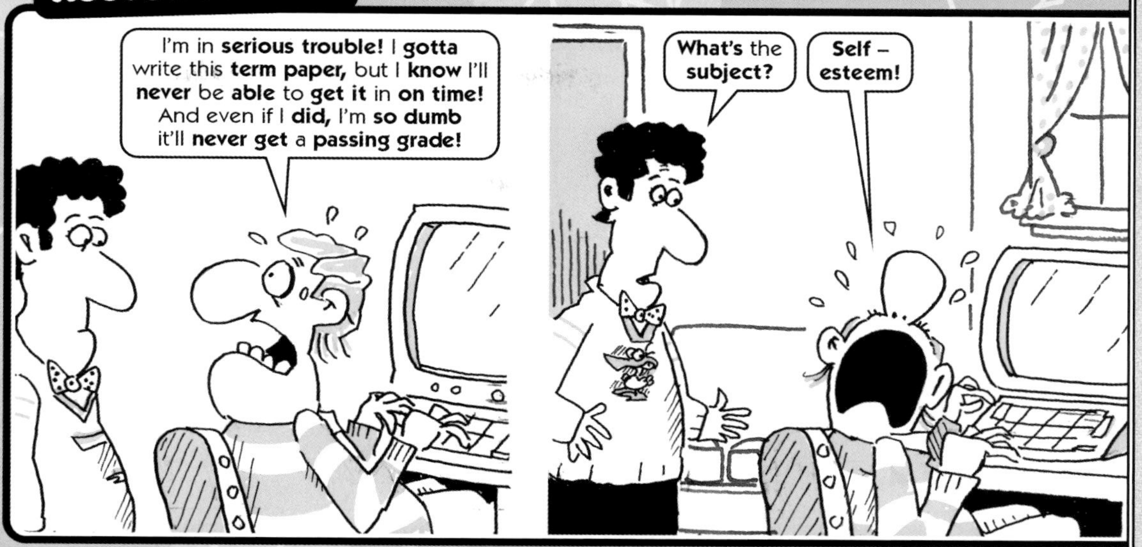
I'm in serious trouble! I gotta write this term paper, but I know I'll never be able to get it in on time! And even if I did, I'm so dumb it'll never get a passing grade!
What's the subject?
Self – esteem!

ARTIST: DUCK EDWING

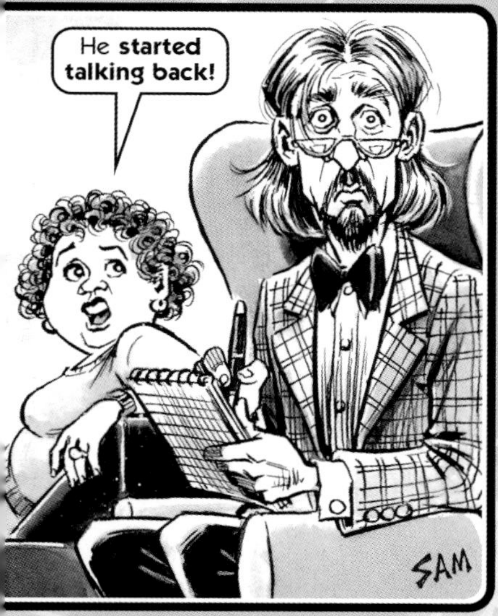
He started talking back!
SAM

EFFICIENCY

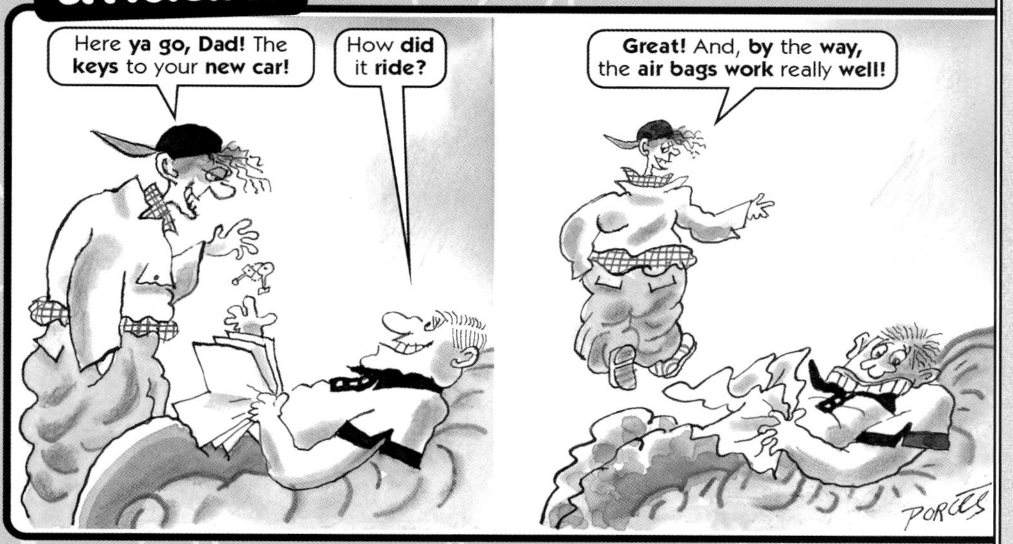
Here ya go, Dad! The keys to your new car!
How did it ride?
Great! And, by the way, the air bags work really well!
PORGES

ARTIST: PAUL PETER PORGES

RESTAURANTS

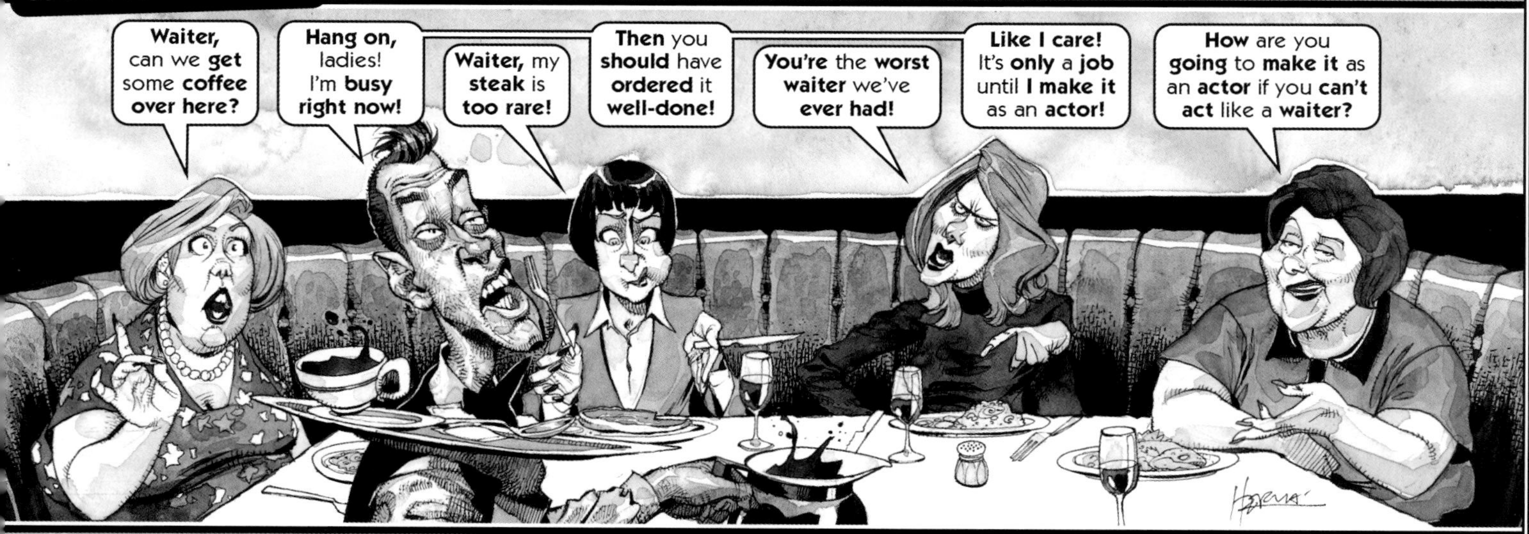
Waiter, can we get some coffee over here?
Hang on, ladies! I'm busy right now!
Waiter, my steak is too rare!
Then you should have ordered it well-done!
You're the worst waiter we've ever had!
Like I care! It's only a job until I make it as an actor!
How are you going to make it as an actor if you can't act like a waiter?

ARTIST: HERMANN MEJIA

EXERCISE

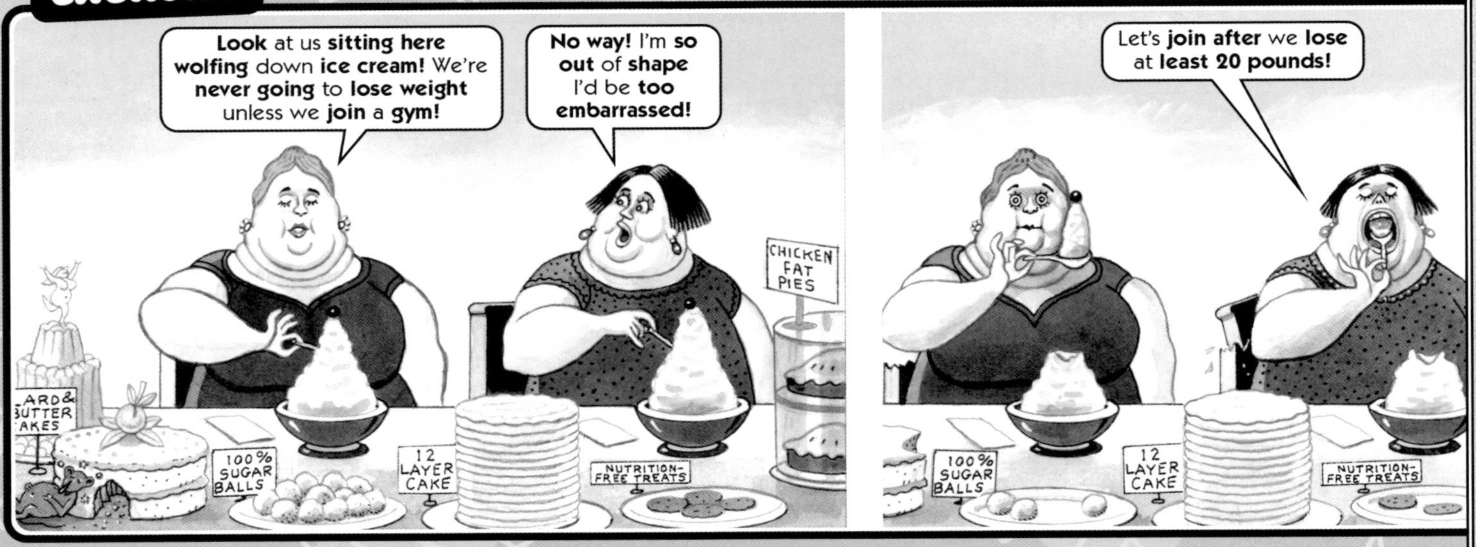
Look at us sitting here wolfing down ice cream! We're never going to lose weight unless we join a gym!
No way! I'm so out of shape I'd be too embarrassed!
CHICKEN FAT PIES
100% SUGAR BALLS
12 LAYER CAKE
NUTRITION-FREE TREATS
Let's join after we lose at least 20 pounds!
100% SUGAR BALLS
12 LAYER CAKE
NUTRITION-FREE TREATS

ARTIST: AL JAFFEE

BELIEFS

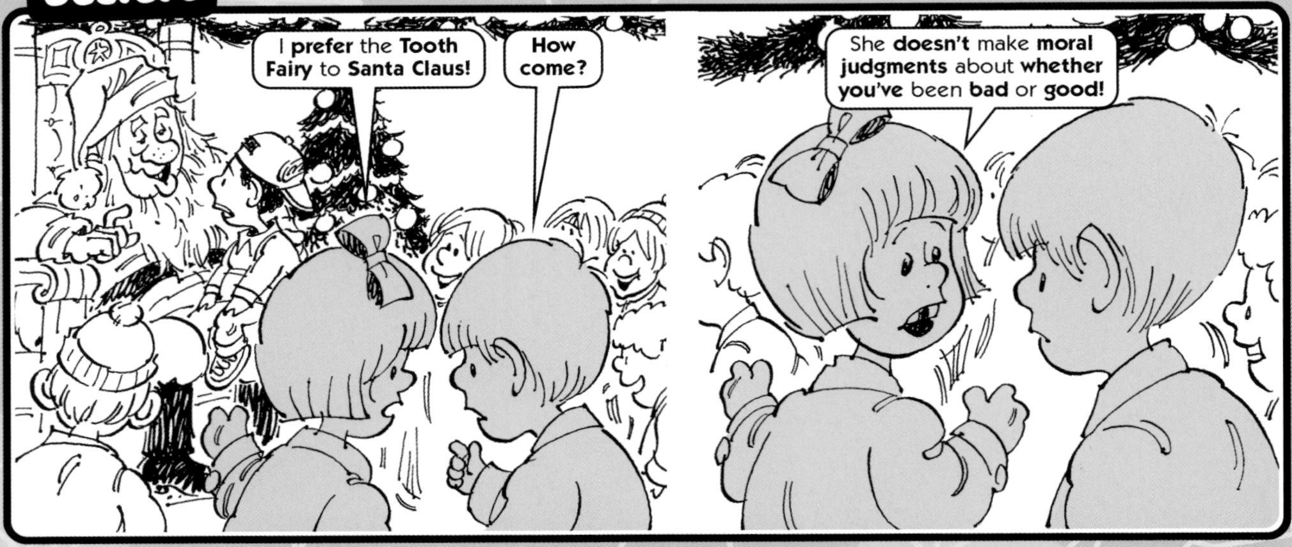
I prefer the Tooth Fairy to Santa Claus!
How come?
She doesn't make moral judgments about whether you've been bad or good!

ARTIST: PAUL COKER

THE OFFICE

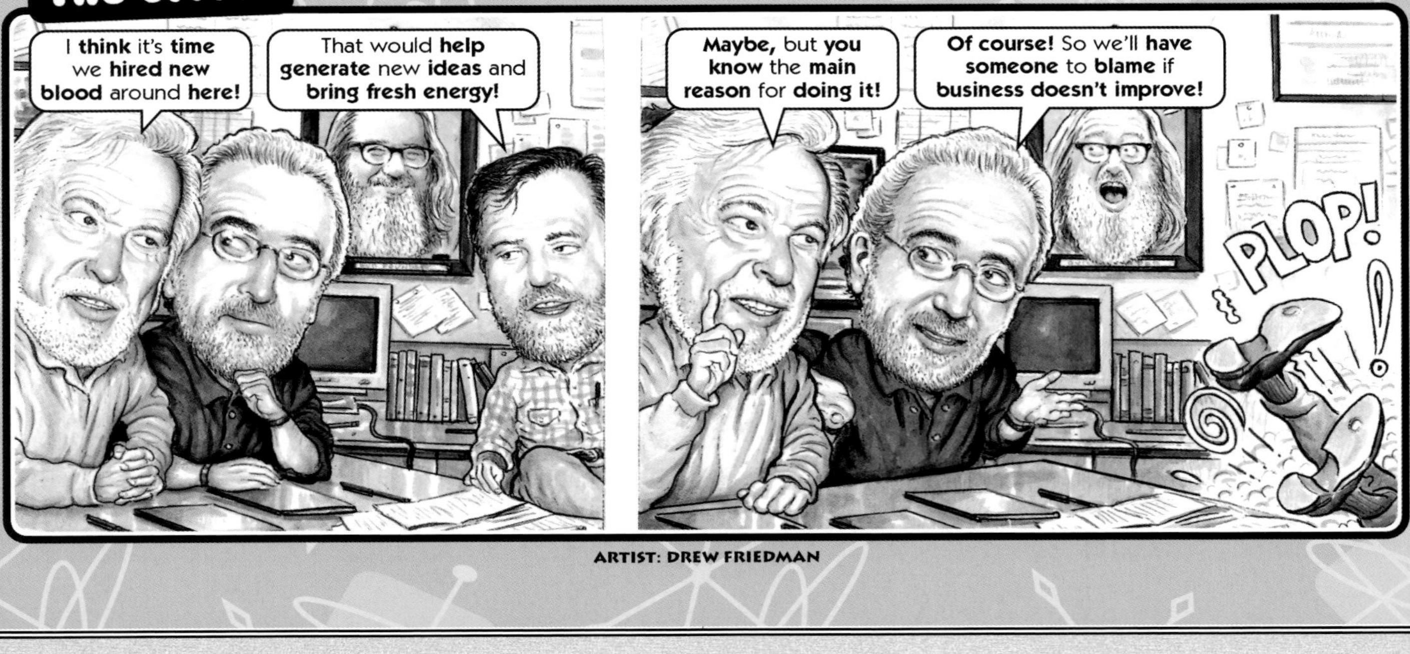
I think it's time we hired new blood around here!
That would help generate new ideas and bring fresh energy!
Maybe, but you know the main reason for doing it!
Of course! So we'll have someone to blame if business doesn't improve!
PLOP!

ARTIST: DREW FRIEDMAN

Dave Berg on *The Simpsons* and *Family Guy*

Dave's influence on subsequent generations is evident in these animated cameos he made on *The Simpsons* (Season 9, episode 1) and *Family Guy* (Season 9, episode 20).

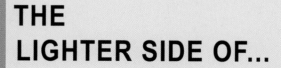

THE LIGHTER SIDE OF...

THE FORCE

ARTIST & WRITER : DAVE BERG

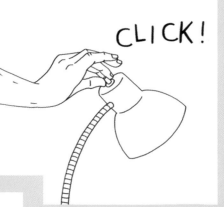

CLICK!

Dad, what are you doing? I need that lamp to study.

Sorry, son. Just trying to be a *light saver.*

BERG'S-EYE REVIEW DEPT. PART II

Since MAD's Usual Gang of Idiots (artists' division) paid tribute to Dave in issue #427, additional artists who were also influenced by "The Lighter Side of..." have appeared in our pages. They also wanted to pay tribute, and so, as an exclusive feature in this book (and using Dave's original dialogue), we present...

More MAD Artists Pay Tribute to The Lighter Side of...

ASSERTIVENESS

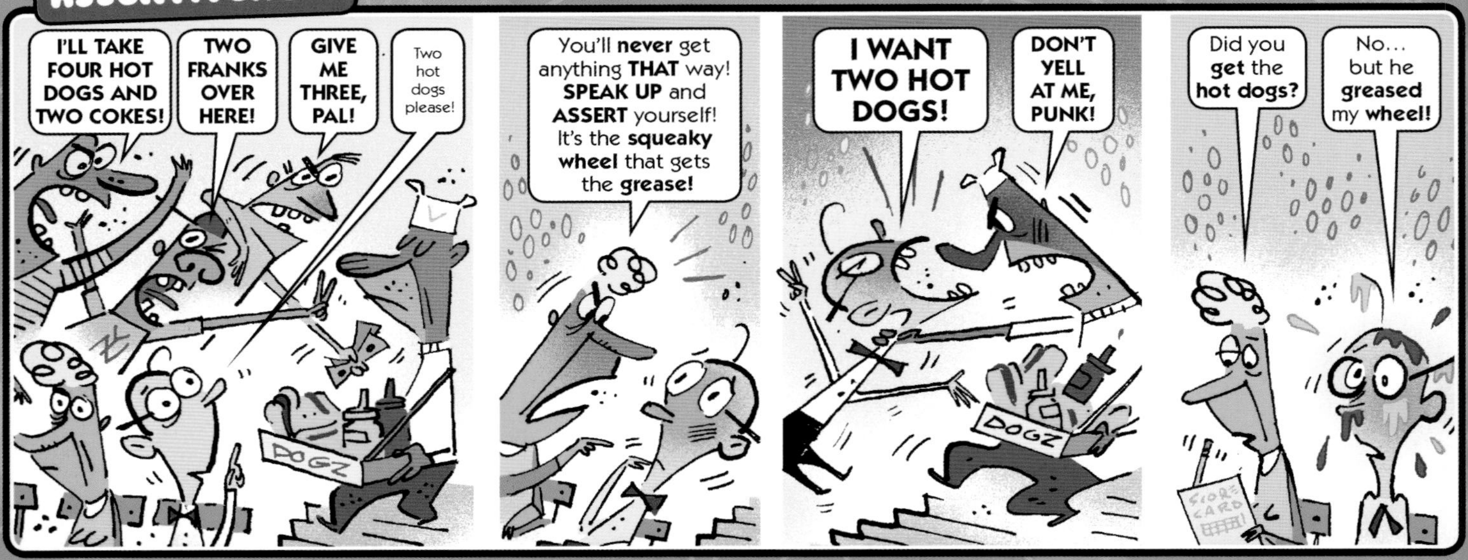

I'LL TAKE FOUR HOT DOGS AND TWO COKES!
TWO FRANKS OVER HERE!
GIVE ME THREE, PAL!
Two hot dogs please!
DOGZ
You'll never get anything THAT way! SPEAK UP and ASSERT yourself! It's the squeaky wheel that gets the grease!
I WANT TWO HOT DOGS!
DON'T YELL AT ME, PUNK!
DOGZ
Did you get the hot dogs?
No... but he greased my wheel!

ARTIST: BOB STAAKE

WINNING A BET

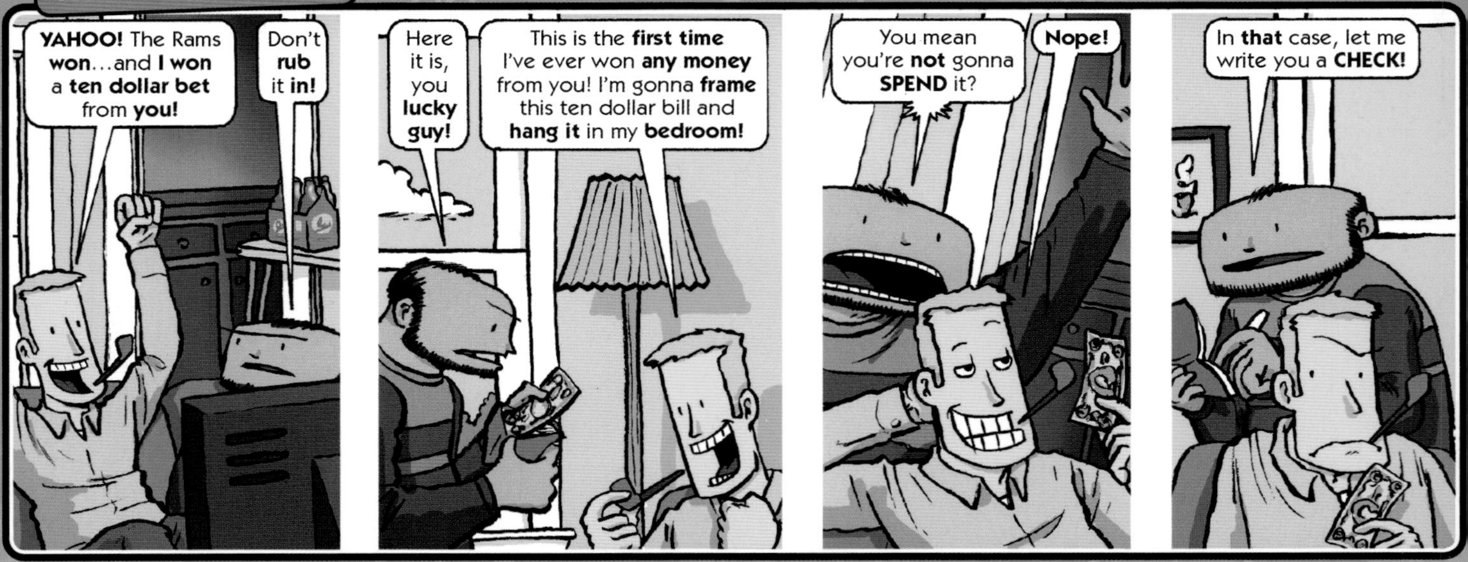

YAHOO! The Rams won...and I won a ten dollar bet from you!
Don't rub it in!
Here it is, you lucky guy!
This is the first time I've ever won any money from you! I'm gonna frame this ten dollar bill and hang it in my bedroom!
You mean you're not gonna SPEND it?
Nope!
In that case, let me write you a CHECK!

ARTIST: CHRISTOPHER BALDWIN

ADVICE

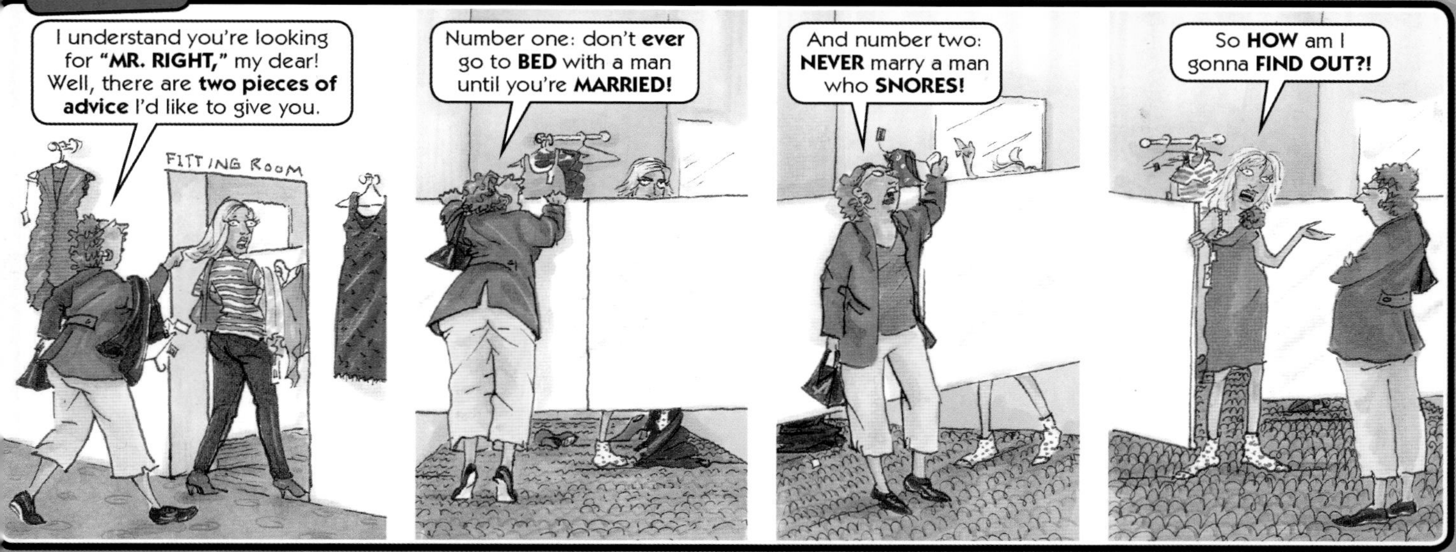

I understand you're looking for "MR. RIGHT," my dear! Well, there are two pieces of advice I'd like to give you.
FITTING ROOM
Number one: don't ever go to BED with a man until you're MARRIED!
And number two: NEVER marry a man who SNORES!
So HOW am I gonna FIND OUT?!

ARTIST: TERESA BURNS PARKHURST

GOOD DEEDS

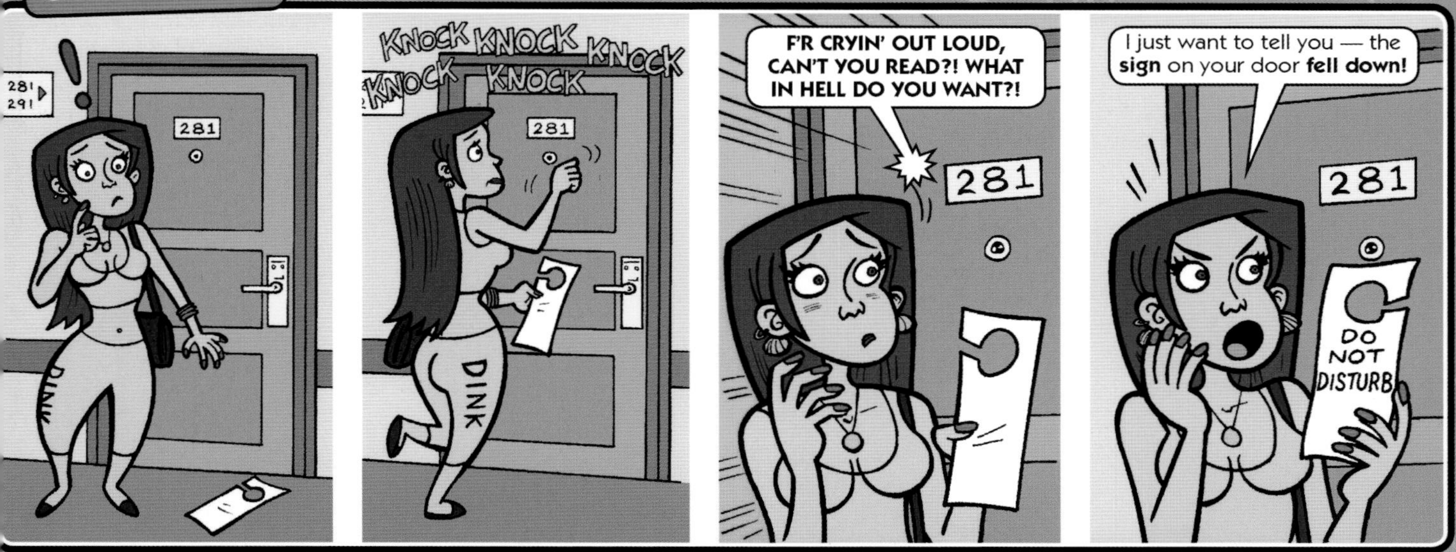

281
291
281
DINK
KNOCK KNOCK KNOCK
KNOCK KNOCK
281
DINK
F'R CRYIN' OUT LOUD, CAN'T YOU READ?! WHAT IN HELL DO YOU WANT?!
281
I just want to tell you — the sign on your door fell down!
281
DO NOT DISTURB

ARTISTS: EVAN DORKIN & SARAH DYER

RULES

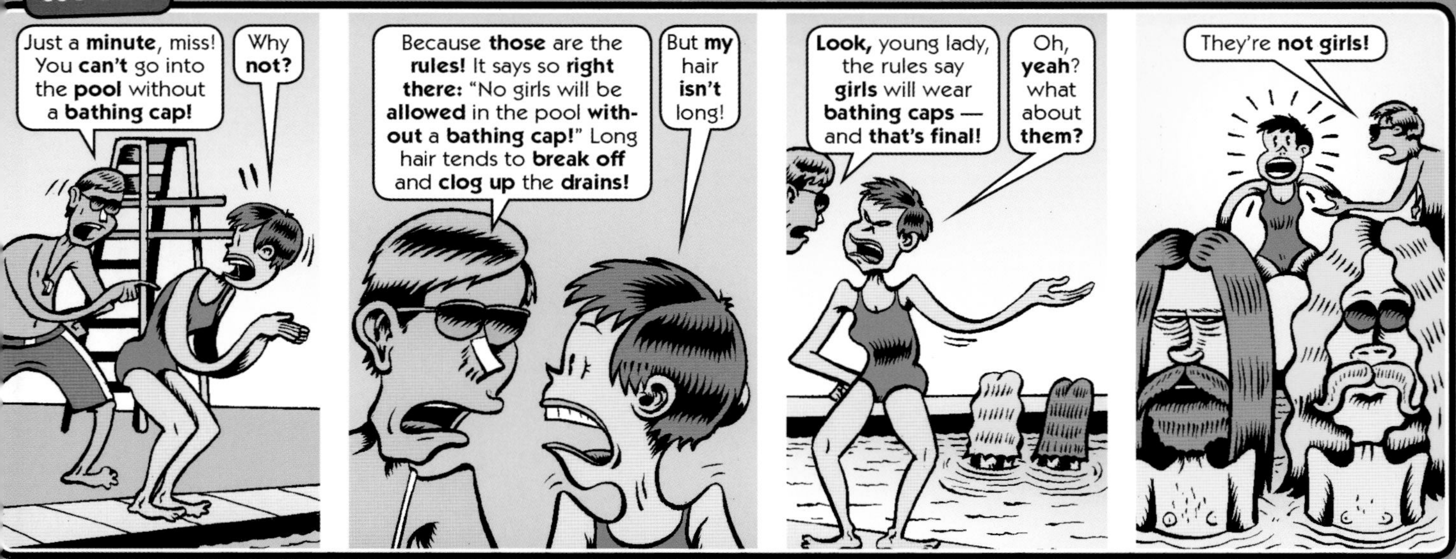

Just a minute, miss! You can't go into the pool without a bathing cap!
Why not?
Because those are the rules! It says so right there: "No girls will be allowed in the pool without a bathing cap!" Long hair tends to break off and clog up the drains!
But my hair isn't long!
Look, young lady, the rules say girls will wear bathing caps — and that's final!
Oh, yeah? what about them?
They're not girls!

ARTIST: PETER BAGGE

CRIME

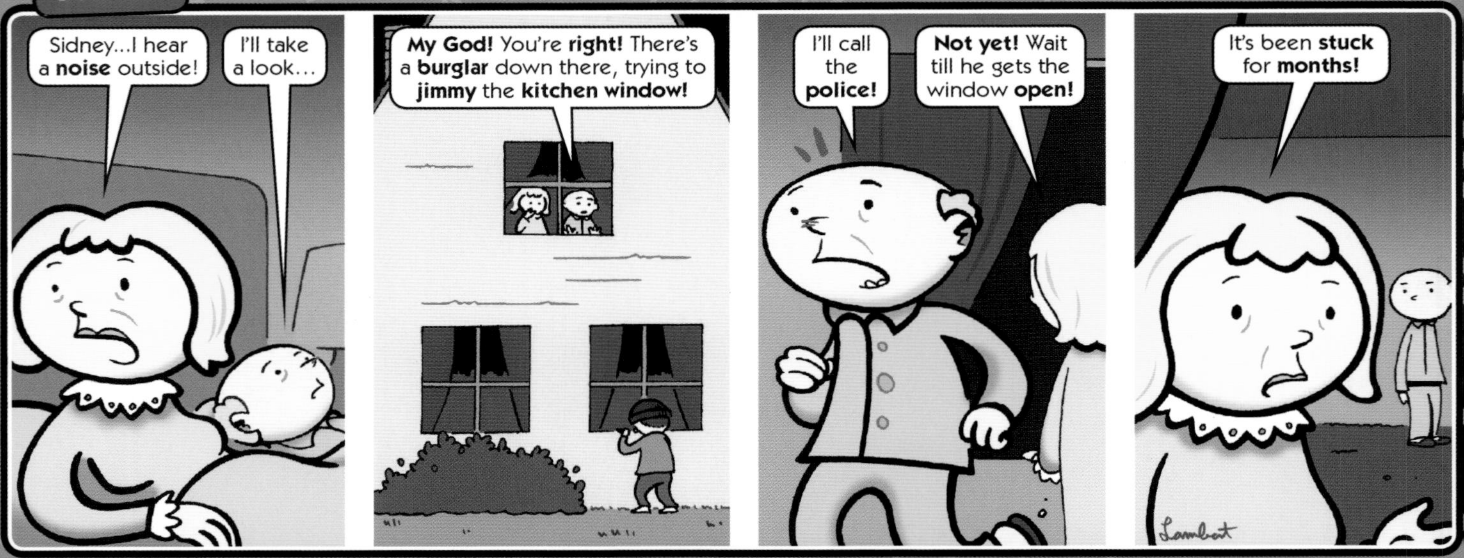

Sidney...I hear a **noise** outside!
I'll take a look...
My God! You're **right!** There's a **burglar** down there, trying to **jimmy** the **kitchen window!**
I'll call the **police!**
Not yet! Wait till he gets the window **open!**
It's been **stuck** for **months!**
Lambert

ARTIST: JACOB LAMBERT

MUSIC

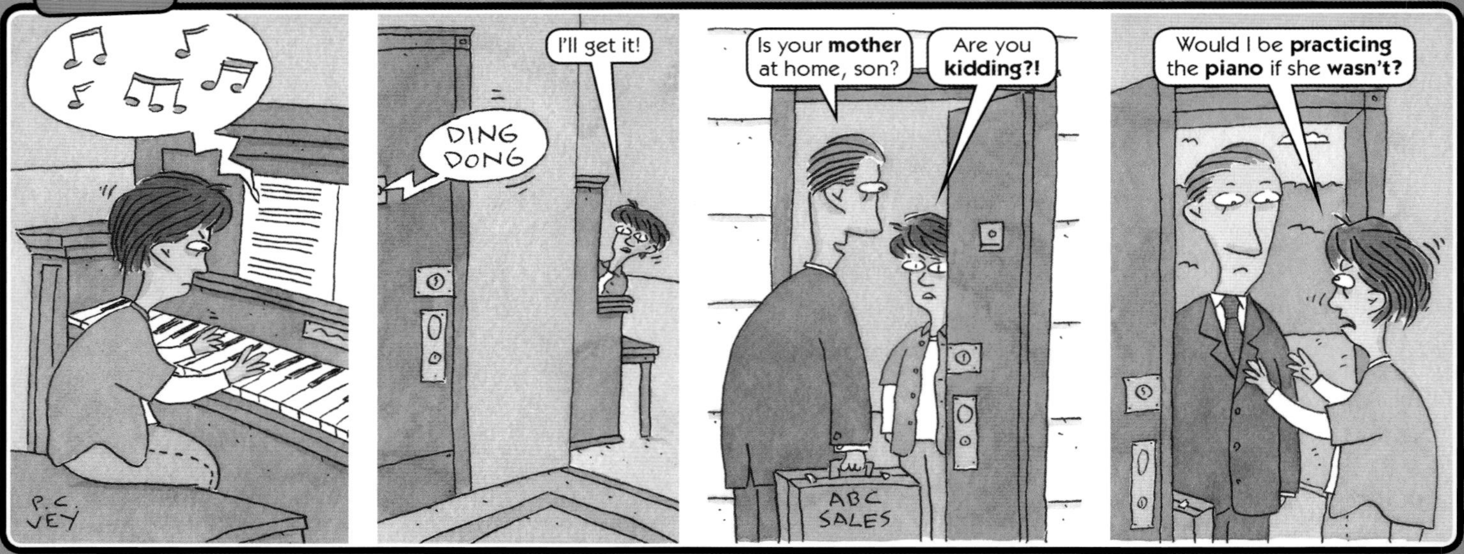

P.C. VEY
DING DONG
I'll get it!
Is your **mother** at home, son?
Are you **kidding?!**
ABC SALES
Would I be **practicing** the **piano** if she **wasn't?**

ARTIST: P.C. VEY

BIG CITIES

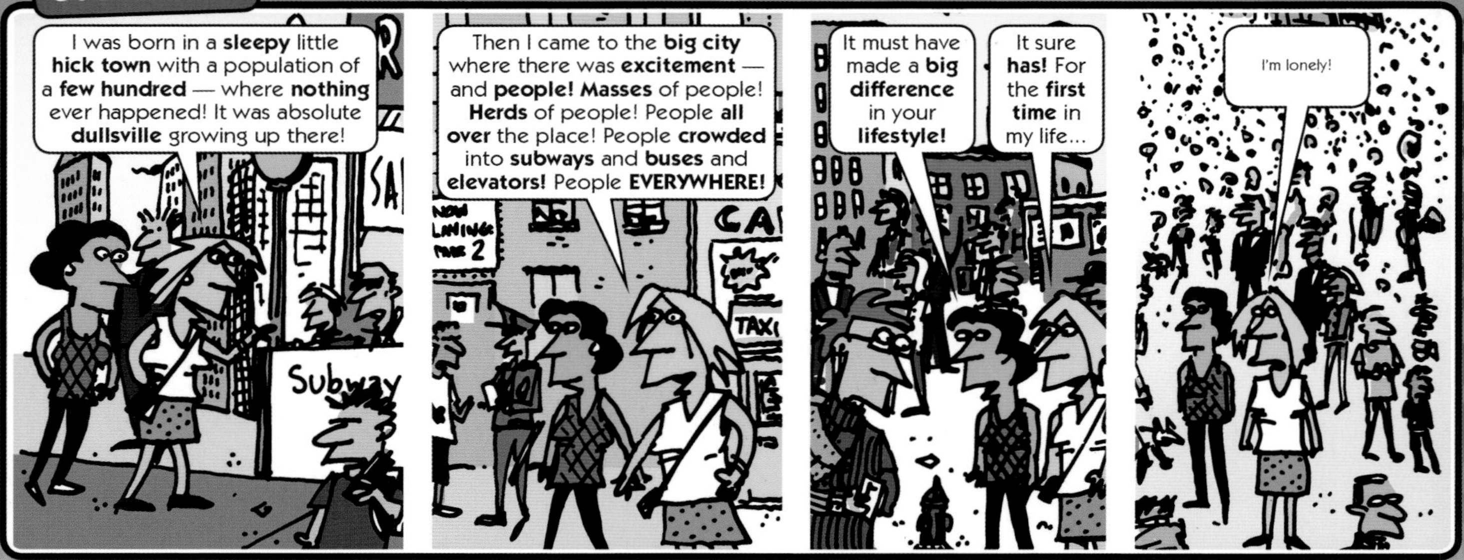

I was born in a **sleepy** little **hick town** with a population of a **few hundred** — where **nothing** ever happened! It was absolute **dullsville** growing up there!
Subway
Then I came to the **big city** where there was **excitement** — and **people! Masses** of people! **Herds** of people! People **all over** the place! People **crowded** into **subways** and **buses** and **elevators!** People **EVERYWHERE!**
TAXI
It must have made a **big difference** in your **lifestyle!**
It sure **has!** For the **first time** in my life...
I'm lonely!

ARTIST: TED RALL

PARTIES

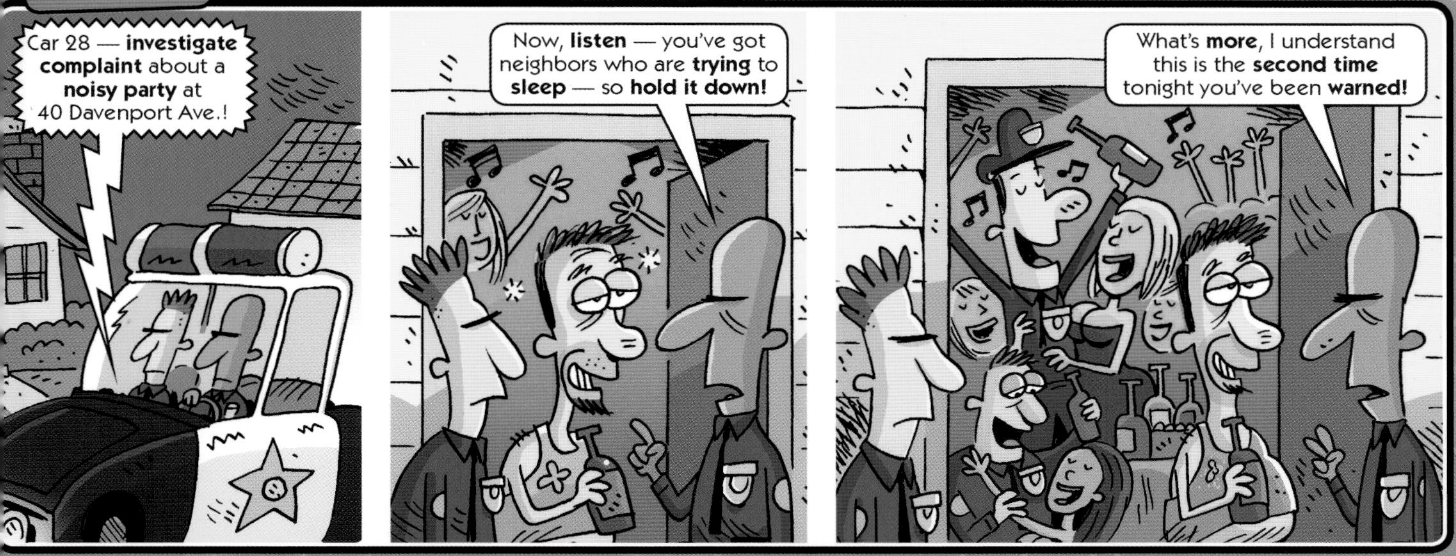
Car 28 — investigate complaint about a noisy party at 40 Davenport Ave.!
Now, listen — you've got neighbors who are trying to sleep — so hold it down!
What's more, I understand this is the second time tonight you've been warned!

ARTIST: SCOTT NICKEL

BABYSITTING

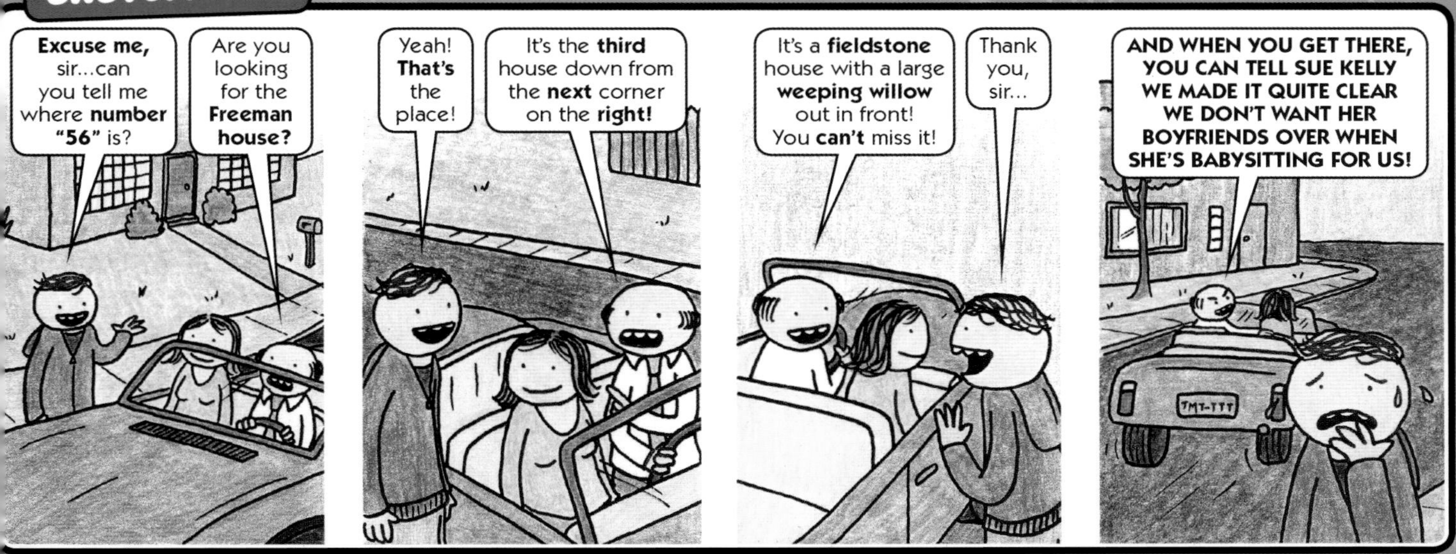
Excuse me, sir...can you tell me where number "56" is?
Are you looking for the Freeman house?
Yeah! That's the place!
It's the third house down from the next corner on the right!
It's a fieldstone house with a large weeping willow out in front! You can't miss it!
Thank you, sir...
AND WHEN YOU GET THERE, YOU CAN TELL SUE KELLY WE MADE IT QUITE CLEAR WE DON'T WANT HER BOYFRIENDS OVER WHEN SHE'S BABYSITTING FOR US!

ARTIST: JOEY ALISON SAYERS

PUNISHMENT

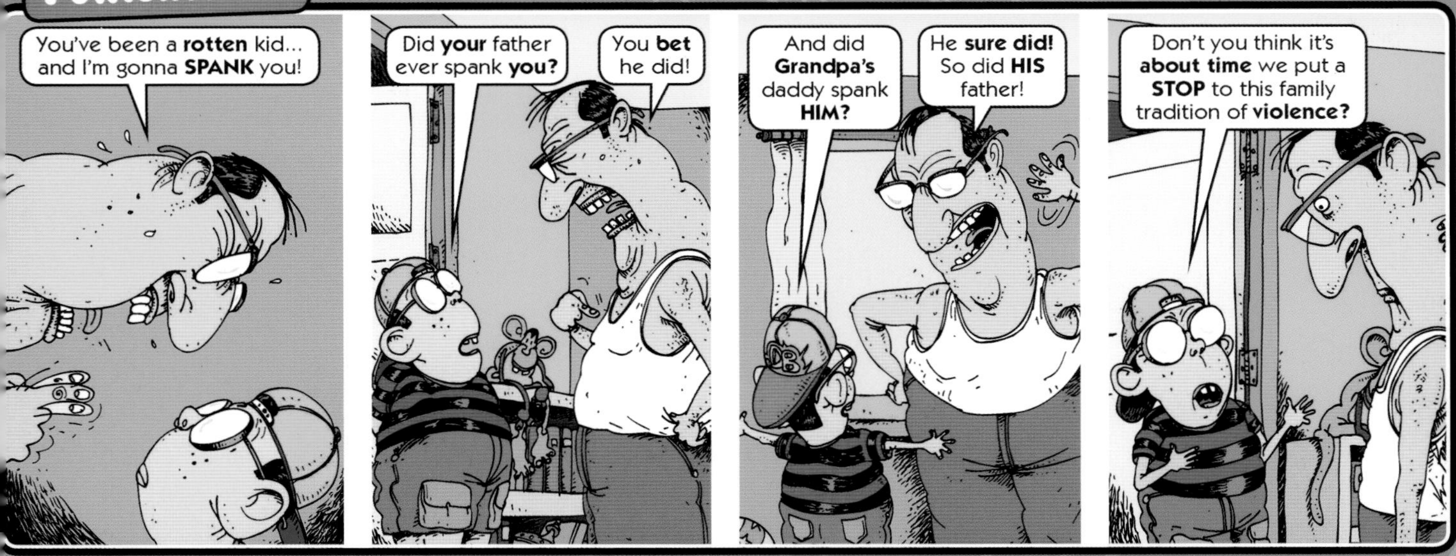
You've been a rotten kid... and I'm gonna SPANK you!
Did your father ever spank you?
You bet he did!
And did Grandpa's daddy spank HIM?
He sure did! So did HIS father!
Don't you think it's about time we put a STOP to this family tradition of violence?

ARTIST: KEVIN POPE

THE OFFICE

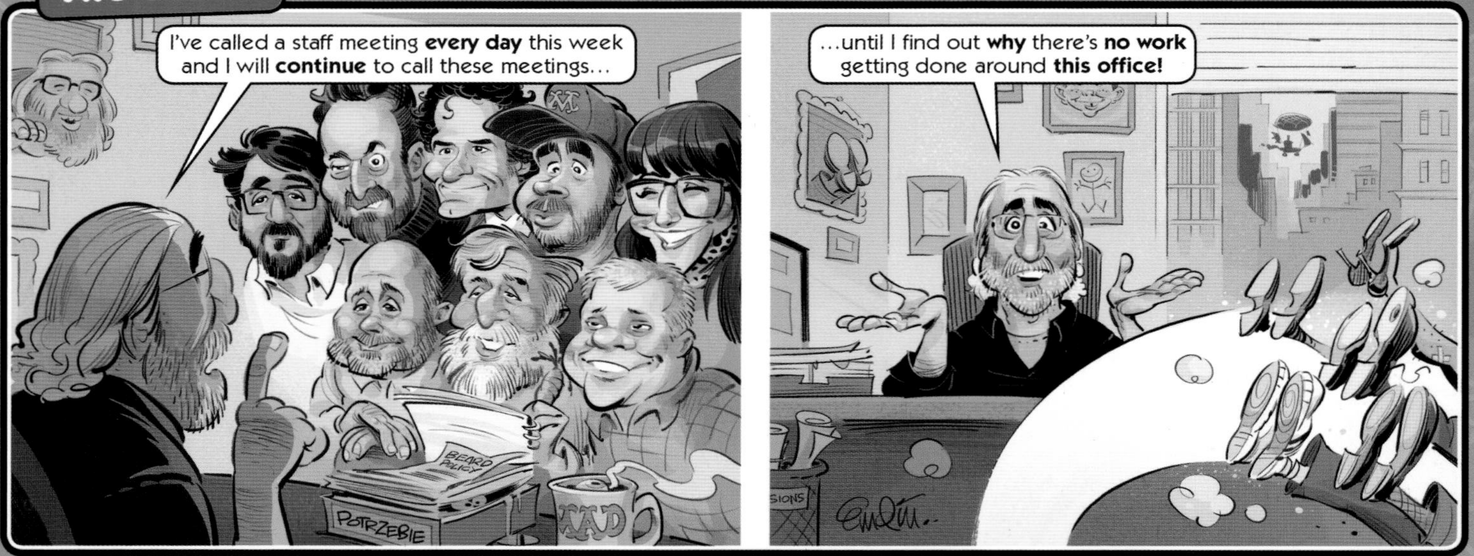
I've called a staff meeting **every day** this week and I will **continue** to call these meetings…
…until I find out **why** there's **no work** getting done around **this office!**
POTRZEBIE

ARTIST: ANTON EMDIN

BAD HABITS

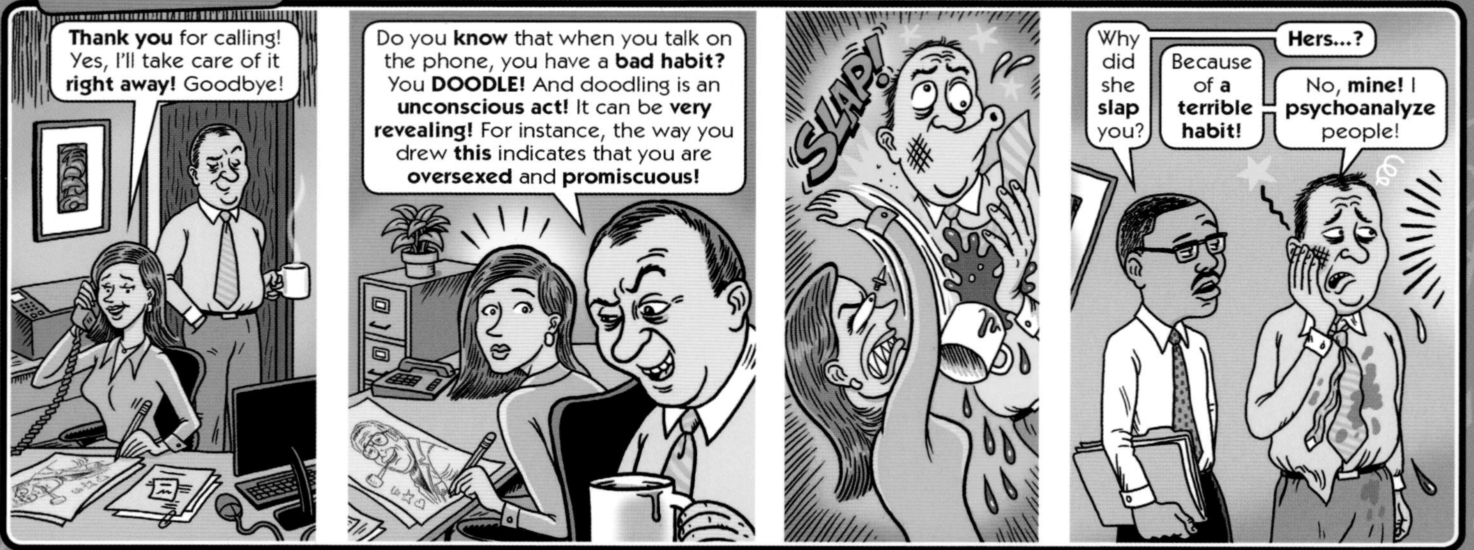
Thank you for calling! Yes, I'll take care of it **right away!** Goodbye!
Do you **know** that when you talk on the phone, you have a **bad habit?** You **DOODLE!** And doodling is an **unconscious act!** It can be **very revealing!** For instance, the way you drew **this** indicates that you are **oversexed** and **promiscuous!**
SLAP!
Why did she **slap** you?
Because of **a terrible habit!**
Hers…?
No, **mine!** I **psychoanalyze** people!

ARTIST: WARD SUTTON

DOCTORS

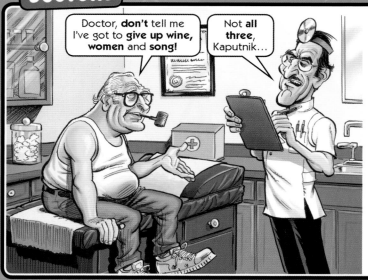

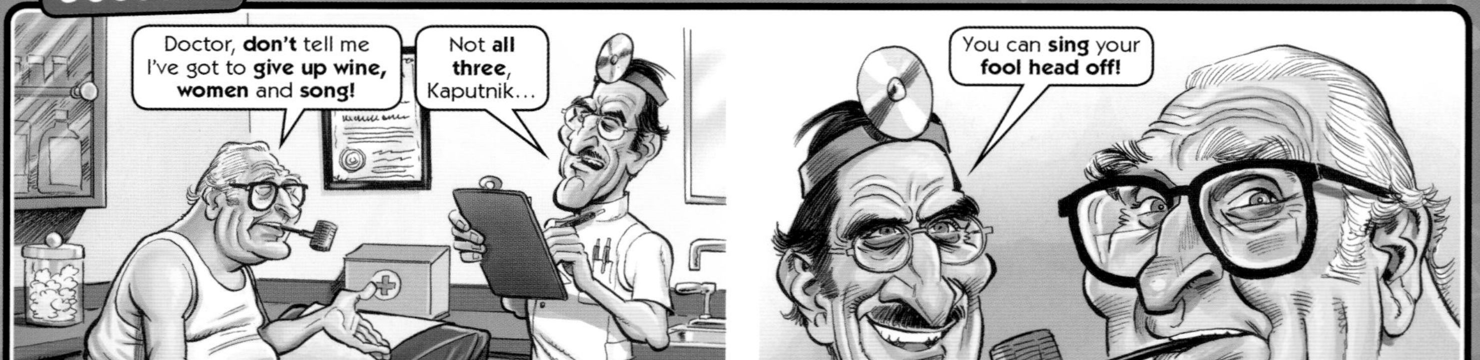
Doctor, **don't** tell me I've got to **give up wine, women** and **song!**
Not **all three**, Kaputnik…
You can **sing** your **fool head off!**

ARTIST: TOM RICHMOND

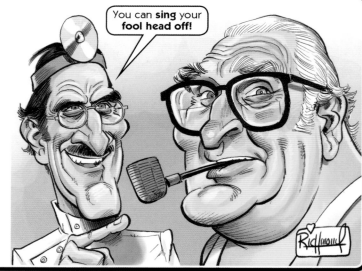

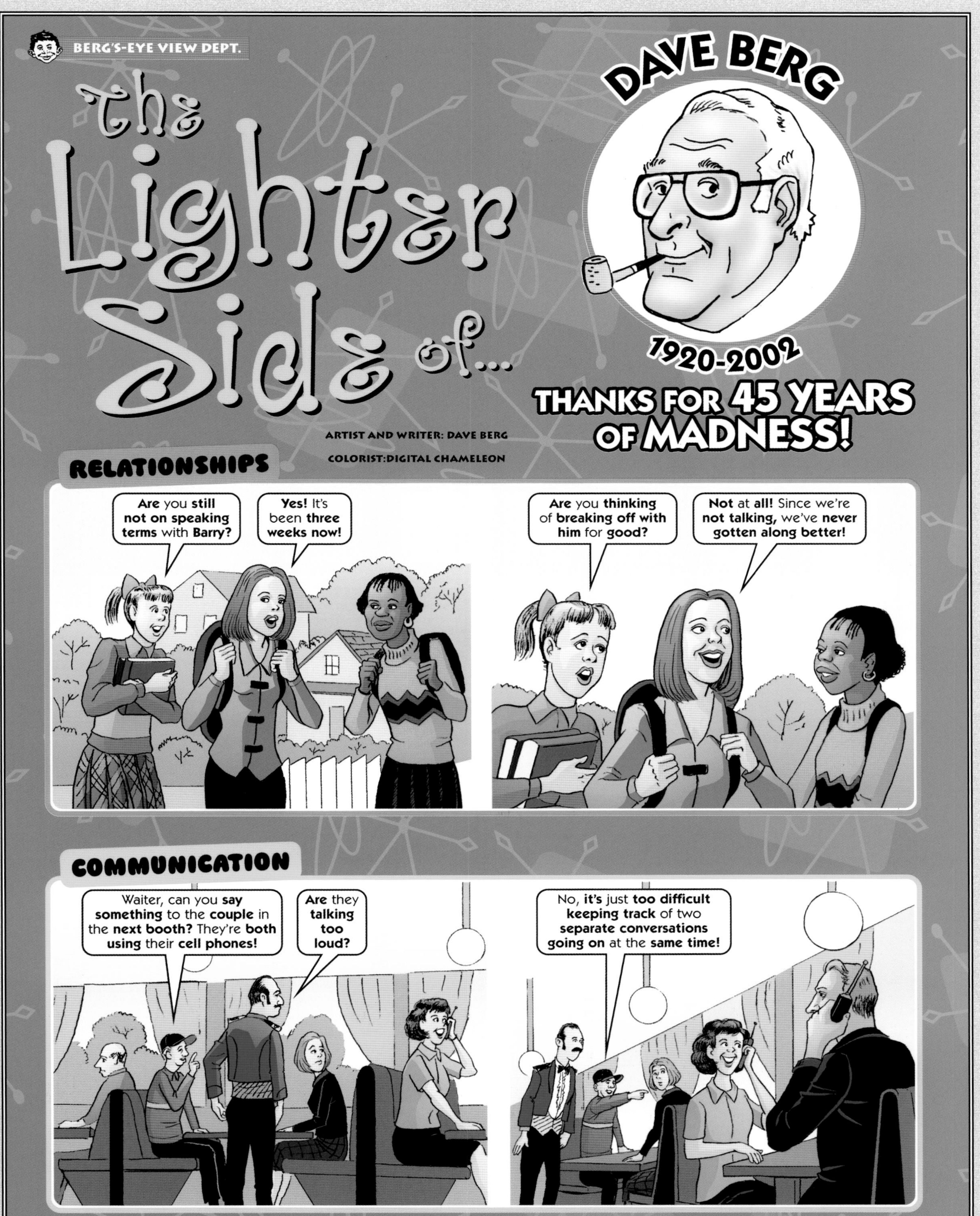
BERG'S-EYE VIEW DEPT.
The Lighter Side of...
DAVE BERG
1920-2002
THANKS FOR 45 YEARS OF MADNESS!
ARTIST AND WRITER: DAVE BERG
COLORIST: DIGITAL CHAMELEON
RELATIONSHIPS
Are you still not on speaking terms with Barry?
Yes! It's been three weeks now!
Are you thinking of breaking off with him for good?
Not at all! Since we're not talking, we've never gotten along better!
COMMUNICATION
Waiter, can you say something to the couple in the next booth? They're both using their cell phones!
Are they talking too loud?
No, it's just too difficult keeping track of two separate conversations going on at the same time!

The final edition of "The Lighter Side of..." written and drawn by Dave Berg

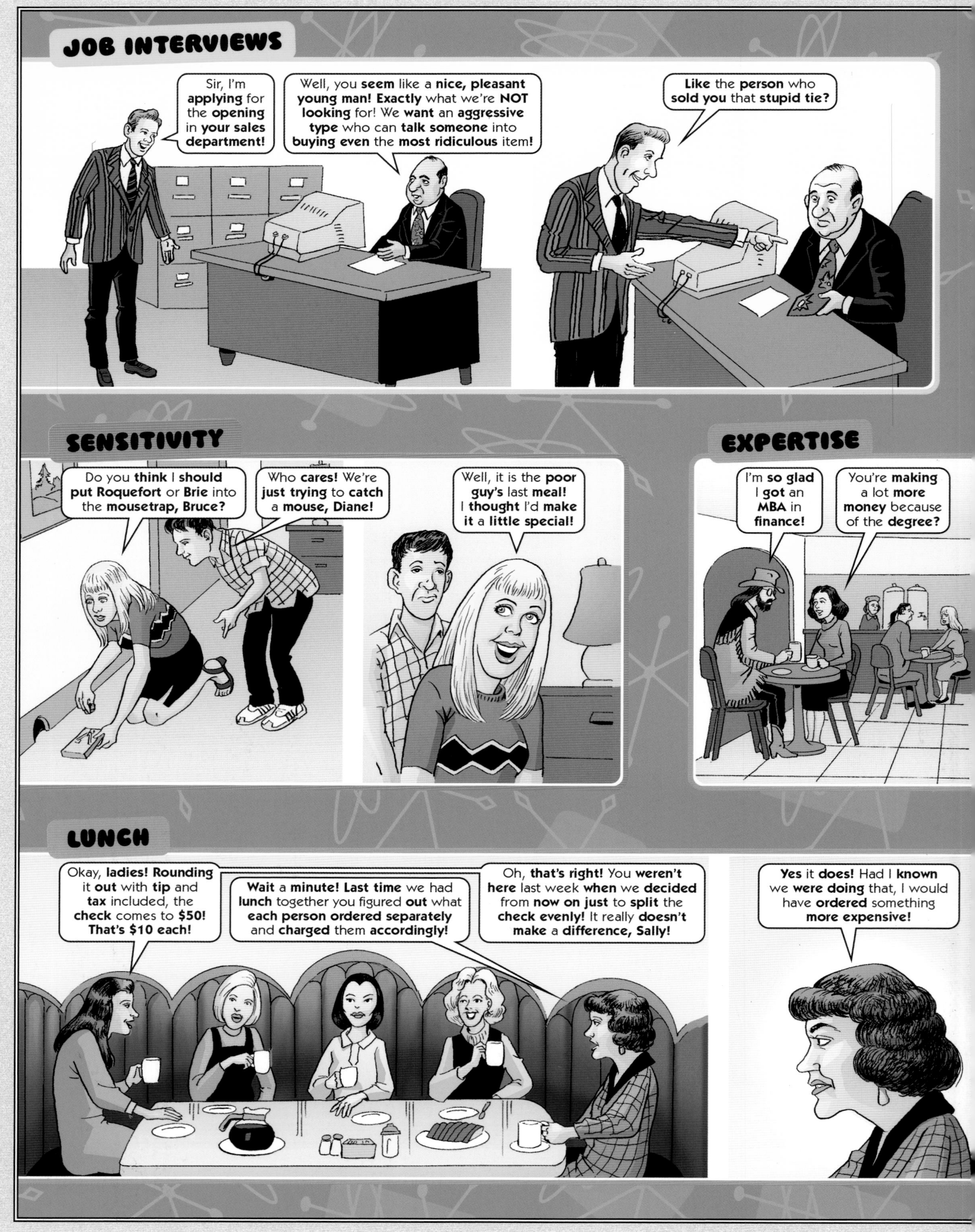
JOB INTERVIEWS
Sir, I'm applying for the opening in your sales department!
Well, you seem like a nice, pleasant young man! Exactly what we're NOT looking for! We want an aggressive type who can talk someone into buying even the most ridiculous item!
Like the person who sold you that stupid tie?
SENSITIVITY
Do you think I should put Roquefort or Brie into the mousetrap, Bruce?
Who cares! We're just trying to catch a mouse, Diane!
Well, it is the poor guy's last meal! I thought I'd make it a little special!
EXPERTISE
I'm so glad I got an MBA in finance!
You're making a lot more money because of the degree?
LUNCH
Okay, ladies! Rounding it out with tip and tax included, the check comes to $50! That's $10 each!
Wait a minute! Last time we had lunch together you figured out what each person ordered separately and charged them accordingly!
Oh, that's right! You weren't here last week when we decided from now on just to split the check evenly! It really doesn't make a difference, Sally!
Yes it does! Had I known we were doing that, I would have ordered something more expensive!

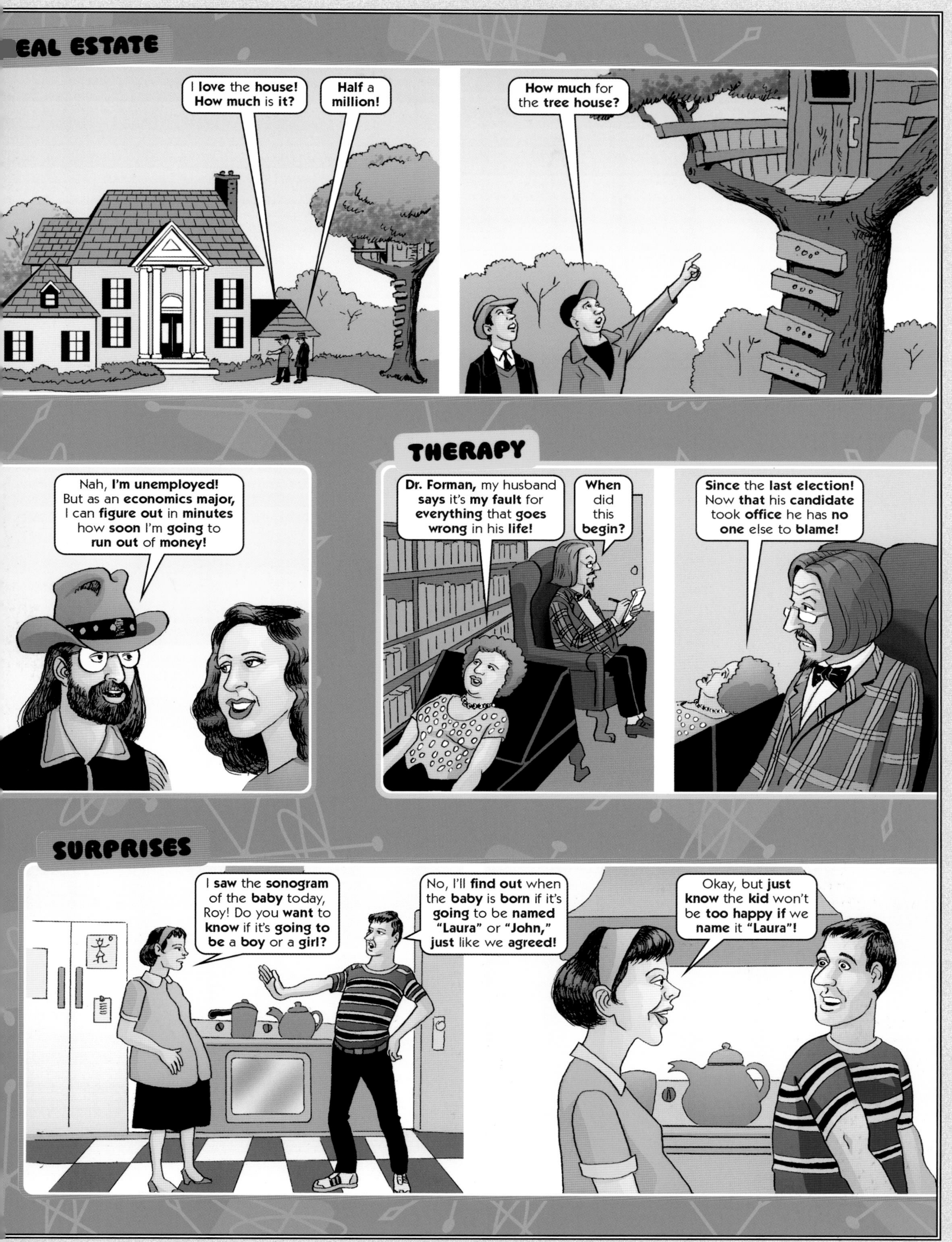
EAL ESTATE
I love the house! How much is it?
Half a million!
How much for the tree house?
Nah, I'm unemployed! But as an economics major, I can figure out in minutes how soon I'm going to run out of money!
THERAPY
Dr. Forman, my husband says it's my fault for everything that goes wrong in his life!
When did this begin?
Since the last election! Now that his candidate took office he has no one else to blame!
SURPRISES
I saw the sonogram of the baby today, Roy! Do you want to know if it's going to be a boy or a girl?
No, I'll find out when the baby is born if it's going to be named "Laura" or "John," just like we agreed!
Okay, but just know the kid won't be too happy if we name it "Laura"!

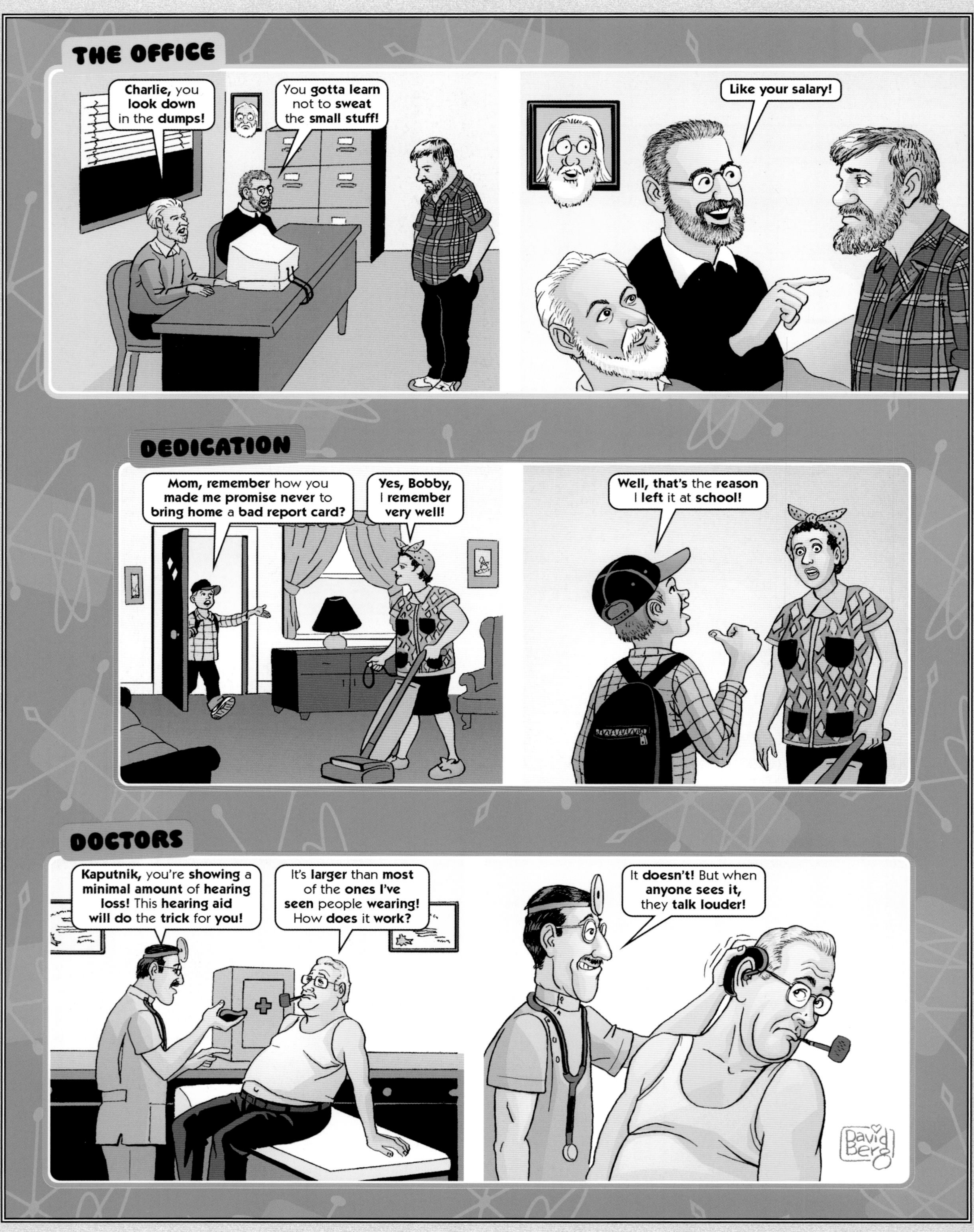
THE OFFICE
Charlie, you look down in the dumps!
You gotta learn not to sweat the small stuff!
Like your salary!
DEDICATION
Mom, remember how you made me promise never to bring home a bad report card?
Yes, Bobby, I remember very well!
Well, that's the reason I left it at school!
DOCTORS
Kaputnik, you're showing a minimal amount of hearing loss! This hearing aid will do the trick for you!
It's larger than most of the ones I've seen people wearing! How does it work?
It doesn't! But when anyone sees it, they talk louder!
David Berg